Introduction

Wittgenstein claimed that his ambition to write a philosophical work constructed entirely of jokes was frustrated when he realized that he had no sense of humour. The editor of a dictionary of humorous quotations, looking back on his final selection, must wonder how many of his choices will convince the reader that he shares Wittgenstein's disability. For the philosopher there was comfort in the thought that no-one *completely* devoid of a sense of humour would be so aware of his limitations. There is also the suspicion, supported by diligent research, that many jokes are indeed fashioned by people who have no sense of humour.

These reassurances are denied to an editor. He is accountable for deciding that every one of roughly 5,000 quotations in this collection is likely to set the table on a roar. His paranoia is increased by the spectrum of attitudes to humour. 'Humour's a funny thing,' says a character in Terry Johnson's play *Dead Funny*. But an old lady coming out of one of Victoria Wood's shows complained within earshot of the star, 'I don't find humour funny.'

'The joy of simple laughter' is another of Terry Johnson's deftly deployed clichés. Laughter is not invariably joyous and what produces it is rarely simple. I make this disclaimer because I have been encouraged by the publishers to make a more personal selection than the compilers of the fourth edition of the *Oxford Dictionary of Quotations* and the *Oxford Dictionary of Modern Quotations*. These were assembled in the former case by recruiting 'a team of distinguished advisers, united by scholarship in particular literary periods and subject fields' who picked their way through 'the *embarras de richesses*' offered by earlier editions; and in the latter by reducing 'a collection of more than 200,000 citations assembled by combing books, magazines, and newspapers'. Both books are 'an objective selection of quotations which are most widely known and used'.

It is impossible to be objective about humour. Therefore although I have combed both dictionaries because they contain so many quotations which are humorous as well as well-known, I have also sought to admit many which gain entrance not because they are well-known but because they are amusing and deserve our better acquaintance.

Chronologically the spread is from the earliest quotations; but I have justified the inclusion of antique saws solely on the grounds that they raise a smile today. Paul Johnson recently suggested in the *Spectator* that the first recorded laughter occurred at the end of the Early Bronze Age, about 2000 BC:

> Significantly it was a woman who laughed. The Book of Genesis tells us
> (xviii. 10 ff.) that, when Sarah overheard the Lord inform her husband

Abraham she was to have a son, 'Sarah laughed within herself, saying, after I am waxed old shall I have pleasure, my lord being old also?'

Johnson's conclusion is that the first joke was female and was about sex. Sarah tried to keep it to herself; but the men accused her of laughing. She denied it, 'for she was afraid'. It may have seemed a good joke to Sarah in 2000 BC but that does not justify its inclusion today. On the other hand some 3,600 years later, Shakespeare's stage direction 'Exit, pursued by a bear' in *The Winter's Tale*, now a mellow 400 years old, still makes me smile—whether he intended it or not. However, there is no room for all the smiles in Shakespeare. I mourn the passing of 'Nay, faith, let me not play a woman: I have a beard coming,' from the *Dream*, which is warm, funny, and well observed; however, it is preserved in the *Oxford Dictionary of Quotations*.

I have not thought it necessary to reopen the ever-raging debate fought over the boundaries between wit and humour. In introducing his *Anthology of Wit*, Guy Boas derives humour from the supposition that human nature was once held to be determined by the physical 'humours' and fluids which make up the body. Imbalance of these fluids produces (as in Ben Jonson's plays) conduct which was freakish, absurd, or whimsical— provoking laughter at the recognizably humorous situation. The word 'wit', however, stems from the Old English *witan* to know, which lent itself flatteringly to the Anglo-Saxon approximation to Parliament, and implied optimistically the exercise there of the intellect. So wit is associated with the mind's contribution to what is amusing. 'Humour', to Boas, 'is the funny situation or object; wit is the fun which a particular mind subjectively perceives on the situation or object.' There is room in this book for both. So what were the criteria for the quotations which survive?

No such book can afford to ignore perennials like Wilde, Mencken, Coward, Parker, Kaufman, and Shaw; Johnny Speight, the creator of *Till Death Do Us Part* (and therefore, in America, of *All in the Family*) grew up reading collections of quotations and concluded that Bernard Shaw was a gag-writer, which fuelled his own ambitions in the field of comedy. Among phrase-makers in recent years Gore Vidal, Tom Stoppard, Alan Bennett, Russell Baker, P. J. O'Rourke, Stephen Fry, and Craig Brown demand inclusion as new hardy annuals. Some writers are consistently witty, some have a happy inspiration. The former earn more entries than the latter. I did not consider it useful to operate a quota system.

The unintentionally humorous can be as diverting and must also be found a place. With its 'Colemanballs' feature *Private Eye* magazine spotlighted for our superior pleasure the pressure under which sports commentators try and sometimes fail to find the right word—though who can be sure whether 'the batsman's Holding, the bowler's Willey' was Brian Johnston's accidental comment or the result of a confrontation for which he had long been lying in wait. In America there is the famous Phil Rizzuto remark when his commentary was interrupted by the news of the Pope's death: 'that puts a damper, even on a Yankee win.' Dan Quayle and George

The Oxford Dictionary of
Humorous
Quotations

The Oxford Dictionary of
Humorous
Quotations

Edited by **Ned Sherrin**

Oxford   New York

OXFORD UNIVERSITY PRESS

Oxford University Press, Walton Street, Oxford OX2 6DP

Oxford New York
Athens Auckland Bangkok Bogota Bombay
Buenos Aires Calcutta Cape Town Dar es Salaam
Delhi Florence Hong Kong Istanbul Karachi
Kuala Lumpur Madras Madrid Melbourne
Mexico City Nairobi Paris Singapore
Taipei Tokyo Toronto
and associated companies in
Berlin Ibadan

Oxford is a trade mark of Oxford University Press

Selection and arrangement © Ned Sherrin. Oxford University Press, 1995
Introduction © Ned Sherrin 1995

First published 1995 by Oxford University Press
First issued as an Oxford University Press paperback 1996

British Library Cataloguing in Publication Data
Data available

Library of Congress Cataloging in Publication Data
The Oxford dictionary of humorous quotations
edited by Ned Sherrin.
p. cm. Includes indexes.
1. Quotations, English. 2. Wit and humor.
I. Sherrin, Ned.
082—dc20   PN6084.H8O94   1995   94–37211
ISBN 0–19–214244–5 (hbk.)
ISBN 0–19–280045–0 (pbk.)

10 9 8 7 6 5 4 3 2

Printed in Great Britain by
Mackays plc
Chatham, Kent

Project Team

Editor	Ned Sherrin
Managing Editor	Elizabeth M. Knowles
Index Editor	Susan Ratcliffe
Quotation Collection	Jean Buchanan, Helen McCurdy, Verity Mason
Quotation Retrieval	Katie Weale
Library Research	Ralph Bates, Marie G. Diaz
Data Capture	Sandra Vaughan
Proofreading	Fabia Claris, Penny Trumble

We are grateful to Melinda Babcock, George Chowdharay-Best, and Jon Ross Simon for additional research

Bush are modern political stars on the unconscious humour circuit. It is hard to do better than Quayle's alleged hesitation on visiting Latin America, 'not having studied Latin', or his insistence on the 'e' at the end of 'potato'.

Political correctness throws up a shoal of examples of unconscious humour, some of which have found a place. I might have found room for excerpts from the reported BBC *Woman's Hour* directive to new presenters in the early 1990s:

> 3. Do not be surprised that a woman has achieved something…4. Do not be surprised that an older person has achieved something…5. Do not be surprised that a black person has achieved something…

but there is a leaden mind behind that directive which does not deserve to be included.

The pronouncements of censors are another rich vein of unconscious humour. In the 1920s Nina Shortt, daughter of a film censor and ex-Home Secretary, Sir Edward Shortt, refused a certificate to Jean Cocteau's avant-garde movie *The Seashell and the Clergyman*:

> [This film] is so cryptic as to be almost meaningless. If there is a meaning, it is doubtless objectionable.

Lord Tyrell, who succeeded Shortt, went one better in 1937:

> We take pride in observing that there is not a single film showing in London today that deals with any of the burning issues of the hour.

The sublimely named Major de Fonblanque Cox combined censorship with dogbreeding. On his appointment he declared:

> No, my boy, let us show clean films in the old country! I shall judge film stories as I would horseflesh, or a dog. I shall look for clean lines everywhere.

There may be less art in this than in the words which the Grossmiths put into Mr Pooter's mouth, 'I left the room with silent dignity but caught my foot in the mat,' but there is no less humour.

Another *Private Eye* feature, 'Pseud's Corner', is based on yet another sort of unconscious humour, I do not think Professor Karl Miller's verdict on the footballer Paul Gascoigne for *The London Review of Books* found its way there, but it deserved to:

> He was a highly charged spectacle on the field of play: fierce and comic, formidable and vulnerable, urchin-like and waiflike, a strong head and torso with comparatively breakable legs, strange-eyed, pink-faced, fair-haired, tense and upright, a priapic monolith in the Mediterranean sun…he is magic, and fairy-tale magic at that.

Of them all, the late Lord Massereene and Ferrard emerges as a new star provider of unintentional amusement, recommending the warning notice, 'Beware of the Agapanthus'.

Quotations are taken from novels, plays, poems, essays, letters, speeches, films, radio and television broadcasts, songs, popular jokes, graffiti, and advertisements, accurately attributed wherever possible. Some have had to fall by the wayside for reasons of space, or because I could not legitimize them. Under the firm but patient guidance of the Dictionary Department at Oxford University Press, I have endeavoured to help their devoted detectives to verify the quotations chosen in original or authoritative sources.

I have found space for some of the best-known catch-phrases which have sprung from radio and television programmes, but sources are so prolific that a general anthology can only hint at the richness—from the inventive conceits of Frank Muir and Denis Norden in *Take It From Here* to the anachronistic whimsies of Ben Elton and Richard Curtis in *Blackadder*. In *Take It From Here* the puns were elaborate, the plotting devious:

> [SILAS THE PURITAN] Thou art spending all the royal coffers on this female
>   person [Nell Gwynne]. But yesterday you sold the Crown Jewels...to buy
>   her a sedan chair with a sunshine roof!
> [KING CHARLES II] So I blued a couple of baubles? 'Tis of no account.
> [SILAS] (*reproachfully*) But you're forever blueing baubles.

In *Blackadder* the humour is starker:

> The Germans are a cruel race. Their operas last for six hours and they have
> no word for fluffy.

Some catch-phrases demand to be included, such as the Chief Whip's notorious response in Michael Dobbs' *House of Cards*:

> You might very well think that. I couldn't possibly comment.

Formula jokes are also generally too plentiful and often too unfunny to earn a place—sick jokes, light-bulb jokes, elephant jokes, and drummer jokes are excluded. I have also resisted the temptation to follow a 1994 trend with the latest fashionable American joke craze, 'Doing the Dozens', allegedly a venerable Afro-American habit of trading insults—preferably about the opponent's mother. For example, 'Your mother is so ugly, when she walks into the bank they turn off the camera,' or 'Your mother is so dumb, she went to the movies and the sign said, "Under 17 not admitted", so she came back with 18 friends.' 'Doing the Dozens' can wait for the slim paperback volume in which these ripostes will doubtless one day be collected by another publisher.

At the moment when I identified a mass-multiplying reproach, 'like turkeys voting for Christmas', a scholarly commentator in the *Independent Magazine* traced the birth of this death-wish simile to the late David Penhaligon who used it to highlight his distaste for the British Lib-Lab pact (1977–8). For Penhaligon it emphasized the Prime Minister's (James Callaghan's) certainty that the Liberals would never vote to bring him down. Callaghan himself plundered it the next year to slight the weak position of Scottish Nationalists. It crossed the Irish Sea when a Fianna Fáil member of the Dáil said that, 'a woman voting for divorce is like turkeys...' Both the Bruges Group of Conservative MPs and Michael Heseltine rented the phrase for their own ends in 1991. Paddy Ashdown, the leader of Penhaligon's old party, grabbed it to pour scorn on rebel Tories during the Maastricht debate. The Tory Party, he said, would not be defeated by its place-preserving backbenchers. For them to bring the Government down, 'would be like turkeys...' he said, 'etc.' The apotheosis of this witfest came when the French awarded a special 'foreign political humour prize' to the British MP Teresa Gorman for trotting out the same rubric, once again in the context of Maastricht. If anyone deserves to accept the prize it is the Widow Penhaligon.

Topicality admitted the inclusion of a borderline case, a version of another cliché-ridden humorous quip which is custom-made for hand-me-down insults. John Major was not being witty or original when he called some of his backbenchers, 'a few apples short of a picnic', but the phrase caught the public fancy. I can't remember whether the ex-chairman of Test Selectors, Ted Dexter, said of someone or was described by someone as being, 'a few roos loose in the top paddock'. 'One brick short of a load' and 'One slice short of a sandwich' are in the same vein: but none of them earns inclusion. Victor Lewis-Smith, describing Lord Rees-Mogg as 'two coupons short of a pop-up toaster', gets nearer with a vivid variation but is still disqualified by the curse of formula. Had he been Prime Minister he might have made it.

The files of the OUP Dictionary Department have inevitably provided a mass of material, all providentially sourced. Sadly many of the contributions derived from my own serendipitizing were lodged solely in the mind which failed to remember where I had found them. However, perhaps I should have let stand more of those remarks at whose birth I was present. One example is Anthony Quinton's impromptu comment as solemn music flooded a BBC studio when we were taken off the air for a news bulletin during the Falklands War. 'I know that tune,' he said, 'it's Sibelius' "You Can't Win 'Em All".' I can't think of a better authority.

In culling the new material the decision to organize the book thematically and not to arrange quotations under author headings was often revealing. In the section on Wealth, for example, some fun is to be had by the witty at the expense of the wealthy; but I relish the petulant note that invades the voices of the rich from Lord Durham (who in the nineteenth century was known as 'King Jog' because he could 'jog along' on £40,000 a year) through Lord Northcliffe (who said that when he wanted a peerage he would 'buy it like an honest man') and Chips Channon (who found it difficult in 1934 to go out shopping and spend less than £200) to Alan Clark (moaning in his diary in 1987 of the £700,000 in his Abbey National Crazy-High-Interest account, 'but what's the use?'). Sadly I could not confirm the Duke of Marlborough's bleat when urged to sack one of his many Viennese pastry-cooks, 'May not a man have a biscuit?'

Looking at other collections, I was frustrated by innumerable headings which yield very few quotations. Here we have a total of 149 classifications, some of which represent the combination of related headings. For example, Truth is linked with Lies rather than sitting unhappily in separate beds, while on the other hand the stage is such a productive source that I have separated Actors and Acting from The Theatre. Appropriate cross-reference entries are supplied, and keyword and author indexes further facilitate the chasing of references. (For a more detailed account, see 'How to Use the Dictionary'.)

I have introduced a large number of quotations from popular songs—so much wit is crammed into the discipline which a lyric writer observes. My selection cannot be comprehensive but it aims to point the road to a Samarkand of riches. Which do you choose from a Sondheim lyric? Look at 'Now', a song from *A Little Night Music*, in which a literary-minded middle-aged husband is trying to decide which gem will turn on his reluctant young wife. I sacrificed:

> The Brontes are grander
> But not very gay.
> Her taste is much blander
> I'm sorry to say,
> But is Hans Christian Ander-
> sen ever risqué?

in favour of:

> And Stendhal would ruin
> The plan of attack,
> As there isn't much blue in
> *The Red and the Black.*

But the whole score is laced with wit.

To backtrack, I was tempted to include the current Professor of Poetry at Oxford's review of Sondheim's *Sweeney Todd* in the *Sunday Times*, 'the worst rhymes in London', along with Dan Quayle's contributions to unconscious humour; but it got away. Coward, Porter, and Hart are dinosaurs in the field but other British and American lyric writers from E. Y. Harburg to Raymond Douglas Davis (The Kinks) deserve a more detailed examination than this book can afford. I hope enough creeps in to point the reader in the right direction.

Songs are easy to source, but an arrangement in themes prompted all sorts of quotations that dance tantalizingly in my magpie memory and have eluded our keenest detectives. Some of recollection's children I cannot legitimize. Some I have had to omit for others more favoured. Here are some of those I mourn:

Lord Thorneycroft's reply to Lord Houghton's letter, 'outlining his massive campaign to put animals into politics':

> Dear Douglas, Thank you for your letter about animals. I do think that the poor creatures have enough to put up with without being put into politics. Yours sincerely...

Nietzsche and Michael Frayn on books:

> Books for general reading always smell badly. The odour of the common people hangs about them. (Nietzsche)

There is something about a blurb-writer paying his respects to a funny book which puts one in mind of a short-sighted Lord Mayor raising his hat to a hippopotamus. (Frayn)

Robert Altman on children:

If you have a child who is seven feet tall, you don't cut off his head or his legs. You buy him a bigger bed and hope he plays basketball.

Evelyn Waugh on class:

No writer before the middle of the nineteenth century wrote about the working-class other than as grotesques or as pastoral decorations. Then when they were given the vote, certain writers started to suck up to them.

Ronald Firbank on the country:

I'd like to spank the white walls of (that shepherd's) cottage.

Antonia Fraser on death:

Once there was a Drag Hunt Ball, just outside Oxford, to which I had unaccountably failed to be asked. I asked God to do something about it, and God recklessly killed poor King George, as a result of which the Hunt Ball was cancelled.

Mickey Rose on dress-sense:

Nobody would wear beige to rob a bank.

Lord Rosebery's advice to Queen Victoria:

There is much exaggeration about the attainments required for a Speaker. All Speakers are highly successful, all Speakers are deeply regretted, and are generally announced to be irreplaceable. But a Speaker is soon found, and found, almost invariably, among the mediocrities of the House.

Bernard Levin on Barbara Cartland's grasp of history:

Miss Cartland insists that Earl Mountbatten helped her with the writing...All that expert help, however, has still not managed to correct her apparent belief that Trafalgar came very shortly after Waterloo; perhaps she has confused English history with the London Underground system.

Lily Tomlin on love:

If love is the answer, could you rephrase the question?

Chekhov on marriage:

If you're afraid of loneliness, don't marry.

Carl Sandburg on murder:

Papa loved Mamma
Mamma loved men
Mamma's in the graveyard
Papa's in the pen.

Thomas Beecham on a fellow-musician:

> Sir Adrian Boult came to see me this morning—positively reeking of Horlicks.

J. G. Saxe on the newspaper world:

> Who would not be an Editor? To write
> The magic 'we' of such enormous might.
> To be so great beyond the common span
> It takes the plural to express the Man.

Senator Wyche Fowler on being asked whether, in 'those permissive sixties', he had smoked a marijuana cigarette:

> Only when committing adultery.

Norman Douglas on Suffolk:

> Land of uncomfortable beds, brown sherry, and Perpendicular Gothic.

The Duke of Devonshire on President Nasser and Anthony Eden:

> The camel that broke the straw's back.

P. G. Wodehouse's Sir Roderick Glossop on religion:

> A lay interest in matters to do with liturgical procedure is invariably a prelude to insanity.

Horace Walpole on Queen Charlotte in her later years:

> I do think the *bloom* of her ugliness is going off.

The Prince of Conti, a noted rake, when he at last became aware of his failing sexual prowess:

> It is time for me to retire. Formerly my civilities were taken for declarations of love. Now my declarations of love are taken for civilities.

W. G. Grace, apologizing for his bad fielding in old age:

> It is the ground, it's too far away.

The President of Cornell University on a proposed sporting fixture:

> I shall not permit thirty men to travel four hundred miles (to Michigan) to agitate a ball of wind.

William Faulkner on Henry James:

> One of the nicest old ladies I ever met.

Edith Sitwell and Herman Mankiewicz on modern writers:

> A lot of people writing poetry today would be better employed keeping rabbits. (Sitwell)

> 'Tell me, do you know any 75 dollar-a-week writers?'
> 'Yes, I know lots of them. but they're all making 1500 dollars a week.' (Mankiewicz)

I found one aspect of the arrangement of previous dictionaries unsympathetic to humorous quotations. It has been customary to print the quote and follow it with the contextual explanation. This is often like giving the punchline of a joke and then adding the premise. Where appropriate I have put the explanation first, for example this quotation from Thomas Gainsborough:

> *On attempting to paint two actors, David Garrick and Samuel Foote:*
>
> Rot them for a couple of rogues, they have everybody's faces but their own.

The learned editor of the *Oxford Dictionary of Quotations* has wisely written, 'Ideally, a quotation should be able to float free from its moorings, remaining detached from its original context.' However, one could compare two extracts from a page opened at random in the fourth edition; while the Wolcott Gibbs quote 'Backward ran sentences until reeled the mind' is arresting enough to stand with the subsequent note ('satirizing the style of *Time* magazine'), André Gide's sigh, '*Hugo — hélas!*' would read more entertainingly if the explanation, 'When asked who was the greatest 19th-century poet' preceded it.

I have tried to resist the temptation to admit anecdote where quotation is the brief. Lord Albemarle might have found a place in the unconscious humour section, but the preamble to his striking sentence is too long and involved:

> *The dancer Maude Allen had been accused of lesbianism in an article entitled 'The Cult of the Clitoris', and Miss Allen sued for libel in a much publicized lawsuit which caught the puzzled attention of Lord Albemarle, who complained:*
>
> I've never heard of this Greek chap Clitoris they're talking about.

However vivid the phrase may be its context is overpoweringly anecdotal. While Lord Macaulay's riposte, aged four, having had hot coffee spilt over his legs, 'Thank you, Madam, the agony is abated,' is a splendid quote preceded to its advantage by a succinct explanation.

I hope that this collection gathers together a vast number of old friends whom it would be disloyal to exclude—conscious that they will still surprise some. I am often astonished at the way an audience can pounce on an over-familiar quip by Coward or Wilde and welcome it as new-minted. It proved particularly enjoyable to hunt for less well-known quotations from established wits. Noel Coward's chestnuts are included, but also his vivid vignette (in spite of Lord Byron's warning, 'Damn description, it is always disgusting'):

> Edith Sitwell, in that great Risorgimento cape of hers, looks as though she were covering a teapot or a telephone.

Less familiar Oscar Wilde contributions include his admonishment to a waiter:

> When I ask for a watercress sandwich, I do not mean a loaf with a field in the middle of it;

his judgement on publishers:

> I suppose all publishers are untrustworthy. They certainly always look it;

and his request to his examiners in his viva at Oxford when he was asked to stop his brilliant translation of the Greek version of the New Testament:

> Oh, do let me go on, I want to see how it ends.

Sydney Smith is sharp on the incongruity of oratorio, 'How absurd to see 500 people fiddling like madmen about Israelites in the Red Sea,' and playful on two Edinburgh women hurling insults at one another across an alleyway, 'Those two women will never agree; they are arguing from different premises.' There is Whistler on the picture of his mother, 'Yes, one does like to make one's mummy just as nice as possible', and Gore Vidal on ex-President Eisenhower, 'reading a speech with his usual sense of discovery'.

Among the modern phrase-makers I enjoy: Jonathan Lynn and Antony Jay in *Yes Minister*:

> I think it will be a clash between the political will and the administrative won't.

Richard Curtis and Ben Elton in *Blackadder*:

> To you, Baldrick, the Renaissance was just something that happened to other people, wasn't it?

Keith Waterhouse in his play *Bookends*:

> Should not the Society of Indexers be known as Indexers, Society of, The?

Joseph O'Connor in his novel *Cowboys and Indians*:

> Buckingham Palace looked a vast doll's house that some bullying skinhead brother had kicked down the Mall.

Clive James writes of John McEnroe that he 'did his complete Krakatoa number', and John Osborne says of his American producer David Merrick that he 'liked writers in the way a snake likes live rabbits'.

Unlikely candidates include: Lord Tennyson's brother, introducing himself to Dante Gabriel Rossetti:

> I am Septimus, the most morbid of the Tennysons.

Rupert Murdoch, asked to explain Page 3:

> I don't know. The editor did it while I was away.

T. E. Lawrence on reading *Lady Chatterley's Lover*:

> Surely the sex business isn't worth all this damned fuss? I've met only a handful of people who cared a biscuit for it.

Samuel Beckett encouraging an actor who lamented, 'I'm failing':

> Go on failing. Only next time, try to fail better.

C. S. Lewis on desire:

> He that but looketh on a plate of ham and eggs to lust after it, hath already committed breakfast with it in his heart.

There are some new Royal quotes, often falling into the category of unconscious humour. 'Aren't we due a royalty statement?' (Charles, Prince of Wales), 'I know no person so perfectly disagreeable and even dangerous as an author' (William IV), and George V, asked which film he would like to see while convalescing, 'Anything except that damned Mouse,' which makes a change from 'Bugger Bognor.' Furthermore, I have tried to add to the files of the OUP some quotations which are less familiar. This has meant casting a wider net over, for instance, North American sources, and again I have tried to balance the quotations which demand inclusion on account of the fame of their authors—Dorothy Parker, Robert Benchley, Mark Twain, Sam Goldwyn, and S. J. Perelman ('God, whom you doubtless remember as that quaint old subordinate of General Douglas MacArthur'), with the words of modern masters. I have taken pleasure in adding:

Mary McGrory on Watergate:

> Haldeman is the only man in America in this generation who let his hair grow for a courtroom appearance.

P. J. O'Rourke on certainty:

> That happy sense of purpose people have when they are standing up for a principle they haven't really been knocked down for yet.

Bill Bryson on childhood:

> I had always thought that once you grew up you could do anything you wanted—stay up all night or eat ice-cream straight out of the container.

The film critic James Agee on *Tycoon*:

> Several tons of dynamite are set off in this picture: none of it under the right people.

Jackie Mason on the English:

> If an Englishman gets run down by a truck he apologizes to the truck.

Woody Allen, Neil Simon, Fran Lebowitz, and Russell Baker appear *passim*, and for a British angle on America, Anthony Burgess supplies, 'the US Presidency is a Tudor monarchy with telephones.' George Bush ('What's wrong with being a boring kind of guy?') and Dan Quayle supply generous helpings of unconscious humour, such as 'Space is almost infinite. As a matter of fact, we think it is infinite' (Quayle), and are convenient targets, as in 'Poor George [Bush], he can't help it—he was born with a silver foot in his mouth' (Ann Richards). Sports writers like Jimmy Cannon are rewarding on their own craft, 'Let's face it, sports writers, we're not hanging around with brain surgeons'; so, sometimes, can sportsmen be, 'If people don't want to come out to the ball park, nobody's going to stop 'em' (Yogi Berra). Canada supplies both the unconscious humour of Brian Mulroney's 'I am not denying anything I did not say,' and, at the other extreme, Robertson Davies:

> I see Canada as a country torn between a very northern, rather extraordinary, mystical spirit which it fears and its desire to present itself to the world as a Scotch banker.

Australia under Paul Keating has been developing a rich vein of humorous invective like the exchange between the Prime Minister and his opponent John Hewson. Keating's comment:

> [John Hewson] is simply a shiver looking for a spine to run up,

is countered by Hewson with:

> I decided the worst thing you can call Paul Keating, quite frankly, is Paul Keating.

Reflecting on the insularity of his homeland, Clive James has written:

> A broad school of Australian writing has based itself on the assumption that Australia not only has a history worth bothering about, but that all the history worth bothering about happened in Australia.

To verify this range of information would not have been possible without the diligent and imaginative work of the Oxford Dictionary Department researchers. However, the responsibility for the taste and the accuracy must be mine, the only caveat being Simon Strunsky's, 'Famous remarks are very seldom quoted correctly.' Above all it is my sense of humour which conditions the final choice and my regret if your favourite humorous quotation is not recorded here or if you pass too many entries without amusement.

NED SHERRIN

August 1994

How to Use the Dictionary

The Oxford Dictionary of Humorous Quotations is organized by themes, such as
**Actors and Acting, The Family, Food and Drink, Love, Travel and
Exploration, The Weather,** and **Writers and Writing**. The themes are placed
in alphabetical order, and within each theme the quotations are arranged
chronologically.

The themes have been chosen to reflect as wide a range of subjects as
possible. Themes such as **Death, Life and Living,** and **Success and Failure**
emphasize the general rather than the particular, but categories such as
Description, Last Words, People and Personalities, and **Towns and Cities** have
a wider coverage of quotations relevant to specific people, places, and events.

Related topics may be covered by a single theme, such as **Behaviour
and Etiquette** and **Crime and Punishment,** and linked opposites may also be
grouped in a single antithetical theme, such as **Heaven and Hell, Trust and
Treachery,** and **Truth and Lies**. A cross-reference from the second element of
the pair appears in the appropriate place in the alphabetic sequence both in
the main text and in the List of Themes, so that **Lies** *see Truth and Lies* will be
found to precede the entry for **Life and Living**.

Where themes are closely related, 'See also' references are given at
the head of a section, immediately following the theme title and preceding
the quotations. **Actors and Acting** thus precedes the direction *See also The
Theatre,* and the heading **The Family** is followed by *See also Children, Parents*.

Each quotation has a marginal note giving the name of the author to
whom the quotation is attributed; dates of birth and death (where known)
are given. In general, the authors' names are given in the form by which
they are best known, so that we have 'Saki' rather than 'H. H. Munro'. If
the authorship is unknown, 'Anonymous' appears.

A source note, usually including the specific date of the quotation,
follows the author information. When the date is uncertain or unknown, and
the quotation cannot be related to a particular event, the author's date of
death has been used to determine the place of the quotation within its theme.
Quotations which are in general currency but which are not at present
traceable to a specific source are indicated by 'attributed' in the source note;
quotations which are popularly attributed to an author but whose
authenticity is doubted are indicated by a note such as 'perhaps apocryphal'.

Contextual information regarded as essential to a full appreciation of
the quotation precedes the relevant text in an italicized note; information
seen as providing helpful amplification follows in the source note.

Allocation of a quotation to an individual theme is inevitably
subjective, but the keyword index makes provision for tracing specific items
other than by theme titles. Citations by named authors may similarly be

traced via the author index. In each case, references show the theme name, sometimes in a shortened form (**Satisfaction** for **Satisfaction and Discontent**; **Theatre** for **The Theatre**), followed by the number of the quotation within the theme: 'Science 7' therefore means the seventh quotation within the theme **Science and Technology**.

List of Themes

Actors and Acting
Advertising
Alcohol
America and Americans
Anger
Animals *see Birds and Animals*
Appearance
Architecture
Argument
Aristocracy
The Armed Forces
Art and Artists
Autobiography *see Biography and Autobiography*

Behaviour and Etiquette
Betting and Gambling
The Bible
Biography and Autobiography
Birds and Animals
The Body
Books
Bores and Boredom
Broadcasting and Television
Bureaucracy
Business and Commerce

Catch-phrases *see Comedy Routines and Catch-phrases*
Censorship
Certainty and Doubt
Character
Children
Choice
Christmas
Cinema and Films
Cities *see Towns and Cities*
Class
Comedy Routines and Catch-phrases
Commerce *see Business and Commerce*

Conversation
Countries and Peoples
The Country
Crime and Punishment
Critics and Criticism

Dance
Death
Debt
Democracy
Description
Despair *see Hope and Despair*
Diaries
Dictionaries
Diplomacy
Discontent *see Satisfaction and Discontent*
Doubt *see Certainty and Doubt*
Dreams *see Sleep and Dreams*
Dress *see Fashion and Dress*
Drink *see Food and Drink*

Economics
Education
Enemies *see Friends and Enemies*
England and the English
Environment *see Nature and the Environment*
Epitaphs
Etiquette *see Behaviour and Etiquette*
Exploration *see Travel and Exploration*

Failure *see Success and Failure*
Fame
The Family
Fashion and Dress
Films *see Cinema and Films*
Flattery *see Praise and Flattery*
Food and Drink
Foolishness and Ignorance
Friends and Enemies
The Future

The Oxford Dictionary of
Humorous
Quotations

Actors and Acting See also *The Theatre*

1 I could play Ercles rarely, or a part to tear a cat in, to make all split.

William Shakespeare 1564–1616: *A Midsummer Night's Dream* (1595–6)

2 I will roar you as gently as any sucking dove; I will roar you as 'twere any nightingale.

William Shakespeare 1564–1616: *A Midsummer Night's Dream* (1595–6)

3 The best actors in the world, either for tragedy, comedy, history, pastoral, pastoral-comical, historical-pastoral, tragical-historical, tragical-comical-historical-pastoral, scene individable, or poem unlimited.

William Shakespeare 1564–1616: *Hamlet* (1601)

4 On the stage he was natural, simple, affecting;
'Twas only that when he was off he was acting.

Oliver Goldsmith 1730–74: of David Garrick; *Retaliation* (1774)

5 I wish sir, you would practise this without me. I can't stay dying here all night.

Richard Brinsley Sheridan 1751–1816: *The Critic* (1779)

6 Language was not powerful enough to describe the infant phenomenon.

Charles Dickens 1812–70: *Nicholas Nickleby* (1839)

7 She's the only sylph I ever saw, who could stand upon one leg, and play the tambourine on her other knee, like a sylph.

Charles Dickens 1812–70: *Nicholas Nickleby* (1839)

Of Creston Clarke as King Lear:
8 He played the King as though under momentary apprehension that someone else was about to play the ace.

Eugene Field 1850–95: review attributed to Field; in *Denver Tribune* c.1880

Of Irving as Mephistopheles in Goethe's Faust:
9 The actor, of course, at moments presents to the eye a remarkably sinister figure. He strikes us, however, as superficial—a terrible fault for an archfiend.

Henry James 1843–1916: *The Scenic Art* (1948)

10 My dear fellow, I never saw anything so funny in my life, and yet it was not in the least bit vulgar.

W. S. Gilbert 1836–1911: of Beerbohm Tree's Hamlet (1892); D. Bispham *A Quaker Singer's Recollections* (1920)

11 I must somewhat tardily acknowledge an invitation to witness a performance at the Royalty Theatre by a Miss Hope Booth, a young lady who cannot sing, dance or speak, but whose appearance suggests that she might profitably spend three or four years in learning these arts, which are useful on the stage.

George Bernard Shaw 1856–1950: *Our Theatre in the Nineties* (1932); review 23 March 1895

12 It is greatly to Mrs Patrick Campbell's credit that, bad as the play was, her acting was worse.

George Bernard Shaw 1856–1950: *Our Theatre in the Nineties* (1932); review of Sardou *Fedora* 1 June 1895

13 [Ellen Terry] never *was* an actress, in the strict sense of the word—only a delightful sort of a creature, symbolizing (what one imagines to have been) Merrie England in the time of Elizabeth.

Max Beerbohm 1872–1956: letter 20 March 1906

To an over-genteel actress in an Egyptian drama:
14 Oh my God! Remember you're in Egypt. The *skay* is only seen in Kensington.

Herbert Beerbohm Tree 1852–1917: M. Peters *Mrs Pat* (1984)

To a motley collection of American females, assembled to play ladies-in-waiting to a queen:

15 Ladies, just a little more virginity, if you don't mind.

Herbert Beerbohm Tree 1852–1917: Alexander Woollcott *Shouts and Murmurs* (1923)

16 I'm out of a job. London wants flappers, and I can't flap.

Mrs Patrick Campbell 1865–1940: of the theatre of 1927; Margot Peters *Mrs Pat* (1984)

17 I acted so tragic the house rose like magic,
The audience yelled 'You're sublime.'
They made me a present of Mornington Crescent
They threw it a brick at a time.

W. F. Hargreaves 1846–1919: 'The Night I Appeared as Macbeth' (1922)

18 This Iago was obviously an intellectual, and refreshingly unlike the usual furtive dog-stealer who would not impose upon the most trustful old lady, not to mention an experienced man of affairs like Othello.

James Agate 1877–1947: of Neil Porter's Iago in 1927; *Brief Chronicles* (1943)

19 This Othello had the naturalness, and the dignity, and the mind of a highly educated Moor, and not of a cultivated English gentleman who wakes up one morning to find that his skin has unexpectedly turned black.

James Agate 1877–1947: of Balliol Holloway's Othello in 1927; *Brief Chronicles* (1943)

Of Katharine Hepburn at a Broadway first night:

20 She ran the whole gamut of the emotions from A to B, and put some distance between herself and a more experienced colleague [Alison Skipworth] lest she catch acting from her.

Dorothy Parker 1893–1967: at the first night of *The Lake* (1933); attributed

The daughter of Sybil Thorndike and Lewis Casson explaining to a telephone enquiry why neither of her charitably inclined parents was at home:

21 Daddy is reading Shakespeare Sonnets to the blind and Mummy's playing Shakespeare to the lepers.

Anne Casson: recounted by Emlyn Williams; James Harding *Emlyn Williams* (1987)

22 Don't put your daughter on the stage, Mrs Worthington,
Don't put your daughter on the stage,
One look at her bandy legs should prove
She hasn't got a chance,
In addition to which
The son of a bitch
Can neither sing nor dance.

Noël Coward 1899–1973: 'Mrs Worthington' (1935)

To Judith Anderson, playing Gertrude to John Gielgud's Hamlet in 1936:

23 Why do you sit on the bed? Only housemaids sit on the bed.

Mrs Patrick Campbell 1865–1940: Margot Peters *Mrs Pat* (1984)

24 She's such a nice woman. If you knew her you'd even admire her acting.

Mrs Patrick Campbell 1865–1940: of another actress; James Agate diary 6 May 1937

25 Tallulah Bankhead barged down the Nile last night as Cleopatra—and sank.

John Mason Brown 1900–69: in *New York Post* 11 November 1937

To Lilian Braithwaite who was playing a part based on Mrs Patrick Campbell, while Mrs Pat herself was about to go off on tour:

26 I hear you are a perfect *tour de force* playing me! And here I am forced to tour!

Mrs Patrick Campbell 1865–1940: Robin May *The Wit of the Theatre* (1969)

27 Tallulah [Bankhead] is always skating on thin ice. Everyone wants to be there when it breaks.

Mrs Patrick Campbell 1865–1940: in *The Times* 13 December 1968

28 She is the great lady of the American stage. Her voice is so beautiful that you won't understand a word she says.

Mrs Patrick Campbell 1865–1940: of another actress; James Agate diary 6 May 1937

29 To control and keep together a troupe of amateur actors is to weave each night a Penelope's web. Unlike professionals, who are seldom prevented from appearing, some of our company were always laid low with unexpected diseases or overwhelmed by accident.

Cecil Beaton 1904–80: diary March 1940

30 He wore a really wonderful wig apparently made out of a discarded tea-cosy, and later a crown like the business part of a permanent-wave machine.

James Agate 1877–1947: review of Ernest Milton's *King John* (1941); *Brief Chronicles* (1943)

Shakespeare is trying to make a start on Love's Labour Won, *but Burbage interrupts him:*

31 'I've been thinking,' he said, 'I'd like to play a Dane— young, intellectual—I see him pale, vacillating, but above everything sad and prone to soliloquy.' 'I know,' said Shakespeare. 'Introspective.'

Caryl Brahms 1901–82 and **S. J. Simon** 1904–48: *No Bed for Bacon* (1941)

32 My only regret in the theatre is that I could never sit out front and watch me.

John Barrymore 1882–1942: Eddie Cantor *The Way I See It* (1959)

33 She was like a sinking ship firing on the rescuers.

Alexander Woollcott 1887–1943: of Mrs Patrick Campbell; *While Rome Burns* (1944) 'The First Mrs Tanqueray'

34 Acting is merely the art of keeping a large group of people from coughing.

Ralph Richardson 1902–83: in *New York Herald Tribune* 19 May 1946

35 One day they may tell you you will not go far,
That night you open and there you are.
Next day on your dressing room
They hang a star!
Let's go on with the show!

Irving Berlin 1888–1989: 'There's No Business Like Show Business' (1946)

36 I thought he was elderly, a cautionary-tale-finger- wagging-oracular Hamlet; rather like a university extension lecturer; a Hamlet in invisible pince-nez.

Neville Cardus 1889–1975: of Forbes-Robertson as Hamlet; *Autobiography* (1947)

37 This Rosalind was a gay and giddy creature—loads of fun, game for any jape, rather like a popular head girl— but a tiring companion, I felt, after a long day.

Kenneth Tynan 1927–80: review of *As You Like It* in 1952; *Curtains* (1961)

38 Shakespeare is so tiring. You never get a chance to sit down unless you're a king.

Josephine Hull 1886–1957: in *Time* 16 November 1953

39 Miss (Maureen) Stapleton played the part as though she had not yet signed her contract with the producer.

George Jean Nathan 1882–1958: review of *The Emperor's Clothes* in 1953; Diana Rigg *No Turn Unstoned* (1982)

40 As Lavinia, Vivien Leigh receives the news that she is about to be ravished on her husband's corpse with little more than the mild annoyance of one who would have preferred Dunlopillo.

Kenneth Tynan 1927–80: review of *Titus Andronicus* in 1955; *Curtains* (1961)

41 As Virgilia in *Coriolanus* she yearns so hungrily that I longed to throw her a fish.

Kenneth Tynan 1927–80: of Claire Bloom in 1955; *Curtains* (1961)

42 Richard Briers played Hamlet like a demented typewriter.

W. A. Darlington 1890–1979: review of a RADA production; Diana Rigg *No Turn Unstoned* (1982)

43 The key to Beatrice Lillie's success is that she ignores her audience. This is an act of daring that amounts to revolution.

Kenneth Tynan 1927–80: in *Holiday* September 1956

44 An actor is a kind of a guy who if you ain't talking about him ain't listening.

George Glass 1910–84: Bob Thomas *Brando* (1973); said to be quoted frequently by Marlon Brando

45 Her affectionate scenes with a young nephew are especially sinister, it being apparent that, given the smallest textual encouragement, Miss Dresdel could and would bite her little friend's arm off at the elbow. It is to the Eumenides and not the humanities that this intimidating actress should confine herself.

Kenneth Tynan 1927–80: of Sonia Dresdel in *Doctor Jo* (1956); Diana Rigg *No Turn Unstoned* (1982)

Gogarty's patient Michael Scott, then an actor, coming to on the operating table, tried weakly to indicate that he was conscious:
46 Nurse, kindly put your hand over that man's mouth; we are not interested in an actor's subconscious.

Oliver St John Gogarty 1878–1957: Ulick O'Connor *Oliver St John Gogarty* (1964)

47 But I have a go, lady, don't I? I 'ave a go. I do.

John Osborne 1929– : *The Entertainer* (1957)

48 Let me know where you are next week! I'll come and see you.

John Osborne 1929– : *The Entertainer* (1957); last lines

49 This Thane of Cawdor would be unnerved by Banquo's valet, never mind Banquo's ghost.

Alan Brien 1925– : of Michael Hordern in *Macbeth* in 1959; Diana Rigg *No Turn Unstoned* (1982)

50 He certainly takes the audience into his confidence, but the process seems to exclude from his confidence everyone else in the cast...[He] behaves throughout in a manner that has nothing to do with acting, although it perfectly hits off the demeanour of a rapscallion uncle dressed up to entertain the children at a Christmas party.

Kenneth Tynan 1927–80: of Charles Laughton as Lear in 1959; *A View of the English Stage* (1975)

51 Massey won't be satisfied until he's assassinated.

George S. Kaufman 1889–1961: on Raymond Massey's success in playing Lincoln; Howard Teichman *George S. Kaufman* (1973)

On the Burton-Taylor Private Lives *in* 1964:
52 He's miscast and she's Miss Taylor.

Emlyn Williams 1905–87: James Harding *Emlyn Williams* (1987)

53 She [Edith Evans] took her curtain calls as though she had just been un-nailed from the cross.

Noël Coward 1899–1973: diary 25 October 1964

54 We're *actors*—we're the opposite of people!...Think, in your head, *now*, think of the most...*private*...*secret*... *intimate* thing you have ever done secure in the knowledge of its privacy...Are you thinking of it?... *Well, I saw you do it!*

Tom Stoppard 1937– : *Rosencrantz and Guildenstern Are Dead* (1967)

When asked to say something terrifying during rehearsals for Peter Brook's Oedipus *in* 1968:
55 We open in two weeks.

John Gielgud 1904– : Peter Hay *Theatrical Anecdotes* (1987)

56 CLAUDETTE COLBERT: I knew these lines backwards last night.
    NOËL COWARD: And that's just the way you're saying them this morning.

Noël Coward 1899–1973: Cole Lesley *The Life of Noel Coward* (1976)

57 LAURENCE HARVEY: Will you call me, Noël?
    NOËL COWARD: I certainly will—many things.

Noël Coward 1899–1973: William Marchant *The Privilege of his Company* (1975)

58 ALISON SKIPWORTH: You forget I've been an actress for forty years.
    MAE WEST: Don't worry, dear. I'll keep your secret.

Mae West 1892–1980: G. Eells and S. Musgrove *Mae West* (1989)

On being refused membership of an exclusive golf-club:
59 I'm *not* an actor, and I enclose my press cuttings to prove it.

Victor Mature 1915– : Ned Sherrin *Cutting Edge* (1984)

60 Like a rat up a rope.

Coral Browne 1913–91: of an over-busy actor; attributed

61 Like acting with 210 pounds of condemned veal.

Coral Browne 1913–91: of a dull actor; attributed

62 Dear Ingrid—speaks five languages and can't act in any of them.

John Gielgud 1904– : of Ingrid Bergman; Ronald Harwood *The Ages of Gielgud* (1984); attributed

On the part of Lear:
63 When you've the strength for it, you're too young; when you've the age you're too old. It's a bugger, isn't it?

Laurence Olivier 1907–89: in *Sunday Telegraph* 4 May 1986

64 I made a great hit in *Macbeth* as the messenger because I took the precaution of running three times round the playground before I made my entrance so that I could deliver the news in a state of exhaustion.

Alec Guinness 1914– : on a school production; John Mortimer *Character Parts* (1986)

65 He brought to every one of his roles this quality of needing the money.

Stephen Fry 1957– and **Hugh Laurie**: *A Bit More Fry and Laurie* (1991)

Advertising

1 The explanation of intuition is the same as that of advertisement: tell a man ten thousand times that Pears Soap is good for the complexion and eventually he will have an intuitive certainty of the fact.

W. Somerset Maugham 1874–1965: *A Writer's Notebook* (1949) written in 1901

2 Advertising may be described as the science of arresting human intelligence long enough to get money from it.

Stephen Leacock 1869–1944: *Garden of Folly* (1924)

3 I think that I shall never see
A billboard lovely as a tree.
Perhaps, unless the billboards fall,
I'll never see a tree at all.

Ogden Nash 1902–71: 'Song of the Open Road' (1933)

4 Advertising is the rattling of a stick inside a swill bucket.

George Orwell 1903–50: attributed

5 [Orson Welles] has a voice of bottled thunder, so deeply encasked that one thinks of those liquor advertisements which boast that not a drop is sold till it's seven years old.

Kenneth Tynan 1927–80: review of *Moby Dick* in 1955; *A View of the English Stage* (1975)

On a consultant who had given a paper 'Advertising in Medicine':
6 It was like listening to a loudspeaker blaring out 'Mum's the word'.

Oliver St John Gogarty 1878–1957: Ulick O'Connor *Oliver St John Gogarty* (1964)

7 The consumer isn't a moron; she is your wife.

David Ogilvy 1911– : *Confessions of an Advertising Man* (1963)

8 While you were out your exterminator called.

Anonymous: heading of leaflet left in a New York letter-box; Sylvia Townsend Warner letter to David Garnett, 12 May 1967

9 Blurbs that appear on the back cover and in the advertisements recommending the book in glowing terms...are written by friends of the author who haven't read the book but owe the poor guy a favour.

Art Buchwald 1925– : *I Never Danced at the White House* (1974)

10 The cheap contractions and revised spellings of the advertising world which have made the beauty of the written word almost unrecognizable—surely any society that permits the substitution of 'kwik' for 'quick' and 'e.z.' for 'easy' does not deserve Shakespeare, Eliot or Michener.

Russell Baker 1925– : column in *New York Times*; Ned Sherrin *Cutting Edge* (1984)

11 Society drives people crazy with lust and calls it advertising.

John Lahr 1941– : in *Guardian* 2 August 1989

Asked why he had made a commercial for American Express:
12 To pay for my American Express.

Peter Ustinov 1921– : in *Ned Sherrin in his Anecdotage* (1993)

Alcohol   See also *Food and Drink*

*The Abbot of Westminster had made a nuisance of himself by
demanding two tuns of wine in payment of a disputed debt:*

1 The Abbot of Westminster is sick...I would he had a tun
of wine, and the cask, in his belly!

John Husee c.1506–48: letter to
Lord Lisle, 21 August 1537, in *Lisle
Letters* (1985)

2 Doth it not show vilely in me to desire small beer?

William Shakespeare 1564–1616:
Henry IV, Part 2 (1597)

3 PORTER: Drink, sir, is a great provoker of three things.
MACDUFF: What three things does drink especially
provoke?
PORTER: Marry, sir, nose-painting, sleep, and urine.
Lechery, sir, it provokes, and unprovokes; it provokes
the desire, but it takes away the performance.

William Shakespeare 1564–1616:
Macbeth (1606)

4 And he that will go to bed sober,
Falls with the leaf still in October.

John Fletcher 1579–1625: *The
Bloody Brother, or Rollo Duke of
Normandy* (with Ben Jonson and
others, performed c.1616)

5 Best while you have it use your breath,
There is no drinking after death.

John Fletcher 1579–1625: *The
Bloody Brother, or Rollo Duke of
Normandy* (with Ben Jonson and
others, performed c.1616)

6 When at dinner and supper, I drank, I know not how, of
my own accord, so much wine, that I was even almost
foxed and my head ached all night. So home.

Samuel Pepys 1633–1703: diary
29 September 1661

Of claret:
7 It would be port if it could.

Richard Bentley 1662–1742: R. C.
Jebb *Bentley* (1902)

8 A bumper of good liquor
Will end a contest quicker
Than justice, judge, or vicar.

Richard Brinsley Sheridan
1751–1816: *The Duenna* (1775)

9 Claret is the liquor for boys; port, for men; but he who
aspires to be a hero (smiling) must drink brandy.

Samuel Johnson 1709–84: James
Boswell *Life of Samuel Johnson* (1791)
7 April 1779

10 It occasionally fell to my lot to convey him home—no
sinecure—for he was so tipsy that I was obliged to put
on his cocked hat for him—to be sure it tumbled off
again and I was not myself so sober as to be able to pick
it up again.

Lord Byron 1788–1824: of Richard
Brinsley Sheridan; 'Detached
Thoughts' 15 October 1821

11 It's my opinion, sir, that this meeting is drunk, sir!

Charles Dickens 1812–70: *Pickwick
Papers* (1837)

12 Champagne certainly gives one werry gentlemanly ideas,
but for a continuance, I don't know but I should prefer
mild hale.

R. S. Surtees 1805–64: *Jorrocks's
Jaunts and Jollities* (1838)

13 'Mrs Harris,' I says, 'leave the bottle on the chimley-
piece, and don't ask me to take none, but let me put my
lips to it when I am so dispoged.'

Charles Dickens 1812–70: *Martin
Chuzzlewit* (1844)

14 Therefore I *do* require it, which I makes confession, to be brought reg'lar and draw'd mild.

Charles Dickens 1812–70: *Martin Chuzzlewit* (1844)

15 'I rather like bad wine,' said Mr Mountchesney; 'one gets so bored with good wine.'

Benjamin Disraeli 1804–81: *Sybil* (1845)

16 Licker talks mighty loud w'en it git loose fum de jug.

Joel Chandler Harris 1848–1908: *Uncle Remus: His Songs and His Sayings* (1880) 'Plantation Proverbs'

17 We drink one another's healths, and spoil our own.

Jerome K. Jerome 1859–1927: *Idle Thoughts of an Idle Fellow* (1886)

18 I'm only a beer teetotaller, not a champagne teetotaller.

George Bernard Shaw 1856–1950: *Candida* (1898)

19 R-E-M-O-R-S-E!
Those dry Martinis did the work for me;
Last night at twelve I felt immense,
Today I feel like thirty cents.
My eyes are bleared, my coppers hot,
I'll try to eat, but I cannot.
It is no time for mirth and laughter,
The cold, grey dawn of the morning after.

George Ade 1866–1944: *The Sultan of Sulu* (1903)

20 Alcohol is a very necessary article...It makes life bearable to millions of people who could not endure their existence if they were quite sober. It enables Parliament to do things at eleven at night that no sane person would do at eleven in the morning.

George Bernard Shaw 1856–1950: *Major Barbara* (1907)

21 I have begged and stolen; and if I never drank, that was only an application of the principle of division of labour to the Shaw clan; for several members of it drank enough for ten.

George Bernard Shaw 1856–1950: preface to *The Autobiography of a Super-tramp* (1908)

22 There is wan thing, an' on'y wan thing, to be said in favour iv dhrink, an' that is that it has caused manny a lady to be loved that otherwise might've died single.

Finley Peter Dunne 1867–1936: *Mr. Dooley Says* (1910)

23 Just a wee deoch-an-doris,
Just a wee yin, that's a'.
Just a wee deoch-an-doris,
Before we gang awa'.
There's a wee wifie waitin',
In a wee but-an-ben;
If you can say
'It's a braw bricht moonlicht nicht',
Ye're a' richt, ye ken.

R. F. Morrison: 'Just a Wee Deoch-an-Doris' (1911); popularized by Harry Lauder

24 There is no such thing [as a Temperance Hotel], you might as well talk of a celibate brothel.

Robert Yelverton Tyrrell 1844–1914: Ulick O'Connor *Oliver St John Gogarty* (1964)

25 And Noah he often said to his wife when he sat down to dine,
'I don't care where the water goes if it doesn't get into the wine.'

G. K. Chesterton 1874–1936: 'Wine and Water' (1914)

26 There are two things that will be believed of any man whatsoever, and one of them is that he has taken to drink.

Booth Tarkington 1869–1946: *Penrod* (1914)

27 Gin was mother's milk to her.

George Bernard Shaw 1856–1950: *Pygmalion* (1916)

28 Let's get out of these wet clothes and into a dry Martini.

Anonymous: line coined in the 1920s by Robert Benchley's press agent and adopted by Mae West in *Every Day's a Holiday* (1937 film)

29 It was my Uncle George who discovered that alcohol was a food well in advance of medical thought.

P. G. Wodehouse 1881–1975: *The Inimitable Jeeves* (1923)

30 Often Daddy sat up very late working on a case of Scotch.

Robert Benchley 1889–1945: *Pluck and Luck* (1925)

31 But I'm not so think as you drunk I am.

J. C. Squire 1884–1958: 'Ballade of Soporific Absorption' (1931)

32 Candy
Is dandy
But liquor
Is quicker.

Ogden Nash 1902–71: 'Reflections on Ice-breaking' (1931)

33 One evening in October, when I was one-third sober,
An' taking home a 'load' with manly pride;
My poor feet began to stutter, so I lay down in the gutter,
And a pig came up an' lay down by my side;
Then we sang 'It's all fair weather when good fellows get together,'
Till a lady passing by was heard to say:
'You can tell a man who "boozes" by the company he chooses'
And the pig got up and slowly walked away.

Benjamin Hapgood Burt 1880–1950: 'The Pig Got Up and Slowly Walked Away' (1933)

34 Prohibition makes you want to cry into your beer and denies you the beer to cry into.

Don Marquis 1878–1937: *Sun Dial Time* (1936)

35 It's a naïve domestic Burgundy without any breeding, but I think you'll be amused by its presumption.

James Thurber 1894–1961: cartoon caption in *New Yorker* 27 March 1937

36 At the present moment, the whole Fleet's lit up. When I say 'lit up', I mean lit up by fairy lamps.

Thomas Woodroofe 1899–1978: engaged to make a live outside broadcast of the Spithead Review, 20 May 1937, Woodroofe was so overcome by his reunion with many old Naval colleagues that the celebrations sabotaged his ability to commentate.

37 You can always tell that the crash is coming when I start getting tender about Our Dumb Friends. Three highballs and I think I'm St Francis of Assisi.

Dorothy Parker 1893–1967: *Here Lies* (1939)

38 Some weasel took the cork out of my lunch.

W. C. Fields 1880–1946: *You Can't Cheat an Honest Man* (1939 film)

39 So make it another old-fashioned, please.
Leave out the cherry,
Leave out the orange,
Leave out the bitters,
Just make it a straight rye!

Cole Porter 1891–1964: 'Make it
Another Old-Fashioned, Please' (1940)

40 At Dirty Dick's and Sloppy Joe's
We drank our liquor straight,
Some went upstairs with Margery,
And some, alas, with Kate.

W. H. Auden 1907–73: 'The Sea
and the Mirror' (1944)

*On being told that the particular drink he was consuming was slow
poison:*
41 So who's in a hurry?

Robert Benchley 1889–1945:
Nathaniel Benchley *Robert Benchley*
(1955)

42 A woman drove me to drink and I never even had the
courtesy to thank her.

W. C. Fields 1880–1946: attributed

43 Anybody who hates dogs and loves whisky can't be all
bad.

W. C. Fields 1880–1946: attributed

44 I exercise strong self-control. I never drink anything
stronger than gin before breakfast.

W. C. Fields 1880–1946: attributed

45 I always keep a supply of stimulant handy in case I see
a snake—which I also keep handy.

W. C. Fields 1880–1946: Corey
Ford *Time of Laughter* (1970);
attributed

46 Love makes the world go round? Not at all. Whisky
makes it go round twice as fast.

Compton Mackenzie 1883–1972:
Whisky Galore (1947)

47 Somewhere in the limbo which divides perfect sobriety
from mild intoxication.

Cyril Asquith 1890–1954: J. A.
Gere and John Sparrow (eds.) *Geoffrey
Madan's Notebooks* (1981)

48 Take the juice of two quarts of whisky.

Eddie Condon 1905–73:
recommended hangover cure; in *New
York Sunday News* 10 June 1951

49 A good general rule is to state that the bouquet is better
than the taste, and vice versa.

Stephen Potter 1900–69: on wine-
tasting; *One-Upmanship* (1952)

50 [An alcoholic:] A man you don't like who drinks as
much as you do.

Dylan Thomas 1914–53:
Constantine Fitzgibbon *Life of Dylan
Thomas* (1965)

51 From the bathing machine came a din
As of jollification within;
It was heard far and wide,
And the incoming tide
Had a definite flavour of gin.

Edward Gorey 1925– : *The Listing
Attic* (1954)

52 Sometimes I have a sherry before dinner.

Charlie Parker 1920–55: a notable
understatement; Bill Crow *Jazz
Anecdotes* (1990)

53 I am prepared to admit some merit in every alcoholic
beverage ever devised by the incomparable brain of man,
and drink them all when the occasions are suitable—
wine with meat, the hard liquors when my so-called soul

H. L. Mencken 1880–1956:
Minority Report (1956)

languishes, beer to let me down gently of an evening. In other words, I am omnibibulous, or, more simply, ombibulous.

54 The Lord above made liquor for temptation
To see if man could turn away from sin.
The Lord above made liquor for temptation—but
With a little bit of luck,
With a little bit of luck,
When temptation comes you'll give right in!

Alan Jay Lerner 1918–86: 'With a Little Bit of Luck' (1956)

55 There is no such thing as a small whisky.

Oliver St John Gogarty 1878–1957: attributed

56 Poe...was perhaps the first great nonstop literary drinker of the American nineteenth century. He made the indulgences of Coleridge and De Quincey seem like a bit of mischief in the kitchen with the cooking sherry.

James Thurber 1894–1961: *Alarms and Diversions* (1957)

57 I don't drink liquor. I don't like it. It makes me feel good.

Oscar Levant 1906–72: in *Time* 5 May 1958

58 A man shouldn't fool with booze until he's fifty; then he's a damn fool if he doesn't.

William Faulkner 1897–1962: James M. Webb and A. Wigfall Green *William Faulkner of Oxford* (1965)

59 If one glass of stout on a Sunday night is not enough, his spiritual home is the bodega.

J. B. Morton 1893–1975: M. Frayn *The Best of Beachcomber* (1963)

60 I have taken more out of alcohol than alcohol has taken out of me.

Winston Churchill 1874–1965: Quentin Reynolds *By Quentin Reynolds* (1964)

61 Was 1 a good year?

Burt Shevelove 1915–82 and **Larry Gelbart** ?1928– : *A Funny Thing Happened on the Way to the Forum* (1962)

62 Oh, I was down by Manly Pier
Drinking tubes of ice-cold beer
With a bucket full of prawns upon me knee.
But when I'd swallowed the last prawn
I had a technicolour yawn
And I chundered in the old Pacific sea.

Barry Humphries 1934– : 'Chunder Down Under' (1964)

On the water content of a glass of whiskey:
63 True, it is nearly impossible to avoid absorbing water in one form or another. But are you quite sane to be paying four shillings for a modest glasheen of it?

Flann O'Brien 1911–66: *Myles Away from Dublin* (1990)

64 One more drink and I'd have been under the host.

Dorothy Parker 1893–1967: Howard Teichman *George S. Kaufman* (1973)

65 An admirable man, who puts down half a bottle of whisky a day and has two convictions for drunken driving, but otherwise a pillar of society.

Alan Bennett 1934– : *Getting On* (1972)

When seriously ill and given a blood transfusion:
66 This must be Fats Waller's blood. I'm getting high.

Eddie Condon 1905–73: Bill Crow *Jazz Anecdotes* (1990)

On being invited by a friend to dine at a Middle Eastern restaurant:

67 The aftertaste of foreign food spoils the clean, pure flavour of gin for hours.

Eddie Condon 1905–73: Bill Crow *Jazz Anecdotes* (1990)

68 A Mr Dewar from somewhere in the British Isles was also in the studio at the time, very welcome indeed, although exhausted at the end of the ceremony.

Eddie Condon 1905–73: record album note; Bill Crow *Jazz Anecdotes* (1990)

69 BRINDLEY: It does say Burgundy on the bottle.
MARKS: It's the old wine ramp, vicar! Cheapish, reddish and Spanish.

Tom Stoppard 1937– : *Where Are They Now?* (1973)

70 He's a terrific drinker. All day. The potting shed's full of his empties. He says they're for weed killer but he's got enough there to defoliate the whole of Sussex.

Alan Ayckbourn 1939– : *Round and Round the Garden* (1975)

71 There's also parsnip or dandelion but this seems to have a slightly better bouquet. The dandelion's all right but I lost the use of one side of my face for about half an hour after I drunk it.

Alan Ayckbourn 1939– : *Table Manners* (1975)

72 Heineken refreshes the parts other beers cannot reach.

Terry Lovelock: slogan for Heineken lager, 1975 onwards

73 You're not drunk if you can lie on the floor without holding on.

Dean Martin 1917– : Paul Dickson *Official Rules* (1978)

74 Sure I eat what I advertise. Sure I eat Wheaties for breakfast. A good bowl of Wheaties with Bourbon can't be beat.

Dizzy Dean: a baseball star's comment; in *Guardian* 23 December 1978 'Sports Quotes of the Year'

75 Watlington, which combined the distinction of being the smallest town in England with having more pubs per head of the population than I believed possible.

John Mortimer 1923– : *Clinging to the Wreckage* (1982)

76 The teacher I most wanted to emulate, however, was single, drank wine and had been gassed in World War I. Of his three admirable traits, there was only one I wanted to copy, and sure enough, to this day, I love the sound of a popping cork.

Russell Baker 1925– . column in *New York Times*; Ned Sherrin *Cutting Edge* (1984)

77 'I've got some wine...' 'Very nice...I wonder how they got the cat to sit on the bottle.'

Stephen Fry 1957– : *The Liar* (1992)

78 I felt that the assortment of tablets that I had been given may have been mis-prescribed, since they seemed to interfere with the pleasant effects of alcohol. In the interests of my health, therefore, I stopped taking them.

Barry Humphries 1934– : *More Please* (1992)

America and Americans See also *Countries and Peoples, Places*

1 America is a model of force and freedom and moderation—with all the coarseness and rudeness of its people.

Lord Byron 1788–1824: letter 12 October 1821

2 I would rather...have a nod from an American, than a snuff-box from an Emperor.

Lord Byron 1788–1824: letter 8 June 1822

3 MRS ALLONBY: They say, Lady Hunstanton, that when good Americans die they go to Paris.

Oscar Wilde 1854–1900: *A Woman of No Importance* (1893)

LADY HUNSTANTON: Indeed? And when bad Americans die,
where do they go to?
LORD ILLINGWORTH: Oh, they go to America.

4 The youth of America is their oldest tradition. It has been
going on now for three hundred years.

Oscar Wilde 1854–1900: *A Woman of No Importance* (1893)

5 Nearly all th' most foolish people in th' counthry an'
manny iv th' wisest goes to Noo York. Th' wise people
ar-re there because th' foolish wint first. That's th' way
th' wise men make a livin'.

Finley Peter Dunne 1867–1936: *Mr. Dooley's Opinions* (1902)

6 Father's name was Hezikiah,
Mother's name was Anna Maria,
Yanks, through and through!
Red White and Blue.

George M. Cohan 1878–1942: 'Yankee Doodle Dandy' (1904)

7 And this is good old Boston,
The home of the bean and the cod,
Where the Lowells talk to the Cabots
And the Cabots talk only to God.

John Collins Bossidy 1860–1928: verse spoken at Holy Cross College alumni dinner in Boston, Massachusetts, 1910

8 He held, too, in his enlightened way, that Americans
have a perfect right to exist. But he did often find himself
wishing Mr Rhodes had not enabled them to exercise
that right in Oxford.

Max Beerbohm 1872–1956: *Zuleika Dobson* (1911)

9 I could come back to America...to die—but never, never
to live.

Henry James 1843–1916: letter to Mrs William James, 1 April 1913

10 The wish to include a glimpse of my personality in
a literary article is low, unworthy, and American.

A. E. Housman 1859–1936: letter 21 September 1921

11 So I really think that American gentlemen are the best
after all, because kissing your hand may make you feel
very very good but a diamond and safire bracelet lasts
forever.

Anita Loos 1893–1981: *Gentlemen Prefer Blondes* (1925)

12 Last Sunday afternoon
I took a trip to Hackensack
But after I gave Hackensack the once-over
I took the next train back.
I happen to like New York.

Cole Porter 1891–1964: 'I Happen to Like New York' (1931)

13 Cities are above
The quarrels that were hapless.
Look who's making love:
St Paul and Minneap'lis!

Ira Gershwin 1896–1983: 'Love is Sweeping the Country' (1931)

14 In the United States there is more space where nobody is
than where anybody is. That is what makes America
what it is.

Gertrude Stein 1874–1946: *The Geographical History of America* (1936)

15 When J. P. Morgan bows, I just nod;
Green Pastures wanted me to play God.
But you've got me down hearted
'Cause I can't get started with you.

Ira Gershwin 1896–1983: 'I Can't Get Started' (1936)

16 Every American woman has two souls to call her own,
the other being her husband's.

James Agate 1877–1947: diary 15 May 1937

17 When I was a boy I was told that anybody could become President. I'm beginning to believe it.

Clarence Darrow 1857–1938: Irving Stone *Clarence Darrow for the Defence* (1941)

18 Broadway's turning into Coney,
Champagne Charlie's drinking gin.
Old New York is new and phoney—
Give it back to the Indians.

Lorenz Hart 1895–1943: 'Give it back to the Indians' (1940)

19 California is a fine place to live—if you happen to be an orange.

Fred Allen 1894–1956: in *American Magazine* December 1945

20 A friend of mine...writes from Austria that she has been raped by 6 Cossacks. (Hard cheese as she is a Lesbian.) Very topical and in the swim of her isn't it. I wrote back and told her what the Americans were like here to cheer her up.

Nancy Mitford 1904–73: letter 3 February 1946

21 Last week, I went to Philadelphia, but it was closed.

W. C. Fields 1880–1946: Richard J. Anobile *Godfrey Daniels* (1975); attributed

22 Your eyes are like the prairie flowers
When they're refreshed by sudden showers,
Next to Texas I love you.

Sammy Cahn 1913– : 'Next to Texas I Love You' (1947)

23 I'm as corny as Kansas in August
I'm as normal as blueberry pie...
...High as a flag on the fourth of July.

Oscar Hammerstein II 1895–1960: 'I'm in Love with a Wonderful Guy' (1949)

24 I like America...
All delegates
From Southern States
Are nervy and distraught.
In New Orleans
The wrought-iron screens
Are dreadfully overwrought...
But—I like America,
Every scrap of it,
All the sentimental crap of it.

Noël Coward 1899–1973: 'I like America' (1949)

25 I met him in Boston
In the native quarter.
He was from Harvard
Just across the border.

Sheldon Harnick 1924– : 'The Boston Beguine' (1952)

26 In America any boy may become President and I suppose it's just one of the risks he takes!

Adlai Stevenson 1900–65: speech in Detroit, 7 October 1952

27 To Americans, English manners are far more frightening than none at all.

Randall Jarrell 1914–65: *Pictures from an Institution* (1954)

28 You're from Big D,
My, oh yes, I mean Big D, little a, double l-a-s
And that spells Dallas, my darlin' darlin' Dallas,
Don't it give you pleasure to confess
That you're from Big D?
My, oh yes!

Frank Loesser 1910–69: 'Big D' (1956)

29 I like to be in America!
O.K. by me in America!
Ev'rything free in America
For a small fee in America!

Stephen Sondheim 1930– :
'America' (1957)

30 The thing that impresses me most about America is the
way parents obey their children.

Edward VIII 1894–1972: in *Look*
5 March 1957

31 I have always liked Americans, and the sort of man that
likes Americans is liable to like Russians.

Claud Cockburn 1904–81:
Crossing the Line (1958)

*Gilbert Harding, applying for a US visa, was irritated by having to fill
in a long form with many questions, including 'Is it your intention to
overthrow the Government of the United States by force?':*
32 Sole purpose of visit.

Gilbert Harding 1907–60: W.
Reyburn *Gilbert Harding* (1978)

33 The Texan turned out to be good-natured, generous and
likable. In three days no one could stand him.

Joseph Heller 1923– : *Catch-22*
(1961)

34 For some guys
The dream is Paris,
But I found a shrine
Where Hollywood Boulevard crosses Vine.

Ervin Drake: 'My Hometown'
(1964)

35 The land of the dull and the home of the literal.

Gore Vidal 1925– : *Reflections
upon a Sinking Ship* (1969)

36 Molasses to
Rum to
Slaves!
'Tisn't morals, 'tis money that saves!
Shall we dance to the sound
Of the profitable pound, in
Molasses and
Rum and
Slaves?

Sherman Edwards: 'Molasses to
Rum' (1969)

37 Once we had a Roosevelt
Praise the Lord!
Now we're stuck with Nixon, Agnew, Ford
Brother, can you spare a rope!

E. Y. Harburg 1898–1981: parody
of 'Brother Can You Spare a Dime?',
written for the *New York Times* at the
time of Watergate

38 If I had to give a definition of capitalism I would say: the
process whereby American girls turn into American
women.

Christopher Hampton 1946– :
Savages (1974)

The universal philosophy of young America:
39 I can do that.

Ed Kleban: song-title (1975)

40 America is a vast conspiracy to make you happy.

John Updike 1932– : *Problems*
(1980) 'How to love America and
Leave it at the Same Time'

41 They're the experts where personality is concerned, the
Americans; they've got it down to a fine art.

Alan Bennett 1934– : *Talking
Heads* (1988)

42 Never criticize Americans. They have the best taste that
money can buy.

Miles Kington 1941– : *Welcome to
Kington* (1989)

43 I have only one firm belief about the American political system, and that is this: God is a Republican and Santa Claus is a Democrat.

P. J. O'Rourke 1947– : *Parliament of Whores* (1991)

44 In the past an American's ears were used to keep his spectacles on; with the universal adoption of the contact lens, it is probable that evolution may well phase out his ears completely over the next hundred years or so.

Stephen Fry 1957– : *Paperweight* (1992)

Anger

1 Whereat, with blade, with bloody blameful blade, He bravely broached his boiling bloody breast.

William Shakespeare 1564–1616: *A Midsummer Night's Dream* (1595–6)

2 Anger makes dull men witty, but it keeps them poor.

Francis Bacon 1561–1626: *Works* (1859) 'Baconiana'

3 I was angry with my friend;
I told my wrath, my wrath did end.
I was angry with my foe:
I told it not, my wrath did grow.

William Blake 1757–1827: 'A Poison Tree' (1794)

4 When angry, count four; when very angry, swear.

Mark Twain 1835–1910: *Pudd'nhead Wilson* (1894)

5 The adjective 'cross' as a description of his Jovelike wrath . . . jarred upon Derek profoundly. It was as though Prometheus, with the vultures tearing his liver, had been asked if he were piqued.

P. G. Wodehouse 1881–1975: *Jill the Reckless* (1922)

6 It's my rule never to lose me temper till it would be dethrimental to keep it.

Sean O'Casey 1880–1964: *The Plough and the Stars* (1926)

7 I wish I knew why the hero [of *Look Back in Anger*] is so dreadfully cross and what about? I should also like to know how, where and why he and his friend run a sweet-stall and if, considering the hero's unparalleled capacity for invective, they ever manage to sell any sweets?

Noël Coward 1899–1973: diary 17 February 1957

8 He never let the sun go down on his wrath, though there were some colourful sunsets while it lasted.

A. A. Thomson: of W. G. Grace; Alan Gibson *The Cricket Captains of England* (1979)

9 I expect to pass through this world but once and therefore if there is anybody that I want to kick in the crutch I had better kick them in the crutch *now*, for I do not expect to pass this way again.

Maurice Bowra 1898–1971: while lunching at the Reform Club with a bishop at the next table; Arthur Marshall *Life's Rich Pageant* (1984)

10 At this present moment, I have a strong urge to go over there, wrap both his legs round his neck and stick his suede shoes in his mouth. But I suppose that would only be termed a temporary solution.

Alan Ayckbourn 1939– : *Sisterly Feelings* (1981)

11 I am stuck in the back of a car with a woman who has the political views of Attila the Hun and I'm about to let her have it between the hat.

Alan Ayckbourn 1939– : *Sisterly Feelings* (1981)

12 McEnroe . . . did his complete Krakatoa number.

Clive James 1939– : of John McEnroe disputing a line call at Wimbledon; in *Observer* 5 July 1981

Animals See *Birds and Animals*

Appearance

1 It is better to be beautiful than to be good. But...it is better to be good than to be ugly.

Oscar Wilde 1854–1900: *The Picture of Dorian Gray* (1891)

2 I always say beauty is only sin deep.

Saki 1870–1916: *Reginald* (1904)

3 He had a thin vague beard—or rather, he had a chin on which a large number of hairs weakly curled and clustered to cover its retreat.

Max Beerbohm 1872–1956: 'Enoch Soames' (1912)

4 I look like an elderly *wasp* in an interesting condition.

Mrs Patrick Campbell 1865–1940: of her appearance in her black and yellow costume for *False Gods* in 1917; Margot Peters *Mrs Pat* (1984)

5 Sure, deck your lower limbs in pants;
Yours are the limbs, my sweeting.
You look divine as you advance—
Have you seen yourself retreating?

Ogden Nash 1902–71: 'What's the Use?' (1940)

His son Ben had expressed his horror of rendering himself conspicuous:

6 Considering that his hair is like that of a gollywog and his clothes noticeable the other end of Trafalgar Square, this is an odd assertion.

Harold Nicolson 1886–1968: diary 21 June 1953

7 In appearance Dior is like a bland country curate made out of pink marzipan.

Cecil Beaton 1904–80: of Christian Dior; *The Glass of Fashion* (1954)

Rupert Hart-Davis's profile of Lady Diana, accompanied by a photograph of her by Douglas Glass, had appeared in the Sunday Times:

8 Glass should be broken, and whoever wrote the praise exhalted [sic].

Diana Cooper 1892–1986: Rupert Hart-Davis letter to George Lyttelton, 15 March 1958

9 I'm tired of all this nonsense about beauty being only skin-deep. That's deep enough. What do you want—an adorable pancreas?

Jean Kerr 1923– : *The Snake has all the Lines* (1958)

To the producer, Jed Harris, at the end of an interview while Harris was in the nude:

10 Jed, your fly is open.

George S. Kaufman 1889–1961: Howard Teichman *George S. Kaufman* (1973)

11 You're welcome to take a bath. You look like the second week of the garbage strike.

Neil Simon 1927– : *The Gingerbread Lady* (1970)

12 Look at this dry pink plate of a face. Why didn't God give me a face on which the skin hangs in genial brown folds, the mouth is firm...but kindly...and with long large ears. Nearly every man of distinction has long ears.

Alan Bennett 1934– : *Getting On* (1972)

13 My face looks like a wedding cake left out in the rain.

W. H. Auden 1907–73: Humphrey Carpenter *W. H. Auden* (1981)

14 Edith Sitwell, in that great Risorgimento cape of hers, looks as though she were covering a teapot or a telephone.

Noël Coward 1899–1973: William Marchant *The Pleasure of his Company* (1975)

15 The most common error made in matters of appearance is the belief that one should disdain the superficial and let the true beauty of one's soul shine through. If there are places on one's body where this is a possibility, you are not attractive—you are leaking.

Fran Lebowitz 1946– : *Metropolitan Life* (1978)

16 I guess a drag queen's like an oil painting: You gotta stand back from it to get the full effect.

Harvey Fierstein 1954– : *Torch Song Trilogy* (1979)

17 No power on earth, however, can abolish the merciless class distinction between those who are physically desirable and the lonely, pallid, spotted, silent, unfancied majority.

John Mortimer 1923– : *Clinging to the Wreckage* (1982)

18 Ronald Reagan doesn't dye his hair, he's just prematurely orange.

Gerald Ford 1909– : attributed

19 He had the sort of face that makes you realise God does have a sense of humour.

Bill Bryson 1951– : *Neither Here Nor There* (1991)

20 My beauty am faded.

Rudolf Nureyev 1939–93: on being rejected by a young man he had tried to pick up; in *Ned Sherrin in his Anecdotage* (1993)

Architecture

On Brighton Pavilion:
1 As if St Paul's had come down and littered.

Sydney Smith 1771–1845: Peter Virgin *Sydney Smith* (1994)

2 Sir Christopher Wren
Said, 'I am going to dine with some men.
If anybody calls
Say I am designing St Paul's.'

Edmund Clerihew Bentley 1875–1956: 'Sir Christopher Wren' (1905)

3 The Pavilion
Cost a million
As a monument to Art,
And the wits here
Say it sits here
Like an Oriental tart!

Noël Coward 1899–1973: on Brighton Pavilion; 'There was Once a Little Village' (1934)

4 Ghastly good taste, or a depressing story of the rise and fall of English architecture.

John Betjeman 1906–84: title of book (1933)

5 The existence of St Sophia is atmospheric; that of St Peter's, overpoweringly, imminently substantial. One is a church to God: the other a salon for his agents. One is consecrated to reality, the other, to illusion. St Sophia in fact is large, and St Peter's is vilely, tragically small.

Robert Byron 1905–41: *The Road to Oxiana* (1937)

6 Whatever may be said in favour of the Victorians, it is pretty generally admitted that few of them were to be trusted within reach of a trowel and a pile of bricks.

P. G. Wodehouse 1881–1975: *Summer Moonshine* (1938)

7 A taste for the grandiose, like a taste for morphia, is, once it has been fully acquired, difficult to keep within limits.

Osbert Lancaster 1908–80: *Homes Sweet Homes* (1939)

8 It's just my colour: it's *beige!*

Elsie Mendl d. 1950: a fashionable interior decorator's first view of the Parthenon; Osbert Sitwell *Rat Week: An Essay on the Abdication* (1986)

9 The physician can bury his mistakes, but the architect can only advise his client to plant vines.

Frank Lloyd Wright 1867–1959: in *New York Times* 4 October 1953

10 I *do* like the mullioned window between the Doric columns—that has a quality of coy desperation, like a spinster gatecrashing a costume ball in a flowered frock.

Tom Stoppard 1937– : *The Dog It Was That Died* (1983)

11 A monstrous carbuncle on the face of a much-loved and elegant friend.

Charles, Prince of Wales 1948– : speech on the proposed extension to the National Gallery, London, 30 May 1984

12 A singularly dreary street. What I would term Victorian Varicose.

Peter Shaffer 1926– : *Lettice and Lovage* (rev. ed. 1989)

13 Washington has lots of those Greek- and Roman-style buildings that practically make you feel like a senator just walking up the steps of them. Senators, in particular, are fond of this feeling, and this is one reason official Washington escaped the worst effects of modern architecture.

P. J. O'Rourke 1947– : *Parliament of Whores* (1991)

14 Architecture offers quite extraordinary opportunities to serve the community, to enhance the landscape, refresh the environment and to advance mankind—the successful architect needs training to overcome these pitfalls however, and start earning some serious money.

Stephen Fry 1957– : *Paperweight* (1992)

Argument

1 Sir Roger told them, with the air of a man who would not give his judgement rashly, that much might be said on both sides.

Joseph Addison 1672–1719: *The Spectator* 20 July 1711

2 Those who in quarrels interpose, Must often wipe a bloody nose.

John Gay 1685–1732: *Fables* (1727) 'The Mastiffs'

3 My uncle Toby would never offer to answer this by any other kind of argument, than that of whistling half a dozen bars of Lillabullero.

Laurence Sterne 1713–68: *Tristram Shandy* (1759–67)

4 And who are you? said he.—Don't puzzle me, said I.

Laurence Sterne 1713–68: *Tristram Shandy* (1759–67)

5 There is no arguing with Johnson; for when his pistol misses fire, he knocks you down with the butt end of it.

Oliver Goldsmith 1730–74: James Boswell *Life of Samuel Johnson* (1934 ed.) 26 October 1769

6 Why, i'faith, I believe I am between *both*.

Richard Brinsley Sheridan
1751–1816: when two royal dukes
walking on either side of him told him
that they were trying to decide if he
was a greater fool or rogue; Walter
Jerrold *Bon-Mots* (1893)

*On seeing two Edinburgh women hurling insults at one another
across an alleyway:*

7 Those two women will never agree; they are arguing
from different premises.

Sydney Smith 1771–1845: Peter
Virgin *Sydney Smith* (1994)

8 I'll not listen to reason...Reason always means what
someone else has got to say.

Elizabeth Gaskell 1810–65:
Cranford (1853)

9 'My idea of an agreeable person,' said Hugo Bohun, 'is
a person who agrees with me.'

Benjamin Disraeli 1804–81:
Lothair (1870)

10 [Logic] is neither a science nor an art, but a dodge.

Benjamin Jowett 1817–93: Lionel
A. Tollemache *Benjamin Jowett* (1895)

11 For scholars to argue against me as Mr Heitland argues
is just the way to foster in me that arrogant temper to
which I owe my deplorable reputation.

A. E. Housman 1859–1936: in
Classical Review 1901

12 Any stigma, as the old saying is, will serve to beat
a dogma.

Philip Guedalla 1889–1944:
Masters and Men (1923)

13 Several excuses are always less convincing than one.

Aldous Huxley 1894–1963: *Point
Counter Point* (1928)

14 JUDGE: What do you suppose I am on the Bench for, Mr
Smith?
SMITH: It is not for me, Your Honour, to attempt to
fathom the inscrutable workings of Providence.

F. E. Smith 1872–1930: Lord
Birkenhead *F. E.* (1959 ed.)

15 You can't turn a thing upside down if there's no theory
about it being the right way up.

G. K. Chesterton 1874–1936:
attributed

16 When two strong men stand face to face, each claiming
to be Major Brabazon-Plank, it is inevitable that there
will be a sense of strain, resulting in a momentary
silence.

P. G. Wodehouse 1881–1975:
Uncle Dynamite (1948)

17 Casuistry has got a bad name in the world, mainly,
I suppose, because of the dubious uses to which it was
put during the Sixteenth and Seventeenth Centuries by
some of its Jesuit practitioners. But it is really a very
useful art.

H. L. Mencken 1880–1956:
Minority Report (1956)

18 It won't upset her. She'll insist on being carried
downstairs to be in at the kill. There's nothing she likes
better than a good row.

Alan Ayckbourn 1939– : *Living
Together* (1975)

19 I had inherited what my father called the art of the
advocate, or the irritating habit of looking for the flaw in
any argument.

John Mortimer 1923– : *Clinging to
the Wreckage* (1982)

20 The first obligation of the demonstrator is to be legible.
Miss Manners cannot sympathize with a cause whose
signs she cannot make out even with her glasses on.

Judith Martin 1938– : 'Advice
from Miss Manners', column in
Washington Post 1979–82

21 I don't take orders from you, you're just a figure-head
and I've seen better ones on the sharp end of a dredger.

Tom Stoppard 1937– : *The Dog It Was That Died* (1983)

22 I think I detect sarcasm. I can't be doing with sarcasm.
You know what they say? Sarcasm is the greatest
weapon of the smallest mind.

Alan Ayckbourn 1939– : *Woman in Mind* (1986)

23 I think it will be a clash between the political will and
the administrative won't.

Jonathan Lynn 1943– and **Anthony Jay** 1930– : *Yes Prime Minister* vol. 2 (1987)

24 You can always reason with a German. You can always
reason with a barnyard animal, too, for all the good it
does.

P. J. O'Rourke 1947– : *Holidays in Hell* (1988)

The Aristocracy See also *Class*

1 I'll purge, and leave sack, and live cleanly, as
a nobleman should do.

William Shakespeare 1564–1616: *Henry IV, Part* 1 (1597)

2 This world consists of men, women, and Herveys.

Lady Mary Wortley Montagu 1689–1762: attributed by Lord Wharncliffe in *Letters and Works of Lady Mary Wortley Montagu* (1837), 'Herveys' being a reference to John Hervey, Baron Hervey of Ickworth, 1696–1743

3 We always feel kindly disposed towards noble authors.

Lord Macaulay 1800–59: in *Edinburgh Review* January 1833

4 They are no members of the common throng;
They are all noblemen who have gone wrong!

W. S. Gilbert 1836–1911: *The Pirates of Penzance* (1879)

5 Hearts just as pure and fair
May beat in Belgrave Square
As in the lowly air
Of Seven Dials.

W. S. Gilbert 1836–1911: *Iolanthe* (1882)

6 Spurn not the nobly born
With love affected,
Nor treat with virtuous scorn
The well-connected.

W. S. Gilbert 1836–1911: *Iolanthe* (1882)

7 There never was a Churchill from John of Marlborough
down that had either morals or principles.

W. E. Gladstone 1809–98: in conversation in 1882, recorded by Captain R. V. Briscoe; R. F. Foster *Lord Randolph Churchill* (1981)

8 I can trace my ancestry back to a protoplasmal
primordial atomic globule. Consequently, my family pride
is something in-conceivable. I can't help it. I was born
sneering.

W. S. Gilbert 1836–1911: *The Mikado* (1885)

9 LORD ILLINGWORTH: A title is really rather a nuisance in
these democratic days. As George Harford I had
everything I wanted. Now I have merely everything
that other people want.

Oscar Wilde 1854–1900: *A Woman of No Importance* (1893)

10 The young Sahib shot divinely, but God was very
merciful to the birds.

Anonymous: G. W. E. Russell *Collections and Recollections* (1898)

*After Lord Dunsany's arrest in 1921 by the Black and Tans, Oliver St
John Gogarty's attempt to console him diverged into a reminder of
a peer's privilege of being hanged with a silken rope and speculation
on the probable elasticity of silk, neither of which were well-received:*

11 There are certain things which are not jokes, Gogarty,
and one of them is my hanging.

Lord Dunsany 1878–1957: Ulick
O'Connor *Oliver St John Gogarty*
(1964)

At the trial by his peers of Lord de Clifford:

12 They were followed by 2 pretty girls who testified. As one
gave her name and address I saw one old Peer raise his
robes, fish out a pencil and, no doubt, note down her
address.

Chips Channon 1897–1958: diary
12 December 1935

13 The Stately Homes of England,
How beautiful they stand,
To prove the upper classes
Have still the upper hand.

Noël Coward 1899–1973: 'The
Stately Homes of England' (1938)

14 We don't represent anybody, it's true,
But that's not a thing to regret;
We can say what we think—and I know one or two
Who've never said anything yet.
While the Commons must bray like an ass every day
To appease their electoral hordes,
We don't say a thing till we've something to say—
There's a lot to be said for the Lords.

A. P. Herbert 1890–1971: *Big Ben*
(1946)

The much-married Duke of Westminster had died the previous day:

15 There was a bad fire next door; lots of smoke, but it
turned out *not* to be the four bereaved Duchesses of
Westminster committing suttee.

Chips Channon 1897–1958: diary
21 July 1953

16 The aristocracy and landed gentry, although Nationally
Entrusted and sadly Thirkellized, are still, thank
goodness, for all their constant complainings of
extinction, visibly and abundantly there.

Osbert Lancaster 1908–80: *All
Done From Memory* (1953)

17 An aristocracy in a republic is like a chicken whose head
has been cut off: it may run about in a lively way, but in
fact it is dead.

Nancy Mitford 1904–73: *Noblesse
Oblige* (1956) 'The English Aristocracy'

*Replying to Harold Wilson's remark (on Home's leading the
Conservatives to victory in the 1963 election) that 'the whole
[democratic] process has ground to a halt with a fourteenth Earl':*

18 As far as the fourteenth earl is concerned, I suppose Mr
Wilson, when you come to think of it, is the fourteenth
Mr Wilson.

Lord Home 1903–95: in *Daily
Telegraph* 22 October 1963

19 At the palace of the Duke of Ferrara,
Who was prematurely deaf but a dear,
At the palace of the Duke of Ferrara
I acquired some position
Plus a tiny Titian...
Liaisons! What's happened to them?

Stephen Sondheim 1930– :
'Liaisons' (1972)

20 I only wish we could have discussed this topic at another time when the doorkeepers' dance was not in the offing.

Lord Massereene and Ferrard 1914–93: speech on the Environmental Protection Bill in the House of Lords, 20 December 1989

The Armed Forces See also War

1 If you would take the pains but to examine the wars of Pompey the Great, you shall find, I warrant you, that there is no tiddle-taddle nor pibble-pabble in Pompey's camp.

William Shakespeare 1564–1616: *Henry V* (1599)

Replying to the Duke of Newcastle, who had complained that General Wolfe was a madman:
2 Mad, is he? Then I hope he will *bite* some of my other generals.

George II 1683–1760: Henry Beckles Willson *Life and Letters of James Wolfe* (1909)

3 No man will be a sailor who has contrivance enough to get himself into a jail; for being in a ship is being in a jail, with the chance of being drowned...A man in a jail has more room, better food, and commonly better company.

Samuel Johnson 1709–84: James Boswell *Life of Samuel Johnson* (1791) 16 March 1759

4 Admirals extolled for standing still, Or doing nothing with a deal of skill.

William Cowper 1731–1800: 'Table Talk' (1782)

5 For a soldier I listed, to grow great in fame, And be shot at for sixpence a-day.

Charles Dibdin 1745–1814: 'Charity' (1791)

6 Ben Battle was a soldier bold, And used to war's alarms: But a cannon-ball took off his legs, So he laid down his arms!

Thomas Hood 1799–1845: 'Faithless Nelly Gray' (1826)

7 For here I leave my second leg, And the Forty-second Foot!

Thomas Hood 1799–1845: 'Faithless Nelly Gray' (1826)

To a general who sent his dispatches from 'Headquarters in the Saddle':
8 The trouble with Hooker is that he's got his headquarters where his hindquarters ought to be.

Abraham Lincoln 1809–65: P. M. Zall *Abe Lincoln Laughing* (1982)

9 Stick close to your desks and never go to sea, And you all may be Rulers of the Queen's Navee!

W. S. Gilbert 1836–1911: *HMS Pinafore* (1878)

10 I'm very good at integral and differential calculus, I know the scientific names of beings animalculous; In short, in matters vegetable, animal, and mineral, I am the very model of a modern Major-General.

W. S. Gilbert 1836–1911: *The Pirates of Penzance* (1879)

11 Though I've belted you and flayed you, By the livin' Gawd that made you, You're a better man than I am, Gunga Din!

Rudyard Kipling 1865–1936: 'Gunga Din' (1892)

12 The uniform 'e wore Was nothin' much before, An' rather less than 'arf o' that be'ind.

Rudyard Kipling 1865–1936: 'Gunga Din' (1892)

13 The General was essentially a man of peace, except in his domestic life.

Oscar Wilde 1854–1900: *The Importance of Being Earnest* (1895)

14 Oh, you are a very poor soldier—a chocolate cream soldier!

George Bernard Shaw 1856–1950: *Arms and the Man* (1898)

15 Your friend the British soldier can stand up to anything except the British War Office.

George Bernard Shaw 1856–1950: *The Devil's Disciple* (1901)

16 When the military man approaches, the world locks up its spoons and packs off its womankind.

George Bernard Shaw 1856–1950: *Man and Superman* (1903)

Replying to a begging letter from Diana Cooper:
17 I do not care a damn for the Westminster Church Mission for Sailors. Sailors ought never to go to church. They ought to go to hell, where it is much more comfortable.

H. G. Wells 1866–1946: Philip Ziegler *Diana Cooper* (1981)

18 [Haig is] brilliant—to the top of his boots.

David Lloyd George 1863–1945: Paul Johnson (ed.) *The Oxford Book of Political Anecdotes* (1986); attributed

19 Napoleon's armies always used to march on their stomachs shouting: 'Vive l'Intérieur!'

W. C. Sellar 1898–1951 and **R. J. Yeatman** 1898–1968: *1066 and All That* (1930)

20 Has anybody seen our ship?
The H.M.S. Peculiar
We've been on shore
For a month or more,
And when we see the Captain we shall get 'what for'.

Noël Coward 1899–1973: 'Has Anybody Seen Our Ship' (1935)

21 Have you had any word
Of that bloke in the 'Third',
Was it Southerby, Sedgwick or Sim?
They had him thrown out of the club in Bombay
For, apart from his mess bills exceeding his pay,
He took to pig-sticking in *quite* the wrong way.
I wonder what happened to him!

Noël Coward 1899–1973: 'I Wonder What Happened to Him' (1945)

22 As for being a General, well at the age of four with paper hats and wooden swords we're all Generals. Only some of us never grow out of it.

Peter Ustinov 1921– : *Romanoff and Juliet* (1956)

23 Colonel Cathcart had courage and never hesitated to volunteer his men for any target available.

Joseph Heller 1923– : *Catch-22* (1961)

24 I had examined myself pretty thoroughly and discovered that I was unfit for military service.

Joseph Heller 1923– : *Catch-22* (1961)

25 Don't talk to me about naval tradition. It's nothing but rum, sodomy, and the lash.

Winston Churchill 1874–1965: Peter Gretton *Former Naval Person* (1968)

A woman to a man:
26 Are you joining the Army? Good, it'll make a woman of you.

Joe Orton 1933–67: *Up Against It*, screenplay written for the Beatles but never filmed

27 I should like to take the opportunity to correct some widespread misconceptions about the part played in the global struggle by the Irish Navy—a force with whom no one, except the patriots afloat, mucked in at all.

Patrick Campbell 1913–80: *The Campbell Companion* (1994) 'Sean Tar Joins Up'

28 Fortunately, the army has had much practice at ignoring impossible instructions.

Michael Green 1927– : *The Boy Who Shot Down an Airship* (1988)

29 My parents were very pleased that I was in the army. The fact that I hated it somehow pleased them even more.

Barry Humphries 1934– : *More Please* (1992)

Art and Artists

On attempting to paint two actors, David Garrick and Samuel Foote:
1 Rot them for a couple of rogues, they have everybody's faces but their own.

Thomas Gainsborough 1727–88: Allan Cunningham *The Lives of the Most Eminent Painters, Sculptors and Architects* (1829)

To a lawyer who had asked him why he laid such stress on 'the painter's eye':
2 The painter's eye is to him what the lawyer's tongue is to you.

Thomas Gainsborough 1727–88: William Hazlitt *Conversations of James Northcote* (1830)

3 There are only two styles of portrait painting; the serious and the smirk.

Charles Dickens 1812–70: *Nicholas Nickleby* (1839)

4 I maintain that two and two would continue to make four, in spite of the whine of the amateur for three, or the cry of the critic for five.

James McNeill Whistler 1834–1903: *Whistler v. Ruskin. Art and Art Critics* (1878)

5 Then a sentimental passion of a vegetable fashion must excite your languid spleen,
An attachment à la Plato for a bashful young potato, or a not too French French bean!
Though the Philistines may jostle, you will rank as an apostle in the high aesthetic band,
If you walk down Piccadilly with a poppy or a lily in your medieval hand.

W. S. Gilbert 1836–1911: *Patience* (1881)

After the death of the outlaw Jesse James relics of his house were sold:
6 His sole work of art, a chromo-lithograph of the most dreadful kind, of course was sold at a price which in Europe only a Mantegna or an undoubted Titian can command!

Oscar Wilde 1854–1900: letter 25 April 1882

7 All that I desire to point out is the general principle that Life imitates Art far more than Art imitates Life.

Oscar Wilde 1854–1900: *Intentions* (1891) 'The Decay of Lying'

On hearing the late Lord Leighton, President of the Royal Academy, praised as a musician, linguist, essayist, and host:
8 Painted, too, didn't he?

James McNeill Whistler 1834–1903: Hesketh Pearson *The Man Whistler* (1952)

9 Yes—one does like to make one's mummy just as nice as possible!

James McNeill Whistler 1834–1903: on his portrait of his mother; E. R. and J. Pennell *The Life of James McNeill Whistler* (1908)

In his case against Ruskin, replying to the question: 'For two days' labour, you ask two hundred guineas?':

10 No, I ask it for the knowledge of a lifetime.

James McNeill Whistler
1834–1903: D. C. Seitz *Whistler Stories* (1913)

To a lady who had been reminded of his work by an 'exquisite haze in the atmosphere':

11 Yes madam, Nature is creeping up.

James McNeill Whistler
1834–1903: D. C. Seitz *Whistler Stories* (1913)

12 The artistic temperament is a disease that afflicts amateurs. It is a disease which arises from men not having sufficient power of expression to utter and get rid of the element of art in their being.

G. K. Chesterton 1874–1936: *Heretics* (1905)

13 Mrs Ballinger is one of the ladies who pursue Culture in bands, as though it were dangerous to meet it alone.

Edith Wharton 1862–1937: *Xingu and Other Stories* (1916)

14 It is a symbol of Irish art. The cracked lookingglass of a servant.

James Joyce 1882–1941: *Ulysses* (1922)

15 The Sheridan stands in the heart of New York's Bohemian and artistic quarter. If you threw a brick from any of its windows, you would be certain to brain some rising young interior decorator, some Vorticist sculptor or a writer of revolutionary *vers libre*.

P. G. Wodehouse 1881–1975: *The Small Bachelor* (1927)

16 As my poor father used to say
In 1863,
Once people start on all this Art
Goodbye, moralitee!

A. P. Herbert 1890–1971: 'Lines for a Worthy Person' (1930)

A few days after the funeral of Sir William Orpen:

17 Our painter! He never got under the surface till he got under the sod.

Oliver St John Gogarty
1878–1957: Ulick O'Connor *Oliver St John Gogarty* (1964)

Of Art Nouveau:

18 Certainly no style seems at first glance to provide a richer field for the investigations of Herr Freud.

Osbert Lancaster 1908–80: *Homes Sweet Homes* (1939)

19 Little bits of porcelain,
Little sticks of Boule
Harmonize with Venuses
Of the Flemish school.

Osbert Lancaster 1908–80: *Homes Sweet Homes* (1939)

20 Mr Landseer whose only merit as a painter was the tireless accuracy with which he recorded the more revoltingly sentimental aspects of the woollier mammals.

Osbert Lancaster 1908–80: *Homes Sweet Homes* (1939)

21 All the arts in America are a gigantic racket run by unscrupulous men for unhealthy women.

Thomas Beecham 1879–1961: in *Observer* 5 May 1946

22 Of course he [William Morris] was a wonderful all-round man, but the act of walking round him has always tired me.

Max Beerbohm 1872–1956: letter to S. N. Behrman c.1953; *Conversations with Max* (1960)

23 There is only one position for an artist anywhere: and that is, upright.

Dylan Thomas 1914–53: *Quite Early One Morning* (1954)

On a South African statue of the Voortrekkers:
24 Patriotism is the last refuge of the sculptor.

William Plomer 1903–73: Rupert Hart-Davis letter to George Lyttelton, 13 October 1956

Comment by an old lady on Epstein's controversial Christ in Majesty:
25 I can never forgive Mr Epstein for his representation of Our Lord. So very un-English!

Anonymous: in *Ned Sherrin in his Anecdotage* (1993)

26 My art belongs to Dada.

Cole Porter 1891–1964: attributed

27 The perfect aesthete logically feels that the artist is strictly a turkish bath attendant.

Flann O'Brien 1911–66: *The Best of Myles* (1968)

28 If a scientist were to cut his ear off, no one would take it as evidence of a heightened sensibility.

Peter Medawar 1915–87: 'J. B. S.' (1968)

On a Constable painting of the Thames:
29 It is as though Constable had taken a long steady appraising stare at Canaletto and then charged straight through him.

Sylvia Townsend Warner 1893–1978: letter 6 February 1969

30 BEAUCHAMP: Secondly!—how can the artist justify himself in the community? ...Donner, why are you trying to be an artist?
DONNER: I heard there were opportunities to meet naked women.

Tom Stoppard 1937– : *Artist Descending a Staircase* (1973)

31 Yes, Frances [his wife] has the most beautiful hands in the world—and someday I'm going to have a bust made of them.

Sam Goldwyn 1882–1974: Michael Freedland *The Goldwyn Touch* (1986)

32 I doubt that art needed Ruskin any more than a moving train needs one of its passengers to shove it.

Tom Stoppard 1937– : in *Times Literary Supplement* 3 June 1977

33 Oh, I wish I could draw. I've always wanted to draw. I'd give my right arm to be able to draw. It must be very relaxing.

Alan Ayckbourn 1939– : *Joking Apart* (1979)

34 [Feydeau] had the great traditional stimulant to the industry of an artist, laziness and debt.

John Mortimer 1923– : *Clinging to the Wreckage* (1982)

35 If you want art to be like ovaltine, then clearly some art is not for you.

Peter Reading 1946– : in *Critics' Forum*, Radio 3, 22 November 1986; attributed

36 There is, perhaps, no more dangerous man in the world than the man with the sensibilities of an artist but without creative talent. With luck such men make wonderful theatrical impresarios and interior decorators, or else they become mass murderers or critics.

Barry Humphries 1934– : *More Please* (1992)

37 Portrait painters tend to regard faces as not very still lives.

Alan Bennett 1934– : *A Question of Attribution* (1989)

Recalling that in the 1970s he used to be asked what were the ingredients for a successful exhibition:
38 You've got to have two out of death, sex and jewels.

Roy Strong 1935– : in *Sunday Times* 23 January 1994

Autobiography See *Biography and Autobiography*

Behaviour and Etiquette

1 I always take blushing either for a sign of guilt, or of ill breeding.

William Congreve 1670–1729: *The Way of the World* (1700)

2 Don't let us be familiar or fond, nor kiss before folks, like my Lady Fadler and Sir Francis: nor go to Hyde-Park together the first Sunday in a new chariot, to provoke eyes and whispers, and then never be seen there together again; as if we were proud of one another the first week, and ashamed of one another ever after...Let us be very strange and well-bred: Let us be as strange as if we had been married a great while, and as well-bred as if we were not married at all.

William Congreve 1670–1729: *The Way of the World* (1700)

3 Suspect all extraordinary and groundless civilities.

Thomas Fuller 1654–1734: *Gnomologia* (1734)

4 Orthodoxy is my doxy; heterodoxy is another man's doxy.

William Warburton 1698–1779: to Lord Sandwich; Joseph Priestley *Memoirs* (1807)

Aged four, having had hot coffee spilt over his legs:
5 Thank you, madam, the agony is abated.

Lord Macaulay 1800–59: G. O. Trevelyan *Life and Letters of Lord Macaulay* (1876)

6 The young ladies entered the drawing-room in the full fervour of sisterly animosity.

R. S. Surtees 1805–64: *Mr Sponge's Sporting Tour* (1853)

7 These sort of boobies think that people come to balls to do nothing but dance; whereas everyone knows that the real business of a ball is either to look out for a wife, to look after a wife, or to look after somebody else's wife.

R. S. Surtees 1805–64: *Mr Facey Romford's Hounds* (1865)

8 Curtsey while you're thinking what to say. It saves time.

Lewis Carroll 1832–98: *Through the Looking-Glass* (1872)

9 It isn't etiquette to cut any one you've been introduced to. Remove the joint.

Lewis Carroll 1832–98: *Through the Looking-Glass* (1872)

10 Duty is what one expects from others, it is not what one does oneself.

Oscar Wilde 1854–1900: *A Woman of No Importance* (1893)

11 It is very vulgar to talk like a dentist when one isn't a dentist. It produces a false impression.

Oscar Wilde 1854–1900: *The Importance of Being Earnest* (1895)

12 It looked bad when the Duke of Fife
Left off using a knife;
But people began to talk
When he left off using a fork.

Edmund Clerihew Bentley 1875–1956: 'The Duke of Fife' (1905)

13 The mayor gave no other answer than that deep guttural grunt which is technically known in municipal interviews as refusing to commit oneself.

Stephen Leacock 1869–1944: *Arcadian Adventures with the Idle Rich* (1914)

14 It is a good rule in life never to apologize. The right sort of people do not want apologies, and the wrong sort take a mean advantage of them.

P. G. Wodehouse 1881–1975: *The Man Upstairs* (1914)

15 I am a woman of the world, Hector; and I can assure you that if you will only take the trouble always to do the perfectly correct thing, and to say the perfectly correct thing, you can do just what you like.

George Bernard Shaw 1856–1950: *Heartbreak House* (1919)

16 You children must be extra polite to strangers because your father's an actor.

Mrs Fields: Dorothy Fields' mother; taped lecture in Caryl Brahms and Ned Sherrin *Song by Song* (1984)

17 I have noticed that the people who are late are often so much jollier than the people who have to wait for them.

E. V. Lucas 1868–1938: *365 Days and One More* (1926)

18 One of those telegrams of which M. de Guermantes had wittily fixed the formula: 'Cannot come, lie follows'.

Marcel Proust 1871–1922: *Le Temps retrouvé* (Time Regained, 1926)

19 HECKLER: We expected a better play.
COWARD: I expected better manners.

Noël Coward 1899–1973: to a heckler in the audience after *Sirocco* (1927) was booed; Sheridan Morley *A Talent to Amuse* (1969)

20 In olden days, a glimpse of stocking
Was looked on as something shocking,
But now, God knows,
Anything goes.

Cole Porter 1891–1964: 'Anything Goes' (1934)

21 Miss Otis regrets she's unable to lunch today, Madam.

Cole Porter 1891–1964: 'Miss Otis Regrets' (1934)

22 I get too hungry for dinner at eight.
I like the theatre, but never come late.
I never bother with people I hate.
That's why the lady is a tramp.

Lorenz Hart 1895–1943: 'The Lady is a Tramp' (1937)

23 I spent two nights at Cap Ferrat with Mr Maugham (who has lost his fine cook) and made a great gaffe. The first evening he asked me what someone was like and I said, 'A pansy with a stammer'. All the Picassos on the wall blanched.

Evelyn Waugh 1903–66: letter to Harold Acton, 14 April 1952

24 I am very sorry to hear that Duff [Cooper] was surprised and grieved to hear that I had detested him for 23 years. I must have nicer manners than people normally credit me with.

Evelyn Waugh 1903–66: letter to Lady Diana Cooper, 29 August 1953

25 Eccentricity, to be socially acceptable, had still to have at least four or five generations of inbreeding behind it.

Osbert Lancaster 1908–80: *All Done From Memory* (1953)

26 You know what charm is: a way of getting the answer yes without having asked any clear question.

Albert Camus 1913–60: *La Chute* (1956)

27 This is a free country, madam. We have a right to share your privacy in a public place.

Peter Ustinov 1921– : *Romanoff and Juliet* (1956)

28 I tried to keep in mind the essential rules of British conduct which the Major had carefully instilled in me:
1. The English never speak to anyone unless they have been properly introduced (except in case of shipwreck).
2. You must never talk about God or your stomach.

Pierre Daninos: *Major Thompson and I* (1957)

29 'What are you doing for dinner tonight?'
'Digesting it.'

George S. Kaufman 1889–1961: to a dinner invitation arriving at 8.30 pm; Howard Teichman *George S. Kaufman* (1973)

30 Manners are especially the need of the plain. The pretty can get away with anything.

Evelyn Waugh 1903–66: in *Observer* 15 April 1962

Somerset Maugham excused his leaving early when dining with Lady Tree by saying, 'I must look after my youth':

31 Next time do bring him. We adore those sort of people.

Lady Tree 1863–1937: in *Ned Sherrin in his Anecdotage* (1993)

On Harold Wilson's 'Lavender List' (the honours list he drew up on resigning the British premiership in 1976):

32 Such a graceful exit. And then he had to go and do this on the doorstep.

John Junor 1919– : in *Observer* 23 December 1990

33 Actually, there is no way of making vomiting courteous. You have to do the next best thing, which is to vomit in such a way that the story you tell about it later will be amusing.

P. J. O'Rourke 1947– : *Modern Manners* (1984)

34 Good manners are a combination of intelligence, education, taste, and style mixed together so that you don't need any of those things.

P. J. O'Rourke 1947– : *Modern Manners* (1984)

35 He describes, I am told, seduction by his father, with whom he had an affair. The trouble with dishing up a story like that in Chapter One, when the final chapter deals with his salt-free diet, is that if the end and the beginning are tasteless, who can be sure about the middle?

Gerald Asher: on the autobiography of Craig Claiborne, the star cookery writer of *The New York Times*; Ned Sherrin *Cutting Edge* (1984)

36 Etiquette, sacred subject of, 1–389.

Judith Martin 1938– : *Miss Manners' Guide to Rearing Perfect Children* (1985); index entry

37 The confessions of error, as jocular as they are suspect, which the upper class have always associated with good manners.

Hugo Young 1938– : in *Guardian* 20 September 1990

38 Sophistication is not an admired quality. Not only at school. Nobody likes it anywhere. In England at any rate.

Stephen Fry 1957– : *The Liar* (1992)

39 After a brief period of anguish over whether or not to sling out the fish-knives, everyone said, 'Oh, stuff it', and heaved a sigh of relief, and the haut-ton was gone for ever.

Alice Thomas Ellis 1932– : in *Independent on Sunday* 2 October 1993

Betting and Gambling

1 I have a notion that gamblers are as happy as most people—being always excited.

Lord Byron 1788–1824: 'Detached Thoughts' 15 October 1821

2 Don't let's go to the dogs tonight,
For mother will be there.

A. P. Herbert 1890–1971: 'Don't Let's Go to the Dogs Tonight' (1926)

3 'You are snatching a hard guy when you snatch Bookie Bob. A very hard guy, indeed. In fact,' I say, 'I hear the softest thing about him is his front teeth.'

Damon Runyon 1884–1946: in *Collier's* 26 September 1931, 'The Snatching of Bookie Bob'

4 I long ago come to the conclusion that all life is 6 to 5 against.

Damon Runyon 1884–1946: in *Collier's* 8 September 1934, 'A Nice Price'

5 Never give a sucker an even break.

W. C. Fields 1880–1946: title of a W. C. Fields film (1941); the catch-phrase (Fields's own) is said to have originated in the musical comedy *Poppy* (1923)

6 I got a horse right here,
The name is Paul Revere,
And here's a guy that says if the weather's clear,
Can do, can do, this guy says the horse can do.

Frank Loesser 1910–69: 'Fugue for Tinhorns' (1950)

7 Not for good old reliable Nathan for it's always just
a short walk,
To the oldest established permanent floating crap game in
New York.

Frank Loesser 1910–69: 'The Oldest Established' (1950)

8 My immediate reward for increasing the tax on bookmaking was major vilification. It was confidently asserted in the bookmakers' circles that my mother and father met only once and then for a very brief period.

George Wigg 1900–83: in 1972, when Chairman of the British Betting Levy Board; Jonathon Green and Don Atyeo (eds.) *The Book of Sports Quotes* (1979)

9 Rowe's Rule: the odds are five to six that the light at the end of the tunnel is the headlight of an oncoming train.

Paul Dickson 1939– : in *Washingtonian* November 1978

10 It's one thing to ask your bank manager for an overdraft to buy 500 begonias for the borders in Haslemere, but quite another to seek financial succour to avail oneself of some of the 5–2 they're offering on Isle de Bourbon for the St Leger.

Jeffrey Bernard 1932– : in *Guardian* 23 December 1978 'Sports Quotes of the Year'

11 Two-up is Australia's very own way of parting a fool and his money.

Germaine Greer 1939– : in *Observer* 1 August 1982

The Bible

1 There's a great text in Galatians,
Once you trip on it, entails
Twenty-nine distinct damnations,
One sure, if another fails.

Robert Browning 1812–89: 'Soliloquy of the Spanish Cloister' (1842)

2 LORD ILLINGWORTH: The Book of Life begins with a man and a woman in a garden.
MRS ALLONBY: It ends with Revelations.

Oscar Wilde 1854–1900: *A Woman of No Importance* (1893)

3 It ain't necessarily so,
It ain't necessarily so—
De t'ings that yo' li'ble
To read in de Bible—
It ain't necessarily so.

Ira Gershwin 1896–1989: 'It Ain't Necessarily So' (1935)

4 A wonderful book, but there are some very queer things in it.

George V 1865–1936: K. Rose *King George V* (1983)

On Moses and the reason why there are only ten commandments:

5 He probably said to himself, 'Must stop or I shall be getting silly.'

Mrs Patrick Campbell 1865–1940: James Agate diary 6 May 1937

6 I read the book of Job last night. I don't think God comes well out of it.

Virginia Woolf 1882–1941: attributed

Biography and Autobiography

1 If a man is to write *A Panegyric* he may keep vices out of sight; but if he professes to write *A Life*, he must represent it as it really was.

Samuel Johnson 1709–84: James Boswell *Life of Samuel Johnson* (1791) 1777

2 I shall not say why and how I became, at the age of fifteen, the mistress of the Earl of Craven.

Harriette Wilson 1789–1846: opening words of *Memoirs* (1825)

3 Sir John Malcolm, whose love passes the love of biographers, and who can see nothing but wisdom and justice in the action of his idol.

Lord Macaulay 1800–59: 'Lord Clive' (1840)

4 Then there is my noble and biographical friend who has added a new terror to death.

Charles Wetherell 1770–1846: on Lord Campbell's *Lives of the Lord Chancellors* being written without the consent of heirs or executors; also attributed to Lord Lyndhurst (1772–1863)

5 Every great man nowadays has his disciples, and it is always Judas who writes the biography.

Oscar Wilde 1854–1900: *Intentions* (1891) 'The Critic as Artist'

6 The Art of Biography
Is different from Geography.
Geography is about Maps,
But Biography is about Chaps.

Edmund Clerihew Bentley 1875–1956: *Biography for Beginners* (1905) introduction

On hearing that Arthur Benson was to write the life of Rossetti:

7 No, no, no, it won't do. *Dear* Arthur, we know just what he can, so beautifully, do, but no, oh no, this is to have the story of a purple man written by a white, or at the most, a pale green man.

Henry James 1843–1916: George Lyttelton letter to Rupert Hart-Davis, 28 February 1957

8 The reminiscences of Mrs Humphrey Ward . . . convinced me that autobiography is a sin.

Harold Laski 1893–1950: letter to Oliver Wendell Holmes, 1 December 1918

9 I write no memoirs. I'm a gentleman. I cannot bring myself to write nastily about persons whose hospitality I have enjoyed.

John Pentland Mahaffy 1839–1919: W. B. Stanford and R. B. McDowell *Mahaffy* (1971)

On Margot Asquith's forthcoming memoirs:

10 As scandal is the second breath of life my name is down for an early copy.

Harold Laski 1893–1950: letter to Oliver Wendell Holmes, 6 March 1920

11 Biography, like big game hunting, is one of the recognized forms of sport, and it is as unfair as only sport can be.

Philip Guedalla 1889–1944: *Supers and Supermen* (1920)

12 Biography should be written by an acute enemy.

Arthur James Balfour 1848–1930: in *Observer* 30 January 1927

13 I never read the life of any important person without discovering that he knew more and could do more than I could ever hope to know or to do in half a dozen lifetimes.

J. B. Priestley 1894–1984: *Apes and Angels* (1928)

14 Every time somebody's Autobiography comes out I turn to the Index to see if my name occurs, and of course it never does.

James Agate 1877–1947: diary 16 September 1932

15 Discretion is not the better part of biography.

Lytton Strachey 1880–1932: Michael Holroyd *Lytton Strachey* (1967)

16 If I write anything of an autobiographical nature, as I have sometimes idly thought of doing, I shall send it to the British Museum to be kept under lock and key for fifty years. There is no biography of Matthew Arnold...in accordance with his own advice; so there certainly need be none of me.

A. E. Housman 1859–1936: letter 14 December 1933

17 Do not send me your manuscript. Worse than the practice of writing books about living men is the conduct of living men in supervising such books.

A. E. Housman 1859–1936: letter to his would-be biographer Houston Martin, 22 March 1936

18 Reformers are always finally neglected, while the memoirs of the frivolous will always eagerly be read.

Chips Channon 1897–1958: diary 7 July 1936

On James Agate's autobiography Ego:
19 I did so enjoy your book. Everything that everybody writes in it is so good.

Mrs Patrick Campbell 1865–1940: James Agate diary 6 May 1937

20 To write one's memoirs is to speak ill of everybody except oneself.

Henri Philippe Pétain 1856–1951: in *Observer* 26 May 1946

21 The reader need not become uneasy; I do not intend to write of the boy that made good.

Neville Cardus 1889–1975: *Autobiography* (1947)

22 If you really want to hear about it, the first thing you'll probably want to know is where I was born, and what my lousy childhood was like, and how my parents were occupied and all before they had me, and all that David Copperfield kind of crap, but I don't feel like going into it.

J. D. Salinger 1919– : *The Catcher in the Rye* (1951)

23 Every autobiography...becomes an absorbing work of fiction, with something of the charm of a cryptogram.

H. L. Mencken 1880–1956: *Minority Report* (1956)

24 An autobiography should give the reader opportunity to point out the author's follies and misconceptions.

Claud Cockburn 1904–81: *Crossing the Line* (1958)

Of a biography of Lord Northcliffe:
25 It weighs too much.

Lord Beaverbrook 1879–1964: A. J. P. Taylor *Letters to Eva* (1991)

26 Only when one has lost all curiosity about the future has one reached the age to write an autobiography.

Evelyn Waugh 1903–66: *A Little Learning* (1964)

27 Autobiography is now as common as adultery and hardly less reprehensible.

John Grigg 1924– : Leon Harris *The Fine Art of Political Wit* (1965); attributed

28 My problem is that I am not frightfully interested in anything, except myself. And of all forms of fiction autobiography is the most gratuitous.

Tom Stoppard 1937– : *Lord Malquist and Mr Moon* (1966)

29 Like all good memoirs it has not been emasculated by considerations of good taste.

Peter Medawar 1915–87: review of James D. Watson *The Double Helix* (1968)

30 An autobiography is an obituary in serial form with the last instalment missing.

Quentin Crisp 1908– : *The Naked Civil Servant* (1968)

31 The purpose of the Presidential Office is not power, or leadership of the Western World, but reminiscence, best-selling reminiscence.

Roger Jellinek 1938– : in *New York Times Book Review* 1969; Jonathon Green (ed.) *A Dictionary of Contemporary Quotations* (1982)

32 Next to the writer of real estate advertisements, the autobiographer is the most suspect of prose artists.

Donal Henahan: in *New York Times* 1977; Jonathon Green (ed.) *A Dictionary of Contemporary Quotations* (1982)

33 I have always liked reading biographies. It is the ideal literary genre for someone too prim, like me, to acknowledge a gossipy interest in the living—don't you *hate* gossips, aren't they *too* awful?—but avid for any nuggets from the private lives of the dead because that is perfectly respectable, an altogether worthy and informative way of spending one's time.

Jill Tweedie 1936–93: *It's Only Me* (1980)

34 Blamelessness runs riot through six hundred pages.

John Vincent 1937– : review of Kenneth Harris's biography of Attlee; in *Sunday Times* 26 September 1982

35 As a devoted reader of autobiographies, I have long since come to dread passages which begin with 'The family hailed originally, I believe, from Cleckheaton', and back we go to the middle of the eighteenth century where, before long, there surges up a frightful old 'Character' called 'Grumps', first cousin to the Starkadders, who becomes the Scourge of Bradford and extremely bad news all over Yorkshire.

Arthur Marshall 1910–89: *Life's Rich Pageant* (1984)

Autographing a book for a dissatisfied customer:
36 CUSTOMER: But usen't you to be J. B. Priestley?
PRIESTLAND: That was a long time ago.

Gerald Priestland 1927–91: *Something Understood* (1986)

37 *Recreations*: growling, prowling, scowling and owling.

Nicholas Fairbairn 1933– : entry in *Who's Who 1990*

38 I used to think I was an interesting person, but I must tell you how sobering a thought it is to realize your life's story fills about thirty-five pages and you have, actually, not much to say.

Roseanne Arnold 1953– : *Roseanne* (1990)

Of political memoirists:
39 It is an exceptionally inadequate ex-minister who fails to secure a six-figure sum for his work, serialization included.

Hugo Young 1938– : in *Guardian* 20 September 1990

40 The first biography of Tennyson to refer to the television soap opera *Neighbours*.

Anonymous: publicity for Michael Thorn's biography of Tennyson (1992); in *Ned Sherrin in his Anecdotage* (1993)

Giles Gordon's father had criticized the length of his son's entry in Who's Who:

41 I've just measured it, with a ruler; it's exactly the same length as my male organ, which I've also just measured.

Giles Gordon 1940– : *Aren't We Due a Royalty Statement?* (1993)

42 *Recreations*: drawing ships, making quips, confounding Whips, scuttling drips.

Nicholas Fairbairn 1933– : entry in *Who's Who* 1994

43 Even when Micheál [MacLíammóir] took in later life to autobiographies, they were about as reliable as his hairpieces.

Sheridan Morley 1941– : in *Sunday Times* 6 February 1994

Birds and Animals

1 If ye could get me a wild Sow and close her in a coffer, or in some other thing to be made for her, and to send her unto me alive, ye should do me as singular and as high a pleasure as is possible to devise.

William Fitzwilliam c.1490–1543: letter to Lord Lisle, 25 November 1534 in *Lisle Letters* (1985)

2 I think Crab my dog be the sourest-natured dog that lives.

William Shakespeare 1564–1616: *The Two Gentlemen of Verona* (1592–3)

3 Commodus killed a camelopardalis or giraffe...the tallest, the most gentle, and the most useless of the large quadrupeds. This singular animal, a native only of the interior parts of Africa, has not been seen in Europe since the revival of letters, and though M. de Buffon...has endeavoured to describe, he has not ventured to delineate the giraffe.

Edward Gibbon 1737–94: *The Decline and Fall of the Roman Empire* (1776–88)

4 The more one gets to know of men, the more one values dogs.

A. Toussenel 1803–85: *L'Esprit des bêtes* (1847); attributed to Mme Roland in the form 'The more I see of men, the more I like dogs'

5 Oh how the family affections combat
Within this heart, and each hour flings a bomb at
My burning soul! Neither from owl or from bat
Can peace be gained until I clasp my wombat.

Dante Gabriel Rossetti 1828–82: on the loss of his pet wombat, and his other pets; 'The Wombat' (1849)

6 Nothing brutalizes people more than cruelty to animals, and to dogs, who are the companions of man, it is especially revolting. The Queen is sorry to say, that she thinks the English are inclined to be more cruel to animals than some other civilized nations are.

Queen Victoria 1819–1901: letter to the Home Secretary, 20 July 1868

7 If I were a cassowary
On the plains of Timbuctoo,
I would eat a missionary,
Cassock, band, and hymn-book too.

Samuel Wilberforce 1805–73: impromptu verse, attributed

8 There was one poor tiger that hadn't *got* a Christian.

Punch 1841–1992: vol. 68 (1875)

9 A hen is only an egg's way of making other eggs.

Samuel Butler 1835–1902: *Life and Habit* (1877)

10 Bred en bawn in a brier-patch!

Joel Chandler Harris 1848–1908:
*Uncle Remus and His Legends of the
Old Plantation* (1881) 'How Mr Rabbit
was too Sharp for Mr Fox'

11 Tar-baby ain't sayin' nuthin', en Brer Fox, he lay low.

Joel Chandler Harris 1848–1908:
*Uncle Remus and His Legends of the
Old Plantation* (1881) 'The Wonderful
Tar-Baby Story'

12 He thought he saw an Elephant,
That practised on a fife:
He looked again, and found it was
A letter from his wife.
'At length I realize,' he said,
'The bitterness of life!'

Lewis Carroll 1832–98: *Sylvie and
Bruno* (1889)

13 I shoot the Hippopotamus
With bullets made of platinum,
Because if I use leaden ones
His hide is sure to flatten 'em.

Hilaire Belloc 1870–1953: 'The
Hippopotamus' (1896)

14 The Tiger, on the other hand, is kittenish and mild,
He makes a pretty play fellow for any little child;
And mothers of large families (who claim to common
　　sense)
Will find a Tiger well repay the trouble and expense.

Hilaire Belloc 1870–1953: 'The
Tiger' (1896)

15 I had an Aunt in Yucatan
Who bought a Python from a man
And kept it for a pet.
She died, because she never knew
These simple little rules and few;—
The Snake is living yet.

Hilaire Belloc 1870–1953: 'The
Python' (1897)

16 They say a reasonable amount o' fleas is good fer
a dog—keeps him from broodin' over bein' a dog, mebbe.

Edward Noyes Westcott
1846–98: *David Harum* (1898)

17 Don't go into Mr McGregor's garden: your father had an
accident there, he was put into a pie by Mrs McGregor.

Beatrix Potter 1866–1943: *The Tale
of Peter Rabbit* (1902)

18 When a man wants to murder a tiger he calls it sport;
when a tiger wants to murder him, he calls it ferocity.

George Bernard Shaw
1856–1950: *Man and Superman* (1903)

19 Oh, a wondrous bird is the pelican!
His beak holds more than his belican.
He takes in his beak
Food enough for a week.
But I'll be darned if I know how the helican.

Dixon Lanier Merritt 1879–1972:
in *Nashville Banner* 22 April 1913

20 My God...The hero is a bee!

Sam Goldwyn 1882–1974: on
reading the synopsis of a story by
Maurice Maeterlinck in 1920; Michael
Freedland *The Goldwyn Touch* (1986)

21 The rabbit has a charming face:
Its private life is a disgrace.
I really dare not name to you
The awful things that rabbits do.

Anonymous: *The Week-End Book*
(1925) 'The Rabbit'

22 Arabs of means rode none but she-camels, since they...
were patient and would endure to march long after they
were worn out, indeed until they tottered with
exhaustion and fell in their tracks and died: whereas the
coarser males grew angry, flung themselves down when
tired, and from sheer rage would die there unnecessarily.

T. E. Lawrence 1888–1935: *Seven
Pillars of Wisdom* (1926)

23 Eeyore, the old grey Donkey, stood by the side of the
stream, and looked at himself in the water. 'Pathetic,' he
said. 'That's what it is. Pathetic.'

A. A. Milne 1882–1956: *Winnie-the-
Pooh* (1926)

24 [Arthur Platt] was a Fellow of the Zoological Society,
frequented its Gardens, and inspired a romantic passion
in their resident population. There was a leopard which
at Platt's approach would almost ooze through the bars
of its cage to establish contact with the beloved object.

A. E. Housman 1859–1936:
preface to Arthur Platt *Nine Essays*
(1927)

25 Canaries, caged in the house, do it,
When they're out of season, grouse do it.

Cole Porter 1891–1964: 'Let's Do It,
Let's Fall in Love' (1928)

26 Pooh began to feel a little more comfortable, because
when you are a Bear of Very Little Brain, and you Think
of Things, you find sometimes that a Thing which
seemed very Thingish inside you is quite different when it
gets out into the open and has other people looking at it.

A. A. Milne 1882–1956: *The House
at Pooh Corner* (1928)

27 I know two things about the horse
And one of them is rather coarse.

Naomi Royde-Smith
c.1875–1964: in *Weekend Book* (1928)

28 The cow is of the bovine ilk;
One end is moo, the other, milk.

Ogden Nash 1902–71: 'The Cow'
(1931)

29 The turtle lives 'twixt plated decks
Which practically conceal its sex.
I think it clever of the turtle
In such a fix to be so fertile.

Ogden Nash 1902–71: 'Autres Bêtes,
Autres Moeurs' (1931)

30 One disadvantage of being a hog is that at any moment
some blundering fool may try to make a silk purse out of
your wife's ear.

J. B. Morton 1893–1975: *By the
Way* (1931)

*The Lindbergh's fierce guard dog, Thor, had shown signs of not caring
for Harold Nicolson:*
31 By the time you get this I shall either be front-page news
or Thor's chum.

Harold Nicolson 1886–1968: letter
to his wife Vita Sackville-West,
30 September 1934

32 The camel has a single hump;
The dromedary, two;
Or else the other way around,
I'm never sure. Are you?

Ogden Nash 1902–71: 'The Camel'
(1936)

33 God in His wisdom made the fly
And then forgot to tell us why.

Ogden Nash 1902–71: 'The Fly'
(1942)

34 A Heron flies in a slow leisurely manner, as if it was
hoping to remember where it's going before it actually
gets there.

Anthony Armstrong 1897–1976:
Good Egg! (1944)

35 Even the rabbits
Inhibit their habits
On Sunday at Cicero Falls.

E. Y. Harburg 1898–1981: 'Sunday at Cicero Falls' (1944)

36 Four legs good, two legs bad.

George Orwell 1903–50: *Animal Farm* (1945)

37 On my 1st night in this utterly luxurious flat I was
woken up by a RAT sitting on my tummy. So like Paris
somehow. It jumped off (when I spoke to it) with exactly
the same amount of noise and impact a great dane
would have made and galloped away over the parquet
like a cart-horse.

Nancy Mitford 1904–73: letter 3 November 1947

38 Rudolph, the Red-Nosed Reindeer
Had a very shiny nose,
And if you ever saw it,
You would even say it glows.

Johnny Marks 1909–85: 'Rudolph, the Red-Nosed Reindeer' (1949)

39 Get out of town!
And he went, with a quack and a waddle and a quack,
In a flurry of eiderdown.

Frank Loesser 1910–69: 'The Ugly Duckling' (1952)

40 A door is what a dog is perpetually on the wrong side of.

Ogden Nash 1902–71: 'A Dog's Best Friend is his Illiteracy' (1953)

41 It's awf'lly bad luck on Diana,
Her ponies have swallowed their bits;
She fished down their throats with a spanner
And frightened them all into fits.

John Betjeman 1906–84: 'Hunter Trials' (1954)

42 Slow but sure the turtle
Enormously fert'le
Lays her eggs by the dozens,
Maybe some are her cousins,
Even the catamount is nonplussed by that amount
It's Spring, Spring, Spring!

Johnny Mercer 1909–76: 'Spring, Spring, Spring' (1954)

Of a dog belonging to the headmaster of Eton:
43 Do you recollect the Alington poodle—exactly like
a typhoid germ magnified.

George Lyttelton 1883–1962: letter to Rupert Hart-Davis, 11 April 1957

44 The Ostrich roams the great Sahara.
Its mouth is wide, its neck is narra.
It has such long and lofty legs,
I'm glad it sits to lay its eggs.

Ogden Nash 1902–71: 'The Ostrich' (1957)

45 Diana gives a terrible account of your cat, such
a wrecker? Alas old animals are so much nicer I love my
cat now, but it took about 8 years.

Nancy Mitford 1904–73: letter to Lady Redesdale, 16 December 1959

46 *Puella Rigensis ridebat*
Quam tigris in tergo vehebat;
Externa profecta,
Interna revecta,
Risusque cum tigre manebat.
There was a young lady of Riga
Who went for a ride on a tiger;
They returned from the ride

Anonymous: R. L. Green (ed.) *A Century of Humorous Verse* (1959)

With the lady inside,
And a smile on the face of the tiger.

47 I am fond of pigs. Dogs look up to us. Cats look down on us. Pigs treat us as equal.   .

Winston Churchill 1874–1965: M. Gilbert *Never Despair* (1988); attributed

Of dogs:
48 It's the one species I wouldn't mind seeing vanish from the face of the earth. I wish they were like the White Rhino—six of them left in the Serengeti National Park, and all males.

Alan Bennett 1934– : *Getting On* (1972)

49 It's from one of those battery farms...A few hens who've earned privileges for good behaviour are allowed out in front of the sheds. Meanwhile the rest are bound and gagged inside.

Alan Bennett 1934– : *Getting On* (1972)

50 The lion and the calf shall lie down together but the calf won't get much sleep.

Woody Allen 1935– : in *New Republic* 31 August 1974

51 That indefatigable and unsavoury engine of pollution, the dog.

John Sparrow 1906–92: letter to *The Times* 30 September 1975

52 Cats and dogs amicably embracing before a grate of glowing coals exist chiefly in the reckless imagination of the greetings card artist, who does nothing for credibility by adding the caption 'Good Pals' in flowing script.

Basil Boothroyd 1910–88: *Let's Move House* (1977)

53 I have had some extremely endearing bulls. I had one Ayrshire bull down in Kent who was extremely friendly. One day he walked into a wedding reception in the village hall. He was, of course, perfectly harmless but caused a bit of a panic. I believe he also knocked over the wedding cake.

Lord Massereene and Ferrard 1914–93: speech on the Wildlife and Countryside Bill, House of Lords 19 February 1981

54 Dogs who earn their living by appearing in television commercials in which they constantly and aggressively demand meat should remember that in at least one Far Eastern country they *are* meat.

Fran Lebowitz 1946– : *Social Studies* (1981)

55 Spiders are the SAS of nature, and will spend hours flying through the air on their ropes, prior to landing and subjecting some hapless insect to savage interrogation. The question they usually ask is: 'Have you any last requests?'

Miles Kington 1941– : *Nature Made Ridiculously Simple* (1983)

56 SUSAN: No, my father didn't approve.
BILL: Of horses?
SUSAN: Of animals. Dogs, cats, hamsters, horses. He had a theory that they gave off diseases...
BILL: Well, he was right, they do. They also give off an awful lot of happiness. Which probably balances it up in the long run. People may catch diseases but at least they die happier.

Alan Ayckbourn 1939– : *Woman in Mind* (1986)

57 To my mind, the only possible pet is a cow. Cows love you...They will listen to your problems and never ask a thing in return. They will be your friends for ever. And

Bill Bryson 1951– : *Neither Here Nor There* (1991)

when you get tired of them, you can kill and eat them.
Perfect.

58 I wouldn't really call it a cushion, Pekingese is a more
common name for them. No, well never mind, he was
very old.

Stephen Fry 1957– : *Paperweight*
(1992)

59 If our history of bear-baiting, pit ponies and ejected
Christmas puppies can honestly be called a great British
love affair with animals then the average praying mantis
and her husband are Darby and Joan.

Stephen Fry 1957– : *Paperweight*
(1992)

*During his time in the Lords the eighth Earl of Arran was concerned
with measures for homosexual reform and the protection of badgers,
interests concisely summed up by a fellow peer:*

60 Teaching people not to bugger badgers and not to badger
buggers.

Anonymous: in *Ned Sherrin in his
Anecdotage* (1993)

The Body See also *Appearance, Description*

1 Thou seest I have more flesh than another man, and
therefore more frailty.

William Shakespeare 1564–1616:
Henry IV, Part 1 (1597)

2 You may know by my size that I have a kind of alacrity
in sinking.

William Shakespeare 1564–1616:
The Merry Wives of Windsor (1597)

To William Cecil, who suffered from gout:

3 My lord, we make use of you, not for your bad legs, but
for your good head.

Elizabeth I 1533–1603: F.
Chamberlin *Sayings of Queen
Elizabeth* (1923)

4 What they call 'heart' lies much lower than the fourth
waistcoat button.

Georg Christoph Lichtenberg
1742–99: notebook (1776–79) in
Aphorisms (1990)

5 And our carcases, which are to rise again, are they
worth raising? I hope, if mine is, that I shall have
a better pair of legs than I have moved on these two-and-
twenty years, or I shall be sadly behind in the squeeze
into Paradise.

Lord Byron 1788–1824: letter
13 September 1811

6 He had but one eye, and the popular prejudice runs in
favour of two.

Charles Dickens 1812–70: *Nicholas
Nickleby* (1839)

7 If you could see my legs when I take my boots off, you'd
form some idea of what unrequited affection is.

Charles Dickens 1812–70: *Dombey
and Son* (1848)

On the probable reaction to the painting of the subjects of Turner's
Girls Surprised while Bathing:

8 I should think devilish surprised to see what Turner has
made of them.

Dante Gabriel Rossetti 1828–82:
O. Doughty *A Victorian Romantic*
(1960)

9 I have a left shoulder-blade that is a miracle of loveliness.
People come miles to see it. My right elbow has
a fascination that few can resist.

W. S. Gilbert 1836–1911: *The
Mikado* (1885)

10 Bah! the thing is not a nose at all, but a bit of primordial
chaos clapped on to my face.

H. G. Wells 1866–1946: *Select
Conversations with an Uncle* (1895)
'The Man with a Nose'

11 His legs, perhaps, were shorter than they should have been.

Lytton Strachey 1880–1932: *Eminent Victorians* (1918) 'Dr Arnold'

12 A bit of talcum
Is always walcum.

Ogden Nash 1902–1971: 'The Baby' (1931)

13 He was built on large lines, and seemed to fill the room to overflowing. In physique he was not unlike what Primo Carnera would have been if Carnera hadn't stunted his growth by smoking cigarettes when a boy.

P. G. Wodehouse 1881–1975: *Mulliner Nights* (1933)

14 What is man, when you come to think upon him, but a minutely set, ingenious machine for turning, with infinite artfulness, the red wine of Shiraz into urine?

Isak Dinesen 1885–1962: *Seven Gothic Tales* (1934) 'The Dreamers'

Warning his young son John to avoid opium on account of its 'terrible binding effect':
15 Have you ever seen the pictures of the wretched poet Coleridge? He smoked opium. Take a look at Coleridge, he was green about the gills and a stranger to the lavatory.

Clifford Mortimer: John Mortimer *Clinging to the Wreckage* (1982)

16 Imprisoned in every fat man a thin one is wildly signalling to be let out.

Cyril Connolly 1903–74: *The Unquiet Grave* (1944)

17 I travel light; as light,
That is, as a man can travel who will
Still carry his body around because
Of its sentimental value.

Christopher Fry 1907– : *The Lady's not for Burning* (1949)

18 In an advanced state of nudity.

Joe Orton 1933–67: *Up Against It*, screenplay written for the Beatles but never filmed

19 I would merely say that if everyone who caught an unlooked-for glimpse of the female bosom chose to publish it in book form, civilization would very shortly grind to a halt.

Alan Bennett 1934– : *Forty Years On* (1969)

20 Like all stout women she is very fat, but then, it would be inconsistent of her to be otherwise, would it not?

Alan Bennett 1934– : *Forty Years On* (1969)

21 The body of a young woman is God's greatest achievement...Of course, He could have built it to last longer but you can't have everything.

Neil Simon 1927– : *The Gingerbread Lady* (1970)

22 There is something between us.

Donald Hall 1928– : 'Breasts' (a one-line poem, 1971)

23 I didn't pay three pounds fifty just to see half a dozen acorns and a chipolata.

Noël Coward 1899–1973: on David Storey's *The Changing Room*; attributed

24 Tragic. And he came through puberty with such flying colours.

Alan Bennett 1934– : *Habeas Corpus* (1973)

25 My brain? It's my second favourite organ.

Woody Allen 1935– and **Marshall Brickman** 1941– : *Sleeper* (1973 film)

THE BODY · BOOKS

26 Obesity is really widespread.

Joseph O. Kern II: Laurence J. Peter (ed.) *Quotations for our Time* (1977)

27 Let's forget the six feet and talk about the seven inches.

Mae West 1892–1980: G. Eells and S. Musgrove *Mae West* (1989)

28 The only hope for someone like me with pigeon toes is that one day, I'll be carried off feet first in a flight of my own fancy.

Alan Ayckbourn 1939– : *Sisterly Feelings* (1981)

29 [Alfred Hitchcock] thought of himself as looking like Cary Grant. That's tough, to think of yourself one way and look another.

Tippi Hedren 1935– : interview in California, 1982; P. F. Boller and R. L. Davis *Hollywood Anecdotes* (1988)

After Richard Burton had left his wife Sybil for Elizabeth Taylor, he periodically turned up for maudlin reunions. At the end of one visit he announced that he must get back to the Dorchester or there would be 'a lot of breast-beating':

30 And indeed, there's quite a lot of breast to beat, isn't there?

Sybil Burton: James Harding *Emlyn Williams* (1987)

31 I'd like to borrow his body for just 48 hours. There are three guys I'd like to beat up and four women I'd like to make love to.

Jim Murray: of Muhammad Ali; attributed

32 Even thin people look fat there [New York], and fat women are always out with handsome men (not like in California, where everyone thinks fat is something you can catch, and therefore is to be avoided).

Roseanne Arnold 1953– : *Roseanne* (1990)

33 I am sitting in bed this morning...my head more full of undesirable fluids than the Cambridge public swimming baths.

Stephen Fry 1957– : *Paperweight* (1992)

Books See also *Dictionaries, Libraries, Literature, Poetry and Poets, Publishing, Writers and Writing*

1 My desire is...that mine adversary had written a book.

Bible: *Job*

2 I hate books; they only teach us to talk about things we know nothing about.

Jean-Jacques Rousseau 1712–78: *Émile* (1762)

3 Digressions, incontestably, are the sunshine;—they are the life, the soul of reading;—take them out of this book for instance,—you might as well take the book along with them.

Laurence Sterne 1713–68: *Tristram Shandy* (1759–67)

4 [ELPHINSTON:] What, have you not read it through? [JOHNSON:] No, Sir, do *you* read books *through*?

Samuel Johnson 1709–84: James Boswell *Life of Samuel Johnson* (1791) 19 April 1773

5 Take care not to understand editions and title-pages too well. It always smells of pedantry, and not always of learning...Beware of the *bibliomanie*.

Lord Chesterfield 1694–1773: *Letters to his Son* (1774)

6 No furniture so charming as books.

Sydney Smith 1771–1845: Lady Holland *Memoir* (1855)

7 'Pilgrim's Progress', about a man that left his family it didn't say why...The statements was interesting, but tough.

Mark Twain 1835–1910: *The Adventures of Huckleberry Finn* (1884)

8 There is no such thing as a moral or an immoral book. Books are well written, or badly written.

Oscar Wilde 1854–1900: *The Picture of Dorian Gray* (1891)

9 One man is as good as another until he has written a book.

Benjamin Jowett 1817–93: Evelyn Abbott and Lewis Campbell (eds.) *Life and Letters of Benjamin Jowett* (1897)

10 The good ended happily, and the bad unhappily. That is what fiction means.

Oscar Wilde 1854–1900: *The Importance of Being Earnest* (1895)

11 'Classic.' A book which people praise and don't read.

Mark Twain 1835–1910: *Following the Equator* (1897)

12 If you don't find it in the Index, look very carefully through the entire catalogue.

Anonymous: in *Consumer's Guide, Sears, Roebuck and Co.* (1897); Donald E. Knuth *Sorting and Searching* (1973)

13 In every first novel the hero is the author as Christ or Faust.

Oscar Wilde 1854–1900: attributed

14 In the old days books were written by men of letters and read by the public. Nowadays books are written by the public and read by anybody.

Oscar Wilde 1854–1900: attributed

15 This left me with only one unprinted masterpiece, my Opus 1, which had cost me an unconscionable quantity of paper, and was called, with merciless fitness, Immaturity. Part of it had by this time been devoured by mice, though even they had not been able to finish it.

George Bernard Shaw 1856–1950: 'Novels of my Nonage' (1901)

16 Synopsis of Previous Chapters: There are no Previous Chapters.

Stephen Leacock 1869–1944: *Nonsense Novels* (1911) 'Gertrude the Governess'

On being lent a hot-from-the-press copy of Lytton Strachey's Eminent Victorians *in 1918:*
17 We are in for a bad time.

G. M. Young 1882–1959: attributed

18 Things were easier for the old novelists who saw people all of a piece. Speaking generally, their heroes were good through and through, their villains wholly bad.

W. Somerset Maugham 1874–1965: *A Writer's Notebook* (1949) written in 1922

Preface to 'second edition':
19 A first edition limited to one copy and printed on rice paper and bound in buck-boards and signed by one of the editors was sold to the other editor, who left it in a taxi somewhere between Piccadilly Circus and the Bodleian.

W. C. Sellar 1898–1951 and **R. J. Yeatman** 1898–1968: *1066 and All That* (1930)

The Editors' acknowledgements:
20 Their thanks are also due to their wife for not preparing the index wrong. There is no index.

W. C. Sellar 1898–1951 and **R. J. Yeatman** 1898–1968: 1066 *and All That* (1930)

21 Of each volume [of Manilius] there were printed 400 copies: only the first is yet sold out, and that took 23 years; and the reason why it took no longer is that it found purchasers among the unlearned, who had heard that it contained a scurrilous preface and hoped to extract from it a low enjoyment.

A. E. Housman 1859–1936: *The Editing of Manilius* (1930)

22 Arrival of Book of the Month choice, and am disappointed. History of a place I am not interested in, by an author I do not like.

E. M. Delafield 1890–1943: *The Diary of a Provincial Lady* (1930)

23 A best-seller is the gilded tomb of a mediocre talent.

Logan Pearsall Smith 1865–1946: *Afterthoughts* (1931) 'Art and Letters'

24 People say that life is the thing, but I prefer reading.

Logan Pearsall Smith 1865–1946: *Afterthoughts* (1931) 'Myself'

25 This is primarily a picture-book and the letterpress is intended to do no more than provide a small mass of information leavened by a large dose of personal prejudice.

Osbert Lancaster 1908–80: *Pillar to Post* (1938)

26 [*The Compleat Angler*] is acknowledged to be one of the world's books. Only the trouble is that the world doesn't read its books, it borrows a detective story instead.

Stephen Leacock 1869–1944: *The Boy I Left Behind Me* (1947)

27 Here again is '*Human Geography*', the fortunate phrase by good old Jean Brunhes, while still young, so fortunate that he lived on it for the rest of his life. It is marvellous what a good title does.

Stephen Leacock 1869–1944: *The Boy I Left Behind Me* (1947)

28 An index is a great leveller.

George Bernard Shaw 1856–1950: G. N. Knight *Indexing* (1979); attributed, perhaps apocryphal

29 What really knocks me out is a book that, when you're all done reading it, you wish the author that wrote it was a terrific friend of yours and you could call him up on the phone whenever you felt like it.

J. D. Salinger 1919– : *Catcher in the Rye* (1951)

30 I am writing a book about the Crusades so *dull* that I can scarcely write it.

Hilaire Belloc 1870–1953: Rupert Hart-Davis letter to George Lyttelton, 25 March 1956

31 When the [Supreme] Court moved to Washington in 1800, it was provided with no books, which probably accounts for the high quality of early opinions.

Robert H. Jackson 1892–1954: *The Supreme Court in the American System of Government* (1955)

32 I opened it at page 96—the secret page on which I write my name to catch out borrowers and book-sharks.

Flann O'Brien 1911–66: *Myles Away from Dublin* (1990)

33 Some savage faculty for observation told him that most respectable and estimable people usually had a lot of books in their houses.

Flann O'Brien 1911–66: *The Best of Myles* (1968)

34 I've just heard on the wireless that there's no point in writing books any more because the electric brain can do it better. I'm all for it so long as I don't have to read the Brain's effusions, don't feel they are made for me.

Nancy Mitford 1904–73: letter 7 October 1967

35 Reading isn't an occupation we encourage among police officers. We try to keep the paper work down to a minimum.

Joe Orton 1933–67: *Loot* (1967)

36 This is not a novel to be tossed aside lightly. It should be thrown with great force.

Dorothy Parker 1893–1967: R. E. Drennan *Wit's End* (1973)

37 I read part of it all the way through.

Sam Goldwyn 1882–1974: N. Zierold *Hollywood Tycoons* (1969)

38 Book—what they make a movie out of for television.

Leonard Louis Levinson:
Laurence J. Peter (ed.) *Quotations for
our Time* (1977)

39 Having been unpopular in high school is not just cause
for book publication.

Fran Lebowitz 1946- :
Metropolitan Life (1978)

Of Hinsley's official history of spies:
40 A book by a committee, for a committee, about
a committee: history without the people.

Maurice Oldfield 1915-81: in
Observer 10 May 1987; attributed

41 One of those big, fat paperbacks, intended to while away
a monsoon or two, which, if thrown with a good
overarm action, will bring a water buffalo to its knees.

Nancy Banks-Smith: review of
television adaptation of M. M. Kaye
The Far Pavilions; in *Guardian*
4 January 1984

On hearing that Watership Down *was a novel about rabbits written
by a civil servant:*
42 I would rather read a novel about civil servants written
by a rabbit.

Craig Brown 1957- : attributed;
probably apocryphal

43 It's very difficult to find a book with no alcohol, no sex
and no reference to men whatever.

Victoria Wood 1953- : *Mens Sana
in Thingummy Doodah* (1990)

44 Should not the Society of Indexers be known as Indexers,
Society of, The?

Keith Waterhouse 1929- :
Bookends (1990)

45 Whenever I am sent a new book on the lively arts, the
first thing I do is look for myself in the index.

Julie Burchill 1960- : *The
Spectator* 16 January 1992

46 A hefty, overblown production whose insane initial price
ensured its arrival in the remainder shops by the direct
route from the warehouse.

Clive James 1939- : *The Dreaming
Swimmer* (1992)

47 Vilely set on what must have been a hand press once
dropped, with unnecessary violence, to partisans in
Yugoslavia.

Clive James 1939- : *The Dreaming
Swimmer* (1992)

48 This is not a book for the pundit, the savant, the serious
student of the political process, or the policy wonk.
Nowhere in these pages are there prescient comments by
men named Kevin, Ed, or Fritz, or barbed asides by
bespectacled women named Ann.

Joe Queenan: *Imperial Caddy*
(1992)

49 There are books you don't read because life is too short
(will *Clarissa* ever seem a temporal bargain against
rereading all Jane Austen?); books whose silly titles put
you off for years (*The Catcher in the Rye* has no faults
except its misleadingly ludic-pastoral title); books you
won't read because some old fool once recommended
them.

Julian Barnes 1946- : in *Daily
Telegraph* 22 January 1994

Bores and Boredom

1 It is to be noted that when any part of this paper appears
dull there is a design in it.

Richard Steele 1672-1729: *The
Tatler* 7 July 1709

2 He was dull in a new way, and that made many people
think him *great*.

Samuel Johnson 1709-84: of
Thomas Gray; James Boswell *Life of
Samuel Johnson* (1791) 28 March 1775

3 He is not only dull in himself, but the cause of dullness in others.

Samuel Foote 1720–77: on a dull law lord; James Boswell *Life of Samuel Johnson* (1934 ed.) 1783

4 In England people actually try to be brilliant at breakfast. That is so dreadful of them! Only dull people are brilliant at breakfast.

Oscar Wilde 1854–1900: *An Ideal Husband* (1895)

5 A bore is a man who, when you ask him how he is, tells you.

Bert Leston Taylor 1866–1901: *The So-Called Human Race* (1922)

6 Dullness is so much stronger than genius because there is so much more of it, and it is better organized and more naturally cohesive *inter se*. So the arctic volcano can do nothing against arctic ice.

Samuel Butler 1835–1902: *Notebooks* (1912)

7 A person who talks when you wish him to listen.

Ambrose Bierce 1842–?1914: definition of a bore; *Cynic's Word Book* (1906)

To a bore at table:
8 Have some tongue, like cures like.

Robert Yelverton Tyrrell 1844–1914: Ulick O'Connor *Oliver St John Gogarty* (1964)

9 He is an old bore. Even the grave yawns for him.

Herbert Beerbohm Tree 1852–1917: of Israel Zangwill; Max Beerbohm *Herbert Beerbohm Tree* (1920)

10 The boredom occasioned by too much restraint is always preferable to that produced by an uncontrolled enthusiasm for a pointless variety.

Osbert Lancaster 1908–80: *Pillar to Post* (1938)

A device used by Wavell, when Viceroy, 'to get him through the tedium of Indian dinner parties':
11 He turns to his female neighbour, when conversation flags, and asks 'If you were not a woman—what animal would you like to be?'

Lord Wavell 1883–1950: Chips Channon diary 7 January 1944

12 Dylan talked copiously, then stopped. 'Somebody's boring me,' he said, 'I think it's me.'

Dylan Thomas 1914–53: Rayner Heppenstall *Four Absentees* (1960)

13 Across the table... loomed the benignant but deadly form of Lord Dunsany, who will bore you to sleep on the subject of rock-salt if you give him a glimpse of an opening.

Rupert Hart-Davis 1907– : letter to George Lyttelton, 26 February 1956

14 A bore is simply a nonentity who resents his humble lot in life, and seeks satisfaction for his wounded ego by forcing himself on his betters.

H. L. Mencken 1880–1956: *Minority Report* (1956)

15 The capacity of human beings to bore one another seems to be vastly greater than that of any other animals. Some of their most esteemed inventions have no other apparent purpose, for example, the dinner party of more than two, the epic poem, and the science of metaphysics.

H. L. Mencken 1880–1956: *Minority Report* (1956)

16 He was not only a bore; he bored for England.

Malcolm Muggeridge 1903–90: of Anthony Eden; *Tread Softly* (1966)

17 I'm really very fond of Tom but he really is terribly heavy going. Like running up hill in roller skates.

Alan Ayckbourn 1939– : *Living Together* (1975)

18 My boredom threshold is low at the best of times but I have spent more time being slowly and excruciatingly bored by children than any other section of the human race.

Jill Tweedie 1936–93: *It's Only Me* (1980)

19 The only rule I have found to have any validity in writing is not to bore yourself.

John Mortimer 1923– : *Clinging to the Wreckage* (1982)

20 I can truthfully say that I have never in my life been bored, however inviting the circumstances. The most severe challenge was, I suppose, provided by the chapel services at Oundle School in the 1920s but even here, though at maximum ennui risk and encased in sombre black and starched collar and feeling fairly Sundayish and dreary, there was always something to activate the imagination.

Arthur Marshall 1910–89: *Life's Rich Pageant* (1984)

21 What's wrong with being a boring kind of guy?

George Bush 1924– : during the campaign for the Republican nomination; in *Daily Telegraph* 28 April 1988

22 Most of my contemporaries at school entered the World of Business, the logical destiny of bores.

Barry Humphries 1934– : *More Please* (1992)

Broadcasting and Television

1 *Television?* The word is half Greek, half Latin. No good can come of it.

C. P. Scott 1846–1932: view of the editor of the *Manchester Guardian*; Asa Briggs *The BBC: the First Fifty Years* (1985)

Edward Boyle's father did not appreciate the somewhat radical tone of J. B. Priestley's wartime broadcasts:

2 The feller sounds as though he's after my dining room clock.

Edward Boyle 1878–1945: in *Ned Sherrin in his Anecdotage* (1993)

3 TV—a clever contraction derived from the words Terrible Vaudeville…we call it a medium because nothing's well done.

Goodman Ace 1899–1982: letter to Groucho Marx, c.1953

4 We hope to amuse the customers with music and with rhyme
But ninety minutes is a long, long time.

Noël Coward 1899–1973: '90 Minutes is a Long, Long Time' (1955); opening song for a CBS television live special starring Noël Coward and Mary Martin

5 Television is for appearing on, not looking at.

Noël Coward 1899–1973: Dick Richards *The Wit of Noël Coward* (1968)

Of television:

6 It used to be that we in films were the lowest form of art. Now we have something to look down on.

Billy Wilder 1906– : A. Madsen *Billy Wilder* (1968)

7 The media. It sounds like a convention of spiritualists.

Tom Stoppard 1937– : *Night and Day* (1978)

8 Perhaps one of the more noteworthy trends of our time is the occupation of buildings accompanied by the taking of hostages. The perpetrators of these deeds are generally motivated by political grievance, social injustice, and the deeply felt desire to see how they look on TV.

Fran Lebowitz 1946– : *Metropolitan Life* (1978)

9 Television is simultaneously blamed, often by the same people, for worsening the world and for being powerless to change it.

Clive James 1939– : *Glued to the Box* (1981); introduction

10 Every time I think that Ned Sherrin is dead I switch on the television and see him in some dreadful, off-colour programme which brings home all too painfully the fact that he is still alive.

Ian Hamilton 1938– : Ned Sherrin *Cutting Edge* (1984); attributed

Of the time when, still on the staff of Oundle School, he started to broadcast:
11 I became the object of some quite friendly publicity, with its attendant misprints ('Arthur Marshall is, of course, a master at a pubic school').

Arthur Marshall 1910–89: *Life's Rich Pageant* (1984)

12 IAN ST JOHN: Is he speaking to you yet?
JIMMY GREAVES: Not yet, but I hope to be incommunicado with him in a very short space of time.

Jimmy Greaves 1940– : Barry Fantoni (ed.) *Private Eye's Colemanballs 2* (1984)

13 9.55 Des O'Connor with Max Bygraves as chief guest; it looks like overkill night, charmwise.

Geoffrey Parsons: TV listings in the *Evening Standard*; Ned Sherrin *Cutting Edge* (1984)

14 Any story that begins with a cancerous giraffe stamping on the genitals of its keeper must surely be marked high for cliché-avoidance.

Russell Davies 1946– : on the televising of Angus Wilson's *The Old Men at the Zoo*; in *Sunday Times* 18 September 1983

On television programmes:
15 I don't mind the quizzes so much as the discussion programmes. The ones where they go, 'Yes, you—the lady with the blotchy neck—do you think they should bring back capital punishment for parking offences?'

Victoria Wood 1953– : *Mens Sana in Thingummy Doodah* (1990)

16 You know daytime television? You know what it's supposed to be for? It's to keep unemployed people happy. It's supposed to stop them running to the social security demanding mad luxuries like cookers and windows.

Victoria Wood 1953– : *Mens Sana in Thingummy Doodah* (1990)

17 The best that can be said for Norwegian television is that it gives you the sensation of a coma without the worry and inconvenience.

Bill Bryson 1951– : *Neither Here Nor There* (1991)

18 A TV station, for a man with the right set of characteristics, is an unbeatable mechanism for accumulating debt.

Clive James 1939– : *The Dreaming Swimmer* (1992)

19 To goad the BBC is a rewarding sport in itself. It makes a tabloid feel like a heavyweight.

Clive James 1939– : *The Dreaming Swimmer* (1992)

20 I don't watch television, I think it destroys the art of talking about oneself.

Stephen Fry 1957– : *Paperweight* (1992)

21 It is astonishing how articulate one can become when alone and raving at a radio. Arguments and counter-arguments, rhetoric and bombast flow from one's lips like scurf from the hair of a bank manager.

Stephen Fry 1957– : *Paperweight* (1992)

22 [Men] are happier with women who make their coffee than make their programmes.

Denise O'Donoghue: G. Kinnock and F. Miller (eds.) *By Faith and Daring* (1993)

Bureaucracy

1 Whatever was required to be done, the Circumlocution Office was beforehand with all the public departments in the art of perceiving—HOW NOT TO DO IT.

Charles Dickens 1812–70: *Little Dorrit* (1857)

2 Official dignity tends to increase in inverse ratio to the importance of the country in which the office is held.

Aldous Huxley 1894–1963: *Beyond the Mexique Bay* (1934)

3 This island is made mainly of coal and surrounded by fish. Only an organizing genius could produce a shortage of coal and fish at the same time.

Aneurin Bevan 1897–1960: speech at Blackpool 24 May 1945; in *Daily Herald* 25 May 1945

Explaining why he performed badly in the Civil Service examinations:
4 I evidently knew more about economics than my examiners.

John Maynard Keynes 1883–1946: Roy Harrod *Life of John Maynard Keynes* (1951)

5 By the time the civil service has finished drafting a document to give effect to a principle, there may be little of the principle left.

Lord Reith 1889–1971: *Into the Wind* (1949)

6 I confidently expect that we [civil servants] shall continue to be grouped with mothers-in-law and Wigan Pier as one of the recognized objects of ridicule.

Edward Bridges 1892–1969: *Portrait of a Profession* (1950)

7 The Pentagon, that immense monument to modern man's subservience to the desk.

Oliver Franks 1905– : in *Observer* 30 November 1952

8 A civil servant doesn't make jokes.

Eugène Ionesco 1912–94: *Tueur sans gages* (The Killer, 1958)

9 The man who is denied the opportunity of taking decisions of importance begins to regard as important the decisions he is allowed to take.

C. Northcote Parkinson 1909–93: *Parkinson's Law* (1958)

10 Perfection of planned layout is achieved only by institutions on the point of collapse.

C. Northcote Parkinson 1909–93: *Parkinson's Law* (1958)

11 Here lies a civil servant. He was civil
To everyone, and servant to the devil.

C. H. Sisson 1914– : *The London Zoo* (1961)

12 May I hasten to support Mrs McGurgle's contention that civil servants are human beings, and must be treated as such?

J. B. Morton 1893–1975: M. Frayn (ed.) *The Best of Beachcomber* (1963)

His secretary had suggested throwing away out-of-date files:
13 A good idea, only be sure to make a copy of everything before getting rid of it.

Sam Goldwyn 1882–1974: Michael Freedland *The Goldwyn Touch* (1986)

14 A memorandum is written not to inform the reader but to protect the writer.

Dean Acheson 1893–1971: in *Wall Street Journal* 8 September 1977

15 MAM: Opportunities calling for devoted self-sacrifice don't turn up every day of the week.

MS CRAIG: Quite. Any really first-rate chance of improving the soul gets snapped up by the social services department.

Alan Bennett 1934– : *Enjoy* (1980)

16 Give a civil servant a good case and he'll wreck it with clichés, bad punctuation, double negatives and convoluted apology.

Alan Clark 1928– : diary 22 July 1983

17 I have the title of Co-ordinator. The lowest rank of technical responsibility. Do you see the hideous subtlety of that position? All the black marks at the bottom rise like damp till they reach me. And those that start at the top are deflected down. I am a sort of elephants' graveyard for every black mark somewhere in motion in the Department.

Tom Stoppard 1937– : *Neutral Ground* (1983)

18 Underneath runs the main current of preoccupation, which is keeping one's nose clean at all times. This means that when things go wrong you have to pass the blame along the line, like pass-the-parcel, till the music stops.

Tom Stoppard 1937– : *Neutral Ground* (1983)

19 The truth in these matters may be stated as a scientific law: 'The persistence of public officials varies inversely with the importance of the matter on which they are persisting.'

Bernard Levin 1928– : *In These Times* (1986)

20 It is characteristic of committee discussions and decisions that every member has a vivid recollection of them and that every member's recollection differs violently from every other member's recollection.

Jonathan Lynn 1943– and **Anthony Jay** 1930– : *Yes Prime Minister* vol. 2 (1987)

21 The actual work of government is too unglamorous for the people who govern us to do. Important elected office-holders and high appointed officials create bureaucratic departments to perform the humdrum tasks of national supervision.

P. J. O'Rourke 1947– : *Parliament of Whores* (1991)

Business and Commerce

1 Go to your business, I say, pleasure, whilst I go to my pleasure, business.

William Wycherley c.1640–1716: *The Country Wife* (1675)

2 Put all your eggs in one basket—and WATCH THAT BASKET.

Mark Twain 1835–1910: *Pudd'nhead Wilson* (1894)

3 Breakages, Limited, the biggest industrial corporation in the country.

George Bernard Shaw 1856–1950: *The Apple Cart* (1930)

4 It's a recession when your neighbour loses his job; it's a depression when you lose yours.

Harry S. Truman 1884–1972: in *Observer* 13 April 1958

5 A: I play it the company way
Where the company puts me, there I'll stay.
B: But what is your point of view?
A: I have no point of view!
Supposing the company thinks...I think so too!

Frank Loesser 1910–69: 'The Company Way' (1962)

6 Accountants are the witch-doctors of the modern world and willing to turn their hands to any kind of magic.

Lord Justice Harman 1894–1970: speech, February 1964; Anthony Sampson *The New Anatomy of Britain* (1971)

7 Could Henry Ford produce the Book of Kells? Certainly not. He would quarrel initially with the advisability of such a project and then prove it was impossible.

Flann O'Brien 1911–66: *Myles Away from Dublin* (1990)

8 GERALD: Is she not connected with Trade?
LADY D: Trade? Nonsense. Her father made a fortune by introducing the corset to the Eskimos. That is not trade. It is philanthropy.

Alan Bennett 1934– : *Forty Years On* (1969)

9 [Commercialism is] doing well that which should not be done at all.

Gore Vidal 1925– : in *Listener* 7 August 1975

Definition of insider trading:
10 Stealing too fast.

Calvin Trillin 1935– : 'The Inside on Insider Trading' (1987)

11 Nothing is illegal if one hundred well-placed business men decide to do it.

Andrew Young 1932– : Morris K. Udall *Too Funny to be President* (1988)

Prediction to Lord Carrington from a colleague on the probable nature of Barclays' board meetings:
12 Like High Mass without the vestments.

Anonymous: Lord Carrington *Reflect on Things Past* (1988)

On his dislike of working in teams:
13 A camel is a horse designed by a committee.

Alec Issigonis 1906–88: in *Guardian* 14 January 1991 'Notes and Queries' (attributed)

14 As a simple countryman, he distrusted the use of money and, finding barter cumbersome, preferred to steal.

Miles Kington 1941– : *Welcome to Kington* (1989)

15 The last stage of fitting the product to the market is fitting the market to the product.

Clive James 1939– : in *Observer* 16 October 1989

16 My first rule of consumerism is never to buy anything you can't make your children carry.

Bill Bryson 1951– : *The Lost Continent* (1989)

17 We even sell a pair of earrings for under £1, which is cheaper than a prawn sandwich from Marks & Spencers. But I have to say the earrings probably won't last as long.

Gerald Ratner 1949– : speech to the Institute of Directors, Albert Hall, 23 April 1991

Censorship

1 No government ought to be without censors: and where the press is free, no one ever will.

Thomas Jefferson 1743–1826: letter to George Washington, 9 September 1792

2 When Zola tried to repopulate France by writing a book in praise of parentage [*Fécondité*, 1899], the only comment made here was that the book could not possibly be translated into English, as its subject was too improper.

George Bernard Shaw 1856–1950: preface to *Getting Married* (1911)

3 Assassination is the extreme form of censorship.

George Bernard Shaw
1856–1950: *The Showing-Up of Blanco Posnet* (1911) 'Limits to Toleration'

4 Everybody favours free speech in the slack moments when no axes are being ground.

Heywood Broun 1888–1939: in *New York World* 23 October 1926

Of the tendency of the Classical Dictionary *to deprave and corrupt:*
5 The boys of Eton must not be encouraged to dress themselves as swans or wild beasts for the purpose of idle and illicit flirtation; but that can be the only effect of these deplorable anecdotes.

A. P. Herbert 1890–1971: *Misleading Cases* (1935)

Of Valentine Ackland's longing to enter the censor's department:
6 She has always been perfectly shameless about reading letters not meant for her, and, as she said, she was ideally suited for the work by never having much inclination to answer letters back.

Sylvia Townsend Warner
1893–1978: letter 17 November 1940

In reply to the question, 'Are dirty jokes permissible, and where should the line be drawn?':
7 Jokes which have to do with the natural functions of the mind and body are permissible, whereas jokes which palliate and condone the infiltration of the normal and healthy by the abnormal and unhealthy are impermissible. This...would seem to let in Rabelais, Montaigne, Swift, Sterne, Smollett, and the Restoration dramatists, while letting out writers of thrillers obnoxious to the police.

James Agate 1877–1947: diary 1 July 1942

On her biography of Madame de Pompadour:
8 *Pompadour* is banned in Ireland. This always happens because one or 2 sentences are objected to, and sometimes one cuts them out in another edition. So I eagerly asked what were the operative paragraphs and was told it was banned because of the title.

Nancy Mitford 1904–73: letter June/July 1954

9 Free speech is not to be regulated like diseased cattle and impure butter. The audience...that hissed yesterday may applaud today, even for the same performance.

William O. Douglas 1898–1980: dissenting opinion in *Kingsley Books, Inc. v. Brown* 1957

10 We are paid to have dirty minds.

John Trevelyan: when British Film Censor; in *Observer* 15 November 1959 'Sayings of the Week'

11 Freedom of the press is guaranteed only to those who own one.

A. J. Liebling 1904–63: 'The Wayward Press: Do you belong in Journalism?' (1960)

On being appointed Irish film censor:
12 I am between the devil and the Holy See...[My task is to prevent] the Californication of Ireland.

James Montgomery: Ulick O'Connor *Oliver St John Gogarty* (1964)

13 I'm all in favour of free expression provided it's kept rigidly under control.

Alan Bennett 1934– : *Forty Years On* (1969)

14 What I am objecting to is the use, absolutely without qualification, of the word, breast.

Alan Bennett 1934– : *Forty Years On* (1969)

15 Anybody who stands up and says total freedom may not be a good thing is immediately swamped with appreciative letters from old ladies whose twin hobbies are prize cucumbers and the castration of sex offenders.

Alan Bennett 1934– : *Getting On* (1972)

16 I dislike censorship. Like an appendix it is useless when inert and dangerous when active.

Maurice Edelman 1911–75: Jonathon Green (ed.) *A Dictionary of Contemporary Quotations* (1982)

17 She insists on all these torrid romances...I have to wrap them round with copies of *Country Life* to carry them home.

Alan Ayckbourn 1939– : *Round and Round the Garden* (1975)

18 My desire to curtail undue freedom of speech extends only to such public areas as restaurants, airports, streets, hotel lobbies, parks, and department stores. Verbal exchanges between consenting adults in private are as of little interest to me as they probably are to them.

Fran Lebowitz 1946– : *Metropolitan Life* (1978)

On the trial for obscenity of Last Exit to Brooklyn:
19 David Sheppard, who had been Captain of the English Cricket Team, also gave evidence to the effect that he had not, metaphorically speaking, held his bat so straight after reading *Last Exit to Brooklyn*, but as he went on to become Bishop of Liverpool the damage, whatever it was, doesn't seem to have been serious.

John Mortimer 1923– : *Clinging to the Wreckage* (1982)

20 Sir Basil Blackwell, the Oxford bookseller, said that he had certainly been depraved by the book [*Last Exit to Brooklyn*], but as he was in his eighties at the time the matter didn't seem to be of great practical significance.

John Mortimer 1923– : *Clinging to the Wreckage* (1982)

21 I suppose that writers should, in a way, feel flattered by the censorship laws. They show a primitive fear and dread at the fearful magic of print.

John Mortimer 1923– : *Clinging to the Wreckage* (1982)

22 A censor is a man who knows more than he thinks you ought to.

Laurence J. Peter 1919– : Jonathon Green (ed.) *A Dictionary of Contemporary Quotations* (1982)

23 Censorship, like charity, should begin at home, but, unlike charity, it should end there.

Clare Boothe Luce 1903–87: Jonathon Green (ed.) *A Dictionary of Contemporary Quotations* (1982)

24 Those unconscionable members of our society who demand that the wireless should be some kind of genteel hermitage upon which the language, idiom and vitality of the world never impinges...Those whose grip upon the world is so tenuous that they can be severely offended by words and phrases and yet remain all unoffended by the injustice, violence and oppression that howls daily about our ears.

Stephen Fry 1957– : *Paperweight* (1992)

Certainty and Doubt See also *Religion*

1 There is something pagan in me that I cannot shake off. In short, I deny nothing, but doubt everything.

Lord Byron 1788–1824: letter 4 December 1811

2 I wish I was as cocksure of anything as Tom Macaulay is of everything.

Lord Melbourne 1779–1848: Lord Cowper *Preface to Lord Melbourne's Papers* (1889)

3 I would earnestly warn you against trying to find out the reason for and explanation of everything...To try and find out the reason for everything is very dangerous and leads to nothing but disappointment and dissatisfaction, unsettling your mind and in the end making you miserable.

Queen Victoria 1819–1901: letter to Princess Victoria of Hesse, 22 August 1883

4 Oh! let us never, never doubt
What nobody is sure about!

Hilaire Belloc 1870–1953: 'The Microbe' (1897)

5 Well, sir, you never can tell. That's a principle in life with me, sir, if you'll excuse my having such a thing, sir.

George Bernard Shaw 1856–1950: *You Never Can Tell* (1898)

Of Thomas Arnold, son of Dr Arnold of Rugby, a notable and frequent nineteenth-century convert:
6 Poor Tom Arnold has lost his faith *again*.

Eliza Conybeare 1820–1903: Rose Macaulay letter to Father Johnson, 8 April 1951

7 Like all weak men he laid an exaggerated stress on not changing one's mind.

W. Somerset Maugham 1874–1965: *Of Human Bondage* (1915)

8 Certitude is not the test of certainty. We have been cocksure of many things that were not so.

Oliver Wendell Holmes Jr. 1841–1935: 'Natural Law' (1918)

9 I do not pretend to know where many ignorant men are sure—that is all that agnosticism means.

Clarence Darrow 1857–1938: speech at the trial of John Thomas Scopes, 15 July 1925; *The World's Most Famous Court Trial* (1925)

When asked whether he really believed a horseshoe hanging over his door would bring him luck:
10 Of course not, but I am told it works even if you don't believe in it.

Niels Bohr 1885–1962: A. Pais *Inward Bound* (1986)

11 All right, have it your own way—you heard a seal bark!

James Thurber 1894–1961: cartoon caption; in *New Yorker* 30 January 1932

W. H. Macaulay had been an atheist from his undergraduate days, but when he was dying his sister was pleased by his response to her mentioning 'God and a future life':
12 Well, there's nothing so rum it might not be true.

William Herrick Macaulay 1853–1936: Rose Macaulay letter to Father Johnson, 30 August 1950

13 ESTRAGON: Charming spot. Inspiring prospects. Let's go.
VLADIMIR: We can't.
ESTRAGON: Why not?
VLADIMIR: We're waiting for Godot.

Samuel Beckett 1906–89: *Waiting for Godot* (1955)

14 One of the thieves was saved. (*Pause*) It's a reasonable percentage.

Samuel Beckett 1906–89: *Waiting for Godot* (1955)

15 A young man who wishes to remain a sound atheist cannot be too careful of his reading.

C. S. Lewis 1898–1963: *Surprised by Joy* (1955)

16 Often undecided whether to desert a sinking ship for one that might not float, he would make up his mind to sit on the wharf for a day.

Lord Beaverbrook 1879–1964: of Lord Curzon; *Men and Power* (1956)

17 I'll give you a definite maybe.

Sam Goldwyn 1882–1974: attributed

18 He used to be fairly indecisive, but now he's not so certain.

Peter Alliss 1931– : Barry Fantoni (ed.) *Private Eye's Colemanballs* 3 (1986)

19 I am not denying anything I did not say.

Brian Mulroney 1939– : in *The Globe and Mail* 18 September 1986

20 The archbishop [Archbishop Runcie] is usually to be found nailing his colours to the fence.

Frank Field 1942– : attributed in *Crockfords 1987/88* (1987); Geoffrey Madan records in his *Notebooks* that Harry Cust made a similar comment on A. J. Balfour's ambiguous attitude to Chamberlain's Protectionist crusade, c.1904.

21 That happy sense of purpose people have when they are standing up for a principle they haven't really been knocked down for yet.

P. J. O'Rourke 1947– : *Give War a Chance* (1992)

Character   See also *Self-Knowledge and Self-Deception*

1 It is like a barber's chair that fits all buttocks.

William Shakespeare 1564–1616: *All's Well that Ends Well* (1603–4)

2 My father named me Autolycus; who being, as I am, littered under Mercury, was likewise a snapper-up of unconsidered trifles.

William Shakespeare 1564–1616: *The Winter's Tale* (1610–11)

3 An unforgiving eye, and a damned disinheriting countenance!

Richard Brinsley Sheridan 1751–1816: *The School for Scandal* (1777)

4 It was one of the deadliest and heaviest feelings of my life to feel that I was no longer a boy.—From that moment I began to grow old in my own esteem—and in my esteem age is not estimable.

Lord Byron 1788–1824: 'Detached Thoughts' 15 October 1821

5 We never knows wot's hidden in each other's hearts; and if we had glass winders there, we'd need keep the shutters up, some on us, I do assure you!

Charles Dickens 1812–70: *Martin Chuzzlewit* (1844)

6 CECIL GRAHAM: What is a cynic?
LORD DARLINGTON: A man who knows the price of everything and the value of nothing.

Oscar Wilde 1854–1900: *Lady Windermere's Fan* (1892)

7 Few things are harder to put up with than the annoyance of a good example.

Mark Twain 1835–1910: *Pudd'nhead Wilson* (1894)

8 I am afraid that he has one of those terribly weak natures that are not susceptible to influence.

Oscar Wilde 1854–1900: *An Ideal Husband* (1895)

9 Slice him where you like, a hellhound is always a hellhound.

P. G. Wodehouse 1881–1975: *The Code of the Woosters* (1938)

10 Then, with that faint fleeting smile playing about his lips, he faced the firing squad; erect and motionless, proud and disdainful, Walter Mitty, the undefeated, inscrutable to the last.

James Thurber 1894–1961: in *New Yorker* 18 March 1939 'The Secret Life of Walter Mitty'

11 There, standing at the piano, was the original good time who had been had by all.

Kenneth Tynan 1927–80: at an Oxford Union Debate, while an undergraduate; attributed (also attributed to Bette Davis of a passing starlet)

12 He's so wet you could shoot snipe off him.

Anthony Powell 1905– : *A Question of Upbringing* (1951)

13 He never failed to seek a peaceful solution of a problem when all other possibilities had failed.

Anonymous: Cecil Roth 'Joseph Herman Hertz' (1959) in *The Dictionary of National Biography*

14 Clevinger was one of those people with lots of intelligence and no brains, and everyone knew it except those who soon found it out. In short, he was a dope.

Joseph Heller 1923– : *Catch-22* (1961)

15 He's too nervous to kill himself. He wears his seat belt in a drive-in movie.

Neil Simon 1927– : *The Odd Couple* (1966)

16 They were both pink and summer puddingish and liable to be swayed by sawney sentimental values.

Noël Coward 1899–1973: of Beverley Nichols and Harold Nicolson; diary 16 October 1966

17 Felix? Playing around? Are you crazy? He wears a vest and galoshes.

Neil Simon 1927– : *The Odd Couple* (1966)

18 You can tell a lot about a fellow's character by his way of eating jellybeans.

Ronald Reagan 1911– : in *New York Times* 15 January 1981

19 A thin, unkempt young man who gives the impression of having inner fires that have been damped by ceaseless disappointment.

Alan Ayckbourn 1939– : *Sisterly Feelings* (1981)

20 I'm told he's [a] decent sort when you get to know him, but no one ever has, so his decency is sort of secret.

Tom Stoppard 1937– : *Neutral Ground* (1983)

21 Claudia's the sort of person who goes through life holding on to the sides.

Alice Thomas Ellis 1932– : *The Other Side of the Fire* (1983)

22 Nice guys, when we turn nasty, can make a terrible mess of it, usually because we've had so little practice, and have bottled it up for too long.

Matthew Parris 1949– : in *The Spectator* 27 February 1993

Children See also *The Family, Parents, Youth*

1 As yet a child, nor yet a fool to fame,
I lisped in numbers, for the numbers came.

Alexander Pope 1688–1744: 'An Epistle to Dr Arbuthnot' (1735)

2 I don't know what Scrope Davies meant by telling you I liked children, I abominate the sight of them so much that I have always had the greatest respect for the character of Herod.

Lord Byron 1788–1824: letter 30 August 1811

3 The place is very well and quiet and the children only scream in a low voice.

Lord Byron 1788–1824: letter 21 September 1813

The nurse, excusing her illegitimate baby:
4 If you please, ma'am, it was a very little one.

Frederick Marryat 1792–1848: *Mr Midshipman Easy* (1836)

5 I only know two sorts of boys. Mealy boys, and beef-faced boys.

Charles Dickens 1812–70: *Oliver Twist* (1838)

6 I s'pect I growed. Don't think nobody never made me.

Harriet Beecher Stowe 1811–96: *Uncle Tom's Cabin* (1852)

7 Speak roughly to your little boy,
And beat him when he sneezes;
He only does it to annoy,
Because he knows it teases.

Lewis Carroll 1832–98: *Alice's Adventures in Wonderland* (1865)

8 I fear the seventh granddaughter and fourteenth grandchild becomes a very uninteresting thing—for it seems to me to go on like the rabbits in Windsor Park!

Queen Victoria 1819–1901: letter to the Crown Princess of Prussia, 10 July 1868

9 Go directly—see what she's doing, and tell her she mustn't.

Punch 1841–1992: vol. 63 (1872)

10 You will find as the children grow up that as a rule children are a bitter disappointment—their greatest object being to do precisely what their parents do not wish and have anxiously tried to prevent.

Queen Victoria 1819–1901: letter to the Crown Princess of Prussia, 5 January 1876

11 Children begin by loving their parents; after a time they judge them; rarely, if ever, do they forgive them.

Oscar Wilde 1854–1900: *A Woman of No Importance* (1893)

12 I call you bad, my little child,
Upon the title page,
Because a manner rude and wild
Is common at your age.

Hilaire Belloc 1870–1953: *A Bad Child's Book of Beasts* (1896); introduction

13 O'er the rugged mountain's brow
Clara threw the twins she nursed,
And remarked, 'I wonder now
Which will reach the bottom first?'

Harry Graham 1874–1936: 'Calculating Clara' (1899)

14 If the literary offspring is not to die young, almost as much trouble must be taken with it as with the bringing up of a physical child. Still, the physical child is the harder work of the two.

Samuel Butler 1835–1902: *Notebooks* (1912)

Jack Llewelyn-Davies, stuffing himself with cakes at tea, was warned by his mother Sylvia, 'You'll be sick tomorrow':
15 I'll be sick tonight.

Jack Llewelyn-Davies 1894–1959: Andrew Birkin *J. M. Barrie and the Lost Boys* (1979); Barrie used the line in *Little Mary* (1903)

16 Children are given us to discourage our better emotions.

Saki 1870–1916: *Reginald* (1904)

At the first night of J. M. Barrie's Peter Pan:
17 Oh, for an hour of Herod!

Anthony Hope 1863–1933: Denis Mackail *The Story of JMB* (1941)

18 A Trick that everyone abhors
In Little Girls is slamming Doors.

Hilaire Belloc 1870–1953: 'Rebecca' (1907)

CHILDREN   58

19 She was not really bad at heart,
But only rather rude and wild:
She was an aggravating child.

Hilaire Belloc 1870-1953: 'Rebecca' (1907)

20 And always keep a-hold of Nurse
For fear of finding something worse.

Hilaire Belloc 1870-1953: 'Jim' (1907)

21 'I—I say, you fellows—'
'Shut up, Bunter.'
'But—but I say—'
'Keep that cush over his chivvy.'
'I—I say—groo—groo—yarooh!'
And Bunter's remarks again tailed off under the cushion.

Frank Richards 1876-1961: in *Magnet* (1909)

22 The fat greedy owl of the Remove.

Frank Richards 1876-1961: 'Billy Bunter' in *Magnet* (1909)

23 The parent who could see his boy as he really is, would shake his head and say: 'Willie is no good; I'll sell him.'

Stephen Leacock 1869-1944: *Essays and Literary Studies* (1916)

24 Children with Hyacinth's temperament don't know better as they grow older; they merely know more.

Saki 1870-1916: *Toys of Peace and Other Papers* (1919)

25 I'll thcream and thcream and thcream till I'm thick.

Richmal Crompton 1890-1969: *Still—William* (1925); Violet Elizabeth Bott's habitual threat

26 Parents—especially step-parents—are sometimes a bit of a disappointment to their children. They don't fulfil the promise of their early years.

Anthony Powell 1905- : *A Buyer's Market* (1952)

Definition of a baby:
27 A loud noise at one end and no sense of responsibility at the other.

Ronald Knox 1888-1957: attributed

28 Timothy Winters comes to school
With eyes as wide as a football-pool,
Ears like bombs and teeth like splinters:
A blitz of a boy is Timothy Winters.

Charles Causley 1917- : 'Timothy Winters' (1957)

29 Every luxury was lavished on you—atheism, breast-feeding, circumcision.

Joe Orton 1933-67: *Loot* (1967)

On being asked what sort of child he was:
30 When paid constant attention, extremely lovable. When not, a pig.

Noël Coward 1899-1973: interview with David Frost in 1969

31 Children always assume the sexual lives of their parents come to a grinding halt at their conception.

Alan Bennett 1934- : *Getting On* (1972)

32 Childhood is Last Chance Gulch for happiness. After that, you know too much.

Tom Stoppard 1937- : *Where Are They Now?* (1973)

33 Children can be awe-inspiringly horrible; manipulative, aggressive, rude, and unfeeling to a point where I often think that, if armed, they would make up the most terrifying fighting force the world has ever seen.

Jill Tweedie 1936-93: *It's Only Me* (1980)

34 Having a baby is like trying to push a grand piano through a transom.

Alice Roosevelt Longworth 1884-1980: Michael Teague *Mrs L* (1981)

35 Ask your child what he wants for dinner only if he's buying.

Fran Lebowitz 1946– : *Social Studies* (1981)

36 Don't bother discussing sex with small children. They rarely have anything to add.

Fran Lebowitz 1946– : *Social Studies* (1981)

37 If men had to have babies, they would only ever have one each.

Diana, Princess of Wales 1961– : while in late pregnancy; in *Observer* 29 July 1984 'Sayings of the Week'

38 All bachelors love dogs, and we would love children just as much if they could be taught to retrieve.

P. J. O'Rourke 1947– : *The Bachelor Home Companion* (1987)

Of the headmistress of his first school, who told his mother 'Michael is a strange child':
39 Thirty years later, it would transpire she was the godmother of my literary agent, but not knowing this at the time I did not hold it against her.

Michael Green 1927– : *The Boy Who Shot Down an Airship* (1988)

40 I had always thought that once you grew up you could do anything you wanted—stay up all night or eat ice-cream straight out of the container.

Bill Bryson 1951– : *The Lost Continent* (1989)

41 There is this horrible idea, beginning with Jean-Jacques Rousseau and still going strong in college classrooms, that natural man is naturally good...Anybody who's ever met a toddler knows this is nonsense.

P. J. O'Rourke 1947– : *Parliament of Whores*

42 When you've seen a nude infant doing a backward somersault you know why clothing exists.

Stephen Fry 1957– : *Paperweight* (1992)

43 With the birth of each child you lose two novels.

Candia McWilliam 1955– : in *Guardian* 5 May 1993

44 Any child with sense knew you didn't involve yourself with the adult world if you weren't absolutely forced to. We lived on our side of a great divide and we crossed it at our peril.

Jill Tweedie 1936–93: *Eating Children* (1993)

Choice

1 Still raise for good the supplicating voice,
   But leave to heaven the measure and the choice.

Samuel Johnson 1709–84: *The Vanity of Human Wishes* (1749)

2 'You oughtn't to yield to temptation.' 'Well, somebody must, or the thing becomes absurd,' said I.

Anthony Hope 1863–1933: *The Dolly Dialogues* (1894)

3 Economy is going without something you do want in case you should, some day, want something you probably won't want.

Anthony Hope 1863–1933: *The Dolly Dialogues* (1894)

George V was asked which film he would like to see while convalescing:
4 Anything except that damned Mouse.

George V 1865–1936: George Lyttelton letter to Rupert Hart-Davis, 12 November 1959

Geoffrey Fisher appeared to disapprove of the choice of Michael Ramsey to succeed him as Archbishop of Canterbury:

5 RAMSEY: Fisher was my headmaster and he has known all my deficiencies for a long time.
MACMILLAN: Well, he is not going to be my headmaster.

Harold Macmillan 1894–1986: Owen Chadwick *Michael Ramsey* (1990)

On the contrast between Alec Douglas-Home and Harold Wilson:
6 Dull Alec versus Smart Alec.

David Frost 1939– : in *That Was The Week That Was* in 1963

On the presidential contest between Gerald Ford and Jimmy Carter:
7 No longer a choice between the lesser of two weevils, you now know that you can't win.

S. J. Perelman 1904–79: letter 18 October 1976

8 More than any other time in history, mankind faces a crossroads. One path leads to despair and utter hopelessness. The other, to total extinction. Let us pray we have the wisdom to choose correctly.

Woody Allen 1935– : *Side Effects* (1980)

9 Place the following in order of importance: (a) Food (b) World peace (c) A Lanceolated Warbler.

Bill Oddie 1941– : *Bill Oddie's Little Black Bird Book* (1980)

10 A compromise in the sense that being bitten in half by a shark is a compromise with being swallowed whole.

P. J. O'Rourke 1947– : *Parliament of Whores*

Christmas

1 I have often thought, says Sir Roger, it happens very well that Christmas should fall out in the Middle of Winter.

Joseph Addison 1672–1719: *The Spectator* 8 January 1712

2 I am a poor man, but I would gladly give ten shillings to find out who sent me the insulting Christmas card I received this morning.

George Grossmith 1847–1912 and **Weedon Grossmith** 1854–1919: *The Diary of a Nobody* (1894)

3 There are six evacuated children in our house. My wife and I hate them so much that we have decided to *take away* something from them for Christmas!

Anonymous: letter from a friend in the country; James Agate diary 22 December 1939

4 A Merry Christmas to all my friends except two.

W. C. Fields 1880–1946: attributed

5 And girls in slacks remember Dad,
And oafish louts remember Mum,
And sleepless children's hearts are glad,
And Christmas-morning bells say 'Come!'
Even to shining ones who dwell
Safe in the Dorchester Hotel.

And is it true? And is it true,
This most tremendous tale of all,
Seen in a stained-glass window's hue,
A Baby in an ox's stall?
The Maker of the stars and sea
Become a Child on earth for me?

John Betjeman 1906–84: 'Christmas' (1954)

6 I'm walking backwards for Christmas
Across the Irish Sea.

Spike Milligan 1918– : 'I'm Walking Backwards for Christmas' (1956)

7 Christmas begins about the first of December with an office party and ends when you finally realize what you spent, around April fifteenth of the next year.

P. J. O'Rourke 1947– : *Modern Manners* (1984)

8 Don't send funny greetings cards on birthdays or at Christmas. Save them for funerals when their cheery effect is needed.

P. J. O'Rourke 1947– : *Modern Manners* (1984)

9 The phone rings and I curse.
Literary editor.
Seasonal verse.

Wendy Cope 1945– : '19th Christmas Poem' (1992)

10 Christmas, that time of year when people descend into the bunker of the family.

Byron Rogers: in *Daily Telegraph* 27 December 1993

Cinema and Films See also *Actors and Acting*

1 'She reads at such a pace,' she complained, 'and when I asked her *where* she had learnt to read so quickly, she replied "On the screens at cinemas."'

Ronald Firbank 1886–1926: *The Flower Beneath the Foot* (1923)

On the take-over of United Artists by Charles Chaplin, Mary Pickford, Douglas Fairbanks and D. W. Griffith:
2 The lunatics have taken charge of the asylum.

Richard Rowland c.1881–1947: Terry Ramsaye *A Million and One Nights* (1926)

3 I'm not very keen on Hollywood. I'd rather have a nice cup of cocoa really.

Noël Coward 1899–1973: letter to his mother, 1931; Cole Lesley *The Life of Noël Coward* (1976)

4 When he meets Garbo in a suit of corduroy,
He gives a little frown
And knocks her down.
Oh dear, oh dear, I'm mad about the boy.

Noël Coward 1899–1973: 'Mad About the Boy' (1932)

5 I didn't have to act in 'Tarzan, the Ape Man'—just said, 'Me Tarzan, you Jane.'

Johnny Weissmuller 1904–84: in *Photoplay Magazine* June 1932 (the words 'Me Tarzan, you Jane' do not occur in the 1932 film)

Of Hollywood:
6 A trip through a sewer in a glass-bottomed boat.

Wilson Mizner 1876–1933: Alva Johnston *The Legendary Mizners* (1953), reworked by Mayor Jimmy Walker into 'A reformer is a guy who rides through a sewer in a glass-bottomed boat'

7 Jack Warner has oilcloth pockets so he can steal soup.

Wilson Mizner 1876–1933: Max Wilk *The Wit and Wisdom of Hollywood* (1972)

8 This might have been good for a picture—except it has too many characters in it.

Wilson Mizner 1876–1933: to Jack Warner, on the LA telephone directory; Max Wilk *The Wit and Wisdom of Hollywood* (1972)

On resigning from the Motion Picture Producers and Distributors of America in 1933:
9 Gentlemen, include me out.

Sam Goldwyn 1882–1974: Michael Freedland *The Goldwyn Touch* (1986)

10 Ah don't believe Ah know which pictures are yours. Do you make the Mickey Mouse brand?

William Faulkner 1897–1962: to Irving Thalberg; Max Wilk *The Wit and Wisdom of Hollywood* (1972)

11 Bring on the empty horses!

Michael Curtiz 1888–1962: said while directing the 1936 film *The Charge of the Light Brigade*; David Niven *Bring on the Empty Horses* (1975)

12 A verbal contract isn't worth the paper it is written on.

Sam Goldwyn 1882–1974: Alva Johnston *The Great Goldwyn* (1937)

13 That's the way with these directors, they're always biting the hand that lays the golden egg.

Sam Goldwyn 1882–1974: Alva Johnston *The Great Goldwyn* (1937)

14 The trouble, Mr Goldwyn, is that you are only interested in art and I am only interested in money.

George Bernard Shaw 1856–1950: telegraphed version of the outcome of a conversation between Shaw and Sam Goldwyn; Alva Johnson *The Great Goldwyn* (1937)

15 The trouble with this business is the dearth of bad pictures.

Sam Goldwyn 1882–1974: after making *The Goldwyn Follies* in 1937; Michael Freedland *The Goldwyn Touch* (1986)

16 Oh come, my love, and join with me
The oldest infant industry.
Come seek the bourne of palm and pearl
The lovely land of Boy-Meets-Girl.
Come grace this lotus-laden shore,
This Isle of Do-What's-Done-Before.
Come, curb the new, and watch the old win,
Out where the streets are paved with Goldwyn.

Dorothy Parker 1893–1967: 'The Passionate Screen Writer to His Love' (1937)

17 Cecil B. de Mille
Rather against his will,
Was persuaded to leave Moses
Out of 'The Wars of the Roses'.

Anonymous: J. W. Carter (ed.) *Clerihews* (1938); attributed to Nicolas Bentley

18 The movies are the only court where the judge goes to the lawyer for advice.

F. Scott Fitzgerald 1896–1940: *The Crack-up* (1945)

19 This is the biggest electric train any boy ever had!

Orson Welles 1915–85: of Hollywood; Leo Rosten *Hollywood* (1941)

20 Disappointed with Edward G. Robinson in *The Sea Wolf*, a psychological film about a rascally captain with a split mind, whereas I had been looking forward to two hundred lashes in Technicolor.

James Agate 1877–1947: diary 27 January 1942

During the making of Lifeboat *in 1944, Mary Anderson asked Hitchcock what he thought her 'best side' for photography was:*

21 My dear, you're sitting on it.

Alfred Hitchcock 1899–1980: D. Spoto *Life of Alfred Hitchcock* (1983)

22 I don't care if it [*The Best Years of Our Lives*, 1946] doesn't make a cent—just so long as every man, woman and child in the country sees it.

Sam Goldwyn 1882–1974: Michael Freedland *The Goldwyn Touch* (1986)

23 GOLDWYN: I hope you didn't think it was too blood and thirsty.
THURBER: Not only did I think so but I was horror and struck.

Sam Goldwyn 1882–1974: of *The Secret Life of Walter Mitty*, Goldwyn's 1947 film of Thurber's story; Michael Freedland *The Goldwyn Touch* (1986)

24 Several tons of dynamite are set off in this picture [*Tycoon*]; none of it under the right people.

James Agee 1909–55: in *The Nation* 14 February 1948

25 Wet, she was a star—dry she ain't.

Joe Pasternak 1901–91: of the swimmer Esther Williams and her 1940s film career; attributed

26 JOE GILLIS: You used to be in pictures. You used to be big.
NORMA DESMOND: I am big. It's the pictures that got small.

Charles Brackett 1892–1969 and **Billy Wilder** 1906– : *Sunset Boulevard* (1950 film)

27 Johnny, it's the usual slashed-wrist shot...Keep it out of focus. I want to win the foreign picture award.

Billy Wilder 1906– : to his lighting cameraman, John Seitz, when filming *Sunset Boulevard* (1950); P. F. Boller and R. L. Davis *Hollywood Anecdotes* (1988)

28 Hollywood is a place where people from Iowa mistake each other for stars.

Fred Allen 1894–1956: Maurice Zolotow *No People like Show People* (1951)

At a dinner party for a number of American guests including John Huston:
29 They talked for *one hour* about a Japanese film and I got in bad from the start by saying I only like historical films with Sacha Guitry dressed up as every king of France in turn.

Nancy Mitford 1904–73: letter 29 May 1952

An assistant director trying to encourage some uninspired extras during the filming of Julius Caesar *(1953):*
30 All right, kids. It's Rome, it's hot and here comes Julius!

Anonymous: recounted by John Gielgud; in *Ned Sherrin in his Anecdotage* (1993)

31 It might be a fight like you see on the screen
A swain getting slain for the love of a Queen,
Some great Shakespearean scene
Where a ghost and a prince meet
And everyone ends as mince-meat...

Howard Dietz 1896–1983: 'That's Entertainment' (1953)

32 Do you have any idea how bad the picture is? I'll tell you. Stay away from the neighbourhood where it's playing—don't even go near that street! It might rain—you could get caught in the downpour, and to keep dry you'd have to go inside the theatre.

Herman J. Mankiewicz 1898–1953: attributed

Adolph Zukor had protested at the escalating costs of The Ten Commandments:
33 What do you want me to do? Stop shooting now and release it as *The Five Commandments*?

Cecil B. De Mille 1881–1959: M. LeRoy *Take One* (1974)

34 Tsar of all the rushes.

B. P. Schulberg D. 1957: of Louis B. Mayer; Norman Zierold *The Hollywood Tycoons* (1969)

35 Hollywood money isn't money. It's congealed snow, melts in your hand, and there you are.

Dorothy Parker 1893–1967: Malcolm Cowley (ed.) *Writers at Work* 1st Series (1958)

When asked what it was like to kiss Marilyn Monroe:
36 It's like kissing Hitler.

Tony Curtis 1925– : A. Hunter *Tony Curtis* (1985)

On Hollywood:
37 The most beautiful slave-quarters in the world.

Moss Hart 1904–61: attributed

38 The question is whether Marilyn [Monroe] is a person at all or one of the greatest Dupont products ever invented. She has breasts like granite and a brain like Swiss cheese, full of holes.

Billy Wilder 1906– : E. Goodman *The Fifty-Year Decline and Fall of Hollywood* (1961)

On Marilyn Monroe's unpunctuality:
39 My Aunt Minnie would always be punctual and never hold up production, but who would pay to see my Aunt Minnie?

Billy Wilder 1906– : P. F. Boller and R. L. Davis *Hollywood Anecdotes* (1988)

40 She is a phenomenon of nature, like Niagara Falls or the Grand Canyon. You can't talk to it. It can't talk to you. All you can do is stand back and be awed by it.

Nunnally Johnson 1897–1977: of Marilyn Monroe; Peter Harry Brown and Patte B. Barham *Marilyn, the Last Take* (1990)

41 I'm not [biting my fingernails]. I'm biting my knuckles. I finished the fingernails months ago.

Joseph L. Mankiewicz 1909– : while directing *Cleopatra* (1963); Dick Sheppard *Elizabeth* (1975)

On nouvelle vague:
42 You watch, the new wave will discover the slow dissolve in ten years or so.

Billy Wilder 1906– : attributed, perhaps apocryphal

On hearing that Ronald Reagan was seeking nomination as Governor of California:
43 No, *no. Jimmy Stewart* for governor—Reagan for his best friend.

Jack Warner 1892–1978: Max Wilk *The Wit and Wisdom of Hollywood* (1972)

44 Oh, it's all right. You make a little money and get caught up on your debts. We're up to 1912 now...

Dorothy Parker 1893–1967: on Hollywood; Max Wilk *The Wit and Wisdom of Hollywood* (1972)

45 The only 'ism' in Hollywood is plagiarism.

Dorothy Parker 1893–1967: attributed

46 They used to shoot her through gauze. You should shoot me through linoleum.

Tallulah Bankhead 1903–68: on Shirley Temple; attributed

47 What they [critics] call dirty in our pictures, they call lusty in foreign films.

Billy Wilder 1906– : A. Madsen *Billy Wilder* (1968)

48 That man's ears make him look like a taxi-cab with both doors open.

Howard Hughes Jr. 1905–76: of Clark Gable; Charles Higham and Joel Greenberg *Celluloid Muse* (1969)

49 Our comedies are not to be laughed at.

Sam Goldwyn 1882–1974: N. Zierold *Hollywood Tycoons* (1969)

50 'Do you have a leading lady for your film?'
'We're trying for the Queen, she sells.'

George Harrison 1943– : at a press conference in the 1960s; Ned Sherrin *Cutting Edge* (1984)

51 It was a cute picture. They used the basic story of *Wuthering Heights* and worked in surfriders.

Neil Simon 1927– : *Last of the Red Hot Lovers* (1970)

52 Behind the phoney tinsel of Hollywood lies the real tinsel.

Oscar Levant 1906–72: Laurence J. Peter (ed.) *Quotations for our Time* (1977)

53 Hollywood is bounded on the north, south, east, and west by agents.

William Fadiman: *Hollywood Now* (1972)

Of one of his own films:
54 It's more than magnificent, it's mediocre.

Sam Goldwyn 1882–1974: attributed, perhaps apocryphal

55 PRODUCTION ASSISTANT: But Mr Goldwyn, you said you wanted a spectacle.
GOLDWYN: Yes, but goddam it, I wanted an intimate spectacle!

Sam Goldwyn 1882–1974: attributed, perhaps apocryphal

56 Do you want me to put my head in a moose?

Sam Goldwyn 1882–1974: Michael Freedland *The Goldwyn Touch* (1986); attributed

57 This business is dog eat dog and nobody is gonna eat me.

Sam Goldwyn 1882–1974: Michael Freedland *The Goldwyn Touch* (1986)

58 Let's have some new clichés.

Sam Goldwyn 1882–1974: attributed, perhaps apocryphal

59 Never let the bastard back into my room again—unless I need him.

Sam Goldwyn 1882–1974: Michael Freedland *The Goldwyn Touch* (1986); attributed, perhaps apocryphal

60 What we need is a story that starts with an earthquake and works its way up to a climax.

Sam Goldwyn 1882–1974: attributed, perhaps apocryphal

61 Pictures are for entertainment, messages should be delivered by Western Union.

Sam Goldwyn 1882–1974: Arthur Marx *Goldwyn* (1976)

62 Anything but Beethoven. Nobody wants to see a movie about a blind composer.

Jack Warner 1892–1978: J. Lawrence *Actor* (1975)

63 I wouldn't say when you've seen one Western you've seen the lot; but when you've seen the lot you get the feeling you've seen one.

Katharine Whitehorn 1926– : *Sunday Best* (1976) 'Decoding the West'

64 Hollywood: They know only one word of more than one syllable here, and that is fillum.

Louis Sherwin: Laurence J. Peter (ed.) *Quotations for our Time* (1977)

65 To Raoul Walsh a tender love scene is burning down a whorehouse.

Jack Warner 1892–1978: P. F. Boller and R. L. Davis *Hollywood Anecdotes* (1988)

66 I can't tell you [the perfect ending to a script]...
I thought of the answer after 5.30.

Norman Krasna 1909–84: to Jack Warner, who imposed a strict nine-to-five-thirty schedule on his scriptwriters; M. Freedland *Warner Brothers* (1983)

67 It's not what I do, but the way I do it. It's not what I say, but the way I say it.

Mae West 1892–1980: G. Eells and S. Musgrove *Mae West* (1989)

Asking Graham Greene to give a final polish to a rewrite of the last part of the screenplay for Ben Hur:
68 You see, we find a kind of anticlimax after the Crucifixion.

Sam Zimbalist: Graham Greene *Ways of Escape* (1980)

69 GEORGES FRANJU: Movies should have a beginning, a middle and an end.
JEAN-LUC GODARD: Certainly. But not necessarily in that order.

Jean-Luc Godard 1930– : in *Time* 14 September 1981

70 The writer, in the eyes of many film producers, still seems to occupy a position of importance somewhere between the wardrobe lady and the tea boy, with this difference: it's often quite difficult to replace the wardrobe lady.

John Mortimer 1923– : *Clinging to the Wreckage* (1982)

71 All Americans born between 1890 and 1945 wanted to be movie stars.

Gore Vidal 1925– : *Pink Triangle and Yellow Star* (1982)

72 Nowadays Mitchum doesn't so much act as point his suit at people.

Russell Davies 1946– : in *Sunday Times* 18 September 1983

73 I like the old masters, by which I mean John Ford, John Ford, and John Ford.

Orson Welles 1915–85: P. F. Boller and R. L. Davis *Hollywood Anecdotes* (1988)

74 Can't act. Slightly bald. Also dances.

Anonymous: studio official's comment on Fred Astaire; Bob Thomas *Astaire* (1985)

75 To work as hard as I've worked to accomplish anything and then have some yo-yo come up and say 'Take off those dark glasses and let's have a look at those blue eyes' is really discouraging.

Paul Newman 1925– : in *Observer* 5 October 1986 'Sayings of the Week'

76 The first nine commandments for a director are 'Thou shalt not bore.' The tenth is 'Thou shalt have the right of final cut.'

Billy Wilder 1906– : attributed, perhaps apocryphal

77 Elizabeth [Taylor] is a wonderful movie actress: she has a deal with the film lab—she gets better in the bath overnight.

Mike Nichols: in *Vanity Fair* June 1994

Cities See *Towns and Cities*

Class See also *The Aristocracy, Snobbery*

1 A branch of one of your antediluvian families, fellows that the flood could not wash away.

William Congreve 1670–1729: *Love for Love* (1695)

2 I came upstairs into the world; for I was born in a cellar.

William Congreve 1670–1729: *Love for Love* (1695)

3 We are all Adam's children but silk makes the difference.

Thomas Fuller 1654–1734: *Gnomologia* (1732)

4 The only infallible rule we know is, that the man who is always talking about being a gentleman never is one.

R. S. Surtees 1805–64: *Ask Mamma* (1858)

5 The so called immorality of the lower classes is not to be named on the same day with that of the higher and highest. This is a thing which makes my blood boil, and they will pay for it.

Queen Victoria 1819–1901: letter to the Crown Princess of Prussia, 26 June 1872

6 Bow, bow, ye lower middle classes!
Bow, bow, ye tradesmen, bow, ye masses.

W. S. Gilbert 1836–1911: *Iolanthe* (1882)

7 All shall equal be.
The Earl, the Marquis, and the Dook,
The Groom, the Butler, and the Cook,
The Aristocrat who banks with Coutts,
The Aristocrat who cleans the boots.

W. S. Gilbert 1836–1911: *The Gondoliers* (1889)

8 When every one is somebodee,
Then no one's anybody.

W. S. Gilbert 1836–1911: *The Gondoliers* (1889)

9 Really, if the lower orders don't set us a good example, what on earth is the use of them?

Oscar Wilde 1854–1900: *The Importance of Being Earnest* (1895)

10 His lordship may compel us to be equal upstairs, but there will never be equality in the servants' hall.

J. M. Barrie 1860–1937: *The Admirable Crichton* (performed 1902)

11 People are fond of blaming valets because no man is a hero to his valet. But it is equally true that no man is a valet to his hero; and the hero, consequently, is apt to blunder very ludicrously about valets, through judging them from an irrelevant standard of heroism.

George Bernard Shaw 1856–1950: preface to *The Irrational Knot* (1905)

12 A gentleman never eats. He breakfasts, he lunches, he dines, but he *never* eats!

Anonymous: Cole Porter's headmaster, c.1910; Caryl Brahms and Ned Sherrin *Song by Song* (1984)

13 He's a gentleman: look at his boots.

George Bernard Shaw 1856–1950: preface to *Pygmalion* (1916)

14 I don't want to talk grammar, I want to talk like a lady.

George Bernard Shaw 1856–1950: *Pygmalion* (1916)

15 Mankind is divisible into two great classes: hosts and guests.

Max Beerbohm 1872–1956: *And Even Now* (1920)

16 Dear me, I never knew that the lower classes had such white skins.

Lord Curzon 1859–1925: K. Rose *Superior Person* (1969)

17 I expect you'll be becoming a schoolmaster, sir. That's what most of the gentlemen does, sir, that gets sent down for indecent behaviour.

Evelyn Waugh 1903–66: *Decline and Fall* (1928)

18 Like many of the Upper Class
He liked the Sound of Broken Glass.

Hilaire Belloc 1870–1953: 'About John' (1930)

19 Boston social zones
Are changing social habits,
And I hear the Cohns
Are taking up the Cabots.

Ira Gershwin 1896–1983: 'Love is Sweeping the Country' (1931)

20 Today it may be three white feathers,
But yesterday it was three brass balls.

Noël Coward 1899–1973: 'Three White Feathers' (1932)

21 Finer things are for the finer folk
Thus society began
Caviare for peasants is a joke
It's too good for the average man.

Lorenz Hart 1895–1943: 'Too Good for the Average Man' (1936)

22 Of all the hokum with which this country [America] is riddled the most odd is the common notion that it is free of class distinctions.

W. Somerset Maugham 1874–1965: *A Writer's Notebook* (1949) written in 1941

23 All men fall into two main divisions: those who value human relationships, and those who value social or financial advancement. The first division are gentlemen; the second division are cads.

Norman Douglas 1868–1952: *An Almanac* (1941)

24 Gentlemen do not take soup at luncheon.

Lord Curzon 1859–1925: E. L. Woodward *Short Journey* (1942)

25 When the idle poor become the idle rich
You'll never know just who is who or who is which.

E. Y. Harburg 1898–1981: 'When the Idle Poor become the Idle Rich' (1947)

26 Impotence and sodomy are socially O.K. but birth control is flagrantly middle-class.

Evelyn Waugh 1903–66: 'An Open Letter'; Nancy Mitford *Noblesse Oblige* (1956)

On a social climber who was becoming notorious for the number of times he had fallen off his horse:
27 Acquired concussion won't open the doors of country houses. The better classes are born concussed.

Oliver St John Gogarty 1878–1957: Ulick O'Connor *Oliver St John Gogarty* (1964)

28 He [Lord Home] is used to dealing with estate workers. I cannot see how anyone can say he is out of touch.

Caroline Douglas-Home 1937– : comment on her father becoming Prime Minister; in *Daily Herald* 21 October 1963

29 If they could see me now,
My little dusty group,
Traipsing 'round this
Million-dollar chicken coop!
I'd hear those thrift shop cats say:
'Brother! Get her!'
Draped on a bedspread made from
Three kinds of fur.

Dorothy Fields 1905–74: 'If my Friends could See Me Now' (1966)

30 The ancient native order [of Irish society] was patriarchal and aristocratic, the people knew their place (i.e. the scullery).

Flann O'Brien 1911–66: *The Hair of the Dogma* (1977)

31 She sits
At The Ritz
With her splits

Stephen Sondheim 1930– : 'Uptown Downtown', song rejected from *Follies* (1971); composer's archive

Of Mum's
And starts to pine
For a Stein
With her Village chums.
But with a Schlitz
In her mitts
Down in Fitz—
Roy's Bar,
She thinks of the Ritz—oh,
It's so
Schizo.

32 The old middle-class male prerogative of being permanently in a most filthy temper.

John Mortimer 1923– : *Clinging to the Wreckage* (1982)

33 If she [Margaret Thatcher] has a weakness, it is for shopkeepers, which probably accounts for the fact that she cannot pass a branch of Marks and Spencer without inviting its manager to join her private office.

Julian Critchley 1930– : *Westminster Blues* (1986)

34 My experience of tattoos is that they're generally confined to the lower echelons, and when I saw his vest it had electrician written all over it.

Alan Bennett 1934– : *Talking Heads* (1988)

35 Q: What rituals does the middle class have?
A: Dinner parties at which nothing can be discussed except mortgages, education and children.

Miles Kington 1941– : *Welcome to Kington* (1989)

36 There are those who think that Britain is a class-ridden society, and those who think it doesn't matter either way as long as you know your place in the set-up.

Miles Kington 1941– : *Welcome to Kington* (1989)

37 People like me never usually meet people like you except in a Crown Court, when you're wearing a wig.

Stephen Fry 1957– : *The Liar* (1992)

38 If you bed people of below-stairs class, they will go to the papers.

Jane Clark: in *Daily Telegraph* 31 May 1994

Comedy Routines and Catch-phrases

1 Meredith, we're in!

Fred Kitchen 1872–1950: catch-phrase originating in *The Bailiff* (1907 stage sketch)

2 Do you suppose I could buy back my introduction to you?

S. J. Perelman 1904–79 et al.: in *Monkey Business* (1931 film)

3 Mind my bike!

Jack Warner 1895–1981: catch-phrase used in the BBC radio series *Garrison Theatre*, 1939 onwards

4 CECIL: After you, Claude.
CLAUDE: No, after you, Cecil.

Ted Kavanagh 1892–1958: catch-phrase in *ITMA* (BBC radio programme, 1939–49)

5 Can I do you now, sir?

Ted Kavanagh 1892–1958: catch-phrase spoken by 'Mrs Mopp' in *ITMA* (BBC radio programme, 1939–49)

6 Don't forget the diver.

Ted Kavanagh 1892–1958: catch-phrase spoken by 'The Diver' in *ITMA* (BBC radio programme, 1939–49)

7 I don't mind if I do.

Ted Kavanagh 1892–1958: catch-phrase spoken by 'Colonel Chinstrap' in *ITMA* (BBC radio programme, 1939–49)

8 I go—I come back.

Ted Kavanagh 1892–1958: catch-phrase spoken by 'Ali Oop' in *ITMA* (BBC radio programme, 1939–49)

9 It's being so cheerful as keeps me going.

Ted Kavanagh 1892–1958: catch-phrase spoken by 'Mona Lott' in *ITMA* (BBC radio programme, 1939–49)

10 ABBOTT: Now, on the St Louis team we have Who's on first, What's on second, I Don't Know is on third. COSTELLO: That's what I want to find out.

Bud Abbott 1895–1974 and **Lou Costello** 1906–59: *Naughty Nineties* (1945)

11 Have you read any good books lately?

Richard Murdoch 1907–90 and **Kenneth Horne** 1900–69: catch-phrase used by Richard Murdoch in radio comedy series *Much-Binding-in-the-Marsh* (started 2 January 1947)

12 Good morning, sir—was there something?

Richard Murdoch 1907–90 and **Kenneth Horne** 1900–69: catch-phrase used by Sam Costa in radio comedy series *Much-Binding-in-the-Marsh* (started 2 January 1947)

13 Ee, it was agony, Ivy.

Ted Ray 1906–77: catch-phrase in *Ray's a Laugh* (BBC radio programme, 1949–61)

14 He's loo-vely, Mrs Hoskin...he's loo-ooo-vely!

Ted Ray 1906–77: catch-phrase in *Ray's a Laugh* (BBC radio programme, 1949–61)

15 SEAGOON: Ying tong iddle I po.

Spike Milligan 1918– : *The Dreaded Batter Pudding Hurler* in *The Goon Show* (BBC radio series) 12 October 1954; catch-phrase also used in *The Ying Tong Song* (1956)

16 Oh, calamity!

Robertson Hare 1891–1979: catch-phrase in *Yours Indubitably* (1956)

17 Seriously, though, he's doing a grand job!

David Frost 1939– : catch-phrase written by Waterhouse and Hall for Roy Kinnear's sketch 'The Safe Comedian', and adopted by David Frost for 'That Was The Week That Was', on BBC Television, 1962–3

18 Hello, I'm Julian and this is my friend, Sandy.

Barry Took and **Marty Feldman** 1933–83: catch-phrase in *Round the Horne* (BBC radio series, 1965–8)

19 Very interesting...but stupid.

Dan Rowan 1922–87 and **Dick Martin** 1923– : catch-phrase in *Rowan and Martin's Laugh-In* (American television series, 1967–73)

20 Nobody expects the Spanish Inquisition! Our chief weapon is surprise—surprise and fear...fear and surprise...our two weapons are fear and surprise—and ruthless efficiency...our *three* weapons are fear and surprise and ruthless efficiency and an almost fanatical devotion to the Pope...our *four*...no...*Amongst* our weapons—amongst our weaponry—are such elements as fear, surprise...I'll come in again.

Graham Chapman 1941–89, **John Cleese** 1939–, et al.: *Monty Python's Flying Circus* (BBC TV programme, 1970)

21 'This one's going to be a real winner,' said C. J. 'I didn't get where I am today without knowing a real winner when I see one.'

David Nobbs 1935– : *The Death of Reginald Perrin* (1975); subsequently a catch-phrase in BBC television series *The Fall and Rise of Reginald Perrin*, 1976–80

22 Eric Sykes had this quick ear and could tell by any inflection I put into a line how to make it a catch phrase—at one time I had more catch phrases than I could handle. I had the whole country saying things like 'I've arrived and to prove it I'm here!' 'A good idea—son' 'Bighead!' 'Dollar lolly'.

Eric Sykes and **Max Bygraves** 1922– : Max Bygraves *I Wanna Tell You a Story!* (1976)

23 'Er indoors.

Leon Griffiths: used in ITV television series *Minder* (1979 onwards) by Arthur Daley (played by George Cole) to refer to his wife

24 So Harry says, 'You don't like me any more. Why not?' And he says, 'Because you've got so terribly pretentious.' And Harry says, 'Pretentious? *Moi?*'

John Cleese 1939– and **Connie Booth**: *Fawlty Towers* (BBC TV programme, 1979)

25 Shome mishtake, shurely?

Anonymous: catch-phrase in *Private Eye* magazine, 1980s

26 Pass the sick bag, Alice.

John Junor 1919– : referring to a canteen lady at the old *Express* building in Fleet Street, who conveyed plates of egg and chips to journalists at their desks; in *Sunday Express* 28 December 1980

27 I have a cunning plan.

Richard Curtis and **Ben Elton** 1959– : *Blackadder II* (1987) television series; Baldrick's habitual overoptimistic promise

28 You might very well think that. I couldn't possibly comment.

Michael Dobbs 1948– : *House of Cards* (televised 1990); the Chief Whip's habitual response to questioning

Conversation See also *Speeches and Speechmaking*

1 Nothing comes amiss to her but speaking commendably of anybody but herself without some tokens of reserve.

Anonymous: in *The Female Tatler* September 1709

2 Faith, that's as well said, as if I had said it myself.

Jonathan Swift 1667–1745: *Polite Conversation* (1738)

3 —d! said my mother, 'what is all this story about?'—'A Cock and a Bull,' said Yorick.

Laurence Sterne 1713–68: *Tristram Shandy* (1759–67)

4 I hate historic talk, and when Charles Fox said something to me once about Catiline's Conspiracy, I withdrew my attention, and thought about Tom Thumb.

Samuel Johnson 1709–84: Hester Lynch Piozzi letter 21 August 1819

5 [Macaulay] has occasional flashes of silence, that make his conversation perfectly delightful.

Sydney Smith 1771–1845: Lady Holland *Memoir* (1855)

6 If you are ever at a loss to support a flagging conversation, introduce the subject of eating.

Leigh Hunt 1784–1859: J. A. Gere and John Sparrow (eds.) *Geoffrey Madan's Notebooks* (1981); attributed

7 'Then you should say what you mean,' the March Hare went on. 'I do,' Alice hastily replied; 'at least—at least I mean what I say—that's the same thing, you know.' 'Not the same thing a bit!' said the Hatter. 'Why, you might just as well say that "I see what I eat" is the same thing as "I eat what I see!" '

Lewis Carroll 1832–98: *Alice's Adventures in Wonderland* (1865)

8 The fun of talk is to find what a man really thinks, and then contrast it with the enormous lies he has been telling all dinner, and, perhaps, all his life.

Benjamin Disraeli 1804–81: *Lothair* (1870)

9 If one hears bad music it is one's duty to drown it in conversation.

Oscar Wilde 1854–1900: *The Picture of Dorian Gray* (1891)

10 Considering how foolishly people act and how pleasantly they prattle, perhaps it would be better for the world if they talked more and did less.

W. Somerset Maugham 1874–1965: *A Writer's Notebook* (1949) written in 1892

11 If one could only teach the English how to talk, and the Irish how to listen, society here would be quite civilized.

Oscar Wilde 1854–1900: *An Ideal Husband* (1895)

12 If one plays good music, people don't listen and if one plays bad music people don't talk.

Oscar Wilde 1854–1900: *The Importance of Being Earnest* (1895)

13 At a dinner party one should eat wisely but not too well, and talk well but not too wisely.

W. Somerset Maugham 1874–1965: *Writer's Notebook* (1949), written in 1896

14 Although there exist many thousand subjects for elegant conversation, there are persons who cannot meet a cripple without talking about feet.

Ernest Bramah 1868–1942: *The Wallet of Kai Lung* (1900)

15 She plunged into a sea of platitudes, and with the powerful breast stroke of a channel swimmer made her confident way towards the white cliffs of the obvious.

W. Somerset Maugham 1874–1965: *A Writer's Notebook* (1949) written in 1919

16 'What ho!' I said.
'What ho!' said Motty.
'What ho! What ho!'
'What ho! What ho! What ho!'
After that it seemed rather difficult to go on with the conversation.

P. G. Wodehouse 1881–1975: *My Man Jeeves* (1919)

On visiting Lord Alfred Douglas:
17 We had resolved not to mention Oscar Wilde, prison, Winston, Robbie Ross or Frank Harris, but we were soon well embarked on all five subjects, though not at once.

Chips Channon 1897–1958: diary 10 October 1942

18 There are two things in ordinary conversation which ordinary people dislike—information and wit.

Stephen Leacock 1869–1944: *The Boy I Left Behind Me* (1947)

19 With first-rate sherry flowing into second-rate whores, And third-rate conversation without one single pause: Just like a young couple Between the wars.

William Plomer 1903–73: 'Father and Son: 1939' (1945)

20 If you have nothing to say, or, rather, something extremely stupid and obvious, say it, but in a 'plonking' tone of voice—i.e. roundly, but hollowly and dogmatically.

Stephen Potter 1900–69: *Lifemanship* (1950)

Commenting that George Bernard Shaw's wife was a good listener:
21 God knows she had plenty of practice.

J. B. Priestley 1894–1984: *Margin Released* (1962)

22 It is clear enough that you are making some distinction in what you said, that there is some nicety of terminology in your words. I can't quite follow you.

Flann O'Brien 1911–66: *The Dalkey Archive* (1964)

23 I've just spent an hour talking to Tallulah for a few minutes.

Fred Keating: Denis Brian *Tallulah, Darling* (1980)

24 How time flies when you's doin' all the talking.

Harvey Fierstein 1954– : *Torch Song Trilogy* (1979)

25 The conversational overachiever is someone whose grasp exceeds his reach. This is possible but not attractive.

Fran Lebowitz 1946– : *Social Studies* (1981)

26 The opposite of talking isn't listening. The opposite of talking is waiting.

Fran Lebowitz 1946– : *Social Studies* (1981)

27 We don't discuss anything anyway. Unless it appears on Patrick's official breakfast-time agenda. And that consists mainly of food. Minutes of the last meal and proposals for the next.

Alan Ayckbourn 1939– : *Sisterly Feelings* (1981)

28 One thing talk can't accomplish, however, is communication. This is because everybody's talking too much to pay attention to what anyone else is saying.

P. J. O'Rourke 1947– : *Modern Manners* (1984)

29 The failure to meet somebody's eyes, if prolonged for an hour or so, is extremely off-putting and discouraging and I warmly recommend it as a weapon.

Arthur Marshall 1910–89: *Life's Rich Pageant* (1984)

30 *You* talked animatedly for some time about language being the aniseed trail that draws the hounds of heaven when the metaphysical fox has gone to earth; he must have thought you were barmy.

Tom Stoppard 1937– : *Jumpers* (rev. ed. 1986)

31 I am quite capable of speaking, unprepared, a sentence containing anything up to forty subordinate clauses all embedded in their neighbours like those wooden Russian dolls, and many a native of these islands, speaking English as to the manner born, has followed me trustingly into the labyrinth only to perish miserably trying to find the way out.

Bernard Levin 1928– : *In These Times* (1986)

32 There is nothing worse than a Jew sitting and listening to a conversation. They nod their heads with a fraudulent air of rabbinical wisdom that makes you want to set about them with staves.

Stephen Fry 1957– : *The Hippopotamus* (1994)

Countries and Peoples See also *Places*

1 I think he bought his doublet in Italy, his round hose in France, his bonnet in Germany, and his behaviour everywhere.

William Shakespeare 1564–1616: *The Merchant of Venice* (1596–8)

2 They order, said I, this matter better in France.

Laurence Sterne 1713–68: opening words of *A Sentimental Journey* (1768)

3 The perpetual lamentations after beef and beer, the stupid bigoted contempt for every thing foreign, and insurmountable incapacity of acquiring even a few words of any language, rendered him like all other English servants, an encumbrance.

Lord Byron 1788–1824: letter 14 January 1811

4 I look upon Switzerland as an inferior sort of Scotland.

Sydney Smith 1771–1845: letter to Lord Holland, 1815

5 Yet, who can help loving the land that has taught us Six hundred and eighty-five ways to dress eggs?

Thomas Moore 1779–1852: *The Fudge Family in Paris* (1818)

In response to the comment, after the failure of the Carbonari uprising, 'Alas! the Italians must now return to making operas':
6 I fear *that* and macaroni are their forte.

Lord Byron 1788–1824: letter 28 April 1821

7 Holland...lies so low they're only saved by being dammed.

Thomas Hood 1799–1845: *Up the Rhine* (1840) 'Letter from Martha Penny to Rebecca Page'

8 Some people...may be Rooshans, and others may be Prooshans; they are born so, and will please themselves. Them which is of other naturs thinks different.

Charles Dickens 1812–70: *Martin Chuzzlewit* (1844)

9 The best thing I know between France and England is— the sea.

Douglas Jerrold 1803–57: *The Wit and Opinions of Douglas Jerrold* (1859) 'The Anglo-French Alliance'

10 Earth is here so kind, that just tickle her with a hoe and she laughs with a harvest.

Douglas Jerrold 1803–57: *The Wit and Opinions of Douglas Jerrold* (1859) 'A Land of Plenty' (Australia)

11 Lump the whole thing! say that the Creator made
Italy from designs by Michael Angelo!

Mark Twain 1835–1910: *The Innocents Abroad* (1869)

12 For he might have been a Roosian,
A French, or Turk, or Proosian,
Or perhaps Ital-ian!
But in spite of all temptations
To belong to other nations,
He remains an Englishman!

W. S. Gilbert 1836–1911: *HMS Pinafore* (1878)

13 I don't like Switzerland: it has produced nothing but
theologians and waiters.

Oscar Wilde 1854–1900: letter from Switzerland, 20 March 1899

*On hearing someone object that the good manners of the French
were all on the surface:*
14 Well, you know, a very good place to have them.

James McNeill Whistler
1834–1903: E. R. and J. Pennell *The Life of James McNeill Whistler* (1908)

15 Cusins is a very nice fellow, certainly: nobody would ever
guess that he was born in Australia.

George Bernard Shaw
1856–1950: *Major Barbara* (1907)

16 The people of Crete unfortunately make more history
than they can consume locally.

Saki 1870–1916: *Chronicles of Clovis* (1911)

17 I was early taught to regard Germany as a very serious
place because I was a little Irish Protestant and knew
that Martin Luther was a German. I therefore concluded
that all Germans went to heaven, an opinion which I no
longer hold with any conviction.

George Bernard Shaw
1856–1950: 'What I Owe to German Culture' (1911)

18 Then brim the bowl with atrabilious liquor!
We'll pledge our Empire vast across the flood:
For Blood, as all men know, than Water's thicker,
But Water's wider, thank the Lord, than Blood.

Aldous Huxley 1894–1963: 'Ninth Philosopher's Song' (1920)

19 I like my 'abroad' to be Catholic and sensual.

Chips Channon 1897–1958: diary 18 January 1924

20 The Dutch in old Amsterdam do it,
Not to mention the Finns,
Folks in Siam do it,
Think of Siamese twins.
Some Argentines, without means, do it,
People say, in Boston, even beans do it
Let's do it, let's fall in love.

Cole Porter 1891–1964: 'Let's Do It, Let's Fall in Love' (1928)

21 To speak with your mouth full
And swallow with greed
Are national traits
Of the travelling Swede.

Duff Cooper 1890–1954: Philip Ziegler *Diana Cooper* (1981)

22 Every wise and thoroughly worldly wench
Knows there's always something fishy about the French!

Noël Coward 1899–1973: 'There's Always Something Fishy about the French' (1933)

23 I don't like Norwegians at all. The sun never sets, the
bar never opens, and the whole country smells of kippers.

Evelyn Waugh 1903–66: letter to Lady Diana Cooper, 13 July 1934

24 When you enter a house you take your shoes off
It's better with your shoes off! . . .

Howard Dietz 1896–1983: 'Get Yourself a Geisha' (1935)

Get yourself a Geisha. The flower of Asia,
She's one with whom to take up.
At night your bed she'll make up,
And she'll be there when you wake up.

25 I gather it has now been decided not to embrace the
Russian bear, but to hold out a hand and accept its paw
gingerly. No more. The worst of both worlds.

Chips Channon 1897–1958: diary
16 May 1939

26 Don't let's be beastly to the Germans
When our Victory is ultimately won.
It was just those nasty Nazis who persuaded them to
fight
And their Beethoven and Bach are really far worse than
their bite,
Let's be meek to them—
And turn the other cheek to them
And try to bring out their latent sense of fun.

Noël Coward 1899–1973: 'Don't
Let's Be Beastly to the Germans'
(1943)

27 Canada keeps up the appeal from its own law courts to
the final decision of the British Privy Council in London.
We get better justice. It must be better because it costs
ten times as much, as our lawyers assure us on their
return from pleading.

Stephen Leacock 1869–1944: *The
Boy I Left Behind Me* (1947)

28 It's like Bob Benchley's remark on India—'India, what
does the name *not* suggest?' To which Benchley himself
gives the answer—'a hell of a lot of things.'

Robert Benchley 1889–1945:
Stephen Leacock *The Boy I Left Behind
Me* (1947); attributed

29 Frogs...are slightly better than Huns or Wops, but
abroad is unutterably bloody and foreigners are fiends.

Nancy Mitford 1904–73: *The
Pursuit of Love* (1945)

30 We sing you the Song of the Rhineland—
Europe's beauty spot...
That wonderful pretzel-and-stein land
Can never be forgot!

Ira Gershwin 1896–1983: 'Song of
the Rhineland' (1945)

31 I'd love to get you
On a slow boat to China,
All to myself, alone.

Frank Loesser 1910–69: 'On a Slow
Boat to China' (1948)

32 In Italy for thirty years under the Borgias they had
warfare, terror, murder, bloodshed—they produced
Michelangelo, Leonardo da Vinci and the Renaissance. In
Switzerland they had brotherly love, five hundred years
of democracy and peace and what did that produce...?
The cuckoo clock.

Orson Welles 1915–85: *The Third
Man* (1949 film); words added by
Welles to Graham Greene's script

*To a Boer who had told her that he could never quite forgive the
British for having conquered his country:*
33 I understand that perfectly. We feel very much the same
in Scotland.

**Queen Elizabeth, the Queen
Mother** 1900– : Elizabeth Longford
(ed.) *The Oxford Book of Royal
Anecdotes* (1989)

34 England and America are two countries divided by
a common language.

George Bernard Shaw
1856–1950: attributed in this and other
forms, but not found in Shaw's
published writings

35 If one had to be foreign it was far better to be German, preferably a Prussian...Indeed, had the Germans only possessed a sense of humour they might almost have qualified as honorary Englishmen.

Osbert Lancaster 1908-80: *All Done From Memory* (1953)

36 And we will all go together when we go— Every Hottentot and every Eskimo.

Tom Lehrer 1928- : 'We Will All Go Together When We Go' (1953)

37 In a bar on the Piccola Marina
Life called to Mrs Wentworth-Brewster,
Fate beckoned her and introduced her
Into a rather queer
Unfamiliar atmosphere...

Just for fun three young sailors from Messina
Bowed low to Mrs Wentworth-Brewster,
Said 'Scusi' and politely goosed her.
Then there was quite a scena.
Her family, in floods of tears, cried,
'Leave these men, Mama.'
She said, 'They're just high-spirited, like all Italians are
And most of them have a great deal more to offer than
      Papa,
In a bar on the Piccola Marina.'

Noël Coward 1899-1973: 'A Bar on the Piccola Marina' (1954)

38 That Britain was no part of Europe was his conviction.

Lord Beaverbrook 1879-1964: of Lord Milner; *Men and Power* (1956)

39 ELIZA: The Rain in Spain stays mainly in the plain.
HIGGINS: By George, she's got it!

Alan Jay Lerner 1918-86: 'The Rain in Spain' (1956)

40 If you come on a camel, you can park it,
So come to the supermarket
And see
Pe-
king.

Cole Porter 1891-1964: 'Come to the Supermarket in Old Peking' (1958)

41 In fact, I'm not really a *Jew*. Just Jew-*ish*. Not the whole hog, you know.

Jonathan Miller 1934- : *Beyond the Fringe* (1960 review) 'Real Class'

42 A country is a piece of land surrounded on all sides by boundaries, usually unnatural.

Joseph Heller 1923- : *Catch*-22 (1961)

43 *Ich bin ein Berliner.*
I am a Berliner.

John F. Kennedy 1917-63: speech in West Berlin, 26 June 1963, *ein Berliner* being the name given in Germany to a doughnut, and the occasion, therefore, of much hilarity

44 How can you govern a country which has 246 varieties of cheese?

Charles de Gaulle 1890-1970: Ernest Mignon *Les Mots du Général* (1962)

Advising Ogden Nash to read V. S. Naipaul's An Area of Darkness:
45 It will save you a great deal of money, because you will most certainly never go to India after reading it.

S. J. Perelman 1904-79: letter to Ogden Nash, 21 June 1965

A reporter had asked Noël Coward to tell her something he had learned in Australia:
46 Kangaroo.

Noël Coward 1899-1973: Sheridan Morley *A Talent to Amuse* (1969)

The French jazz critic Hugues Panassie had given Condon a generally favourable notice:

47 I don't see why we need a Frenchman to come over here and tell us how to play American music. I wouldn't think of going to France and telling him how to jump on a grape.

Eddie Condon 1905–73: Bill Crow *Jazz Anecdotes* (1990)

48 All my wife has ever taken from the Mediterranean— from that whole vast intuitive culture—are four bottles of Chianti to make into lamps.

Peter Shaffer 1926– : *Equus* (1973)

49 They're Germans. Don't mention the war.

John Cleese 1939– and **Connie Booth**: *Fawlty Towers* (BBC TV programme, 1975)

50 I have to spend so much time explaining to Americans that I am not English and to Englishmen that I am not American that I have little time left to be Canadian...(On second thought, I am a true cosmopolitan—unhappy anywhere.)

Laurence J. Peter 1919– : *Quotations for our Time* (1977)

51 No matter how politely or distinctly you ask a Parisian a question he will persist in answering you in French.

Fran Lebowitz 1946– : *Metropolitan Life* (1978)

52 LOUISE: You were champion of all Finland?
SVEN: Well. Nearly all Finland. There were some parts of Finland that didn't compete. Let us say, most of Finland.

Alan Ayckbourn 1939– : *Joking Apart* (1979)

53 It's where they commit suicide and the king rides a bicycle, Sweden.

Alan Bennett 1934– : *Enjoy* (1980)

54 Sweden boasts some fine modern architecture plus a free-wheeling attitude towards personal morality.

Alan Bennett 1934– : *Enjoy* (1980)

55 'We went in [to the European Community],' he said, 'to screw the French by splitting them off from the Germans. The French went in to protect their inefficient farmers from commercial competition. The Germans went in to cleanse themselves of genocide and apply for readmission to the human race.'

Jonathan Lynn 1943– and **Antony Jay** 1930– : *Yes, Minister* vol. 2 (1982)

56 Australia is a huge rest home, where no unwelcome news is ever wafted on to the pages of the worst newspapers in the world.

Germaine Greer 1939– : in *Observer* 1 August 1982

57 Paris last year. Wonderful town but the French are awful, the waiters and so on, they're tip mad.

Tom Stoppard 1937– : *Neutral Ground* (1983)

58 Canadians are Americans with no Disneyland.

Margaret Mahy 1937– : *The Changeover* (1984)

59 We did have a form of Afro-Asian studies which consisted of colouring bits of the map red to show the British Empire.

Michael Green 1927– : *The Boy Who Shot Down an Airship* (1988)

60 I see Canada as a country torn between a very northern, rather extraordinary, mystical spirit which it fears and its desire to present itself to the world as a Scotch banker.

Robertson Davies 1913– : *The Enthusiasms of Robertson Davies* (1990)

61 That's the main trouble with the two nations: bad Brits are snobs, bad Americans are slobs.

Peter Shaffer 1926– : *Whom Do I Have the Honour of Addressing?* (1990)

62 Germans are flummoxed by humour, the Swiss have no concept of fun, the Spanish think there is nothing at all ridiculous about eating dinner at midnight, and the Italians should never, ever have been let in on the invention of the motor car.

Bill Bryson 1951– : *Neither Here Nor There* (1991)

63 Just as America had, in Bernard Shaw's perception, moved from barbarism to decadence without an intervening period of civilization, Australian humour had somehow skipped the ironic and gone from folksy to camp.

Barry Humphries 1934– : *More Please* (1992)

64 [The Commonwealth] is a largely meaningless relic of Empire—like the smile on the face of the Cheshire Cat which remains when the cat has disappeared.

Nigel Lawson 1932– : in *Ned Sherrin in his Anecdotage* (1993)

The Country

1 Very few people have settled entirely in the country but have grown at length weary of one another. The lady's conversation generally falls into a thousand impertinent effects of idleness, and the gentleman falls in love with his dogs and horses, and out of love with every thing else.

Lady Mary Wortley Montagu 1689–1762: letter to Edward Wortley Montague, 12 August 1712

2 He likes the country, but in truth must own, Most likes it, when he studies it in town.

William Cowper 1731–1800: 'Retirement' (1782)

3 God made the country, and man made the town.

William Cowper 1731–1800: *The Task* (1785)

4 I have no relish for the country; it is a kind of healthy grave.

Sydney Smith 1771–1845: letter to Miss G. Harcourt, 1838

5 Anybody can be good in the country.

Oscar Wilde 1854–1900: *The Picture of Dorian Gray* (1891)

6 Sylvia...was accustomed to nothing much more sylvan than 'leafy Kensington'. She looked on the country as something excellent and wholesome in its way, which was apt to become troublesome if you encouraged it overmuch.

Saki 1870–1916: *The Chronicles of Clovis* (1911)

7 The Farmer will never be happy again; He carries his heart in his boots; For either the rain is destroying his grain Or the drought is destroying his roots.

A. P. Herbert 1890–1971: 'The Farmer' (1922)

8 In a mountain greenery Where God paints the scenery—.

Lorenz Hart 1895–1943: 'Mountain Greenery' (1926)

9 Farming, that's the fashion, Farming, that's the passion Of our great celebrities of today. Kit Cornell is shellin' peas, Lady Mendl's climbin' trees,

Cole Porter 1891–1964: 'Farming' (1941)

Dear Mae West is at her best in the hay...

The natives think it's utterly utter
When Margie Hart starts churning her butter...

Miss Elsa Maxwell, so the folks tattle,
Got well-goosed while dehorning her cattle...

Liz Whitney has, on her bin of manure, a
Clip designed by the Duke of Verdura,
Farming is so charming, they all say.

10 So *that's* what hay looks like.

Queen Mary 1867–1953: said at Badminton House, where she was evacuated during the Second World War; James Pope-Hennessy *Life of Queen Mary* (1959)

11 June is bustin' out all over
The sheep aren't sleepin' any more!
All the rams that chase the ewe sheep
Are determined there'll be new sheep
And the ewe sheep aren't even keepin' score!

Oscar Hammerstein II 1895–1960: 'June is Bustin' Out All Over' (1945)

12 What do we see at once but a little robin! There is no need to burst into tears fotherington-tomas swete tho he be. Nor to buzz a brick at it, molesworth 2.

Geoffrey Willans 1911–58 and **Ronald Searle** 1920– : a nature walk at St Custards; *Down with Skool!* (1953)

13 Having always been told that living at Crowborough was 'living in the country' I wrongly identified English country life with interminable calls on elderly ladies whose favourite topic was the servant problem.

Tom Driberg 1905–76: *The Best of Both Worlds* (1953)

14 A farm is an irregular patch of nettles bounded by short-term notes, containing a fool and his wife who didn't know enough to stay in the city.

S. J. Perelman 1904–79: *The Most of S. J. Perelman* (1959) 'Acres and Pains'

15 According to recent figures compiled by trained statisticians working under filtered oatmeal, the first thing ninety-four per cent of the population does on acquiring a country place is to build some sort of swimming pool. The other six per cent instantly welshes on the deal and stops payment.

S. J. Perelman 1904–79: *The Most of S. J. Perelman* (1959) 'Acres and Pains'

16 Hey, buds below, up is where to grow,
Up with which below can't compare with.
Hurry! It's lovely up here! *Hurry!*

Alan Jay Lerner 1918–86: 'It's Lovely Up Here' (1965)

17 It is no good putting up notices saying 'Beware of the bull' because very rude things are sometimes written on them. I have found that one of the most effective notices is 'Beware of the Agapanthus'.

Lord Massereene and Ferrard 1914–93: speech on the Wildlife and Countryside Bill, House of Lords 16 December 1980

18 Very occasionally you will come across things that can move about, but not very freely. This is almost certain to be a tethered goat, a wounded animal or something stuck in a cobweb. Whichever it is, obey the country code and leave well alone; they are private property, belonging respectively to a *Guardian* reader, the RSPCA and a spider.

Miles Kington 1941– : *Nature Made Ridiculously Simple* (1983)

19 You don't get nice trees in other places, not the variety. Nice trees are taken for granted in England. Yes, awfully fond of trees, damned fond...Carol's got a tree, you know—her own. I actually *bought* her a tree for her birthday.

Tom Stoppard 1937– : *Neutral Ground* (1983)

20 Whose woods are whose everybody knows exactly, and everybody knows who got them rezoned for a shopping mall and who couldn't get the financing to begin construction and why it was he couldn't get it.

P. J. O'Rourke 1947– : on a traditional New England community, with reference to Robert Frost's 'Whose woods these are I think I know'; *Parliament of Whores* (1991)

21 We didn't have any cutesy-artsy objections to seeing trees cut down. It's a lot easier to shoot a deer on a 350-yard par-four fairway than it is in the deep woods.

P. J. O'Rourke 1947– : *Parliament of Whores* (1991)

22 I wish I was a provincial poet,
Writing a lot about nature,
Whenever I thought about London poets,
I'd mutter darkly, 'I hate yer.'

Wendy Cope 1945– : 'Pastoral' (1992)

23 'You are a pretty urban sort of person though, wouldn't you say?'
'Only nor'nor'east,' I said. 'I know a fox from a fax-machine.'

Stephen Fry 1957– : *The Hippopotamus* (1994)

Crime and Punishment See also *The Law and Lawyers*

1 The most peaceable way for you, if you do take a thief, is, to let him show himself what he is and steal out of your company.

William Shakespeare 1564–1616: *Much Ado About Nothing* (1598–9)

2 I grow, I prosper;
Now, gods, stand up for bastards!

William Shakespeare 1564–1616: *King Lear* (1605–6)

3 Thwackum was for doing justice, and leaving mercy to heaven.

Henry Fielding 1707–54: *Tom Jones* (1749)

Of a burglar:
4 He found it inconvenient to be poor.

William Cowper 1731–1800: 'Charity' (1782)

5 It's over, and can't be helped, and that's one consolation, as they always says in Turkey, ven they cuts the wrong man's head off.

Charles Dickens 1812–70: *Pickwick Papers* (1837)

6 Thou shalt not steal; an empty feat,
When it's so lucrative to cheat.

Arthur Hugh Clough 1819–61: 'The Latest Decalogue' (1862)

7 But when our neighbours do wrong, we sometimes feel the fitness of making them smart for it, whether they have repented or not.

Oliver Wendell Holmes Jr. 1841–1935: *The Common Law* (1881)

8 As some day it may happen that a victim must be found, I've got a little list—I've got a little list
Of society offenders who might well be under ground
And who never would be missed—who never would be missed!

W. S. Gilbert 1836–1911: *The Mikado* (1885)

9 Awaiting the sensation of a short, sharp shock,
From a cheap and chippy chopper on a big black block.

W. S. Gilbert 1836–1911: *The Mikado* (1885)

10 Something lingering, with boiling oil in it, I fancy.

W. S. Gilbert 1836–1911: *The Mikado* (1885)

11 If a man can't forge his own will, whose will can he forge?

W. S. Gilbert 1836–1911: *Ruddigore* (1887)

12 It is quite a three-pipe problem, and I beg that you won't speak to me for fifty minutes.

Arthur Conan Doyle 1859–1930: *The Adventures of Sherlock Holmes* (1892) 'The Red-Headed League'

13 'Excellent,' I cried. 'Elementary,' said he.

Arthur Conan Doyle 1859–1930: *The Memoirs of Sherlock Holmes* (1894) 'The Crooked Man'. 'Elementary, my dear Watson' is not found in any book by Conan Doyle

14 Thieves respect property. They merely wish the property to become their property that they may more perfectly respect it.

G. K. Chesterton 1874–1936: *The Man who was Thursday* (1908)

15 It was beautiful and simple as all truly great swindles are.

O. Henry 1862–1910: *Gentle Grafter* (1908) 'Octopus Marooned'

16 What is robbing a bank compared with founding a bank?

Bertolt Brecht 1898–1956: *Die Dreigroschenoper* (1928)

A prisoner before Mr Justice Darling objected to being called 'a professional crook':
17 PRISONER: I've only done two jobs, and each time I've been nabbed.
   LORD DARLING: It has never been suggested that you are successful in your profession.

Lord Darling 1849–1936: Edward Maltby *Secrets of a Solicitor* (1929)

Reply to a prison visitor who asked if he were sewing:
18 No, reaping.

Horatio Bottomley 1860–1933: S.T. Felstead *Horatio Bottomley* (1936)

19 Since it is probable that any book flying a bullet in its title is going to produce a corpse sooner or later—here it is.

Caryl Brahms 1901–82 and **S. J. Simon** 1904–48: *A Bullet in the Ballet* (1937)

20 When their lordships asked Bacon
   How many bribes he had taken
   He had at least the grace
   To get very red in the face.

Edmund Clerihew Bentley 1875–1956: 'Bacon' (1939)

21 He would be astounded if you told him he was a crook. He honestly looks upon a fifty-fifty proposition as seventy-five for himself and twenty-five for the other fellow.

W. Somerset Maugham 1874–1965: *A Writer's Notebook* (1949) written in 1941

22 Major Strasser has been shot. Round up the usual suspects.

Julius J. Epstein 1909– : *Casablanca* (1942 film)

23 Three juvenile delinquents,
   Juvenile delinquents,
   Happy as can be—we
   Waste no time
   On the wherefores and whys of it;
   We like crime
   And that's about the size of it.

Noël Coward 1899–1973: 'Three Juvenile Delinquents' (1949)

24 Here in our city
We're all of us pretty
Well sure that vice
Will in a trice
Be bundled out of sight,
Old men in lobbies
With dubious hobbies
Can still get the deuce of a fright
In London at night.

Noël Coward 1899–1973: 'London at Night' (1953)

25 Let it appear in a criminal trial that the accused is
a Sunday-school superintendent, and the jury says guilty
almost automatically.

H. L. Mencken 1880–1956: *Minority Report* (1956)

26 The Warden threw a party at the county jail,
The prison band was there an' they began to wail.
The brass band was jumpin' an' the joint began to swing
You should have heard those knocked out jail birds sing.

Jerry Leiber 1933– and **Mike Stoller** 1933– : 'Jailhouse Rock' (1957)

27 In sentencing a man for one crime, we may well be
putting him beyond the reach of the law in respect of
those crimes which he has not yet had an opportunity to
commit. The law, however, is not to be cheated in this
way. I shall therefore discharge you.

N. F. Simpson 1919– : *One Way Pendulum* (1960)

28 She starts to tell me how she's...married to an Italian
with four restaurants on Long Island and right away
I dig he's in with the mob. I mean one restaurant, you're
in business, four restaurants it's the Mafia.

Neil Simon 1927– : *The Gingerbread Lady* (1970)

29 The only time I fired a catapult as a boy was at
a sparrow in London. I got into awful trouble. It went
through somebody's bathroom window and hit an old
man on the head while he was in the bath. My father
got blamed.

Lord Massereene and Ferrard 1914–93: speech on the Wildlife and Countryside Bill, House of Lords 27 January 1981

John Mortimer had been defending an East End totter (a rag-and-bone collector) on a charge of attempted murder:
30 As I thought, as usual, of all the things I might have
said, art took its revenge on life. 'Your Mr Rumpole
could've got me out of this,' the totter said, 'so why the
hell can't you?'

John Mortimer 1923– : *Clinging to the Wreckage* (1982)

31 I'm trusting in the Lord and a good lawyer.

Oliver North 1943– : in *Observer* 7 December 1986 'Sayings of the Week'

32 When I heard the words criminal investigation my
mindset changed considerably.

Oliver North 1943– : in *New York Times* 10 July 1987 'Quotation of the Day'

33 These Nazi war criminals are getting so old anyway,
what would you do with them? Shorten one leg on their
walker? Put a frog in their colostomy bag? Stick
a playing card in their wheelchair spokes so they make
a lot of noise and are easier for Mossad to find?

P. J. O'Rourke 1947– : *Give War a Chance* (1992)

34 She thanks the one man, small boy and dog that are the hapless art and antique squad at Scotland Yard for generous help (hollow laughter now quite uncontrollable).

Brian Sewell: review of Shirley Conran *Tiger Eyes* in *Daily Telegraph* 11 June 1994

Critics and Criticism

1 At ev'ry word a reputation dies.

Alexander Pope 1688–1744: *The Rape of the Lock* (1714)

2 As learned commentators view
In Homer more than Homer knew.

Jonathan Swift 1667–1745: 'On Poetry' (1733)

3 Criticism is a study by which men grow important and formidable at very small expense.

Samuel Johnson 1709–84: *The Idler* 9 June 1759

4 Full many a gallant man lies slain
On Waterloo's ensanguined plain,
But none by bullet or by shot
Fell half so flat as Walter Scott.

Anonymous: comment on Scott's poem 'The Field of Waterloo' (1815), sometimes attributed to Thomas Erskine; Una Pope-Hennessy *The Laird of Abbotsford* (1932)

5 Send me no more reviews of any kind.—I will read no more of evil or good in that line.—Walter Scott has not read a review of *himself* for *thirteen years*.

Lord Byron 1788–1824: letter to his publisher John Murray, 3 November 1821

6 He took the praise as a greedy boy takes apple pie, and the criticism as a good dutiful boy takes senna-tea.

Lord Macaulay 1800–59: of Bulwer Lytton, whose novels he had criticized; letter 5 August 1831

7 I never read a book before reviewing it; it prejudices a man so.

Sydney Smith 1771–1845: H. Pearson *The Smith of Smiths* (1934)

8 You know who the critics are? The men who have failed in literature and art.

Benjamin Disraeli 1804–81: *Lothair* (1870)

9 The lot of critics is to be remembered by what they failed to understand.

George Moore 1852–1933: *Impressions and Opinions* (1891) 'Balzac'

10 There is a sort of savage nobility about his firm reliance on his own bad taste.

A. E. Housman 1859–1936: of Richard Bentley's edition of *Paradise Lost*; 'Introductory Lecture' (1892)

John Churton Collins, a rival of Edmund Gosse, launched a bitter critical attack on him. When Gosse took tea with Tennyson he found an ally who defined Collins as:
11 A louse in the locks of literature.

Alfred, Lord Tennyson
1809–92: Evan Charteris *Life and Letters of Sir Edmund Gosse* (1931)

12 WILDE: I shall always regard you as the best critic of my plays.
TREE: But I have never criticized your plays.
WILDE: That's why.

Oscar Wilde 1854–1900: conversation with Beerbohm Tree after the first-night success of *A Woman of No Importance*; Hesketh Pearson *Beerbohm Tree* (1956)

13 Criticism is not only medicinally salutary: it has positive popular attractions in its cruelty, its gladiatorship, and the gratification given to envy by its attacks on the great, and to enthusiasm by its praises.

George Bernard Shaw 1856–1950: preface to *Plays Unpleasant* (1898)

14 One must have a heart of stone to read the death of Little Nell without laughing.

Oscar Wilde 1854–1900: Ada Leverson *Letters to the Sphinx* (1930)

15 Mr Owen's innovations, so far as I can see, have only one merit, which certainly, in view of their character, is a merit of some magnitude: they are few.

A. E. Housman 1859–1936: in *Classical Review* 1903

16 This method answers the purpose for which it was devised; it saves lazy editors from working and stupid editors from thinking.

A. E. Housman 1859–1936: 'The Editing of Manilius' (1903)

17 I have always thought it was a sound impulse by which he [Kipling] was driven to put his 'Recessional' into the waste-paper basket, and a great pity that Mrs Kipling fished it out and made him send it to *The Times*.

Max Beerbohm 1872–1956: letter 30 October 1913

18 The original Greek is of great use in elucidating Browning's translation of the *Agamemnon*.

Robert Yelverton Tyrrell 1844–1914: habitual remark to students; Ulick O'Connor *Oliver St John Gogarty* (1964)

19 Progress through its clumsy and invertebrate sentences is like plodding over a ploughed field of clay.

A. E. Housman 1859–1936: in *Cambridge Review* 1915

20 My dear Sir: I have read your play. Oh, my dear Sir! Yours faithfully.

Herbert Beerbohm Tree 1852–1917: rejecting a play; Peter Hay *Theatrical Anecdotes* (1987)

21 Reviewing here [in Baltimore] is a hazardous occupation. Once I spoke harshly of an eminent American novelist, and he retaliated by telling a very charming woman that I was non compos penis. In time she came to laugh at him as a liar.

H. L. Mencken 1880–1956: letter to Hugh Walpole, 1922

22 The scratching of pimples on the body of the bootboy at Claridges.

Virginia Woolf 1882–1941: of James Joyce's *Ulysses*; letter to Lytton Strachey, 24 April 1922

23 Last year I gave several lectures on 'Intelligence and the Appreciation of Music Among Animals'. Today I am going to speak to you about 'Intelligence and the Appreciation of Music Among Critics'. The subject is very similar.

Erik Satie 1866–1925: Nat Shapiro (ed.) *An Encyclopedia of Quotations about Music* (1978)

24 And it is that word 'hummy', my darlings, that marks the first place in 'The House at Pooh Corner' at which Tonstant Weader fwowed up.

Dorothy Parker 1893–1967: review in *New Yorker* 20 October 1928

25 [Jeanne Aubert's] husband, if you can believe the papers, recently pled through the French courts that he be allowed to restrain his wife from appearing on the stage. Professional or not, the man is a dramatic critic.

Dorothy Parker 1893–1967: in *New Yorker* February 1931; Dorothy Hart *Thou Swell, Thou Witty* (1976)

26 The *Times* critic said that the author was entitled to telescope history and re-interpret it. I think I must now write a play to prove that Nero went behind the scenes at circuses for intellectual conversation, and another to show that fire descended upon Sodom because the inhabitants refused to pay poll-tax.

James Agate 1877–1947: diary 11 September 1934

27 For 18 years he *started the day* by reading a French novel (in preparation for his history of them) an act so unnatural to man as to amount almost to genius.

Stephen Potter 1900–69: of the critic G.E. B. Saintsbury; *The Muse in Chains* (1937)

28 Never pay any attention to what critics say...A statue has never been set up in honour of a critic!

Jean Sibelius 1865–1957: Bengt de Törne *Sibelius: A Close-Up* (1937)

29 About one thing I am determined. This is not to be afraid of saying No to pretentious rubbish because fifty years ago Clement Scott made a fool of himself over Ibsen.

James Agate 1877–1947: diary 24 December 1939

30 He takes the long review of things;
He asks and gives no quarter.
And you can sail with him on wings
Or read the book. It's shorter.

David McCord 1897– : 'To A Certain Most Certainly Certain Critic' (1945)

31 Hebrews 13.8. [Jesus Christ, the same yesterday, and today, and forever.]

Robert Benchley 1889–1945: summing up the long-running 1920s Broadway hit *Abie's Irish Rose*; Peter Hay *Theatrical Anecdotes* (1987)

32 GLAND: I would say it's somehow redolent, and full of vitality.
 HILDA: Well, I would say it's got about as much life in it as a potted shrimp.
 GLAND: Well, I think we're probably both trying to say the same thing in different words.

Henry Reed 1914–86: *The Primal Scene, as it were* (1958 radio play)

33 It would be unfair to suggest that one of the most characteristic sounds of the English Sunday is the sound of Harold Hobson barking up the wrong tree.

Penelope Gilliatt 1933– : in *Encore* November–December 1959

34 Critics are like eunuchs in a harem; they know how it's done, they've seen it done every day, but they're unable to do it themselves.

Brendan Behan 1923–64: Jonathon Green (ed.) *A Dictionary of Contemporary Quotations* (1982)

35 A critic is a man who knows the way but can't drive the car.

Kenneth Tynan 1927–80: in *New York Times Magazine* 9 January 1966

36 Dr Leavis believed he could identify a woman writer by her style, even though necessarily all that she wrote must have been a parody of some man's superior achievement. After all, there was not much wrong with Virginia Woolf except that she was a woman.

Germaine Greer 1939– : *The Female Eunuch* (1970)

37 Hard to lay down and easy not to pick up.

Malcolm Cowley 1898–1989: of John O'Hara's novels; Laurence J. Peter (ed.) *Quotations for our Time* (1977)

38 Mr Julian Symons is a hack journalist half as old as time. He was one of Colley Cibber's friends...Permanent fringe to whatever is the current fringe, I believe Mr Symons's competence is the detective story.

Gore Vidal 1925– : in *The Spectator* 23 October 1982

39 She also writes with the authority and easy confidence of someone who knows that she is very well known indeed to those few who know her.

Gore Vidal 1925– : of Midge Decter; *Pink Triangle and Yellow Star* (1984)

40 Critics search for ages for the wrong word which, to give them credit, they eventually find.

Peter Ustinov 1921– : Ned Sherrin *Cutting Edge* (1984)

41 *Non, je suis critique.*

Harold Hobson 1904– : to Jean Genet, who, misinterpreting Hobson's admiration, had asked *'Alors, monsieur, est-ce que vous êtes pédéraste?'*; in Ned Sherrin in his *Anecdotage* (1993)

42 CRITIC: I'm so terribly clever, you see. That's one of the things I really admire about myself. I have this extraordinary ability to see, after the event, why something didn't work, and communicate it so wittily. I really am fabulous.

Stephen Fry 1957– and **Hugh Laurie**: *A Bit More Fry and Laurie* (1991)

43 'The polecat [in Saki's *Sredni Vashtar*] is a phallic symbol, do we think?'
'Honestly, dear,' said Gary, 'you're so obsessed, you'd think a *penis* was phallic.'

Stephen Fry 1957– : *The Liar* (1991)

44 A bad review may spoil your breakfast but you shouldn't allow it to spoil your lunch.

Kingsley Amis 1922–95. Giles Gordon *Aren't We Due a Royalty Statement?* (1993); attributed

45 When I read something saying I've not done anything as good as *Catch-22* I'm tempted to reply, 'Who has?'

Joseph Heller 1923– : in *The Times* 9 June 1993

Explaining why Vikram Seth's A Suitable Boy *had not been shortlisted for the* 1993 *Booker Prize:*
46 All the wrong bits are in and the right bits are out.

Lord Gowrie 1939– : in *Guardian* 9 March 1994

47 The only passage in the book worth reading is at the very end, where she acknowledges the technical help of a duchess, a marchioness, a baroness and even poor Bruce Chatwin.

Brian Sewell: review of Shirley Conran *Tiger Eyes* in *Daily Telegraph* 11 June 1994

Dance

1 Will you, won't you, will you, won't you, will you join the dance?

Lewis Carroll 1832–98: *Alice's Adventures in Wonderland* (1865)

2 I wish I could shimmy like my sister Kate,
She shivers like the jelly on a plate.

Armand J. Piron: 'Shimmy like Kate' (1919)

3 Everyone else at the table had got up to dance, except him and me. There I was, trapped. Trapped like a trap in a trap.

Dorothy Parker 1893–1967: *After Such Pleasures* (1933)

The ballet designer Benois:
4 Benois...If 'e come.

Caryl Brahms 1901–82 and **S. J. Simon** 1904–48: *A Bullet in the Ballet* (1937)

5 Cheek to Cheek
Toes to Toes
Here's a dance you can do on a dime
Knees to Knees
Nose to Nose
Slowly move, and you're doin' 'The Slime'.

Jerry Leiber 1933– : 'The Slime' (1942)

6 Though no one ever could be keener
Than little Nina
On quite a number
Of very eligible men who did the Rhumba
When they proposed to her she simply left them flat.
She said that love should be impulsive
But not compulsive
And syncopation
Has a discouraging effect on procreation
And that she'd rather read a book—and that was that!

Noël Coward 1899–1973: 'Nina' (1945)

7 We are told that her supporting company are all relations, and I dare say they do better than yours or mine would under the circumstances.

Caryl Brahms 1901–82: of Carmen Armaya's Spanish Gypsy Dancers at the Prince's Theatre; in *Evening Standard* 1948

8 [Dancing is] a perpendicular expression of a horizontal desire.

George Bernard Shaw 1856–1950: in *New Statesman* 23 March 1962

9 If the Louvre custodian can,
If the Guard Republican can,
If Van Gogh and Matisse and Cézanne can,
Baby, you can can-can too...

Lovely Duse in Milan can,
Lucien Guitry and Réjane can,
Sarah Bernhardt upon a divan can,
Baby, you can can-can too.

Cole Porter 1891–1964: 'Can-Can' (1953)

10 Miles of cornfields, and ballet in the evening.

Alan Hackney: of Russia; *Private Life* (1958) (later filmed as *I'm All Right Jack*, 1959)

11 I made the little buggers hop.

Thomas Beecham 1879–1961: on conducting the Diaghilev Ballet; attributed

12 No. You see there are portions of the human anatomy which would keep swinging after the music had finished.

Robert Helpmann 1909–86: reply to question on whether the fashion for nudity would extend to dance; Elizabeth Salter *Helpmann* (1978)

13 Stately as a galleon, I sail across the floor,
Doing the Military Two-step, as in the days of yore...
So gay the band,
So giddy the sight,
Full evening dress is a must,
But the zest goes out of a beautiful waltz
When you dance it bust to bust.

Joyce Grenfell 1910–79: 'Stately as a Galleon' (1978)

Death See also *Epitaphs, Last Words, Murder*

1 One dies only once, and it's for such a long time!

Molière 1622–73: *Le Dépit amoureux* (performed 1656, published 1662)

2 Not louder shrieks to pitying heav'n are cast,
When husbands or when lapdogs breathe their last.

Alexander Pope 1688–1744: *The Rape of the Lock* (1714)

3 But thousands die, without or this or that,
Die, and endow a college, or a cat.

Alexander Pope 1688–1744:
Epistles to Several Persons 'To Lord
Bathurst' (1733)

4 Here am I, dying of a hundred good symptoms.

Alexander Pope 1688–1744: to
George, Lord Lyttelton, 15 May 1744

5 He makes a very handsome corpse and becomes his coffin
prodigiously.

Oliver Goldsmith 1730–74: *The
Good-Natured Man* (1768)

During his last illness:
6 If Mr Selwyn calls again, show him up: if I am alive
I shall be delighted to see him; and if I am dead he
would like to see me.

Lord Holland 1705–74: J. H. Jesse
*George Selwyn and his
Contemporaries* (1844)

7 Depend upon it, Sir, when a man knows he is to be
hanged in a fortnight, it concentrates his mind
wonderfully.

Samuel Johnson 1709–84: James
Boswell *Life of Samuel Johnson* (1791)
19 September 1777

8 In this world nothing can be said to be certain, except
death and taxes.

Benjamin Franklin 1706–90:
letter to Jean Baptiste Le Roy,
13 November 1789

9 We met...Dr Hall in such very deep mourning that
either his mother, his wife, or himself must be dead.

Jane Austen 1775–1817: letter to
Cassandra Austen, 17 May 1799

10 His death, which happened in his berth,
At forty-odd befell:
They went and told the sexton, and
The sexton tolled the bell.

Thomas Hood 1799–1845:
'Faithless Sally Brown' (1826)

11 Swans sing before they die: 'twere no bad thing
Should certain persons die before they sing.

Samuel Taylor Coleridge
1772–1834: 'On a Volunteer Singer'
(1834)

12 He'd make a lovely corpse.

Charles Dickens 1812–70: *Martin
Chuzzlewit* (1844)

13 The best of us being unfit to die, what an inexpressible
absurdity to put the worst to death!

Nathaniel Hawthorne 1804–64:
diary 13 October 1851

14 Bombazine would have shown a deeper sense of her loss.

Elizabeth Gaskell 1810–65:
Cranford (1853)

15 Thou shalt not kill; but need'st not strive
Officiously to keep alive.

Arthur Hugh Clough 1819–61:
'The Latest Decalogue' (1862)

16 Take away that emblem of mortality.

Benjamin Disraeli 1804–81: on
being offered an air cushion to sit on,
1881; Robert Blake *Disraeli* (1966)

17 But there, everything has its drawbacks, as the man said
when his mother-in-law died, and they came down upon
him for the funeral expenses.

Jerome K. Jerome 1859–1927:
Three Men in a Boat (1889)

18 One can survive everything nowadays, except death, and
live down anything except a good reputation.

Oscar Wilde 1854–1900: *A Woman
of No Importance* (1893)

19 The report of my death was an exaggeration.

Mark Twain 1835–1910: in *New
York Journal* 2 June 1897 (usually
quoted 'Reports of my death have
been greatly exaggerated')

During the Boxer rising it was erroneously reported that those besieged in the Legation quarter of Peking, including the Times *correspondent Dr Morrison, had been massacred. Morrison cabled the paper:*

20 Have just read obituary in the Times. Kindly adjust pay to suit.

George Ernest Morrison
1862–1920: Claud Cockburn *In Time of Trouble* (1956); attributed

21 'There's been an accident,' they said,
'Your servant's cut in half; he's dead!'
'Indeed!' said Mr Jones, 'and please,
Send me the half that's got my keys.'

Harry Graham 1874–1936: 'Mr Jones' (1899)

22 Billy, in one of his nice new sashes,
Fell in the fire and was burnt to ashes;
Now, although the room grows chilly,
I haven't the heart to poke poor Billy.

Harry Graham 1874–1936: 'Tender-Heartedness' (1899)

At the mention of a huge fee for a surgical operation:
23 Ah, well, then, I suppose that I shall have to die beyond my means.

Oscar Wilde 1854–1900: R. H. Sherard *Life of Oscar Wilde* (1906)

Of the wallpaper in the room where he was dying:
24 One of us must go.

Oscar Wilde 1854–1900: attributed, probably apocryphal

25 Alas! Lord and Lady Dalhousie are dead, and buried at last,
Which causes many people to feel a little downcast.

William McGonagall
c.1825–1902: 'The Death of Lord and Lady Dalhousie'

26 Beautiful Railway Bridge of the Silv'ry Tay!
Alas, I am very sorry to say
That ninety lives have been taken away
On the last Sabbath day of 1879,
Which will be remembered for a very long time.

William McGonagall
c.1825–1902: 'The Tay Bridge Disaster'

On returning his ticket for Irving's funeral:
27 Literature, alas, has no place in his death as it had no place in his life. Irving would turn in his coffin if I came, just as Shakespeare will turn in his coffin when Irving comes.

George Bernard Shaw
1856–1950: letter November 1905

28 What I like about Clive
Is that he is no longer alive.
There is a great deal to be said
For being dead.

Edmund Clerihew Bentley
1875–1956: 'Clive' (1905)

29 I refused to attend his funeral, but I wrote a very nice letter explaining that I approved of it.

Mark Twain 1835–1910: on hearing of the death of a corrupt politician; James Munson (ed.) *The Sayings of Mark Twain* (1992)

30 I detest life-insurance agents; they always argue that I shall some day die, which is not so.

Stephen Leacock 1869–1944: *Literary Lapses* (1910)

31 Lord Finchley tried to mend the Electric Light
Himself. It struck him dead: And serve him right!
It is the business of the wealthy man
To give employment to the artisan.

Hilaire Belloc 1870–1953: 'Lord Finchley' (1911)

32 Waldo is one of those people who would be enormously improved by death.

Saki 1870–1916: *Beasts and Super-Beasts* (1914)

33 Death is the most convenient time to tax rich people.

David Lloyd George 1863–1945: in *Lord Riddell's Intimate Diary of the Peace Conference and After, 1918–23* (1933)

34 When I am dead, I hope it may be said:
'His sins were scarlet, but his books were read.'

Hilaire Belloc 1870–1953: 'On His Books' (1923)

Before his death, Lord Curzon had informed his second wife of his arrangements for her burial in the family vault at Kedleston, when he 'placing his hand on one of the niches, said "This, Gracie dearest, is reserved for you."' In fact he had already placed in the niche 'a large Foreign Office envelope on which he had scrawled in blue pencil':
35 Reserved for the second Lady Curzon.

Lord Curzon 1859–1925: Harold Nicolson diary 13 January 1934

36 You're here to stay until the rustle in your dying throat relieves you!

H. M. Walker: addressed to Laurel and Hardy in *Beau Hunks* (1931 film; re-named *Beau Chumps* for British audiences)

37 Ain't it grand to be blooming well dead?

Leslie Sarony 1897–1985: title of song (1932)

On being told by Robert Benchley that Calvin Coolidge had died:
38 DOROTHY PARKER: How can they tell?
ROBERT BENCHLEY: He had an erection.

Dorothy Parker 1893–1967: Ned Sherrin in *The Listener* 8 January 1987; Benchley's final remark vouched for by his grandson Peter on the authority of Benchley's widow.

39 I still go up my 44 stairs two at a time, but that is in hopes of dropping dead at the top.

A. E. Housman 1859–1936: letter to Laurence Housman, 9 June 1935

40 Death and taxes and childbirth! There's never any convenient time for any of them.

Margaret Mitchell 1900–49: *Gone with the Wind* (1936)

On spiritualism:
41 I always knew the living talked rot, but it's nothing to the rot the dead talk.

Margot Asquith 1864–1945: Chips Channon diary 20 December 1937

42 He was just teaching me my death duties.

Lady Tree 1863–1937: on her deathbed, having been visited by her solicitor to put her affairs in order; in *Ned Sherrin in his Anecdotage* (1993)

43 Guns aren't lawful;
Nooses give;
Gas smells awful;
You might as well live.

Dorothy Parker 1893–1967: 'Résumé' (1937)

44 Drink and dance and laugh and lie
Love, the reeling midnight through
For tomorrow we shall die!
(But, alas, we never do.)

Dorothy Parker 1893–1967: 'The Flaw in Paganism' (1937)

45 Either he's dead, or my watch has stopped.

Groucho Marx 1895–1977: in *A Day at the Races* (1937 film; script by Robert Pirosh, George Seaton, and George Oppenheimer)

46 Early to rise and early to bed makes a male healthy and wealthy and dead.

James Thurber 1894–1961: 'The Shrike and the Chipmunks'; in *New Yorker* 18 February 1939

47 Just think who we'd have been seen dead with!

Rebecca West 1892–1983: postcard to Noël Coward, on discovery in 1945 that their names had both been on the Nazi blacklist for arrest and probable execution

48 At his funeral in Omaha he filled the church to capacity. He was a draw right to the finish.

Jack Hurley: after the death of the boxer Vince Foster in 1949; Jonathon Green and Don Atyeo (eds.) *The Book of Sports Quotes* (1979)

49 There is to be a public lying-in-state for Gertie [Lawrence], in which she will wear the pink dress in which she danced the polka in *The King and I*. Vulgarity can go no further.

Noël Coward 1899–1973: diary 8 September 1952

50 The babe with a cry brief and dismal,
Fell into the water baptismal;
Ere they gathered its plight,
It had sunk out of sight,
For the depth of the font was abysmal.

Edward Gorey 1925– : *The Listing Attic* (1954)

51 The only thing that really saddens me over my demise is that I shall not be here to read the nonsense that will be written about me...There will be lists of apocryphal jokes I never made and gleeful misquotations of words I never said. *What* a pity I shan't be here to enjoy them!

Noël Coward 1899–1973: diary 19 March 1955

52 When I die I want to decompose in a barrel of porter and have it served in all the pubs in Dublin. I wonder would they know it was me?

J. P. Donleavy 1926– : *Ginger Man* (1955)

53 BLUEBOTTLE: You rotten swines. I told you I'd be deaded.

Spike Milligan 1918– : *The Hastings Flyer* in *The Goon Show* (BBC radio series) 3 January 1956

On a deceased judge with indeterminate sexual characteristics:
54 He died of an undelivered judgment.

Oliver St John Gogarty 1878–1957: Ulick O'Connor *Oliver St John Gogarty* (1964)

55 Well, it only proves what they always say—give the public something they want to see, and they'll come out for it.

Red Skelton 1913– : comment on crowds attending the funeral of the movie tycoon Harry Cohn on 2 March 1958

56 When I came back to Dublin, I was courtmartialled in my absence and sentenced to death in my absence, so I said they could shoot me in my absence.

Brendan Behan 1923–64: *Hostage* (1958)

57 [Death is] nature's way of telling you to slow down.

Anonymous: American life insurance proverb, in *Newsweek* 25 April 1960

On how he would kill himself:
58 With kindness.

George S. Kaufman 1889–1961: Howard Teichman *George S. Kaufman* (1973)

On his deathbed, asked by an acquaintance how he was:
59 Hovering between wife and death.

James Montgomery: Ulick O'Connor *Oliver St John Gogarty* (1964)

60 I have nothing against undertakers personally. It's just that I wouldn't want one to bury my sister.

Jessica Mitford 1917– : in *Saturday Review* 1 February 1964

61 V. hard on my poor old dad that he died too soon—if murder had been allowed when he was in his prime our home would have been like the last act of *Othello* almost daily.

Nancy Mitford 1904–73: letter 17 December 1969

When ex-President Eisenhower's death prevented her photograph appearing on the cover of Newsweek:
62 Fourteen heart attacks and he had to die in my week. In MY week.

Janis Joplin 1943–70: in *New Musical Express* 12 April 1969

63 The thought of death has now become a part of my life. I read the obituaries every day just for the satisfaction of not seeing my name there.

Neil Simon 1927– : *Last of the Red Hot Lovers* (1970)

64 I read the *Times* and if my name is not in the obits I proceed to enjoy the day.

Noël Coward 1899–1973: attributed

65 I'm amazed he was such a good shot.

Noël Coward 1899–1973: on being told that his accountant had blown his brains out; in *Ned Sherrin's Theatrical Anecdotes* (1991)

66 Canon Throbbing, no dish it's true, but with a brilliant future on both sides of the grave.

Alan Bennett 1934– : *Habeas Corpus* (1973)

67 I don't want to achieve immortality through my work... I want to achieve it through not dying.

Woody Allen 1935– : Eric Lax *Woody Allen and his Comedy* (1975)

68 It's not that I'm afraid to die. I just don't want to be there when it happens.

Woody Allen 1935– : *Death* (1975)

69 Jimmy Hoffa's most valuable contribution to the American labour movement came at the moment he stopped breathing—on July 30th, 1975.

Don E. Moldea: *The Hoffa Wars* (1978)

70 The cemetery is a sort of Mayfair of the dead, the most expensive real estate in Buenos Aires.

Robert Robinson 1927– : of the Recoleta Cemetery in Buenos Aires; in *The Times* 22 July 1978

71 Death has got something to be said for it:
There's no need to get out of bed for it;
Wherever you may be,
They bring it to you, free.

Kingsley Amis 1922–95: 'Delivery Guaranteed' (1979)

72 True you can't take it with you, but then, that's not the place where it comes in handy.

Brendan Francis: Jonathon Green (ed.) *A Dictionary of Contemporary Quotations* (1982)

73 [Memorial services are the] cocktail parties of the geriatric set.

Ralph Richardson 1902–83: Ruth Dudley Edwards *Harold Macmillan* (1983)

74 Suicide is no more than a trick played on the calendar.

Tom Stoppard 1937– : *The Dog It Was That Died* (1983)

Of Truman Capote's death:
75 Good career move.

Gore Vidal 1925– : attributed

76 Guns are always the best method for a private suicide. They are more stylish looking than single-edged razor blades and natural gas has got so expensive. Drugs are too chancy. You might miscalculate the dosage and just have a good time.

P. J. O'Rourke 1947– : *Modern Manners* (1984)

77 There is nothing like a morning funeral for sharpening the appetite for lunch.

Arthur Marshall 1910–89: *Life's Rich Pageant* (1984)

78 Death is always a great pity of course but it's not as though the alternative were immortality.

Tom Stoppard 1937– : *Jumpers* (rev. ed. 1986)

79 Grief-stricken people do not expect to emerge from the Chapel of Rest to find grown men skulking in the rhododendrons with tab-ends in their mouths. If the hearse drivers must smoke then facilities should be provided.

Alan Bennett 1934– : *Talking Heads* (1988)

80 Even death is unreliable: instead of zero it may be some ghastly hallucination, such as the square root of minus one.

Samuel Beckett 1906–89: attributed

81 Regret to inform you Hand that rocked the cradle kicked the bucket.

Anonymous: reported telegram; in *Ned Sherrin in his Anecdotage* (1993)

Debt See also *Money, Poverty*

1 One must have some sort of occupation nowadays. If I hadn't my debts I shouldn't have anything to think about.

Oscar Wilde 1854–1900: *A Woman of No Importance* (1893)

2 Cohen owes me ninety-seven dollars.

Irving Berlin 1888–1989; song-title (1913)

3 The National Debt is a very Good Thing and it would be dangerous to pay it off, for fear of Political Economy.

W. C. Sellar 1898–1951 and **R. J. Yeatman** 1898–1968: *1066 and All That* (1930)

On the subject of war debts incurred by England and others:
4 They hired the money, didn't they?

Calvin Coolidge 1872–1933: John H. McKee *Coolidge: Wit and Wisdom* (1933)

5 When creditors press you for debts that you cannot pay…remember that the position of a destitute person is impregnable: the County Court judge will not commit you under a judgment summons unless the creditor can

George Bernard Shaw 1856–1950: letter to Kerree Collins, 1938

prove that you have the means to pay. Maintain an
insouciant dignity, and announce your condition frankly.

6 My feet want to dance in the sun.
My head wants to rest in the shade.
The Lord says, 'Go out and have fun'.
But the Landlord says,
'Your rent ain't paid.'

E. Y. Harburg 1898–1981:
'Necessity' (1947)

7 If the spoken word is repeated often enough, it is
eventually written and thus made permanent...Many
a decent man who has written a bad cheque knows the
truth of that.

Flann O'Brien 1911–66: *Myles
Away from Dublin* (1990)

8 [My father] taught me two things about bills; always
query them and never pay till you have no alternative.

Miles Kington 1941– : *Welcome to
Kington* (1989)

Democracy See also *Government, Politics*

*A voter canvassed by Wilkes had declared that he would sooner vote
for the devil:*

1 And if your friend is not standing?

John Wilkes 1727–97: Raymond
Postgate *'That Devil Wilkes'* (1956 rev.
ed.)

2 A majority is always the best repartee.

Benjamin Disraeli 1804–81:
Tancred (1847)

3 I always voted at my party's call,
And I never thought of thinking for myself at all.

W. S. Gilbert 1836–1911: *HMS
Pinafore* (1878)

4 Democracy means simply the bludgeoning of the people
by the people for the people.

Oscar Wilde 1854–1900: *Sebastian
Melmoth* (1891)

5 Democracy is the name we give the people whenever we
need them.

Robert, Marquis de Flers
1872–1927 and **Armand de
Caillavet** 1869–1915: *L'habit vert*
(1913)

6 Democracy is the theory that the common people know
what they want, and deserve to get it good and hard.

H. L. Mencken 1880–1956: *A
Little Book in C major* (1916)

7 The worst thing I can say about democracy is that it has
tolerated the Right Honourable Gentleman [Neville
Chamberlain] for four and a half years.

Aneurin Bevan 1897–1960: speech
in the House of Commons 23 July
1929

8 Most of His Majesty's judges are much better fitted for the
making of laws than the queer and cowardly rabble who
are elected to Parliament for that purpose by the fantastic
machinery of universal suffrage.

A. P. Herbert 1890–1971:
Misleading Cases (1935)

9 Elections are won by men and women chiefly because
most people vote against somebody rather than for
somebody.

Franklin P. Adams 1881–1960:
Nods and Becks (1944)

10 Democracy is the recurrent suspicion that more than half
of the people are right more than half of the time.

E. B. White 1899–1985: in *New
Yorker* 3 July 1944

11 All animals are equal but some animals are more equal
than others.

George Orwell 1903–50: *Animal
Farm* (1945)

12 Hell, I never vote *for* anybody. I always vote *against*.

W. C. Fields 1880–1946: Robert Lewis Taylor *W. C. Fields* (1950)

On the death of a supporter of Proportional Representation:
13 He has joined what even he would admit to be the majority.

John Sparrow 1906–92: J. A. Gere and John Sparrow (eds.) *Geoffrey Madan's Notebooks* (1981)

14 Under democracy one party always devotes its energies to trying to prove that the other party is unfit to rule—and both commonly succeed and are right.

H. L. Mencken 1880–1956: *Minority Report* (1956)

15 Democracy means government by discussion, but it is only effective if you can stop people talking.

Clement Attlee 1883–1967: speech at Oxford, 14 June 1957

On John F. Kennedy's electoral victory:
16 I must say the Senator's victory in Wisconsin was a triumph for democracy. It proves that a millionaire has just as good a chance as anybody else.

Bob Hope 1903– : TV programme (1960); William Robert Faith *Bob Hope* (1983)

17 There was no telling what people might find out once they felt free to ask whatever questions they wanted to.

Joseph Heller 1923– : *Catch-22* (1961)

18 It's not the voting that's democracy, it's the counting.

Tom Stoppard 1937– : *Jumpers* (1972)

19 Every government is a parliament of whores. The trouble is, in a democracy the whores are us.

P. J. O'Rourke 1947– : *Parliament of Whores* (1991)

Description

1 Damn description, it is always disgusting.

Lord Byron 1788–1824: letter 6 August 1809

2 Like the silver plate on a coffin.

John Philpot Curran 1750–1817: describing Robert Peel's smile; quoted by Daniel O'Connell, House of Commons 26 February 1835

3 The ministers [on the Treasury Bench] reminded me of one of those marine landscapes not very uncommon on the coast of South America. You behold a range of exhausted volcanoes. Not a flame flickers on a single pallid crest.

Benjamin Disraeli 1804–81: speech at Manchester, 3 April 1872

4 She fitted into my biggest armchair as if it had been built round her by someone who knew they were wearing armchairs tight about the hips that season.

P. G. Wodehouse 1881–1975: *My Man Jeeves* (1919)

5 Diana Manners has no heart but her brains are in the right place.

Cyril Asquith 1890–1954: J. A. Gere and John Sparrow (eds.) *Geoffrey Madan's Notebooks* (1981)

6 Monsignor was forty-four then, and bustling—a trifle too stout for symmetry, with hair the colour of spun gold, and a brilliant, enveloping personality. When he came into a room clad in his full purple regalia from thatch to toe, he resembled a Turner sunset.

F. Scott Fitzgerald 1896–1940: *This Side of Paradise* (1921)

7 I turned to Aunt Agatha, whose demeanour was now rather like that of one who, picking daisies on the

P. G. Wodehouse 1881–1975: *The Inimitable Jeeves* (1923)

railway, has just caught the down express in the small of
the back.

8 Housman's cap, like a damp bun or pad of waste which
engine-drivers clean their hands on.

A. C. Benson 1862–1925: J. A. Gere
and John Sparrow (eds.) *Geoffrey
Madan's Notebooks* (1981)

9 You are so graceful, have you wings?
You have a faceful of nice things
You have no speaking voice, dear...
With every word it sings.

Lorenz Hart 1895–1943: 'Thou
Swell' (1927)

10 [The baby] romped on my lap like a short stout salmon.

Sylvia Townsend Warner
1893–1978: diary 13 October 1929

11 Rudyard Kipling's eyebrows are very odd indeed! They
curl up black and furious like the moustache of
a Neapolitan tenor.

Harold Nicolson 1886–1968: diary
8 January 1930

12 The Cavaliers (Wrong but Wromantic) and the
Roundheads (Right but Repulsive).

W. C. Sellar 1898–1951 and **R. J.
Yeatman** 1898–1968: *1066 and All
That* (1930)

13 The Right Hon. was a tubby little chap who looked as if
he had been poured into his clothes and had forgotten to
say 'When!'

P. G. Wodehouse 1881–1975: *Very
Good, Jeeves* (1930)

14 Though I yield to no one in my admiration for Mr
Coolidge, I do wish he did not look as if he had been
weaned on a pickle.

Anonymous: remark recorded in
Alice Roosevelt Longworth *Crowded
Hours* (1933)

15 We also saw Haworth, which surpassed even my appetite
for gloomy churchyards. Glutted, is the only word for it.

Sylvia Townsend Warner
1893–1978: letter 26 September 1935

16 Roderick Spode? Big chap with a small moustache and
the sort of eye that can open an oyster at sixty paces?

P. G. Wodehouse 1881–1975: *The
Code of the Woosters* (1938)

17 A rose-red sissy half as old as time.

William Plomer 1903–73: 'Playboy
of the Demi-World: 1938' (1945)

18 General de Gaulle is again pictured in our newspapers,
looking as usual like an embattled codfish. I wish he
could be filleted and put quietly away in a refrigerator.

Sylvia Townsend Warner
1893–1978: letter to Nancy Cunard,
1 September 1948

19 'It's no good your saying a *word*,' his face tells us, 'I will
not be eaten with a plastic spoon.'

Kenneth Tynan 1927–80: of
Stanley Parker's resemblance to
strawberry ice-cream; in *Cherwell*
14 June 1948

20 I don't think I have ever seen a Silver Band so
nonplussed. It was as though a bevy of expectant wolves
had overtaken a sleigh and found no Russian peasant on
board.

P. G. Wodehouse 1881–1975:
Uncle Dynamite (1948)

21 His appearance with his large features and rich mane of
hair suggested the attempt of some archaic sculptor only
acquainted with sheep to achieve a lion by hearsay.

Osbert Lancaster 1908–80: *All
Done From Memory* (1953)

22 The Henry Fondas lay on the evening like a damp
mackintosh.

Noël Coward 1899–1973: diary
8 May 1960

After a party given by Dorothy Parker:

23 The less I behave like Whistler's Mother the night before, the more I look like her the morning after.

Tallulah Bankhead 1903–68: R. E. Drennan *Wit's End* (1973)

24 A day away from Tallulah is like a month in the country.

Howard Dietz 1896–1983: *Dancing in the Dark* (1974)

25 A high altar on the move.

Elizabeth Bowen 1899–1973: of Edith Sitwell; V. Glendinning *Edith Sitwell* (1981)

26 His smile bathed us like warm custard.

Basil Boothroyd 1910–88: *Let's Move House* (1977)

27 Springing from the grassroots of the country clubs of America.

Alice Roosevelt Longworth 1884–1980: of Wendell Willkie; Michael Teague *Mrs L* (1981)

28 *Minder* ... has been particularly nutritious lately, with George Cole's portrayal of Arthur Daley attaining such depths of seediness that a flock of starlings could feed off him.

Clive James 1939– : in *Observer* 28 February 1982

29 The place smelt of apple-scented air freshener, not like apples, but like a committee's idea of what apples smell like.

Joseph O'Connor 1963– : *Cowboys and Indians* (1992)

30 Buckingham Palace looked a vast doll's house that some bullying skinhead big brother had kicked down the Mall.

Joseph O'Connor 1963– : *Cowboys and Indians* (1992)

31 A man who so much resembled a Baked Alaska—sweet, warm and gungy on the outside, hard and cold within.

Francis King 1923– : of C. P. Snow; *Yesterday Came Suddenly* (1993)

32 Her face showed the kind of ferocious disbelief with which Goneril must have taken the news that her difficult old father King Lear had decided to retire and move in with her.

Frank Muir 1920– : *The Walpole Orange* (1993)

Despair See *Hope and Despair*

Diaries

1 A page of my Journal is like a cake of portable soup. A little may be diffused into a considerable portion.

James Boswell 1740–95: *Journal of a Tour to the Hebrides* (1785)

2 I never travel without my diary. One should always have something sensational to read in the train.

Oscar Wilde 1854–1900: *The Importance of Being Earnest* (1895)

Laski had been reading the Life of Sir Henry Wilson, *in which he thought the Field-Marshal 'to have revealed his own foolishness in his diary about as fully as a man can':*

3 It is a fair proposition, I think, that the diaries of men who enjoy their own nudity ought not to be published unless they are as interesting as Pepys. Otherwise it is really too distressing for the observer.

Harold Laski 1893–1950: letter to Oliver Wendell Holmes, 23 October 1927

4 What is more dull than a discreet diary? One might just as well have a discreet soul.

Chips Channon 1897–1958: diary 26 July 1935

5 I always say, keep a diary and some day it'll keep you.

Mae West 1892–1980: *Every Day's a Holiday* (1937 film)

6 Now that I am finishing the damned thing I realise that diary-writing isn't wholly good for one, that too much of it leads to living for one's diary instead of living for the fun of living as ordinary people do.

James Agate 1877–1947: letter 7 December 1946

7 I regret, dear journal, this unworthy, sordid preoccupation with money, but I have worked hard all my life, I am £15,000 overdrawn in London, I am fifty-five years old and I fully intend to end my curious days in as much comfort, peace and luxury as I can get.

Noël Coward 1899–1973: diary 15 April 1955

8 To write a diary every day is like returning to one's own vomit.

Enoch Powell 1912– : interview in *Sunday Times* 6 November 1977

9 I have decided to keep a full journal, in the hope that my life will perhaps seem more interesting when it is written down.

Sue Townsend 1946– : *Adrian Mole: The Wilderness Years* (1993)

Dictionaries

1 *Lexicographer.* A writer of dictionaries, a harmless drudge.

Samuel Johnson 1709–84: *A Dictionary of the English Language* (1755)

2 They are strange beings, these lexicographers.

John Brown 1810–82: *Horae Subsecivae* (rev. ed. 1884)

Henry Liddell (1811–98) and Robert Scott (1811–87) were co-authors of the Greek Lexicon *(1843), Liddell being in the habit of ascribing to his co-author usages which he criticized in his pupils, and which they said that they had culled from the* Lexicon:

3 Two men wrote a lexicon, Liddell and Scott;
Some parts were clever, but some parts were not.
Hear, all ye learned, and read me this riddle,
How the wrong part wrote Scott, and the right part wrote Liddell.

Edward Waterfield: L. E. Tanner *Westminster School: A History* (1934)

4 I hope you're not getting that deplorable habit of picking phrases out of newspapers and using them without knowing what they mean. A good thing to do is to read two pages of the *New Oxford Dictionary* every day. You get the exact derivations of all words and their differing shades of meaning at different periods. An excellent habit.

Henry Cockburn: advice to his son Claud; Claud Cockburn *In Time of Trouble* (1956)

5 The Dictionary has not attempted to rival some of its predecessors in deliberate humour...Such rare occasions for a smile as may be found in it are unintentional.

W. A. Craigie 1867–1967: of the *New English Dictionary*; in *The Periodical* 15 February 1928

6 I've been in *Who's Who*, and I know what's what, but it'll be the first time I ever made the dictionary.

Mae West 1892–1980: letter to the RAF, early 1940s, on having an inflatable life jacket named after her

7 Like Webster's Dictionary, we're Morocco bound.

Johnny Burke 1908–64: *The Road to Morocco* (1942 film), title song

8 A bad business, opening dictionaries; a thing I very rarely do. I try to make it a rule never to open my mouth, dictionaries, or hucksters' shops.

Flann O'Brien 1911–66: *The Best of Myles* (1968)

9 I suppose that so long as there are people in the world, they will publish dictionaries defining what is unknown in terms of something equally unknown.

Flann O'Brien 1911–66: *Myles Away from Dublin* (1990)

Of his coinage of the phrase 'life's rich pageant':
10 As far as I know, I didn't borrow the words from anywhere else and no less a body than the compilers of *The Oxford Dictionary of Quotations* have since taken an interest in the matter. They have finally decided that the phrase, such as it is, was my own invention and it is to be credited to me. Let me assure you that this small feather in my cap has not gone, so to speak, to my head.

Arthur Marshall 1910–89: *Life's Rich Pageant* (1984)

11 Short dictionaries should be improved because they are intended for people who actually need help.

William Empson 1906–84: attributed

12 Big dictionaries are nothing but storerooms with infrequently visited and dusty corners.

Richard W. Bailey 1939– : *Images of English* (1991)

13 I reach for the *Architect's Dictionary*, Volume One 'Asbestos to Balsa wood girders', and look up the word 'aesthetic'. I find this entry: 'aesthetic, obs. vulg. orig. unknown.' That could describe a modern architect couldn't it? Obs. vulg. orig. unknown. Obscene, vulgar bastard.

Stephen Fry 1957– : *Paperweight* (1992)

Diplomacy See also *Politics*

1 An ambassador is an honest man sent to lie abroad for the good of his country.

Henry Wotton 1568–1639: written in the album of Christopher Fleckmore in 1604

2 Lord Palmerston, with characteristic levity had once said that only three men in Europe had ever understood [the Schleswig-Holstein question], and of these the Prince Consort was dead, a Danish statesman (unnamed) was in an asylum, and he himself had forgotten it.

Lord Palmerston 1784–1865: R. W. Seton-Watson *Britain in Europe* 1789–1914 (1937)

After the United States joined Britain and her Allies in World War One, Churchill was asked what he thought of 'those splendid Americans':
3 What do you expect me to do? Kiss them on all four cheeks?

Winston Churchill 1874–1965: K. Halle *The Irrepressible Churchill* (1985)

On the Hoare-Laval pact:
4 Sam Hoare was certified by his doctors as unfit for public business, and on his way to the sanatorium he stops off in Paris and allows Laval to do him down.

Harold Nicolson 1886–1968: diary 12 December 1935

R. A. Butler had asked whether he and Maisky could use Channon's house in Belgrave Square for a secret meeting:
5 I never thought that the Russian Ambassador would ever cross my threshold; I checked up on the snuff-boxes on my return but did not notice anything missing.

Chips Channon 1897–1958: diary 28 November 1939

Of a meeting with the Russians, when Vyshinsky began 'I have my instructions':

6 Well, I have no instructions other than those which I give myself. Clearly therefore we are not discussing on the same level and I had better turn you over to my deputy.

Ernest Bevin 1881–1951: at the Peace Conference in Paris, 1946; Harold Nicolson *Diaries* (1980)

On the Council of Europe:

7 If you open that Pandora's Box, you never know what Trojan 'orses will jump out.

Ernest Bevin 1881–1951: Roderick Barclay *Ernest Bevin and the Foreign Office* (1975)

On the life of a Foreign Secretary:

8 Forever poised between a cliché and an indiscretion.

Harold Macmillan 1894–1986: in *Newsweek* 30 April 1956

9 A diplomat these days is nothing but a head-waiter who's allowed to sit down occasionally.

Peter Ustinov 1921– : *Romanoff and Juliet* (1956)

10 There cannot be a crisis next week. My schedule is already full.

Henry Kissinger 1923– : in *New York Times Magazine* 1 June 1969

11 The chief distinction of a diplomat is that he can say no in such a way that it sounds like yes.

Lester Bowles Pearson 1897–1972: a Canadian Prime Minister's view; Geoffrey Pearson *Seize the Day* (1993)

12 The French are masters of 'the dog ate my homework' school of diplomatic relations.

P. J. O'Rourke 1947– : *Holidays in Hell* (1988)

13 In return for a handsomely bound facsimile of Palestrina's music, the Vicar of God was rewarded with a signed photograph of the Grocer and a gramophone record of himself conducting an orchestra.

Nicholas Shakespeare 1957– : at a meeting between the Pope and Edward Heath; in *The Spectator* 19/26 December 1992

14 There is a story that when Mrs Thatcher first met Gorbachev he gave her a ball-point and she offered him Labour-voting Scotland.

Nicholas Shakespeare 1957– : in *The Spectator* 19/26 December 1992

15 The Prime Minister rather enjoyed being led up the garden path by the Taoiseach, but she didn't much like the garden when she got there.

Anonymous: unnamed civil servant on negotiations between Margaret Thatcher and Charles Haughey; in *Daily Telegraph* 14 August 1993

Discontent See *Satisfaction and Discontent*

Dreams See *Sleep and Dreams*

Dress See *Fashion and Dress*

Economics See also *Money*

1 No real English gentleman, in his secret soul, was ever sorry for the death of a political economist.

Walter Bagehot 1826–77: *Estimates of some Englishmen and Scotchmen* (1858) 'The First Edinburgh Reviewers'

2 Nothink for nothink 'ere, and precious little for sixpence.

Punch 1841–1992: vol. 57 (1869)

3 John Stuart Mill,
By a mighty effort of will,
Overcame his natural *bonhomie*
And wrote 'Principles of Political Economy'.

Edmund Clerihew Bentley
1875–1956: 'John Stuart Mill' (1905)

4 Political Economy has, quite obviously, turned out to be
the Idiot Boy of the Scientific Family; all the more pitiful,
as having been so bright at first; put up on a chair to
recite by old Dr Adam Smith and Mr Ricardo—and then
somehow went wrong.

Stephen Leacock 1869–1944: *The Boy I Left Behind Me* (1947)

5 If economists could manage to get themselves thought of
as humble, competent people, on a level with dentists,
that would be splendid!

John Maynard Keynes
1883–1946: 'Economic Possibilities for
our Grandchildren'; David Howell
Blind Victory (1986)

6 Expenditure rises to meet income.

C. Northcote Parkinson 1909– :
The Law and the Profits (1960)

7 People don't realize that the Victorian age was simply an
interruption in British history...It's exciting living on the
edge of bankruptcy.

Harold Macmillan 1894–1986: in
conversation in 1961; Anthony
Sampson *Macmillan* (1967)

8 In '29 when the banks went bust,
Our coins still read 'In God We Trust'.

E. Y. Harburg 1898–1981: 'Federal
Reserve' (1965)

9 Greed—for lack of a better word—is good. Greed is right.
Greed works.

Stanley Weiser and **Oliver
Stone** 1946– : *Wall Street* (1987 film)

10 Trickle-down theory—the less than elegant metaphor
that if one feeds the horse enough oats, some will pass
through to the road for the sparrows.

J. K. Galbraith 1908– : *The
Culture of Contentment* (1992)

Education

1 [JOHNSON:] I had no notion that I was wrong or
          irreverent to my tutor.
[BOSWELL:] That, Sir, was great fortitude of mind.
[JOHNSON:] No, Sir; stark insensibility.

Samuel Johnson 1709–84: James
Boswell *Life of Samuel Johnson* (1791)
31 October 1728

Of Cambridge University:
2 This place is the Devil, or at least his principal residence,
they call it the University, but any other appellation
would have suited it much better, for study is the last
pursuit of the society; the Master eats, drinks, and sleeps,
the Fellows drink, dispute and pun, the employments of
the undergraduates you will probably conjecture without
my description.

Lord Byron 1788–1824: letter
23 November 1805

3 EDUCATION.—At Mr Wackford Squeers's Academy,
Dotheboys Hall, at the delightful village of Dotheboys,
near Greta Bridge in Yorkshire, Youth are boarded,
clothed, booked, furnished with pocket-money, provided
with all necessaries, instructed in all languages living
and dead, mathematics, orthography, geometry,
astronomy, trigonometry, the use of the globes, algebra,
single stick (if required), writing, arithmetic, fortification,
and every other branch of classical literature. Terms,

Charles Dickens 1812–70: *Nicholas
Nickleby* (1839)

twenty guineas per annum. No extras, no vacations, and
diet unparalleled.

4 C-l-e-a-n, clean, verb active, to make bright, to scour.
W-i-n, win, d-e-r, der, winder, a casement. When the
boy knows this out of the book, he goes and does it.

Charles Dickens 1812–70: *Nicholas
Nickleby* (1839)

5 Soap and education are not as sudden as a massacre, but
they are more deadly in the long run.

Mark Twain 1835–1910: *A Curious
Dream* (1872) 'Facts concerning the
Recent Resignation'

*In his viva at Oxford Wilde was required to translate a passage from
the Greek version of the New Testament. Having acquitted himself
well, he was stopped:*
6 Oh, do let me go on, I want to see how it ends.

Oscar Wilde 1854–1900: James
Sutherland (ed.) *The Oxford Book of
Literary Anecdotes* (1975)

7 MRS CHEVELEY: The higher education of men is what
I should like to see. Men need it so sadly.
LADY MARKBY: They do, dear. But I am afraid such
a scheme would be quite unpractical. I don't think
man has much capacity for development. He has got
as far as he can, and that is not far, is it?

Oscar Wilde 1854–1900: *An Ideal
Husband* (1895)

8 I was not unpopular [at school]...It is Oxford that has
made me insufferable.

Max Beerbohm 1872–1956: *More*
(1899) 'Going Back to School'

9 Very nice sort of place, Oxford, I should think, for people
that like that sort of place. They teach you to be
a gentleman there. In the Polytechnic they teach you to
be an engineer or such like.

George Bernard Shaw
1856–1950: *Man and Superman* (1903)

10 He who can, does. He who cannot, teaches.

George Bernard Shaw
1856–1950: *Man and Superman* (1903)
'Maxims: Education'

11 The clever men at Oxford
Know all that there is to be knowed.
But they none of them know one half as much
As intelligent Mr Toad!

Kenneth Grahame 1859–1932:
The Wind in the Willows (1908)

12 No academic person is ever voted into the chair until he
has reached an age at which he has forgotten the
meaning of the word 'irrelevant'.

Francis M. Cornford 1874–1943:
Microcosmographia Academica (1908)

13 Good gracious, you've got to educate him first. You can't
expect a boy to be vicious till he's been to a good school.

Saki 1870–1916: *Reginald in Russia*
(1910)

14 [He] was about to open his lecture, when one of his
students rose in his seat and asked a question. It is
a practice...which, I need hardly say, we do not
encourage; the young man, I believe, was a newcomer in
the philosophy class.

Stephen Leacock 1869–1944:
*Arcadian Adventures with the Idle
Rich* (1914)

15 Gentlemen: I have not had your advantages. What poor
education I have received has been gained in the
University of Life.

Horatio Bottomley 1860–1933:
speech at the Oxford Union,
2 December 1920

16 That state of resentful coma that...dons dignify by the name of research.

Harold Laski 1893–1950: letter to Oliver Wendell Holmes, 10 October 1922

17 Most people tire of a lecture in ten minutes; clever people can do it in five. Sensible people never go to lectures at all.

Stephen Leacock 1869–1944: *My Discovery of England* (1922)

18 In examinations those who do not wish to know ask questions of those who cannot tell.

Walter Raleigh 1861–1922: *Laughter from a Cloud* (1923) 'Some Thoughts on Examinations'

Replying to Woodrow Wilson's 'And what in your opinion is the trend of the modern English undergraduate?':
19 Steadily towards drink and women, Mr President.

F. E. Smith 1872–1930: attributed

20 Ev'ry pedagogue
Goes to bed agog at night—
Doing Collegiana....

Dorothy Fields 1905–74: 'Collegiana' (1924)

When asked, while an undergraduate at Oxford, what he did for his college:
21 I drink for it.

Evelyn Waugh 1903–66: attributed

22 'We class schools, you see, into four grades: Leading School, First-rate School, Good School, and School. Frankly,' said Mr Levy, 'School is pretty bad.'

Evelyn Waugh 1903–66: *Decline and Fall* (1928)

23 Any one who has been to an English public school will always feel comparatively at home in prison. It is the people brought up in the gay intimacy of the slums, Paul learned, who find prison so soul-destroying.

Evelyn Waugh 1903–66: *Decline and Fall* (1928)

24 *Educ*: during the holidays from Eton.

Osbert Sitwell 1892–1969: entry in *Who's Who* (1929)

25 Do not on any account attempt to write on both sides of the paper at once.

W. C. Sellar 1898–1951 and **R. J. Yeatman** 1898–1968: *1066 and All That* (1930) 'Test Paper 5'

26 For every person who wants to teach there are approximately thirty who don't want to learn—much.

W. C. Sellar 1898–1951 and **R. J. Yeatman** 1898–1968: *And Now All This* (1932) introduction

27 Education in those elementary subjects which are ordinarily taught to our defenceless children, as reading, writing, and arithmetic.

A. P. Herbert 1890–1971: *Misleading Cases* (1935)

28 'Didn't Frankenstein get married?'
'Did he?' said Eggy. 'I don't know. I never met him. Harrow man, I expect.'

P. G. Wodehouse 1881–1975: *Laughing Gas* (1936)

29 Oxford's instinctive hatred of any branch of education which is directly useful, superficially easy, or attractive, which above all has connections with universities younger than itself.

Stephen Potter 1900–69: *The Muse in Chains* (1937)

30 A pretty example he sets to this Infants' Bible Class of which he speaks! A few years of sitting at the feet of Harold Pinker and imbibing his extraordinary views on morality and ethics, and every bally child on the list will

P. G. Wodehouse 1881–1975: *The Code of the Woosters* (1938)

be serving a long stretch at Wormwood Scrubs for
blackmail.

31 It was then that Mr Furriskey surprised and, indeed,   **Flann O'Brien** 1911–66: *At Swim-*
delighted his companions, not to mention our two   *Two-Birds* (1939)
friends, by a little act which at once demonstrated his
resource and his generous urge to spread enlightenment.
With the end of his costly malacca cane, he cleared away
the dead leaves at his feet and drew the outline of three
dials or clock faces on the fertile soil...How to read the
gas-meter, he announced.

32 Exeter is the second oldest college in Oxford—unless you   **Eric Arthur Barber** 1888–1965:
count lodging houses, in which case it is the fourth.   the Rector of Exeter's welcoming
speech to undergraduates in 1951

33 I don't think one 'comes down' from Jimmy's university.   **John Osborne** 1929– : *Look Back*
According to him, it's not even red brick, but white tile.   *in Anger* (1956)

34 Who walks in the classroom cool and slow?   **Jerry Leiber** 1933– and **Mike**
Who calls his English teacher Daddy-O?   **Stoller** 1933– : 'Charlie Brown' (1959)

35 To me education is a leading out of what is already there   **Muriel Spark** 1918– : *The Prime of*
in the pupil's soul. To Miss Mackay it is a putting in of   *Miss Jean Brodie* (1961)
something that is not there, and that is not what I call
education, I call it intrusion.

36 I am putting old heads on your young shoulders...all my   **Muriel Spark** 1918– : *The Prime of*
pupils are the crème de la crème.   *Miss Jean Brodie* (1961)

37 Assistant masters came and went...Some liked little boys   **Evelyn Waugh** 1903–66: *A Little*
too little and some too much.   *Learning* (1964)

38 The development of the body could be secured without   **Flann O'Brien** 1911–66: *The Best of*
oppressing minorities or waging war, and such   *Myles* (1968)
development inculcated sportsmanship and manliness.
The Boy Scout movement was a case in point.

39 I read Shakespeare and the Bible and I can shoot dice.   **Tallulah Bankhead** 1903–68:
That's what I call a liberal education.   attributed

40 Someone once said, Rumbold, that education is what is   **Alan Bennett** 1934– : *Forty Years*
left when you have forgotten all you have ever learned.   *On* (1969)
You appear to be trying to circumvent the process by
learning as little as possible.

41 FRANKLIN: Have you ever thought, Headmaster, that   **Alan Bennett** 1934– : *Forty Years*
your standards might perhaps be a little out of date?   *On* (1969)
HEADMASTER: Of course they're out of date. Standards are
always out of date. That is what makes them
standards.

42 At school I never minded the lessons. I just resented   **John Mortimer** 1923– : *A Voyage*
having to work terribly hard at playing.   *Round My Father* (1971)

43 Beauty school report   **Jim Jacobs** and **Warren Casey**:
No graduation day for you   'Beauty School Dropout' (1972)
Beauty school dropout
Mixed your mid-terms and flunked shampoo.

44 Education with socialists, it's like sex, all right so long as   **Alan Bennett** 1934– : *Getting On*
you don't have to pay for it.   (1972)

45 I went to public school, of course. But looking back on it, I think it may have been Borstal.

Alan Bennett 1934– : *Getting On* (1972)

46 The Socratic method is a game at which only one (the professor) can play.

Ralph Nader 1934– : Joel Seligman *The High Citadel* (1978)

47 HELEN: …Does your wife teach as well?
ERIC: Who? Oh yes…
HELEN: Isn't that extraordinary? You know, they always come in pairs. Don't you find that? Teachers. Like Noah's Ark.

Alan Ayckbourn 1939– : *Ten Times Table* (1979)

48 I think Patrick plans to wean our child straight on to calculators.

Alan Ayckbourn 1939– : *Sisterly Feelings* (1981)

49 If you are truly serious about preparing your child for the future, don't teach him to subtract—teach him to deduct.

Fran Lebowitz 1946– : *Social Studies* (1981)

50 Stand firm in your refusal to remain conscious during algebra. In real life, I assure you, there is no such thing as algebra.

Fran Lebowitz 1946– : *Social Studies* (1981)

51 The head boy at Harrow survived the war to become an English butler in Hollywood, a profession for which his education had prepared him admirably.

John Mortimer 1923– : *Clinging to the Wreckage* (1982)

52 Drugs have taught an entire generation of English kids the metric system.

P. J. O'Rourke 1947– : *Modern Manners* (1984, UK ed.)

53 What training is, I wonder, given to school bursars? Is there a Dehumanising Cabinet (patent applied for) in which they spend an hour each day?

Arthur Marshall 1910–89: *Life's Rich Pageant* (1984)

54 The schoolteacher is certainly underpaid as a childminder, but ludicrously overpaid as an educator.

John Osborne 1929– : in *Observer* 21 July 1985 'Sayings of the Week'

55 Common to all staff was a conviction that they could have done better outside education. The teachers believed in a mysterious world outside the school called 'business' where money was handed out freely.

Michael Green 1927– : *The Boy Who Shot Down an Airship* (1988)

56 I think I should feel considerably less rotten than I do this morning had I not learned all my anatomy from Arthur Mee's *Children's Encyclopaedia*. Never mind Ignatius Loyola, is my view: give a child to Arthur Mee until it is seven years old, and it will be his forever.

Alan Coren 1938– : *Seems Like Old Times* (1989)

57 In my day, the principal concerns of university students were sex, smoking dope, rioting and learning. Learning was something you did only when the first three weren't available.

Bill Bryson 1951– : *The Lost Continent* (1989)

58 As one who has spent his entire life, man, boy and raving old dotard, in and out of educational establishments I am the last person to offer any useful advice about them. Better leave that to politicians with no education, sense or commitment. They at least can bring an empty mind to the problem.

Stephen Fry 1957– : *Paperweight* (1992)

59 At the University, I saw many men I knew doing courses only to gratify their parents or, as the phrase went, 'to get something solid behind them.' There was a moral

Barry Humphries 1934– : *More Please* (1992)

virtue in suppressing all real talent; in flying in the face
of impulse and vocation and doing something, instead,
which was completely repugnant. That made parents
happy.

60 The competitive spirit is an ethos which it is the business
of universities such as the one in which I have the
honour to move and work, to subdue and neutralise.

Stephen Fry 1957– : *Paperweight*
(1992)

61 Liberals have invented whole college majors—
psychology, sociology, women's studies—to prove that
nothing is anybody's fault.

P. J. O'Rourke 1947– : *Give War a Chance* (1992)

Enemies   See *Friends and Enemies*

England and the English   See also *Countries and Peoples, Places*

1 But 'tis the talent of our English nation,
Still to be plotting some new reformation.

John Dryden 1631–1700: 'The
Prologue at Oxford, 1680'

2 But we, brave Britons, foreign laws despised,
And kept unconquered, and uncivilized.

Alexander Pope 1688–1744: *An
Essay on Criticism* (1711)

3 The English are busy; they don't have time to be polite.

Montesquieu 1689–1755: *Pensées et
fragments inédits…* (1901)

4 I think for my part one half of the nation is mad—and
the other not very sound.

Tobias Smollett 1721–71: *The
Adventures of Sir Launcelot Greaves*
(1762)

5 Now hang it! quoth I, as I looked towards the French
coast—a man should know something of his own
country too, before he goes abroad.

Laurence Sterne 1713–68: *Tristram
Shandy* (1759–67)

6 As an Englishman does not travel to see Englishmen,
I retired to my room.

Laurence Sterne 1713–68: *A
Sentimental Journey* (1768)

7 For 'tis a low, newspaper, humdrum, lawsuit
Country.

Lord Byron 1788–1824: *Don Juan*
(1819–24)

8 What a pity it is that we have no amusements in
England but vice and religion!

Sydney Smith 1771–1845: Hesketh
Pearson *The Smith of Smiths* (1934)

9 What two ideas are more inseparable than Beer and
Britannia?

Sydney Smith 1771–1845: Hesketh
Pearson *The Smith of Smiths* (1934)

10 No little lily-handed baronet he,
A great broad-shouldered genial Englishman,
A lord of fat prize-oxen and of sheep,
A raiser of huge melons and of pine,
A patron of some thirty charities,
A pamphleteer on guano and on grain.

Alfred, Lord Tennyson
1809–92: *The Princess* (1847)

11 There is in the Englishman a combination of qualities,
a modesty, an independence, a responsibility, a repose,
combined with an absence of everything calculated to
call a blush into the cheek of a young person, which one
would seek in vain among the Nations of the Earth.

Charles Dickens 1812–70: *Our
Mutual Friend* (1865)

12 He is an Englishman!
For he himself has said it,

W. S. Gilbert 1836–1911: *HMS
Pinafore* (1878)

And it's greatly to his credit,
That he is an Englishman!

13 You should study the Peerage, Gerald...It is the best
thing in fiction the English have ever done.

Oscar Wilde 1854–1900: *A Woman of No Importance* (1893)

14 He is a typical Englishman, always dull and usually
violent.

Oscar Wilde 1854–1900: *An Ideal Husband* (1895)

15 Englishmen never will be slaves: they are free to do
whatever the Government and public opinion allow them
to do.

George Bernard Shaw
1856–1950: *Man and Superman* (1903)

16 An Englishman thinks he is moral when he is only
uncomfortable.

George Bernard Shaw
1856–1950: *Man and Superman* (1903)

17 We English are of course the chosen race; but we should
be none the worse for a little intellectual apprehension.

A. C. Benson 1862–1925: *From a College Window* (1906)

18 In England it is very dangerous to have a sense of
humour.

E. V. Lucas 1868–1938: *365 Days and One More* (1926)

19 Any who have heard that sound will shrink at the
recollection of it; it is the sound of English county
families baying for broken glass.

Evelyn Waugh 1903–66: *Decline and Fall* (1928)

20 I like a man to be a clean, strong, upstanding
Englishman who can look his gnu in the face and put an
ounce of lead in it.

P. G. Wodehouse 1881–1975: *Mr. Mulliner Speaking* (1929)

21 The Roman Conquest was, however, a *Good Thing*, since
the Britons were only natives at the time.

W. C. Sellar 1898–1951 and **R. J. Yeatman** 1898–1968: *1066 and All That* (1930)

22 What Englishman will give his mind to politics as long as
he can afford to keep a motor car?

George Bernard Shaw
1856–1950: *The Apple Cart* (1930)

23 Mad dogs and Englishmen
Go out in the midday sun.
The Japanese don't care to,
The Chinese wouldn't dare to,
The Hindus and Argentines sleep firmly from twelve to
    one,
But Englishmen detest a siesta.
In the Philippines, there are lovely screens
To protect you from the glare;
In the Malay states, they have hats like plates
Which the Britishers won't wear.
At twelve noon, the natives swoon,
And no further work is done;
But mad dogs and Englishmen go out in the midday sun.

Noël Coward 1899–1973: 'Mad Dogs and Englishmen' (1931)

24 The truth is that every Englishman's house is his
hospital, particularly the bathroom. Patent medicine is
the English patent.

Oliver St John Gogarty
1878–1957: *As I Was Going Down Sackville Street* (1937)

25 Stiff upper lip! Stout fella!
Carry on, old fluff!
Chin up! Keep muddling through!
Stiff upper lip! Stout fella!

Ira Gershwin 1896–1989: 'Stiff Upper Lip' (1937)

When the going's rough—
Pip-pip to Old Man Trouble—and a toodle-oo, too!

26 This Englishwoman is so refined
She has no bosom and no behind.

Stevie Smith 1902–71: 'This Englishwoman' (1937)

27 Let us pause to consider the English,
Who when they pause to consider themselves they get all
    reticently thrilled and tinglish,
Because every Englishman is convinced of one thing, viz.:
That to be an Englishman is to belong to the most
    exclusive club there is.

Ogden Nash 1902–71: 'England Expects' (1938)

28 Other nations use 'force'; we Britons alone use 'Might'.

Evelyn Waugh 1903–66: *Scoop* (1938)

29 The old English belief that if a thing is unpleasant it is
automatically good for you.

Osbert Lancaster 1908–80: *Homes Sweet Homes* (1939)

30 Think of what our Nation stands for,
Books from Boots' and country lanes,
Free speech, free passes, class distinction,
Democracy and proper drains.
Lord, put beneath Thy special care
One-eighty-nine Cadogan Square.

John Betjeman 1906–84: 'In Westminster Abbey' (1940)

31 Good evening, England. This is Gillie Potter speaking to
you in English.

Gillie Potter 1887–1975: *Heard at Hogsnorton* (opening words of broadcasts, 6 June 1946 and 11 November 1947)

32 An Englishman, even if he is alone, forms an orderly
queue of one.

George Mikes 1912– : *How to be an Alien* (1946)

33 You never find an Englishman among the under-dogs—
except in England, of course.

Evelyn Waugh 1903–66: *The Loved One* (1948)

34 Not to be English was for my family so terrible
a handicap as almost to place the sufferer in the
permanent invalid class.

Osbert Lancaster 1908–80: *All Done From Memory* (1953)

35 Contrary to popular belief, English women do not wear
tweed nightgowns.

Hermione Gingold 1897–1987: in *Saturday Review* 16 April 1955

36 The English can be explained by their Anglo-Saxon
heritage and the influence of the Methodists. But I prefer
to explain them in terms of tea, roast beef and rain. A
people is first what it eats, drinks and gets pelted with.

Pierre Daninos: *Major Thompson and I* (1957)

37 He was born an Englishman and remained one for years.

Brendan Behan 1923–64: *Hostage* (1958)

38 The English may not like music, but they absolutely love
the noise it makes.

Thomas Beecham 1879–1961: in *New York Herald Tribune* 9 March 1961

39 It is hard to tell where the MCC ends and the Church of
England begins.

J. B. Priestley 1894–1984: in *New Statesman* 20 July 1962

40 Even crushed against his brother in the Tube, the
average Englishman pretends desperately that he is alone.

Germaine Greer 1939– : *The Female Eunuch* (1970)

41 If an Englishman gets run down by a truck he apologizes to the truck.

Jackie Mason 1931– : in *Independent* 20 September 1990

42 We really *like* dowdiness in England. It's absolutely incurable in us, I believe.

Peter Shaffer 1926– : *Whom Do I Have the Honour of Addressing?* (1990)

43 Trotter was thought of with the kind of contempt and revulsion young Englishmen of the right type reserve for the sick, the mad, the poor and the old.

Stephen Fry 1957– : *The Liar* (1991)

44 Larkin was so English that he didn't even care much about Britain, and he rarely mentioned it.

Clive James 1939– : *The Dreaming Swimmer* (1992)

Environment See *Nature and the Environment*

Epitaphs See also *Death*

1 Whoever treadeth on this stone
I pray you tread most neatly
For underneath this stone do lie
Your honest friend
WILL WHEATLEY.

Anonymous: gravestone at Stepney, London, 10 November 1683; Fritz Spiegl (ed.) *A Small Book of Grave Humour* (1971)

2 In bloom of life
She's snatched from hence
She had not room
To make defence;
For Tiger fierce
Took life away,
And here she lies
In a bed of clay
Until the Resurrection Day.

Anonymous: gravestone in Malmesbury churchyard to Hannah Twynnoy, who had been attacked by an escaped tiger from a travelling circus in 1703

3 He gave the little wealth he had
To build a house for fools and mad;
And showed, by one satiric touch,
No nation wanted it so much.

Jonathan Swift 1667–1745: 'Verses on the Death of Dr Swift' (1731)

4 Poor Pope will grieve a month, and Gay
A week, and Arbuthnot a day.
St John himself will scarce forbear
To bite his pen, and drop a tear.
The rest will give a shrug, and cry,
'I'm sorry—but we all must die!'

Jonathan Swift 1667–1745: 'Verses on the Death of Dr Swift' (1731)

5 Under this stone, Reader, survey
Dead Sir John Vanbrugh's house of clay.
Lie heavy on him, Earth! for he
Laid many heavy loads on thee!

Abel Evans 1679–1737: 'Epitaph on Sir John Vanbrugh, Architect of Blenheim Palace'

6 Here lies Fred,
Who was alive and is dead:
Had it been his father,
I had much rather;
Had it been his brother,
Still better than another;
Had it been his sister,

Anonymous: epitaph for Frederick, Prince of Wales, killed by a cricket ball in 1751; Horace Walpole *Memoirs of George II* (1847)

No one would have missed her;
Had it been the whole generation,
Still better for the nation:
But since 'tis only Fred,
Who was alive and is dead,—
There's no more to be said.

7 Here Skugg
Lies snug
As a bug
In a rug.

Benjamin Franklin 1706–90:
letter to Georgiana Shipley on the
death of her squirrel, 26 September
1772

8 Here lies Nolly Goldsmith, for shortness called Noll,
Who wrote like an angel, but talked like poor Poll.

David Garrick 1717–79:
'Impromptu Epitaph' (written 1773/4)

9 John Adams lies here, of the parish of Southwell,
A carrier who carried his can to his mouth well;
He carried so much, and he carried so fast,
He could carry no more—so was carried at last;
For the liquor he drank, being too much for one,
He could not carry off—so he's now carri-on.

Lord Byron 1788–1824: 'Epitaph on
John Adams of Southwell, a Carrier
who Died of Drunkenness' (1807)

10 Here lies a poor woman who always was tired,
For she lived in a place where help wasn't hired.
Her last words on earth were, Dear friends I am going
Where washing ain't done nor sweeping nor sewing,
And everything there is exact to my wishes,
For there they don't eat and there's no washing of
    dishes...
Don't mourn for me now, don't mourn for me never,
For I'm going to do nothing for ever and ever.

Anonymous: epitaph in Bushey
churchyard, before 1860; destroyed by
1916

11 Here lie I, Martin Elginbrodde:
Hae mercy o' my soul, Lord God;
As I wad do, were I Lord God,
And ye were Martin Elginbrodde.

George MacDonald 1824–1905:
David Elginbrod (1863)

12 There was a poor poet named Clough,
Whom his friends all united to puff,
But the public, though dull,
Had not such a skull
As belonged to believers in Clough.

Algernon Charles Swinburne
1837–1909: *Essays and Studies* (1875)

On the death of US President Warren G. Harding:
13 The only man, woman or child who wrote a simple
declarative sentence with seven grammatical errors is
dead.

e. e. cummings 1894–1962:
attributed

14 Here lies W. C. Fields. I would rather be living in
Philadelphia.

W. C. Fields 1880–1946: suggested
epitaph for himself; in *Vanity Fair*
June 1925

15 Here lies Mr Chesterton,
who to heaven might have gone,
but didn't, when he heard the news
that the place was run by Jews.

Humbert Wolfe 1886–1940: 'G. K.
Chesterton' (1925)

16 Excuse My Dust.

Dorothy Parker 1893–1967: suggested epitaph for herself; Alexander Woollcott *While Rome Burns* (1934) 'Our Mrs Parker'

Epitaph for a waiter:
17 By and by
God caught his eye.

David McCord 1897– : 'Remainders' (1935)

18 Poor G.K.C., his day is past—
Now God will know the truth at last.

E. V. Lucas 1868–1938: mock epitaph for G. K. Chesterton; Dudley Barker *G. K. Chesterton* (1973)

19 His friends he loved. His direst earthly foes—
Cats—I believe he did but feign to hate.
My hand will miss the insinuated nose,
Mine eyes the tail that wagged contempt at Fate.

William Watson 1858–1936: 'An Epitaph'

20 Beneath this slab
John Brown is stowed.
He watched the ads,
And not the road.

Ogden Nash 1902–71: 'Lather as You Go' (1942)

Suggested epitaph for an unnamed movie queen whose love-life had been notorious:
21 She sleeps alone at last.

Robert Benchley 1889–1945: attributed

Epitaph for Maurice Bowra:
22 Without you, Heaven would be too dull to bear,
And Hell would not be Hell if you are there.

John Sparrow 1906–92: in *Times Literary Supplement* 30 May 1975

Etiquette See *Behaviour and Etiquette*

Exploration See *Travel and Exploration*

Failure See *Success and Failure*

Fame

1 I was unwise enough to be photographed in bed wearing a Chinese dressing-gown and an expression of advanced degeneracy.

Noël Coward 1899–1973: on being photographed everywhere after the success of *The Vortex* in 1924; *Present Indicative* (1937)

On being asked what it was like to be famous:
2 It's like having a string of pearls given you. It's nice, but after a while, if you think of it at all, it's only to wonder if they're real or cultured.

W. Somerset Maugham 1874–1965: *A Writer's Notebook* (1949) written in 1941

3 A celebrity is a person who works hard all his life to become well known, and then wears dark glasses to avoid being recognized.

Fred Allen 1894–1956: Laurence J. Peter (ed.) *Quotations for our Time* (1977)

4 Well, not exactly a big star...But I once had a sandwich named after me at the Stage Delicatessen.

Neil Simon 1927– : *The Gingerbread Lady* (1970)

5 A very quiet and tasteful way to be famous is to have a famous relation. Then you can not only be nothing, you can do nothing, too.

P. J. O'Rourke 1947– : *Modern Manners* (1984)

6 It must be unnerving to be so famous that you know they are going to come in the moment you croak and hang velvet cords across all the doorways and treat everything with reverence. Think of the embarrassment if you left a copy of *Reader's Digest Condensed Books* on the bedside table.

Bill Bryson 1951– : *The Lost Continent* (1989)

7 Oh, the self-importance of fading stars. Never mind, they will be black holes one day.

Jeffrey Bernard 1932– : in *The Spectator* 18 July 1992

8 You can't shame or humiliate modern celebrities. What used to be called shame and humiliation is now called publicity.

P. J. O'Rourke 1947– : *Give War a Chance* (1992)

9 The best fame is a writer's fame: it's enough to get a table at a good restaurant, but not enough that you get interrupted when you eat.

Fran Lebowitz 1946– : in *Observer* 30 May 1993 'Sayings of the Week'

The Family See also *Children, Parents*

1 It is a wise father that knows his own child.

William Shakespeare 1564–1616: *The Merchant of Venice* (1596–8)

2 Am not I consanguineous? am I not of her blood?

William Shakespeare 1564–1616: *Twelfth Night* (1601)

3 John Donne, Anne Donne, Un-done.

John Donne 1572–1631: in a letter to his wife, on being dismissed from the service of his father-in-law, Sir George More; in Izaak Walton *The Life of Dr Donne* (first printed in *LXXX Sermons*, 1640)

4 My sister and my sister's child,
Myself and children three,
Will fill the chaise; so you must ride
On horseback after we.

William Cowper 1731–1800: 'John Gilpin' (1785)

5 I should, many a good day, have blown my brains out, but for the recollection that it would have given pleasure to my mother-in-law; and, even *then*, if I could have been certain to haunt her...

Lord Byron 1788–1824: letter 28 January 1817

6 If a man's character is to be abused, say what you will, there's nobody like a relation to do the business.

William Makepeace Thackeray 1811–63: *Vanity Fair* (1847–8)

7 Accidents will occur in the best-regulated families.

Charles Dickens 1812–70: *David Copperfield* (1850)

8 'Never was born!' persisted Topsy... 'never had no father, nor mother, nor nothin'. I was raised by a speculator, with lots of others.'

Harriet Beecher Stowe 1811–96: *Uncle Tom's Cabin* (1852)

9 A man...is *so* in the way in the house!

Elizabeth Gaskell 1810–65: *Cranford* (1853)

10 If you must go flopping yourself down, flop in favour of your husband and child, and not in opposition to 'em.

Charles Dickens 1812–70: *A Tale of Two Cities* (1859)

11 Your sister is given to government.

Charles Dickens 1812–70: *Great Expectations* (1861)

12 I am Septimus, the most morbid of the Tennysons.

Septimus Tennyson 1815–66: introducing himself to Dante Gabriel Rossetti; Peter Levi *Tennyson* (1993)

13 I find it difficult to take much interest in a man whose father was a dragon.

Dante Gabriel Rossetti 1828–82: apologizing for his inability to appreciate William Morris's epic poem *Sigurd the Volsung* (1876); Osbert Sitwell *Noble Essences* (1950)

14 All happy families resemble one another, but each unhappy family is unhappy in its own way.

Leo Tolstoy 1828–1910: *Anna Karenina* (1875–7)

15 And so do his sisters, and his cousins and his aunts!
His sisters and his cousins,
Whom he reckons up by dozens,
And his aunts!

W. S. Gilbert 1836–1911: *HMS Pinafore* (1878)

16 I'm Charley's aunt from Brazil—where the nuts come from.

Brandon Thomas 1856–1914: *Charley's Aunt* (1892)

17 After a good dinner one can forgive anybody, even one's own relations.

Oscar Wilde 1854–1900: *A Woman of No Importance* (1893)

18 Fathers should be neither seen nor heard. That is the only proper basis for family life.

Oscar Wilde 1854–1900: *An Ideal Husband* (1895)

19 To lose one parent, Mr Worthing, may be regarded as a misfortune; to lose both looks like carelessness.

Oscar Wilde 1854–1900: *The Importance of Being Earnest* (1895)

20 Few misfortunes can befall a boy which bring worse consequences than to have a really affectionate mother.

W. Somerset Maugham 1874–1965: *A Writer's Notebook* (1949), written in 1896

21 Familiarity breeds contempt—and children.

Mark Twain 1835–1910: *Notebooks* (1935)

22 As a rule, you see, I'm not lugged into Family Rows. On the occasions when Aunt is calling to Aunt like mastodons bellowing across primeval swamps and Uncle James's letter about Cousin Mabel's peculiar behaviour is being shot round the family circle...the clan has a tendency to ignore me.

P. G. Wodehouse 1881–1975: *The Inimitable Jeeves* (1923)

23 We must all be very kind to Auntie Jessie,
For she's never been a Mother or a Wife,
You mustn't throw your toys at her
Or make a vulgar noise at her,
She hasn't led a very happy life.

Noël Coward 1899–1973: 'We Must All be Very Kind to Auntie Jessie' (c.1924)

24 To my daughter Leonora without whose never-failing sympathy and encouragement this book would have been finished in half the time.

P. G. Wodehouse 1881–1975: dedication to *The Heart of a Goof* (1926)

25 To your tents, O Israel!

Lord Rosebery 1847–1929: to his wife's Rothschild relations one evening at Mentmore; Robert Rhodes James *Rosebery* (1963); perhaps apocryphal

Questionnaire for would-be Kings in the Wars of the Roses:
26 What have you done with your mother? (If *Nun*, write *None*.)

W. C. Sellar 1898–1951 and **R. J. Yeatman** 1898–1968: *1066 and All That* (1930)

27 One would be in less danger
From the wiles of the stranger
If one's own kin and kith
Were more fun to be with.

Ogden Nash 1902–71: 'Family Court' (1931)

28 I suppose that the high-water mark of my youth in Columbus, Ohio, was the night the bed fell on my father.

James Thurber 1894–1961: *My Life and Hard Times* (1933)

29 We do everything alike
We look alike, we dress alike,
We walk alike, we talk alike,
and what is more we hate each other very much.

Howard Dietz 1896–1983: 'Triplets' (1937)

30 There came from without the hoof-beats of a galloping relative and Aunt Dahlia whizzed in.

P. G. Wodehouse 1881–1975: *The Code of the Woosters* (1938)

31 It is no use telling me that there are bad aunts and good aunts. At the core, they are all alike. Sooner or later, out pops the cloven hoof.

P. G. Wodehouse 1881–1975: *The Code of the Woosters* (1938)

32 Parentage is a very important profession, but no test of fitness for it is ever imposed in the interest of the children.

George Bernard Shaw 1856–1950: *Everybody's Political What's What?* (1944)

33 T'Morra, t'morra,
Lookin' for t'morra,
My aunt became a spinster that way.

E. Y. Harburg 1898–1981: 'T'Morra' (1944)

34 I'm off to see if X Mansions is really razed to the ground, as I have an uncle who lives there and I know I'm in his will!

Ernest Thesiger 1879–1961: during the war; in *Ned Sherrin in his Anecdotage* (1993)

35 What fun—dear little Sidney
Produced a spectacular stone in his kidney,
He's had eleven
So God's in His heaven
And that is the end of the news.

Noël Coward 1899–1973: 'That is the End of the News' (1945)

36 He will be six foot two,
My son-in-law;
His haircut will be crew,
My son-in-law.

Ira Gershwin 1896–1983: 'My Son-in-Law' (1946)

37 What is wrong with a little incest? It is both handy and cheap.

James Agate 1877–1947: on *The Barretts of Wimpole Street*; attributed, perhaps apocryphal

38 It was that strange, almost unearthly light which comes into the eyes of wronged uncles when they see a chance of getting a bit of their own back from erring nephews.

P. G. Wodehouse 1881–1975: *Uncle Dynamite* (1948)

39 Valentine [Ackland] has just been stretched on a different type of filial rack. Her mother has just been broadcast: in a BBC feature programme about the WVS. It was indescribably awful—two and a half minutes of vertiginous embarrassment, followed by a pat on the back from Wilfred Pickles. What one goes through!

Sylvia Townsend Warner 1893–1978: letter to Nancy Cunard, 17 July 1948

40 My grandfather had displayed that Jovelike side to his character of which his family were always nervously aware.

Osbert Lancaster 1908–80: *All Done From Memory* (1953)

41 My father is a bastard
My Ma's an S.O.B.
My Grandpa's always plastered
My Grandma pushes tea
My sister wears a moustache
My brother wears a dress
Goodness gracious, that's why I'm a mess.

Stephen Sondheim 1930– : 'Gee, Officer Krupke' (1957)

Of his appointment of his brother Robert:
42 I see nothing wrong with giving Robert some legal experience as Attorney General before he goes out to practice law.

John F. Kennedy 1917–63: Bill Adler *The Complete Kennedy Wit* (1967)

43 'It wouldn't hurt us to be nice, would it?'
'That depends on your threshold of pain.'

George S. Kaufman 1889–1961: on being told his aunt was coming to visit; Howard Teichman *George S. Kaufman* (1973)

44 Bury her naked? My own mum? It's a Freudian nightmare.

Joe Orton 1933–67: *Loot* (1967)

45 *Chutzpa* is that quality enshrined in a man who, having killed his mother and father, throws himself on the mercy of the court as an orphan.

Leo Rosten 1908– : *The Joys of Yiddish* (1968)

46 Uncle Carl Laemmle,
Has a very large faemmle.

Ogden Nash 1902–71: of a Hollywood mogul much given to nepotism; Philip French *The Movie Moguls* (1969)

47 NORMAN: She's stuck here, all on her own, day after day looking after that old sabre-toothed bat upstairs...
SARAH: Will you not refer to Mother like that.

Alan Ayckbourn 1939– : *Living Together* (1975)

48 And my parents finally realize that I'm kidnapped and they snap into action immediately: They rent out my room.

Woody Allen 1935– : Eric Lax *Woody Allen and his Comedy* (1975)

49 My mother lost her memory. I think.

Alan Bennett 1934– : *Enjoy* (1980)

50 Could you possibly whistle your father and put him back on his lead, please.

Alan Ayckbourn 1939– : *Sisterly Feelings* (1981)

51 There is usually something pretty odd about sisters that come in triplicate. Consider pretty little Cinderella and her ugly and dance-mad relations. Consider Chekhov's trio, high and dry in the provinces and longing gloomily for Moscow. Consider Macbeth's friends, bent keenly over

Arthur Marshall 1910–89: *Life's Rich Pageant* (1984)

the cauldron and intent on passing that Culinary Test for
the Advanced Student.

52 A home keeps you from living with your parents.

P. J. O'Rourke 1947– : *The Bachelor Home Companion* (1987)

53 Children from the age of five to ten should watch more
television. Television depicts adults as rotten SOB's, given
to fistfights, gunplay, and other mayhem. Kids who
believe this about grownups aren't likely to argue about
bedtime.

P. J. O'Rourke 1947– : *The Bachelor Home Companion* (1987)

54 Everybody knows how to raise children, except the
people who have them.

P. J. O'Rourke 1947– : *The Bachelor Home Companion* (1987)

55 Daughters are best. They don't migrate.

Alan Bennett 1934– : *Talking Heads* (1988)

56 He's been had up for exposing himself in Sainsbury's
doorway. As Mother said, 'Tesco, you could understand
it.'

Alan Bennett 1934– : *Talking Heads* (1988)

57 We have become a grandmother.

Margaret Thatcher 1925– : in *The Times* 4 March 1989

58 You know what they say, if at first you don't succeed,
you're not the eldest son.

Stephen Fry 1957– : *Paperweight* (1992)

59 If Gloria hadn't divorced me she might never have
become her own daughter-in-law.

Cy Howard: of his former wife, Gloria Grahame, who had married her former stepson; in *Ned Sherrin in his Anecdotage* (1993)

Fashion and Dress

1 I must to the barber's, monsieur, for methinks I am
marvellous hairy about the face.

William Shakespeare 1564–1616: *A Midsummer Night's Dream* (1595–6)

2 She wears her clothes, as if they were thrown on her
with a pitchfork.

Jonathan Swift 1667–1745: *Polite Conversation* (1738)

3 It is charming to totter into vogue.

Horace Walpole 1717–97: letter to George Selwyn, 2 December 1765

Lord Charles Russell had appeared incorrectly dressed at a Court Ball:
4 Good evening, sir, I suppose you are the regimental
doctor.

George IV 1762–1830: Michael Hill (ed.) 'Right Royal Remarks' (unpublished compilation); in *Ned Sherrin in his Anecdotage* (1993)

5 You should never have your best trousers on when you
go out to fight for freedom and truth.

Henrik Ibsen 1828–1906: *An Enemy of the People* (1882)

6 She wore far too much rouge last night, and not quite
enough clothes. That is always a sign of despair in
a woman.

Oscar Wilde 1854–1900: *An Ideal Husband* (1895)

To Ada Leverson, who with her husband visited Wilde on the morning he left Pentonville:
7 How marvellous of you to know exactly the right hat to
wear at seven o'clock in the morning to meet a friend
who has been away.

Oscar Wilde 1854–1900: Rupert Hart-Davis (ed.) *Selected Letters of Oscar Wilde* (1979)

8 Her frocks are built in Paris, but she wears them with a strong English accent.

Saki 1870–1916: *Reginald* (1904)

To Sir Frederick Ponsonby, who had proposed accompanying him in a tail-coat:
9 I thought everyone must know that a *short* jacket is always worn with a silk hat at a private view in the morning.

Edward VII 1841–1910: Philip Magnus *Edward VII* (1964)

Lord Harris appeared at Ascot in a brown bowler:
10 Goin' rattin', 'Arris?

Edward VII 1841–1910: Michael Hill 'Right Royal Remarks' (unpublished compilation); in *Ned Sherrin in his Anecdotage* (1993)

11 His socks compelled one's attention without losing one's respect.

Saki 1870–1916: *Chronicles of Clovis* (1911)

12 A silk dress in four sections, and shoes with high heels that would have broken the heart of John Calvin.

Stephen Leacock 1869–1944: *Arcadian Adventures with the Idle Rich* (1914)

13 Satan himself can't save a woman who wears thirty-shilling corsets under a thirty-guinea costume.

Rudyard Kipling 1865–1936: *Debits and Credits* (1926)

14 I guess I'll have to change my plan
I should have realized there'd be another man
Why did I buy those blue pyjamas
Before the big affair began?
I guess I'll have to change my plan.

Howard Dietz 1896–1983: 'I Guess I'll Have to Change My Plan' (1929)

Of Asquith's first wife:
15 She lived in Hampstead and had no clothes.

Margot Asquith 1864–1945: Chips Channon diary 31 October 1937

16 When he buys his ties he has to ask if gin will make them run.

F. Scott Fitzgerald 1896–1940: *Notebooks* (1978)

Of Dior's New Look:
17 Clothes by a man who doesn't know women, never had one, and dreams of being one!

Coco Chanel 1883–1971: in *Vanity Fair* June 1994

On being asked what she wore in bed:
18 Chanel No. 5.

Marilyn Monroe 1926–62: Pete Martin *Marilyn Monroe* (1956)

On being told that several of his fly-buttons were undone:
19 No matter. The dead bird does not leave the nest.

Winston Churchill 1874–1965: Rupert Hart-Davis letter to George Lyttelton, 5 January 1957

20 If Botticelli were alive today he'd be working for *Vogue*.

Peter Ustinov 1921– : in *Observer* 21 October 1962 'Sayings of the Week'

21 The hats were nearly all as though made by somebody who had once heard about flowers but never seen one— huge muffs of horror.

Nancy Mitford 1904–73: of Princess Alexandra's wedding; letter 28 April 1963

Of the appearance of Princess Margaret at Princess Alexandra's wedding:
22 Unspeakable, like a hedgehog all in primroses.

Nancy Mitford 1904–73: letter 28 April 1963

23 He thinks he is a flower to be looked at
And when he pulls his frilly nylon pants right up tight
He feels a dedicated follower of fashion.

Raymond Douglas Davies:
'A Dedicated Follower
of Fashion' (1966)

When a waiter at Buckingham Palace spilled soup on her dress:
24 Never darken my Dior again!

Beatrice Lillie 1894–1989: *Every Other Inch a Lady* (1973)

25 I am not...totally unreceptive to colour providing it makes its appearance quietly, deferentially, and without undue fanfare.

Fran Lebowitz 1946– : *Metropolitan Life* (1978)

26 There are easier things in this life than being a drag queen. But, I ain't got no choice. Try as I may, I just can't walk in flats.

Harvey Fierstein 1954– : *Torch Song Trilogy* (1979)

27 The officers of this branch of the Force [the Obscene Publications Squad at Scotland Yard] have a discouraging club tie, on which a book is depicted being cut in half by a larger pair of scissors.

John Mortimer 1923– : *Clinging to the Wreckage* (1982)

28 The only really firm rule of taste about cross dressing is that neither sex should ever wear anything they haven't yet figured out how to go to the bathroom in.

P. J. O'Rourke 1947– : *Modern Manners* (1984)

29 Wearing a hat implies that you are bald if you are a man and that your hair is dirty if you are a woman.

P. J. O'Rourke 1947– : *Modern Manners* (1984)

30 You've got so much ice on your hands I could skate on them.

John Curry 1949–94: to Liberace; Ned Sherrin *Cutting Edge* (1984)

31 I had spent the whole of my savings...on a suit for the wedding—a remarkable piece of apparel with lapels that had been modelled on the tail fins of a 1957 Coupe de Ville and trousers so copiously flared that when I walked you didn't see my legs move.

Bill Bryson 1951– : *Neither Here Nor There* (1991)

Films   See *Cinema and Films*

Flattery   See *Praise and Flattery*

Food and Drink   See also *Alcohol*

1 You won't be surprised that diseases are innumerable—count the cooks.

Seneca c.4 BC–AD 65: *Epistles*

2 Methinks I have a great desire to a bottle of hay: good hay, sweet hay, hath no fellow.

William Shakespeare 1564–1616: *A Midsummer Night's Dream* (1595–6)

3 A plague o' these pickle herring!

William Shakespeare 1564–1616: *Twelfth Night* (1601)

4 Cheese it is a peevish elf
It digests all things but itself.

John Ray 1627–1705: *English Proverbs* (1670)

5 Of soup and love, the first is the best.

Thomas Fuller 1654–1732: *Gnomologia* (1732)

6 The vulgar boil, the learned roast, an egg.

Alexander Pope 1688–1744: *Imitations of Horace* (1738)

7 We could not have had a better dinner had there been a *Synod of Cooks*.

Samuel Johnson 1709–84: James Boswell *Life of Samuel Johnson* (1791) 5 August 1763

8 A cucumber should be well sliced, and dressed with pepper and vinegar, and then thrown out, as good for nothing.

Samuel Johnson 1709–84: James Boswell *Journal of a Tour to the Hebrides* (1785) 5 October 1773

9 Heaven sends us good meat, but the Devil sends cooks.

David Garrick 1717–79: 'On Doctor Goldsmith's Characteristical Cookery' (1777)

10 I never see an egg brought on my table but I feel penetrated with the wonderful change it would have undergone but for my gluttony; it might have been a gentle useful hen, leading her chickens with a care and vigilance which speaks shame to many women.

St John de Crévecoeur 1735–1813: *Letters from an American Farmer* (1782)

11 Then my stomach must digest its waistcoat.

Richard Brinsley Sheridan 1751–1816: when told that drinking would ruin the coat of his stomach; in *Sheridaniana* (1826)

12 The mountain sheep are sweeter,
But the valley sheep are fatter;
We therefore deemed it meeter
To carry off the latter.

Thomas Love Peacock 1785–1866: 'The War-Song of Dinas Vawr' (1823)

13 The discovery of a new dish does more for the happiness of mankind than the discovery of a new star.

Anthelme Brillat-Savarin 1755–1826: *Physiologie du Goût* (1826)

14 Anyone who tells a lie has not a pure heart, and cannot make a good soup.

Ludwig van Beethoven 1770–1827: Ludwig Nohl *Beethoven Depicted by his Contemporaries* (1880)

15 The divine took his seat at the breakfast-table, and began to compose his spirits by the gentle sedative of a large cup of tea, the demulcent of a well-buttered muffin, and the tonic of a small lobster.

Thomas Love Peacock 1785–1866: *Crotchet Castle* (1831)

16 It's a wery remarkable circumstance...that poverty and oysters always seem to go together.

Charles Dickens 1812–70: *Pickwick Papers* (1837)

17 Please, sir, I want some more.

Charles Dickens 1812–70: *Oliver Twist* (1838)

18 'It's very easy to talk,' said Mrs Mantalini. 'Not so easy when one is eating a demnition egg,' replied Mr Mantalini; 'for the yolk runs down the waistcoat, and yolk of egg does not match any waistcoat but a yellow waistcoat, demmit.'

Charles Dickens 1812–70: *Nicholas Nickleby* (1839)

19 United Metropolitan Improved Hot Muffin and Crumpet Baking and Punctual Delivery Company.

Charles Dickens 1812–70: *Nicholas Nickleby* (1839)

20 Subdue your appetites my dears, and you've conquered human natur.

Charles Dickens 1812–70: *Nicholas Nickleby* (1839)

21 If there is a pure and elevated pleasure in this world it is a roast pheasant with bread sauce. Barn door fowls for dissenters but for the real Churchman, the thirty-nines time articled clerk—the pheasant, the pheasant.

Sydney Smith 1771–1845: letter to R. H. Barham, 15 November 1841

22 I'll fill hup the chinks wi' cheese.

R. S. Surtees 1805–64: *Handley Cross* (1843)

23 Serenely full, the epicure would say,
Fate cannot harm me, I have dined to-day.

Sydney Smith 1771–1845: Lady Holland *Memoir* (1855) 'Receipt for a Salad'

24 'Take some more tea,' the March Hare said to Alice, very earnestly. 'I've had nothing yet,' Alice replied in an offended tone, 'so I can't take more.' 'You mean you can't take *less*,' said the Hatter: 'it's very easy to take *more* than nothing.'

Lewis Carroll 1832–98: *Alice's Adventures in Wonderland* (1865)

25 'There's nothing like eating hay when you're faint'...
'I didn't say there was nothing *better*,' the King replied,
'I said there was nothing *like* it.'

Lewis Carroll 1832–98: *Through the Looking-Glass* (1872)

26 He said, 'I look for butterflies
That sleep among the wheat:
I make them into mutton-pies,
And sell them in the street.'

Lewis Carroll 1832–98: *Through the Looking-Glass* (1872)

27 I had never had a piece of toast
Particularly long and wide,
But fell upon the sanded floor,
And always on the buttered side.

James Payn 1830–98: in *Chambers's Journal* 2 February 1884

To a waiter:
28 When I ask for a watercress sandwich, I do not mean a loaf with a field in the middle of it.

Oscar Wilde 1854–1900: Max Beerbohm letter to Reggie Turner, 15 April 1893

29 Cauliflower is nothing but cabbage with a college education.

Mark Twain 1835–1910: *Pudd'nhead Wilson* (1894)

30 Botticelli isn't a wine, you Juggins! Botticelli's a *cheese*!

Punch 1841–1992: vol. 106 (1894)

31 BISHOP: I'm afraid you've got a bad egg, Mr Jones.
CURATE: Oh no, my Lord, I assure you! Parts of it are excellent!

Punch 1841–1992: vol. 109 (1895)

32 People often feed the hungry so that nothing may disturb their own enjoyment of a good meal.

W. Somerset Maugham 1874–1965: *A Writer's Notebook* (1949) written in 1896

33 The healthy stomach is nothing if not conservative. Few radicals have good digestions.

Samuel Butler 1835–1902: *Notebooks* (1912)

34 Look here, Steward, if this is coffee, I want tea; but if this is tea, then I wish for coffee.

Punch 1841–1992: vol. 123 (1902)

35 The cook was a good cook, as cooks go; and as good cooks go, she went.

Saki 1870–1916: *Reginald* (1904)

36 It is said that the effect of eating too much lettuce is 'soporific'.

Beatrix Potter 1866–1943: *The Tale of the Flopsy Bunnies* (1909)

37 Roast Beef, Medium, is not only a food. It is a philosophy.

Edna Ferber 1887–1968: foreword to *Roast Beef, Medium* (1911)

38 Good to eat, and wholesome to digest, as a worm to a toad, a toad to a snake, a snake to a pig, a pig to a man, and a man to a worm.

Ambrose Bierce 1842–c.1914: on the cycle of digestion; *The Enlarged Devil's Dictionary* (1967)

39 One of the sauces which serve the French in place of a state religion.

Ambrose Bierce 1842–c.1914: on mayonnaise; *The Enlarged Devil's Dictionary* (1967)

40 When the Reverend Mr. Dumfarthing sternly refused tea as a pernicious drink weakening to the system, the Anglican rector was too ignorant of the presbyterian system to know well enough to give him Scotch whisky.

Stephen Leacock 1869–1944: *Arcadian Adventures with the Idle Rich* (1914)

41 Tea, although an Oriental,
Is a gentleman at least.
Cocoa is a cad and coward
Cocoa is a vulgar beast.

G. K. Chesterton 1874–1936: 'A Song of Right and Wrong' (1914)

42 'But why should you want to shield him?' cried Egbert; 'the man is a common murderer.' 'A common murderer, possibly, but a very uncommon cook.'

Saki 1870–1916: *Beasts and Super-Beasts* (1914)

43 The boy flew at the oranges with the enthusiasm of a ferret finding the rabbit family at home after a long day of fruitless subterranean research.

Saki 1870–1916: *The Toys of Peace* (1919)

44 What with excellent browsing and sluicing and cheery conversation and what-not, the afternoon passed quite happily.

P. G. Wodehouse 1881–1975: *My Man Jeeves* (1919)

45 I was so darned sorry for poor old Corky that I hadn't the heart to touch my breakfast. I told Jeeves to drink it himself.

P. G. Wodehouse 1881–1975: *My Man Jeeves* (1919)

46 Mr Leopold Bloom ate with relish the inner organs of beasts and fowls. He liked thick giblet soup, nutty gizzards, a stuffed roast heart, liverslices fried with crustcrumbs, fried hencod's roes. Most of all he liked grilled mutton kidneys which gave to his palate a fine tang of faintly scented urine.

James Joyce 1882–1941: *Ulysses* (1922)

47 When I makes tea I makes tea, as old mother Grogan said. And when I makes water I makes water...*Begob, ma'am*, says Mrs Cahill, *God send you don't make them in the one pot.*

James Joyce 1882–1941: *Ulysses* (1922)

48 Does the spearmint lose its flavour on the bedpost overnight?

Billy Rose 1899–1966 and **Marty Bloom**: title of song (1924); revived in 1959 by Lonnie Donegan with the title 'Does your chewing-gum lose its flavour on the bedpost overnight?'

49 Day will break and you'll awake and start to bake a sugar cake for all the boys to see.

Irving Caesar 1895– : 'Tea for Two' (1925)

50 Ask for heron's eggs whipped with wine into an amber foam.

Ronald Firbank 1886–1926: when asked by a friend what to order in a Lyons teashop; Mervyn Horder *Ronald Firbank: Memoirs and Critiques* (1977)

51 The lunches of fifty-seven years had caused his chest to slip down into the mezzanine floor.

P. G. Wodehouse 1881–1975: *The Heart of a Goof* (1926)

52 You are offered a piece of bread and butter that feels like a damp handkerchief and sometimes, when cucumber is added to it, like a wet one.

Compton Mackenzie 1883–1972: *Vestal Fire* (1927)

53 MOTHER: It's broccoli, dear.
CHILD: I say it's spinach, and I say the hell with it.

E. B. White 1899–1985: cartoon caption in *New Yorker* 8 December 1928

54 I've had a taste of society
And society has had a taste of me.

Cole Porter 1891–1964: the oyster ending up back in the sea after a day of social climbing; 'The Tale of the Oyster' (1929)

55 Be content to remember that those who can make omelettes properly can do nothing else.

Hilaire Belloc 1870–1953: *A Conversation with a Cat* (1931)

56 'Turbot, Sir,' said the waiter, placing before me two fishbones, two eyeballs, and a bit of black mackintosh.

Thomas Earle Welby 1881–1933: *The Dinner Knell* (1932) 'Birmingham or Crewe?'

57 Long as there is chicken and gravy on your rice
Ev'rything is nice.

Johnny Mercer 1909–76: 'Lazybones' (1932)

58 Beulah, peel me a grape.

Mae West 1892–1980: in *I'm No Angel* (1933 film)

59 The tragedy of English cooking is that 'plain' cooking cannot be entrusted to 'plain' cooks.

Countess Morphy fl. 1930–50: *English Recipes* (1935)

60 Like cannibalism, a matter of taste.

G. K. Chesterton 1874–1936: attributed, perhaps apocryphal

61 You like potato and I like po-tah-to,
You like tomato and I like to-mah-to;
Potato, po-tah-to, tomato, to-mah-to—
Let's call the whole thing off!

Ira Gershwin 1896–1983: 'Let's Call the Whole Thing Off' (1937)

62 It just proves that fifty million Frenchmen can't be wrong. They eat horses instead of ride them.

Cole Porter 1891–1964: having been crippled in a riding accident in 1937; G. Eells *The Life that Late He Led* (1967)

63 Last night we went to a Chinese dinner at six and a French dinner at nine, and I can feel the sharks' fins navigating unhappily in the Burgundy.

Peter Fleming 1907–71: letter from Yunnanfu, 20 March 1938

64 The ham roll consisted of greasy pie dough of the sort contained in five-cent pork pies. Imbedded rubber-like in this were strips of fried ham tasting slightly of kerosine. Over the pasty lay an inch of Dole's Hawaiian shredded pineapple. The vegetables were a stone-cold, glass-hard roast potato, some billiard-green string beans out of a can and floating in a water sauce, and two spoonfuls of tuna-fish salad using hemp instead of lettuce.

S. J. Perelman 1904–79: letter 4 December 1939

65 And now with some pleasure I find that it's seven; and must cook dinner. Haddock and sausage meat. I think it is true that one gains a certain hold on sausage and haddock by writing them down.

Virginia Woolf 1882–1941: diary 8 March 1941

66 Sir Walter Raleigh gripped his seat under the table. He had sailed halfway round the world to find this root, he had faced great perils to bring it back, he had withstood the blandishments of the most expert cajolers at Court, and had not even hinted at the secret of its flavour, he had changed his chef six times, and now Elizabeth of England was tasting it.
He looked at her.
Elizabeth of England spat.
'Not enough salt,' she said.

Caryl Brahms 1901–82 and **S. J. Simon** 1904–48: *No Bed for Bacon* (1941)

67 Parsley
Is gharsley.

Ogden Nash 1902–71: 'Further Reflections on Parsley' (1942)

68 Cook my own lunch—a thing I have not done for twenty years. Pork Chop. Looking for guidance in my Electrical Cookery Book, I turn up the letter 'P', and find any amount of instruction about Peach Gâteau, Petits Fours, Pineapple Soufflée, Pound Cake, and Prairie Oysters, but not a word about Pork Chops.

James Agate 1877–1947: diary 18 April 1943

69 Cannibalism went right out as soon as the American canned food came in.

Stephen Leacock 1869–1944: *The Boy I Left Behind Me* (1947)

70 We lived for days on nothing but food and water.

W. C. Fields 1880–1946: attributed

71 Fish fuck in it.

W. C. Fields 1880–1946: on being asked why he never drank water; attributed

72 I'll take a lemonade!...In a dirty glass!

Norman Panama 1914– and **Melvin Frank** 1913–88: in *Road to Utopia* (1946 film; words spoken by Bob Hope)

73 Sue wants a barbecue, Sam wants to boil a ham, Grace votes for bouillabaisse stew,
Jake wants a weeny-bake, steak and a layer cake,
He'll get a tummy ache too.

Johnny Mercer 1909–76: 'In the Cool, Cool, Cool of the Evening' (1951)

74 There is no danger of my getting scurvy [while in England], as I have to consume at least two gin-and-limes every evening to keep the cold out.

S. J. Perelman 1904–79: letter 13 December 1953

75 It's all right, the white wine came up with the fish.

Herman J. Mankiewicz 1898–1953: at a formal dinner at the home of the producer Arthur Hornblow Jr., having left the dinner table to be sick; Max Wilk *The Wit and Wisdom of Hollywood* (1972); also claimed by Howard Dietz.

On returning from a trip to Russia:
76 I brought buckets of caviare and asked all the greediest people I know. They sat in a holy circle and never spoke to me once, except to say, in loud asides, that the others were making pigs of themselves.

Nancy Mitford 1904–73: letter 20 June 1954

77 Open up the caviare
And say Thank God.

Noël Coward 1899–1973: 'Alice is At It Again' (1954)

78 And the sooner the tea's out of the way, the sooner we can get out the gin, eh?

Henry Reed 1914–86: *Private Life of Hilda Tablet* (1954 radio play)

79 Dinner at the Huntercombes' possessed 'only two dramatic features—the wine was a farce and the food a tragedy'.

Anthony Powell 1905– : *The Acceptance World* (1955)

80 [Cheese is] milk's leap toward immortality.

Clifton Fadiman 1904– : *Any Number Can Play* (1957)

81 Have an egg roll, Mr Goldstone,
Have a napkin, have a chopstick, have a chair!
Have a sparerib, Mr Goldstone—
Any sparerib that I can spare, I'd be glad to share!

Stephen Sondheim 1930– : 'Mr Goldstone, I Love You' (1959)

Of a pre-Christmas dinner to which Nancy Mitford took her guest Maurice Bowra:

82 The dinner was: cold TINNED ham and cold hard mince pies. Then we sang carols which was rather fun I'm bound to say. Bring me flesh and *bring me wine*. Poor Maurice's tenor boomed in vain—not a drop.

Nancy Mitford 1904–73: letter 3 January 1962

83 The test of a cook is how she boils an egg. My boiled eggs are FANTASTIC, FABULOUS. Sometimes as hard as a 100 carat diamond, or again soft as a feather bed, or running like a cooling stream, they can also burst like fireworks from their shells and take on the look and rubbery texture of a baby octopus. Never a dull egg, with me.

Nancy Mitford 1904–73: letter 3 October 1963

84 Take away that pudding—it has no theme.

Winston Churchill 1874–1965: Lord Home *The Way the Wind Blows* (1976)

85 The best number for a dinner party is two—myself and a dam' good head waiter.

Nubar Gulbenkian 1896–1972: in *Daily Telegraph* 14 January 1965

86 'For what we are about to receive,
Oh Lord, 'tis Thee we thank,'
Said the cannibal as he cut a slice
Of the missionary's shank.

E. Y. Harburg 1898–1981: 'The Realist' (1965)

87 OSCAR: I got brown sandwiches and green sandwiches...
Well, what do you say?
MURRAY: What's the green?
OSCAR: It's either very new cheese or very old meat.

Neil Simon 1927– : *The Odd Couple* (1966)

88 Lunch Hollywood-style—a hot dog and vintage wine.

Harry Kurnitz 1907–68: Max Wilk *The Wit and Wisdom of Hollywood* (1971)

89 Where else can you see, at a table for six, six grey suits?

Seymour Britchky: of the men at '21'; *The Restaurants of New York* (1974 ed.)

90 The lard starts forming on the guest even before he gets out of his car, and by the time he rises flushed from the table, he can be used to baste an ox.

S. J. Perelman 1904–79: letter 1975

91 Salad. I can't bear salad. It grows while you're eating it, you know. Have you noticed? You start one side of your

Alan Ayckbourn 1939– : *Living Together* (1975)

plate and by the time you've got to the other, there's
a fresh crop of lettuce taken root and sprouted up.

92 What I always say about your salads, Annie, is that
I may not enjoy eating them but I learn an awful lot
about insect biology.

Alan Ayckbourn 1939– : *Table Manners* (1975)

93 'Can I have a table near the floor?'
'Certainly, I'll have the waiter saw the legs off.'

Groucho Marx 1895–1977: attributed

94 A gourmet can tell from the flavour whether
a woodcock's leg is the one on which the bird is
accustomed to roost.

Lucius Beebe 1902– : Laurence J. Peter (ed.) *Quotations for our Time* (1977)

95 Shake and shake
The catsup bottle,
None will come,
And then a lot'll.

Richard Armour: Laurence J. Peter (ed.) *Quotations for our Time* (1977)

96 Large, naked, raw carrots are acceptable as food only to
those who live in hutches eagerly awaiting Easter.

Fran Lebowitz 1946– : *Metropolitan Life* (1978)

97 Food is an important part of a balanced diet.

Fran Lebowitz 1946– : *Metropolitan Life* (1978)

98 Shepherd's pie peppered with actual shepherd on top.

Stephen Sondheim 1930– : one of Mrs Lovett's variations on Sweeney Todd's human meat pies; 'A Little Priest' (1979)

99 Louise doesn't claim to be anything of a cook...She
really doesn't see eye to eye with a stove at all.

Alan Ayckbourn 1939– : *Joking Apart* (1979)

100 BRENDA: It's all sort of gritty this sandwich.
RALPH: Gritty, is it? Never mind, it's probably been
dropped somewhere. It's good for you, grit. They give
it to hens.

Alan Ayckbourn 1939– : *Sisterly Feelings* (1981)

101 Some of the waiters discuss the menu with you as if they
were sharing wisdom picked up in the Himalayas.

Seymour Britchky: *The Restaurants of New York* (1981 ed.)

102 One cannot imagine Mr Jenkins sending a task force
anywhere except to a good restaurant.

Alan Watkins 1933– : on Roy Jenkins at the time of the Falklands War; in *Observer* 20 June 1982

103 [Seaweed's] only natural enemies are children, who try
to turn it into weather-forecasting devices, and the
Welsh, who try to turn it into bread. Both attempts are
disastrously unsuccessful.

Miles Kington 1941– : *Nature Made Ridiculously Simple* (1983)

On snails:
104 The theory behind their presence in restaurants is that
they have a lovely delicate flavour of garlic, butter and
parsley, but in my experience this comes simply from
adding parsley, garlic and butter. If you eat snails
without the added delicacies you are in for a shock. That
is why I admire thrushes so much.

Miles Kington 1941– : *Nature Made Ridiculously Simple* (1983)

105 What proper man would plump for bints
Ahead of After-Eight thin mints?
True pleasure for a man of parts
Is tarts in him, not him in tarts.

Clive James 1939– : Ned Sherrin *Cutting Edge* (1984)

106 A number of other remarkable things show up in holiday dinners, such as...pies made out of something called 'mince', although if anyone has ever seen a mince in its natural state he did not live to tell about it.

P. J. O'Rourke 1947– : *Modern Manners* (1984)

107 As to those who can find it in them to employ the doubtlessly useful word 'brunch', do they, I wonder, ever up-grade it to 'bruncheon'? This is the kind of question that I ponder on while waiting for the kettle to boil. The active mind is never at rest.

Arthur Marshall 1910–89: *Life's Rich Pageant* (1984)

108 For the edible and the readable we give thanks to God, the Author of Life.

Mervyn Stockwood 1913– : grace for a literary lunch, in Ned Sherrin *Cutting Edge* (1984)

109 I could never understand what Sir Godfrey Tearle saw in Jill Bennett, until I saw her at the Caprice eating corn-on-the-cob.

Coral Browne 1913–91: on a romance between a young actress and a Grand Old Man of the theatre; attributed

110 You know that really was quite the most appalling meal I've ever tasted. I'd forgotten how bad she was. Burnt Earl Grey omelettes. It's almost an art form to mistreat food in that way.

Alan Ayckbourn 1939– : *Woman in Mind* (1986)

111 A fruit is a vegetable with looks and money. Plus, if you let fruit rot, it turns into wine, something Brussels sprouts never do.

P. J. O'Rourke 1947– : *The Bachelor Home Companion* (1987)

112 Never serve oysters in a month that has no paycheck in it.

P. J. O'Rourke 1947– : *The Bachelor Home Companion* (1987)

113 Boiled lamb brisket...is either the national dish or just what everything in Australia tastes like.

P. J. O'Rourke 1947– : *Holidays in Hell* (1988)

114 [England] is the only country in the world where the food is more dangerous than sex. I mean, a hard cheese will kill you, but a soft cheese will kill you in *seconds*.

Jackie Mason 1931– : in *Independent* 17 February 1989

115 My grandmother...about as bad a cook as you can be without actually being hazardous.

Bill Bryson 1951– : *The Lost Continent* (1989)

116 JACKIE: Pity there's no such thing as Sugar Replacement Therapy.
VICTORIA: There is. It's called chocolate.

Victoria Wood 1953– : *Mens Sana in Thingummy Doodah* (1990)

117 I had left home (like all Jewish girls) in order to eat pork and take birth control pills. When I first shared an intimate evening with my husband, I was swept away by the passion (so dormant inside myself) of a long and tortured existence. The physical cravings I had tried so hard to deny, finally and ultimately sated...But enough about the pork.

Roseanne Arnold 1953– : *Roseanne* (1990)

118 Trouble is meat and drink to Dad. Isn't it Dad? Meat and drink. Well, no meat—we've given up due to the cruelty.

Victoria Wood 1953– : *Mens Sana in Thingummy Doodah* (1990)

119 Mashed figs—a foodstuff that only your grandmother would eat, and only then because she couldn't find her dentures.

Bill Bryson 1951– : *Neither Here Nor There* (1991)

120 I ordered the only alcoholic thing on the menu, which was a low alcohol lager called Germania. This was 0.5% alcohol, which meant that I would have had to drink roughly 10 pints to loosen up, and another 64 pints if I wanted to become involved in a fist fight with a fishfinger. My wife later said that it was the first meal she had ever eaten with me where I didn't grow happier as it went on, and this may have had something to do with it.

Craig Brown 1957– : *Craig Brown's Greatest Hits* (1993)

121 The burger was horrid, thin and bitty like a Pekingese's tongue.

Craig Brown 1957– : *Craig Brown's Greatest Hits* (1993)

Watching the TV chef Michael Barry prepare a venison dish:
122 Bambi—see the movie! Eat the cast!

Henry Kelly: in *Daily Telegraph* 26 February 1994

Foolishness and Ignorance

1 He does it with a better grace, but I do it more natural.

William Shakespeare 1564–1616: *Twelfth Night* (1601)

2 I believe they talked of me, for they laughed consumedly.

George Farquhar 1678–1707: *The Beaux' Stratagem* (1707)

3 Fools have this happiness—to be easy with themselves, and let other people blush for 'em.

Anonymous: in *The Female Tatler* July–August 1709

4 How haughtily he lifts his nose,
To tell what every schoolboy knows.

Jonathan Swift 1667–1745: 'The Journal' (1727)

On being asked why he had defined pastern as the 'knee' of a horse:
5 Ignorance, madam, pure ignorance.

Samuel Johnson 1709–84: James Boswell *Life of Samuel Johnson* (1791) 1755

6 The worst of Warburton is, that he has a rage for saying something, when there's nothing to be said.

Samuel Johnson 1709–84: James Boswell *Life of Samuel Johnson* (1791) 1758

7 'A soldier,' cried my Uncle Toby, interrupting the corporal, 'is no more exempt from saying a foolish thing, Trim, than a man of letters.'—'But not so often, an' please your honour,' replied the corporal.

Laurence Sterne 1713–68: *Tristram Shandy* (1759–67)

8 How much a dunce that has been sent to roam
Excels a dunce that has been kept at home?

William Cowper 1731–1800: 'The Progress of Error' (1782)

Sheridan's son Tom announced that when he became an MP he would proclaim his independence of party by writing 'To Let' on his forehead:
9 And, under that, Tom, write 'unfurnished'.

Richard Brinsley Sheridan 1751–1816: Walter Jerrold *Bon-Mots* (1893)

10 The Cardinal [at Ravenna] is at his wit's end—it is true—that he had not far to go.

Lord Byron 1788–1824: letter 22 July 1820

11 Mr Kremlin himself was distinguished for ignorance, for he had only one idea,—and that was wrong.

Benjamin Disraeli 1804–81: *Sybil* (1845)

12 Major Yammerton was rather a peculiar man, inasmuch as he was an ass, without being a fool.

R. S. Surtees 1805–64: *Ask Mamma* (1858)

In response to the comment on another lawyer, 'It may be doubted whether any man of our generation has plunged more deeply into the sacred fount of learning':
13 Or come up drier.

Abraham Lincoln 1809–65: Leon Harris *The Fine Art of Political Wit* (1965)

14 Hain't we got all the fools in town on our side? and ain't that a big enough majority in any town?

Mark Twain 1835–1910: *The Adventures of Huckleberry Finn* (1884)

15 The idiot who praises, with enthusiastic tone,
All centuries but this, and every country but his own.

W. S. Gilbert 1836–1911: *The Mikado* (1885)

16 Ignorance is like a delicate exotic fruit; touch it and the bloom is gone. The whole theory of modern education is radically unsound. Fortunately, in England, at any rate, education produces no effect whatsoever.

Oscar Wilde 1854–1900: *The Importance of Being Earnest* (1895)

17 The public is soon disarmed. This planet is largely inhabited by parrots, and it is easy to disguise folly by giving it a fine name.

A. E. Housman 1859–1936: 'The Editing of Manilius' (1903)

18 Man is without any doubt the most interesting fool there is. Also the most eccentric. He hasn't a single written law, in his Bible or out of it, which has any but one purpose and intention—to *limit or defeat a law of God.*

Mark Twain 1835–1910: *Letters from the Earth* (1905–09)

19 Better to keep your mouth shut and appear stupid than to open it and remove all doubt.

Mark Twain 1835–1910: James Munson (ed.) *The Sayings of Mark Twain* (1992); attributed, perhaps apocryphal

On the suggestion that Ellen Terry had rejected a play by James 'because she did not think the part suited her':
20 Think? Think? How should the poor, toothless, chattering hag THINK?

Henry James 1843–1916: Edmund Gosse letter 14 April 1920

21 McIlwain asked a student the other day what he knew of St Petersburg and got for an answer that it was founded in the winter by St Peter. Do you wonder that Bolshevism triumphs?

Harold Laski 1893–1950: letter to Oliver Wendell Holmes, 1 December 1918

22 You know everybody is ignorant, only on different subjects.

Will Rogers 1879–1935: in *New York Times* 31 August 1924

23 *New Year Resolutions*
1. To refrain from saying witty, unkind things, unless they are really witty and irreparably damaging.
2. To tolerate fools more gladly, provided this does not encourage them to take up more of my time.

James Agate 1877–1947: diary 2 January 1942

24 The Lord made Adam,
The Lord made Eve,
He made 'em both a little naïve.

E. Y. Harburg 1898–1981: 'The Begat' (1947)

25 As any fule kno.

Geoffrey Willans 1911–58 and **Ronald Searle** 1920– : *Down with Skool!* (1953)

26 A man may be a fool and not know it, but not if he is married.

H. L. Mencken 1880–1956: Laurence J. Peter (ed.) *Quotations for our Time* (1977)

27 You've heard of people living in a fool's paradise? Well, Leonora has a duplex there.

George S. Kaufman 1889–1961: of Leonora Corbett; Howard Teichman *George S. Kaufman* (1973)

28 Oh, innocent victims of Cupid,
Remember this terse little verse;
To let a fool kiss you is stupid,
To let a kiss fool you is worse.

E. Y. Harburg 1898–1981: 'Inscriptions on a Lipstick' (1965)

29 Had your forefathers, Wiglesworth, been as stupid as you are, the human race would never have succeeded in procreating itself.

Alan Bennett 1934– : *Forty Years On* (1969)

30 A bishop wrote gravely to the *Times* inviting all nations to destroy 'the formula' of the atomic bomb. There is no simple remedy for ignorance so abysmal.

Peter Medawar 1915–87: *The Hope of Progress* (1972)

31 When a line of action is said to be supported 'by all responsible men' it is nearly always dangerous or foolish.

Harold Macmillan 1894–1986: *The Past Masters* (1975)

32 I sometimes wonder if the manufacturers of foolproof items keep a fool or two on their payroll to test things.

Alan Coren 1938– : *Seems Like Old Times* (1989)

33 What a waste it is to lose one's mind, or not to have a mind. How true that is.

Dan Quayle 1947– : speech to the United Negro College Fund, whose slogan is 'a mind is a terrible thing to waste'; in *The Times* 26 May 1989

34 Seriousness is stupidity sent to college.

P. J. O'Rourke 1947– : *Give War a Chance* (1992)

35 I could name eight people—half of those eight are barmy. How many apples short of a picnic?

John Major 1943– : on Tory critics, 19 September 1993

Friends and Enemies

1 I do not love thee, Dr Fell.
The reason why I cannot tell;
But this I know, and know full well,
I do not love thee, Dr Fell.

Thomas Brown 1663–1704: written while an undergraduate at Christ Church, Oxford, of which Dr Fell was Dean

2 We were in some little time fixed in our seats, and sat with that dislike which people not too good-natured usually conceive of each other at first sight.

Richard Steele 1672–1729: *The Spectator* 1 August 1711

3 People wish their enemies dead—but I do not; I say give them the gout, give them the stone!

Lady Mary Wortley Montagu 1689–1762: W. S. Lewis et al. (eds.) *Horace Walpole's Correspondence* (1973)

4 If it is abuse,—why one is always sure to hear of it from one damned goodnatured friend or another!

Richard Brinsley Sheridan 1751–1816: *The Critic* (1779)

5 I detest him more than cold boiled veal.

Lord Macaulay 1800–59: of the Tory essayist and politician John Wilson Croker; letter 5 August 1831

6 A man cannot be too careful in the choice of his
enemies.

Oscar Wilde 1854–1900: *The Picture of Dorian Gray* (1891)

7 I find that forgiving one's enemies is a most curious
morbid pleasure; perhaps I should check it.

Oscar Wilde 1854–1900: letter ?20 April 1894

8 It takes your enemy and your friend, working together,
to hurt you to the heart: the one to slander you and the
other to get the news to you.

Mark Twain 1835–1910: *Following the Equator* (1897)

9 *I* go to the OP club [a theatrical society where he would
have faced a hostile audience]? I should be like a poor
lion in a den of Daniels.

Oscar Wilde 1854–1900: Ford Madox Ford *Return to Yesterday* (1931)

10 He [Bernard Shaw] hasn't an enemy in the world, and
none of his friends like him.

Oscar Wilde 1854–1900: George Bernard Shaw *Sixteen Self Sketches* (1949)

11 A person whom we know well enough to borrow from,
but not well enough to lend to. A degree of friendship
called slight when its object is poor or obscure, and
intimate when he is rich or famous.

Ambrose Bierce 1842–*c*.1914: definition of an acquaintance; *The Cynic's Word Book* (1906)

12 Greater love than this, he said, no man hath that a man
lay down his wife for his friend. Go thou and do likewise.
Thus, or words to that effect, saith Zarathustra, sometime
regius professor of French letters to the university of
Oxtail.

James Joyce 1882–1941: *Ulysses* (1922)

13 I may be wrong, but I have never found deserting friends
conciliates enemies.

Margot Asquith 1864–1945: *Lay Sermons* (1927)

14 Any kiddie in school can love like a fool,
But hating, my boy, is an art.

Ogden Nash 1902–71: 'Plea for Less Malice Toward None' (1933)

15 Scratch a lover, and find a foe.

Dorothy Parker 1893–1967: 'Ballade of a Great Weariness' (1937)

Of a rival:
16 Such a clever actress. Pity she does her hair with Bovril.

Mrs Patrick Campbell 1865–1940: in *Ned Sherrin in his Anecdotage* (1993); attributed

17 I am gratified when a friend slaps me on the back and
tells me I'm a fine fellow, but I do a little resent it when
with his other hand he picks my pocket.

W. Somerset Maugham 1874–1965: *A Writer's Notebook* (1949) written in 1941

18 To find a friend one must close one eye. To keep him—
two.

Norman Douglas 1868–1952: *Almanac* (1941)

19 [Friends are] God's apology for relations.

Hugh Kingsmill 1889–1949: Michael Holroyd *The Best of Hugh Kingsmill* (1970)

20 I cannot love people in the country, I discover, because
there is always this danger that they may be
acquaintances, with all the perils and choleras of
acquaintance implicit in them.

Sylvia Townsend Warner 1893–1978: letter 10 June 1950

On Harold Macmillan's sacking seven of his Cabinet on 13 July 1962:

21 Greater love hath no man than this, that he lay down his friends for his life.

Jeremy Thorpe 1929– : D. E. Butler and Anthony King *The General Election of 1964* (1965)

22 Money couldn't buy friends but you got a better class of enemy.

Spike Milligan 1918– : *Puckoon* (1963)

23 Unfortunately we have little in common except a mutual knowledge of a story by Charlotte Yonge in which the hero is an albino curate with eyes like rubies. This is cordial, but not enough.

Sylvia Townsend Warner 1893–1978: letter 31 October 1967

24 You had only two friends in the world, and having killed one you can't afford to irritate the other.

Tom Stoppard 1937– : *Artist Descending a Staircase* (1973)

25 There is nothing like sexual frustration to give warmth to friendship, which flourishes in prisons, armies, on Arctic expeditions and did well in wartime Oxford.

John Mortimer 1923– : *Clinging to the Wreckage* (1982)

26 It may be more difficult to make new friends as you get older but it is some consolation to know how easy it is to lose them when you are young.

Jeffrey Bernard 1932– : in *The Spectator* 17 August 1985

27 I am a hoarder of two things: documents and trusted friends.

Muriel Spark 1918– : *Curriculum Vitae* (1992)

The Future See also *Past and Present*

1 That period of time in which our affairs prosper, our friends are true, and our happiness is assured.

Ambrose Bierce 1842–c.1914: *The Cynic's Word Book* (1906)

2 Cheer up! the worst is yet to come!

Philander Chase Johnson 1866–1939: in *Everybody's Magazine* May 1920

3 Posterity is as likely to be wrong as anybody else.

Heywood Broun 1888–1939: *Sitting on the World* (1924)

4 This very remarkable man
Commends a most practical plan:
You can do what you want
If you don't think you can't,
So don't think you can't think you can.

Charles Inge 1868–1957: 'On Monsieur Coué' (1928)

5 I never think of the future. It comes soon enough.

Albert Einstein 1879–1955: interview given on the *Belgenland*, December 1930

6 Lord Kelvin presently ratified this. Being Scotch, he didn't mind damnation and he gave the sun and the whole solar system only ninety million years more to live.

Stephen Leacock 1869–1944: *The Boy I Left Behind Me* (1947)

7 The bridge to the future is the phallus.

D. H. Lawrence 1885–1930: *Sex, Literature and Censorship* (1955)

8 In our little house, the question was whether the war would break out first, or the revolution. This was around 1910.

Claud Cockburn 1904–81: *In Time of Trouble* (1956)

9 You can only predict things after they have happened.

Eugène Ionesco 1912–94: *Le Rhinocéros* (1959)

10 Fascism is not in itself a new order of society. It is the future refusing to be born.

Aneurin Bevan 1897–1960: Leon Harris *The Fine Art of Political Wit* (1965)

11 Soon we'll be sliding down the razor-blade of life.

Tom Lehrer 1928– : 'Bright College Days' (c.1960)

12 Why should I write for posterity?
What, if I may be free
To ask a ridiculous question,
Has posterity done for me?

E. Y. Harburg 1898–1981: 'Posterity is Right Around the Corner' (1976)

13 ANDERSON: Tomorrow is another day, McKendrick.
MCKENDRICK: Tomorrow, in my experience, is usually the same day.

Tom Stoppard 1937– : *Professional Foul* (1978)

Gambling See *Betting and Gambling*

Games See *Sports and Games*

Gardens and Gardening

1 'I distinguish the picturesque and the beautiful, and I add to them, in the laying out of the grounds, a third and distinct character, which I call *unexpectedness*.'
'Pray, Sir,' said Mr Milestone, 'by what name do you distinguish this character, when a person walks round the grounds for a second time?'

Thomas Love Peacock 1785–1866: *Headlong Hall* (1816)

2 Gr-r-r—there go, my heart's abhorrence!
Water your damned flower-pots, do!
If hate killed men, Brother Lawrence,
God's blood, would not mine kill you!

Robert Browning 1812–89: 'Soliloquy of the Spanish Cloister' (1842)

3 'I want to be a lawn.' Greta Garbo.

W. C. Sellar 1898–1951 and **R. J. Yeatman** 1898–1968: *Garden Rubbish* (1930); chapter heading

4 'A garden is a loathsome thing—so what? Capt. W. D. Pontoon.

W. C. Sellar 1898–1951 and **R. J. Yeatman** 1898–1968: *Garden Rubbish* (1930); chapter heading

5 'All really grim gardeners possess a keen sense of humus.' Capt. W. D. Pontoon.

W. C. Sellar 1898–1951 and **R. J. Yeatman** 1898–1968: *Garden Rubbish* (1930); chapter heading

6 I contend that Titania remains fairy in spite of the fact that, when Shakespeare's gardening fit is on, she talks pure Mr Middleton.

James Agate 1877–1947: diary 3 January 1943 (Mr Middleton was the popular wireless gardener)

7 Irish gardens beat *all* for horror. With 19 gardeners, Lord Talbot of Malahide has produced an affair exactly like a suburban golf course.

Nancy Mitford 1904–73: letter 24 May 1965

8 Perennials are the ones that grow like weeds, biennials are the ones that die this year instead of next and hardy annuals are the ones that never come up at all.

Katharine Whitehorn 1926– : *Observations* (1970)

9 One thimbleful of water every blue moon does not constitute expertise. Otherwise we should all be fellows of the Royal Horticultural Society.

Alan Bennett 1934– : *Getting On* (1972)

10 A delectable sward, shaved as close as a bridegroom and looking just as green.

Basil Boothroyd 1910–88: *Let's Move House* (1977)

11 Laid to lawn? This is laid to adventure playground.

Basil Boothroyd 1910–88: *Let's Move House* (1977)

12 I was dosing the greenfly...with that frightfully good aerosol defoliant that Picarda got the recipe for from some boffin on the run from Porton Down.

Richard Ingrams 1937– and **John Wells** 1936– : *The Other Half* (1981); 'Dear Bill' letters

13 I will keep returning to the virtues of sharp and swift drainage, whether a plant prefers to be wet or dry...I would have called this book Better Drains, but you would never have bought it or borrowed it for bedtime.

Robin Lane Fox 1946– : *Better Gardening* (1982)

14 Mad fools of gardeners go out in the pouring rain
To prove they're Anglo-Saxon
They rarely put their macks on;
Each puts on rubber boots and squelches through moist
   terrain,
Then leaves the mud and silt on
The Wilton.

Alan Melville 1910–83: *Gnomes and Gardens* (1983)

15 When you get down to it, as sooner or later you must, gardening is a long-drawn-out war of attrition against the elements, a tripartite agreement involving the animal, insect and bird worlds, and the occasional sheer perversity of Nature.

Alan Melville 1910–83: *Gnomes and Gardens* (1983)

16 Everyone had a Japanese maple, although after Pearl Harbour most of these were patriotically poisoned, ringbarked and extirpated.

Barry Humphries 1934– : *More Please* (1992)

The Generation Gap See also *Children, Parents*

1 When I was your age...I had been an inconsolable widower for three months, and was already paying my addresses to your admirable mother.

Oscar Wilde 1854–1900: *An Ideal Husband* (1895)

2 The young have aspirations that never come to pass, the old have reminiscences of what never happened.

Saki 1870–1916: *Reginald* (1904)

3 When I was a boy of 14, my father was so ignorant I could hardly stand to have the old man around. But when I got to be 21, I was astonished at how much the old man had learned in seven years.

Mark Twain 1835–1910: attributed in *Reader's Digest* September 1939, but not traced in his works

4 The denunciation of the young is a necessary part of the hygiene of older people, and greatly assists the circulation of their blood.

Logan Pearsall Smith 1865–1946: *Afterthoughts* (1931) 'Age and Death'

5 There is more felicity on the far side of baldness than young men can possibly imagine.

Logan Pearsall Smith 1865–1946: *Afterthoughts* (1931) 'Age and Death'

6 It is the one war in which everyone changes sides.

Cyril Connolly 1903–74: Tom Driberg speech in House of Commons, 30 October 1959

7 Time is the one thing you have got. If there's one thing I envy you for, it's not your cool and your easy birds... it's time.

Alan Bennett 1934– : *Getting On* (1972)

8 What is a teenager in San Francisco to rebel against, for pity's sake? Their parents are all so busy trying to be non-judgemental, it's no wonder they take to dyeing their hair green.

Molly Ivins 1944– : in *Dallas Times Herald* 3 February 1987

9 So what are we going to do with our pricey ancestors? I really can't think of anything. Except maybe we could hunt them down and kill them. The government could sell licenses and old-bat stamps.

P. J. O'Rourke 1947– : *Parliament of Whores* (1991)

10 Remember the battle between the generations twenty-some years ago? Remember all the screaming at the dinner table about haircuts and getting jobs and the American dream? Well, our parents won. They're out there living the American dream on some damned golf course, and we're stuck with the jobs and haircuts.

P. J. O'Rourke 1947– : *Parliament of Whores* (1991)

11 Two things my parents did for me as a child stand head and shoulders above what parents usually do for their children. They had me in Egypt and they set me a vivid example of everything I didn't want to be when I grew up.

Jill Tweedie 1936–93: *Eating Children* (1993)

God See also *Religion*

Boswell's daughter had concluded that God did not exist:
1 I looked into Cambrai's *Education of a Daughter*, hoping to have found some simple argument for the being of God. But it is taken for granted.

James Boswell 1740–95: diary 20 December 1779

2 God will not always be a Tory.

Lord Byron 1788–1824: letter 2 February 1821

3 God will pardon me, it is His trade.

Heinrich Heine 1797–1856: on his deathbed, in Alfred Meissner *Heinrich Heine. Erinnerungen* (1856)

4 Thou shalt have one God only; who Would be at the expense of two?

Arthur Hugh Clough 1819–61: 'The Latest Decalogue' (1862)

To an undergraduate trying to excuse himself from attendance at early morning chapel on the plea of loss of faith:
5 You will find God by tomorrow morning, or leave this college.

Benjamin Jowett 1817–93: Kenneth Rose *Superior Person* (1969)

Replying to the Master of Trinity College Cambridge, H. M. Butler, who in proposing the health of the College had said that 'it was well to remember that, at this moment, both the Sovereign and the Prime Minister are Trinity men':
6 The Master should have added that he can go further, for it is obvious that the affairs of the world are built upon the momentous fact that God also is a Trinity man.

Augustine Birrell 1850–1933: Harold Laski letter to Oliver Wendell Holmes, 4 December 1926

7 An apology for the Devil: It must be remembered that we have only heard one side of the case. God has written all the books.

Samuel Butler 1835–1902: *Notebooks* (1912)

8 Only one thing, is impossible for God: to find any sense in any copyright law on the planet.

Mark Twain 1835–1910: Notebook 23 May 1903

9 God was left out of the Constitution but was furnished a front seat on the coins of the country.

Mark Twain 1835–1910: *Mark Twain in Eruption* (1940)

10 It was a divine sermon. For it was like the peace of God—which passeth all understanding. And like his mercy, it seemed to endure for ever.

Henry Hawkins 1817–1907: of an Assize sermon; Gordon Lang *Mr Justice Avory* (1935)

11 The great act of faith is when a man decides he is not God.

Oliver Wendell Holmes Jr. 1841–1935: letter to William James, 24 March 1907

12 These damned mystics with a private line to God ought to be compelled to disconnect. I cannot see that they have done anything save prevent necessary change.

Harold Laski 1893–1950: letter to Oliver Wendell Holmes, 29 January 1919

13 I agree with you as to those who tell you they are in on the ground floor with God.

Oliver Wendell Holmes Jr. 1841–1935: letter to Harold Laski, 1 February 1919

14 How odd
Of God
To choose
The Jews.

William Norman Ewer 1885–1976: *Week-End Book* (1924)

15 But not so odd
As those who choose
A Jewish God,
But spurn the Jews.

Cecil Browne 1932– : reply to verse by William Norman Ewer.

16 Not odd
Of God:
Goyim
Annoy 'im.

Anonymous: in *Leo Rosten's Book of Laughter* (1986)

17 There once was a man who said, 'God
Must think it exceedingly odd
If he finds that this tree
Continues to be
When there's no one about in the Quad.'

Ronald Knox 1888–1957: Langford Reed *Complete Limerick Book* (1924)

18 Dear Sir,
Your astonishment's odd:
I am always about in the Quad.
And that's why the tree
Will continue to be,
Since observed by
Yours faithfully,
God.

Anonymous: reply to verse by Ronald Knox; Langford Reed *Complete Limerick Book* (1924)

Birrell once saw a man treat George Eliot rudely:

19 I sat down in a corner and prayed to God to blast him. God did nothing, and ever since I have been an agnostic.

Augustine Birrell 1850–1933: Harold Laski letter to Oliver Wendell Holmes, 21 January 1928

20 I don't believe in God because I don't believe in Mother Goose.

Clarence Darrow 1857–1938: speech in Toronto in 1930

21 Those who set out to serve both God and Mammon soon discover that there is no God.

Logan Pearsall Smith 1865–1946: *Afterthoughts* (1931) 'Other People'

22 We have read with particular repugnance the record of the alleged god, Zeus, whose habit it was to assume the shape of swans, bulls, and other animals, and, thus disguised, to force his attentions upon defenceless females of good character.

A. P. Herbert 1890–1971: *Misleading Cases* (1935)

23 I don't know why it is that the religious never ascribe common sense to God.

W. Somerset Maugham 1874–1965: *A Writer's Notebook* (1949) written in 1941

24 God, whom you doubtless remember as that quaint old subordinate of General Douglas MacArthur.

S. J. Perelman 1904–79: letter to Mel Elliott, 24 April 1951

25 It is impossible to imagine the universe run by a wise, just and omnipotent God, but it is quite easy to imagine it run by a board of gods. If such a board actually exists it operates precisely like the board of a corporation that is losing money.

H. L. Mencken 1880–1956: *Minority Report* (1956)

26 The chief contribution of Protestantism to human thought is its massive proof that God is a bore.

H. L. Mencken 1880–1956: *Minority Report* (1956)

27 Let us pray to God…the bastard! He doesn't exist!

Samuel Beckett 1906–89: *Endgame* (1958)

28 The lifelong trust he had placed in the wisdom and justice of an immortal, omnipotent, omniscient, humane, universal, anthropomorphic, English-speaking, Anglo-Saxon, pro-American God…had begun to waver.

Joseph Heller 1923– : *Catch-22* (1961)

29 Forgive, O Lord, my little jokes on Thee
And I'll forgive Thy great big one on me.

Robert Frost 1874–1963: 'Cluster of Faith' (1962)

30 Did God who gave us flowers and trees,
Also provide the allergies?

E. Y. Harburg 1898–1981: 'A Nose is a Nose is a Nose' (1965)

31 God can stand being told by Professor Ayer and Marghanita Laski that He doesn't exist.

J. B. Priestley 1894–1984: in *Listener* 1 July 1965

On being asked if he believed in God:
32 We've never been intimate.

Noël Coward 1899–1973: in an interview with David Frost in 1969

33 CLAIRE: How do you know you're…God?
EARL OF GURNEY: Simple. When I pray to Him I find I'm talking to myself.

Peter Barnes 1931– : *The Ruling Class* (1969)

Ogden Nash had had his car broken into in Boston:
34 I'd expect to be robbed in Chicago
But not in the land of the cod,
So I hope that the Cabots and Lowells
Will mention the matter to God.

Ogden Nash 1902–71: David Frost and Michael Shea *The Mid-Atlantic Companion* (1986)

35 For ten years of my life, three times a day, I thanked the Lord for what I was about to receive and thanked him

Tom Stoppard 1937– : *Where Are They Now?* (1973)

again for what I had just received, and then we lost
touch—and I suddenly thought, *where is He now?*

36 If only God would give me some clear sign! Like making
a large deposit in my name at a Swiss bank.

Woody Allen 1935– : 'Selections
from the Allen Notebooks' in *New
Yorker* 5 November 1973

37 God is not dead but alive and working on a much less
ambitious project.

Anonymous: graffito quoted in
Guardian 26 November 1975

38 If it turns out that there is a God, I don't think that he's
evil. But the worst that you can say about him is that
basically he's an underachiever.

Woody Allen 1935– : *Love and
Death* (1975 film)

39 God is silent, now if only we can get Man to shut up.

Woody Allen 1935– :
'Remembering Needleman' (1976)

40 I imagine when it comes to the next prayer book...God
will be written in the lower case to banish any lurking
sense of inferiority his worshippers might feel.

Alan Bennett 1934– : *The Old
Country* (1978)

41 God, to whom, if he existed, I felt I should have nothing
very polite to say.

John Mortimer 1923– : *Clinging to
the Wreckage* (1982)

On readings in the school chapel:
42 Why was almost everybody in the Old Testament
permanently ratty and disagreeable, with God (whom we
were constantly thanking for this or that) by far the
rattiest of the lot? It didn't make sense then and, by
golly, it makes a great deal less now.

Arthur Marshall 1910–89: *Life's
Rich Pageant* (1984)

43 Satan probably wouldn't have talked so big if God had
been his wife.

P. J. O'Rourke 1947– : *Modern
Manners* (1984)

44 Our only hope rests on the off-chance that God does
exist.

Alice Thomas Ellis 1932– :
Unexplained Laughter (1985)

45 'I always think Graham would have made a good
parson...only he doesn't believe in God.' 'That's no
handicap these days.'

Alan Bennett 1934– : *Talking
Heads* (1988)

46 The peculiar, even unsatisfactory system whereby God
never communicated direct with his chosen people but
preferred to give the Israelite leaders an off-the-record
briefing.

Miles Kington 1941– : *Welcome to
Kington* (1989)

47 If I were Her what would really piss me off the worst is
that they cannot even get My gender right for
Christsakes.

Roseanne Arnold 1953– :
Roseanne (1990)

48 God is an elderly or, at any rate, middle-aged male,
a stern fellow, patriarchal rather than paternal and
a great believer in rules and regulations.

P. J. O'Rourke 1947– : *Parliament
of Whores* (1991)

49 Santa Claus is preferable to God in every way but one:
There is no such thing as Santa Claus.

P. J. O'Rourke 1947– : *Parliament
of Whores* (1991)

50 I do not have the ear of the Almighty, and I shrink from
guessing His plans for this world; but there must be a file
somewhere in the heavenly archives marked 'Total
destruction by Fire/Brimstone/Plague/Flood/Great

Bernard Levin 1928– : *If You
Want My Opinion* (1992)

Beast/Other', and I have an uneasy feeling He may be about to blow the dust off it.

51 Zeus, 'the God of wine and whoopee'.

Garrison Keillor 1942– : *The Book of Guys* (1994)

Gossip

1 I know that's a secret, for it's whispered every where.

William Congreve 1670–1729: *Love for Love* (1695)

2 They come together like the Coroner's Inquest, to sit upon the murdered reputations of the week.

William Congreve 1670–1729: *The Way of the World* (1700)

3 Here is the whole set! a character dead at every word.

Richard Brinsley Sheridan 1751–1816: *The School for Scandal* (1777)

4 I'm called away by particular business—but I leave my character behind me.

Richard Brinsley Sheridan 1751–1816: *The School for Scandal* (1777)

5 You have dished me up, like a savoury omelette, to gratify the appetite of the reading rabble for gossip.

Thomas Love Peacock 1785–1866: *Crotchet Castle* (1831)

6 There is only one thing in the world worse than being talked about, and that is not being talked about.

Oscar Wilde 1854–1900: *The Picture of Dorian Gray* (1891)

7 It is perfectly monstrous the way people go about, nowadays, saying things against one behind one's back that are absolutely and entirely true.

Oscar Wilde 1854–1900: *A Woman of No Importance* (1893)

8 She proceeds to dip her little fountain-pen filler into pots of oily venom and to squirt this mixture at all her friends.

Harold Nicolson 1886–1968: of the society hostess Mrs Ronnie Greville; diary 20 July 1937

9 It's the gossip columnist's business to write about what is none of his business.

Louis Kronenberger 1904– : *The Cart and the Horse* (1964)

10 Everyone is so anaesthetized by scandal that if it turned out that Richard Nixon was the illegitimate son of Golda Meir, it wouldn't make the front pages.

Gore Vidal 1925– : attributed

11 Can you suggest any suitable aspersions to spread abroad about Mrs Thatcher? It is idle to suggest she has unnatural relations with Mrs Barbara Castle; what is needed is something socially lower: that she eats asparagus with knife and fork, or serves instant mash potatoes.

Sylvia Townsend Warner 1893–1978: letter 29 January 1976

12 A secret in the Oxford sense: you may tell it to only one person at a time.

Oliver Franks 1905– : in *Sunday Telegraph* 30 January 1977

13 I hate to spread rumours, but what else can one do with them?

Amanda Lear: in an interview in 1978; Jonathon Green (ed.) *A Dictionary of Contemporary Quotations* (1978)

14 If you haven't got anything good to say about anyone come and sit by me.

Alice Roosevelt Longworth 1884–1980: maxim embroidered on a cushion; Michael Teague *Mrs L: Conversations with Alice Roosevelt Longworth* (1981)

15 Gossip is what you say about the objects of flattery when they aren't present.

P. J. O'Rourke 1947– : *Modern Manners* (1984)

16 Never gossip about people you don't know. This deprives simple artisans like Truman Capote of work. The best subject of gossip is someone you and your audience love dearly. The enjoyment of gossip is thus doubled: To the delight of disapprobation is added the additional delight of pity.

P. J. O'Rourke 1947– : *Modern Manners* (1984)

Government See also *Democracy, Politics*

Criticism of an opposition motion to declare general warrants illegal, 17 February 1764:
1 If I was a Judge, I should pay no more regard to this resolution than to that of a drunken porter.

Fletcher Norton 1716–1789: Horace Walpole *Memoirs of the Reign of George III* (1845)

2 What an augmentation of the field for jobbing, speculating, plundering, office-building and office-hunting would be produced by an assumption of all the state powers into the hands of the general government.

Thomas Jefferson 1743–1826: letter 13 August 1800

3 There is, in fact, no law or government at all [in Italy]; and it is wonderful how well things go on without them.

Lord Byron 1788–1824: letter 2 January 1821

Of the difference between Cabinet ministers and staff officers:
4 They agree to what I say in the morning, and then in the evening they start up with some crotchet which deranges the whole plan. I have not been used to that in all the early part of my life.

Duke of Wellington 1769–1852: letter January 1828; Elizabeth Longford *Pillar of State* (1972)

5 The Government should take a firm, bold line. This delay—this uncertainty, by which, abroad, we are losing our prestige and our position, while Russia is advancing and will be before Constantinople in no time! Then the Government will be fearfully blamed and the Queen so humiliated that she thinks she would abdicate at once. Be bold!

Queen Victoria 1819–1901: letter to Lord Beaconsfield, 27 June 1877

6 The House of Peers, throughout the war,
Did nothing in particular,
And did it very well.

W. S. Gilbert 1836–1911: *Iolanthe* (1882)

7 Ambassadors cropped up like hay,
Prime Ministers and such as they
Grew like asparagus in May,
And dukes were three a penny.

W. S. Gilbert 1836–1911: *The Gondoliers* (1889)

8 But the privilege and pleasure
That we treasure beyond measure
Is to run on little errands for the Ministers of State.

W. S. Gilbert 1836–1911: *The Gondoliers* (1889)

9 Now that the House of Commons is trying to become useful, it does a great deal of harm.

Oscar Wilde 1854–1900: *An Ideal Husband* (1895)

10 The art of government is the organization of idolatry.

George Bernard Shaw 1856–1950: *Man and Superman* (1903) 'Maxims: Idolatry'

11 'Do you pray for the senators, Dr Hale?' 'No, I look at the senators and I pray for the country.'

Edward Everett Hale 1822–1909: Van Wyck Brooks *New England Indian Summer* (1940)

12 We all know that Prime Ministers are wedded to the truth, but like other married couples they sometimes live apart.

Saki 1870–1916: *The Unbearable Bassington* (1912)

13 It was in dealing with the early feminist that the Government acquired the tact and skilfulness with which it is now handling Ireland.

Rebecca West 1892–1983: in *Daily News* 7 August 1916

14 I work for a Government I despise for ends I think criminal.

John Maynard Keynes 1883–1946: letter to Duncan Grant, 15 December 1917

15 Like Odysseus, the President [Woodrow Wilson] looked wiser when he was seated.

John Maynard Keynes 1883–1946: *The Economic Consequences of the Peace* (1919)

16 And they that rule in England,
In stately conclaves met,
Alas, alas for England
They have no graves as yet.

G. K. Chesterton 1874—1936: 'Elegy in a Country Churchyard' (1922)

17 This high official, all allow,
Is grossly overpaid;
There wasn't any Board, and now
There isn't any Trade.

A. P. Herbert 1890–1971: 'The President of the Board of Trade' (1922)

On the prospect (disapproved of by George V) of meeting Lenin and Trotsky, compared with the Turkish representative Sami Bey 'a man who I understand has grown tired of affairs with women and has lately taken up unnatural sexual intercourse':

18 I do not think that there is very much to choose between these persons whom I am forced to meet from time to time in Your Majesty's service.

David Lloyd George 1863–1945: to George V; Frances Stevenson diary 3 February 1922

19 He [Calvin Coolidge] slept more than any other President, whether by day or by night. Nero fiddled, but Coolidge only snored.

H. L. Mencken 1880–1956: in *American Mercury* April 1933

20 As for the House of Commons, my Lords, the House of Commons be blowed!
Lord Lick, Lord Arrowroot, Lord Pullover, and Lord Laburnum (with some hesitation) concurred.

A. P. Herbert 1890–1971: *Misleading Cases* (1935)

21 One of these days the people of Louisiana are going to get good government—and they aren't going to like it.

Huey Long 1893–1935: attributed

22 The policy of the Government is not to reduce the speed of motor cars (for that would be fantastic and fatal), but to increase the speed of pedestrians. It is hoped to

A. P. Herbert 1890–1971: *Misleading Cases* (1935)

educate the pedestrian to such a degree of alertness and alacrity that he will at last approximate to the hen.

23 People must not do things for fun. We are not here for fun. There is no reference to fun in any Act of Parliament.

A. P. Herbert 1890–1971: *Uncommon Law* (1935) 'Is it a Free Country?'

24 Democracy means government by the uneducated, while aristocracy means government by the badly educated.

G. K. Chesterton 1874–1936: in *New York Times* 1 February 1931

25 The distinguished patients wanted two things—a quick hypodermic to end the pain and a course of treatment to cure the disease. They wanted them in a hurry. We gave them both. And now some of the patients seem to be doing very nicely. Some of them are even well enough to throw their crutches at the doctor!

Franklin D. Roosevelt 1882–1945: campaign speech in Chicago; in *New York Times* 15 October 1936

26 Distrust of authority should be the first civic duty.

Norman Douglas 1868–1952: *An Almanac* October (1941)

27 A government which robs Peter to pay Paul can always depend on the support of Paul.

George Bernard Shaw 1856–1950: *Everybody's Political What's What?* (1944)

28 A wartime Minister of Information is compelled, in the national interest, to such continuous acts of duplicity that even his natural hair must grow to resemble a wig.

Claud Cockburn 1904–81: of Brendan Bracken; *Crossing the Line* (1958)

29 Are you labouring under the impression that I read these memoranda of yours? I can't even lift them.

Franklin D. Roosevelt 1882–1945: to Leon Henderson; J. K. Galbraith *Ambassador's Journal* (1969)

30 Those who want the Government to regulate matters of the mind and spirit are like men who are so afraid of being murdered that they commit suicide to avoid assassination.

Harry S. Truman 1884–1972: address at the National Archives, Washington, D.C., 15 December 1952

31 I like a lot of Republicans...Indeed, there are some I would trust with anything—anything, that is, except public office.

Adlai Stevenson 1900–65: in *New York Times* 15 August 1952

32 Whenever Republicans talk of cutting taxes first and discussing national security second, they remind me of the very tired, rich man who said to his chauffeur, 'Drive off that cliff, James, I want to commit suicide.'

Adlai Stevenson 1900–65: in the presidential campaign of 1952; Bill Adler *The Stevenson Wit* (1966)

33 We are a government of laws. Any laws some government hack can find to louse up a man who's down.

Murray Kempton 1917– : in *New York Post* 21 December 1955

34 The kind of man who wants the government to adopt and enforce his ideas is always the kind of man whose ideas are idiotic.

H. L. Mencken 1880–1956: *Minority Report* (1956)

35 The worst government is often the most moral. One composed of cynics is often very tolerant and humane. But when fanatics are on top there is no limit to oppression.

H. L. Mencken 1880–1956: *Minority Report* (1956)

The White House in the time of President Eisenhower:
36 The Tomb of the Well-Known Soldier.

Emlyn Williams 1905–87: James Harding *Emlyn Williams* (1987)

37 Office hours are from 12 to 1 with an hour off for lunch.

George S. Kaufman 1889–1961: of the US Senate; Howard Teichman *George S. Kaufman* (1973)

38 Members [of civil service orders] rise from CMG (known sometimes in Whitehall as 'Call Me God') to the KCMG ('Kindly Call Me God') to—for a select few governors and super-ambassadors—the GCMG ('God Calls Me God').

Anthony Sampson 1926– : *Anatomy of Britain* (1962)

39 The House of Lords, an illusion to which I have never been able to subscribe—responsibility without power, the prerogative of the eunuch throughout the ages.

Tom Stoppard 1937– : *Lord Malquist and Mr Moon* (1966)

40 There are two reasons for making an appointment. Either there was nobody else; or there *was* somebody else.

Lord Normanbrook 1902–67: Anthony Sampson *The Changing Anatomy of Britain* (1982)

41 The first requirement of a statesman is that he be dull.

Dean Acheson 1893–1971: in *Observer* 21 June 1970

42 No patent medicine was ever put to wider and more varied use than the Fourteenth Amendment.

William O. Douglas 1898–1980: Hugo Black Jr. *My Father: A Remembrance* (1975)

Of the House of Commons:
43 The longest running farce in the West End.

Cyril Smith 1928– : *Big Cyril* (1977)

44 I don't mind how much my Ministers talk, so long as they do what I say.

Margaret Thatcher 1925– : in *Observer* 27 January 1980

45 That loyal retainer of the Chase Manhattan Bank, the American president.

Gore Vidal 1925– : in *Esquire* August 1980

Alan Clark, then a Parliamentary Under-Secretary at the Department of Employment, asked Douglas Hogg, then a junior Whip, how he was 'keeping all the new boys in order':
46 By offering them your job.

Douglas Hogg 1945– : Alan Clark diary 28 July 1983

47 Back in the East you can't do much without the right papers, but *with* the right papers you can do *anything.* They *believe* in papers. Papers are power.

Tom Stoppard 1937– : *Neutral Ground* (1983)

48 Like most Chief Whips he [Michael Jopling] knew who the shits were.

Alan Clark 1928– : diary 17 June 1987

49 The Republicans are the party that says government doesn't work and then gets elected and proves it.

P. J. O'Rourke 1947– : *Holidays in Hell* (1988)

50 Feeling good about government is like looking on the bright side of any catastrophe. When you quit looking on the bright side, the catastrophe is still there.

P. J. O'Rourke 1947– : *Parliament of Whores* (1991)

51 Whatever it is that the government does, sensible Americans would prefer that the government does it to somebody else. This is the idea behind foreign policy.

P. J. O'Rourke 1947– : *Parliament of Whores* (1991)

52 Today's ministers are not permitted to accept gifts over the value of £125, but how rarely does their own generosity even approach this sum.

Nicholas Shakespeare 1957– : in *The Spectator* 19/26 December 1992

53 Office tends to confer a dreadful plausibility on even the most negligible of those who hold it.

Mark Lawson: Joe Queenan *Imperial Caddy* (1992); introduction

54 We already have a sabbatical system. It's called opposition, and I've had enough of it.

Nigel Lawson 1932– : on being told by an American professor of politics that he needed a sabbatical; Greg Knight *Parliamentary Sauce* (1993); attributed

Handwriting

Of Foreign Office handwriting:

1 Iron railings leaning out of the perpendicular.

Lord Palmerston 1784–1865: J. A. Gere and John Sparrow (eds.) *Geoffrey Madan's Notebooks* (1981)

2 Indistinct and very small handwriting, like this draft, in very pale ink, has become the habit...Unfortunately, Lord Rosebery himself is the very worst offender. The Queen (whose eyesight has become very faulty, and has not yet got glasses to suit) can hardly read them at all.

Queen Victoria 1819–1901: letter to Sir Henry Ponsonby, 21 December 1894

3 I know that handwriting...I remember it perfectly. The ten commandments in every stroke of the pen, and the moral law all over the page.

Oscar Wilde 1854–1900: *An Ideal Husband* (1895)

4 As regards the mode of copying: of course it is too long for any amanuensis to attempt: and your own handwriting, dear Robbie, in your last letter seems specially designed to remind me that the task is not to be yours.

Oscar Wilde 1854–1900: letter to Robert Ross from Reading Prison, 1 April 1897

5 No individual word was decipherable, but, with a bold reader, groups could be made to conform to a scheme based on probabilities.

Edith Œ. Somerville 1858–1949 and **Martin Ross** 1862–1915: *In Mr Knox's Country* (1915)

6 The dawn of legibility in his handwriting has revealed his utter inability to spell.

Ian Hay 1876–1952: attributed; perhaps used in a dramatization of *The Housemaster* (1938)

7 That exquisite handwriting like a fly which has been trained at the Russian ballet.

James Agate 1877–1947: of George Bernard Shaw's handwriting; diary 22 September 1944

8 Did you ever get a letter from Monty James? I once had a note from him inviting us to dinner—we guessed that the time was 8 and not 3, as it appeared to be, but all we could tell about the day was that it was not Wednesday.

George Lyttelton 1883–1962: letter to Rupert Hart-Davis, 9 November 1955

9 I never saw Monty James's writing but doubt whether he can have been more illegible than Lady Colefax: the only hope of deciphering *her* invitations, someone said, was to pin them up on the wall and *run* past them!

Rupert Hart-Davis 1907– : letter to George Lyttelton, 13 November 1955

10 I do apologise for writing by hand—and so badly. I shall soon be like Helen Thomas, notoriously illegible. In her last letter only two words stood out plain: 'Blood pressure'. Subsequent research demonstrated that what she had actually written was 'Beloved friends'.

Sylvia Townsend Warner 1893–1978: letter 21 June 1963

Happiness and Unhappiness   See also *Hope and Despair*

1 Let us have wine and women, mirth and laughter,
   Sermons and soda-water the day after.

   Lord Byron 1788–1824: *Don Juan* (1819–24)

2 Life would be very pleasant if it were not for its enjoyments.

   R. S. Surtees 1805–64: *Mr Facey Romford's Hounds* (1865)

3 Let us all be happy, and live within our means, even if we have to borrer the money to do it with.

   Artemus Ward 1834–67: *Artemus Ward in London* (1867)

4 When constabulary duty's to be done,
   A policeman's lot is not a happy one.

   W. S. Gilbert 1836–1911: *The Pirates of Penzance* (1879)

5 A cigarette is the perfect type of a perfect pleasure. It is exquisite, and it leaves one unsatisfied. What more can one want?

   Oscar Wilde 1854–1900: *The Picture of Dorian Gray* (1891)

6 From the standpoint of pure reason, there are no good grounds to support the claim that one should sacrifice one's own happiness to that of others.

   W. Somerset Maugham 1874–1965: *A Writer's Notebook* (1949) written in 1896

7 MEDVEDENKO: Why do you wear black all the time?
   MASHA: I'm in mourning for my life, I'm unhappy.

   Anton Chekhov 1860–1904: *The Seagull* (1896)

8 I can imagine no more comfortable frame of mind for the conduct of life than a humorous resignation.

   W. Somerset Maugham 1874–1965: *A Writer's Notebook* (1949) written in 1903

9 There are two tragedies in life. One is not to get your heart's desire. The other is to get it.

   George Bernard Shaw 1856–1950: *Man and Superman* (1903)

10 But a lifetime of happiness! No man alive could bear it: it would be hell on earth.

   George Bernard Shaw 1856–1950: *Man and Superman* (1903)

11 He's simply got the instinct for being unhappy highly developed.

   Saki 1870–1916: *Chronicles of Clovis* (1911)

12 All the things I really like to do are either illegal, immoral, or fattening.

   Alexander Woollcott 1887–1943: R. E. Drennan *Wit's End* (1973)

13 Men are the only animals who devote themselves to making one another unhappy. It is, I suppose, one of their godlike qualities. Jahweh, as the Old Testament shows, spends a large part of His time trying to ruin the business and comfort of all other Gods.

   H. L. Mencken 1880–1956: *Minority Report* (1956)

14 The fact that I have no remedy for the sorrows of the world is no reason for my accepting yours. It simply supports the strong probability that yours is a fake.

   H. L. Mencken 1880–1956: *Minority Report* (1956)

15 MRS BAKER is a woman who has managed to find a little misery in the best of things. Sorrow and trouble are the only things that can make her happy.

   Neil Simon 1927– : *Come Blow Your Horn* (1961)

16 You have flair...It's handed out at birth...And as always happens in these cases, it's always given to the very people who in my opinion do least to earn it. It's taken me forty-two years to think of that and I'm very depressed.

   Alan Ayckbourn 1939– : *Joking Apart* (1979)

17 LEN: Try and cheer her up a bit, will you?
MELVYN: Why?
LEN: Because she's like a mourner peeling onions, that's
why.

Alan Ayckbourn 1939– : *Sisterly Feelings* (1981)

18 VICTORIA: Of course we can manage. Jesus managed.
JACKIE: When?
VICTORIA: In the wilderness. I mean he managed for forty
days and forty nights, but did he have a good time?
Did he send a postcard home saying, 'Wish you were
here, the weather is fabulous'? No. He was miserable.
If he'd had a fortnight in a stationary caravan at
Cleethorpes there'd be no such thing as Lent.

Victoria Wood 1953– : *Mens Sana in Thingummy Doodah* (1990)

19 No pleasure is worth giving up for the sake of two more
years in a geriatric home in Weston-super-Mare.

Kingsley Amis 1922–95: in *The Times* 21 June 1994; attributed

Health See *Sickness and Health*

Heaven and Hell

1 All are inclined to believe what they covet, from
a lottery-ticket up to a passport to Paradise,—in which,
from description, I see nothing very tempting.

Lord Byron 1788–1824: diary 27 November 1813

2 My idea of heaven is, eating *pâté de foie gras* to the sound
of trumpets.

Sydney Smith 1771–1845: view ascribed by Smith to his friend Henry Luttrell; Peter Virgin *Sydney Smith* (1994)

3 I always say, as you know, that if my fellow citizens
want to go to Hell I will help them. It's my job.

Oliver Wendell Holmes Jr. 1841–1935: letter to Harold Laski, 4 March 1920

4 If Max [Beaverbrook] gets to Heaven he won't last long.
He will be chucked out for trying to pull off a merger
between Heaven and Hell ... after having secured
a controlling interest in key subsidiary companies in both
places, of course.

H. G. Wells 1866–1946: A. J. P. Taylor *Beaverbrook* (1972)

*Of Lord Curzon, who at the age of thirty-nine had been created
Viceroy of India:*
5 For all the rest of his life Curzon was influenced by his
sudden journey to heaven at the age of thirty-nine, and
then by his return seven years later to earth, for the
remainder of his mortal existence.

Lord Beaverbrook 1879–1964: *Men and Power* (1956)

6 The Devil himself had probably re-designed Hell in the
light of information he had gained from observing airport
layouts.

Anthony Price 1928– : *The Memory Trap* (1989)

History

1 The one duty we owe to history is to rewrite it.

Oscar Wilde 1854–1900: *Intentions* (1891) 'The Critic as Artist' pt. 1

2 To give an accurate and exhaustive account of the period
would need a far less brilliant pen than mine.

Max Beerbohm 1872–1956: in *Yellow Book* (1895)

3 SWINDON: What will history say?
BURGOYNE: History, sir, will tell lies as usual.

George Bernard Shaw
1856–1950: *The Devil's Disciple* (1901)

4 An account, mostly false, of events, mostly unimportant, which are brought about by rulers, mostly knaves, and soldiers, mostly fools.

Ambrose Bierce 1842–c.1914: definition of history; *The Cynic's Word Book* (1906)

5 History is more or less bunk.

Henry Ford 1863–1947: in *Chicago Tribune* 25 May 1916

6 Human history becomes more and more a race between education and catastrophe.

H. G. Wells 1866–1946: *Outline of History* (1920)

7 History repeats itself. Historians repeat each other.

Philip Guedalla 1889–1944: *Supers and Supermen* (1920) 'Some Historians'

8 Thanks for *Dethronements*, though I do not think it one of your good books...I do not believe that any of the people resembled or resemble your figures; and in the second dialogue the falsification of history is quite awful.

A. E. Housman 1859–1936: 1922 letter to his brother Laurence Housman, 5 December 1922

9 Histories have previously been written with the object of exalting their authors. The object of this History is to console the reader. *No other history does this.*

W. C. Sellar 1898–1951 and **R. J. Yeatman** 1898–1968: *1066 and All That* (1930)

10 History is not what you thought. *It is what you can remember.*

W. C. Sellar 1898–1951 and **R. J. Yeatman** 1898–1968: *1066 and All That* (1930) 'Compulsory Preface'

11 AMERICA was thus clearly top nation, and History came to a .

W. C. Sellar 1898–1951 and **R. J. Yeatman** 1898–1968: *1066 and All That* (1930)

12 People who make history know nothing about history. You can see that in the sort of history they make.

G. K. Chesterton 1874–1936: J. A. Gere and John Sparrow (eds.) *Geoffrey Madan's Notebooks* (1981)

13 It is a fair summary of history to say that the safeguards of liberty have been forged in controversies involving not very nice people.

Felix Frankfurter 1882–1965: dissenting opinion in *United States v. Rabinowitz* 1950

The accession of Elizabeth II had been greeted with numerous articles on 'the new Elizabethan Age':

14 We are in for the undoing of all the work of recent historians who have exposed the wickedness of Elizabeth Tudor. It has begun today in all weekly papers. Rebunking.

Evelyn Waugh 1903–66: letter to Lady Diana Cooper, February 1952

15 History started badly and hav been geting steadily worse.

Geoffrey Willans 1911–1958 and **Ronald Searle** 1920– : *Down with Skool!* (1953)

At a Press Conference celebrating the completion of his A Study of History, *a journalist had asked 'what purpose had impelled him to devote thirty-five years of his life to this single great work':*

16 Curiosity.

Arnold Toynbee 1889–1975: Harold Nicolson diary 12 October 1954

17 Human blunders usually do more to shape history than human wickedness.

A. J. P. Taylor 1906–90: *The Origins of the Second World War* (1961)

18 He majored in English history, which was a mistake. 'English history!' roared the silver-maned senator from his state indignantly. 'What's the matter with American history? American history is as good as any history in the world!'

Joseph Heller 1923– : *Catch-22* (1961)

19 Like most of those who study history, he [Napoleon III] learned from the mistakes of the past how to make new ones.

A. J. P. Taylor 1906–90: in *Listener* 6 June 1963

20 History gets thicker as it approaches recent times.

A. J. P. Taylor 1906–90: *English History 1914–45* (1965), bibliography

21 History teaches us that men and nations behave wisely once they have exhausted all other alternatives.

Abba Eban 1915– : speech in London 16 December 1970

22 History, like wood, has a grain in it which determines how it splits; and those in authority, besides trying to shape and direct events, sometimes find it more convenient just to let them happen.

Malcolm Muggeridge 1903–90: *The Infernal Grove* (1975)

23 This we learn from Watergate
That almost any creep'll
Be glad to help the Government
Overthrow the people.

E. Y. Harburg 1898–1981: 'History Lesson' (1976)

On being asked what would have happened in 1963, had Khrushchev and not Kennedy been assassinated:
24 With history one can never be certain, but I think I can safely say that Aristotle Onassis would not have married Mrs Khrushchev.

Gore Vidal 1925– : in *Sunday Times* 4 June 1989

25 A broad school of Australian writing has based itself on the assumption that Australia not only has a history worth bothering about, but that all the history worth bothering about happened in Australia.

Clive James 1939– : *The Dreaming Swimmer* (1992)

Holidays

1 I don't think we can do better than 'Good old Broadstairs'.

George Grossmith 1847–1912 and **Weedon Grossmith** 1854–1919: *The Diary of a Nobody* (1894)

2 There's sand in the porridge and sand in the bed, And if this is pleasure we'd rather be dead.

Noël Coward 1899–1973: 'The English Lido' (1928)

3 Cannot avoid contrasting deliriously rapid flight of time when on a holiday with very much slower passage of days, and even hours, in other and more familiar surroundings.

E. M. Delafield 1890–1943: *The Diary of a Provincial Lady* (1930)

4 The Victorians had not been anxious to go away for the weekend. The Edwardians, on the contrary, were nomadic.

T. H. White 1906–64: *Farewell Victoria* (1933)

5 I suppose we all have our recollections of our earlier holidays, all bristling with horror.

Flann O'Brien 1911–66: *Myles Away from Dublin* (1990)

6 A weekend in the country
With the panting
And the yawns

Stephen Sondheim 1930– : 'A Weekend in the Country' (1972)

With the crickets and the pheasants
And the orchards and the hay,
With the servants and the peasants,
We'll be laying our plans
While we're playing croquet
For a weekend in the country
So inactive one has to lie down.
A weekend in the country
Where we're twice as upset
As in town.

7 All through the night there's a friendly receptionist
Welcome to Holiday Inn.

Dorothy Fields 1905–74:
'Welcome to Holiday Inn' (1973)

8 I wish I'd given Spain a miss this year—I nearly plumped
for a crochet week in Rhyl. I was going to have a stab at
a batwing blouson.

Victoria Wood 1953– : *Mens Sana
in Thingummy Doodah* (1990)

9 I did advertise for a holiday companion—capable widow,
no sense of humour, some knowledge of haemorrhoids
preferred—not a reply.

Victoria Wood 1953– : *Mens Sana
in Thingummy Doodah* (1990)

The Home and Housework

1 I have heard of a man who had a mind to sell his house,
and therefore carried a piece of brick in his pocket, which
he shewed as a pattern to encourage purchasers.

Jonathan Swift 1667–1745: *The
Drapier's Letters* (1724)

2 Love and a cottage! Eh, Fanny! Ah, give me indifference
and a coach and six!

George Colman, the Elder
1732–94 and **David Garrick**
1717–79: *The Clandestine Marriage*
(1766)

3 Thus first necessity invented stools,
Convenience next suggested elbow-chairs,
And luxury the accomplished sofa last.

William Cowper 1731–1800: *The
Task* (1785)

*On being encountered drinking a glass of wine in the street, while
watching his theatre, the Drury Lane, burn down, on 24 February
1809:*
4 A man may surely be allowed to take a glass of wine by
his own fireside.

Richard Brinsley Sheridan
1751–1816: T. Moore *Life of Sheridan*
(1825)

5 The premises are so delightfully extensive, that two
people might live together without ever seeing, hearing,
or meeting.

Lord Byron 1788–1824: of
Newstead Abbey; letter 30 (31?)
August 1811

6 Mrs Crupp had indignantly assured him that there
wasn't room to swing a cat there; but, as Mr Dick justly
observed to me, sitting down on the foot of the bed,
nursing his leg, 'You know, Trotwood, I don't want to
swing a cat. I never do swing a cat. Therefore, what does
that signify to *me!*'

Charles Dickens 1812–70: *David
Copperfield* (1850)

On a guest who had outstayed his welcome:
7 There is a mad artist named Inchbold,
With whom you must be at a pinch bold:
Or you may as well score

Dante Gabriel Rossetti 1828–82:
limerick written c.1870

The brass plate on your door
With the name of J. W. Inchbold.

8 What's the good of a home if you are never in it?

George Grossmith 1847–1912 and
Weedon Grossmith 1854–1919:
The Diary of a Nobody (1894)

9 The great advantage of a hotel is that it's a refuge from
home life.

George Bernard Shaw
1856–1950: *You Never Can Tell* (1898)

10 I want a house that has got over all its troubles; I don't
want to spend the rest of my life bringing up a young
and inexperienced house.

Jerome K. Jerome 1859–1927:
They and I (1909)

11 Home life as we understand it is no more natural to us
than a cage is natural to a cockatoo.

George Bernard Shaw
1856–1950: *Getting Married* (1911)
preface 'Hearth and Home'

12 Hatred of domestic work is a natural and admirable
result of civilization.

Rebecca West 1892–1983: in *The
Freewoman* 6 June 1912

13 The national sport of England is obstacle racing. People
fill their rooms with useless and cumbersome furniture,
and spend the rest of their lives in trying to dodge it.

Herbert Beerbohm Tree
1852–1917: Hesketh Pearson *Beerbohm
Tree* (1956)

14 My old man said, 'Follow the van,
Don't dilly-dally on the way!'
Off went the cart with the home packed in it,
I walked behind with my old cock linnet.
But I dillied and dallied, dallied and dillied,
Lost the van and don't know where to roam.

Charles Collins: 'Don't Dilly-Dally
on the Way' (1919, with Fred Leigh);
popularized by Marie Lloyd

15 Tho' the pipes that supply the bathroom burst
And the lavatory makes you fear the worst,
It was used by Charles the First
Quite informally,
And later by George the Fourth
On a journey North.

Noël Coward 1899–1973: 'The
Stately Homes of England' (1938)

16 Though the fact that they have to be rebuilt
And frequently mortgaged to the hilt
Is inclined to take the gilt
Off the gingerbread,
And certainly damps the fun
Of the eldest son.

Noël Coward 1899–1973: 'The
Stately Homes of England' (1938)

17 Although very few people are actually called upon to live
in palaces a very large number are unwilling to admit
the fact.

Osbert Lancaster 1908–80:
Homes Sweet Homes (1939)

18 They tell me there is no more toilet paper in the house.
How can I be expected to act a romantic part and
remember to order TOILET PAPER!

Mrs Patrick Campbell
1865–1940: Margot Peters *Mrs Pat*
(1984)

19 Housewife. You know—sleep-in maids.

Neil Simon 1927– : *Come Blow
Your Horn* (1961)

20 You know why I really left home? I don't want to have
milk and cake standing over the sink any more. I want
to sit in a chair and eat like real people.

Neil Simon 1927– : *Come Blow
Your Horn* (1961)

21 All I need is room enough to lay a hat and a few friends.
Dorothy Parker 1893–1967: R. E. Drennan *Wit's End* (1973)

22 Is that bottle just going to sit up there or are you going to turn it into a lamp?
Neil Simon 1927– : *Last of the Red Hot Lovers* (1970)

23 It looks different when you're sober. I thought I had twice as much furniture.
Neil Simon 1927– : *The Gingerbread Lady* (1970)

24 On moving house, the first candidates for the dustbin are your rose-coloured glasses with special hindsight attachment.
Basil Boothroyd 1910–88: *Let's Move House* (1977)

25 This is not the definitive work on house-moving. I'm not up to it. Gibbon might have been. Macaulay. They covered things in depth. Myself, like the removal men, I'm only scratching the surface.
Basil Boothroyd 1910–88: *Let's Move House* (1977)

26 Conran's Law of Housework—it expands to fill the time available plus half an hour.
Shirley Conran 1932– : *Superwoman* 2 (1977)

27 Cockroaches have been given a bad rap. They don't bite, smell, or get into your booze. Would that all houseguests were as well behaved.
P. J. O'Rourke 1947– : *The Bachelor Home Companion* (1987)

28 Keeping house is as unpleasant and filthy as coal mining, and the pay's a lot worse.
P. J. O'Rourke 1947– : *The Bachelor Home Companion* (1987)

29 Curtains in orange nylon and no place mats, there's not even the veneer of civilization.
Alan Bennett 1934– : *Talking Heads* (1988)

30 Everything's getting on top of me. I can't switch off. I've got a self-cleaning oven—I have to get up in the night to see if it's doing it.
Victoria Wood 1953– : *Mens Sana in Thingummy Doodah* (1990)

31 There's no greater bliss in life than when the plumber eventually comes to unblock your drains. No writer can give that sort of pleasure.
Victoria Glendinning 1937– : in *Observer* 3 January 1993

Hope and Despair   See also *Happiness and Unhappiness, Satisfaction and Discontent*

1 'Blessed is the man who expects nothing, for he shall never be disappointed' was the ninth beatitude.
Alexander Pope 1688–1744: letter to Fortescue, 23 September 1725

2 He told me, only the other day, that it was provided for. That was Mr Micawber's expression, 'Provided for.'
Charles Dickens 1812–70: *David Copperfield* (1850)

3 I have known him come home to supper with a flood of tears, and a declaration that nothing was now left but a jail; and go to bed making a calculation of the expense of putting bow-windows to the house, 'in case anything turned up,' which was his favourite expression.
Charles Dickens 1812–70: *David Copperfield* (1850)

4 'Do you know what a pessimist is?' 'A man who thinks everybody is as nasty as himself, and hates them for it.'
George Bernard Shaw 1856–1950: *An Unsocial Socialist* (1887)

5 A minor form of despair, disguised as a virtue.
Ambrose Bierce 1842–c.1914: definition of patience; *The Devil's Dictionary* (1911)

6 We seek to find peace of mind in the word, the formula, the ritual. The hope is an illusion.

Benjamin N. Cardozo 1870–1938: *The Growth of the Law* (1924)

7 an optimist is a guy
that has never had
much experience.

Don Marquis 1878–1937: *archy and mehitabel* (1927) 'certain maxims of archy'

8 but wotthehell
archy wotthehell
it s cheerio
my deario that
pulls a lady through.

Don Marquis 1878–1937: *archy and mehitabel* (1927) 'cheerio my deario'

9 but wotthehell archy wotthehell
jamais triste archy jamais triste
that is my motto.

Don Marquis 1878–1937: *archy and mehitabel* (1927) 'mehitabel sees paris'

10 Why, even the janitor's wife
Has a perfectly good love life
And here am I
Facing tomorrow
Alone with my sorrow
Down in the depths on the ninetieth floor.

Cole Porter 1891–1964: 'Down in the Depths' (1936)

11 There are bad times just around the corner,
There are dark clouds travelling through the sky
And it's no good whining
About a silver lining
For we know from experience that they won't roll by,
With a scowl and a frown
We'll keep our peckers down
And prepare for depression and doom and dread,
We're going to unpack our troubles from our old kitbag
And wait until we drop down dead.

Noël Coward 1899–1973: 'There are Bad Times Just Around the Corner' (1953)

12 It's always hard to see hope with a hangover.

P. J. O'Rourke 1947– : *Holidays in Hell* (1988)

13 It drives me to a frothing frenzy when politicians return from inner cities saying, 'What the people of this town need is Hope', as if we could all respond with a glad cry of 'No sooner said than done old sport,' as we gather up a handful of Hope from the sideboard, stuff it into a Jiffy-bag and send it off to Liverpool 8 by the First Class post. What these bleeding hearts mean is Money, but they're too greasy to say so.

Stephen Fry 1957– : *The Hippopotamus* (1994)

Housework See *The Home and Housework*

The Human Race

1 This world is a comedy to those that think, a tragedy to those that feel.

Horace Walpole 1717–97: letter to Anne, Countess of Upper Ossory, 16 August 1776

2 Men have an extraordinarily erroneous opinion of their position in nature; and the error is ineradicable.

W. Somerset Maugham
1874–1965: *A Writer's Notebook* (1949) written in 1896

3 Certainty generally is illusion, and repose is not the destiny of man.

Oliver Wendell Holmes Jr.
1841–1935: 'The Path of the Law' (1897)

4 Man is the Only Animal that Blushes. Or needs to.

Mark Twain 1835–1910: *Following the Equator* (1897)

5 That habit of treading in ruts and trooping in companies which men share with sheep.

A. E. Housman 1859–1936: 'The Editing of Juvenal' (1905)

6 The only man who wasn't spoilt by being lionized was Daniel.

Herbert Beerbohm Tree
1852–1917: Hesketh Pearson *Beerbohm Tree* (1956)

7 I wish I loved the Human Race;
I wish I loved its silly face;
I wish I liked the way it walks;
I wish I liked the way it talks;
And when I'm introduced to one
I wish I thought *What Jolly Fun!*

Walter Raleigh 1861–1922: 'Wishes of an Elderly Man' (1923)

8 'Have you ever seen Spode eat asparagus?'
'No.'
'Revolting. It alters one's whole conception of Man as Nature's last word.'

P. G. Wodehouse 1881–1975: *The Code of the Woosters* (1938)

9 Well, of course, people are only human...But it really does not seem much for them to be.

Ivy Compton-Burnett
1884–1969: *A Family and a Fortune* (1939)

10 Man is a beautiful machine that works very badly. He is like a watch of which the most that can be said is that its cosmetic effect is good.

H. L. Mencken 1880–1956: *Minority Report* (1956)

11 Man is one of the toughest of animated creatures. Only the anthrax bacillus can stand so unfavourable an environment for so long a time.

H. L. Mencken 1880–1956: *Minority Report* (1956)

12 The human race has probably never produced a wholly admirable man. Such trite examples as Lincoln, Washington, Goethe and the holy saints are obviously very lame candidates. Even Jesus fails to meet any rational specification.

H. L. Mencken 1880–1956: *Minority Report* (1956)

13 The history of human calumny is largely a series of breaches of good manners.

Tom Stoppard 1937– : *Professional Foul* (1978)

14 He's an animal lover...People he don't like so much.

Tom Stoppard 1937– : *Neutral Ground* (1983)

15 Man is the only creature that seems to have the time and energy to pump all his sewage out to sea, and then go swimming in it.

Miles Kington 1941– : *Nature Made Ridiculously Simple* (1983)

16 Reality is something the human race doesn't handle very well.

Gore Vidal 1925– : in *Radio Times* 3 January 1990

17 We used to build civilizations. Now we build shopping malls.

Bill Bryson 1951– : *Neither Here Nor There* (1991)

18 Nobody's perfect. Now and then, my pet,
You're almost human. You could make it yet.

Wendy Cope 1945– : 'Faint Praise' (1992)

19 I'm dealing in rock'n'roll. I'm, like, I'm not a bona fide human being.

Phil Spector 1940– : attributed

Humility See *Pride and Humility*

Humour See also *Wit and Wordplay*

1 It's an odd job, making decent people laugh.

Molière 1622–73: *La Critique de l'école des femmes* (1663)

2 The end of satire is reformation, and this would be of more force than your societies for that purpose, were it duly observed and hearkened to, without being misconstrued defamation.

Anonymous: in *The Female Tatler* October 1709

3 Among all kinds of writing, there is none in which authors are more apt to miscarry than in works of humour, as there is none in which they are more ambitious to excel.

Joseph Addison 1672–1719: *The Spectator* 10 April 1711

4 A joke's a very serious thing.

Charles Churchill 1731–64: *The Ghost* (1763)

5 Laughter is pleasant, but the exertion is too much for me.

Thomas Love Peacock 1785–1866: *Nightmare Abbey* (1818)

6 That joke was lost on the foreigner—guides cannot master the subtleties of the American joke.

Mark Twain 1835–1910: *The Innocents Abroad* (1869)

7 A difference of taste in jokes is a great strain on the affections.

George Eliot 1819–80: *Daniel Deronda* (1876)

8 'Tis ever thus with simple folk—an accepted wit has but to say 'Pass the mustard', and they roar their ribs out!

W. S. Gilbert 1836–1911: *The Yeoman of the Guard* (1888)

9 She had a penetrating sort of laugh. Rather like a train going into a tunnel.

P. G. Wodehouse 1881–1975: *The Inimitable Jeeves* (1923)

10 Everything is funny as long as it is happening to Somebody Else.

Will Rogers 1879–1935: *The Illiterate Digest* (1924) 'Warning to Jokers: lay off the prince'

11 I did not intend to write a funny book, at first. I did not know I was a humorist. I have never been sure about it. In the middle ages, I should probably have gone about preaching and got myself burnt or hanged.

Jerome K. Jerome 1859–1927: *My Life and Times* (1926)

12 Without humour you cannot run a sweetie-shop, let alone a nation.

John Buchan 1875–1940: *Castle Gay* (1930)

Returning for his twenty-fifth homecoming at Harvard in 1937, he told underclassmen:

13 I feel as I always have, except for an occasional heart attack.'

Robert Benchley 1889–1945: Groucho Marx *Grouchophile* (1976)

14 Madeleine Bassett laughed the tinkling, silvery laugh that had got her so disliked by the better element.

P. G. Wodehouse 1881–1975: *The Code of the Woosters* (1938)

15 What do you mean, funny? Funny-peculiar or funny ha-ha?

Ian Hay 1876–1952: *The Housemaster* (1938)

16 My idea of an ideal programme would be a show where I would have all the questions and some other bastard would have to figure out the funny answers.

Groucho Marx 1895–1977: letter 10 October 1940

To a tiresome dinner partner:
17 Do you know why God withheld the sense of humour from women?...That we may love you instead of laughing at you.

Mrs Patrick Campbell 1865–1940: Margot Peters *Mrs Pat* (1984)

18 By good rights, great humorists ought to be gentle, agreeable people to meet, with a breadth of view and a kindly tolerance of trifles—such as they show in print. Mostly they are not.

Stephen Leacock 1869–1944: *The Boy I Left Behind Me* (1947)

19 In Milwaukee last month a man died laughing over one of his own jokes. That's what makes it so tough for us outsiders. We have to fight home competition.

Robert Benchley 1889–1945: R. E. Drennan *Wit's End* (1973)

20 The funniest thing about comedy is that you never know why people laugh. I know *what* makes them laugh but trying to get your hands on the *why* of it is like trying to pick an eel out of a tub of water.

W. C. Fields 1880–1946: Richard J. Anobile *A Flask of Fields* (1972)

21 Good taste and humour...are a contradiction in terms, like a chaste whore.

Malcolm Muggeridge 1903–90: in *Time* 14 September 1953

22 Laughter would be bereaved if snobbery died.

Peter Ustinov 1921– : in *Observer* 13 March 1955

23 Reality goes bounding past the satirist like a cheetah laughing as it lopes ahead of the greyhound.

Claud Cockburn 1904–81: *Crossing the Line* (1958)

24 There are those who, in their pride and their innocence, dedicate their careers to writing humorous pieces. Poor dears, the world is stacked against them from the start, for everybody in it has the right to look at their work and say, 'I don't think that's funny.'

Dorothy Parker 1893–1967: introduction to *The Most of S. J. Perelman* (1959)

25 Humour is emotional chaos remembered in tranquillity.

James Thurber 1894–1961: in *New York Post* 29 February 1960

26 A sober God-fearing man whose idea of a good joke was to lie about his age.

Joseph Heller 1923– : *Catch-22* (1961)

27 Another day gone and no jokes.

Flann O'Brien 1911–66: *The Best of Myles* (1968)

28 Mark my words, when a society has to resort to the lavatory for its humour, the writing is on the wall.

Alan Bennett 1934– : *Forty Years On* (1969)

29 Comedy, like sodomy, is an unnatural act.

Marty Feldman 1933–83: in *The Times* 9 June 1969

30 [Comedy is] the kindly contemplation of the incongruous.

P. G. Wodehouse 1881–1975: attributed

31 The marvellous thing about a joke with a double meaning is that it can only mean one thing.

Ronnie Barker 1929– : *Sauce* (1977)

32 I knew nothing about farce until I read [Feydeau's] *Puce à l'Oreille*, and had no idea what a deadly serious business it is.

John Mortimer 1923– : *Clinging to the Wreckage* (1982)

33 The role of humour is to make people fall down and writhe on the Axminster, and that is the top and bottom of it.

Alan Coren 1938– : *Seems Like Old Times* (1989)

34 When you tell an Iowan a joke, you can see a kind of race going on between his brain and his expression.

Bill Bryson 1951– : *The Lost Continent* (1989)

35 Humour is, by its nature, more truthful than factual.

P. J. O'Rourke 1947– : *Parliament of Whores* (1991)

36 Freud's theory was that when a joke opens a window and all those bats and bogeymen fly out, you get a marvellous feeling of relief and elation. The trouble with Freud is that he never had to play the old Glasgow Empire on a Saturday night after Rangers and Celtic had both lost.

Ken Dodd 1931– : in *Guardian* 30 April 1991 (quoted in many, usually much contracted, forms since the mid-1960s)

37 It's certainly easy to mock some things…Oddly enough though I've never found it easy to mock anything of value. Only things that are tawdry and fatuous—perhaps it's just me.

Stephen Fry 1957– : *The Liar* (1992)

38 It is easy to forget that the most important aspect of comedy, after all, its great saving grace, is its ambiguity. You can simultaneously laugh at a situation, *and* take it seriously.

Stephen Fry 1957– : *Paperweight* (1992)

39 We often laughed at others in our house, and I picked up the craft of being polite while people were present and laughing later if there was anything to laugh about.

Muriel Spark 1918– : *Curriculum Vitae* (1992)

40 All humour is based on hostility—that's why World War Two was funny.

Neil Simon 1927– : *Laughter on the 23rd Floor* (1993)

41 The world dwindles daily for the humorist…Jokes are fast running out, for a joke must transform real life in some perverse way, and real life has begun to perform the same operation perfectly professionally upon itself.

Craig Brown 1957– : *Craig Brown's Greatest Hits* (1993)

42 Life is a campus: in a Greenwich Village bookstore, looking for a New Yorker collection, I asked of an earnest-looking assistant where I might find the humour section. Peering over her granny glasses, she enquired, 'Humour studies would that be, sir?'

Keith Waterhouse 1929– : in *The Spectator* 15 January 1994

43 As humourless a lump of dough as ever held a torchlight vigil outside the South African Embassy or stuck an AIDS awareness ribbon on an unwilling first-nighter.

Stephen Fry 1957– : *The Hippopotamus* (1994)

Hypocrisy

1 Of all the cants which are canted in this canting world,—though the cant of hypocrites may be the worst,—the cant of criticism is the most tormenting!

Laurence Sterne 1713–68: *Tristram Shandy* (1759–67)

The hypocritical Quaker, Ephraim Smooth, hears violin music:

2 I must shut my ears. The man of sin rubbeth the hair of the horse to the bowels of the cat.

John O'Keeffe 1747–1833: *Wild Oats* (1791)

3 In England the only homage which they pay to Virtue— is hypocrisy.

Lord Byron 1788–1824: letter 11 May 1821

4 We are so very 'umble.

Charles Dickens 1812–70: *David Copperfield* (1850)

5 He combines the manners of a Marquis with the morals of a Methodist.

W. S. Gilbert 1836–1911: *Ruddigore* (1887)

6 I hope you have not been leading a double life, pretending to be wicked and being really good all the time. That would be hypocrisy.

Oscar Wilde 1854–1900: *The Importance of Being Earnest* (1895)

Speaking against the Welsh Disestablishment Bill, F. E. Smith had called it 'a Bill which has shocked the conscience of every Christian community in Europe':

7 It would greatly, I must own,
Soothe me, Smith!
If you left this theme alone,
Holy Smith!
For your legal cause or civil
You fight well and get your fee!
For your God or dream or devil
You will answer, not to me.
Talk about the pews and steeples
and the Cash that goes therewith!
But the souls of Christian people...
Chuck it, Smith!

G. K. Chesterton 1874–1936: 'Antichrist, or the Reunion of Christendom: An Ode' (1912)

8 All Reformers, however strict their social conscience, live in houses just as big as they can pay for.

Logan Pearsall Smith 1865–1946: *Afterthoughts* (1931) 'Other People'

9 Most people sell their souls, and live with a good conscience on the proceeds.

Logan Pearsall Smith 1865–1946: *Afterthoughts* (1931) 'Other People'

10 Hypocrisy is not generally a social sin, but a virtue.

Judith Martin 1938– : *Miss Manners' Guide to Rearing Perfect Children* (1985)

11 When the moment came to pull the lever which dropped Mr Hawke through the trap-door to the waiting crocodiles, Mr Keating did not pretend to share their tears.

Clive James 1939– : *The Dreaming Swimmer* (1992)

12 There are moments when we in the British press can show extraordinary sensitivity; these moments usually coincide with the death of a proprietor, or a proprietor's wife.

Craig Brown 1957– : *Craig Brown's Greatest Hits* (1993)

Ideas

1 He can compress the most words into the smallest ideas better than any man I ever met.

Abraham Lincoln 1809–65: of another Illinois lawyer; Leon Harris *The Fine Art of Political Wit* (1965)

2 The chief end of man is to frame general ideas—and . . .
no general idea is worth a damn.

Oliver Wendell Holmes Jr.
1841–1935: letter to Morris R. Cohen,
12 April 1915

3 There are some ideas so wrong that only a very
intelligent person could believe in them.

George Orwell 1903–50: attributed

4 A household where a total unawareness of the world of
ideas not only existed but was regarded as a matter for
congratulation.

Osbert Lancaster 1908–80: *All
Done From Memory* (1953)

5 It is better to entertain an idea than to take it home to
live with you for the rest of your life.

Randall Jarrell 1914–65: *Pictures
from an Institution* (1954)

6 I had a monumental idea this morning, but I didn't like
it.

Sam Goldwyn 1882–1974: N.
Zierold *Hollywood Tycoons* (1969)

7 A small intellectual idea, the kind of notion that might
occur to a man in his bath and be forgotten in the
business of drying between his toes.

Tom Stoppard 1937– : *Artist
Descending a Staircase* (1973)

8 The average Englishman, you see, is not interested in
ideas . . . You could shove a slice of the Communist
Manifesto in the Queen's Speech and no one would turn
a hair. Least of all, I suspect, HMQ.

Alan Bennett 1934– : *An
Englishman Abroad* (1989)

9 An original idea. That can't be too hard. The library
must be full of them.

Stephen Fry 1957– : *The Liar* (1991)

Ignorance See *Foolishness and Ignorance*

Insults and Invective

1 BEATRICE: I wonder that you will still be talking, Signior
Benedick: nobody marks you.
BENEDICK: What! my dear Lady Disdain, are you yet
living?

William Shakespeare 1564–1616:
Much Ado About Nothing (1598–9)

2 A cherub's face, a reptile all the rest.

Alexander Pope 1688–1744: of
Lord Hervey; 'An Epistle to Dr
Arbuthnot' (1735)

3 Let Sporus tremble—'What? that thing of silk,
Sporus, that mere white curd of ass's milk?
Satire or sense, alas! can Sporus feel?
Who breaks a butterfly upon a wheel?'

Alexander Pope 1688–1744: of
Lord Hervey; 'An Epistle to Dr
Arbuthnot' (1735)

4 A brain of feathers, and a heart of lead.

Alexander Pope 1688–1744: *The
Dunciad* (1742)

5 A wit with dunces, and a dunce with wits.

Alexander Pope 1688–1744: *The
Dunciad* (1742)

6 This man [Lord Chesterfield] I thought had been a Lord
among wits; but, I find, he is only a wit among Lords.

Samuel Johnson 1709–84: James
Boswell *Life of Samuel Johnson* (1791)
(1754)

7 Is not a Patron, my Lord, one who looks with unconcern
on a man struggling for life in the water, and, when he
has reached ground, encumbers him with help? The
notice which you have been pleased to take of my

Samuel Johnson 1709–84: letter to
Lord Chesterfield, 7 February 1755;
James Boswell *Life of Samuel Johnson*
(1791)

labours, had it been early, had it been kind; but it has been delayed till I am indifferent, and cannot enjoy it; till I am solitary, and cannot impart it; till I am known, and do not want it.

8 Sir, you have but two topics, yourself and me. I am sick of both.

Samuel Johnson 1709–84: James Boswell *Life of Samuel Johnson* (1791) May 1776

9 [EARL OF SANDWICH:] 'Pon my soul, Wilkes, I don't know whether you'll die upon the gallows or of the pox.
[WILKES:] That depends, my Lord, whether I first embrace your Lordship's principles, or your Lordship's mistresses.

John Wilkes 1727–97: Charles Petrie *The Four Georges* (1935); probably apocryphal

10 Science is his forte, and omniscience his foible.

Sydney Smith 1771–1845: of William Whewell, master of Trinity College, Cambridge; Isaac Todhunter *William Whewell* (1876)

On a proposal to surround St Paul's with a wooden pavement:
11 Let the Dean and Canons lay their heads together and the thing will be done.

Sydney Smith 1771–1845: H. Pearson *The Smith of Smiths* (1934)

12 He has to learn that petulance is not sarcasm, and that insolence is not invective.

Benjamin Disraeli 1804–81: of Sir Charles Wood; speech, House of Commons 16 December 1852

Henry Clay of Virginia unexpectedly moved out of the way of his political rival, John Randolph of Roanoke:
13 JOHN RANDOLPH: I never sidestep skunks.
HENRY CLAY: I always do.

Henry Clay 1777–1852: Robert V. Remini *Henry Clay* (1991)

14 He has all the characteristics of a dog except loyalty.

Sam Houston 1793–1863: of Thomas Jefferson Green; Leon Harris *The Fine Art of Political Wit* (1965)

15 A sophistical rhetorician, inebriated with the exuberance of his own verbosity.

Benjamin Disraeli 1804–81: of Gladstone; in *The Times* 29 July 1878

16 I regard you with an indifference closely bordering on aversion.

Robert Louis Stevenson 1850–94: *New Arabian Nights* (1882)

17 Don't look at me, Sir, with—ah—in that tone of voice.

Punch 1841–1992: vol. 87 (1884)

18 What time he can spare from the adornment of his person he devotes to the neglect of his duties.

William Hepworth Thompson 1810–86: of Richard Jebb, later Professor of Greek at Cambridge; M. R. Bobbit *With Dearest Love to All* (1960)

19 CECILY: When I see a spade I call it a spade.
GWENDOLEN: I am glad to say that I have never seen a spade.

Oscar Wilde 1854–1900: *The Importance of Being Earnest* (1895)

At the Trinity Dublin high table, of his rival, Provost Traill, who was presiding:
20 A beast. But fortunately a deaf beast.

John Pentland Mahaffy 1839–1919: W. B. Stanford and R. B. McDowell *Mahaffy* (1971)

21 Stoeber's mind, though that is no name to call it by, was one which turned as unswervingly to the false, the

A. E. Housman 1859–1936: 'The Editing of Manilius' (1903)

meaningless, the unmetrical, and the ungrammatical, as the needle to the pole.

When pressed by a gramophone company for a written testimonial:

22 Sirs, I have tested your machine. It adds a new terror to life and makes death a long-felt want.

Herbert Beerbohm Tree 1852–1917: Hesketh Pearson *Beerbohm Tree* (1956)

23 A very weak-minded fellow I am afraid, and, like the feather pillow, bears the marks of the last person who has sat on him!

Earl Haig 1861–1928: of Lord Derby; letter to Lady Haig, 14 January 1918

24 The affair between Margot Asquith and Margot Asquith will live as one of the prettiest love stories in all literature.

Dorothy Parker 1893–1967: review of Margot Asquith's *Lay Sermons*; in *New Yorker* 22 October 1927

25 JUDGE: You are extremely offensive, young man.
SMITH: As a matter of fact, we both are, and the only difference between us is that I am trying to be, and you can't help it.

F. E. Smith 1872–1930: Lord Birkenhead *Earl of Birkenhead* (1933)

On being approached by the secretary of the Athenaeum, which he had been in the habit of using as a convenience on the way to his office:

26 Good God, do you mean to say this place is a club?

F. E. Smith 1872–1930: attributed

27 Mr. Welles's Brutus is like an obstetrician who very seriously visits a lady in order to placate her nerves.

Mrs Patrick Campbell 1865–1940: of Orson Welles's production of *Julius Caesar*; Margot Peters *Mrs Pat* (1984)

28 Lillian Gish may be a charming person, but she is not Ophelia. She comes on stage as if she had been sent for to sew rings on the new curtains.

Mrs Patrick Campbell 1865–1940: Margot Peters *Mrs Pat* (1984)

29 [*The Sun Also Rises* is about] bullfighting, bullslinging, and bull—.

Zelda Fitzgerald 1900–47: Marion Meade *What Fresh Hell Is This?* (1988)

30 Ettie [Lady Desborough] is an ox: she will be made into Bovril when she dies.

Margot Asquith 1864–1945: Jeanne Mackenzie *Children of the Souls* (1986)

31 Lord Birkenhead is very clever but sometimes his brains go to his head.

Margot Asquith 1864–1945: in *Listener* 11 June 1953 'Margot Oxford' by Lady Violet Bonham Carter

32 The *t* is silent, as in *Harlow*.

Margot Asquith 1864–1945: to Jean Harlow, who had been mispronouncing her first name

Bishop Henson, who greatly disliked his dean, Welldon, was asked during a discussion of odd old sayings whether he had ever seen pigs in clover:

33 Well, no, not exactly—though I have seen the Dean of Durham in bed.

Herbert Hensley Henson 1863–1947: George Lyttelton letter to Rupert Hart-Davis, 29 November 1957

34 NANCY ASTOR: If I were your wife I would put poison in your coffee!
WINSTON CHURCHILL: And if I were your husband I would drink it.

Nancy Astor 1879–1964: Consuelo Vanderbilt Balsan *Glitter and Gold* (1952)

35 [Clement Attlee is] a modest man who has a good deal to be modest about.

Winston Churchill 1874–1965: in *Chicago Sunday Tribune Magazine of Books* 27 June 1954

36 Every other inch a gentleman.

Rebecca West 1892–1983: of Michael Arlen; Victoria Glendinning *Rebecca West* (1987)

37 The truckman, the trashman and the policeman on the block may call me Alice but you may not.

Alice Roosevelt Longworth 1884–1980: to Senator Joseph McCarthy; Michael Teague *Mrs. L* (1981)

38 Some men are born mediocre, some men achieve mediocrity, and some men have mediocrity thrust upon them. With Major Major it had been all three.

Joseph Heller 1923– : *Catch-22* (1961)

39 I didn't know he'd been knighted. I knew he'd been doctored.

Thomas Beecham 1879–1961: on Malcolm Sargent's knighthood; attributed

40 Such cruel glasses.

Frankie Howerd 1922–92: of Robin Day; in *That Was The Week That Was* (BBC television series, from 1963)

41 I married beneath me, all women do.

Nancy Astor 1879–1964: in *Dictionary of National Biography* 1961–1970 (1981)

42 BESSIE BRADDOCK: Winston, you're drunk. CHURCHILL: Bessie, you're ugly. But tomorrow I shall be sober.

Winston Churchill 1874–1965: an exchange with the Labour MP Bessie Braddock; J. L. Lane (ed.) *Sayings of Churchill* (1992)

43 A sheep in sheep's clothing.

Winston Churchill 1874–1965: of Clement Attlee; Lord Home *The Way the Wind Blows* (1976)

44 The majority of the members of the Irish parliament are professional politicians, in the sense that otherwise they would not be given jobs minding mice at crossroads.

Flann O'Brien 1911–66: *The Hair of the Dogma* (1977)

45 Guido Natso is natso guido.

Dorothy Parker 1893–1967: Ned Sherrin *Cutting Edge* (1984); attributed

To Clare Boothe Luce, who had stood aside for her saying, 'Age before Beauty':
46 Pearls before swine.

Dorothy Parker 1893–1967: R. E. Drennan *Wit's End* (1973)

47 I never forget a face, but in your case I'll be glad to make an exception.

Groucho Marx 1895–1977: Leo Rosten *People I have Loved, Known or Admired* (1970) 'Groucho'

48 Diana Rigg is built like a brick mausoleum with insufficient flying buttresses.

John Simon 1925– : review of *Abelard and Heloise* in 1970; Diana Rigg *No Turn Unstoned* (1982)

49 Frazier is so ugly that he should donate his face to the US Bureau of Wild Life.

Muhammad Ali 1942– : in *Guardian* 23 December 1972 'Sports Quotes of the Year'

50 He played too much football without a helmet.

Lyndon Baines Johnson 1908–73: of Gerald Ford; Denys Cook *Presidents of the USA* (1981)

51 So dumb he can't fart and chew gum at the same time.

Lyndon Baines Johnson 1908–73: of Gerald Ford; Richard Reeves *A Ford, not a Lincoln* (1975)

On being criticized by Geoffrey Howe:
52 Like being savaged by a dead sheep.

Denis Healey 1917– : speech, House of Commons 14 June 1978

53 ERIC: Philippa happens to be very good with children.
HELEN: Presumably why she lives with you.

Alan Ayckbourn 1939– : *Ten Times Table* (1979)

54 He's thick enough to start a timber yard but he moves like the clappers.

Alan Ayckbourn 1939– : *Sisterly Feelings* (1981)

55 She's all right to look at but intellectually I don't reckon she can tell her fishcakes from her falsies.

Alan Ayckbourn 1939– : *Sisterly Feelings* (1981)

56 Never strike anyone so old, small, or weak that verbal abuse would have sufficed.

P. J. O'Rourke 1947– : *Modern Manners* (1984)

57 'With respect, Prime Minister, I think you should know that the DES will react with some caution to this rather novel proposal.' This was the language of war! Humphrey had all guns blazing. I've never heard such abusive language from him.

Jonathan Lynn 1943– and **Anthony Jay** 1930– : *Yes Prime Minister* vol. 2 (1987)

58 The 'g' is silent—the only thing about her that is.

Julie Burchill 1960– : of Camille Paglia; in *The Spectator* 16 January 1992

59 I used to think it a pity that her mother rather than she had not thought of birth control.

Muriel Spark 1918– : of Marie Stopes; *Curriculum Vitae* (1992)

60 If you say a modern celebrity is an adulterer, a pervert and a drug addict, all it means is that you've read his autobiography.

P. J. O'Rourke 1947– : *Give War a Chance* (1992)

61 This little flower, this delicate little beauty, this cream puff, is supposed to be beyond personal criticism…He is simply a shiver looking for a spine to run up.

Paul Keating 1944– : of John Hewson, the Australian Liberal leader; in *Ned Sherrin in his Anecdotage* (1993)

62 I decided the worst thing you can call Paul Keating, quite frankly, is Paul Keating.

John Hewson 1946– : the Australian Liberal leader on the Labour Prime Minister; Michael Gordon *A Question of Leadership* (1993)

63 Littlejohn, who in the farmyard of humanity would surely occupy a sty.

Matthew Norman: of a TV talk show host; television review in *Evening Standard* 11 June 1994

Intelligence and Intellectuals See also *The Mind*

1 But—Oh! ye lords of ladies intellectual,
Inform us truly, have they not hen-pecked you all?

Lord Byron 1788–1824: *Don Juan* (1819–24)

2 I have nothing to declare except my genius.

Oscar Wilde 1854–1900: at the New York Custom House; Frank Harris *Oscar Wilde* (1918)

3 Genius is one per cent inspiration, ninety-nine per cent perspiration.

Thomas Alva Edison 1847–1931: said *c*.1903; in *Harper's Monthly Magazine* September 1932

4 Men of genius are so few that they ought to atone for their fewness by being at any rate ubiquitous.

Max Beerbohm 1872–1956: letter to W. B. Yeats, 11 July 1911

5 No one in this world, so far as I know—and I have searched the records for years, and employed agents to help me—has ever lost money by underestimating the intelligence of the great masses of the plain people.

H. L. Mencken 1880–1956: in *Chicago Tribune* 19 September 1926

6 What is a highbrow? He is a man who has found something more interesting than women.

Edgar Wallace 1875–1932: in *New York Times* 24 January 1932

7 'Jeeves is a wonder.'
'A marvel.'
'What a brain.'
'Size nine-and-a-quarter, I should say.'
'He eats a lot of fish.'

P. G. Wodehouse 1881–1975: *Thank You, Jeeves* (1934)

8 'Well, I think you're a pig.'
'A pig, maybe, but a shrewd, levelheaded pig. I wouldn't touch the project with a bargepole.'

P. G. Wodehouse 1881–1975: *The Code of the Woosters* (1938)

9 Cleverness is a quality that, in architecture no less than in life, we have always been notorious for regarding with ill-concealed dislike.

Osbert Lancaster 1908–80: *Pillar to Post* (1938)

10 With the thoughts I'd be thinkin'
I could be another Lincoln,
If I only had a brain.

E. Y. Harburg 1898–1981: 'If I Only Had a Brain' (1939)

11 Zip! Walter Lippman wasn't brilliant today,
Zip! Will Saroyan ever write a great play?
Zip! I was reading Schopenhauer last night.
Zip! And I think that Schopenhauer was right!

Lorenz Hart 1895–1943: 'Zip' (1940), satirizing the intellectual pretensions of Gypsy Rose Lee

12 To the man-in-the-street, who, I'm sorry to say,
Is a keen observer of life,
The word 'Intellectual' suggests straight away
A man who's untrue to his wife.

W. H. Auden 1907–73: *New Year Letter* (1941)

Replying to Oliver St John Gogarty's suggestion that to recognize their own immortality during their lifetime was an attribute of great artists:

13 What about Marie Corelli gliding down the Avon in a gondola with her parasol?

George Bernard Shaw 1856–1950: Ulick O'Connor *Oliver St John Gogarty* (1964)

14 A genius. An I.Q. of 170. Same as her weight.

Neil Simon 1927– : *Come Blow Your Horn* (1961)

15 You can persuade a man to believe almost anything provided he is clever enough, but it is much more difficult to persuade someone less clever.

Tom Stoppard 1937- :
Professional Foul (1978)

16 I know I've got a degree. Why does that mean I have to spend my life with intellectuals? I've got a life-saving certificate but I don't spend my evenings diving for a rubber brick with my pyjamas on.

Victoria Wood 1953- : *Mens Sana in Thingummy Doodah* (1990)

17 Bush had also spent some time actually conversing with Quayle; it is impossible to believe that this fine, upstanding, well-read Yale graduate would not have noticed that Quayle's membership in the Great Books Club seemed to have lapsed after that initial ten-day introductory offer.

Joe Queenan: *Imperial Caddy* (1992)

Invective See *Insults and Invective*

Ireland and the Irish See also *Countries and Peoples, Places*

Denying that he was Irish:
1 Because a man is born in a stable, that does not make him a horse.

Duke of Wellington 1769–1852: Paul Johnson (ed.) *The Oxford Book of Political Anecdotes* (1986)

2 An Irishman's heart is nothing but his imagination.

George Bernard Shaw 1856–1950: *John Bull's Other Island* (1907)

3 The Irish, he says, don't care for clean government; they want Irish government.

Stephen Leacock 1869–1944: *Arcadian Adventures with the Idle Rich* (1914)

4 Lady Conyngham is giving them all lunch at Slane for a visit to Newgrange, which is described as a pre-Christian cemetery, but this would be misleading except to us who know that the suggestion of subsequent Christianity is unfounded.

Oliver St John Gogarty 1878–1957: letter to Lady Leslie about the guests for the Taillteann Games, 1924; Ulick O'Connor *Oliver St John Gogarty* (1964)

5 Gladstone...spent his declining years trying to guess the answer to the Irish Question; unfortunately whenever he was getting warm, the Irish secretly changed the Question.

W. C. Sellar 1898–1951 and **R. J. Yeatman** 1898–1968: *1066 and All That* (1930)

On being asked why J. P. Mahaffy had chosen to stay in Dublin:
6 He was Provost. He was knighted. What Fellow in Oxford can be knighted without being benighted first?

Oliver St John Gogarty 1878–1957: Ulick O'Connor *Oliver St John Gogarty* (1964)

7 Where would the Irish be without someone to be Irish at?

Elizabeth Bowen 1899–1973: *The House in Paris* (1935)

8 [In Ireland] they're working hard to restore the old Gaelic. If they're not careful, they'll learn to speak it and then they'll be sorry.

Stephen Leacock 1869–1944: *The Boy I Left Behind Me* (1947)

9 We rose to bring about Eutopia,
But all we got was Dev's myopia.

Oliver St John Gogarty
1878–1957: letter to James
Montgomery; Ulick O'Connor *Oliver St
John Gogarty* (1964)

10 I put myself in the position of St Patrick. What would he
say to it? When he visited Ireland, there was no word in
the Irish language to express sobriety.

Oliver St John Gogarty
1878–1957: speech in the Irish Senate;
Ulick O'Connor *Oliver St John Gogarty*
(1964)

11 PAT: He was an Anglo-Irishman.
MEG: In the blessed name of God what's that?
PAT: A Protestant with a horse.

Brendan Behan 1923–64: *Hostage*
(1958)

12 I founded the Rathmines branch of the Gaelic League.
Having nothing to say, I thought at that time that it was
important to revive a distant language in which
absolutely nothing could be said.

Flann O'Brien 1911–66: *The Best of
Myles* (1968)

13 Our ancestors believed in magic, prayers, trickery,
browbeating and bullying: I think it would be fair to sum
that list up as 'Irish politics'.

Flann O'Brien 1911–66: *The Hair of
the Dogma* (1977)

14 He'd...settled into a life of Guinness, sarcasm and late
late nights, the kind of life that American academics
think real Dubliners lead.

Joseph O'Connor 1963– :
Cowboys and Indians (1991)

Journalism See *News and Journalism*

Language and Languages See also *Words*

1 Egad I think the interpreter is the hardest to be
understood of the two!

Richard Brinsley Sheridan
1751–1816: *The Critic* (1779)

2 'Do you spell it with a "V" or a "W"?' inquired the
judge. 'That depends upon the taste and fancy of the
speller, my Lord,' replied Sam [Weller].

Charles Dickens 1812–70: *Pickwick
Papers* (1837)

On being told there was no English word equivalent to sensibilité:
3 Yes we have. Humbug.

Lord Palmerston 1784–1865:
attributed

4 They spell it Vinci and pronounce it Vinchy; foreigners
always spell better than they pronounce.

Mark Twain 1835–1910: *The
Innocents Abroad* (1869)

5 Speak in French when you can't think of the English for
a thing.

Lewis Carroll 1832–98: *Through
the Looking-Glass* (1872)

6 Though 'Bother it' I may
Occasionally say,
I never use a big, big D—

W. S. Gilbert 1836–1911: *HMS
Pinafore* (1878)

7 I once heard a Californian student in Heidelberg say, in
one of his calmest moods, that he would rather decline
two drinks than one German adjective.

Mark Twain 1835–1910: *A Tramp
Abroad* (1880)

8 When you're lying awake with a dismal headache, and
repose is taboo'd by anxiety,
I conceive you may use any language you choose to
indulge in, without impropriety.

W. S. Gilbert 1836–1911: *Iolanthe*
(1882)

9 Good intentions are invariably ungrammatical.

Oscar Wilde 1854–1900: attributed

10 Is there no Latin word for Tea? Upon my soul, if I had known that I would have let the vulgar stuff alone.

Hilaire Belloc 1870–1953: 'On Tea' (1908)

On the first-person plural pronoun:
11 Only presidents, editors, and people with tapeworms have the right to use the editorial 'we'.

Mark Twain 1835–1910: attributed

12 Enormous romping vitality and a love for the beauty of language in which one would believe more thoroughly if she did not so frequently split her infinitives neatly down the middle.

Rebecca West 1892–1983: of the novelist Marjorie Bowen in 1915; *The Young Rebecca* (1982)

13 Remember that you are a human being with a soul and the divine gift of articulate speech: that your native language is the language of Shakespeare and Milton and The Bible; and don't sit there crooning like a bilious pigeon.

George Bernard Shaw 1856–1950: *Pygmalion* (1916)

14 The minute a phrase becomes current it becomes an apology for not thinking accurately to the end of the sentence.

Oliver Wendell Holmes Jr. 1841–1935: letter to Harold Laski, 2 July 1917

15 An unalterable and unquestioned law of the musical world required that the German text of French operas sung by Swedish artists should be translated into Italian for the clearer understanding of English-speaking audiences.

Edith Wharton 1862–1937: *The Age of Innocence* (1920)

16 The slang with which Mr Simpson now and then defiles his pen is probably slang which he heard in his cradle and believed in his innocence to be English.

A. E. Housman 1859–1936: in *Cambridge Review* 1923

17 'Basta!' his master replied, with all the brilliant glibness of the Berlitz-school.

Ronald Firbank 1886–1926: *The Flower Beneath the Foot* (1923)

18 My spelling is Wobbly. It's good spelling but it Wobbles, and the letters get in the wrong places.

A. A. Milne 1882–1956: *Winnie-the-Pooh* (1926)

19 I hear it's the Hebrew in Heaven, sir. Spanish is seldom spoken.

Ronald Firbank 1886–1926: *Concerning the Eccentricities of Cardinal Pirelli* (1926)

20 Weep not for little Léonie
Abducted by a French Marquis!
Though loss of honour was a wrench
Just think how it's improved her French.

Harry Graham 1874–1936: 'Compensation' (1930)

21 Since they are not in constant attendance at the cinema their speech is uncorrupted by the slang or accent of Chicago.

A. P. Herbert 1890–1971: *Misleading Cases* (1935)

22 Backward ran sentences until reeled the mind.

Wolcott Gibbs 1902–58: in *New Yorker* 28 November 1936 'Time... Fortune...Life...Luce' (satirizing the style of *Time* magazine)

23 KENNETH: If you're so hot, you'd better tell me how to say she has ideas above her station.
BRIAN: Oh, yes, I forgot. It's fairly easy, old boy. *Elle a des idées au-dessus de sa gare.*

Terence Rattigan 1911–77: *French without Tears* (1937)

KENNETH: You can't do it like that. You can't say *au-dessus de sa gare*. It isn't that sort of station.

Dennis Wheatley had told Humbert Wolfe that his novels had been translated into 'every European language except one':
24 HUMBERT WOLFE: I can't think which.
PAMELA FRANKAU: English!

Pamela Frankau 1908–67: James Agate diary 10 April 1938

25 'Feather-footed through the plashy fen passes the questing vole'...'Yes,' said the Managing Editor. 'That must be good style.'

Evelyn Waugh 1903–66: *Scoop* (1938)

26 JOSEPHINE BAKER: Donnez-moi une tasse de café, s'il vous plait.
MARY CAMPBELL: Honey, talk out of the mouth you was born with.

Mary Campbell: exchange between Josephine Baker, who had moved to France from America, and who was staying with Lorenz Hart's parents, and Mary Campbell, who was the Harts' cook; Samuel Marx and Jan Clayton *Rodgers and Hart* (1975)

27 Albanian...a language that sounded comic with all its pffts, pees, wees, pings and fitts.

Cecil Beaton 1904–80: diary August 1940

28 The subjunctive mood is in its death throes, and the best thing to do is to put it out of its misery as soon as possible.

W. Somerset Maugham 1874–1965: *A Writer's Notebook* (1949) written in 1941

On speaking French fluently rather than correctly:
29 It's nerve and brass, *audace* and disrespect, and leaping-before-you-look and what-the-hellism, that must be developed.

Diana Cooper 1892–1986: Philip Ziegler *Diana Cooper* (1981)

30 Would you convey my compliments to the purist who reads your proofs and tell him or her that I write in a sort of broken-down patois which is something like the way a Swiss waiter talks, and that when I split an infinitive, God damn it, I split it so it will stay split.

Raymond Chandler 1888–1959: letter to Edward Weeks, 18 January 1947

31 This is the sort of English up with which I will not put.

Winston Churchill 1874–1965: Ernest Gowers *Plain Words* (1948) 'Troubles with Prepositions'

32 Where in this small-talking world can I find
A longitude with no platitude?

Christopher Fry 1907– : *The Lady's not for Burning* (1949)

33 Orchestras only need to be sworn at, and a German is consequently at an advantage with them, as English profanity, except in America, has not gone beyond the limited terminology of perdition.

George Bernard Shaw 1856–1950: Harold Schonberg *The Great Conductors* (1967)

34   I hope
I've done nothing so monosyllabic as to cheat,
A spade is never so merely a spade as the word
Spade would imply.

Christopher Fry 1907– : *Venus Observed* (1950)

35 There even are places where English completely disappears.
In America, they haven't used it for years!
Why can't the English teach their children how to speak?

Alan Jay Lerner 1918–86: 'Why Can't the English?' (1956)

When Khrushchev began banging his shoe on the desk:

36 Perhaps we could have a translation, I could not quite follow.

Harold Macmillan 1894–1986: during his speech to the United Nations, 29 September 1960

37 Waiting for the German verb is surely the ultimate thrill.

Flann O'Brien 1911–66: *The Hair of the Dogma* (1977)

38 It is worth remembering that if Irish were to die completely, the standard of English here, both in the spoken and written word, would sink to a level probably as low as that obtaining in England and it would stop there only because it could go no lower.

Flann O'Brien 1911–66: *The Best of Myles* (1968)

39 Don't swear, boy. It shows a lack of vocabulary.

Alan Bennett 1934– : *Forty Years On* (1969)

40 The sentence, that dignified entity with subject and predicate, is shortly to be made illegal. It probably already is in Torremolinos.

Alan Bennett 1934– : *Getting On* (1972)

41 It has never occurred to Anderson that one foreign language can be translated into another. He assumes that every strange tongue exists only by virtue of its not being English.

Tom Stoppard 1937– : *Where Are They Now?* (1973)

42 Anglish is what we don' know
Spanglish is langlish we know.

Dorothy Fields 1905–74: 'Spanglish' (1973)

43 Sentence structure is innate but whining is acquired.

Woody Allen 1935– : 'Remembering Needleman' (1976)

44 Even now a team of linguists is at work translating Don Revie's writings on the game [football] from the original gibberish into Arabic.

Michael Parkinson 1935– : in *Guardian* 24 December 1977 'Sports Quotes of the Year'

45 Linguistic analysis. A lot of chaps pointing out that we don't always mean what we say, even when we manage to say what we meant.

Tom Stoppard 1937– : *Professional Foul* (1978)

46 The letter is written in the tongue of the Think Tanks, a language more difficult to master than Basque or Navaho and spoken only where strategic thinkers clump together in Institutes.

Russell Baker 1925– : in *New York Times* 8 April 1981

47 There's no such thing as a foreign language. The world is just filled with people who grunt and squeak instead of speaking sensibly. But since it's impossible to figure out what French people are saying, we'll never know for sure.

P. J. O'Rourke 1947– : *Modern Manners* (1984)

48 Save the gerund and screw the whale.

Tom Stoppard 1937– : *The Real Thing* (1988 rev. ed.)

49 Lyrically passionate writing should always be resisted, especially by the writer. A real idea slows you down, by demanding that you make yourself as plain as possible.

Clive James 1939– : *The Dreaming Swimmer* (1992)

50 Every sentence he [George Bush] manages to utter scatters its component parts like pond water from a verb chasing its own tail.

Clive James 1939– : *The Dreaming Swimmer* (1992)

51 Stars, Charlie had noticed before, always spoke slowly. Listening to Warren Beatty being interviewed was like waiting for speech to finish being invented.

Ray Connally: *Shadows on a Wall* (1994)

Last Words See also *Death*

1 This is no time for making new enemies.

Voltaire 1694–1778: on being asked to renounce the Devil, on his deathbed; attributed

2 They couldn't hit an elephant at this distance.

John Sedgwick d. 1864: immediately prior to being killed by enemy fire at the battle of Spotsylvania in the American Civil War, May 1864; Robert E. Denney *The Civil War Years* (1992)

3 Die, my dear Doctor, that's the last thing I shall do!

Lord Palmerston 1784–1865: E. Latham *Famous Sayings and their Authors* (1904)

4 I will not go down to posterity talking bad grammar.

Benjamin Disraeli 1804–81: while correcting proofs of his last Parliamentary speech, 31 March 1881; Robert Blake *Disraeli* (1966)

5 No it is better not. She would only ask me to take a message to Albert.

Benjamin Disraeli 1804–81: near death, declining a proposed visit from Queen Victoria; Robert Blake *Disraeli* (1966)

6 If this is dying, then I don't think much of it.

Lytton Strachey 1880–1932: Michael Holroyd *Lytton Strachey* (1967)

On his deathbed in 1936, when someone remarked 'Cheer up, your Majesty, you will soon be at Bognor again':
7 Bugger Bognor.

George V 1865–1936: Kenneth Rose *King George V* (1983); attributed

Lady Eldon had suggested that she should read to him from his own New Testament:
8 No...Awfully jolly of you to suggest it, though.

Ronald Knox 1888–1957: Evelyn Waugh *Life of Ronald Knox*

9 The present civilization is riddled by the do-ers and the done-by. Do you know what George Sand said as she lay dying? *Laissez verdurer. Idiots* suppose that she was giving directions about her grave.

Sylvia Townsend Warner 1893–1978: letter 21 February 1972

The Law and Lawyers See also *Crime and Punishment*

1 The first thing we do, let's kill all the lawyers.

William Shakespeare 1564–1616: *Henry VI, Part 2* (1592)

2 Here [in Paris] they hang a man first, and try him afterwards.

Molière 1622–73: *Monsieur de Pourceaugnac* (1670)

3 Johnson observed, that 'he did not care to speak ill of any man behind his back, but he believed the gentleman was an *attorney.*'

Samuel Johnson 1709–84: James Boswell *Life of Samuel Johnson* (1791) 1770

The judge Sir James Mansfield had suggested that the Court might sit on Good Friday:

4 If your Lordship pleases. But your Lordship will be the first judge who has done so since Pontius Pilate.

William Davy d. 1780: Edward Parry *The Seven Lamps of Advocacy* (1923); the Court did *not* sit

5 Poor fellow, I suppose he fancied he was on the bench.

Richard Brinsley Sheridan 1751–1816: on hearing that a judge had slept through his play *Pizarro;* Walter Jerrold *Bon-Mots* (1893)

6 'Little to do, and plenty to get, I suppose?' said Sergeant Buzfuz, with jocularity. 'Oh, quite enough to get, sir, as the soldier said ven they ordered him three hundred and fifty lashes,' replied Sam. 'You must not tell us what the soldier, or any other man, said, sir,' interposed the judge; 'it's not evidence.'

Charles Dickens 1812–70: *Pickwick Papers* (1837)

7 Battledore and shuttlecock's a wery good game, vhen you an't the shuttlecock and two lawyers the battledores, in which case it gets too excitin' to be pleasant.

Charles Dickens 1812–70: *Pickwick Papers* (1837)

8 'If the law supposes that,' said Mr Bumble... 'the law is a ass—a idiot.'

Charles Dickens 1812–70: *Oliver Twist* (1838)

9 Whatever fees we [Judge Logan and I] earn at a distance, if not paid *before,* we notice we never hear of after the work is done. We therefore, are growing a little sensitive on the point.

Abraham Lincoln 1809–65: letter 2 November 1842

10 Some circumstantial evidence is very strong, as when you find a trout in the milk.

Henry David Thoreau 1817–62: diary 11 November 1850

11 The one great principle of the English law is, to make business for itself.

Charles Dickens 1812–70: *Bleak House* (1853)

12 Laws and institutions are constantly tending to gravitate. Like clocks, they must be occasionally cleansed, and wound up, and set to true time.

Henry Ward Beecher 1813–87: *Life Thoughts* (1858)

13 I always approach Judge [Lemuel] Shaw as a savage approaches his fetish, knowing that he is ugly but feeling that he is great.

Rufus Choate 1799–1859: Van Wyck Brooks *The Flowering of New England* (1936)

14 The lawyer's vacation is the space between the question put to a witness and his answer!

Rufus Choate 1799–1859: *Works of Rufus Choate* (1862)

15 A jury too frequently have at least one member, more ready to hang the panel than to hang the traitor.

Abraham Lincoln 1809–65: letter 12 June 1863

Bethell affected not to recognize Lord Campbell, the newly appointed Lord Chancellor, whom he encountered enveloped in a huge fur coat:

16 I beg your pardon, My Lord. I mistook you for the Great Seal.

Richard Bethell 1800–73: J. B. Atlay *Victorian Chancellors* (1908)

17 When I was a lad I served a term
As office boy to an Attorney's firm.
I cleaned the windows and I swept the floor,

W. S. Gilbert 1836–1911: *HMS Pinafore* (1878)

And I polished up the handle of the big front door.
I polished up that handle so carefullee
That now I am the Ruler of the Queen's Navee!

18 What chance has the ignorant, uncultivated liar against
the educated expert? What chance have I...against
a lawyer?

Mark Twain 1835–1910: 'On the
Decay of the Art of Lying' (1882)

19 The Law is the true embodiment
Of everything that's excellent.
It has no kind of fault or flaw,
And I, my Lords, embody the Law.

W. S. Gilbert 1836–1911: *Iolanthe*
(1882)

20 The only regret she [Queen Victoria] feels about the
decision is that so wicked a woman should escape by
a mere legal quibble! The law is not a moral profession
she must say.

Queen Victoria 1819–1901: on the
commutation of Mrs Maybrick's death
sentence; letter to Sir Henry Ponsonby,
22 August 1889

21 However harmless a thing is, if the law forbids it most
people will think it wrong.

W. Somerset Maugham
1874–1965: *A Writer's Notebook* (1949)
written in 1896

22 There is a little shilling book—ninepence for cash—called
Every Man his own Lawyer. If my friends had only sent it
to me, or even read it themselves, all this trouble,
expense, and worry would have been saved.

Oscar Wilde 1854–1900: on the
settlement to be made with his wife;
letter to Robert Ross from Reading
Prison, 1 April 1897

23 To succeed in other trades, capacity must be shown; in
the law, concealment of it will do.

Mark Twain 1835–1910: *Following
the Equator* (1897)

24 Judges commonly are elderly men, and are more likely to
hate at sight any analysis to which they are not
accustomed, and which disturbs repose of mind, than to
fall in love with novelties.

Oliver Wendell Holmes Jr.
1841–1935: in *Harvard Law Review*
1899

25 I noticed the burst of applause when Judge O'Brien got
up to speak, and I knew that he was either an
exceedingly able man or else that a lot of you practise in
his court...One speaker got up here and urged you to be
honest, and there was no response.

Mark Twain 1835–1910: speech to
Society of Medical Jurisprudence
8 March 1902

*When Knox was Attorney General Theodore Roosevelt requested
a legal justification for his acquisition of the Panama Canal:*

26 Oh, Mr President, do not let so great an achievement
suffer from any taint of legality.

Philander C. Knox 1853–1921:
Tyler Dennett *John Hay: From Poetry
to Politics*

27 Whenever a copyright law is to be made or altered, then
the idiots assemble.

Mark Twain 1835–1910: Notebook
23 May 1903

28 As it was once put to me, always remember that [as
a barrister] you are in the position of a cabman on the
rank, bound to answer the first hail.

Ralph Neville: in *The Times*
16 June 1913

29 I don't know as I want a lawyer to tell me what I cannot
do. I hire him to tell me how to do what I want to do.

J. P. Morgan 1837–1913: Ida M.
Tarbell *The Life of Elbert H. Gary*
(1925)

30 Courtroom—A place where Jesus Christ and Judas
Iscariot would be equals, with the betting odds in favour
of Judas.

H. L. Mencken 1880–1956:
'Sententiae' (1916)

31 Injustice is relatively easy to bear; what stings is justice.

H. L. Mencken 1880–1956:
Prejudices, Third Series (1922)

32 I have always noticed that any time a man can't come and settle with you without bringing his lawyer, why, look out for him.

Will Rogers 1879–1935: 'Slipping the Lariat Over' 14 January 1923

33 Of course, people are getting smarter nowadays; they are letting lawyers instead of their conscience be their guides.

Will Rogers 1879–1935: 'How to Stop the Bootleggin'' 8 April 1923

34 The Polis as Polis, in this city, is Null an' Void!

Sean O'Casey 1880–1964: *Juno and the Paycock* (1925)

35 [A jury consists of] twelve men of limited information and intelligence, chosen precisely because of their lack of intellectual resilience.

H. L. Mencken 1880–1956: *Notes on Democracy* (1926)

36 JUDGE WILLIS: Mr Smith, have you ever heard of a saying by Bacon—the great Bacon—that youth and discretion are ill-wed companions?
SMITH: Indeed I have, your Honour; and has your Honour ever heard of a saying by Bacon—the great Bacon—that a much talking Judge is like an ill-tuned cymbal?

F. E. Smith 1872–1930: Lord Birkenhead *F. E.* (1959)

37 JUDGE: I have read your case, Mr Smith, and I am no wiser now than I was when I started.
SMITH: Possibly not, My Lord, but far better informed.

F. E. Smith 1872–1930: Lord Birkenhead *F. E.* (1959)

38 Let's find out what everyone is doing,
And then stop everyone from doing it.

A. P. Herbert 1890–1971: 'Let's Stop Somebody from Doing Something' (1930)

39 Often he would tell me of his triumphs and I must have been very young when he said, 'Remarkable win today, old boy. Only evidence of adultery we had was a pair of footprints upside down on the dashboard of an Austin Seven parked in Hampstead Garden Suburb.'

Clifford Mortimer: John Mortimer *Clinging to the Wreckage* (1982)

40 Equity does not demand that its suitors shall have led blameless lives.

Louis Brandeis 1856–1941: in *Loughran v. Loughran* 1934

41 An illustration which should be intelligible to the most bovine member of the jury, and may even penetrate to the slumbering consciousness of the fourth gentleman from the left in the back row.

A. P. Herbert 1890–1971: *Misleading Cases* (1935)

42 In view of the delicate character of the question, I propose, with your permission, to write it down in invisible ink and hand it to the witness in a sealed box.

A. P. Herbert 1890–1971: *Misleading Cases* (1935)

43 One of those fogs of ambiguity so dear to the laws of England.

A. P. Herbert 1890–1971: *Misleading Cases* (1935)

44 The general mass, if they consider the law at all, regard it as they regard some monster at the Zoo.

A. P. Herbert 1890–1971: *Misleading Cases* (1935)

45 We find for the defendant, much as we dislike him.

A. P. Herbert 1890–1971: *Misleading Cases* (1935)

46 Went down and spoke at some lawyers' meeting last
night. They didn't think much of my little squib
yesterday about driving the shysters out of their
profession. They seemed to kinder doubt just who would
have to leave.

Will Rogers 1879–1935: 'Mr. Rogers
is Hob Nobbing With Leaders of the
Bar'

An attempt is made to write a cheque on a cow:
47 'Was the cow crossed?'
'No, your worship, it was an open cow.'

A. P. Herbert 1890–1971:
Uncommon Law (1935) 'The
Negotiable Cow'

On hearing that his son John wished to become a writer:
48 Have some consideration for your unfortunate wife.
You'll be sitting around the house all day wearing
a dressing-gown, brewing tea and stumped for words.
You'll be far better off in the law. That's the great thing
about the law, it gets you out of the house.

Clifford Mortimer: John
Mortimer *Clinging to the Wreckage*
(1982)

49 Mr Justice Cocklecarrot began the hearing of a very
curious case yesterday. A Mrs Tasker is accused of
continually ringing the doorbell of a Mrs Renton, and
then, when the door is opened, pushing a dozen red-
bearded dwarfs into the hall and leaving them there.

J. B. Morton 1893–1975: *Diet of
Thistles* (1938)

50 Reform! Reform! Aren't things bad enough already?

Mr Justice Astbury 1860–1939:
attributed

51 When I make a mistake, it's a beaut.

Fiorello H. La Guardia
1882–1947: on his appointment of
Herbert O'Brien as a judge; William
Manners *Patience and Fortitude* (1976)

52 The art of cross-examination is not the art of examining
crossly. It's the art of leading the witness through a line
of propositions he agrees to until he's forced to agree to
the *one fatal question*.

Clifford Mortimer: John
Mortimer *Clinging to the Wreckage*
(1982)

53 There's a lot of law at the end of a nightstick.

Grover A. Whalen 1886–1962:
Quentin Reynolds *Courtroom* (1950)

54 Sue me, sue me
Shoot bullets through me
I love you.

Frank Loesser 1910–69: 'Sue Me'
(1950)

55 I always feel that there should be some comfort derived
from any question from the bench. It is clear proof that
the inquiring Justice is not asleep.

Robert H. Jackson 1892–1954:
'Advocacy before the Supreme Court:
Suggestions for Effective Presentation'
(1951)

Of Judges Learned and Augustus Hand:
56 Quote Learned, and follow 'Gus'.

Robert H. Jackson 1892–1954:
Hershel Shanks *The Art and Craft of
Judging* (1968)

57 The penalty for laughing in the courtroom is six months
in jail: if it were not for this penalty, the jury would
never hear the evidence.

H. L. Mencken 1880–1956:
Andrew and Jonathan Roth *Devil's
Advocates* (1989)

58 Yes, I could have been a judge but I never had the Latin,
never had the Latin for the judging, I just never had

Peter Cook 1937–95: *Beyond the
Fringe* (1961 revue)

sufficient of it to get through the rigorous judging exams.
They're noted for their rigour. People come staggering
out saying, 'My God, what a rigorous exam'—and so
I became a miner instead.

59 The sound of tireless voices is the price we pay for the
right to hear the music of our own opinions.

Adlai Stevenson 1900–65: *The
Guide to American Law* (1984)

60 Policemen, like red squirrels, must be protected.

Joe Orton 1933–67: *Loot* (1967)

61 This contract is so one-sided that I am surprised to find it
written on both sides of the paper.

Lord Evershed 1899–1966: Lord
Denning *Closing Chapter* (1983)

62 There are a lot of mediocre judges and people and
lawyers, and they are entitled to a little representation
[on the Supreme Court], aren't they? We can't have all
Brandeises, Frankfurters, and Cardozos.

Roman L. Hruska 1904– : in *New
York Times* 17 March 1970

63 No brilliance is needed in the law. Nothing but common
sense, and relatively clean finger nails.

John Mortimer 1923– : *A Voyage
Round My Father* (1971)

64 I get paid for seeing that my clients have every break the
law allows. I have knowingly defended a number of
guilty men. But the guilty never escape unscathed. My
fees are sufficient punishment for anyone.

F. Lee Bailey 1933– : in *Los
Angeles Times* 9 January 1972

65 The Court's opinion will accomplish the seemingly
impossible feat of leaving this area of the law more
confused than it found it.

William H. Rehnquist 1924– :
dissenting opinion in *Roe v. Wade*
1973

66 Haldeman is the only man in America in this generation
who let his hair grow for a courtroom appearance.

Mary McGrory 1918– : on the
Watergate hearings; in *Washington
Star* 12 November 1974

67 'The building is named for the late Christopher Columbus
Langdell, who was the dean of Harvard Law School in
the late nineteenth century. Dean Langdell is best known
as the inventor of the Socratic method.'
David lowered his hand and looked sincerely at the
building.
'May he rot in hell,' David said.

Scott Turow 1949– : *One L* (1977)

68 Did you mail that cheque to the Judge?

Roy M. Cohn 1927–86: spoken to
an aide, at breakfast with Ned Sherrin,
1978

69 At last we have a woolsack on the Woolsack.

Norman St John Stevas 1929– :
on Lord Dilhorne's appointment as
Lord Chancellor; attributed

70 If you want to get ahead in this world get a lawyer—not
a book.

Fran Lebowitz 1946– : on self-
help books; *Social Studies* (1981)

71 No one has felt the full glory of a barrister's life who has
not, in wig and gown, been called to the podium in the
committee room of the House of Lords by an official in
full evening dress and, on a wet Monday morning,
lectured five elderly Law Lords in lounge suits on the
virtues of masturbation.

John Mortimer 1923– : *Clinging to
the Wreckage* (1982)

72 A British criminal trial is not primarily an investigation to discover the truth, although truth may sometimes be disinterred by chance.

John Mortimer 1923– : *Clinging to the Wreckage* (1982)

73 As a moth is drawn to the light, so is a litigant drawn to the United States. If he can only get his case into their courts, he stands to win a fortune. At no cost to himself; and at no risk of having to pay anything to the other side.

Lord Denning 1899– : *Smith Kline & French Laboratories Ltd. v. Bloch* 1983

74 Lawyers charge a fortune to handle a bond offering. You know what it takes to handle a bond offering? The mental capacities of a filing cabinet.

Jimmy Breslin 1929– : in *Legal Times* 17 January 1983

75 I don't want to know what the law is, I want to know who the judge is.

Roy M. Cohn 1927–86: in *New York Times Book Review* 3 April 1988

76 Legal writing is one of those rare creatures, like the rat and the cockroach, that would attract little sympathy even as an endangered species.

Richard Hyland 1949– : 'A Defense of Legal Writing' (1986)

77 When I'm sitting [on the Woolsack] I amuse myself by saying 'Bollocks!' *sotto voce* to the Bishops.

Lord Hailsham 1907– : in an interview; John Mortimer *Character Parts* (1986)

78 [Irritable judges] suffer from a bad case of premature adjudication.

John Mortimer 1923– : in *Listener* 22 January 1987

On being told to allow his client, Oliver North, to object for himself if he wished, at the Iran-Contra hearings:
79 I'm not a potted plant...I'm here as the lawyer. That's my job.

Brendan V. Sullivan 1942– : in *New York Times* 10 July 1987

On the award of £600,000 libel damages to Sonia Sutcliffe against Private Eye:
80 If this is justice, I am a banana.

Ian Hislop 1960– : in *Guardian* 25 May 1989

Question in a Christmas quiz:
81 Imagine you are the defence counsel for the late Robert Maxwell. Try and persuade a jury that your client is not megalomaniacally insane.

Stephen Fry 1957– : *Paperweight* (1992)

Leisure See *Work and Leisure*

Letters and Letter-writing

1 I have made this [letter] longer than usual, only because I have not had the time to make it shorter.

Blaise Pascal 1623–62: *Lettres Provinciales* (1657)

2 WITWOUD: Madam, do you pin up your hair with all your letters?
MILLAMANT: Only with those in verse, Mr Witwoud. I never pin up my hair with prose.

William Congreve 1670–1729: *The Way of the World* (1700)

3 I am not a cautious letter-writer and generally say what comes uppermost at the moment.

Lord Byron 1788–1824: letter to Mary Shelley, 9 October 1822

4 [Charles Lamb's] sayings are generally like women's letters; all the pith is in the postscript.

William Hazlitt 1778–1830: *Conversations of James Northcote* (1826–7)

5 Sir, My pa requests me to write to you, the doctors considering it doubtful whether he will ever recuvver the use of his legs which prevents his holding a pen.

Charles Dickens 1812–70: *Nicholas Nickleby* (1839)

Wilde had sent a letter on 'Fashion in Dress' to the Daily Telegraph, *but explained in a covering letter to the proprietor:*
6 I don't wish to sign my name, though I am afraid everybody will know who the writer is: one's style is one's signature always.

Oscar Wilde 1854–1900: letter 2 February 1891

Wilde had been greatly disappointed by Robert Louis Stevenson's Vailima Letters:
7 I see that romantic surroundings are the worst surroundings possible for a romantic writer. In Gower Street Stevenson could have written a new *Trois Mousquetaires*. In Samoa he wrote letters to *The Times* about Germans.

Oscar Wilde 1854–1900: letter to Robert Ross from Reading Prison, 6 April 1897

Circular sent out to forestall unwanted visitors:
8 Mr J. Ruskin is about to begin a work of great importance and therefore begs that in reference to calls and correspondence you will consider him dead for the next two months.

John Ruskin 1819–1900: attributed

9 The applicant may publish the songs so far as I am concerned, but I had rather you should tell her so, as I do not want to write letters to a lady whose name is Birdie.

A. E. Housman 1859–1936: letter to his publisher Grant Richards, 1 March 1904

Responding to a savage review by Rudolph Louis in Münchener Neueste Nachrich *7 February 1906:*
10 I am sitting in the smallest room of my house. I have your review before me. In a moment it will be behind me.

Max Reger 1873–1916: Nicolas Slonimsky *Lexicon of Musical Invective* (1953)

11 It is wonderful how much news there is when people write every other day; if they wait for a month, there is nothing that seems worth telling.

O. Douglas 1877–1948: *Penny Plain* (1920)

12 Dear 338171 (May I call you 338?).

Noël Coward 1899–1973: letter to T. E. Lawrence, 25 August 1930

13 Regarding yours, dear Mrs Worthington, of Wednesday the 23rd.

Noël Coward 1899–1973: 'Mrs Worthington' (1935)

Formula with which to return unsolicited manuscripts:
14 Mr James Agate regrets that he has no time to bother about the enclosed in which he has been greatly interested.

James Agate 1877–1947: diary 3 January 1936

15 I have no need of your God-damned sympathy. I only wish to be entertained by some of your grosser reminiscences.

Alexander Woollcott 1887–1943: letter to Rex O'Malley, 1942

16 Laura's repeated assurances to me that she had both replied to your letter and that she was about to do so are, I think, characteristic of a mind at bay.

S. J. Perelman 1904–79: 1948 letter 17 October 1948

17 The English social mill grinds slowly, it's all done with correspondence, and you can't find out people's phone numbers.

S. J. Perelman 1904–79: letter 13 December 1953

18 It would have been less heterodox
If he had put the letter in the letter-o-box.

Brian Brindley: the Babes-in-the-Wood discovering a letter pinned to a tree by Robin Hood, in an Oxford pantomime in 1953; Ned Sherrin *Cutting Edge* (1984)

19 A man seldom puts his authentic self into a letter. He writes it to amuse a friend or to get rid of a social or business obligation, which is to say, a nuisance.

H. L. Mencken 1880–1956: *Minority Report* (1956)

20 I go downstairs to get the mail…Nine press releases, four screening notices, two bills, an invitation to a party in honor of a celebrated heroin addict, a final disconnect notice from New York Telephone, and three hate letters from *Mademoiselle* readers.

Fran Lebowitz 1946– : *Metropolitan Life* (1978)

Libraries See also *Books*

1 What a sad want I am in of libraries, of books to gather facts from! Why is there not a Majesty's library in every county town? There is a Majesty's jail and gallows in every one.

Thomas Carlyle 1795–1881. diary 18 May 1832; J. A. Froude *Carlyle's Early Life* (1890)

2 Th' first thing to have in a libry is a shelf. Fr'm time to time this can be decorated with lithrachure. But th' shelf is th' main thing.

Finley Peter Dunne 1867–1936: *Mr Dooley Says* (1910)

3 'Our library,' said the president, 'two hundred thousand volumes!' 'Aye,' said the minister, 'a powerful heap of rubbish, I'll be bound!'

Stephen Leacock 1869–1944: *Arcadian Adventures with the Idle Rich* (1914)

4 Headnotes arranged vertically make a digest. Headnotes arranged horizontally make a textbook. Textbooks arranged alphabetically make an encyclopedia. Every few years some investigator has to disintegrate one of these works into its constituent atoms, add some more headnotes from recent decisions, stir well, and give us the latest book on the subject. And so law libraries grow.

Zechariah Chafee Jr. 1885–1957: in *Harvard Law Review* 1917

5 Mr Cobb took me into his library and showed me his books, of which he had a complete set.

Ring Lardner 1885–1933: R. E. Drennan *Wit's End* (1973)

6 There is nowhere in the world where sleep is so deep as in the libraries of the House of Commons.

Chips Channon 1897–1958: diary 16 December 1937

7 E. W. B. Nicholson [Bodley's Librarian] spending three days at the London Docks, watching outgoing ships, after losing a book from Bodley, which was afterwards discovered slightly out of place on the shelf.

Falconer Madan 1851–1935: J. A. Gere and John Sparrow (eds.) *Geoffrey Madan's Notebooks* (1981)

8 Those dreadful detective stories. Another corpse in the library this evening. Really, you know, too much of

Flann O'Brien 1911–66: *The Best of Myles* (1968)

a good thing. Fourth this week. No doubt trouble is
shortage of libraries.

9 REG: Yes, I thought you said you had a—librarians'
conference.
NORMAN: It's been cancelled.
REG: When?
NORMAN: About ten seconds ago. Due to lack of interest.
REG: Funny lot these librarians.

Alan Ayckbourn 1939– : *Living
Together* (1975)

10 RUTH: They'll sack you.
NORMAN: They daren't. I reorganized the Main Index.
When I die, the secret dies with me.

Alan Ayckbourn 1939– : *Round
and Round the Garden* (1975)

11 It's your wishy-washy liberal attitude—video machines
and Asian novels here, taped reminiscences there—mark
my words, John, make people welcome in the library and
it's the thin end of the bookmark.

Victoria Wood 1953– : *Mens Sana
in Thingummy Doodah* (1990)

12 This is the dreariest library in the whole world. They
haven't got anything new. I think they're waiting for the
Domesday Book to come out in paperback.

Victoria Wood 1953– : *Mens Sana
in Thingummy Doodah* (1990)

13 It's a copyright library, you see, so they get a copy of
everything published. Everything…Centuries of
pornography up to the present day.

Stephen Fry 1957– : *The Liar* (1991)

14 If you file your waste-paper basket for 50 years, you
have a public library.

Tony Benn 1925– : in *Daily
Telegraph* 5 March 1994

Lies See *Truth and Lies*

Life and Living

1 Above all, gentlemen, not the slightest zeal.

**Charles-Maurice de
Talleyrand** 1754–1838: P. Chasles
*Voyages d'un critique à travers la vie
et les livres* (1868)

2 'Sairey,' says Mrs Harris, 'sech is life. Vich likeways is
the hend of all things!'

Charles Dickens 1812–70: *Martin
Chuzzlewit* (1844)

3 It's as large as life, and twice as natural!

Lewis Carroll 1832–98: *Through
the Looking-Glass* (1872)

4 Life is just one damned thing after another.

Elbert Hubbard 1859–1915: in
Philistine December 1909, (often
attributed to Frank Ward O'Malley)

5 What a queer thing Life is! So unlike anything else, don't
you know, if you see what I mean.

P. G. Wodehouse 1881–1975: *My
Man Jeeves* (1919)

6 E. F. Benson never lived his life at all; only stayed with it
and lunched with it.

A. C. Benson 1862–1925: J. A. Gere
and John Sparrow (eds.) *Geoffrey
Madan's Notebooks* (1981)

7 As life goes on, don't you find that all you need is about
two real friends, a regular supply of books, and a Peke?

P. G. Wodehouse 1881–1975:
letter 28 October 1930

8 It's a funny old world—a man's lucky if he gets out of it alive.

Walter de Leon and **Paul M. Jones**: *You're Telling Me* (1934 film); spoken by W. C. Fields

9 Laugh it off, laugh it off; it's all part of life's rich pageant.

Arthur Marshall 1910–89: *The Games Mistress* (recorded monologue, 1937)

10 If *A* is a success in life, then *A* equals *x* plus *y* plus *z*. Work is *x*; *y* is play; and *z* is keeping your mouth shut.

Albert Einstein 1879–1955: in *Observer* 15 January 1950

11 Cocaine habit-forming? Of course not. I ought to know. I've been using it for years.

Tallulah Bankhead 1903–68: *Tallulah* (1952)

12 Oh, isn't life a terrible thing, thank God?

Dylan Thomas 1914–53: *Under Milk Wood* (1954)

13 Moderation in all things. Not too much of life. It often lasts too long.

H. L. Mencken 1880–1956: *Minority Report* (1956)

14 Life, you know, is rather like opening a tin of sardines. We are all of us looking for the key. And, I wonder, how many of you here tonight have wasted years of your lives looking behind the kitchen dressers of this life for that key. I know I have. Others think they've found the key, don't they? They roll back the lid of the sardine tin of life, they reveal the sardines, the riches of life, therein, and they get them out, they enjoy them. But, you know, there's always a little bit in the corner you can't get out. I wonder—I wonder, is there a little bit in the corner of your life? I know there is in mine.

Alan Bennett 1934– : in *Beyond the Fringe* (1961 revue)

15 Life is a Cabaret, old chum
Come to the Cabaret.

Fred Ebb: 'Cabaret' (1965)

16 Life goes on even for those of us who are divorced, broke and sloppy.

Neil Simon 1927– : *The Odd Couple* (1966)

17 Life is a gamble at terrible odds—if it was a bet, you wouldn't take it.

Tom Stoppard 1937– : *Rosencrantz and Guildenstern are Dead* (1967)

18 The only thing I regret about my life is the length of it. If I had to live my life again I'd make all the same mistakes—only sooner.

Tallulah Bankhead 1903–68: Laurence J. Peter (ed.) *Quotations for our Time* (1977)

19 I *love* living. I have some problems with my *life*, but living is the best thing they've come up with so far.

Neil Simon 1927– : *Last of the Red Hot Lovers* (1970)

20 I don't honestly think you can possibly share a small tent for any length of time with someone who's ebullient.

Alan Ayckbourn 1939– : *Living Together* (1975)

21 Life is something to do when you can't get to sleep.

Fran Lebowitz 1946– : *Metropolitan Life* (1978)

22 Life is a shit sandwich and every day you take another bite.

Joe Schmidt: a pro football player's view; Jonathon Green and Don Atyeo (eds.) *The Book of Sports Quotes* (1979)

23 Alun's life was coming to consist more and more exclusively of being told at dictation speed what he knew.

Kingsley Amis 1922–95: *The Old Devils* (1986)

24 Brought up in the provinces in the forties and fifties one learned early the valuable lesson that life is generally something that happens elsewhere.

Alan Bennett 1934- : introduction to *Talking Heads* (1988)

25 Life is a sexually transmitted disease.

Anonymous: graffito found on the London Underground

26 Life, if you're fat, is a minefield—you have to pick your way, otherwise you blow up.

Miriam Margolyes: in *Observer* 9 June 1991

27 ...There's no need to worry— Whatever you do, life is hell.

Wendy Cope 1945- : 'Advice to Young Women' (1992)

Literature See also *Books, Poetry and Poets, Writers and Writing*

1 I should have no objection to this method, but that I think it must smell too strong of the lamp.

Laurence Sterne 1713-68: *Tristram Shandy* (1759-67)

2 'The whole of this unfortunate business,' said Dr Lyster, 'has been the result of PRIDE AND PREJUDICE.'

Fanny Burney 1752-1840: *Cecilia* (1782)

3 I hate things all fiction...there should always be some foundation of fact for the most airy fabric—and pure invention is but the talent of a liar.

Lord Byron 1788-1824: letter to his publisher John Murray, 2 April 1817

4 We learn from Horace, Homer sometimes sleeps; We feel without him: Wordsworth sometimes wakes.

Lord Byron 1788-1824: *Don Juan* (1819-24)

5 He has one eminent merit—that of being an enthusiastic admirer of mine—so that I may be the Hero of a novel yet, under the name of Delamere or Mortimer. Only think what an honour.

Lord Macaulay 1800-59: of Bulwer Lytton; letter 5 August 1831

6 'What is the use of a book', thought Alice, 'without pictures or conversations?'

Lewis Carroll 1832-98: *Alice's Adventures in Wonderland* (1865)

7 A literary man—*with* a wooden leg.

Charles Dickens 1812-70: *Our Mutual Friend* (1865)

8 It takes a great deal of history to produce a little literature.

Henry James 1843-1916: *Hawthorne* (1879)

9 When I want to read a novel, I write one.

Benjamin Disraeli 1804-81: W. Monypenny and G. Buckle *Life of Benjamin Disraeli* (1920)

10 Meredith's a prose Browning, and so is Browning.

Oscar Wilde 1854-1900: *Intentions* (1891) 'The Critic as Artist'

11 Nearly all our best men are dead! Carlyle, Tennyson, Browning, George Eliot!—I'm not feeling very well myself.

Punch 1841-1992: vol. 104 (1893)

12 The literary gift is a mere accident—is as often bestowed on idiots who have nothing to say worth hearing as it is denied to strenuous sages.

Max Beerbohm 1872-1956: letter to George Bernard Shaw, 21 September 1903

13 Remote and ineffectual Don That dared attack my Chesterton.

Hilaire Belloc 1870-1953: 'Lines to a Don' (1910)

14 A swear-word in a rustic slum A simple swear-word is to some, To Masefield something more.

Max Beerbohm 1872-1956: *Fifty Caricatures* (1912)

15 Literature's always a good card to play for Honours. It makes people think that Cabinet ministers are educated.

Arnold Bennett 1867–1931: *The Title* (1918)

16 The cheerful clatter of Sir James Barrie's cans as he went round with the milk of human kindness.

Philip Guedalla 1889–1944: *Supers and Supermen* (1920) 'Some Critics'

17 The work of Henry James has always seemed divisible by a simple dynastic arrangement into three reigns: James I, James II, and the Old Pretender.

Philip Guedalla 1889–1944: *Supers and Supermen* (1920) 'Some Critics'

18 From the moment I picked up your book until I laid it down, I was convulsed with laughter. Some day I intend reading it.

Groucho Marx 1895–1977: a blurb written for S. J. Perelman's 1928 book *Dawn Ginsberg's Revenge*

19 You praise the firm restraint with which they write—
I'm with you there, of course:
They use the snaffle and the curb all right,
But where's the bloody horse?

Roy Campbell 1901–57: 'On Some South African Novelists' (1930)

20 A novelist must preserve a childlike belief in the importance of things which common sense considers of no great consequence.

W. Somerset Maugham 1874–1965: *A Writer's Notebook* (1949) written in 1933

21 How rare, how precious is frivolity! How few writers can prostitute all their powers! They are always implying, 'I am capable of higher things.'

E. M. Forster 1879–1970: *Abinger Harvest* (1936)

22 If, with the literate, I am
Impelled to try an epigram,
I never seek to take the credit;
We all assume that Oscar said it.

Dorothy Parker 1893–1967: 'A Pig's-Eye View of Literature' (1937)

23 The play was consumed in wholesome fashion by large masses in places of public resort; the novel was self-administered in private.

Flann O'Brien 1911–66: *At Swim-Two-Birds* (1939)

24 And I'll stay off Verlaine too; he was always chasing Rimbauds.

Dorothy Parker 1893–1967: 'The Little Hours' (1939)

25 All I want is a modest place in Mr X's *Good Reading*, Miss Y's *Good Writing*, and that new edition of *One Thousand Best Bits of Recent Prose*.

James Agate 1877–1947: diary 21 August 1941

26 The magazine was a transformed resurrection of an older college publication, that had died from sheer bulk, the kind of literary dropsy that attacks the writing of professors.

Stephen Leacock 1869–1944: *The Boy I Left Behind Me* (1947)

27 If my books had been any worse, I should not have been invited to Hollywood, and if they had been any better, I should not have come.

Raymond Chandler 1888–1959: letter to Charles W. Morton, 12 December 1945

28 I have only ever read one book in my life, and that is *White Fang*. It's so frightfully good I've never bothered to read another.

Nancy Mitford 1904–1973: *Love in a Cold Climate* (1949); Uncle Matthew's view of literature

29 I have known her pass the whole evening without mentioning a single book, or *in fact anything unpleasant*, at all.

Henry Reed 1914–86: *A Very Great Man Indeed* (1953)

30 The mama of dada.

Clifton Fadiman 1904– : of Gertrude Stein; *Party of One* (1955)

31 He knew everything about literature except how to enjoy it.

Joseph Heller 1923– : *Catch-22* (1961)

32 You're familiar with the tragedies of antiquity, are you? The great homicidal classics?

Tom Stoppard 1937– : *Rosencrantz and Guildenstern are Dead* (1967)

33 I was a frequent visitor for I was distantly related to the Woolf family through some Alsatian cousins.

Alan Bennett 1934– : *Forty Years On* (1969)

34 In view of her penchant
For something romantic,
De Sade is too trenchant
And Dickens too frantic,
And Stendhal would ruin
The plan of attack
As there isn't much blue in
The Red and the Black.

Stephen Sondheim 1930– : 'Now' (1972)

35 We were put to Dickens as children but it never quite took. That unremitting humanity soon had me cheesed off.

Alan Bennett 1934– : *The Old Country* (1978)

36 Dr Weiss, at forty, knew that her life had been ruined by literature.

Anita Brookner 1938– : *A Start in Life* (1981)

On literature as taught in school:
37 Schoolteachers seemed determined to persuade me that 'classic' is a synonym for 'narcotic'.

Russell Baker 1925– : in *New York Times* 14 April 1982

38 Every quarter century, like clockwork, there is a Peacock revival. The great tail feathers unfurl in all their Pavonian splendor, and like-minded folk delight in the display; and that's the end of that for the next twenty-five years.

Gore Vidal 1925– : *Pink Triangle and Yellow Star* (1982)

39 Any writer worth his salt knows that only a small proportion of literature does more than partly compensate people for the damage they have suffered in learning to read.

Rebecca West 1892–1983: Peter Vansittart *Path from a White Horse* (1985), author's note

40 The cure for mixed metaphors, I have always found, is for the patient to be obliged to draw a picture of the result.

Bernard Levin 1928– : *In These Times* (1986)

41 In stories saying it brings it on. So if you get the heroine saying, 'I don't suppose I shall ever be happy', then you can bank on it there's happiness just around the corner. That's the rule in novels. Whereas in life you can say you're never going to be happy and you never are happy, and saying it doesn't make a ha'porth of difference.

Alan Bennett 1934– : *Talking Heads* (1988)

42 Here is that marriage of style and content we look for in all great writing. A shatteringly vulgar and worthless life captured in shatteringly vulgar and worthless prose.

Stephen Fry 1957– : *Paperweight* (1992)

Living See *Life and Living*

Love See also *Marriage, Sex*

1 I was adored once too.

> William Shakespeare 1564–1616: *Twelfth Night* (1601)

2 Love is the fart
Of every heart:
It pains a man when 'tis kept close,
And others doth offend, when 'tis let loose.

> John Suckling 1609–42: 'Love's Offence' (1646)

3 Out upon it, I have loved
Three whole days together;
And am like to love three more,
If it prove fair weather.

Time shall moult away his wings,
Ere he shall discover
In the whole wide world again
Such a constant lover.

> John Suckling 1609–42: 'A Poem with the Answer' (1659)

4 If this be not love, it is madness, and then it is pardonable.

> William Congreve 1670–1729: *The Old Bachelor* (1693)

5 How happy could I be with either,
Were t'other dear charmer away!

> John Gay 1685–1732: *The Beggar's Opera* (1728)

6 Would I were free from this restraint,
Or else had hopes to win her;
Would she could make of me a saint,
Or I of her a sinner.

> William Congreve 1670–1729: 'Pious Selinda Goes to Prayers' (song)

7 What is commonly called love, namely the desire of satisfying a voracious appetite with a certain quantity of delicate white human flesh.

> Henry Fielding 1707–54: *Tom Jones* (1749)

8 Did you ever hear of Captain Wattle?
He was all for love, and a little for the bottle.

> Charles Dibdin 1745–1814: 'Captain Wattle and Miss Roe' (1797)

9 The magic of first love is our ignorance that it can ever end.

> Benjamin Disraeli 1804–81: *Henrietta Temple* (1837)

10 Oh, Mrs Corney, what a prospect this opens! What a opportunity for a jining of hearts and house-keepings!

> Charles Dickens 1812–70: *Oliver Twist* (1838)

11 There are strings . . . in the human heart that had better not be wibrated.

> Charles Dickens 1812–70: *Barnaby Rudge* (1841)

12 Barkis is willin'.

> Charles Dickens 1812–70: *David Copperfield* (1850)

13 Love's like the measles—all the worse when it comes late in life.

> Douglas Jerrold 1803–57: *The Wit and Opinions of Douglas Jerrold* (1859) 'Love'

14 So I fell in love with a rich attorney's
Elderly ugly daughter.

> W. S. Gilbert 1836–1911: *Trial by Jury* (1875)

15 Bed. No woman is worth more than a fiver unless you're in love with her. Then she's worth all she costs you.

> W. Somerset Maugham 1874–1965: *A Writer's Notebook* (1949) written in 1903

16 Women who love the same man have a kind of bitter freemasonry.

Max Beerbohm 1872–1956: *Zuleika Dobson* (1911)

17 A quietly silly woman, Madame Ruiz was often obliged to lament the absence of intellect at her door: accounting for it as the consequence of a weakness for Negroes, combined with a hopeless passion for the Regius Professor of Greek at Oxford.

Ronald Firbank 1886–1926: *Sorrow in Sunlight* (1924)

18 Love's a disease. But curable.

Rose Macaulay 1881–1958: *Crewe Train* (1926)

19 Another bride, another June,
Another sunny honeymoon,
Another season, another reason,
For makin' whoopee!

Gus Kahn 1886–1941: 'Makin' Whoopee' (1928)

20 With love to lead the way,
I've found more clouds of grey
Than any Russian play
Could guarantee...
...When ev'ry happy plot
Ends with the marriage knot—
And there's no knot for me.

Ira Gershwin 1896–1989: 'But Not For Me' (1930)

21 Make love to every woman you meet. If you get five percent on your outlays it's a good investment.

Arnold Bennett 1867–1931: Laurence J. Peter (ed.) *Quotations for our Time* (1977)

22 Love is sweeping the country;
Waves are hugging the shore;
All the sexes
From Maine to Texas
Have never known such love before.

Ira Gershwin 1896–1983: 'Love is Sweeping the Country' (1931)

23 I get no kick from champagne,
Mere alcohol doesn't thrill me at all,
So tell me why should it be true
That I get a kick out of you?

Cole Porter 1891–1964: 'I Get a Kick Out of You' (1934)

24 Four be the things I'd been better without:
Love, curiosity, freckles, and doubt.

Dorothy Parker 1893–1967: 'Inventory' (1937)

25 Oh, life is a glorious cycle of song,
A medley of extemporanea;
And love is a thing that can never go wrong;
And I am Marie of Roumania.

Dorothy Parker 1893–1967: 'Comment' (1937)

26 The broken dates,
The endless waits,
The lovely loving and the hateful hates,
The conversation and the flying plates—
I wish I were in love again.

Lorenz Hart 1895–1943: 'I Wish I Were in Love Again' (1937)

27 When love congeals
It soon reveals
The faint aroma of performing seals,
The double crossing of a pair of heels.
I wish I were in love again!

Lorenz Hart 1895–1943: 'I Wish I Were in Love Again' (1937)

28 Holding hands at midnight
'Neath a starry sky...
Nice work if you can get it,
And you can get it if you try.

Ira Gershwin 1896–1989: 'Nice Work If You Can Get It' (1937)

29 Most gentlemen don't like love,
They just like to kick it around.

Cole Porter 1891–1964: 'Most Gentlemen don't like Love' (1938)

30 The ability to make love frivolously is the chief characteristic which distinguishes human beings from beasts.

Heywood Broun 1888–1939: Howard Teichman *George S. Kaufman* (1973)

31 Tell me, George, if you had to do it all over would you fall in love with yourself again.

Oscar Levant 1906–72: to George Gershwin; David Ewen *The Story of George Gershwin* (1943)

32 Miss Joan Hunter Dunn, Miss Joan Hunter Dunn,
How mad I am, sad I am, glad that you won.
The warm-handled racket is back in its press,
But my shock-headed victor, she loves me no less.

John Betjeman 1906–84: 'A Subaltern's Love-Song' (1945)

33 When I'm not near the girl I love,
I love the girl I'm near.
...When I can't fondle the hand I'm fond of
I fondle the hand at hand.

E. Y. Harburg 1898–1981: 'When I'm Not Near the Girl I Love' (1947)

34 Love is the delusion that one woman differs from another.

H. L. Mencken 1880–1956: *Chrestomathy* (1949)

35 You ain't nothin' but a hound dog,
Quit snoopin' round my door
You can wag your tail but I ain't gonna feed you no more.

Jerry Leiber 1933– and **Mike Stoller** 1933– : 'Hound Dog' (1956)

36 We men have got love well weighed up; our stuff
Can get by without it.
Women don't seem to think that's good enough;
They write about it.

Kingsley Amis 1922–95: 'A Bookshop Idyll' (1956)

37 There are various ways of mending a broken heart, but perhaps going to a learned conference is one of the more unusual.

Barbara Pym 1913–80: *No Fond Return of Love* (1961)

38 In the spring a young man's fancy lightly turns to thoughts of love;
And in summer,
and in autumn,
and in winter—
See above.

E. Y. Harburg 1898–1981: 'Tennyson Anyone?' (1965)

39 ELAINE: *Romantic?* In your mother's clean apartment with two glasses from Bloomingdale's and your rubbers dripping on the newspaper?
BARNEY: It was my belief that romance is inspired by the participants and not the accoutrements.

Neil Simon 1927– : *Last of the Red Hot Lovers* (1970)

40 They made love as though they were an endangered species.

Peter de Vries 1910–93: Laurence J. Peter (ed.) *Quotations for our Time* (1977)

41 Love conquers all things—except poverty and toothache.

Mae West 1892–1980: attributed

*Advising someone rejected in love to be cheerful, forgiving, and
unavailable:*

42 Such behaviour will have two rewards. First, it will take
the sufferer's mind off suffering and begin the recovery.
Second, it will make the former lover worry that this
supposed act of cruelty was actually a relief to the person
it should have hurt. That hurts.

Judith Martin 1938– : 'Advice
from Miss Manners', column in
Washington Post 1979–82

43 LILL: He loves me. He's just waiting till the children are
settled.
VICTORIA: What in—sheltered housing?

Victoria Wood 1953– : *Mens Sana
in Thingummy Doodah* 1990

44 I'm afraid I was very much the traditionalist. I went
down on one knee and dictated a proposal which my
secretary faxed over straight away.

Stephen Fry 1957– and **Hugh
Laurie**: *A Bit More Fry and Laurie*
(1991)

45 1 Don't see him. Don't phone or write a letter.
2 The easy way: get to know him better.

Wendy Cope 1945– : 'Two Cures
for Love' (1992)

46 My heart has made its mind up
And I'm afraid it's you.

Wendy Cope 1945– : 'Valentine'
(1992)

47 My father was a man as unacquainted with love as
a Scots pine tree and what's wrong with that? It makes
a change, these days, when love slops out all over the
place from any old bucket.

Jill Tweedie 1936–93: *Eating
Children* (1993)

Marriage See also *Love, Sex*

1 Yblessed be god that I have wedded fyve!
Welcome the sixte, whan that evere he shal.

Geoffrey Chaucer c.1343–1400:
The Canterbury Tales 'The Wife of
Bath's Prologue'

2 Who weddeth or he be wise shall die ere he thrive.

John Heywood c.1497–c.1580: *A
Dialogue of Proverbs* (1546)

3 Kiss me Kate, we will be married o' Sunday.

William Shakespeare 1564–1616:
The Taming of the Shrew (1592)

4 I will do anything, Nerissa, ere I will be married to
a sponge.

William Shakespeare 1564–1616:
The Merchant of Venice (1596–8)

5 Many a good hanging prevents a bad marriage.

William Shakespeare 1564–1616:
Twelfth Night (1601)

6 A young man married is a man that's marred.

William Shakespeare 1564–1616:
All's Well that Ends Well (1603–4)

7 My wife, who, poor wretch, is troubled with her lonely
life.

Samuel Pepys 1633–1703: diary
19 December 1662

8 Strange to say what delight we married people have to
see these poor fools decoyed into our condition.

Samuel Pepys 1633–1703: diary
25 December 1665

9 But for marriage 'tis good for nothing, but to make
friends fall out.

Thomas Shadwell c.1642–92: *The
Sullen Lovers* (1668)

10 'Tis my maxim, he's a fool that marries, but he's
a greater that does not marry a fool.

William Wycherley c.1640–1716:
The Country Wife (1675)

11 Courtship to marriage, as a very witty prologue to a very
dull play.

William Congreve 1670–1729: *The
Old Bachelor* (1693)

12 SHARPER: Thus grief still treads upon the heels of
    pleasure:
    Married in haste, we may repent at leisure.
    SETTER: Some by experience find those words mis-placed:
    At leisure married, they repent in haste.

William Congreve 1670–1729: *The Old Bachelor* (1693)

13 Tho' marriage makes man and wife one flesh, it leaves
    'em still two fools.

William Congreve 1670–1729: *The Double Dealer* (1694)

14 Nay, for my part I always despised Mr Tattle of all
    things; nothing but his being my husband could have
    made me like him less.

William Congreve 1670–1729: *Love for Love* (1695)

15 LADY BRUTE: 'Tis a hard fate I should not be believed.
    SIR JOHN: 'Tis a damned atheistical age, wife.

John Vanbrugh 1664–1726: *The Provoked Wife* (1697)

16 Here lies my wife; here let her lie!
    Now she's at peace and so am I.

John Dryden 1631–1700: epitaph; attributed but not traced in his works

17 Ay, ay, I have experience: I have a wife, and so forth.

William Congreve 1670–1729: *The Way of the World* (1700)

18 These articles subscribed, if I continue to endure you
    a little longer, I may by degrees dwindle into a wife.

William Congreve 1670–1729: *The Way of the World* (1700)

19 I don't think matrimony consistent with the liberty of the
    subject.

George Farquhar 1678–1707: *The Twin Rivals* (1703)

20 They dream in courtship, but in wedlock wake.

Alexander Pope 1688–1744: *Translations from Chaucer* (1714)

21 POLLY: Then all my sorrows are at an end.
    MRS PEACHUM: A mighty likely speech, in troth, for
    a wench who is just married!

John Gay 1685–1732: *The Beggar's Opera* (1728)

22 Do you think your mother and I should have lived
    comfortably so long together, if ever we had been
    married?

John Gay 1685–1732: *The Beggar's Opera* (1728)

23 The comfortable estate of widowhood, is the only hope
    that keeps up a wife's spirits.

John Gay 1685–1732: *The Beggar's Opera* (1728)

24 His designs were strictly honourable, as the phrase is;
    that is, to rob a lady of her fortune by way of marriage.

Henry Fielding 1707–54: *Tom Jones* (1749)

25 I...chose my wife, as she did her wedding gown, not for
    a fine glossy surface, but such qualities as would wear
    well.

Oliver Goldsmith 1730–74: *The Vicar of Wakefield* (1766)

26 It seemed to me pretty plain, that they had more of love
    than matrimony in them.

Oliver Goldsmith 1730–74: *The Vicar of Wakefield* (1766)

27 My brother Toby, quoth she, is going to be married to
    Mrs Wadman. Then he will never, quoth my father, lie
    diagonally in his bed again as long as he lives.

Laurence Sterne 1713–68: *Tristram Shandy* (1759–67)

Of a man who remarried immediately after the death of a wife with whom he had been unhappy:
28 The triumph of hope over experience.

Samuel Johnson 1709–84: James Boswell *Life of Samuel Johnson* (1791) 1770

29 'Tis safest in matrimony to begin with a little aversion.

Richard Brinsley Sheridan
1751–1816: *The Rivals* (1775)

30 One day at Streatham...a young gentleman called to him suddenly, and I suppose he thought disrespectfully, in these words: 'Mr Johnson, would you advise me to marry?' 'I would advise no man to marry, Sir,' returns for answer in a very angry tone Dr Johnson, 'who is not likely to propagate understanding.'

Samuel Johnson 1709–84: Hester Lynch Piozzi *Anecdotes of...Johnson* (1786)

31 It is a truth universally acknowledged, that a single man in possession of a good fortune, must be in want of a wife.

Jane Austen 1775–1817: *Pride and Prejudice* (1813)

32 I am about to be married—and am of course in all the misery of a man in pursuit of happiness.

Lord Byron 1788–1824: letter 15 October 1814

33 I have great hopes that we shall love each other all our lives as much as if we had never married at all.

Lord Byron 1788–1824: letter to Annabella Milbanke, 5 December 1814

34 Marriage may often be a stormy lake, but celibacy is almost always a muddy horsepond.

Thomas Love Peacock 1785–1866: *Melincourt* (1817)

35 I am not at all the sort of person you and I took me for.

Jane Carlyle 1801–66: letter to Thomas Carlyle, 7 May 1822

36 Marriage is a feast where the grace is sometimes better than the dinner.

Charles Caleb Colton 1780–1832: *Lacon* (1822)

37 Wishing each other, not divorced, but dead;
They lived respectably as man and wife.

Lord Byron 1788–1824: *Don Juan* (1819–24)

38 Think you, if Laura had been Petrarch's wife,
He would have written sonnets all his life?

Lord Byron 1788–1824: *Don Juan* (1819–24)

39 A man cannot marry before he has studied anatomy and has dissected at the least one woman.

Honoré de Balzac 1799–1850: *Physiology of Marriage* (1904)

40 The most happy marriage I can picture or imagine to myself would be the union of a deaf man to a blind woman.

Samuel Taylor Coleridge 1772–1834: Thomas Allsop *Letters, Conversations, and Recollections of S. T. Coleridge* (1836)

41 Ven you're a married man, Samivel, you'll understand a good many things as you don't understand now; but vether it's worth while goin' through so much to learn so little, as the charity-boy said ven he got to the end of the alphabet, is a matter o' taste.

Charles Dickens 1812–70: *Pickwick Papers* (1837)

42 Love matches are formed by people who pay for a month of honey with a life of vinegar.

Countess of Blessington 1789–1849: *Desultory Thoughts and Reflections* (1839)

43 Advice to persons about to marry.—'Don't.'

Punch 1841–1992: vol. 8 (1845)

44 I want you to assist me in forcing her on board the lugger; once there, I'll frighten her into marriage.

John Benn Johnstone 1803–91: *The Gipsy Farmer* (performed 1845); since quoted 'Once aboard the lugger and the maid is mine'

45 My definition of marriage...it resembles a pair of shears, so joined that they cannot be separated; often moving in

Sydney Smith 1771–1845: Lady Holland *Memoir* (1855)

opposite directions, yet always punishing anyone who
comes between them.

46 A woman with fair opportunities and without a positive
hump, may marry whom she likes.

**William Makepeace
Thackeray** 1811–63: *Vanity Fair*
(1847–8)

47 It's my old girl that advises. She has the head. But
I never own to it before her. Discipline must be
maintained.

Charles Dickens 1812–70: *Bleak
House* (1853)

48 I revere the memory of Mr F. as an estimable man and
most indulgent husband, only necessary to mention
Asparagus and it appeared or to hint at any little delicate
thing to drink and it came like magic in a pint bottle it
was not ecstasy but it was comfort.

Charles Dickens 1812–70: *Little
Dorrit* (1857)

49 Kissing don't last: cookery do!

George Meredith 1828–1909: *The
Ordeal of Richard Feverel* (1859)

50 He is dreadfully married. He's the most married man
I ever saw in my life.

Artemus Ward 1834–67: *Artemus
Ward's Lecture* (1869) 'Brigham
Young's Palace'

51 I have always thought that every woman should marry,
and no man.

Benjamin Disraeli 1804–81:
Lothair (1870)

52 Even quarrels with one's husband are preferable to the
ennui of a solitary existence.

Elizabeth Patterson Bonaparte
1785–1879: view of the estranged
American wife of Napoleon
Bonaparte's brother Jerome; Eugene L.
Didier *The Life and Letters of Madame
Bonaparte* (1879)

53 BISHOP: Who is it that sees and hears all we do, and
before whom even I am but as a crushed worm?
PAGE: The Missus, my Lord.

Punch 1841–1992: vol. 79 (1880)

54 No man is regular in his attendance at the House of
Commons until he is married.

Benjamin Disraeli 1804–81:
Hesketh Pearson *Dizzy* (1951)

55 It was very good of God to let Carlyle and Mrs Carlyle
marry one another and so make only two people
miserable instead of four.

Samuel Butler 1835–1902: letter
21 November 1884

56 WIFE OF TWO YEARS STANDING: Oh yes! I'm sure he's not
so fond of me as at first. He's away so much, neglects
me dreadfully, and he's so cross when he comes home.
What *shall* I do?
WIDOW: Feed the brute!

Punch 1841–1992: vol. 89 (1885)

57 The world has grown suspicious of anything that looks
like a happily married life.

Oscar Wilde 1854–1900: *Lady
Windermere's Fan* (1892)

58 Twenty years of romance make a woman look like
a ruin; but twenty years of marriage make her
something like a public building.

Oscar Wilde 1854–1900: *A Woman
of No Importance* (1893)

59 *Once Upon a Time* was dreadful. Since the appearance of
Tree in pyjamas there has been the greatest sympathy for
Mrs Tree. It throws a lurid light on the difficulties of their
married life.

Oscar Wilde 1854–1900: letter
?April 1894

60 In married life three is company and two none.

Oscar Wilde 1854–1900: *The Importance of Being Earnest* (1895)

The Lord Chief Justice, Lord Russell, was once asked by a lady what was the maximum punishment for bigamy:

61 Two mothers-in-law.

Lord Russell of Killowen 1832–1900: Edward Abinger *Forty Years at the Bar* (1930)

62 The awe and dread with which the untutored savage contemplates his mother-in-law are amongst the most familiar facts of anthropology.

James George Frazer 1854–1941: *The Golden Bough* (2nd ed., 1900)

63 If it were not for the presents, an elopement would be preferable.

George Ade 1866–1944: *Forty Modern Fables* (1901)

64 There once was an old man of Lyme
Who married three wives at a time,
When asked 'Why a third?'
He replied, 'One's absurd!
And bigamy, Sir, is a crime!'

William Cosmo Monkhouse 1840–1901: *Nonsense Rhymes* (1902)

65 It is a woman's business to get married as soon as possible, and a man's to keep unmarried as long as he can.

George Bernard Shaw 1856–1950: *Man and Superman* (1903)

66 Marriage is popular because it combines the maximum of temptation with the maximum of opportunity.

George Bernard Shaw 1856–1950: *Man and Superman* (1903) 'Maxims: Marriage'

67 My wife's gone to the country
Hooray! Hooray!
She thought it best, I need a rest,
That's why she's gone away.

Irving Berlin 1888–1989 and **George Whiting**: 'My Wife's Gone To The Country' (1910)

68 Hogamus, higamous
Man is polygamous
Higamus, hogamous
Woman monogamous.

William James 1842–1910: in *Oxford Book of Marriage* (1990)

69 When two people are under the influence of the most violent, most insane, most delusive, and most transient of passions, they are required to swear that they will remain in that excited, abnormal, and exhausting condition continuously until death do them part.

George Bernard Shaw 1856–1950: preface to *Getting Married* (1911)

70 I'm Henery the Eighth, I am!
Henery the Eighth, I am, I am!
I got married to the widow next door,
She's been married seven times before.
Every one was a Henery,
She wouldn't have a Willie or a Sam.
I'm her eighth old man named Henery
I'm Henery the Eighth, I am!

Fred Murray: 'I'm Henery the Eighth, I Am!' (1911)

71 What God hath joined together no man ever shall put asunder: God will take care of that.

George Bernard Shaw 1856–1950: *Getting Married* (1911)

72 They stood before the altar and supplied
The fire themselves in which their fat was fried.

Ambrose Bierce 1842–c.1914: *The Enlarged Devil's Dictionary* (1967)

73 He also reminded her that she was at a time of life when she could hardly expect to pick and choose, and that her spiritual condition was one of, at least, great uncertainty. These combined statements are held, under the law of Scotland at any rate, to be equivalent to an offer of marriage.

Stephen Leacock 1869–1944: *Arcadian Adventures with the Idle Rich* (1914)

74 Being a husband is a whole-time job. That is why so many husbands fail. They cannot give their entire attention to it.

Arnold Bennett 1867–1931: *The Title* (1918)

75 Chumps always make the best husbands. When you marry, Sally, grab a chump. Tap his forehead first, and if it rings solid, don't hesitate. All the unhappy marriages come from the husbands having brains.

P. G. Wodehouse 1881–1975: *The Adventures of Sally* (1920)

76 A husband is what is left of a lover, after the nerve has been extracted.

Helen Rowland 1875–1950: *A Guide to Men* (1922)

77 There are men who fear repartee in a wife more keenly than a sword.

P. G. Wodehouse 1881–1975: *Jill the Reckless* (1922)

78 Death and marriage are raging through this College with such fury that I ought to be grateful for having escaped both.

A. E. Housman 1859–1936: letter 29 May 1925

79 Did you ever look through a microscope at a drop of pond water? You see plenty of love there. All the amoebae getting married. I presume they think it very exciting and important. We don't.

Rose Macaulay 1881–1958: *Crewe Train* (1926)

80 Marriage isn't a word...it's a *sentence*!

King Vidor 1895–1982: in *The Crowd* (1928 film)

81 I've been married six months. She looks like a million dollars, but she only knows a hundred and twenty words and she's only got two ideas in her head.

Eric Linklater 1899–1974: *Juan in America* (1931)

82 By god, D. H. Lawrence was right when he had said there must be a dumb, dark, dull, bitter belly-tension between a man and a woman, and how else could this be achieved save in the long monotony of marriage?

Stella Gibbons 1902–89: *Cold Comfort Farm* (1932)

83 Save your money, dress better and catch a better husband.

Evelyn Waugh 1903–66: advising Nancy Mitford to get rid of her first lover, Hamish St Clair-Erskine; Harold Acton *Nancy Mitford* (1975)

On being asked if he and Mrs Nicolson (Vita Sackville-West) had ever collaborated on anything:
84 Yes, we have two sons.

Harold Nicolson 1886–1968: diary 2 March 1933

85 That's my first wife up there and this is the *present* Mrs Harris.

James Thurber 1894–1961: cartoon caption in *New Yorker* 16 March 1933

86 The deep, deep peace of the double-bed after the hurly-burly of the chaise-longue.

Mrs Patrick Campbell 1865–1940: Alexander Woollcott *While Rome Burns* (1934) 'The First Mrs Tanqueray'

87 Holy deadlock.

> **A. P. Herbert** 1890–1971: title of
> novel (1934)

88 It is probably no mere chance that in legal textbooks the problems relating to married women are usually considered immediately after the pages devoted to idiots and lunatics.

> **A. P. Herbert** 1890–1971:
> *Misleading Cases* (1935)

89 The critical period in matrimony is breakfast-time.

> **A. P. Herbert** 1890–1971:
> *Uncommon Law* (1935) 'Is Marriage
> Lawful?'

90 It feels so fine to be a bride,
And how's the groom? Why, he's slightly fried,
It's delightful, it's delicious, it's de-lovely.

> **Cole Porter** 1891–1964: 'It's De-
> lovely' (1936)

91 There is no more sombre enemy of good art than the pram in the hall.

> **Cyril Connolly** 1903–74: *Enemies
> of Promise* (1938)

92 Marriage is a bribe to make a housekeeper think she's a householder.

> **Thornton Wilder** 1897–1975: *The
> Merchant of Yonkers* (1939)

93 HE: Have you heard Professor Munch
Ate his wife and divorced his lunch?
SHE: Well, did you evah!
What a swell party this is.

> **Cole Porter** 1891–1964: 'Well, Did
> You Evah!' (1939)

94 I married many men,
A ton of them,
And yet I was untrue to none of them
Because I bumped off ev'ry one of them
To keep my love alive.
Sir Paul was frail,
He looked a wreck to me.
At night he was a horse's neck to me.
So I performed an appendectomy
To keep my love alive.

> **Lorenz Hart** 1895–1943: 'To Keep
> My Love Alive' (1943)

95 [Izaak Walton] seems to have borne married life easily as a basis (as with some among us now) from which to go fishing.

> **Stephen Leacock** 1869–1944: *The
> Boy I Left Behind Me* (1947)

96 'Vladimir,' said Natasha, 'do you love me?' 'Toujours,' said Stroganoff, with wariness. An unusual emotion for a honeymooning husband when this particular question crops up. But Stroganoff was lying in the upper berth of a railway compartment and Natasha was in the lower berth so the question could not be an overture to a delightful interlude but merely the prelude to some less delightful demand.

> **Caryl Brahms** 1901–82 and **S. J.
> Simon** 1904–48: *Six Curtains for
> Stroganova* (1945)

97 Imagine signing a lease together;
And hanging a Matisse together;
Being alone and baking bread together.
Reading the *New Yorker* in bed together!
Starting a family tree together!
Voting for the GOP together!

> **Ira Gershwin** 1896–1983: 'There's
> Nothing Like Marriage for People'
> (1946)

98 She very soon married this short young man
Who talked about soldiers all day

> **Noël Coward** 1899–1973:
> 'Josephine' (1946)

But who wasn't above
Making passionate love
In a coarse, rather Corsican way.

99 I'm a maid who would marry
And will take with no qualm
Any Tom, Dick or Harry,
Any Harry, Dick or Tom.

When courting his future wife (whom he married in 1949):
100 I would worship the ground you walk on, Audrey, if you
only lived in a better neighbourhood.

101 Translations (like wives) are seldom strictly faithful if
they are in the least attractive.

102 Bachelors know more about women than married men. If
they did not they would be married too.

103 No matter how happily a woman may be married, it
always pleases her to discover that there is a nice man
who wishes she were not.

On questioning a witness in the divorce court:
104 I always ask a husband, or a wife, as the case may be, is
there anything you have done in the course of your
married life of which you are now thoroughly ashamed?
The witness usually finds that a tricky one to answer.

*Agreeing with the comment, at her remarriage to Alan Campbell in
1950, that some of those present had not spoken to each other for
years:*
105 Including the bride and groom.

106 A husband should not insult his wife publicly, at parties.
He should insult her in the privacy of the home.

107 Love and marriage, love and marriage,
Go together like a horse and carriage.

108 To keep your marriage brimming
With love in the loving cup,
Whenever you're wrong, admit it,
Whenever you're right, shut up.

109 I'm getting married in the morning!
Ding dong! The bells are gonna chime.
Pull out the stopper!
Let's have a whopper!
But get me to the church on time!

To his wife Vita Sackville-West:
110 A crushed life is what I lead, similar to that of the hen
you ran over the other day.

111 GERRY: We can't get married at all...I'm a man.
OSGOOD: Well, nobody's perfect.

Cole Porter 1891–1964: 'Tom, Dick
or Harry' (1948)

Billy Wilder 1906– : M. Zolotow
Billy Wilder in Hollywood (1977)

Roy Campbell 1901–57: in *Poetry
Review* June–July 1949

H. L. Mencken 1880–1956:
Chrestomathy (1949)

H. L. Mencken 1880–1956:
Chrestomathy (1949)

Clifford Mortimer: John
Mortimer *Clinging to the Wreckage*
(1982)

Dorothy Parker 1893–1967:
Marion Meade *What Fresh Hell Is
This?* (1988)

James Thurber 1894–1961: *Thurber
Country* (1953)

Sammy Cahn 1913– : 'Love and
Marriage' (1955)

Ogden Nash 1902–71: 'A Word to
Husbands' (1957)

Alan Jay Lerner 1918–86: 'Get Me
to the Church on Time' (1956)

Harold Nicolson 1886–1968: diary
8 October 1958

Billy Wilder 1906– and **I. A. L.
Diamond** 1915–88: *Some Like It Hot*
(1959 film; closing words)

112 A man in love is incomplete until he has married. Then he's finished.

Zsa Zsa Gabor 1919– : in *Newsweek* 28 March 1960

113 When you were 26, 27, 28, even 29, you were a bachelor. But now you're over thirty and you're still not married, so you're a bum and that's all there is to it.

Neil Simon 1927– : *Come Blow Your Horn* (1961)

114 One doesn't have to get anywhere in a marriage. It's not a public conveyance.

Iris Murdoch 1919– : *A Severed Head* (1961)

115 PAUL: You want me to be rich and famous, don't you? CORRIE: During the day. At night I want you to be here and sexy.

Neil Simon 1927– : *Barefoot in the Park* (1964)

116 Take care of him. And make him feel important. And if you can do that, you'll have a happy and wonderful marriage. Like two out of every ten couples.

Neil Simon 1927– : *Barefoot in the Park* (1964)

117 My wife was an immature woman...I would be home in the bathroom, taking a bath, and my wife would walk in whenever she felt like it and sink my boats.

Woody Allen 1935– : 'I Had a Rough Marriage' (monologue, 1964)

118 It was partially my fault that we got divorced...I tended to place my wife under a pedestal.

Woody Allen 1935– : 'I Had a Rough Marriage' (monologue, 1964)

119 FELIX: Oh, I'm awfully sorry. (*Sighs.*) It's a terrible thing, isn't it? Divorce. GWENDOLEN: It can be...if you haven't got the right solicitor.

Neil Simon 1927– : *The Odd Couple* (1966)

120 I love to cry at weddings, anybody's weddings anytime! ...anybody's weddings just so long as it's not mine!

Dorothy Fields 1905–74: 'I Love to Cry at Weddings' (1966)

121 Don't worry, if you keep him long enough he'll come back in style.

Dorothy Parker 1893–1967: to another long-suffering wife; attributed

122 The great secret of a successful marriage is to treat all disasters as incidents and none of the incidents as disasters.

Harold Nicolson 1886–1968: Jonathon Green (ed.) *A Dictionary of Contemporary Quotations* (1982)

123 The concerts you enjoy together
Neighbours you annoy together
Children you destroy together,
That keep marriage intact.

Stephen Sondheim 1930– : 'The Little Things You Do Together' (1970)

124 'It was she as set her bonnet at him!' cried Mrs Williams, who had never yet let her husband finish a sentence since his 'I will' at Trinity Church, Plymouth Dock, in 1782 [eighteen years before].

Patrick O'Brian 1914– : *Master and Commander* (1970)

125 Do you know what the rate of literacy is in the United States? Eighty-six percent. Do you know how many married people have committed adultery? Eighty-seven percent. This is the only country in the world that has more cheaters than readers.

Neil Simon 1927– : *Last of the Red Hot Lovers* (1970)

126 'Suffer the little children to come unto me.' You might know Jesus wasn't married.

Alan Bennett 1934– : *Getting On* (1972)

127 'What are your views on marriage?'
'Rather garbled.'

Noël Coward 1899–1973: in *Ned Sherrin's Theatrical Anecdotes* (1991); attributed

128 I've known for years our marriage has been a mockery. My body lying there night after night in the wasted moonlight. I know now how the Taj Mahal must feel.

Alan Bennett 1934– : *Habeas Corpus* (1973)

129 Mention of divorce and avenues open up all round.

Alan Bennett 1934– : *Habeas Corpus* (1973)

130 Bigamy is having one husband too many. Monogamy is the same.

Anonymous: Erica Jong *Fear of Flying* (1973)

131 A fate worse than marriage. A sort of eternal engagement.

Alan Ayckbourn 1939– : *Living Together* (1975)

132 Is that how you've seen us for five years? A legal contract? Some marriage. No confetti please—just throw sealing wax and red tape. Do you take this woman, hereinafter called the licensee of the first party...

Alan Ayckbourn 1939– : *Table Manners* (1975)

133 Every woman should marry an archaeologist because she grows increasingly attractive to him as she grows increasingly to resemble a ruin.

Agatha Christie 1890–1976: Russell H. Fitzgibbon *The Agatha Christie Companion* (1980); attributed, perhaps apocryphal

When asked how many husbands she had had:
134 You mean apart from my own?

Zsa Zsa Gabor 1919– : K. Edwards *I Wish I'd Said That* (1976)

135 Marriage is a wonderful invention; but, then again, so is a bicycle repair kit.

Billy Connolly 1942– : Duncan Campbell *Billy Connolly* (1976)

136 Marriage is a great institution, but I'm not ready for an institution yet.

Mae West 1892–1980: Laurence J. Peter (ed.) *Quotations for our Time* (1977); attributed

On hearing that marriage depends 'on what you both put into it':
137 It's all right for him and his 'what you put into it'. I've flung the lot in and it's disappeared without trace.

Alan Ayckbourn 1939– : *Sisterly Feelings* (1981)

138 Never marry a man who hates his mother, because he'll end up hating you.

Jill Bennett 1931–90: in *Observer* 12 September 1982 'Sayings of the Week'

139 He taught me housekeeping; when I divorce I keep the house.

Zsa Zsa Gabor 1919– : of her fifth husband; Ned Sherrin *Cutting Edge* (1984)

140 At the end of dinner it used to be that the men would retire to the billiard room and the women would go into the parlour. Men and women no longer separate after dinner, however. They now separate after twenty years of apparently happy marriage.

P. J. O'Rourke 1947– : *Modern Manners* (1984)

141 Children must be considered in a divorce—considered valuable pawns in the nasty legal and financial contest that is about to ensue.

P. J. O'Rourke 1947– : *Modern Manners* (1984)

142 Staying married may have long-term benefits. You can elicit much more sympathy from friends over a bad marriage than you ever can from a good divorce.

P. J. O'Rourke 1947– : *Modern Manners* (1984)

143 To Wanda, the only item of essential equipment—apart
from a Rolex watch (boiled in a stew by Afghans to test
its waterproof qualities)—not lost, stolen or simply worn
out in the course of some thirty years of travel together.

Eric Newby 1919– : *On the Shores
of the Mediterranean* (1984);
dedication to his wife

144 [Marriage is] the only war where one sleeps with
the enemy.

Anonymous: Mexican
saying; Ned Sherrin *Cutting Edge*
(1984)

*To her husband, who had asked the age of a flirtatious starlet with
noticeably thick legs:*

145 For God's sake, Walter, why don't you chop off her legs
and read the rings?

Carol Matthau: Truman Capote
Answered Prayers (1986)

146 One of those looks which only a quarter-century of
wedlock can adequately marinate.

Alan Coren 1938– : *Seems Like Old
Times* (1989)

147 It was an absolute mésalliance, the Barking Labour Party
and Tom [Driberg, the constituency's MP]—it was like
Zsa Zsa Gabor marrying Freddie Ayer.

Ian Mikardo: Francis Wheen *Tom
Driberg* (1990)

148 Another woman has said that I ruined her marriage,
which is quite simply not true. No woman in her right
mind would jeopardize a happy marriage by going to bed
with me, but have any women got a right mind?

Jeffrey Bernard 1932– : in *The
Spectator* 18 July 1992

149 We remain very married.

Richard Gere and **Cindy
Crawford**: in *The Times* 6 May 1994;
full-page advertisement following
rumours of their separation

Medicine See also *Sickness and Health*

1 Your said medicine hath done me little honesty, for it
made me piss my bed this night, for the which my wife
hath sore beaten me, and saying it is children's parts to
bepiss their bed. Ye have made me such a pisser that
I dare not this day go abroad.

Lord Edmund Howard
*c.*1478/80–1539: letter to Lady Lisle,
*c.*1533–35; *Lisle Letters* (1985)

2 GRONTE: It seems to me you are locating them wrongly:
the heart is on the left and the liver is on the right.
SGANARELLE: Yes, in the old days that was so, but we
have changed all that, and we now practise medicine
by a completely new method.

Molière 1622–73: *Le Médecin malgré
lui* (1667)

3 Cured yesterday of my disease,
I died last night of my physician.

Matthew Prior 1664–1721: 'The
Remedy Worse than the Disease'
(1727)

4 And, on the label of the stuff,
He wrote this verse;
Which one would think was clear enough,
And terse:—
When taken,
To be well shaken.

George Colman the Younger
1762–1836: 'The Newcastle
Apothecary' (1797)

5 In disease Medical Men guess: if they cannot ascertain
a disease, they call it nervous.

John Keats 1795–1821: J. A. Gere
and John Sparrow (eds.) *Geoffrey
Madan's Notebooks* (1981); attributed

*Epigram on Dr John Lettsom, who would sign his prescriptions
'I. Lettsom':*

6 Whenever patients come to I,
I physics, bleeds, and sweats 'em;
If after that they choose to die,
What's that to me!—*I letts 'em.*

Thomas Erskine 1750–1823:
Poetical Works (1823)

7 Meaty jelly, too, especially when a little salt, which is the
case when there's ham, is mellering to the organ.

Charles Dickens 1812–70: *Our
Mutual Friend* (1865)

8 Physicians of the Utmost Fame
Were called at once; but when they came
They answered, as they took their Fees,
'There is no Cure for this Disease.'

Hilaire Belloc 1870–1953: 'Henry
King' (1907)

9 There would never be any public agreement among
doctors if they did not agree to agree on the main point
of the doctor being always in the right.

George Bernard Shaw
1856–1950: preface to *The Doctor's
Dilemma* (1911)

10 There is at bottom only one genuinely scientific
treatment for all diseases, and that is to stimulate the
phagocytes.

George Bernard Shaw
1856–1950: *The Doctor's Dilemma*
(1911)

11 The desire to take medicine is perhaps the greatest
feature which distinguishes man from animals.

William Osler 1849–1919: H.
Cushing *Life of Sir William Osler* (1925)

12 Sir Roderick Glossop...is always called a nerve specialist,
because it sounds better, but everybody knows that he's
really a sort of janitor to the looney-bin.

P. G. Wodehouse 1881–1975: *The
Inimitable Jeeves* (1923)

13 He said my bronchial tubes were entrancing,
My epiglottis filled him with glee,
He simply loved my larynx
And went wild about my pharynx,
But he never said he loved me.

Cole Porter 1891–1964: 'The
Physician' (1933)

14 Your other recipe, a cold douche after my warm bath, is
impracticable, because my bath is cold.

A. E. Housman 1859–1936: letter
to Percy Withers, 30 December 1934

*On a trip to Thorpe Bay Agate realized that he had left his 'asthma
stuff' behind:*

15 I just can't bear to run short of
Acetylmethyldimethyloxamidphenylhydrazine.

James Agate 1877–1947: diary
9 April 1937

16 The medics can now stretch your life out an additional
dozen years but they don't tell you that most of these
years are going to be spent flat on your back while some
ghoul with thick glasses and a matted skull peers at you
through a machine that's hot out of 'Space Patrol'.

Groucho Marx 1895–1977: letter
23 December 1954

17 All the errors that lead to burst appendixes are made by
family doctors. The patient usually is sick enough to call
for help, but by the time he gets to the specialist he is too
far gone for it.

H. L. Mencken 1880–1956:
Minority Report (1956)

18 Medicine never really got anywhere until it threw
metaphysics overboard. Find me a medical man who still
toys with it, and I'll show you a quack. He may be,
perhaps, what is called an ethical quack, but he is still
a quack.

H. L. Mencken 1880–1956:
Minority Report (1956)

Of a famous surgeon who was the defeated defendant in a divorce action:

19 He is the only person who made his fortune with the knife, and lost it with his fork.

Oliver St John Gogarty 1878–1957: Ulick O'Connor *Oliver St John Gogarty* (1964)

20 As for consulting a dentist regularly, my punctuality practically amounted to a fetish. Every twelve years I would drop whatever I was doing and allow wild Caucasian ponies to drag me to a reputable orthodontist.

S. J. Perelman 1904–79: *The Most of S. J. Perelman* (1959) 'Dental or Mental, I Say It's Spinach'

21 Hungry Joe collected lists of fatal diseases and arranged them in alphabetical order so that he could put his finger without delay on any one he wanted to worry about.

Joseph Heller 1923– : *Catch-22* (1961)

22 A psychiatrist is a man who goes to the Folies-Bergère and looks at the audience.

Mervyn Stockwood 1913– : in *Observer* 15 October 1961

23 The kind of doctor I want is one who, when he's not examining me, is home studying medicine.

George S. Kaufman 1889–1961: Howard Teichman *George S. Kaufman* (1973)

24 Hark! the herald angels sing!
Beecham's Pills are just the thing,
Two for a woman, one for a child...
Peace on earth and mercy mild!

Thomas Beecham 1879–1961: advertising jingle devised for his father, but not used; Neville Cardus *Sir Thomas Beecham* (1961)

25 I came in here in all good faith to help my country. I don't mind giving a reasonable amount [of blood], but a pint...why that's very nearly an armful. I'm sorry. I'm not walking around with an empty arm for anybody.

Ray Galton 1930– and **Alan Simpson** 1929– : *The Blood Donor* (1961 television programme, words spoken by Tony Hancock)

26 Randolph Churchill went into hospital...to have a lung removed. It was announced that the trouble was not 'malignant'...it was a typical triumph of modern science to find the only part of Randolph that was not malignant and remove it.

Evelyn Waugh 1903–66: 'Irregular Notes 1960–65'; diary March 1964

27 I fear that being a patient in any hospital in Ireland calls for two things—holy resignation and an iron constitution.

Flann O'Brien 1911–66: *Myles Away from Dublin* (1990)

28 Any man who goes to a psychiatrist should have his head examined.

Sam Goldwyn 1882–1974: Norman Zierold *Moguls* (1969)

29 I can't stand whispering. Every time a doctor whispers in the hospital, next day there's a funeral.

Neil Simon 1927– : *The Gingerbread Lady* (1970)

30 That is an appliance for forcing beef tea down the noses of unsuspecting invalids. It hasn't quite found its place yet.

Alan Bennett 1934– : *Getting On* (1972)

31 The longer I practise medicine the more convinced I am there are only two types of cases: those that involve taking the trousers off and those that don't.

Alan Bennett 1934– : *Habeas Corpus* (1973)

32 Medicinal discovery,
It moves in mighty leaps,
It leapt straight past the common cold
And gave it us for keeps.

Pam Ayres 1947– : 'Oh no, I got a cold' (1976)

33 She has her high days and low days, a bit like the church. It depends what miracle drug the doctor's currently got her on.

Alan Ayckbourn 1939– : *Joking Apart* (1979)

34 Dr Sillitoes's got him on tablets for depression. It's not mental, in fact it's quite widespread. A lot of better-class people get it apparently.

Alan Bennett 1934– : *Enjoy* (1980)

35 No herb ever cures anything, it is only *said* to cure something. This is always based on the testimony of somebody called Cuthbert who died in 1678. No one ever says what he died of.

Miles Kington 1941– : *Nature Made Ridiculously Simple* (1983)

36 'Night starvation' was the classic thirties disease. It was invented by the makers of Horlicks, who, having thought up an illness that didn't exist, claimed to cure it by guaranteeing deep sleep ('ordinary sleep is not enough').

Michael Green 1927– : *The Boy Who Shot Down an Airship* (1988)

37 I do wish the more suspicious of our GPs would stop feeling nervously for their wallets every time I mention the word reform.

Kenneth Clarke 1940– : after-dinner speech, when Minister of Health, to the Royal College of General Practitioners, 9 March 1989

38 JACKIE: It's a shame you didn't soak your feet in a bowl of surgical spirit as I think I suggested earlier.
VICTORIA: Have you tried buying enough surgical spirit to fill a bowl? The woman in Boots thought I was a wino having a cocktail party. I had to buy a toilet-roll holder just to prove I wasn't homeless.

Victoria Wood 1953– : *Mens Sana in Thingummy Doodah* (1990)

39 A cousin of mine who was a casualty surgeon in Manhattan tells me that he and his colleagues had a one-word nickname for bikers: Donors. Rather chilling.

Stephen Fry 1957– : *Paperweight* (1992)

Men See also *Men and Women*

1 God made him, and therefore let him pass for a man.

William Shakespeare 1564–1616: *The Merchant of Venice* (1596–8)

2 To be a well-favoured man is the gift of fortune; but to write and read comes by nature.

William Shakespeare 1564–1616: *Much Ado About Nothing* (1598–9)

3 You men are unaccountable things; mad till you have your mistresses, and then stark mad till you are rid of 'em again.

John Vanbrugh 1664–1726: *The Provoked Wife* (1697)

4 Francesca di Rimini, miminy, piminy,
Je-ne-sais-quoi young man!

W. S. Gilbert 1836–1911: *Patience* (1881)

5 A greenery-yallery, Grosvenor Gallery,
Foot-in-the-grave young man!

W. S. Gilbert 1836–1911: *Patience* (1881)

6 Man is Nature's sole mistake!

W. S. Gilbert 1836–1911: *Princess Ida* (1884)

7 There is something positively brutal about the good temper of most modern men.

Oscar Wilde 1854–1900: *A Woman of No Importance* (1893)

8 You cannot make a man by standing a sheep on its hind-legs. But by standing a flock of sheep in that position you can make a crowd of men.

Max Beerbohm 1872–1956: *Zuleika Dobson* (1911)

9 The follies which a man regrets most, in his life, are
those which he didn't commit when he had the
opportunity.

Helen Rowland 1875–1950: *A
Guide to Men* (1922)

10 He's an oul' butty o' mine—oh, he's a darlin' man,
a daarlin' man.

Sean O'Casey 1880–1964: *Juno
and the Paycock* (1925)

11 Faded boys, jaded boys, come what may,
Art is our inspiration,
And as we are the reason for the 'Nineties' being gay,
We all wear a green carnation.

Noël Coward 1899–1973: 'Green
Carnation' (1929)

12 There is nothing about which men lie so much as about
their sexual powers. In this at least every man is, what
in his heart he would like to be, a Casanova.

W. Somerset Maugham
1874–1965: *A Writer's Notebook* (1949)
written in 1941

13 A hard man is good to find.

Mae West 1892–1980: attributed

14 They say that men suffer,
As badly, as long.
I worry, I worry,
In case they are wrong.

Wendy Cope 1945– : 'I Worry'
(1992)

15 Being all-rite is a dismal way to spend your life, and guys
are not equipped for it anyway. We are lovers and artists
and adventurers, meant to be noble, free-ranging, and
foolish, like dogs, not competing for a stamp of approval,
Friend of Womanhood.

Garrison Keillor 1942– : *The Book
of Guys* (1994)

16 Years ago, manhood was an opportunity for
achievement, and now it is a problem to be overcome.

Garrison Keillor 1942– : *The Book
of Guys* (1994)

Men and Women See also *Men, Women and Woman's Role*

1 Say that she rail; why then I'll tell her plain
She sings as sweetly as a nightingale:
Say that she frown; I'll say she looks as clear
As morning roses newly washed with dew:
Say she be mute and will not speak a word;
Then I'll commend her volubility,
And say she uttereth piercing eloquence.

William Shakespeare 1564–1616:
The Taming of the Shrew (1592)

2 Lord! I could not endure a husband with a beard on his
face: I had rather lie in the woollen.

William Shakespeare 1564–1616:
Much Ado About Nothing (1598–9)

3 OPHELIA: 'Tis brief, my lord.
HAMLET: As woman's love.

William Shakespeare 1564–1616:
Hamlet (1601)

4 A mistress should be like a little country retreat near the
town, not to dwell in constantly, but only for a night
and away.

William Wycherley c.1640–1716:
The Country Wife (1675)

5 Won't you come into the garden? I would like my roses
to see you.

Richard Brinsley Sheridan
1751–1816: to a young lady; attributed

6 ''Cos a coachman's a privileged indiwidual,' replied Mr
Weller, looking fixedly at his son. ''Cos a coachman may
do vithout suspicion wot other men may not; 'cos
a coachman may be on the wery amicablest terms with
eighty mile o' females, and yet nobody think that he ever
means to marry any vun among them.'

Charles Dickens 1812–70: *Pickwick
Papers* (1837)

7 Remember, it is as easy to marry a rich woman as a poor woman.

William Makepeace Thackeray 1811-63: *Pendennis* (1848-50)

8 Yes, I am a fatal man, Madame Fribsbi. To inspire hopeless passion is my destiny.

William Makepeace Thackeray 1811-63: *Pendennis* (1848-50)

9 Only the male intellect, clouded by sexual impulse, could call the undersized, narrow-shouldered, broad-hipped, and short-legged sex the fair sex.

Arthur Schopenhauer 1788-1860: 'On Women' (1851), tr. E. Belfort Bax

10 'Tis strange what a man may do, and a woman yet think him an angel.

William Makepeace Thackeray 1811-63: *The History of Henry Esmond* (1852)

11 Werther had a love for Charlotte
Such as words could never utter;
Would you know how first he met her?
She was cutting bread and butter.

William Makepeace Thackeray 1811-63: 'Sorrows of Werther' (1855)

12 Being kissed by a man who *didn't* wax his moustache was—like eating an egg without salt.

Rudyard Kipling 1865-1936: *The Story of the Gadsbys* (1889) 'Poor Dear Mamma'

13 A man can be happy with any woman as long as he does not love her.

Oscar Wilde 1854-1900: *The Picture of Dorian Gray* (1891)

14 All women become like their mothers. That is their tragedy. No man does. That's his.

Oscar Wilde 1854-1900: *The Importance of Being Earnest* (1895); the same words occur in dialogue form in *A Woman of No Importance* (1893)

15 No man in his heart is quite so cynical as a well-bred woman.

W. Somerset Maugham 1874-1965: *A Writer's Notebook* (1949) written in 1896

16 The only way for a woman to provide for herself decently is for her to be good to some man that can afford to be good to her.

George Bernard Shaw 1856-1950: *Mrs Warren's Profession* (1898)

17 You think that you are Ann's suitor; that you are the pursuer and she the pursued...Fool: it is you who are the pursued, the marked down quarry, the destined prey.

George Bernard Shaw 1856-1950: *Man and Superman* (1903)

18 A bunch of the boys were whooping it up in the Malamute saloon;
The kid that handles the music-box was hitting a jag-time tune;
Back of the bar, in a solo game, sat Dangerous Dan McGrew,
And watching his luck was his light-o'-love, the lady that's known as Lou.

Robert W. Service 1874-1958: 'The Shooting of Dan McGrew' (1907)

19 Like all young men, you greatly exaggerate the difference between one young woman and another.

George Bernard Shaw 1856-1950: *Major Barbara* (1907)

20 An anti-feminist too uninteresting to be really dangerous.

Rebecca West 1892-1983: of Sir William Anson in 1912; *The Young Rebecca* (1982)

On being asked 'what is the difference between man and woman' by an advocate of women's rights:

21 I can't conceive.

John Pentland Mahaffy
1839–1919: Ulick O'Connor *Oliver St John Gogarty* (1964)

22 Some ninety hours afterwards the said young novice brought into the world the Blessed St Elizabeth Bathilde, who, by dint of skipping, changed her sex at the age of forty and became a man.

Ronald Firbank 1886–1926: *Valmouth* (1919)

23 So then he said that he used to be a member of the choir himself, so who was he to cast the first rock at a girl like I.

Anita Loos 1893–1981: *Gentlemen Prefer Blondes* (1925)

24 I killin' meself workin', an' he sthruttin' about from mornin' till night like a paycock!

Sean O'Casey 1880–1964: *Juno and the Paycock* (1925)

25 Too many rings around Rosie
Never got Rosie a ring.

Irving Caesar 1895– : 'Too Many Rings around Rosie' (1925)

26 Brought up in an epoch when ladies apparently rolled along on wheels, Mr Quarles was peculiarly susceptible to calves.

Aldous Huxley 1894–1963: *Point Counter Point* (1928)

27 I should like you all to know,
I'm a famous gigolo.
And of lavender, my nature's got just a dash in it.
As I'm slightly undersexed,
You will always find me next
To some dowager who's wealthy rather than passionate.

Cole Porter 1891–1964: 'I'm a Gigolo' (1929)

28 AMANDA: I've been brought up to believe that it's beyond the pale, for a man to strike a woman.
ELYOT: A very poor tradition. Certain women should be struck regularly, like gongs.

Noël Coward 1899–1973: *Private Lives* (1930)

29 When women go wrong, men go right after them.

Mae West 1892–1980: in *She Done Him Wrong* (1933 film)

30 Some get a kick from cocaine.
I'm sure that if I took even one sniff
That would bore me terrific'ly too,
Yet I get a kick out of you.

Cole Porter 1891–1964: 'I Get a Kick out of You' (1934)

31 A man in the house is worth two in the street.

Mae West 1892–1980: in *Belle of the Nineties* (1934 film)

32 You're the Nile,
You're the Tow'r of Pisa,
You're the smile
On the Mona Lisa.
I'm a worthless check, a total wreck, a flop,
But if, baby, I'm the bottom
You're the top!

Cole Porter 1891–1964: 'You're the Top' (1934)

33 A relic of the excellent but now, alas! almost extinct tradition that man is a superior being to woman, so that a male servant, as such, is accounted a luxury.

A. P. Herbert 1890–1971: *Misleading Cases* (1935)

34 A fine romance with no kisses.
A fine romance, my friend, this is.
We should be like a couple of hot tomatoes,
But you're as cold as yesterday's mashed potatoes.

Dorothy Fields 1905–74: 'A Fine
Romance' (1936)

35 Give a man a free hand and he'll try to put it all over
you.

Mae West 1892–1980: in *Klondike
Annie* (1936 film)

36 Men seldom make passes
At girls who wear glasses.

Dorothy Parker 1893–1967: 'News
Item' (1937)

37 Woman lives but in her lord;
Count to ten, and man is bored.
With this the gist and sum of it,
What earthly good can come of it?

Dorothy Parker 1893–1967:
'General Review of the Sex Situation'
(1937)

38 You yawn at one another,
You treat him like a brother!
He treats you like his mother!
When there's no doubt the fire's out
A lady needs a change!

Dorothy Fields 1905–74: 'The Lady
Needs a Change' (1939)

39 Take him, I won't put a price on him
Take him, he's yours
Take him, pyjamas look nice on him
But how he snores!

Lorenz Hart 1895–1943: 'Take Him'
(1940)

40 I'm wild again,
Beguiled again,
A simpering, whimpering child again—
Bewitched, bothered and bewildered am I.
Couldn't sleep
And wouldn't sleep
Until I could sleep where I shouldn't sleep—
Bewitched, bothered and bewildered am I.

...I'll sing to him,
Each spring to him,
And worship the trousers that cling to him
Bewitched, bothered and bewildered am I.

...Romance—finis;
Your chance—finis;
Those ants that invaded my pants—finis—
Bewitched, bothered and bewildered no more.

Lorenz Hart 1895–1943:
'Bewitched, Bothered and Bewildered'
(1940)

*An unknown woman wrote to Shaw suggesting that as he had the
greatest brain in the world, and she the most beautiful body, they
ought to produce the most perfect child:*

41 What if the child inherits my body and your brains?

George Bernard Shaw
1856–1950: Hesketh Pearson *Bernard
Shaw* (1942)

42 The female [yellowhammer] is not quite so bright as the
male. This is also frequently noticeable in humans.

Anthony Armstrong 1897–1976:
Good Egg! (1944)

43 We sat in the car park till twenty to one
And now I'm engaged to Miss Joan Hunter Dunn.

John Betjeman 1906–84: 'A
Subaltern's Love-Song' (1945)

44 I hate men.
I can't abide 'em even now and then.

Cole Porter 1891–1964: 'I Hate Men'
(1948)

Than ever marry one of them, I'd rest a virgin rather,
For husbands are a boring lot and only give you bother.
Of course, I'm awfly glad that Mother had to marry
    Father,
But I hate men.

45 If a custom-tailored vet
    Asks me out for something wet,
    When the vet begins to pet, I cry 'Hooray!'
    But I'm always true to you, darlin', in my fashion,
    Yes, I'm always true to you, darlin', in my way.

Cole Porter 1891–1964: 'Always True to You in my Fashion' (1948)

46 He tells you when you've got on too much lipstick,
    And helps you with your girdle when your hips stick.

Ogden Nash 1902–71: 'The Perfect Husband' (1949)

47 The breeze is chasing the zephyr,
    The moon is chasing the sea,
    The bull is chasing the heifer,
    But nobody's chasing me...

    Ravel is chasing Debussy,
    The aphis chases the pea,
    The gander's chasing the goosey,
    But nobody's goosing me.

Cole Porter 1891–1964: 'Nobody's Chasing Me' (1950)

48 When you meet a gent paying all sorts of rent
    For a flat that would flatten the Taj Mahal,
    Call it sad, call it funny
    But it's better than even money
    That the guy's only doing it for some doll.

Frank Loesser 1910–69: 'Guys and Dolls' (1950)

49 But let a woman in your life
    And your serenity is through!
    She'll redecorate your home
    From the cellar to the dome;
    Then get on to the enthralling
    Fun of overhauling
    You.

Alan Jay Lerner 1918–86: 'I'm an Ordinary Man' (1956)

50 Brother, do you know a nicer occupation,
    Matter of fact, neither do I,
    Than standing on the corner
    Watching all the girls go by?

Frank Loesser 1910–69: 'Standing on the Corner' (1956)

51 Yes, why can't a woman be more like a man?
    Men are so honest, so thoroughly square;
    Eternally noble, historically fair;
    Who when you win will always give your back a pat—
    Why can't a woman be like that?

Alan Jay Lerner 1918–86: 'A Hymn to Him' (1956)

52 You've got to understand, in a way a thirty-three-year-
    old guy is a lot younger than a twenty-four-year-old girl.
    That is, he may not be ready for marriage yet.

Neil Simon 1927– : Come Blow Your Horn (1961)

53 Oh! to be loved by a man I respect,
    To bask in the glow of his perfectly understandable
    neglect.

Frank Loesser 1910–69: 'Happy to Keep his Dinner Warm' (1961)

54 Whatever women do they must do twice as well as men
    to be thought half as good. Luckily, this is not difficult.

Charlotte Whitton 1896–1975: in *Canada Month* June 1963

55 Our days will be so ecstatic
    Our nights will be so exotic
    For I'm a neurotic erratic
    And you're an erratic erotic.

E. Y. Harburg 1898–1981:
'Courtship in Greenwich Village'
(1965)

56 In Europe, when a rich woman has an affair with
    a conductor, they have a baby. In America, she endows
    an orchestra for him.

Edgar Varèse 1885–1965: Herman
G. Weinberg *Saint Cinema* (1970)

57 The minute you walked in the joint,
    I could see you were a man of distinction,
    A real big spender.
    Good looking, so refined,
    Say, wouldn't you like to know what's going on in my
        mind?
    So let me get right to the point.
    I don't pop my cork for every guy I see.
    Hey! big spender, spend a little time with me.

Dorothy Fields 1905–1974: 'Big
Spender' (1966)

58 All women dress like their mothers, that is their tragedy.
    No man ever does. That is his.

Alan Bennett 1934– : *Forty Years
On* (1969)

*Asked by the gossip columnist Hedda Hopper how she knew so much
about men:*

59 Baby, I went to night school.

Mae West 1892–1980: Max Wilk *The
Wit and Wisdom of Hollywood* (1972)

60 If men could get pregnant, abortion would be
    a sacrament.

Florynce Kennedy 1916– : 'The
Verbal Karate of Florynce R. Kennedy'
(1973)

61 He claims that women can be divided into two groups—
    the ones you stroke and the ones you swipe. There has
    been some research done on this and it's been discovered
    quite recently that they are actually a little more
    complex.

Alan Ayckbourn 1939– : *Round
and Round the Garden* (1975)

62 Some women...enjoy tremendously being told they look
    a mess—and they actually thrill to the threat of physical
    violence. I've never met one that does, mind you, but
    they probably do exist. In books. By men.

Alan Ayckbourn 1939– : *Round
and Round the Garden* (1975)

63 Woe betide the man who dares to pay a woman
    a compliment today...Forget the flowers, the chocolates,
    the soft word—rather woo her with a self-defence
    manual in one hand and a family planning leaflet in the
    other.

Alan Ayckbourn 1939– : *Round
and Round the Garden* (1975)

64 Is that a gun in your pocket, or are you just glad to see
    me?

Mae West 1892–1980: Joseph
Weintraub *Peel Me a Grape* (1975),
usually quoted 'Is that a pistol in your
pocket...'

65 The best way to hold a man is in your arms.

Mae West 1892–1980: Joseph
Weintraub *Peel Me a Grape* (1975)

66 A man has one hundred dollars and you leave him with
    two dollars, that's subtraction.

Mae West 1892–1980: Joseph
Weintraub *Peel Me a Grape* (1975)

*Approaching an unwelcoming Greta Garbo and peering up under the
brim of her floppy hat:*

67 Pardon me, Ma'am...I thought you were a guy I knew
in Pittsburgh.

Groucho Marx 1895–1977: David
Niven *Bring on the Empty Horses*
(1975)

68 The female sex has no greater fan than I, and I have the
bills to prove it.

Alan Jay Lerner 1918–86: *The
Street Where I Live* (1978)

69 Being a woman is of special interest only to aspiring male
transsexuals. To actual women, it is merely a good
excuse not to play football.

Fran Lebowitz 1946– :
Metropolitan Life (1978)

70 Always suspect any job men willingly vacate for women.

Jill Tweedie 1936–93: *It's Only Me*
(1980)

71 In the past a man was expected to give his seat on a bus
to a woman. Today it would be much more courteous for
that man to give her his job.

P. J. O'Rourke 1947– : *Modern
Manners* (1984)

72 There is one thing women can never take away from
men. We die sooner.

P. J. O'Rourke 1947– : *Modern
Manners* (1984)

73 You are the wife of an academic. That means you are
twice removed from the centre of events.

Tom Stoppard 1937– : *Jumpers*
(rev. ed. 1986)

74 There are so many kinds of awful men—
One can't avoid them all. She often said
She'd never make the same mistake again:
She always made a new mistake instead.

Wendy Cope 1945– : 'Rondeau
Redoublé' (1986)

75 LILL: Marcus prefers petite women.
VICTORIA: Yes, because they're easier to tread on.

Victoria Wood 1953– : *Mens Sana
in Thingummy Doodah* (1990)

76 He thinks I can't do anything. When he was in ceiling
tiles he used to look up to me, but now he's in contract
carpeting he treats me like underlay.

Victoria Wood 1953– : *Mens Sana
in Thingummy Doodah* (1990)

77 Women tend not to dress up in leather aprons and nail
each other to coffee tables in their spare time.

Julie Burchill 1960– : in *The
Spectator* 16 January 1992

78 From my experience of life I believe my personal motto
should be 'Beware of men bearing flowers.'

Muriel Spark 1918– : *Curriculum
Vitae* (1992)

*A fellow Congressman attacked a piece of women's rights legislation
with the words, 'I've always thought of women as kissable, cuddly,
and smelling good':*

79 That's what I feel about men. I only hope you haven't
been disappointed as often as I have.

Millicent Fenwick 1910– : in *Ned
Sherrin in his Anecdotage* (1993)

80 I suppose true sexual equality will come when a general
called Anthea is found having an unwise lunch with
a young, unreliable male model from Spain.

John Mortimer 1923– : in *The
Spectator* 26 March 1994

Middle Age See also *Old Age, Youth*

1 Thirty-five is a very attractive age. London society is full
of women of the very highest birth who have, of their
own free choice, remained thirty-five for years.

Oscar Wilde 1854–1900: *The
Importance of Being Earnest* (1895)

2 Nobody loves a fairy when she's forty.

Arthur W. D. Henley: Title of
song (1934)

3 I have a bone to pick with Fate.
Come here and tell me, girlie,
Do you think my mind is maturing late,
Or simply rotted early?

Ogden Nash 1902–71: 'Lines on Facing Forty' (1942)

4 Years ago we discovered the exact point, the dead centre of middle age. It occurs when you are too young to take up golf and too old to rush up to the net.

Franklin P. Adams 1881–1960: *Nods and Becks* (1944)

5 As we get older we do not get any younger.
Seasons return, and today I am fifty-five,
And this time last year I was fifty-four,
And this time next year I shall be sixty-two.

Henry Reed 1914–86: 'Chard Whitlow (Mr Eliot's Sunday Evening Postscript)' (1946)

6 When I was cuter,
Each night meant another suitor,
I sleep easier now.

Cole Porter 1891–1964: 'I Sleep Easier Now' (1950)

7 When I was young I hoped that one day I should be able to go into a post office to buy a stamp without feeling nervous and shy: now I realize that I never shall.

Edmund Blunden 1896–1974: Rupert Hart-Davis letter to George Lyttelton, 5 August 1956

8 From birth to 18 a girl needs good parents. From 18 to 35, she needs good looks. From 35 to 55, good personality. From 55 on, she needs good cash.

Sophie Tucker 1884–1966: Michael Freedland *Sophie* (1978)

9 You are thirty-two. You are rapidly approaching the age when your body, whether it embarrasses you or not, begins to embarrass other people.

Alan Bennett 1934– : *Getting On* (1972)

10 Maturity is a high price to pay for growing up.

Tom Stoppard 1937– : *Where Are They Now?* (1973)

Stage direction:
11 Sven enters. He is thirty, already trying hard to be fifty.

Alan Ayckbourn 1939– : *Joking Apart* (1979)

12 Middle is a dispiritingly practical age. There is a tendency to sift through unfulfilled dreams and begin chucking out the wilder ones.

Alan Coren 1938– : *Seems Like Old Times* (1989)

13 When grown-ups pretend they are in playschool they are either trying to cheat you or are terrified to death.

P. J. Kavanagh 1931– : in *The Spectator* 5 December 1992

14 After forty a woman has to choose between losing her figure or her face. My advice is to keep your face, and stay sitting down.

Barbara Cartland 1901– : Libby Purves 'Luncheon à la Cartland'; in *The Times* 6 October 1993

The Mind   See also *Intelligence and Intellectuals*

1 O Lord, Sir—when a heroine goes mad she always goes into white satin.

Richard Brinsley Sheridan 1751–1816: *The Critic* (1779)

2 Not body enough to cover his mind decently with; his intellect is improperly exposed.

Sydney Smith 1771–1845: Lady Holland *Memoir* (1855)

3 I must have a prodigious quantity of mind; it takes me as much as a week, sometimes, to make it up.

Mark Twain 1835–1910: *The Innocents Abroad* (1869)

4 An apparatus with which we think that we think.

Ambrose Bierce 1842–?1914: definition of the brain; *Cynic's Word Book* (1906)

5 Dr Tayler's thoughts are very white and pure, recalling in their disorder a draper's shop on the last day of a great white sale.

Rebecca West 1892–1983: in *The Clarion* 7 March 1913

6 'Do you know if there was any insanity in her family?' 'Insanity? No, I never heard of any. Her father lives in West Kensington, but I believe he's sane on all other subjects.'

Saki 1870–1916: *Beasts and Super-Beasts* (1914)

7 'I am inclined to think—' said I [Dr Watson]. 'I should do so,' Sherlock Holmes remarked, impatiently.

Arthur Conan Doyle 1859–1930: *The Valley of Fear* (1915)

8 There was only one catch and that was Catch-22, which specified that a concern for one's own safety in the face of dangers that were real and immediate was the process of a rational mind...Orr would be crazy to fly more missions and sane if he didn't, but if he was sane he had to fly them. If he flew them he was crazy and didn't have to; but if he didn't want to he was sane and had to.

Joseph Heller 1923– : *Catch-22* (1961)

9 If I am out of my mind, it's all right with me, thought Moses Herzog.

Saul Bellow 1915– : *Herzog* (1961) opening sentence

10 Sir Myles is a person of unsound mind, having regard to his *post mortem* re-appearance in the face of present taxation levels and general social instability.

Flann O'Brien 1911–66: *The Best of Myles* (1968)

11 A neurosis is a secret you don't know you're keeping.

Kenneth Tynan 1927–80: Kathleen Tynan *Life of Kenneth Tynan* (1987)

12 The asylums of this country are full of the sound of mind disinherited by the out of pocket.

Alan Bennett 1934– : *The Madness of George III* (performed 1991)

Mistakes and Misfortunes

1 Misery acquaints a man with strange bedfellows.

William Shakespeare 1564–1616: *The Tempest* (1611)

When the news that Sheridan's Drury Lane theatre was on fire reached the House of Commons, on 24 February 1809, a motion was made to adjourn the debate on the campaign in Spain:
2 Whatever might be the extent of the individual calamity, I do not consider it of a nature worthy to interrupt the proceedings on so great a national question.

Richard Brinsley Sheridan 1751–1816: speech, House of Commons 24 February 1809

3 Of all the horrid, hideous notes of woe,
Sadder than owl-songs or the midnight blast,
Is that portentous phrase, 'I told you so.'

Lord Byron 1788–1824: *Don Juan* (1819–24)

4 He has gone to the demnition bow-wows.

Charles Dickens 1812–70: *Nicholas Nickleby* (1839)

5 If Gladstone fell into the Thames, that would be misfortune; and if anybody pulled him out, that, I suppose, would be a calamity.

Benjamin Disraeli 1804–81: Leon Harris *The Fine Art of Political Wit* (1965)

6 I left the room with silent dignity, but caught my foot in the mat.

George Grossmith 1847–1912 and **Weedon Grossmith** 1854–1919: *The Diary of a Nobody* (1894)

7 Instead of being arrested, as we stated, for kicking his wife down a flight of stairs and hurling a lighted kerosene lamp after her, the Revd James P. Wellman died unmarried four years ago.

Anonymous: from an American newspaper, quoted by Burne-Jones in a letter to Lady Horner; J. A. Gere and John Sparrow (eds.) *Geoffrey Madan's Notebooks* (1981)

8 The younger Van Eyck
Was christened Jan, and not Mike,
The thought of this curious mistake
Often kept him awake.

Edmund Clerihew Bentley
1875–1956: 'Van Eyck' (1905)

9 Calamities are of two kinds: misfortune to ourselves, and good fortune to others.

Ambrose Bierce 1842–*c*.1914: *The Cynic's Word Book* (1906)

Edith Evans repeatedly inserted the word 'very' into a line of Hay Fever:

10 No, no, Edith. The line is, 'You can see as far as Marlow on a clear day.' On a *very* clear day you can see Marlow *and* Beaumont and Fletcher.

Noël Coward 1899–1973: Cole Lesley *The Life of Noël Coward* (1976)

11 George the Third
Ought never to have occurred.
One can only wonder
At so grotesque a blunder.

Edmund Clerihew Bentley
1875–1956: 'George the Third' (1929)

12 *For* Pheasant *read* Peasant, throughout.

W. C. Sellar 1898–1951 and **R. J. Yeatman** 1898–1968: *1066 and All That* (1930); errata

13 I hope you will give up the New Party. If you must burn your fingers in public life, go to a bright and big blaze.

Lord Beaverbrook 1879–1964: letter to Harold Nicolson, 25 June 1931

14 Something nasty in the woodshed.

Stella Gibbons 1902–89: *Cold Comfort Farm* (1932)

15 now and then
there is a person born
who is so unlucky
that he runs into accidents
which started to happen
to somebody else.

Don Marquis 1878–1937: *archys life of mehitabel* (1933) 'archy says'

16 My only solution for the problem of habitual accidents... is to stay in bed all day. Even then, there is always the chance that you will fall out.

Robert Benchley 1889–1945: *Chips off the old Benchley* (1949) 'Safety Second'

17 Two Archbishops and the Bishop of Durham hold office 'by Divine Providence': all others by 'Divine Permission'. Hensley Henson [Bishop of Durham 1920–39] added that some bishops do so by Divine Inadvertence.

Herbert Hensley Henson 1863–1947: J. A. Gere and John Sparrow (eds.) *Geoffrey Madan's Notebooks* (1981)

18 Higgledy—Piggledy
Andrea Doria
Lines in the name of this
Glorious boat.
As I sit writing these
Non-navigational
Verses a—CRASH! BANG! BLURP!
GLUB...(end of quote).

John Hollander 1929– : 'Last Words' (1966)

19 It was clear to me that I had plunged the pedal extremity into the ordure. The gamma quotient was stepped up from the head of the table and D.T. was once again reduced to a small smouldering heap of ash on the dining room chair.

Richard Ingrams 1937– and **John Wells** 1936– : *Down the Hatch* (1985); 'Dear Bill' letters

20 My misdeeds are accidental happenings and merely the result of having been in the wrong bar or bed at the wrong time, say most days between midday and midnight.

Jeffrey Bernard 1932– : in *The Spectator* 18 July 1992

Money See also *Debt, Poverty, Wealth*

1 Money, wife, is the true fuller's earth for reputations, there is not a spot or a stain but what it can take out.

John Gay 1685–1732: *The Beggar's Opera* (1728)

2 The elegant simplicity of the three per cents.

Lord Stowell 1745–1836: Lord Campbell *Lives of the Lord Chancellors* (1857)

3 Annual income twenty pounds, annual expenditure nineteen nineteen six, result happiness. Annual income twenty pounds, annual expenditure twenty pounds ought and six, result misery.

Charles Dickens 1812–70: *David Copperfield* (1850)

4 Economy was always 'elegant', and money-spending always 'vulgar' and ostentatious—a sort of sour-grapeism, which made us very peaceful and satisfied.

Elizabeth Gaskell 1810–65: *Cranford* (1853)

5 The shares are a penny, and ever so many are taken by Rothschild and Baring,
And just as a few are allotted to you, you awake with a shudder despairing.

W. S. Gilbert 1836–1911: *Iolanthe* (1882)

6 I'm tired of Love: I'm still more tired of Rhyme.
But Money gives me pleasure all the time.

Hilaire Belloc 1870–1953: 'Fatigued' (1923)

7 'My boy,' he says, 'always try to rub up against money, for if you rub up against money long enough, some of it may rub off on you.'

Damon Runyon 1884–1946: in *Cosmopolitan* August 1929, 'A Very Honourable Guy'

8 But I never worshipped the Golden Calf.

William Wedgwood Benn 1877–1960: when Lloyd George referred to him as 'this pocket edition of Moses'; speech in House of Commons, 7 November 1929

9 'First you schange me schmall scheque?' 'No.'

Caryl Brahms 1901–82 and **S. J. Simon** 1904–48: *A Bullet in the Ballet* (1937)

To Joynson-Hicks, who had acquired his double-barrelled surname through marriage with an heiress:
10 On the spur of the moment I can think of no better example of unearned increment than the hyphen in the right honourable gentleman's name.

David Lloyd George 1863–1945: Leon Harris *The Fine Art of Political Wit* (1965)

11 Men are more often bribed by their loyalties and ambitions than money.

Robert H. Jackson 1892–1954: dissenting opinion in *United States v. Wunderlich* 1951

12 I like Chopin and Bizet, and the voice of Doris Day,
Gershwin songs and old forgotten carols.
But the music that excels is the sound of oil wells
As they slurp, slurp, slurp into the barrels.

My little home will be quaint as an old parasol,
Instead of fitted carpets I'll have money wall to wall.
I want an old-fashioned house
With an old-fashioned fence
And an old-fashioned millionaire.

Marve Fisher: 'An Old-Fashioned Girl' (1954)

13 When you don't have any money, the problem is food.
When you have money, it's sex. When you have both
it's health.

J. P. Donleavy 1926– : *The Ginger Man* (1955)

14 A bank is a place that will lend you money if you can
prove that you don't need it.

Bob Hope 1903– : Alan Harrington *Life in the Crystal Palace* (1959)

15 Money, it turned out, was exactly like sex, you thought
of nothing else if you didn't have it and thought of other
things if you did.

James Baldwin 1924–87: in *Esquire* May 1961 'Black Boy looks at the White Boy'

16 If a man runs after money, he's money-mad; if he keeps
it, he's a capitalist; if he spends it, he's a playboy; if he
doesn't get it, he's a ne'er-do-well; if he doesn't try to get
it, he lacks ambition. If he gets it without working for it,
he's a parasite; and if he accumulates it after a lifetime of
hard work, people call him a fool who never got
anything out of life.

Vic Oliver 1898–1964: Laurence J. Peter (ed.) *Quotations for our Time* (1977)

17 There's only one thing to do with loose change of course.
Tighten it.

Flann O'Brien 1911–66: *The Best of Myles* (1968)

18 Money is better than poverty, if only for financial
reasons.

Woody Allen 1935– : *Without Feathers* (1976) 'Early Essays'

19 Money won't buy happiness, but it will pay the salaries
of a large research staff to study the problem.

Bill Vaughan: Laurence J. Peter (ed.) *Quotations for Our Time* (1977)

20 Money is what you'd get on beautifully without if only
other people weren't so crazy about it.

Margaret Case Harriman: Laurence J. Peter (ed.) *Quotations for our Time* (1977)

21 You can't put your VISA bill on your American Express
card.

P. J. O'Rourke 1947– : *The Bachelor Home Companion* (1987)

Morality See also *Virtue and Vice*

1 Dost thou think, because thou art virtuous, there shall be
no more cakes and ale?

William Shakespeare 1564–1616: *Twelfth Night* (1601)

2 BELINDA: Ay, but you know we must return good for evil.
LADY BRUTE: That may be a mistake in the translation.

John Vanbrugh 1664–1726: *The Provoked Wife* (1697)

3 I am all for morality now—and shall confine myself
henceforward to the strictest adultery—which you will
please recollect is all that that virtuous wife of mine has
left me.

Lord Byron 1788–1824: letter 29 October 1819

Asking Robbie Ross to keep away from the scandal-touched Reggie Turner:

4 He is very weak and you, if I remember rightly, are wicked.

Max Beerbohm 1872–1956: letter Spring 1895

5 Nowadays, with our modern mania for morality, everyone has to pose as a paragon of purity, incorruptibility, and all the other seven deadly virtues— and what is the result? You all go over like ninepins— one after the other.

Oscar Wilde 1854–1900: *An Ideal Husband* (1895)

6 On an occasion of this kind it becomes more than a moral duty to speak one's mind. It becomes a pleasure.

Oscar Wilde 1854–1900: *The Importance of Being Earnest* (1895)

7 When a stupid man is doing something he is ashamed of, he always declares that it is his duty.

George Bernard Shaw 1856–1950: *Caesar and Cleopatra* (1901)

8 I don't believe in morality. I am a disciple of Bernard Shaw.

George Bernard Shaw 1856–1950: *The Doctor's Dilemma* (1911)

9 The nation's morals are like its teeth: the more decayed they are the more it hurts to touch them.

George Bernard Shaw 1856–1950: preface to *The Shewing-up of Blanco Posnet* (1911)

10 People will do things from a sense of duty which they would never attempt as a pleasure.

Saki 1870–1916: *The Chronicles of Clovis* (1911)

11 I have to live for others and not for myself: that's middle-class morality.

George Bernard Shaw 1856–1950: *Pygmalion* (1916)

12 PICKERING: Have you no morals, man?
DOOLITTLE: Can't afford them, Governor.

George Bernard Shaw 1856–1950: *Pygmalion* (1916)

13 I'm one of the undeserving poor...up agen middle-class morality all the time...What is middle-class morality? Just an excuse for never giving me anything.

George Bernard Shaw 1856–1950: *Pygmalion* (1916)

14 There is such a thing as letting one's aesthetic sense override one's moral sense...I believe you would have condoned the South Sea Bubble and the persecution of the Albigenses if they had been carried out in effective colour schemes.

Saki 1870–1916: *The Toys of Peace* (1919)

15 If people want a sense of purpose, they should get it from their archbishops. They should not hope to receive it from their politicians.

Harold Macmillan 1894–1986: in conversation 1963; Henry Fairlie *The Life of Politics* (1968)

16 To be absolutely honest, what I feel really bad about is that I don't feel worse. That's the ineffectual liberal's problem in a nutshell.

Michael Frayn 1933– : in *Observer* 8 August 1965

17 My father, to whom I owe so much, never told me the difference between right and wrong: now, I think that's why I remain so greatly in his debt.

John Mortimer 1923– : *Clinging to the Wreckage* (1982)

18 There's nothing wrong with being innocent or high-minded
But I'm glad you're not.

Wendy Cope 1945– : 'From June to December' (1986)

19 The principle feature of contemporary American
liberalism is sanctimoniousness. By loudly denouncing all
bad things—war and hunger and date rape—liberals
testify to their own terrific goodness. More importantly,
they promote themselves to membership in a self-
selecting elite of those who care deeply about such
things.

P. J. O'Rourke 1947– : *Give War a Chance* (1992)

20 I probably have a different sense of morality to most
people.

Alan Clark 1928– : in *The Times* 2 June 1994

Murder

1 I met Murder on the way—
He had a mask like Castlereagh.

Percy Bysshe Shelley 1792–1822: 'The Mask of Anarchy' (1819)

2 When the peremptory challenges were all exhausted,
a jury of twelve men were empaneled—a jury who swore
that they had neither heard, read, talked about nor
expressed an opinion concerning a murder which the
very cattle in the corrals, the Indians in the sage-brush
and the stones in the street were cognizant of!

Mark Twain 1835–1910: *Roughing It* (1872)

3 By the argument of counsel it was shown that at half-
past ten in the morning on the day of the murder, ..
[the defendant] became insane, and remained so for
eleven and a half hours exactly.

Mark Twain 1835–1910: 'A New Crime' (1875)

After another Jack the Ripper murder:
4 All these courts must be lit, and our detectives improved.
They are not what they should be.

Queen Victoria 1819–1901: letter to Lord Salisbury, 10 November 1888

5 Lizzie Borden took an axe
And gave her mother forty whacks;
When she saw what she had done
She gave her father forty-one!

Anonymous: popular rhyme in circulation after the acquittal of Lizzie Borden, in June 1893, from the charge of murdering her father and stepmother at Fall River, Massachusetts on 4 August 1892

6 It was not until several weeks after he had decided to
murder his wife that Dr Bickleigh took any active steps in
the matter. Murder is a serious business.

Francis Iles 1893–1970: *Malice Aforethought* (1931)

7 The Stately Homes of England,
Tho' rather in the lurch,
Provide a lot of chances
For Psychical Research—
There's the ghost of a crazy younger son
Who murdered, in thirteen fifty-one,
An extremely rowdy Nun
Who resented it,
And people who come to call
Meet her in the hall.

Noël Coward 1899–1973: *The Stately Homes of England* (1938)

8 You can't chop your poppa up in Massachusetts,
Not even if it's planned as a surprise
No you can't chop your poppa up in Massachusetts
You know how neighbours love to criticize.

Michael Brown: 'Lizzie Borden' (1952)

9 We'll murder them all amid laughter and merriment,
Except for a few we'll take home to experiment.
My pulse will be quickenin' with each drop of strychnine
   we feed to a pigeon.
(It just takes a smidgin!)
To poison a pigeon in the park.

Tom Lehrer 1928– : 'Poisoning Pigeons in the Park' (1953)

10 You can always count on a murderer for a fancy prose style.

Vladimir Nabokov 1899–1977: *Lolita* (1955)

11 Television has brought back murder into the home—where it belongs.

Alfred Hitchcock 1899–1980: in *Observer* 19 December 1965

On being asked whether he thought that Dr John Bodkin Adams, acquitted of murdering an elderly female patient, had actually been guilty:

12 He must have had quite a lot of explaining to do to the recording angel.

Lord Hailsham 1907– : in an interview; John Mortimer *Character Parts* (1986)

13 BONES: This is a British murder inquiry and some degree of justice must be seen to be more or less done.
ARCHIE: I must say I find your attitude lacking in flexibility.

Tom Stoppard 1937– : *Jumpers* (rev. ed. 1986)

14 On the whole I am against mass murder: I rarely commit it myself, and often find myself quite out of sympathy with those who make a habit of it.

Bernard Levin 1928– : *In These Times* (1986)

Music and Musicians See also *Songs and Singing*

1 I have a reasonable good ear in music: let us have the tongs and the bones.

William Shakespeare 1564–1616: *A Midsummer Night's Dream* (1595–6)

2 Music helps not the toothache.

George Herbert 1593–1633: *Outlandish Proverbs* (1640)

On the performance of a celebrated violinist:

3 Difficult do you call it, Sir? I wish it were impossible.

Samuel Johnson 1709–84: William Seward *Supplement to the Anecdotes of Distinguished Persons* (1797)

4 A carpenter's hammer, in a warm summer noon, will fret me into more than midsummer madness. But those unconnected, unset sounds are nothing to the measured malice of music.

Charles Lamb 1775–1834: *Elia* (1823)

5 Some cry up Haydn, some Mozart,
Just as the whim bites; for my part
I care not a farthing candle
For either of them, or for Handel.

Charles Lamb 1775–1834: 'Free Thoughts on Several Eminent Composers' (1830)

6 Dumb as a drum vith a hole in it, sir.

Charles Dickens 1812–70: *Pickwick Papers* (1837)

7 A pianoforte is a harp in a box.

Leigh Hunt 1784–1859: *The Seer* (1840)

8 Nothing can be more disgusting than an oratorio. How absurd to see 500 people fiddling like madmen about Israelites in the Red Sea!

Sydney Smith 1771–1845: Hesketh Pearson *The Smith of Smiths* (1934)

9 I love Wagner, but the music I prefer is that of a cat hung up by its tail outside a window and trying to stick to the panes of glass with its claws.

Charles Baudelaire 1821–67: Nat Shapiro (ed.) *An Encyclopedia of Quotations about Music* (1978)

10 Wagner has lovely moments but awful quarters of an hour.

Gioacchino Rossini 1792–1868: to Emile Naumann, April 1867

11 It is a music one must hear several times. I am not going again.

Gioacchino Rossini 1792–1868: of *Tannhäuser*; L. de Hegermann-Lindencrone *In the Courts of Memory* (1912)

12 Then they began to sing
That extremely lovely thing,
'*Scherzando! ma non troppo ppp.*'

W. S. Gilbert 1836–1911: 'Story of Prince Agib' (1869)

13 What I love best about music is the women who listen to it.

Jules Goncourt 1830–70: Nat Shapiro (ed.) *An Encyclopedia of Quotations about Music* (1978)

14 'Tis wonderful how soon a piano gets into a log hut on the frontier.

Ralph Waldo Emerson 1803–82: 'Civilization' (1870)

15 A squeak's heard in the orchestra
The leader draws across
The intestines of the agile cat
The tail of the noble hoss.

G. T. Lanigan 1845–86: *The Amateur Orlando* (1875)

Printed notice in an American dancing saloon:
16 Please do not shoot the pianist. He is doing his best.

Anonymous: Oscar Wilde *Impressions of America* 'Leadville' (*c.*1882–3)

17 I only know two tunes. One of them is 'Yankee Doodle' and the other isn't.

Ulysses S. Grant 1822–85: Nat Shapiro (ed.) *An Encyclopedia of Quotations about Music* (1978)

18 The music-hall singer attends a series
Of masses and fugues and 'ops'
By Bach, interwoven
With Spohr and Beethoven,
At classical Monday Pops.

W. S. Gilbert 1836–1911: *The Mikado* (1885)

19 If one will only take the precaution to go in long enough after it commences and to come out long before it is over you will not find it wearisome.

George Bernard Shaw 1856–1950: of Gounod's *La Rédemption*; in *The World* 22 February 1893

20 Musical people are so absurdly unreasonable. They always want one to be perfectly dumb at the very moment when one is longing to be absolutely deaf.

Oscar Wilde 1854–1900: *An Ideal Husband* (1895)

21 I assure you that the typewriting machine, when played with expression, is not more annoying than the piano when played by a sister or near relation.

Oscar Wilde 1854–1900: letter to Robert Ross from Reading Prison, 1 April 1897

22 Hell is full of musical amateurs: music is the brandy of the damned.

George Bernard Shaw 1856–1950: *Man and Superman* (1903)

23 [The piano is] a parlour utensil for subduing the impenitent visitor. It is operated by depressing the keys of the machine and the spirits of the audience.

Ambrose Bierce 1842–*c.*1914: *The Enlarged Devil's Dictionary* (1967)

24 I'm told that Saint-Saëns has informed a delighted public that since the war began he has composed music for the stage, melodies, an elegy and a piece for the trombone. If he'd been making shell-cases instead it might have been all the better for music.

Maurice Ravel 1875–1937: letter to Jean Marnold, 7 October 1916

25 Classic music is th'kind that we keep thinkin'll turn into a tune.

Frank McKinney Hubbard 1868–1930: *Comments of Abe Martin and His Neighbors* (1923)

26 I have been told that Wagner's music is better than it sounds.

Bill Nye 1850–96: Mark Twain *Autobiography* (1924)

27 If I had the power, I would insist on all oratorios being sung in the costume of the period—with a possible exception in the case of *The Creation*.

Ernest Newman 1868–1959: in *New York Post* 1924; Nat Shapiro (ed.) *An Encyclopedia of Quotations about Music* (1978)

28 Ravel refuses the Legion of Honour, but all his music accepts it.

Erik Satie 1866–1925: Jean Cocteau *Le Discours d'Oxford* (1956)

29 Tchaikovsky thought of committing suicide for fear of being discovered as a homosexual, but today, if you are a composer and *not* homosexual, you might as well put a bullet through your head.

Sergei Diaghilev 1872–1929: Vernon Duke *Listen Here!* (1963)

30 Extraordinary how potent cheap music is.

Noël Coward 1899–1973: *Private Lives* (1930)

31 Jazz will endure, just as long as people hear it through their feet instead of their brains.

John Philip Sousa 1854–1932: Nat Shapiro (ed.) *An Encyclopedia of Quotations about Music* (1978)

32 Gentlemen in the clarinet department, how can you resist such an impassioned appeal from the second violins? Give them an answer, I beg you!

Thomas Beecham 1879–1961: Bernard Shore *The Orchestra Speaks* (1938)

33 Slap that bass—
Use it like a tonic.
Slap that bass
Keep your Philharmonic.
Zoom, zoom, zoom—
And the milk and honey'll flow!

Ira Gershwin 1896–1989: 'Slap that Bass' (1937)

34 HAMMERSTEIN: Here is a story laid in China about an Italian told by an Irishman. What kind of music are you going to write?
KERN: It'll be good Jewish music.'

Jerome Kern 1885–1945: in the 1930s, discussing with Oscar Hammerstein II a musical to be based on Donn Byrne's novel *Messer Marco Polo*; Gerald Bordmin *Jerome Kern* (1980)

35 Mine was the kind of piece in which nobody knew what was going on, including the composer, the conductor, and the critics. Consequently I got pretty good notices.

Oscar Levant 1906–72: *A Smattering of Ignorance* (1940)

36 What a terrible revenge by the culture of the Negroes on that of the whites!

Ignacy Jan Paderewski 1860–1941: of jazz; Nat Shapiro (ed.) *An Encyclopedia of Quotations about Music* (1978)

37 The music teacher came twice each week to bridge the awful gap between Dorothy and Chopin.

George Ade 1866–1944: Nat Shapiro (ed.) *An Encyclopedia of Quotations about Music* (1978)

38 I am one of the three worst pianists in the world at the present time. The others are James Agate and somebody whose name I am not at liberty to mention—he is a very famous pianist.

Neville Cardus 1889–1975: *Autobiography* (1947)

Lady Cunard had attempted to insist that Sir Thomas should use a score for Götterdämmerung *on the grounds that he did not know the rhythmical changes:*

39 There are no rhythmical changes in *Götterdämmerung*...It goes on and on from half-past five till midnight like a damned old cart-horse.

Thomas Beecham 1879–1961: Neville Cardus *Autobiography* (1947)

40 I wish I could write librettos for the rest of my life. It is the purest of human pleasures, a heavenly hermaphroditism of being both writer and musician. No wonder that selfish beast Wagner kept it all to himself.

Sylvia Townsend Warner 1893–1978: letter 7 April 1949

41 I absolutely forbid such outrage. If *Pygmalion* is not good enough for your friends with its own verbal music...let them try Mozart's *Cosi Fan Tutti*, or at least Offenbach's *Grand Duchess*.

George Bernard Shaw 1856–1950: refusing to allow a musical based on *Pygmalion*; Caryl Brahms and Ned Sherrin *Song by Song* (1984)

42 You are there and I am here; but where is Beethoven?

Artur Schnabel 1882–1951: to his conductor during a Beethoven rehearsal; Nat Shapiro (ed.) *An Encyclopedia of Quotations about Music* (1978)

43 There is no doubt that the first requirement for a composer is to be dead.

Arthur Honegger 1892–1955: *Je suis compositeur* (1951)

44 Applause is a receipt, not a note of demand.

Artur Schnabel 1882–1951: in *Saturday Review of Literature* 29 September 1951

45 Of course we've all *dreamed* of reviving the *castrati*; but it's needed Hilda to take the first practical steps towards making them a reality...She's drawn up a list of well-known singers who she thinks would benefit...It's only a question of getting them to agree.

Henry Reed 1914–86: *Private Life of Hilda Tablet* (1954)

46 Playing 'Bop' is like scrabble with all the vowels missing.

Duke Ellington 1899–1974: in *Look* 10 August 1954

47 I would like to thank Beethoven, Brahms, Wagner, Strauss, Rimsky-Korsakov.

Dmitri Tiomkin 1899–1979: Oscar acceptance speech for the score of *The High and the Mighty* in 1955; Nat Shapiro (ed.) *An Encyclopedia of Quotations about Music* (1978)

A trumpet player had been suggested with the endorsement 'he's a nice guy':

48 Nice guys are a dime a dozen! Get me a prick that can play!

Tommy Dorsey 1905–56: Bill Crow *Jazz Anecdotes* (1990)

49 After I die, I shall return to earth as the doorkeeper of a bordello and I won't let one of you in.

Arturo Toscanini 1867–1957: to his orchestra during a difficult rehearsal; Nat Shapiro (ed.) *An Encyclopedia of Quotations about Music* (1978)

50 If you play that score one more time before we open, people are going to think we're doing a revival.

George S. Kaufman 1889–1961: to George Gershwin; Howard Teichman *George S. Kaufman* (1973)

Beecham heard that Malcolm Sargent, whose nickname was 'Flash Harry', was conducting concerts in Japan:
51 Ah!—Flash in Japan.

Thomas Beecham 1879–1961: Harold Atkins and Archie Newman *Beecham Stories* (1978)

52 Cor Anglais! Kindly give me some indication of your presence at four bars after Letter G!

Thomas Beecham 1879–1961: H. Proctor-Gregg *Sir Thomas Beecham* (1978)

Reply to an inquiry whether the piano should be moved offstage after a pianist's particularly uninspired performance:
53 Oh, leave it on. Anyway, it will probably slink off by itself.

Thomas Beecham 1879–1961: Harold Atkins and Archie Newman *Beecham Stories* (1978)

54 Don't look now, Mr Pougnet, but I believe we're being followed.

Thomas Beecham 1879–1961: to Jean Pougnet, the violinist, as the playing of the orchestra began to improve; Harold Atkins and Archie Newman *Beecham Stories* (1978)

55 Barbirolli has done splendid work with the Hallé since they brought him back from New York...a good strong, north of England orchestra, masculine and vigorous... Barbirolli has worked wonders with the Hallé. He has transformed it into the finest chamber orchestra in the country.

Thomas Beecham 1879–1961: Neville Cardus *Sir Thomas Beecham* (1961)

56 What can you do with it?—It's like a lot of yaks jumping about.

Thomas Beecham 1879–1961: on the third movement of Beethoven's Seventh Symphony; Harold Atkins and Archie Newman *Beecham Stories* (1978)

57 Festivals are for the purpose of attracting trade to the town. What that has to do with music I don't know.

Thomas Beecham 1879–1961: Harold Atkins and Archie Newman *Beecham Stories* (1978)

58 A musicologist is a man who can read music but can't hear it.

Thomas Beecham 1879–1961: H. Proctor-Gregg *Beecham Remembered* (1976)

59 In the first movement alone, of the Seventh Symphony [by Bruckner], I took note of six pregnancies and at least four miscarriages.

Thomas Beecham 1879–1961: Harold Atkins and Archie Newman *Beecham Stories* (1978)

60 The musical equivalent of the Towers of St Pancras Station.

Thomas Beecham 1879–1961: describing Elgar's 1st Symphony; Neville Cardus *Sir Thomas Beecham* (1961)

Describing the harpsichord:
61 Like two skeletons copulating on a corrugated tin roof.

Thomas Beecham 1879–1961: Harold Atkins and Archie Newman *Beecham Stories* (1978)

To a cellist:
62 Madam, you have between your legs an instrument capable of giving pleasure to thousands—and all you can do is scratch it.

Thomas Beecham 1879–1961: attributed

63 There are two golden rules for an orchestra: start together and finish together. The public doesn't give a damn what goes on in between.

Thomas Beecham 1879–1961: Harold Atkins and Archie Newman *Beecham Stories* (1978)

64 Why do we have to have all these third-rate foreign conductors around—when we have so many second-rate ones of our own?

Thomas Beecham 1879–1961: L. Ayre *Wit of Music* (1966)

65 I know two kinds of audiences only—one coughing, and one not coughing.

Artur Schnabel 1882–1951: *My Life and Music* (1961)

66 'What do you think of Beethoven?'
'I love him, especially his poems.'

Ringo Starr 1940– : at a press conference during the Beatles' first American tour in 1964; Hunter Davies *The Beatles* (1985)

67 He uses music as an accompaniment to his conducting.

Oscar Levant 1906–72: of Leonard Bernstein; *Memoirs of an Amnesiac* (1965)

68 Leonard Bernstein has been disclosing musical secrets that have been known for over four hundred years.

Oscar Levant 1906–72: *Memoirs of an Amnesiac* (1965)

69 If you're in jazz and more than ten people like you, you're labelled commercial.

Herbie Mann 1930– : Henry Pleasants *Serious Music and all that Jazz!* (1969)

70 I prefer to face the wrath of the police than the wrath of Sir John Barbirolli.

Anonymous: a member of the Hallé orchestra on a speeding charge; Ned Sherrin *Cutting Edge* (1984)

When asked what jazz is:
71 If you still have to ask…shame on you.

Louis Armstrong 1901–71: Max Jones et al. *Salute to Satchmo* (1970) (sometimes quoted 'Man, if you gotta ask you'll never know')

72 Satisfied great success.

Igor Stravinsky 1882–1971: reply to telegram from Billy Rose, suggesting that reorchestration by Robert Russell Bennett might make a ballet which was 'a great success' even more successful; in *Ned Sherrin in his Anecdotage* (1993)

73 All music is folk music, I ain't never heard no horse sing a song.

Louis Armstrong 1901–71: in *New York Times* 7 July 1971

74 To the social-minded, a definition for Concert is: that which surrounds an intermission.

Ned Rorem 1923– : *The Final Diary* (1974)

75 I don't like composers who think. It gets in the way of their plagiarism.

Howard Dietz 1896–1983: *Dancing in the Dark* (1974)

76 The tuba is certainly the most intestinal of instruments— the very lower bowel of music.

Peter de Vries 1910–93: *The Glory of the Hummingbird* (1974)

77 There's no need for Peter Pears
To give himself airs.
He has them written
By Benjamin Britten.

Anonymous: a verse from *Punch*; in *Ned Sherrin in his Anecdotage* (1993)

78 On matters of intonation and technicalities I am more than a martinet—I am a martinetissimo!

Leopold Stokowski 1882–1977: Nat Shapiro (ed.) *An Encyclopedia of Quotations about Music* (1978)

79 I don't like my music, but what is my opinion against that of millions of others.

Frederick Loewe 1904–88: Nat Shapiro (ed.) *An Encyclopedia of Quotations about Music* (1978)

80 I hate music, especially when it's played.

Jimmy Durante 1893–1980: Nat Shapiro (ed.) *An Encyclopedia of Quotations about Music* (1978)

81 *Parsifal* is the kind of opera that starts at six o'clock. After it has been going three hours, you look at your watch and it says 6.20.

David Randolph 1914– : Nat Shapiro (ed.) *An Encyclopedia of Quotations about Music* (1978)

Asked how he could play so well when he was loaded:
82 I practise when I'm loaded.

Zoot Sims 1925–85: Bill Crow *Jazz Anecdotes* (1990)

83 If you can imagine a man having a vasectomy without anaesthetic to the sound of frantic sitar-playing, you will have some idea of what popular Turkish music is like.

Bill Bryson 1951– : *Neither Here Nor There* (1991)

84 It's the building. That acoustic would make a fart sound like a sevenfold Amen.

David Willcocks 1919– : on King's College Chapel; in *Ned Sherrin in his Anecdotage* (1993)

Names

Fashionable children's names of which Camden disapproved:
1 The new names, Free-gift, Reformation, Earth, Dust, Ashes...which have lately been given by some to their children.

William Camden 1551–1623: *Remains* (1605)

Wondering why, since he was Irish, he was not O'Sheridan:
2 For in truth we owe everybody.

Richard Brinsley Sheridan 1751–1816: Walter Jerrold *Bon-Mots* (1893)

3 If you should have a boy do not christen him John...'Tis a bad name and goes against a man. If my name had been Edmund I should have been more fortunate.

John Keats 1795–1821: letter to his sister-in-law, 13 January 1820

4 Obadiah Bind-their-kings-in-chains-and-their-nobles-with-links-of-iron.

Lord Macaulay 1800–59: 'The Battle of Naseby' (1824), fictitious author's name

5 'You mustn't mention the Shah out loud.'...'We had better call him Marjoribanks, if we want to remember who we mean.'

Robert Byron 1905–41: *The Road to Oxiana* (1937)

On being asked by William Carlos Williams how he had chosen the name 'West':

6 Horace Greeley said, 'Go West, young man. So I did.'

Nathanael West 1903–40: Jay Martin *Nathanael West* (1970)

7 They *will* call me Mrs Pat. I can't stand it. The 'Pat' is the last straw that breaks the Campbell's back.

Mrs Patrick Campbell 1865–1940: attributed

8 *Yossarian*—the very sight of the name made him shudder. There were so many esses in it. It just had to be subversive.

Joseph Heller 1923– : *Catch-22* (1961)

9 It was an odious, alien, distasteful name, that just did not inspire confidence. It was not at all like such clean, crisp, honest, American names as Cathcart, Peckem and Dreedle.

Joseph Heller 1923– : *Catch-22* (1961)

10 Every Tom, Dick and Harry is called Arthur.

Sam Goldwyn 1882–1974: to Arthur Hornblow, who was planning to name his son Arthur; Michael Freedland *The Goldwyn Touch* (1986)

11 SARAH: It's me that's left looking stupid in front of the headmistress when you forget the names of our own children—
REG: That was only once.

Alan Ayckbourn 1939– : *Table Manners* (1975)

12 Cats' names are more for human benefit. They give one a certain degree more confidence that the animal belongs to you.

Alan Ayckbourn 1939– : *Table Manners* (1975)

13 No, I'm breaking it in for a friend.

Groucho Marx 1895–1977: when asked if Groucho were his real name; attributed

14 There was a valid reason for giving it [the Livingstone daisy] an ordinary name: its proper one is mesembryanthemum, and no-one wants to spend a lifetime trying to pronounce that sort of thing, let alone trying to spell it.

Alan Melville 1910–83: *Gnomes and Gardens* (1983)

Nature and the Environment

1 On seeing Niagara Falls, Mahler exclaimed: 'Fortissimo at last!'

Gustav Mahler 1860–1911: K. Blaukopf *Gustav Mahler* (1973)

2 Every year, in the fulness o' summer, when the sukebind hangs heavy from the wains...'tes the same. And when the spring comes her hour is upon her again. 'Tes the hand of Nature and we women cannot escape it.

Stella Gibbons 1902–89: *Cold Comfort Farm* (1932)

3 What do we chop, when we chop a tree? A thousand things that you daily see.

E. Y. Harburg 1898–1981: 'Song of the Woodman' (1936)

A baby's crib, the poet's chair,
The soap box down in Union Square.
A pipe for Dad, a bat for brother,
An extra broom for dear old mother.

4 I find it hard to accept, difficult to swallow, the new term
'ecology' which has come to us...It sounds a little too
much like being sick.

Stephen Leacock 1869–1944: *The Boy I Left Behind Me* (1947)

5 BRICK: Well, they say nature hates a vacuum, Big Daddy.
BIG DADDY: That's what they say, but sometimes I think
that a vacuum is a hell of a lot better than some of
the stuff that nature replaces it with.

Tennessee Williams 1911–83: *Cat on a Hot Tin Roof* (1955)

6 Man he eat the barracuda,
Barracuda eat the bass
Bass he eat the little flounder,
'Cause the flounder lower class.
Little flounder eat the sardine
That's nature's plan.
Sardine eat the little worm,
Little worm eat man.

E. Y. Harburg 1898–1981: 'For Every Fish' (1957)

7 [Richard Nixon is] the kind of politician who would cut
down a redwood tree, and then mount the stump and
make a speech on conservation.

Adlai Stevenson 1900–65: Fawn M. Brodie *Richard Nixon* (1983)

On the possibility of golden plover being mistaken for grouse:
8 From a gastronomic point of view—that may be the
wrong word—the golden plover are very good to eat but
we must not think of our stomachs, but of conservation.

Lord Massereene and Ferrard 1914–93: speech on the Wildlife and Countryside Bill, House of Lords 2 February 1981

On the Falklands campaign, 1982:
9 It is exciting to have a real crisis on your hands, when
you have spent half your political life dealing with
humdrum issues like the environment.

Margaret Thatcher 1925– : speech to Scottish Conservative Party conference, 14 May 1982

10 Whenever nature creates something that cannot possibly
be confused with something else, it immediately creates
something very like it; if nature abhors a vacuum, it
simply loathes and hates an unmistakable species.

Miles Kington 1941– : *Nature Made Ridiculously Simple* (1983)

11 The only place you can wake up in the morning and
hear the birds coughing in the trees.

Joe Frisco: of Hollywood; attributed

12 Beware pathetic fallacy. Man's confident assumption that
his environment is so sympathetic to his moods as to kick
in with complimentary props when he requires them
bespeaks the kind of arrogance that invites come-
uppance.

Alan Coren 1938– : *Seems Like Old Times* (1989)

13 Worship of nature may be ancient, but seeing nature as
cuddlesome, hug-a-bear and too cute for words is strictly
a modern fashion.

P. J. O'Rourke 1947– : *Parliament of Whores* (1991)

14 One green bottle
Drop it in the bank...
Heaps of bottles
And yesterday's a blank

Wendy Cope 1945– : 'A Green Song' (1992)

But we'll save the planet,
Tinkle, tinkle, clank!

15 Gladioli, especially flesh-pink ones, were the floral
symbols of respectability, success and thrusting,
unquestioning optimism.

Barry Humphries 1934– : *More Please* (1992)

16 I now promise that I will publicly eat an entire dolphin
without salt, when the last Green is stuffed with broccoli,
spinach, lettuce and dandelion-leaves, and boiled in
a very large bio-degradable iron cauldron, not that
anyone would notice a difference in the nonsense he
would be spouting, boiled or raw.

Bernard Levin 1928– : *If You Want My Opinion* (1992)

News and Journalism

1 The newspapers! Sir, they are the most villainous—
licentious—abominable—infernal—Not that I ever read
them—No—I make it a rule never to look into
a newspaper.

Richard Brinsley Sheridan 1751–1816: *The Critic* (1779)

2 Thou god of our idolatry, the press...
Thou fountain, at which drink the good and wise;
Thou ever-bubbling spring of endless lies;
Like Eden's dread probationary tree,
Knowledge of good and evil is from thee.

William Cowper 1731–1800: 'The Progress of Error' (1782)

3 A would-be satirist, a hired buffoon,
A monthly scribbler of some low lampoon,
Condemned to drudge, the meanest of the mean,
And furbish falsehoods for a magazine.

Lord Byron 1788–1824: of journalists; 'English Bards and Scotch Reviewers' (1809)

4 For a slashing article, sir, there's nobody like the
Capting.

William Makepeace Thackeray 1811–63: *Pendennis* (1848–50)

5 None of the worst French novels from which careful
parents try to protect their children can be as bad as
what is daily brought and laid upon the breakfast-table of
every educated family in England, and its effect must be
most pernicious to the public morals of the country.

Queen Victoria 1819–1901: of the reporting of divorce cases in the press; letter to the Lord Chancellor, 26 December 1859

6 'I believe that nothing in the newspapers is ever true,'
said Madame Phoebus. 'And that is why they are so
popular,' added Euphrosyne, 'the taste of the age being
decidedly for fiction.'

Benjamin Disraeli 1804–81: *Lothair* (1870)

7 There are laws to protect the freedom of the press's
speech, but none that are worth anything to protect the
people from the press.

Mark Twain 1835–1910: 'License of the Press' (1873)

8 Newspapers, even, have degenerated. They may now be
absolutely relied upon.

Oscar Wilde 1854–1900: *The Decay of Lying* (1891)

The difference between journalism and literature:
9 Journalism is unreadable, and literature is not read.

Oscar Wilde 1854–1900: 'The Critic as Artist' (1891)

Of the Daily Mail:

10 By office boys for office boys.

Lord Salisbury 1830–1903: H. Hamilton Fyfe *Northcliffe, an Intimate Biography* (1930)

11 There is a journalistic curse of Eve. The woman who writes is always given anti-feminist books to review.

Rebecca West 1892–1983: in *The Clarion* 21 November 1913

12 Journalism largely consists in saying 'Lord Jones Dead' to people who never knew that Lord Jones was alive.

G. K. Chesterton 1874–1936: *Wisdom of Father Brown* (1914)

13 Editor: a person employed by a newspaper, whose business it is to separate the wheat from the chaff, and to see that the chaff is printed.

Elbert Hubbard 1859–1915: *The Roycroft Dictionary* (1914)

14 When a dog bites a man, that is not news, because it happens so often. But if a man bites a dog, that is news.

John B. Bogart 1848–1921: F. M. O'Brien *The Story of the* [New York] *Sun* (1918); often attributed to Charles A. Dana

15 More like a gentleman than a journalist.

J. B. Priestley 1894–1984: of Bruce Richmond, editor of *The Times Literary Supplement*; letter to Edward Davison, 23 June 1924

16 You should always believe all you read in the newspapers, as this makes them more interesting.

Rose Macaulay 1881–1958: *A Casual Commentary* (1926)

17 I think it well to remember that, when writing for the newspapers, we are writing for an elderly lady in Hastings who has two cats of which she is passionately fond. Unless our stuff can successfully compete for her interest with those cats, it is no good.

Willmott Lewis 1877–1950: Claud Cockburn *In Time of Trouble* (1957)

18 'We look forward keenly to the appearance of their last work.'—*Review of Reviews of Reviews*.

W. C. Sellar 1898–1951 and **R. J. Yeatman** 1898–1968: *1066 and All That* (1930)

19 You cannot hope
to bribe or twist,
thank God! the
British journalist.
But, seeing what
the man will do
unbribed, there's
no occasion to.

Humbert Wolfe 1886–1940: 'Over the Fire' (1930)

20 Power without responsibility: the prerogative of the harlot throughout the ages.

Rudyard Kipling 1865–1936: summing up the view of Lord Beaverbrook, who had said to Kipling: 'What I want is power. Kiss 'em one day and kick 'em the next'; Stanley Baldwin, Kipling's cousin, subsequently obtained permission to use the phrase in a speech in London on 18 March 1931; in *Kipling Journal* December 1971

On being asked whether George Mair had been a fastidious journalist:

21 He once telephoned a semicolon from Moscow.

James Bone: James Agate diary 31 October 1935

22 If a newspaper prints a sex crime, it is smut: but when the *New York Times* prints it it is a sociological study.

Adolph S. Ochs 1858–1935: Laurence J. Peter (ed.) *Quotations for our Time* (1977)

23 The witness replied that his leading articles [in *The Observer*] were half-way between a cold bath and a religious exercise, and that this was the place which they occupied, very fitly, in the life of the nation.

A. P. Herbert 1890–1971: *Misleading Cases* (1935)

24 Sticks nix hick pix.

Anonymous: front-page headline on the lack of enthusiasm for farm dramas among rural populations; in *Variety* 17 July 1935

25 Where it will all end, knows God!

Wolcott Gibbs 1902–58: in *New Yorker* 28 November 1936 (satirizing the style of *Time* magazine)

26 The art of newspaper paragraphing is to stroke a platitude until it purrs like an epigram.

Don Marquis 1878–1937: E. Anthony *O Rare Don Marquis* (1962)

27 *The Beast* stands for strong mutually antagonistic governments everywhere...Self-sufficiency at home, self-assertion abroad.

Evelyn Waugh 1903–66: *Scoop* (1938)

28 Up to a point, Lord Copper.

Evelyn Waugh 1903–66: *Scoop* (1938)

29 There is, of course, a certain amount of drudgery in newspaper work, just as there is in teaching classes, tunnelling into a bank, or being President of the United States. I suppose that even the most pleasurable of imaginable occupations, that of batting baseballs through the windows of the R.C.A. building, would pall a little as the days ran on.

James Thurber 1894–1961: *The Thurber Carnival* (1945)

30 More than one newspaper has been ruined by the brilliant writer in the editor's chair.

Lord Camrose 1879–1954: Leonard Russell et al. *The Pearl of Days: An Intimate Memoir of the Sunday Times* (1972)

On being telephoned by the Sunday Express *to ask what was his main wish for 1956:*

31 Not to be telephoned by the *Sunday Express* when I am busy.

Harold Nicolson 1886–1968: diary 29 December 1955

J. B. Morton held that the readers of the Daily Express *were unable to distinguish between his 'Beachcomber' column and the rest of the paper, as on one occasion he received six letters disputing the accuracy of his invented Stop Press report:*

32 *Stop Press.* At 3.55 pm yesterday there was a heavy fall of green Chartreuse over South Croydon.

J. B. Morton 1893–1975: Rupert Hart-Davis letter to George Lyttelton, 5 February 1956

33 It was mimeographed in dark brown ink on buff-coloured foolscap. It was not merely noticeable, it was unquestionably the nastiest-looking bit of work that ever dropped on to a breakfast-table.

Claud Cockburn 1904–81: of his periodical *The Week; In Time of Trouble* (1956)

34 When newspapers became solvent they lost a good deal of their old venality, but at the same time they became increasingly cautious, for capital is always timid.

H. L. Mencken 1880–1956: *Minority Report* (1956)

The words with which Cockburn claimed to have won a competition at The Times *for the dullest headline:*
35 Small earthquake in Chile. Not many dead.

Claud Cockburn 1904–81: *In Time of Trouble* (1956)

36 It is part of the social mission of every great newspaper to provide a refuge and a home for the largest possible number of salaried eccentrics.

Lord Thomson of Fleet 1894–1976: in *Observer* 22 November 1959 'Sayings of the Week'

37 I read the newspapers avidly. It is my one form of continuous fiction.

Aneurin Bevan 1897–1960: in *The Times* 29 March 1960

38 Freedom of the press in Britain means freedom to print such of the proprietor's prejudices as the advertisers don't object to.

Hannen Swaffer 1879–1962: Tom Driberg *Swaff* (1974)

39 SIXTY HORSES WEDGED IN CHIMNEY
The story to fit this sensational headline has not turned up yet.

J. B. Morton 1893–1975: Michael Frayn (ed.) *The Best of Beachcomber* (1963)

40 Accuracy to a newspaper is what virtue is to a lady; but a newspaper can always print a retraction.

Adlai Stevenson 1900–65: *The Wit and Wisdom of Adlai Stevenson* (1965)

41 People don't actually read newspapers. They get into them every morning, like a hot bath.

Marshall McLuhan 1911–80: in 1965; Jonathon Green (ed.) *A Dictionary of Contemporary Quotations* (1982)

42 The aim of so much journalism is to exploit the moral prejudices of the reader, to say nothing of those of the proprietor.

Gore Vidal 1925– : in *Nova* 1969; Jonathon Green (ed.) *A Dictionary of Contemporary Quotations* (1982)

Explaining the craft of sports writers:
43 We work in the toy department.

Jimmy Cannon 1910–73: Michael Parkinson *Sporting Lives* (1993)

44 Let's face it, sports writers, we're not hanging around with brain surgeons.

Jimmy Cannon 1910–73: attributed

45 The first law of journalism—to confirm existing prejudice rather than contradict it.

Alexander Cockburn 1941– : in 1974; Jonathon Green *Says Who?* (1988)

46 Working for [C. P.] Scott [of the *Manchester Guardian*] was like waltzing with some sedate old dowager at a mayoral reception in Manchester; for Beaverbrook, like taking the floor in a night-club in the early hours of the morning, when everyone is more or less drunk.

Malcolm Muggeridge 1903–90: *The Infernal Grove* (1975)

47 Comment is free but facts are on expenses.

Tom Stoppard 1937– : *Night and Day* (1978)

48 I'm with you on the free press. It's the newspapers
I can't stand.

Tom Stoppard 1937– : *Night and
Day* (1978)

49 I never read the papers. I haven't read a paper since
I married. I rely on Sven to tell me if there's a war
broken out. No, I think there's far too much going on
already without reading about it as well.

Alan Ayckbourn 1939– : *Joking
Apart* (1979)

50 Rock journalism is people who can't write interviewing
people who can't talk for people who can't read.

Frank Zappa 1940–93: Linda Botts
Loose Talk (1980)

51 Whenever I see a newspaper I think of the poor trees. As
trees they provide beauty, shade and shelter. But as
paper all they provide is rubbish.

Yehudi Menuhin 1916– :
Jonathon Green (ed.) *Contemporary
Quotations* (1982)

52 Viewing with dismay the conditions in somebody else's
backyard is the speciality of the *New York Times*.

John Crosby 1912– : Jonathon
Green (ed.) *A Dictionary of
Contemporary Quotations* (1982)

*On the support given him by Oundle and its then headmaster, Dr
Fisher, and his wife:*

53 Even when I began to write for the *New Statesman* they
did not flinch. Could steadfastness go further?

Arthur Marshall 1910–89: *Life's
Rich Pageant* (1984)

54 No self-respecting fish would be wrapped in a Murdoch
newspaper.

Mike Royko 1932– : before
resigning from the Chicago *Sun-Times*
when the paper was sold to Rupert
Murdoch in 1984; Karl E. Meyer (ed.)
Pundits, Poets, and Wits (1990)

55 If you are Editor [of *The Times*] you can never get away
for an evening. It's worse than a herd of dairy cows.

Alan Clark 1928– : diary 6 June
1984

56 A newspaper which weighs as much as the *Oxford
Dictionary of Quotations* and a very large haddock.

Bernard Levin 1928– : of the
Sunday edition of the *New York Times*;
In These Times (1986)

57 At certain times each year, we journalists do almost
nothing except apply for the Pulitzers and several dozen
other major prizes. During these times you could walk
right into most newsrooms and commit a multiple axe
murder naked, and it wouldn't get reported in the paper
because the reporters and editors would all be too busy
filling out prize applications.

Dave Barry 1948– : in *Miami
Herald* 29 March 1987

58 If you lose your temper at a newspaper columnist, he'll
be rich, or famous, or both.

James Hagerty 1936– : the view of
President Eisenhower's press secretary;
Jonathon Green *Says Who?* (1988)

59 I like to do my principal research in bars, where people
are more likely to tell the truth or, at least, lie less
convincingly than they do in briefings and books.

P. J. O'Rourke 1947– : *Holidays in
Hell* (1988)

60 I'm just waiting for the paper coming. Not that there's
much in it. The correspondence I initiated on the length
of the Archbishop of Canterbury's hair seems to have
gone off the boil.

Alan Bennett 1934– : *Talking
Heads* (1988)

61 So many journalists have infiltrated the catering side to
expose airport security, your lunch is probably being

Victoria Wood 1953– : *Mens Sana
in Thingummy Doodah* (1990)

cobbled together by two feature writers from the
Independent.

Of a batch of German weekly magazines:
62 There was nothing pornographic about them...They just
covered sex the way British magazines cover gardening.

Bill Bryson 1951– : *Neither Here Nor There* (1991)

63 I am a journalist and, under the modern journalist's code
of Olympian objectivity (and total purity of motive), I am
absolved of responsibility. We journalists don't have to
step on roaches. All we have to do is turn on the kitchen
light and watch the critters scurry.

P. J. O'Rourke 1947– : *Parliament of Whores* (1991)

64 You are misunderstood, maligned, viewed by the press as
a Pulitzer Prize ready to be won.

Lawton Chiles: speech to the Florida legislature on the problems of investigative journalism for politicians; in *St Petersburg (Florida) Times* 6 March 1991

Of Andrew Neil in relation to Rupert Murdoch:
65 He would like to think that he has a mind of his own.
But the pilot-fish, though it might feel that it is leading
the shark, is just riding in its pressure wave.

Clive James 1939– : *The Dreaming Swimmer* (1992)

66 Max Hastings, when he was made editor of the *Daily
Telegraph,* managed, with infinite tact, to bring it at least
into the 20th century, though it is true that he had one
unique advantage, which was that roughly a third of his
regular readers were dead, and indeed buried, or at least
embalmed, thus being in no position to complain.

Bernard Levin 1928– : *If You Want My Opinion* (1992)

67 Not only is this [the Gulf War] the first live televised war,
it's also the first war ever covered by sober journalists.

P. J. O'Rourke 1947– : *Give War a Chance* (1992)

Asked why he had allowed Page 3 to develop:
68 I don't know. The editor did it when I was away.

Rupert Murdoch 1931– : in *Guardian* 25 February 1994

Old Age See also *Middle Age, Youth*

1 A good old man, sir; he will be talking: as they say,
'when the age is in, the wit is out.'

William Shakespeare 1564–1616: *Much Ado About Nothing* (1598–9)

2 When men grow virtuous in their old age, they only
make a sacrifice to God of the devil's leavings.

Alexander Pope 1688–1744: *Miscellanies* (1727) 'Thoughts on Various Subjects'

3 Amidst the mortifying circumstances attendant upon
growing old, it is something to have seen the *School for
Scandal* in its glory.

Charles Lamb 1775–1834: *Elia* (1823)

To a young diplomat who boasted of his ignorance of whist:
4 What a sad old age you are preparing for yourself.

Charles-Maurice de Talleyrand 1754–1838: J. Amédée Pichot *Souvenirs Intimes sur M. de Talleyrand* (1870)

5 He who anticipates his century is generally persecuted
when living, and is always pilfered when dead.

Benjamin Disraeli 1804–81: *Vivian Grey* (1826)

6 'You are old, Father William,' the young man said,
'And your hair has become very white;
And yet you incessantly stand on your head—
Do you think, at your age, it is right?'

Lewis Carroll 1832–98: *Alice's Adventures in Wonderland* (1865)

7 I'll tell thee everything I can:
There's little to relate.
I saw an aged, aged man,
A-sitting on a gate.

Lewis Carroll 1832–98: *Through the Looking-Glass* (1872)

8 W'en folks git ole en strucken wid de palsy, dey mus speck ter be laff'd at.

Joel Chandler Harris 1848–1908: *Nights with Uncle Remus* (1883)

9 I've got to take under my wing,
Tra la,
A most unattractive old thing,
Tra la,
With a caricature of a face.

W. S. Gilbert 1836–1911: *The Mikado* (1885)

10 One should never make one's début with a scandal. One should reserve that to give an interest to one's old age.

Oscar Wilde 1854–1900: *The Picture of Dorian Gray* (1891)

11 The reflective sadness that steals over an elderly man when he sits in the leather arm-chair of a comfortable club smoking a good cigar and musing on the decadence of the present day.

Stephen Leacock 1869–1944: *Arcadian Adventures with the Idle Rich* (1914)

12 Mr Salteena was an elderly man of 42.

Daisy Ashford 1881–1972: *The Young Visiters* (1919)

13 Methus'lah live nine hundred years,
Methus'lah live nine hundred years
But who calls dat livin'
When no gal'll give in
To no man what's nine hundred years?

Ira Gershwin 1896–1989: 'It Ain't Necessarily So' (1935)

14 All I have to live on now is macaroni and memorial services.

Margot Asquith 1864–1945: Chips Channon diary 16 September 1943

15 Experience teaches that no man improves much after 60, and that after 65 most of them deteriorate in a really alarming manner. I could give an autobiographical example, but refrain on the advice of counsel.

H. L. Mencken 1880–1956: in *Baltimore Sun* 7 November 1948

16 Though well stricken in years the old blister becomes on these occasions as young as he feels, which seems to be about twenty-two.

P. G. Wodehouse 1881–1975: *Uncle Dynamite* (1948)

A final letter to a young correspondent, a year before his death:
17 Dear Elise,
Seek younger friends; I am extinct.

George Bernard Shaw 1856–1950: letter 1949

Of an elderly guest:
18 Talk about over 70. She can do 8 times more than I can and reduces me to a pudding of exhaustion.

Nancy Mitford 1904–73: letter 15 October 1953

19 To me old age is always fifteen years older than I am.

Bernard Baruch 1870–1965: in *Newsweek* 29 August 1955

20 How foolish to think that one can ever slam the door in the face of age. Much wiser to be polite and gracious and ask him to lunch in advance.

Noël Coward 1899–1973: diary 3 June 1956

21 H: We met at nine
  G: We met at eight
  H: I was on time
  G: No, you were late
  H: Ah yes! I remember it well.

Alan Jay Lerner 1918–86: 'I Remember It Well' (1957)

22 As I grow older and older,
  And totter towards the tomb,
  I find that I care less and less
  Who goes to bed with whom.

Dorothy L. Sayers 1893–1957: 'That's Why I Never Read Modern Novels'; Janet Hitchman *Such a Strange Lady* (1975)

23 The fountain of youth is dull as paint.
  Methuselah is my favourite saint.
  I've never been so comfortable before.
  Oh I'm so glad I'm not young any more.

Alan Jay Lerner 1918–86: 'I'm Glad I'm Not Young Any More' (1957)

24 The late sixties is rather late to be orphaned.

Noël Coward 1899–1973: on Clifton Webb's grief at his mother's death; diary 21 October 1960

25 Before I go to meet my Maker,
  I want to use the salt left in my shaker.
  I want to find out if it's true
  The Blue Danube is really blue,
  Before I kiss the world goodbye.

Howard Dietz 1896–1983: 'Before I Kiss the World Goodbye' (1963)

26 If only the stubborn old mule [Edith Evans] had taken my original advice and studied the words meticulously *before* we went into rehearsal, she would have saved herself a lot of nervousness, frustration and panic and me many hours of irritation. However, that is all part of the gay, mad world of powder and paint. I seem to be doomed to sit patient and still, watching elderly actresses forgetting their lines.

Noël Coward 1899–1973: diary 4 October 1964

In his old age Churchill overheard one of two new MPs whisper to the other, 'They say the old man's getting a bit past it':
27 And they say the old man's getting deaf as well.

Winston Churchill 1874–1965: K. Halle *The Irrepressible Churchill* (1985)

28 At forty I lost my illusions,
  At fifty I lost my hair,
  At sixty my hope and teeth were gone,
  And my feet were beyond repair.
  At eighty life has clipped my claws,
  I'm bent and bowed and cracked;
  But I can't give up the ghost because
  My follies are intact.

E. Y. Harburg 1898–1981: 'Gerontology or Springtime for Senility' (1965)

29 When our organs have been transplanted
  And the new ones made happy to lodge in us,
  Let us pray one wish be granted—
  We retain our zones erogenous.

E. Y. Harburg 1898–1981: 'Seated One Day at the Organ' (1965)

30 I zeroed in and discovered I was easily the most decrepit. (Just funning, of course, show me a pretty woman and I immediately break into a lively hoedown, followed by Cheyne-Stokes breathing.)

S. J. Perelman 1904–79: letter 27 January 1966

31 Being an old maid is like death by drowning, a really
delightful sensation after you cease to struggle.

Edna Ferber 1887–1968: R. E.
Drennan *Wit's End* (1973)

32 The House of Lords is a perfect eventide home.

Baroness Stocks 1891–1975: *My
Commonplace Book* (1970)

Note left for traffic warden on illegally parked car:
33 Dearest Warden. Front tooth broken off; look like
81-year-old pirate, so at dentist 19a. Very old—
very lame—no metras [sic].

Diana Cooper 1892–1986: Philip
Ziegler *Diana Cooper* (1981)

34 Growing old is like being increasingly penalized for
a crime you haven't committed.

Anthony Powell 1905– :
Temporary Kings (1973)

On reaching the age of 100*:*
35 If I'd known I was gonna live this long, I'd have taken
better care of myself.

Eubie Blake 1883–1983: in *Observer*
13 February 1983 'Sayings of the
Week'; also claimed by Adolph Zukor
on reaching 100

Of Prince Philip on his sixty-fifth birthday:
36 A snappish OAP with a temper like an arthritic corgi.

Jean Rook 1931–91: in *Daily Express*
10 June 1986

37 In England, you see, age wipes the slate clean...If you
live to be ninety in England and can still eat a boiled egg
they think you deserve the Nobel Prize.

Alan Bennett 1934– : *An
Englishman Abroad* (1989)

38 There are now more than thirty-one million 'older
Americans' (the term preferred by run-to-seed specimens
who are sixty-five or more). They outnumber teenagers.

P. J. O'Rourke 1947– : *Parliament
of Whores* (1991)

39 There's one more terrifying fact about old people: I'm
going to be one soon.

P. J. O'Rourke 1947– : *Parliament
of Whores* (1991)

40 Here I sit, alone and sixty,
Bald, and fat, and full of sin,
Cold the seat and loud the cistern,
As I read the Harpic tin.

Alan Bennett 1934– : 'Place Names
of China'

41 I don't need you to remind me of my age, I have
a bladder to do that for me.

Stephen Fry 1957– : *Paperweight*
(1992)

Parents See also *Children, The Family*

1 I wish either my father or my mother, or indeed both of
them, as they were in duty both equally bound to it, had
minded what they were about when they begot me.

Laurence Sterne 1713–68: *Tristram
Shandy* (1759–67)

*On hearing a report that his son Charles James Fox was to be
married:*
2 He will be obliged to go to bed at least one night of his
life.

Lord Holland 1705–74: Christopher
Hobhouse *Fox* (1934)

3 I did not throw myself into the struggle for life: I threw
my mother into it. I was not a staff to my father's old
age: I hung on to his coat tails.

George Bernard Shaw
1856–1950: preface to *The Irrational
Knot* (1905)

4 And her mother came too!

Dion Titheradge: title of song
(1921)

5 Mom and Pop were just a couple of kids when they got married. He was eighteen, she was sixteen, and I was three.

Billie Holiday 1915–59: *Lady Sings the Blues* (1958) opening words

6 In case it is one of mine.

Augustus John 1878–1961: patting children in Chelsea on the head as he passed by; Michael Holroyd *Augustus John* (1975)

7 I can't help it. I like things clean. Blame it on my mother. I was toilet trained at five months old.

Neil Simon 1927– : *The Odd Couple* (1966)

8 A Jewish man with parents alive is a fifteen-year-old boy, and will remain a fifteen-year-old boy until *they die!*

Philip Roth 1933– : *Portnoy's Complaint* (1967)

9 In our society mothers take the place elsewhere occupied by the Fates, the System, Negroes, Communism or Reactionary Imperialist Plots; mothers go on getting blamed until they're eighty, but shouldn't take it personally.

Katharine Whitehorn 1926– : *Observations* (1970)

10 They fuck you up, your mum and dad.
They may not mean to, but they do.
They fill you with the faults they had
And add some extra, just for you.

Philip Larkin 1922–85: 'This Be The Verse' (1974)

11 Parents should conduct their arguments in quiet, respectful tones, but in a foreign language. You'd be surprised what an inducement that is to the education of children.

Judith Martin 1938– : 'Advice from Miss Manners', column in *Washington Post* 1979–82

12 Because of their size, parents may be difficult to discipline properly.

P. J. O'Rourke 1947– : *Modern Manners* (1984)

13 Parents should be given only a modest and sensible allowance. And they should be encouraged to save up for things. This builds character. It also helps pay for the funeral.

P. J. O'Rourke 1947– : *Modern Manners* (1984)

14 The value to a child of poor role models is also underestimated. Parents have the idea that it is their duty to set a good example, never realizing that a bad one will do just as well, indeed better.

Jill Tweedie 1936–93: *Eating Children* (1993)

Past and Present See also *The Future*

1 It used to be a good hotel, but that proves nothing—I used to be a good boy.

Mark Twain 1835–1910: *The Innocents Abroad* (1869)

2 The rule is, jam to-morrow and jam yesterday—but never jam today.

Lewis Carroll 1832–98: *Through the Looking-Glass* (1872)

3 It was in the flood-tide of chivalry. Knighthood was in the pod.

Stephen Leacock 1869–1944: *Nonsense Novels* (1911) 'Guido the Gimlet of Ghent'

4 I do not know which makes a man more conservative— to know nothing but the present, or nothing but the past.

John Maynard Keynes 1883–1946: *The End of Laissez-Faire* (1926)

5 What a Royal Academy,
  Too Alma-Tademy,
  Practical, mystical,
  Over-artistical,
  Highly pictorial,
  Albert Memorial
  Century this has been.

Noël Coward 1899–1973: 'What a Century' (1953)

6 They spend their time mostly looking forward to the past.

John Osborne 1929– : *Look Back in Anger* (1956)

7 Stolen, perhaps, by Nicholas Udall, the Headmaster [of Eton] who stole the college plate, was homosexual, went to gaol, and on coming out was made Headmaster of Westminster. Those were the days!

George Lyttelton 1883–1962: letter to Rupert Hart-Davis, 17 September 1958

8 There's a million more important things going on in the world today. New countries are being born. They're getting ready to send men to the moon. I just can't get excited about making wax fruit.

Neil Simon 1927– : *Come Blow Your Horn* (1961)

9 It is the spirit of the age to believe that any fact, no matter how suspect, is superior to any imaginative exercise, no matter how true.

Gore Vidal 1925– : in *Encounter* December 1967

10 Nostalgia isn't what it used to be.

Anonymous: graffito (taken as title of book by Simone Signoret, 1978)

11 Hindsight is always twenty-twenty.

Billy Wilder 1906– : J. R. Columbo *Wit and Wisdom of the Moviemakers* (1979)

12 'The first ten million years were the worst,' said Marvin, 'and the second ten million years, they were the worst too. The third ten million I didn't enjoy at all. After that I went into a bit of a decline.'

Douglas Adams 1952– : *Restaurant at the End of the Universe* (1980)

13 I've always felt that the past was over and that somehow I'd missed it. Now it's starting all over again.

Alan Bennett 1934– : *Enjoy* (1980)

14 Industrial archaeology…believes that a thing that doesn't work any more is far more interesting than a thing that still works.

Miles Kington 1941– : *Nature Made Ridiculously Simple* (1983)

15 Victorians such as my grandmother always assumed, along with dreary old Isaac Watts who left us in 1748 and not one moment too soon, that Satan finds some mischief still for idle hands to do.

Arthur Marshall 1910–89: *Life's Rich Pageant* (1984)

16 We all live in the twentieth century. Well, I don't live in the twentieth century.

Dan Quayle 1947– : Joe Queenan *Imperial Caddy* (1992)

17 Weren't the eighties grand? Cash grew on trees or, anyway, coca bushes. The rich roamed the land in vast herds hunted by proud, free tribes of investment brokers who lived a simple life in tune with money.

P. J. O'Rourke 1947– : introduction to the second edition of *The Bachelor Home Companion* (1993)

People and Personalities

1 That great Cham of literature, Samuel Johnson.

Tobias Smollett 1721–71: letter to John Wilkes, 16 March 1759

2 He is a person of very *epic* appearance—and has a fine head as far as the outside goes—and wants nothing but taste to make the inside equally attractive.

Lord Byron 1788–1824: of Southey; letter 30 September 1813

3 Daniel Webster struck me much like a steam-engine in trousers.

Sydney Smith 1771–1845: Lady Holland *Memoir* (1855)

4 He [Macaulay] is like a book in breeches.

Sydney Smith 1771–1845: Lady Holland *Memoir* (1855)

To a gentleman who had accosted him in the street saying, 'Mr Jones, I believe?':
5 If you believe that, you'll believe anything.

Duke of Wellington 1769–1852: Elizabeth Longford *Pillar of State* (1972); George Jones RA (1786–1869), painter of military subjects, bore a striking resemblance to Wellington

It was suggested to Disraeli that his attacks on John Bright were too harsh as Bright was a self-made man:
6 I know he is and he adores his maker.

Benjamin Disraeli 1804–81: Leon Harris *The Fine Art of Political Wit* (1965)

7 A man of great common sense and good taste, meaning thereby a man without originality or moral courage.

George Bernard Shaw 1856–1950: *Notes to Caesar and Cleopatra* (1901) 'Julius Caesar'

8 Das Kapital...is the book of a man [Karl Marx] who took no part in normal German or English society, and wrote of Capitalists and Workmen like a Class War Correspondent and not like a fellow creature.

George Bernard Shaw 1856–1950: 'What I owe to German Culture' (1911)

9 Byron!—he would be all forgotten today if he had lived to be a florid old gentleman with iron-grey whiskers, writing very long, very able letters to *The Times* about the Repeal of the Corn Laws.

Max Beerbohm 1872–1956: *Zuleika Dobson* (1911)

On Vita Sackville-West's appearance in a tableau vivant:
10 Dear old Vita, all aqua, no vita, was as heavy as frost.

Margot Asquith 1864–1945: Philip Ziegler *Diana Cooper* (1981)

11 Her conception of God was certainly not orthodox. She felt towards Him as she might have felt towards a glorified sanitary engineer; and in some of her speculations she seems hardly to distinguish between the Deity and the Drains.

Lytton Strachey 1880–1932: of Florence Nightingale; *Eminent Victorians* (1918)

On the vegetarian George Bernard Shaw:
12 If you give him meat no woman in London will be safe.

Mrs Patrick Campbell 1865–1940: Frank Harris *Contemporary Portraits* (1919)

13 Shaw, with incredibly brilliant insolence, began to prove that Foreign Secretaries are by definition cynical and corrupt. Poor Austen, of course, tried to riposte; but he was like an elephant trying to catch an exceedingly agile wasp.

Harold Laski 1893–1950: of an encounter between Bernard Shaw and Austen Chamberlain; letter to Oliver Wendell Holmes, 3 July 1926

14 It was like watching someone organize her own immortality. Every phrase and gesture was studied. Now and again, when she said something a little out of the ordinary, she wrote it down herself in a notebook.

Harold Laski 1893–1950: of Virginia Woolf; letter to Oliver Wendell Holmes, 30 November 1930

15 [James Joyce] has the most lovely voice I know—liquid and soft with undercurrents of gurgle.

Harold Nicolson 1886–1968: letter to his wife Vita Sackville-West, 4 February 1934

On being told by George Bernard Shaw that Mussolini was a greater man than Napoleon:
16 The man's a fraud, a mountebank, a megaphone. He doesn't amount to anything more than a black-shirted bullfrog croaking away in the mud.

J. B. Priestley 1894–1984: interview with H. G. Wells, 5 September 1934; Vincent Brome *J. B. Priestley* (1988)

17 She [Dorothy Parker] is so odd a blend of Little Nell and Lady Macbeth. It is not so much the familiar phenomenon of a hand of steel in a velvet glove as a lacy sleeve with a bottle of vitriol concealed in its folds.

Alexander Woollcott 1887–1943: *While Rome Burns* (1934)

18 Use your commonsense, avoid logic, love your fellow men, have a profound faith in your own people, cultivate the hide of a rhinoceros.

Stanley Baldwin 1867–1947: advice to would-be public figures; speech broadcast 6 March 1934

19 He's always backing into the limelight.

Lord Berners 1883–1950: of T. E. Lawrence; oral tradition

20 Any man who hates dogs and babies can't be all bad.

Leo Rosten 1908– : of W. C. Fields, and often attributed to him; speech at Masquers' Club dinner, 16 February 1939

21 One would have disliked him [Lord Kitchener] intensely if one had not happened to like him.

Margot Asquith 1864–1945: Chips Channon diary 18 September 1939

22 In her early days she had that beatific expression characteristic of Victorian prettiness—like a sheep painted by Raphael.

James Agate 1877–1947: of Lillie Langtry; diary 10 April 1940

23 This was an actress who, for twenty years, had the world at her feet. She kicked it away, and the ball rolled out of her reach.

James Agate 1877–1947: of Mrs Patrick Campbell; diary 12 April 1940

24 I view this able and energetic man with some detachment. He is loyal to his own career but only incidentally to anything or anyone else.

Hugh Dalton 1887–1962: of Richard Crossman; diary 17 September 1941

25 Nothing ever made me more doubtful of T. E. Lawrence's genuineness than that he so heartily trusted two persons whom I knew to be bogus.

W. Somerset Maugham 1874–1965: *A Writer's Notebook* (1949) written in 1941

26 Everything about Leslie [Howard] was English—his manner, look, talk, pipe, slacks, and golf-jacket. He was of Hungarian extraction.

James Agate 1877–1947: diary 5 June 1943

27 Diana [Manners]'s main faults are that she takes money from men and spends her day powdering her face till she looks like a bled pig.

Margot Asquith 1864–1945: Philip Ziegler *Diana Cooper* (1981)

Asked if she really had nothing on in the [calendar] *photograph:*
28 I had the radio on.

Marilyn Monroe 1926–62: in *Time* 11 August 1952

29 All my books [are] by his bed and when he gets to a daring passage he washes it down with Deuteronomy!

Nancy Mitford 1904–73: of Lord Montgomery; letter 19 October 1953

30 He fell in love with himself at first sight and it is a passion to which he has always remained faithful.

Anthony Powell 1905– : *The Acceptance World* (1955)

31 A reader who really follows him starts out in the Nineteenth Century and lands in the Thirteenth.

H. L. Mencken 1880–1956: of G. K. Chesterton; *Minority Report* (1956)

32 The laugh in mourning.

Oliver St John Gogarty 1878–1957: of Eamonn de Valera; Ulick O'Connor *Oliver St John Gogarty* (1964)

33 The triumph of sugar over diabetes.

George Jean Nathan 1882–1958: of J. M. Barrie; Robin May *The Wit of the Theatre* (1969)

34 He [André Gide] was very bald...with...the general look of an elderly fallen angel travelling incognito.

Peter Quennell 1905– : *The Sign of the Fish* (1960)

35 He came to see me this morning—positively reeking of Horlicks.

Thomas Beecham 1879–1961: of Adrian Boult; Ned Sherrin *Cutting Edge* (1984)

36 What, when drunk, one sees in other women, one sees in Garbo sober.

Kenneth Tynan 1927–80: *Curtains* (1961)

37 Forty years ago he was Slightly in *Peter Pan*, and you might say that he has been wholly in *Peter Pan* ever since.

Kenneth Tynan 1927–80: of Noël Coward; *Curtains* (1961)

38 She had much in common with Hitler, only no moustache.

Noël Coward 1899–1973: of Mary Baker Eddy; diary 16 July 1962

Calling on Lord Beaverbrook at Arlington House in St James's, Randolph Churchill was told by Beaverbrook's butler 'The lord is out walking in the park':
39 On the lake, I presume.

Randolph Churchill 1911–68: in *Ned Sherrin in his Anecdotage* (1993)

40 Of course, I believe in the Devil. How otherwise would I account for the existence of Lord Beaverbrook?

Evelyn Waugh 1903–66: L. Gourlay *The Beaverbrook I Knew* (1984)

41 Her interest in native things and people was not healthy when demented Black and Tans were at large and unused to making fine distinctions.

Flann O'Brien 1911–66: of Lady Gregory; *Myles Away from Dublin* (1990)

42 Shyness had always been a disease with him [T. E. Lawrence], and it was shyness and a longing for anonymity that made him disguise himself. Clad in the magnificent white silk robes of an Arab prince, with in his belt the short curved, gold sword of the Ashraf

Alan Bennett 1934– : *Forty Years On* (1969)

descendants of the Prophet, he hoped to pass unnoticed through London. Alas, he was mistaken.

43 Picasso [attending a party given by the Duff Coopers at the British Embassy in Paris] looking like some strange wild ape who had strayed into a film-set where the ball on the eve of the Battle of Waterloo was being filmed.

Malcolm Muggeridge 1903–90: *The Infernal Grove* (1975)

44 There were three things that Chico was always on—a phone, a horse or a broad.

Groucho Marx 1895–1977: Ned Sherrin *Cutting Edge* (1984)

45 I am a life-enhancing pessimist.

J. B. Priestley 1894–1984: *Instead of the Trees* (1977)

46 [Charles Laughton] walks top-heavily, like a salmon standing on its tail.

Kenneth Tynan 1927–80: *Profiles* (ed. Kathleen Tynan, 1989)

47 A triumph of the embalmer's art.

Gore Vidal 1925– : of Ronald Reagan; in *Observer* 26 April 1981

48 That's the trouble with Anthony—half mad baronet, half beautiful woman.

R. A. Butler 1902–82: of Anthony Eden; attributed

49 Not a fun person really.

Arthur Marshall 1910–89: of Isaac Watts; *Life's Rich Pageant* (1984)

50 People shouldn't be treated like objects. They aren't that valuable.

P. J. O'Rourke 1947– : *Modern Manners* (1984)

51 A magnificent sight presents itself: Barbara Cartland wearing an electric pink chiffon dress, with false eyelashes, as thick as those caterpillars that give you a rash if you handle them, was draped on the central staircase with her dress arranged like a caricature of the celebrated Cecil Beaton photograph of the Countess of Jersey.

Alan Clark 1928– : diary 12 May 1984

52 The only Greek Tragedy I know.

Billy Wilder 1906– : of Spyros Skouras, Head of Fox Studios; attributed, perhaps apocryphal

53 He [Kenneth Baker] looked like…the cat who had not only got the cream, but cornered the market in cream futures.

William Keegan 1938– : in *Observer* 13 December 1987

54 Her shrill contralto could be heard urging friend and foe to go over the top. There is a quality to that gritty voice which…amounts to the infliction of pain.

Julian Critchley 1930– : of Margaret Thatcher; Kenneth Harris *Thatcher* (1988)

55 Poor George, he can't help it—he was born with a silver foot in his mouth.

Ann Richards 1933– : of George Bush; keynote speech at the Democratic convention, in *Independent* 20 July 1988

56 Like a Goth swaggering around Rome wearing an onyx toilet seat for a collar, he exudes self-confidence.

Clive James 1939– : of Rupert Murdoch; in *Observer* 16 October 1989

57 A First Minister whose self-righteous stubbornness has not been equalled, save briefly by Neville Chamberlain, since Lord North.

Roy Jenkins 1920– : of Mrs Thatcher; in *Observer* 11 March 1990

58 Everyone with any sense and experience in life would rather take his fellows one by one than in a crowd.

P. J. O'Rourke 1947– : *Parliament of Whores* (1991)

Crowds are noisy, unreasonable and impatient. They can
trample you easier than a single person can. And
a crowd will never buy you lunch.

59 Up to his death three years earlier she had been living
with Lord Alfred Douglas, the fatal lover of Oscar Wilde,
an arrangement which I imagine would satisfy any
woman's craving for birth control.

Muriel Spark 1918– : of Marie
Stopes; *Curriculum Vitae* (1992)

On imitating Harold Macmillan:
60 Talk as though you have a cathedral in your mouth.

Peter Ustinov 1921– : attributed

61 A big cat detained briefly in a poodle parlour, sharpening
her claws on the velvet.

Matthew Parris 1949– : of Lady
Thatcher in the House of Lords; *Look
Behind You!* (1993)

Peoples See *Countries and Peoples*

Philosophy

1 I have tried too in my time to be a philosopher; but,
I don't know how, cheerfulness was always breaking in.

Oliver Edwards 1711–91: James
Boswell *Life of Samuel Johnson*
(1934 ed.) 17 April 1778

2 The philosopher is like a mountaineer who has with
difficulty climbed a mountain for the sake of the sunrise,
and arriving at the top finds only fog; whereupon he
wanders down again. He must be an honest man if he
doesn't tell you that the spectacle was stupendous.

W. Somerset Maugham
1874–1965: *A Writer's Notebook* (1949)
written in 1896

3 Sometimes I sits and thinks, and then again I just sits.

Punch 1841–1992: vol. 131 (1906)

4 Philosophy consists very largely of one philosopher
arguing that all others are jackasses. He usually proves
it, and I should add that he usually proves that he is one
himself.

H. L. Mencken 1880–1956:
Minority Report (1956)

5 To take a gloomy view of life is not part of my
philosophy; to laugh at the idiocies of my fellow
creatures is. However, at this particular moment I cannot
find so much to laugh at as I would like.

Noël Coward 1899–1973: diary
21 July 1963

6 Apart from the known and the unknown, what else is
there?

Harold Pinter 1930– : *The
Homecoming* (1965)

On the speaker's choice of subject at university:
7 Almost everyone who didn't know what to do, did
philosophy. Well, that's logical.

Tom Stoppard 1937– : *Albert's
Bridge* (1969)

8 If rationality were the criterion for things being allowed
to exist, the world would be one gigantic field of soya
beans.

Tom Stoppard 1937– : *Jumpers*
(rev. ed. 1986)

Places See also *America, Countries, England, Ireland, Scotland, Towns and Cities, Wales*

1 Mulberry Garden, now the only place of refreshment
about the town for persons of the best quality to be
exceedingly cheated at.

John Evelyn 1620–1706: diary
10 May 1654

2 Kent, sir—everybody knows Kent—apples, cherries, hops, and women.

Charles Dickens 1812–70: *Pickwick Papers* (1837)

3 I ascertained by looking down from Wenlock Edge that Hughley Church could not have had much of a steeple. But as I had already composed the poem and could not invent another name that sounded so nice, I could only deplore that the church at Hughley should follow the bad example of the church at Brou, which persists in standing on a plain after Matthew Arnold has said that it stands among mountains.

A. E. Housman 1859–1936: letter to Laurence Housman, 5 October 1896

4 Addresses are given to us to conceal our whereabouts.

Saki 1870–1916: *Reginald in Russia* (1910)

5 For Cambridge people rarely smile,
Being urban, squat, and packed with guile.

Rupert Brooke 1887–1915: 'The Old Vicarage, Grantchester' (1915)

6 Very flat, Norfolk.

Noël Coward 1899–1973: *Private Lives* (1930)

7 There's a famous seaside place called Blackpool,
That's noted for fresh air and fun,
And Mr and Mrs Ramsbottom
Went there with young Albert, their son.

Marriott Edgar 1880–1951: 'The Lion and Albert' (1932)

Of Herat:
8 Here at last is Asia without an inferiority complex.

Robert Byron 1905–41: *The Road to Oxiana* (1937)

9 Stayed at the Randolph at Oxford. It is always good to return to places in which one has been thoroughly miserable. I hated Oxford—the rudest, meanest, sub-normallest hole I have ever struck.

James Agate 1877–1947: diary 26 April 1942

10 The Pacific Ocean was a body of water surrounded on all sides by elephantiasis and other dread diseases.

Joseph Heller 1923– : *Catch-22* (1961)

11 BASIL: May I ask what you were hoping to see out of a Torquay bedroom window? Sydney Opera House, perhaps? The Hanging Gardens of Babylon? Herds of wildebeeste sweeping majestically...

John Cleese 1939– and **Connie Booth**: *Fawlty Towers* (1979) 'Communication Problems'

12 The [Sydney] Opera House is a dud...It looks like a portable typewriter full of oyster shells, and to the contention that it echoes the sails of yachts on the harbour I can only point out that the yachts on the harbour don't waste any time echoing opera houses.

Clive James 1939– : *Flying Visits* (1984)

13 He was glued to Soho, a fairly common but chronic attachment some of us formed. There is no known cure for it except the road to Golders Green.

Jeffrey Bernard 1932– : in *The Spectator* 8 March 1986

14 I had forgotten just how flat and empty it [middle America] is. Stand on two phone books almost anywhere in Iowa and you get a view.

Bill Bryson 1951– : *The Lost Continent* (1989)

15 Hammerfest...seemed an agreeable enough town in a thank-you-God-for-not-making-me-live-here sort of way.

Bill Bryson 1951– : *Neither Here Nor There* (1991)

16 They used to say that Cambridge was the first stopping place for the wind that swept down from the Urals: in the thirties that was as true of the politics as the weather.

Stephen Fry 1957– : *The Liar* (1991)

Poetry and Poets See also *Literature, Writers and Writing*

1 'By God,' quod he, 'for pleynly, at a word,
Thy drasty rymyng is nat worth a toord!'

Geoffrey Chaucer c.1343–1400: *The Canterbury Tales* 'Sir Thopas'

2 Dr Donne's verses are like the peace of God; they pass all understanding.

James I 1566–1625: remark recorded by Archdeacon Plume (1630–1704)

3 All that is not prose is verse; and all that is not verse is prose.

Molière 1622–73: *Le Bourgeois Gentilhomme* (1671)

4 M. JOURDAIN: What? when I say: 'Nicole, bring me my slippers, and give me my night-cap,' is that prose?
PHILOSOPHY TEACHER: Yes, Sir.
M. JOURDAIN: Good heavens! For more than forty years I have been speaking prose without knowing it.

Molière 1622–73: *Le Bourgeois Gentilhomme* (1671)

5 So poetry, which is in Oxford made
An art, in London only is a trade.

John Dryden 1631–1700: 'Prologue to the University of Oxon...at the Acting of *The Silent Woman*' (1673)

6 Sir, I admit your gen'ral rule
That every poet is a fool:
But you yourself may serve to show it,
That every fool is not a poet.

Alexander Pope 1688–1744: 'Epigram from the French' (1732)

7 And he, whose fustian's so sublimely bad,
It is not poetry, but prose run mad.

Alexander Pope 1688–1744: 'An Epistle to Dr Arbuthnot' (1735)

8 While pensive poets painful vigils keep,
Sleepless themselves, to give their readers sleep.

Alexander Pope 1688–1744: *The Dunciad* (1742)

On the relative merits of two minor poets:
9 Sir, there is no settling the point of precedency between a louse and a flea.

Samuel Johnson 1709–84: James Boswell *Life of Samuel Johnson* (1791) 1783

10 I have but with some difficulty *not* added any more to this snake of a poem [*The Giaour*]—which has been lengthening its rattles every month.

Lord Byron 1788–1824: letter 26 August 1813

11 The Edinburgh praises Jack Keats or Ketch or whatever his names are;—why his is the Onanism of poetry.

Lord Byron 1788–1824: letter to his publisher John Murray, 4 November 1820

12 What is a modern poet's fate?
To write his thoughts upon a slate;
The critic spits on what is done,
Gives it a wipe—and all is gone.

Thomas Hood 1799–1845: 'A Joke', in Hallam Tennyson *Alfred Lord Tennyson* (1897); not found in Hood's *Complete Works*

Laman Blanchard, a young poet, had submitted some verses entitled 'Orient Pearls at Random Strung' to Household Words:
13 Dear Blanchard, too much string—Yours. C.D.

Charles Dickens 1812–70: Frederick Locker-Lampson *My Confidences* (1896)

14 '*I* can repeat poetry as well as other folk if it comes to that—' 'Oh, it needn't come to that!' Alice hastily said.

Lewis Carroll 1832–98: *Through the Looking-Glass* (1872)

Lewis Morris had asked for advice in dealing with the conspiracy of silence surrounding his name in connection with the laureateship after Tennyson's death:
15 Join it.

Oscar Wilde 1854–1900: Walter Jerrold *A Book of Famous Wits* (1912)

The nineteenth-century headmaster of Eton:
16 I wish Shelley had been at Harrow.

James John Hornby 1826–1909: Henry S. Salt *Percy Bysshe Shelley* (1896)

17 All bad poetry springs from genuine feeling.

Oscar Wilde 1854–1900: 'The Critic as Artist' (1891)

18 Mr Stone's hexameters are verses of no sort, but prose in ribands.

A. E. Housman 1859–1936: in *Classical Review* 1899

19 I made my then famous declaration (among 100 people) 'I am a Socialist, an Atheist and a Vegetarian' (ergo, a true Shelleyan), whereupon two ladies who had been palpitating with enthusiasm for Shelley under the impression that he was a devout Anglican, resigned on the spot.

George Bernard Shaw 1856–1950: letter 1 March 1908

20 In barrenness, at any rate, I hold a high place among English poets, excelling even Gray.

A. E. Housman 1859–1936: letter 28 February 1910

21 The European view of a poet is not of much importance unless the poet writes in Esperanto.

A. E. Housman 1859–1936: in *Cambridge Review* 1915

22 Immature poets imitate; mature poets steal.

T. S. Eliot 1888–1965: *The Sacred Wood* (1920) 'Philip Massinger'

23 I may as well tell you, here and now, that if you are going about the place thinking things pretty, you will never make a modern poet. Be poignant, man, be poignant!

P. G. Wodehouse 1881–1975: *The Small Bachelor* (1927)

24 Of all the literary scenes
Saddest this sight to me:
The graves of little magazines
Who died to make verse free.

Keith Preston 1884–1927: 'The Liberators'

25 I did not begin to write poetry in earnest until the really emotional part of my life was over; and my poetry, so far as I could make out, sprang chiefly from physical conditions, such as a relaxed sore throat during my most prolific period.

A. E. Housman 1859–1936: letter 5 February 1933

On being asked by Stephen Spender in the 1930s how best a poet could serve the Communist cause:
26 Go to Spain and get killed. The movement needs a Byron.

Harry Pollitt 1890–1960: Frank Johnson *Out of Order* (1982); attributed, perhaps apocryphal

27 Europe has not as yet recovered from the Renaissance, nor has English poetry recovered from Alexander Pope.

Oliver St John Gogarty 1878–1957: *As I Was Going Down Sackville Street* (1937)

28 Writing a book of poetry is like dropping a rose petal down the Grand Canyon and waiting for the echo.

Don Marquis 1878–1937: E. Anthony *O Rare Don Marquis* (1962)

29 Mr Spender... writes mediocre verse, as do a multitude of quite decent young men. No particular shame attaches to that. But a group of his friends seem to have conspired to make a booby of him. At a guess, I should say that the literature they have produced about him is, in bulk, about ten times his own work. That is shockingly bad for a man still young, alive and, I fear, productive.

Evelyn Waugh 1903–66: of Stephen Spender; letter in *The Spectator*, 21 April 1939

The young Stephen Spender had told Eliot of his wish to become a poet:

30 I can understand your wanting to write poems, but I don't quite know what you mean by 'being a poet'...

T. S. Eliot 1888–1965: Stephen Spender *World within World* (1951)

31 Peotry is sissy stuff that rhymes. Weedy people sa la and fie and swoon when they see a bunch of daffodils.

Geoffrey Willans 1911–58 and **Ronald Searle** 1920– : *Down with Skool!* (1953)

32 Poetry is the only art people haven't yet learnt to consume like soup.

W. H. Auden 1907–73: in *New York Times* 1960; Jonathon Green (ed.) *A Dictionary of Contemporary Quotations* (1982)

33 It is being said of a certain poet that though he tortures the English language, he has never yet succeeded in forcing it to reveal its meaning.

J. B. Morton 1893–1975: Michael Frayn (ed.) *The Best of Beachcomber* (1963)

34 I'd as soon write free verse as play tennis with the net down.

Robert Frost 1874–1963: Edward Lathem *Interviews with Robert Frost* (1966)

35 I picture him as short and tan.
We'd meet, perhaps, in Hindustan.
I'd say, with admirable *élan*,
'Ah, Anantanarayanan—'.

John Updike 1932– : 'I Missed His Book, But I Read His Name' (1964)

36 For years a secret shame destroyed my peace—
I'd not read Eliot, Auden or MacNeice.
But then I had a thought that brought me hope—
Neither had Chaucer, Shakespeare, Milton, Pope.

Justin Richardson: 'Take Heart, Illiterates' (1966)

37 There are the women whose husbands I meet on
aeroplanes
Who close their briefcases and ask, 'What are *you* in?'
I look in their eyes, I tell them I am in poetry....

Donald Hall 1928– : 'To a Waterfowl' (1971)

38 The notion of expressing sentiments in short lines having similar sounds at their ends seems as remote as mangoes on the moon.

Philip Larkin 1922–85: letter to Barbara Pym, 22 January 1975

39 My favourite poem is the one that starts 'Thirty days hath September' because it actually tells you something.

Groucho Marx 1895–1977: Ned Sherrin *Cutting Edge* (1984); attributed

On poetry:

40 Generally speaking, it is inhumane to detain a fleeting insight.

Fran Lebowitz 1946– : *Metropolitan Life* (1978)

41 [Ian Hamilton] now knows every widow of the late poet
Robert Lowell.

Gore Vidal 1925– : in *The Spectator*
23 October 1982

42 I used to think all poets were Byronic—
Mad, bad and dangerous to know.
And then I met a few. Yes it's ironic—
I used to think all poets were Byronic.
They're mostly wicked as a ginless tonic
And wild as pension plans.

Wendy Cope 1945– : 'Triolet'
(1986)

Of a poetry reading:
43 The audience swelled to six in the end and we all
huddled in a corner.

P. J. Kavanagh 1931– : in *The
Spectator* 5 December 1992

44 Sometimes poetry is emotion recollected in a highly
emotional state.

Wendy Cope 1945– : 'An
Argument with Wordsworth' (1992)

45 There was a young man called MacNabbiter
Who had an organ of prodigious diameter.
But it was not the size
That gave girls the surprise,
'Twas his rhythm—Iambic Pentameter.

Anonymous: in *Ned Sherrin in his
Anecdotage* (1993)

Politicians See also *Politics*

1 DEMOSTHENES: The Athenians will kill thee, Phocion,
should they go crazy.
PHOCION: But they will kill thee, should they come to
their senses.

Phocion c.402–317 BC: Plutarch *Life
of Phocion and Cato the Younger*
(Loeb ed., 1919)

2 In good King Charles's golden days,
When loyalty no harm meant;
A furious High-Churchman I was,
And so I gained preferment.
Unto my flock I daily preached,
Kings are by God appointed,
And damned are those who dare resist,
Or touch the Lord's Anointed.
And this is law, I will maintain,
Unto my dying day, Sir,
That whatsoever King shall reign,
I will be the Vicar of Bray, sir!

Anonymous: *British Musical
Miscellany* (1734) 'The Vicar of Bray'

On the younger Pitt's maiden speech:
3 Not merely a chip of the old 'block', but the old block
itself.

Edmund Burke 1729–97: N. W.
Wraxall *Historical Memoirs of My Own
Time* (1904 ed.)

4 Pitt is to Addington
As London is to Paddington.

George Canning 1770–1827: 'The
Oracle' (c.1803)

*Disraeli was asked on what, offering himself for Marylebone, he
intended to stand:*
5 On my head.

Benjamin Disraeli 1804–81: *Lord
Beaconsfield's Correspondence with
his Sister 1832–1852* (1886)

6 The right hon. Gentleman caught the Whigs bathing, and walked away with their clothes.

Benjamin Disraeli 1804–81: speech, House of Commons 28 February 1845 (on Sir Robert Peel's abandoning protection in favour of free trade, traditionally the policy of the [Whig] Opposition)

7 I never saw so many shocking bad hats in my life.

Duke of Wellington 1769–1852: on seeing the first Reformed Parliament; W. Fraser *Words on Wellington* (1889)

8 At the best only ginger-beer and not champagne, and now an old painted pantaloon, very deaf, very blind, and with false teeth which would fall out of his mouth when speaking if he did not hesitate and halt so in his talk.

Benjamin Disraeli 1804–81: of Palmerston in 1855; Algernon Cecil *Queen Victoria and her Prime Ministers* (1953)

9 Palmerston is now seventy. If he could prove evidence of his potency in his electoral address he'd sweep the country.

Benjamin Disraeli 1804–81: to the suggestion that a Palmerston romance should be made public; Hesketh Pearson *Dizzy* (1951); attributed, probably apocryphal

10 Mr Speaker, the Honourable Gentleman has conceived three times and brought forth nothing.

Stephen A. Douglas 1813–61: when Lincoln, making his first speech in the Illinois legislature, had three times begun 'Mr Speaker, I conceive'; Leon Harris *The Fine Art of Political Wit* (1965)

11 Many a time have I stood on one side of the counter and sold whiskey to Mr Douglas, but the difference between us now is this. I have left my side of the counter, but Mr Douglas still sticks to his as tenaciously as ever.

Abraham Lincoln 1809–65: during a debate with Stephen A. Douglas in 1858; Leon Harris *The Fine Art of Political Wit* (1965)

12 For the purposes of recreation he [Gladstone] has selected the felling of trees, and we may usefully remark that his amusements, like his politics, are essentially destructive...The forest laments in order that Mr Gladstone may perspire.

Lord Randolph Churchill 1849–94: speech on Financial Reform, delivered in Blackpool, 24 January 1884

13 If the country doesn't go to the dogs or the Radicals, we shall have you Prime Minister, some day.

Oscar Wilde 1854–1900: *An Ideal Husband* (1895)

14 McKinley has no more backbone than a chocolate éclair!

Theodore Roosevelt 1858–1919: Harry Thurston Peck *Twenty Years of the Republic* (1906)

15 Sir! you have disappointed us!
We had intended you to be
The next Prime Minister but three:
The stocks were sold; the Press was squared;
The Middle Class was quite prepared.
But as it is!...My language fails!
Go out and govern New South Wales!

Hilaire Belloc 1870–1953: 'Lord Lundy' (1907)

16 God Almighty was satisfied with Ten Commandments.
Mr Wilson requires Fourteen Points.

Georges Clemenceau 1841–1929:
during the Peace Conference
negotiations in 1919; Leon Harris *The
Fine Art of Political Wit* (1965)

17 They [parliament] are a lot of hard-faced men who look
as if they had done very well out of the war.

Stanley Baldwin 1867–1947: J. M.
Keynes *Economic Consequences of the
Peace* (1919)

18 Well, it was the best I could do, seated as I was between
Jesus Christ and Napoleon Bonaparte.

David Lloyd George 1863–1945:
on the outcome of the Peace
Conference negotiations in
1919 between himself, Woodrow
Wilson, and Georges Clemenceau;
Leon Harris *The Fine Art of Political
Wit* (1965)

19 To represent Chamberlain as an injured man, and
Balfour as the man who injured him, is like saying that
Christ crucified Pontius Pilate.

A. E. Housman 1859–1936: letter
7 December 1922

On being asked what place Arthur Balfour would have in history:
20 He will be just like the scent on a pocket handkerchief.

David Lloyd George 1863–1945:
Thomas Jones diary 9 June 1922

*When in 1924 Baldwin offered Churchill the position of Chancellor of
the Exchequer with the words, 'Will you go to the Treasury?', Churchill
replied, 'This fulfils my ambition. I still have my father's robes as
Chancellor. I shall be proud to serve you in this splendid Office.' He
recorded however that he would have liked to give a rather more brief
reply:*
21 Will a bloody duck swim?

Winston Churchill 1874–1965:
Martin Gilbert *Winston S. Churchill*
(1976)

22 A good politician is quite as unthinkable as an honest
burglar.

H. L. Mencken 1880–1956:
Prejudices 4th series (1925)

23 It is fitting that we should have buried the Unknown
Prime Minister [Bonar Law] by the side of the Unknown
Soldier.

Herbert Asquith 1852–1928:
Robert Blake *The Unknown Prime
Minister* (1955)

24 Austen [Chamberlain] always played the game, and he
always lost it.

F. E. Smith 1872–1930: Lord
Beaverbrook *Men and Power* (1956)

After forming the National Government, 25 August 1931:
25 Tomorrow every Duchess in London will be wanting to
kiss me!

Ramsay MacDonald 1866–1937:
Viscount Snowden *An Autobiography*
(1934)

26 I remember, when I was a child, being taken to the
celebrated Barnum's circus, which contained an
exhibition of freaks and monstrosities, but the exhibit on
the programme which I most desired to see was the one
described as 'The Boneless Wonder'. My parents judged
that that spectacle would be too revolting and
demoralizing for my youthful eyes, and I have waited 50
years to see the boneless wonder sitting on the Treasury
Bench.

Winston Churchill 1874–1965: of
Ramsay Macdonald; speech in the
House of Commons 28 January 1931

27 did you ever
  notice that when
  a politician
  does get an idea
  he usually
  gets it all wrong.

Don Marquis 1878–1937: *archys life of mehitabel* (1933) 'archygrams'

On being asked immediately after the Munich crisis if he were not worn out by the late nights:
28 No, not exactly. But it spoils one's eye for the high birds.

Lord Halifax 1881–1959: Paul Johnson (ed.) *The Oxford Book of Political Anecdotes* (1986)

On being asked by C. E. Joad if he did not think that Neville Chamberlain's mind had broadened recently:
29 Yes, in the same way that a darning needle is broader than a sewing-needle.

Harold Nicolson 1886–1968: Nigel Nicolson (ed.) *Diaries and Letters of Harold Nicolson* (1966) vol. 1; introduction

30 He had the geniality of the politician who for years has gone out of his way to be cordial with everyone he meets.

W. Somerset Maugham 1874–1965: *A Writer's Notebook* (1949) written in 1938

31 He may be a son of a bitch, but he's our son of a bitch.

Franklin D. Roosevelt 1882–1945: on President Somoza of Nicaragua, 1938; Jonathon Green *The Book of Political Quotes* (1982)

32 He might make an adequate Lord Mayor of Birmingham in a lean year.

David Lloyd George 1863–1945: of Neville Chamberlain; Leon Harris *The Fine Art of Political Wit* (1965)

33 In the depths of that dusty soul is nothing but abject surrender.

Winston Churchill 1874–1965: of Neville Chamberlain; Leon Harris *The Fine Art of Political Wit* (1965)

34 Listening to a speech by Chamberlain is like paying a visit to Woolworth's: everything in its place and nothing above sixpence.

Aneurin Bevan 1897–1960: Michael Foot *Aneurin Bevan* (1962) vol.1

Churchill responding to a report from Anthony Eden:
35 As far as I can see you have used every cliché except 'God is Love' and 'Please adjust your dress before leaving'.

Winston Churchill 1874–1965: attributed in *Life* 9 December 1940 (when this story was repeated in the *Daily Mirror*, Churchill denied that it was true)

36 Beaverbrook is so pleased to be in the Government that he is like the town tart who has finally married the Mayor!

Beverley Baxter 1891–1964: Chips Channon diary 12 June 1940

37 The rich man's Roosevelt, the simple barefoot boy from Wall Street.

Harold Ickes 1874–1952: of Wendell Willkie, Republican presidential candidate in 1940; Leon Harris *The Fine Art of Political Wit* (1965)

38 a politician is an arse upon which everyone has sat except a man.

e. e. cummings 1894–1962: *1 x 1* (1944)

39 Like the little man on top of the wedding cake.

Harold Ickes 1874–1952: of Thomas Dewey, Republican presidential candidate in 1948; Leon Harris *The Fine Art of Political Wit* (1965); also attributed to Alice Roosevelt Longworth

40 [Churchill] would make a drum out of the skin of his mother in order to sound his own praises.

David Lloyd George 1863–1945: Paul Johnson (ed.) *The Oxford Book of Political Anecdotes* (1986)

41 [Neville Chamberlain] saw foreign policy through the wrong end of a municipal drainpipe.

David Lloyd George 1863–1945: Leon Harris *The Fine Art of Political Wit* (1965); also attributed to Churchill

42 He has sat on the fence so long that the iron has entered his soul.

David Lloyd George 1863–1945: of Sir John Simon; Leon Harris *The Fine Art of Political Wit* (1965)

43 He [Lloyd George] can't see a belt without hitting below it.

Margot Asquith 1864–1945: in *Listener* 11 June 1953 'Margot Oxford' by Lady Violet Bonham Carter

44 If there had been any formidable body of cannibals in the country he would have promised to provide them with free missionaries fattened at the taxpayer's expense.

H. L. Mencken 1880–1956: of Harry Truman's success in the 1948 presidential campaign; in *Baltimore Sun* 7 November 1948

45 If he ever went to school without any boots it was because he was too big for them.

Ivor Bulmer-Thomas 1905–93: referring to Harold Wilson in a speech at the Conservative Party Conference; in *Manchester Guardian* 13 October 1949

46 The candle in that great turnip has gone out.

Winston Churchill 1874–1965: on the death of Stanley Baldwin; Harold Nicolson diary 17 August 1950

Attlee is said to have remarked that Herbert Morrison was his own worst enemy:
47 Not while I'm alive he ain't.

Ernest Bevin 1881–1951: Paul Johnson (ed.) *The Oxford Book of Political Anecdotes* (1986), introduction; also attributed to Bevin of Aneurin Bevan

48 There but for the grace of God, goes God.

Winston Churchill 1874–1965: of Stafford Cripps; P. Brendon *Churchill* (1984)

49 If I talk over people's heads, Ike must talk under their feet.

Adlai Stevenson 1900–65: during the Presidential campaign of 1952; Bill Adler *The Stevenson Wit* (1966)

50 Always threatening resignation, he never signed off.

Lord Beaverbrook 1879–1964: of Lord Derby; *Men and Power* (1956)

51 Few thought he was even a starter
There were many who thought themselves smarter
But he ended PM

Clement Attlee 1883–1967: describing himself; letter to Tom Attlee, 8 April 1956

CH and OM
An earl and a knight of the garter.

Of Eisenhower's presidential campaign in 1956:

52 The General has dedicated himself so many times he
must feel like the cornerstone of a public building.

Adlai Stevenson 1900–65: Leon
Harris *The Fine Art of Political Wit*
(1965)

53 He [Aneurin Bevan] enjoys prophesying the imminent fall
of the capitalist system and is prepared to play a part,
any part, in its burial, except that of mute.

Harold Macmillan 1894–1986:
Michael Foot *Aneurin Bevan* (1962)

54 I am not going to spend any time whatsoever in
attacking the Foreign Secretary...If we complain about
the tune, there is no reason to attack the monkey when
the organ grinder is present.

Aneurin Bevan 1897–1960: during
a debate on the Suez crisis, House of
Commons 16 May 1957

55 A politician is a man who understands government, and
it takes a politician to run a government. A statesman is
a politician who's been dead 10 or 15 years.

Harry S. Truman 1884–1972: in
New York World Telegram and Sun
12 April 1958

56 The right kind of leader for the Labour Party...a
desiccated calculating machine.

Aneurin Bevan 1897–1960:
generally taken as referring to Hugh
Gaitskell, although Bevan specifically
denied it in an interview with Robin
Day on 28 April 1959; Michael Foot
Aneurin Bevan (1973) vol. 2

57 I have recently been travelling round the world—on your
behalf, and at your expense—visiting some of the chaps
with whom I hope to be shaping your future. I went first
to Germany, and there I spoke with the German Foreign
Minister, Herr...Herr and there, and we exchanged
many frank words in our respective languages.

Peter Cook 1937–95: as Harold
Macmillan; in *Beyond the Fringe* (1961
revue)

58 The British House of Lords is the British Outer Mongolia
for retired politicians.

Tony Benn 1925– : in *Observer*
4 February 1962

59 [Lloyd George] did not seem to care which way he
travelled providing he was in the driver's seat.

Lord Beaverbrook 1879–1964: *The
Decline and Fall of Lloyd George*
(1963)

60 QUESTION: What are the desirable qualifications for any
young man who wishes to become a politician?
MR CHURCHILL: It is the ability to foretell what is going to
happen tomorrow, next week, next month, and next
year. And to have the ability afterwards to explain
why it didn't happen.

Winston Churchill 1874–1965: B.
Adler *Churchill Wit* (1965)

61 Higgledy-Piggledy
Benjamin Harrison
Twenty-third President,
Was, and, as such,
Served between Clevelands, and
Save for this trivial
Idiosyncrasy
Didn't do much.

John Hollander 1929– : 'Historical
Reflections' (1966)

62 It was hard to listen to Goldwater and realize that a man could be half Jewish and yet sometimes appear twice as dense as the normal Gentile.

I. F. Stone 1907– : of Senator Goldwater during the 1968 presidential campaign; Jonathon Green (ed.) *A Dictionary of Contemporary Quotations* (1982)

63 Any political party that can't cough up anything better than a treacherous brain-damaged old vulture like Hubert Humphrey deserves every beating it gets. They don't hardly make 'em like Hubert any more—but just to be on the safe side, he should be castrated anyway.

Hunter S. Thompson 1939– : *Fear and Loathing: On the Campaign Trail* (1973)

64 It was not until his campaign collapsed and his ex-staffers felt free to talk that I learned that working for Big Ed [Muskie] was something like being locked in a rolling boxcar with a vicious 200-pound water rat

Hunter S. Thompson 1939– : *Fear and Loathing: On the Campaign Trail* (1973)

65 The average footslogger in the New South Wales Right... generally speaking carries a dagger in one hand and a Bible in the other and doesn't put either to really elegant use.

Neville Wran: in 1973; Michael Gordon *A Question of Leadership* (1993)

66 I worship the quicksand he walks in.

Art Buchwald 1925– : of Richard Nixon (later also applied to Jimmy Carter); Jonathon Green (ed.) *The Book of Political Quotes* (1982)

67 If he were any dumber, he'd be a tree.

Barry Goldwater 1909– : of Senator William Scott of Virginia in 1976; Jonathon Green (ed.) *The Book of Political Quotes* (1982)

68 It is not necessary that every time he rises he should give his famous imitation of a semi-house-trained polecat.

Michael Foot 1913– : of Norman Tebbit; speech in the House of Commons 2 March 1978

69 He is not well suited to the small-scale plot.

Barry Jones 1920– : of Gough Whitlam in 1978; Jonathon Green (ed.) *The Book of Political Quotes* (1982)

70 [Richard Crossman] has the jovial garrulity and air of witty indiscretion that shows he intends to give nothing away.

Tina Brown 1953– : *Loose Talk* (1979)

71 Richard Nixon impeached himself. He gave us Gerald Ford as his revenge.

Bella Abzug 1920– : in *Rolling Stone*; Linda Botts *Loose Talk* (1980)

72 We're realists. It doesn't make much difference between Ford and Carter. Carter is your typical smiling, brilliant, backstabbing, bull-shitting, Southern nut cutter.

Lane Kirkland: Jonathon Green (ed.) *The Book of Political Quotes* (1982)

73 I would not want Jimmy Carter and his men put in charge of snake control in Ireland.

Eugene McCarthy 1916– : Jonathon Green (ed.) *The Book of Political Quotes* (1982)

74 Hubert Humphrey talks so fast that listening to him is like trying to read *Playboy* magazine with your wife turning over the pages.

Barry Goldwater 1909– : Jonathon Green (ed.) *A Dictionary of Contemporary Quotations* (1982)

75 There he sits, like a very old beast of the jungle or veldt, turning his great sad eyes now this way, now that, in an attempt to locate his enemies, and contemplating the while whether to take evasive action or mount a counter-attack.

Alan Watkins 1933– : of William Whitelaw at the Conservative Party Conference; in *Observer* 10 October 1982

76 A politician is a man who can be verbose in fewer words than anyone else.

Peter de Vries 1910–93: Jonathon Green (ed.) *The Book of Political Quotes* (1982)

77 I am the very master of the multipurpose metaphor,
I put them into speeches which I always feel the better for.
The speed of my delivery is totally vehicular,
I'm burning with a passion about nothing in particular.
I'm well acquainted too with matters technological,
I'm able to explain myself in phrases tautological.
My language is poetical and full of hidden promises...
It's like the raging torrent of a thousand Dylan Thomases.

Alistair Beaton: 'I am the very Model...', sung by Pooh-Bach (*Minister for everything else. Formerly Neil Kinnock*) in Ned Sherrin and Alistair Beaton *The Metropolitan Mikado* (1985)

78 Ronald Reagan, the President who never told bad news to the American people.

Garrison Keillor 1942– : *We Are Still Married* (1989), introduction

79 Reagan was probably the first modern president to treat the post as a part-time job, one way of helping to fill the otherwise blank days of retirement.

Simon Hoggart 1946– : *America* (1990)

80 Consider the vice-president, George Bush, a man so bedevilled by bladder problems that he managed, for the last eight years, to be in the men's room whenever an important illegal decision was made.

Barbara Ehrenreich 1941– : *The Worst Years of Our Lives* (1991)

81 Politicians *are* interested in people. Not that this is always a virtue. Dogs are interested in fleas.

P. J. O'Rourke 1947– : *Parliament of Whores* (1991)

82 In our own country, the Republic has been governed by Andrew Johnson, an ineffective drunk; Warren Harding, an ineffective drunk; and Gerald Ford, who didn't even need to be a drunk to be ineffective.

Joe Queenan: *Imperial Caddy* (1992)

83 Rum fellow, that Saddam [Hussein]. He's wearing an Eton Ramblers' tie.

Lord Home 1903–95: while watching television; in *Ned Sherrin in his Anecdotage* (1993)

84 From time to time in these pages, I like to parody the memoirs of politicians, highlighting their conceit, their pomposity, their simple delight in themselves. Over the past couple of years, the job has become abominably hard, for each politician seems far more adept at parodying himself than I could ever hope to be.

Craig Brown 1957– : *Craig Brown's Greatest Hits* (1993)

Politics See also *Democracy, Diplomacy, Government, Politicians*

1 [BOSWELL:] So, Sir, you laugh at schemes of political improvement.
[JOHNSON:] Why, Sir, most schemes of political improvement are very laughable things.

Samuel Johnson 1709–84: James Boswell *Life of Samuel Johnson* (1791) 26 October 1769

2 A little rebellion now and then is a good thing.

Thomas Jefferson 1743–1826: letter to James Madison, 30 January 1787

3 I have no consistency, except in politics; and *that* probably arises from my indifference on the subject altogether.

Lord Byron 1788–1824: letter 16 January 1814

4 From politics, it was an easy step to silence.

Jane Austen 1775–1817: *Northanger Abbey* (1818)

5 The nearest thing to a Tory in disguise is a Whig in office.

Benjamin Disraeli 1804–81: speech at High Wycombe in 1832; Hesketh Pearson *Dizzy* (1951)

6 Tory and Whig in turns shall be my host,
I taste no politics in boiled and roast.

Sydney Smith 1771–1845: letter to John Murray, November 1834

7 'It's always best on these occasions to do what the mob do.' 'But suppose there are two mobs?' suggested Mr Snodgrass. 'Shout with the largest,' replied Mr Pickwick.

Charles Dickens 1812–70: *Pickwick Papers* (1837)

8 The duty of an Opposition [is] very simple...to oppose everything, and propose nothing.

Lord Derby 1799–1869: quoting 'Mr Tierney, a great Whig authority'; House of Lords 4 June 1841

9 'A sound Conservative government,' said Taper, musingly. 'I understand: Tory men and Whig measures.'

Benjamin Disraeli 1804–81: *Coningsby* (1844)

10 'I am all for a religious cry,' said Taper. 'It means nothing, and, if successful, does not interfere with business when we are in.'

Benjamin Disraeli 1804–81: *Coningsby* (1844)

11 Minorities...are almost always in the right.

Sydney Smith 1771–1845: H. Pearson *The Smith of Smiths* (1934)

12 A Conservative Government is an organized hypocrisy.

Benjamin Disraeli 1804–81: speech, House of Commons 17 March 1845; Bagehot, quoting Disraeli in *The English Constitution* (1867) 'The House of Lords', elaborated on the theme with the words 'so much did the ideas of its "head" differ from the sensations of its "tail"'

13 Revolutions are not made with rosewater.

Anonymous: used by Disraeli in speech at High Wycombe in 1847; Hesketh Pearson *Dizzy* (1951)

14 Men destined to the highest places should beware of badinage...An insular country subject to fogs, and with a powerful middle class, requires grave statesmen.

Benjamin Disraeli 1804–81: *Endymion* (1880)

15 What we call public opinion is generally public sentiment.

Benjamin Disraeli 1804–81: speech in House of Commons, 3 August 1880

16 I often think it's comical
How Nature always does contrive
That every boy and every gal,
That's born into the world alive,

W. S. Gilbert 1836–1911: *Iolanthe* (1882)

Is either a little Liberal,
Or else a little Conservative!

17 When in that House MPs divide,
If they've a brain and cerebellum too,
They have to leave that brain outside,
And vote just as their leaders tell 'em to.

W. S. Gilbert 1836–1911: *Iolanthe*
(1882)

18 The prospect of a lot
Of dull MPs in close proximity,
All thinking for themselves is what
No man can face with equanimity.

W. S. Gilbert 1836–1911: *Iolanthe*
(1882)

19 CHILD: Mamma, are Tories born wicked, or do they grow
wicked afterwards?
MOTHER: They are born wicked, and grow worse.

Anonymous: G. W. E. Russell
Collections and Recollections (1898)

20 A statesman who is enamoured of existing evils, as
distinguished from the Liberal, who wishes to replace
them with others.

Ambrose Bierce 1842–c.1914:
definition of a Conservative; *The
Cynic's Word Book* (1906)

21 He knows nothing; and he thinks he knows everything.
That points clearly to a political career.

George Bernard Shaw
1856–1950: *Major Barbara* (1907)

22 Practical politics consists in ignoring facts.

Henry Brooks Adams 1838–1918:
The Education of Henry Adams (1907)

23 That any sane nation, having observed that you could
provide for the supply of bread by giving bakers
a pecuniary interest in baking for you, should go on to
give a surgeon a pecuniary interest in cutting off your
leg, is enough to make one despair of political humanity.

George Bernard Shaw
1856–1950: preface to *The Doctor's
Dilemma* (1911)

24 A strife of interests masquerading as a contest of
principles. The conduct of public affairs for private
advantage.

Ambrose Bierce 1842–c.1914: *The
Enlarged Devil's Dictionary* (1967)

25 Anarchism is a game at which the police can beat you.

George Bernard Shaw
1856–1950: *Misalliance* (1914)

26 If you want to succeed in politics, you must keep your
conscience well under control.

David Lloyd George 1863–1945:
Lord Riddell diary 23 April 1919

27 The more you read and observe about this Politics thing,
you got to admit that each party is worse than the other.

Will Rogers 1879–1935: *The
Illiterate Digest* (1924)

28 There are three classes which need sanctuary more than
others—birds, wild flowers, and Prime Ministers.

Stanley Baldwin 1867–1947: in
Observer 24 May 1925

29 Nature has no cure for this sort of madness [Bolshevism],
though I have known a legacy from a rich relative work
wonders.

F. E. Smith 1872–1930: *Law, Life
and Letters* (1927)

30 [The War Office kept three sets of figures:] one to mislead
the public, another to mislead the Cabinet, and the third
to mislead itself.

Herbert Asquith 1852–1928:
Alistair Horne *Price of Glory* (1962)

31 Testators would do well to provide some indication of the
particular Liberal Party which they have in mind, such
as a telephone number or a Christian name.

A. P. Herbert 1890–1971:
Misleading Cases (1935)

32 I never dared be radical when young
For fear it would make me conservative when old.

Robert Frost 1874–1963:
'Precaution' (1936)

33 Sing us a song
Of social significance.
All other tunes are taboo
It must be packed with social fact
Or we won't love you!

Harold Rome 1908– : 'Sing a Song of Social Significance' (1937)

34 It's not cricket to picket.

Harold Rome 1908– : song-title (1937)

35 A liberal is a man who leaves the room before the fight begins.

Heywood Broun 1888–1939: R. E. Drennan *Wit's End* (1973)

36 When the political columnists say 'Every thinking man' they mean themselves, and when candidates appeal to 'Every intelligent voter' they mean everybody who is going to vote for them.

Franklin P. Adams 1881–1960: *Nods and Becks* (1944)

To Franklin Roosevelt on the likely duration of the Yalta conference with Stalin:

37 I do not see any other way of realizing our hopes about World Organization in five or six days. Even the Almighty took seven.

Winston Churchill 1874–1965: *The Second World War* (1954) vol. 6

38 Conservatives do not believe that the political struggle is the most important thing in life...The simplest of them prefer fox-hunting—the wisest religion.

Lord Hailsham 1907– : *The Case for Conservatism* (1947)

39 Fat filibusterers begat
Income tax adjusterers begat
'Twas Natchaler and Natchaler to
Begat
And sometimes a bachelor, he begat...

E. Y. Harburg 1898–1981: 'The Begat' (1947)

40 My God! They've shot our fox!

Nigel Birch 1906–81: on hearing of the resignation of Hugh Dalton, Chancellor of the Exchequer in the Labour Government, 13 November 1947

41 We all know why Blue Streak was kept on although it was an obvious failure. It was to save the Minister of Defence's face. We are, in fact, looking at the most expensive face in history. Helen of Troy's face, it is true, may only have launched a thousand ships, but at least they were operational.

Harold Wilson 1916–95: to Duncan Sandys in 1951; Leon Harris *The Fine Art of Political Wit* (1965)

42 I will make a bargain with the Republicans. If they will stop telling lies about Democrats, we will stop telling the truth about them.

Adlai Stevenson 1900–65: speech during 1952 Presidential campaign; Leon Harris *The Fine Art of Political Wit* (1965)

43 We know what happens to people who stay in the middle of the road. They get run down.

Aneurin Bevan 1897–1960: in *Observer* 6 December 1953

44 As socialists we want a socialist world not because we have the conceit that men would thereby be more happy...but because we feel the moral imperative in life itself to raise the human condition even if this should ultimately mean no more than that man's suffering has been lifted to a higher level.

Norman Mailer 1923– : 'David Riesman Reconsidered' (1954)

45 Damn it all, you can't have the crown of thorns *and* the thirty pieces of silver.

Aneurin Bevan 1897–1960: on his position in the Labour Party, *c*.1956; Michael Foot *Aneurin Bevan* (1973) vol. 2

46 It is always important in conflict to prove to the satisfaction of all the people on your side that the enemy is not only out to steal your land, or your cattle, or your market for cheap cotton goods, but is at the same time vicious and, as the Irish say, 'an affront to God'.

Claud Cockburn 1904–81: *Crossing the Line* (1958)

47 Politics is the diversion of trivial men who, when they succeed at it, become important in the eyes of more trivial men.

George Jean Nathan 1882–1958: attributed

Statement at London airport on leaving for a Commonwealth tour, 7 January 1958, following the resignation of the Chancellor of the Exchequer and others:

48 I thought the best thing to do was to settle up these little local difficulties, and then turn to the wider vision of the Commonwealth.

Harold Macmillan 1894–1986: in *The Times* 8 January 1958

49 Men enter local politics solely as a result of being unhappily married.

C. Northcote Parkinson 1909–93 : *Parkinson's Law* (1958)

50 DEALER: How about Dave Zimmerman?
BEN: Davie's too bright.
2: What about Walt Gustafson?
BEN: Walt died last night.
3: How about Frank Monohan?
4: What about George Gale?
BEN: Frank ain't a citizen
    And George is in jail.
5: We could run Al Wallenstein.
BEN: He's only twenty three.
DEALER: How about Ed Peterson?
2: You idiot, that's me!
ALL: Politics and Poker...

Sheldon Harnick 1924– : 'Politics and Poker' (1959)

51 There are two ways of getting into the Cabinet—you can crawl in or kick your way in.

Aneurin Bevan 1897–1960: attributed

52 Vote for the man who promises least; he'll be the least disappointing.

Bernard Baruch 1870–1965: Meyer Berger *New York* (1960)

53 He was a long-limbed farmer, a God-fearing, freedom-loving, law-abiding rugged individualist who held that federal aid to anyone but farmers was creeping socialism.

Joseph Heller 1923– : *Catch-22* (1961)

54 As usual the Liberals offer a mixture of sound and original ideas. Unfortunately none of the sound ideas is original and none of the original ideas is sound.

Harold Macmillan 1894–1986: speech to London Conservatives, 7 March 1961

To Winston Churchill, who had complained that a matter had been raised several times in Cabinet:

55 A monologue is not a decision.

Clement Attlee 1883–1967: Francis Williams *A Prime Minister Remembers* (1961)

56 A liberal is a man too broadminded to take his own side in a quarrel.

Robert Frost 1874–1963: Jonathon Green (ed.) *A Dictionary of Contemporary Quotations* (1982)

57 Gratitude is not a normal feature of political life.

Lord Kilmuir 1900–67: *Political Adventure* (1964)

58 Politics are almost as exciting as war and quite as dangerous. In war you can only be killed once, but in politics—many times.

Winston Churchill 1874–1965: attributed

59 I have never found in a long experience of politics that criticism is ever inhibited by ignorance.

Harold Macmillan 1894–1986: Leon Harris *The Fine Art of Politcal Wit* (1965)

60 An independent is a guy who wants to take the politics out of politics.

Adlai Stevenson 1900–65: Bill Adler *The Stevenson Wit* (1966)

61 *Je suis Marxiste—tendance Groucho.*
I am a Marxist—of the Groucho tendency.

Anonymous: slogan found at Nanterre in Paris, 1968

62 Think of it! A second Chamber selected by the Whips. A seraglio of eunuchs.

Michael Foot 1913– : speech in the House of Commons 3 February 1969

63 The Tory Party only panics in a crisis.

Iain Macleod 1913–70: attributed

64 It has always seemed to me more artistic, when the curtain falls on the last performance, to accept the inevitable *E finita la commedia*. It is tempting, perhaps, but unrewarding to hang about the greenroom after final retirement from the stage.

Harold Macmillan 1894–1986: *At the End of the Day* (1973)

65 'Ominous' is not quite the right word for a situation where one of the most consistently unpopular politicians in American history [Richard Nixon] suddenly skyrockets to folk hero status while his closest advisers are being caught almost daily in nazi-style gigs that would have embarrassed Martin Bormann.

Hunter S. Thompson 1939– : *Fear and Loathing: On the Campaign Trail* (1973)

66 Once the toothpaste is out of the tube, it is awfully hard to get it back in.

H. R. Haldeman 1929–93: to John Dean; *Hearings Before the Select Committee on Presidential Campaign Activities of US Senate: Watergate and Related Activities* (1973)

67 M is for Marx
and Movement of Masses
and Massing of Arses
and Clashing of Classes.

Cyril Connolly 1903–74: 'Where Engels Fears to Tread'

68 I'm not going to rearrange the furniture on the deck of the Titanic.

Rogers Morton 1914–79: having lost five of the last six primaries as President Ford's campaign manager; in *Washington Post* 16 May 1976

Annotation to a ministerial brief, said to have been read out inadvertently in the House of Lords:
69 This is a rotten argument, but it should be good enough for their lordships on a hot summer afternoon.

Anonymous: Lord Home *The Way the Wind Blows* (1976)

70 Politics is supposed to be the second oldest profession. I have come to realize that it bears a very close resemblance to the first.

Ronald Reagan 1911– : at a conference in Los Angeles, 2 March 1977

71 Have you ever seen a candidate talking to a rich person on television?

Art Buchwald 1925– : Laurence J. Peter (ed.) *Quotations for our Time* (1977)

72 The US presidency is a Tudor monarchy plus telephones.

Anthony Burgess 1917–93: George Plimpton (ed.) *Writers at Work* 4th Series (1977)

On the quality of debate in the House of Lords:
73 It is, I think, good evidence of life after death.

Donald Soper 1903– : in *Listener* 17 August 1978

74 There are three bodies no sensible man directly challenges: the Roman Catholic Church, the Brigade of Guards and the National Union of Mineworkers.

Harold Macmillan 1894–1986: *Observer* 22 February 1981

75 In politics you must always keep running with the pack. The moment that you falter and they sense that you are injured, the rest will turn on you like wolves.

R. A. Butler 1902–82: Dennis Walters *Not Always with the Pack* (1989)

On his failure to become Conservative leader:
76 It is less important to have the majority of MPs on your side than not to have a hard-core minority against you.

R. A. Butler 1902–82: attributed

77 The only safe pleasure for a parliamentarian is a bag of boiled sweets.

Julian Critchley 1930– : in *Listener* 10 June 1982

78 Labour is led by an upper-class public school man, the Tories by a self-made grammar school lass who worships her creator, though she is democratic enough to talk down to anyone.

Austin Mitchell 1934– : *Westminster Man* (1982)

79 The Labour Party is going around stirring up apathy.

William Whitelaw 1918– : recalled by Alan Watkins as a characteristic 'Willieism', in *Observer* 1 May 1983

80 BLAIR: Everybody knows their safe house. Red Square we call it.
HOGBIN: We call it Dunkremlin.

Tom Stoppard 1937– : *The Dog It Was That Died* (1983)

On privatization:
81 First of all the Georgian silver goes, and then all that nice furniture that used to be in the saloon. Then the Canalettos go.

Harold Macmillan 1894–1986: speech to the Tory Reform Group, 8 November 1985

82 If you want to rise in politics in the United States there is one subject you must stay away from, and that is politics.

Gore Vidal 1925– : in *Observer* 28 June 1987 'Sayings of the Week'

83 There's nothing so improves the mood of the Party as the imminent execution of a senior colleague.

Alan Clark 1928– : diary 13 July 1990

84 There are no true friends in politics. We are all sharks circling, and waiting, for traces of blood to appear in the water.

Alan Clark 1928– : diary 30 November 1990

85 Politics are, like God's infinite mercy, a last resort.

P. J. O'Rourke 1947– : *Parliament of Whores* (1991)

86 Since when was fastidiousness a quality useful for political advancement?

Bernard Levin 1928– : *If You Want My Opinion* (1992)

Nigel Nicolson, who in 1956 abstained from voting with the Government on the Suez Crisis and subsequently lost his seat, reflecting on the Maastricht vote:

87 One final tip to rebels: always have a second profession in reserve.

Nigel Nicolson 1917– : in *The Spectator* 7 November 1992

88 Being an MP is the sort of job all working-class parents want for their children—clean, indoors and no heavy lifting.

Diane Abbott 1953– : in *Observer* 30 January 1994 'Sayings of the Week'

89 Being an MP feeds your vanity and starves your self-respect.

Matthew Parris 1949– : in *The Times* 9 February 1994

On the contest for the Labour leadership, during a debate between himself, Tony Blair, and Margaret Beckett:

90 We're in danger of loving ourselves to death.

John Prescott 1938– : in *Observer* 19 June 1994 'Sayings of the Week'

Poverty See also *Debt, Money*

1 LABRAX: One letter more than a medical man, that's what I am.
GRIPUS: Then you're a mendicant?
LABRAX: You've hit the point.

Plautus *c.*250–184 BC: *Rudens*

2 Come away; poverty's catching.

Aphra Behn 1640–89: *The Rover* (1681)

3 I am pent up in frowzy lodgings, where there is not room enough to swing a cat.

Tobias Smollett 1721–71: *Humphry Clinker* (1771)

4 The murmuring poor, who will not fast in peace.

George Crabbe 1754–1832: 'The Newspaper' (1785)

5 Poverty is no disgrace to a man, but it is confoundedly inconvenient.

Sydney Smith 1771–1845: J. Potter Briscoe *Sydney Smith: His Wit and Wisdom* (1900)

6 How to live well on nothing a year.

William Makepeace Thackeray 1811–63: *Vanity Fair* (1847–8)

7 Up and down the City Road,
In and out the Eagle,
That's the way the money goes—
Pop goes the weasel!

W. R. Mandale: 'Pop Goes the Weasel' (1853); also attributed to Charles Twiggs

8 He was a gentleman who was generally spoken of as having nothing a-year, paid quarterly.

R. S. Surtees 1805–64: *Mr Sponge's Sporting Tour* (1853)

9 As for the virtuous poor, one can pity them, of course, but one cannot possibly admire them.

Oscar Wilde 1854–1900: *Sebastian Melmoth* (1891)

10 There seems to be much more in the New Testament in praise of poverty than we like to acknowledge.

Benjamin Jowett 1817–93: Kenneth Rose *Superior Person* (1969)

11 I have no money at all: I live, or am supposed to live, on a few francs a day...Like dear St Francis of Assisi I am wedded to Poverty: but in my case the marriage is not a success.

Oscar Wilde 1854–1900: letter June 1899

12 The greatest of evils and the worst of crimes is poverty... our first duty—a duty to which every other consideration should be sacrificed—is not to be poor.

George Bernard Shaw 1856–1950: *Major Barbara* (1907) preface

13 You may tempt the upper classes
With your villainous demi-tasses,
But: Heaven will protect a working-girl!

Edgar Smith 1857–1938: 'Heaven Will Protect the Working-Girl' (1909)

14 It's no disgrace t'be poor, but it might as well be.

Frank McKinney Hubbard 1868–1930: *Short Furrows* (1911)

15 Gee, I'd like to see you looking swell, Baby,
Diamond bracelets Woolworth doesn't sell, Baby,
Till that lucky day, you know darned well, Baby
I can't give you anything but love.

Dorothy Fields 1905–74: 'I Can't Give You Anything But Love' (1928)

16 Look at me. Worked myself up from nothing to a state of extreme poverty.

S. J. Perelman 1904–1979 *et al.*: in *Monkey Business* (1931 film)

17 How can I ever start
To tell what's in my heart
At the sight of a dime
Of a shiny new dime.

Harold Rome 1908– : 'The Face on the Dime' (1946)

18 What throws a monkey wrench in
A fella's good intention?
That nasty old invention—
Necessity!

E. Y. Harburg 1898–1981: 'Necessity' (1947)

19 If only Bapu [Gandhi] knew the cost of setting him up in poverty!

Sarojini Naidu 1879–1949: A. Campbell-Johnson *Mission with Mountbatten* (1951)

20 Anyone who has ever struggled with poverty knows how extremely expensive it is to be poor.

James Baldwin 1924–87: *Nobody Knows My Name* (1961) 'Fifth Avenue, Uptown: a letter from Harlem'

21 Do you think Oxfam ever return anything? Oxfam graciously acknowledges the receipt of your gift but feel they must return this pair of your old knickers as they would only aggravate the situation.

Alan Bennett 1934– : *Getting On* (1972)

22 He [Bill Bryson's father] was a child of the Depression and where capital outlays were involved he always wore the haunted look of a fugitive who had just heard bloodhounds in the distance.

Bill Bryson 1951– : *The Lost Continent* (1989)

Power

1 He seemed much greater than a private citizen while he still was a private citizen, and by everyone's consent capable of reigning if only he had not reigned.

Tacitus AD 56–after 117: of the Emperor Galba, quoted by Denis Healey in allusion to John Major; *Histories*

2 Whatever happens we have got
The Maxim Gun, and they have not.

Hilaire Belloc 1870–1953: *The Modern Traveller* (1898)

3 The Pope! How many divisions has *he* got?

Joseph Stalin 1879–1953: on being asked to encourage Catholicism in Russia by way of conciliating the Pope, 13 May 1935

4 So long as men worship the Caesars and Napoleons, Caesars and Napoleons will duly arise and make them miserable.

Aldous Huxley 1894–1963: *Ends and Means* (1937)

5 I'll make him an offer he can't refuse.

Mario Puzo 1920– : *The Godfather* (1969)

6 Children and zip fasteners do not respond to force... Except occasionally.

Katharine Whitehorn 1926– : *Observations* (1970)

7 Anybody that wants the presidency so much that he'll spend two years organizing and campaigning for it is not to be trusted with the office.

David Broder 1929– : in *Washington Post* 18 July 1973

8 I don't want loyalty. I want *loyalty*. I want him to kiss my ass in Macy's window at high noon and tell me it smells like roses. I want his pecker in my pocket.

Lyndon Baines Johnson 1908–73: David Halberstam *The Best and the Brightest* (1972)

9 Better to have him inside the tent pissing out, than outside pissing in.

Lyndon Baines Johnson 1908–73: of J. Edgar Hoover; David Halberstam *The Best and the Brightest* (1972)

10 She [Margaret Thatcher] has been beastly to the Bank of England, has demanded that the BBC 'set its house in order' and tends to believe the worst of the Foreign and Commonwealth Office. She cannot see an institution without hitting it with her handbag.

Julian Critchley 1930– : in *The Times* 21 June 1982

11 If you were handed power on a plate you'd be left fighting over the plate.

Tom Stoppard 1937– : *Squaring the Circle* (1984)

12 I have been warned by someone I am unable to name, to wit a certain person of the female gender who must be obeyed, that if I put anything in writing whatsoever I will be deemed to have committed a criminal libel and left to rot away my few remaining days in the Tower of London.

Richard Ingrams 1937– and **John Wells** 1936– : *Down the Hatch* (1985) 'Dear Bill' letters

13 Eight years of playing second fiddle is not doing me any good.

Paul Keating 1944– : to Bob Hawke in 1988; Michael Gordon *A Question of Leadership* (1993)

14 A generation of citizens who buy red leather combination locked attaché cases and heated trouser presses while remaining ignorant of the metrical constitution of *The Faerie Queene* is not one ready to lead the world.

Stephen Fry 1957– : *Paperweight* (1992)

Praise and Flattery

1 Consider with yourself what your flattery is worth before you bestow it so freely.

Samuel Johnson 1709–84: to Hannah More; James Boswell *Life of Johnson* (1791)

2 We authors, Ma'am.

Benjamin Disraeli 1804–81: to Queen Victoria after the publication of *Leaves from the Journal of our Life in the Highlands* in 1868; Elizabeth Longford *Victoria R.I.* (1964); attributed

3 Your Majesty is the head of the literary profession.

Benjamin Disraeli 1804–81: to Queen Victoria after the publication of *Leaves from the Journal of our Life in the Highlands* (1868); Hesketh Pearson *Dizzy* (1951); attributed

4 I used your soap two years ago; since then I have used no other.

Punch 1841–1992: vol. 86 (1884)

5 What really flatters a man is that you think him worth flattering.

George Bernard Shaw 1856–1950: *John Bull's Other Island* (1907)

6 Arnold Bennett said to me [Geoffrey Madan], the most tremendous compliment ever paid to him was Lord Beaverbrook's saying: 'Arnold, you're a hard man.'

Lord Beaverbrook 1879–1964: J. A. Gere and John Sparrow (eds.) *Geoffrey Madan's Notebooks* (1981)

7 You're the top! You're the Coliseum,
You're the top! You're the Louvre Museum,
You're a melody
From a symphony by Strauss,
You're a Bendel bonnet,
A Shakespeare sonnet,
You're Mickey Mouse!

Cole Porter 1891–1964: 'You're the Top' (1934)

8 I suppose flattery hurts no one, that is, if he doesn't inhale.

Adlai Stevenson 1900–65: television broadcast, 30 March 1952

9 If you are flattering a woman, it pays to be a little more subtle. You don't have to bother with men, they believe any compliment automatically.

Alan Ayckbourn 1939– : *Round and Round the Garden* (1975)

Prejudice and Tolerance

1 Without the aid of prejudice and custom, I should not be able to find my way across the room.

William Hazlitt 1778–1830: 'On Prejudice' (1830)

2 Tolerance is only another name for indifference.

W. Somerset Maugham 1874–1965: *A Writer's Notebook* (1949) written in 1896

Insisting that King Kalakua of the Sandwich Islands should take precedence over the Crown Prince of Germany:
3 Either the brute is a king or else he is an ordinary black nigger and if he is not a king, why is he here?

Edward VII 1841–1910: Michael Hill (ed.) 'Right Royal Remarks' (unpublished compilation); in *Ned Sherrin in his Anecdotage* (1993)

4 I don't like men who live, by choice, out of their own country. I don't like interior decorators. I don't like Germans. I don't like buggers and I don't like Christian Scientists.

Duff Cooper 1890–1954: Philip Ziegler *Diana Cooper* (1981)

5 His face shining like Moses, his teeth like the Ten
   Commandments, all broken.

Herbert Beerbohm Tree
1852–1917: of the great Jewish actor,
Israel Zangwill; Hesketh Pearson
Beerbohm Tree (1956)

*Helen Ogden Mills Reid, sister of the anti-British owner of the
Chicago Tribune, encountered Churchill at a White House lunch in
1943 and immediately attacked him on the grounds of Britain's
treatment of India:*

6 Before we proceed further let us get one thing clear. Are
   we talking about the brown Indians in India, who have
   multiplied alarmingly under the benevolent British rule?
   Or are we speaking of the red Indians in America who,
   I understand, are almost extinct?

Winston Churchill 1874–1965: G.
Pawle *The War and Colonel Warden*
(1963)

7 'It's powerful,' he said.
   'What?'
   'That one drop of Negro blood—because just *one* drop of
   black blood makes a man coloured. *One* drop—you are
   a Negro!'

Langston Hughes 1902–67:
Simple Takes a Wife (1953)

8 You gotta say this for the white race—its self-confidence
   knows no bounds. Who else could go to a small island in
   the South Pacific where there's no poverty, no crime, no
   unemployment, no war and no worry—and call it
   a 'primitive society'?

Dick Gregory 1932– : *From the
Back of the Bus* (1962)

9 Wouldn't it be a hell of a thing if all this was burnt cork
   and you people were being tolerant for nothing?

Dick Gregory 1932– : *Nigger*
(1965)

10 Being a star has made it possible for me to get insulted in
   places where the average Negro could never *hope* to go
   and get insulted.

Sammy Davis Jnr. 1925–90: *Yes
I Can* (1965)

11 The South African police would leave no stone unturned
   to see that nothing disturbed the even terror of their
   lives.

Tom Sharpe 1928– : *Indecent
Exposure* (1973)

12 I have a distinct impression that the anthropologists'
   version of that famous quote from Alexander Pope's
   essay runs: 'The proper study of mankind is *black* man,
   or if not actually black, at least poor and a long way off.'

Jill Tweedie 1936–93: *It's Only Me*
(1980)

*Christopher Isherwood had tried to point out to a young Jewish film
producer that in German concentration camps, Jews wore yellow stars
while homosexuals wore pink triangles, and that Hitler had killed six
hundred thousand homosexuals. The young man was not impressed,
pointing out that Hitler had killed six million Jews:*

13 What are you? In real estate?

Christopher Isherwood
1904–86: Gore Vidal *Pink Triangle and
Yellow Star* (1982)

*On Norman Podhoretz's criticism of homosexual women at the Island
of Pines:*

14 Well, if I were a dyke and a pair of Podhoretzes came
   waddling towards me on the beach, copies of Leviticus
   and Freud in hand, I'd get in touch with the nearest
   Alsatian dealer pronto.

Gore Vidal 1925– : *Pink Triangle
and Yellow Star* (1982)

15 If there were any of Australia's original inhabitants living in Melbourne they were kept well out of the way of nice people; unless, of course, they could sing.

Barry Humphries 1934– : *More Please* (1992)

Present See *Past and Present*

Pride and Humility

1 But be not afraid of greatness: some men are born great, some achieve greatness, and some have greatness thrust upon them.

William Shakespeare 1564–1616: *Twelfth Night* (1601)

2 He does smile his face into more lines than are in the new map with the augmentation of the Indies.

William Shakespeare 1564–1616: *Twelfth Night* (1601)

3 She thus advises thee that sighs for thee. Remember who commended thy yellow stockings, and wished to see thee ever cross-gartered.

William Shakespeare 1564–1616: *Twelfth Night* (1601)

4 Every day when he looked into the glass, and gave the last touch to his consummate toilette, he offered his grateful thanks to Providence that his family was not unworthy of him.

Benjamin Disraeli 1804–81: *Lothair* (1870)

5 I am the Dean of Christ Church, Sir:
There's my wife; look well at her.
She's the Broad and I'm the High;
We are the University.

Cecil Spring-Rice 1859–1918: *The Masque of Balliol* (composed by and current among members of Balliol College, Oxford, in the 1870s); the first couplet was unofficially altered to: 'I am the Dean, and this is Mrs Liddell; / She the first, and I the second fiddle.'

6 The cross of the Legion of Honour has been conferred upon me. However, few escape that distinction.

Mark Twain 1835–1910: *A Tramp Abroad* (1880)

7 Of all my verse, like not a single line;
But like my title, for it is not mine.
That title from a better man I stole;
Ah, how much better, had I stol'n the whole!

Robert Louis Stevenson 1850–94: *Underwoods* (1887) foreword

8 Charity, dear Miss Prism, charity! None of us are perfect. I myself am peculiarly susceptible to draughts.

Oscar Wilde 1854–1900: *The Importance of Being Earnest* (1895)

9 His opinion of himself, having once risen, remained at 'set fair'.

Arnold Bennett 1867–1931: *The Card* (1911)

10 Do you imagine I am going to pronounce the name of my beautiful theatre in a hired cab?

Herbert Beerbohm Tree 1852–1917: refusing to give directions to His Majesty's theatre to a cab-driver; Neville Cardus *Sir Thomas Beecham* (1961)

11 When I pass my name in such large letters I blush, but at the same time instinctively raise my hat.

Herbert Beerbohm Tree 1852–1917: Hesketh Pearson *Beerbohm Tree* (1956)

12 We have the highest authority for believing that the meek shall inherit the earth; though I have never found any particular corroboration of this aphorism in the records of Somerset House.

F. E. Smith 1872–1930:
Contemporary Personalities (1924)
'Marquess Curzon'

On stepping from his bath in the presence of a startled President Roosevelt:
13 The Prime Minister has nothing to hide from the President of the United States.

Winston Churchill 1874–1965: as recalled by Roosevelt's son in *Churchill* (BBC television series presented by Martin Gilbert, 1992)

14 I have often wished I had time to cultivate modesty... But I am too busy thinking about myself.

Edith Sitwell 1887–1964: in *Observer* 30 April 1950

15 Modest? My word, no...He was an all-the-lights-on man.

Henry Reed 1914–86: *A Very Great Man Indeed* (1953 radio play) in *Hilda Tablet and Others*

16 In 1969 I published a small book on Humility. It was a pioneering work which has not, to my knowledge, been superseded.

Lord Longford 1905– : in *The Tablet* 22 January 1994

On being asked to name the best living author writing in English:
17 No one working in the English language now comes close to my exuberance, my passion, my fidelity to words.

Jeanette Winterson 1959– : in *Sunday Times* 13 March 1994

Progress See also *Science and Technology*

1 The civilized man has built a coach, but has lost the use of his feet.

Ralph Waldo Emerson 1803–82: 'Self-Reliance' (1841)

2 Now, *here*, you see, it takes all the running *you* can do, to keep in the same place. If you want to get somewhere else, you must run at least twice as fast as that!

Lewis Carroll 1832–98: *Through the Looking-Glass* (1872)

3 A swell house with...all the modern inconveniences.

Mark Twain 1835–1910: *Life on the Mississippi* (1883)

4 All progress is based upon a universal innate desire on the part of every organism to live beyond its income.

Samuel Butler 1835–1902: *Notebooks* (1912)

5 You can't say civilization don't advance, however, for in every war they kill you in a new way.

Will Rogers 1879–1935: in *New York Times* 23 December 1929

6 They all laughed at Christopher Columbus
When he said the world was round
They all laughed when Edison recorded sound
They all laughed at Wilbur and his brother
When they said that man could fly;
They told Marconi
Wireless was a phony—
It's the same old cry!

Ira Gershwin 1896–1989: 'They All Laughed' (1937)

7 Mechanics, not microbes, are the menace to civilization.

Norman Douglas 1868–1952: introduction to *The Norman Douglas Limerick Book* (1967)

8 The cry was for vacant freedom and indeterminate progress: *Vorwärts! Avanti! Onwards! Full speed ahead!*,

George Santayana 1863–1952: *My Host the World* (1953)

without asking whether directly before you was not
a bottomless pit.

9 Don't get smart alecksy,
With the galaxy
Leave the atom alone.

E. Y. Harburg 1898–1981: 'Leave
the Atom Alone' (1957)

10 Push de button!
Up de elevator!
Push de button!
Out de orange juice!
Push de button!
From refrigerator
Come banana short-cake and frozen goose!

E. Y. Harburg 1898–1981: 'Push de
Button' (1957)

11 Everywhere one looks, decadence. I saw a bishop with
a moustache the other day.

Alan Bennett 1934– : *Forty Years
On* (1969)

12 Is this what we were promised when we emerged from
the Dark Ages? Is this Civilization? I'm only thankful
Kenneth Clark isn't here to see it.

Alan Bennett 1934– : *Habeas
Corpus* (1973)

13 You started something which you can't stop. You want
a self-limiting revolution but it's like trying to limit
influenza.

Tom Stoppard 1937– : *Squaring
the Circle* (1984)

14 To you, Baldrick, the Renaissance was just something
that happened to other people, wasn't it?

Richard Curtis and **Ben Elton**
1959– : *Blackadder II* (1987) television
series

Publishing

1 The poem will please if it is lively—if it is stupid it will
fail—but I will have none of your damned cutting and
slashing.

Lord Byron 1788–1824: letter to his
publisher John Murray, 6 April 1819

*At a literary dinner during the Napoleonic Wars, Thomas Campbell
proposed a toast to Napoleon:*
2 Gentlemen, you must not mistake me. I admit that the
French Emperor is a tyrant. I admit he is a monster.
I admit that he is the sworn foe of our nation, and, if
you will, of the whole human race. But, gentlemen, we
must be just to our great enemy. We must not forget that
he once shot a bookseller.

Thomas Campbell 1777–1844: G.
O. Trevelyan *The Life of Lord Macaulay*
(1876)

3 Now Barabbas was a publisher.

Thomas Campbell 1777–1844:
attributed, in Samuel Smiles *A
Publisher and his Friends: Memoir and
Correspondence of the late John
Murray*; also attributed, wrongly, to
Byron

4 A new firm of publishers has written to me proposing to
publish 'the successor' of *A Shropshire Lad*. But as they
don't also offer to write it, I have had to put them off.

A. E. Housman 1859–1936: letter
to Laurence Housman, 5 October 1896

5 Times have changed since a certain author was executed
for murdering his publisher. They say that when the
author was on the scaffold he said goodbye to the

J. M. Barrie 1860–1937: speech at
Aldine Club, New York, 5 November
1896

minister and to the reporters, and then he saw some
publishers sitting in the front row below, and to them he
did not say goodbye. He said instead, 'I'll see you later.'

6 I suppose publishers are untrustworthy. They certainly
always look it.

Oscar Wilde 1854–1900: letter
February 1898

7 I have seen enough of my publishers to know that they
have no ideas of their own about literature save what
they can clutch at as believing it to be a straight tip from
a business point of view.

Samuel Butler 1835–1902:
Notebooks (1912)

8 All a publisher has to do is write cheques at intervals,
while a lot of deserving and industrious chappies rally
round and do the real work.

P. G. Wodehouse 1881–1975: *My
Man Jeeves* (1919)

9 The illustrations, which are far more numerous and less
apposite than comports with the dignity of history, may
be imputed to the publishers, for publishers seek to
attract readers whom authors would wish to repel.

A. E. Housman 1859–1936:
Cambridge Review 1923

10 One envies a publisher because of course he can help
himself cheaply to anything he produces. To listen to
these two Macmillans one might imagine that their
publishing business was almost run at a loss and that the
authors got away with the swag! Being an author in
a very mild way I hold a contrary view.

Cuthbert Morley Headlam
1876–1964: diary 10 April 1932

11 There is some kind of notion abroad that because a book
is humorous the publisher has to be funnier and madder
than hell in marketing it.

S. J. Perelman 1904–79: letter to
Bennett Cerf, 23 July 1937

12 You cannot or at least you should not try to argue with
authors. Too many are like children whose tears can
suddenly be changed to smiles if they are handled in the
right way.

Michael Joseph 1897–1958: a
publisher's view; *The Adventure of
Publishing* (1949)

13 Being published by the Oxford University Press is rather
like being married to a duchess: the honour is almost
greater than the pleasure.

G. M. Young 1882–1959: Rupert
Hart-Davis letter to George Lyttelton,
29 April 1956

14 Publishers regard writers as vain, petty, juvenile, and
thoroughly impossible...So there's no use in attempting
to be reasonable with them, or trying to prove that you,
as a writer, are a person with a sense of dignity who's
merely interested in their merchandising your work,
a job they frequently aren't equipped to do by any
business standards.

S. J. Perelman 1904–79: letter
22 November 1956

15 The publishers contend that you only advertise a book to
any extent *after* it's beginning to sell, which is certainly
Alice-in-Wonderland thinking.

S. J. Perelman 1904–79: letter
22 November 1956

16 English publishers being what they are (i.e., chary about
wasting stamps), I never get to find out what the press
says about any book of mine until years later, and then
only in red ink on the publisher's statement.

S. J. Perelman 1904–79: letter
7 January 1960

On being sent the manuscript of Travels with my Aunt, *Greene's American publishers had cabled, 'Terrific book, but we'll need to change the title':*

17 No need to change title. Easier to change publishers.

Graham Greene 1904–91: telegram to his American publishers in 1968; Giles Gordon *Aren't We Due a Royalty Statement?* (1993)

18 It circulated for five years, through the halls of fifteen publishers, and finally ended up with the Vanguard Press which, as you can see, is rather deep into the alphabet.

Patrick Dennis: Laurence J. Peter (ed.) *Quotations for our Time* (1977)

19 A publisher who writes is like a cow in a milk bar.

Arthur Koestler 1905–83: Jonathon Green (ed.) *A Dictionary of Contemporary Quotations* (1982)

20 I always thought Barabbas was a much misunderstood man...

Peter Grose: a publisher's view; letter 25 May 1983

21 The relationship of an agent to a publisher is that of a knife to a throat.

Marvin Josephson: an American agent's view; Ned Sherrin *Cutting Edge* (1984)

22 An author who shouts 'You mean bastard' at a publisher is not going to be popular. However, I do have the satisfaction of having been rude to some of the most famous publishers in London.

Michael Green 1927– : *The Boy Who Shot Down an Airship* (1988)

23 If I had been someone not very clever, I would have done an easier job like publishing. That's the easiest job I can think of.

A. J. Ayer 1910–89: attributed

24 Four happy publishers
Out on a spree.
Someone had to pay the bill
And then there were three.

Wendy Cope 1945– : 'Two Hand-Rhymes for Grown-ups' (1992)

25 The ever-increasing dullness and oddity of Oxford books is an old favourite among humorists, who are always trying to think up new and hilariously tedious 'The Oxford Book of...' titles.

Craig Brown 1957– : *Craig Brown's Greatest Hits* (1993)

Leading item on the autumn list of 'a new publishing house that would be sure to fail':

26 *Canada, Our Good Neighbour to the North.*

Robert Gottlieb: in Ned Sherrin in his *Anecdotage* (1993)

27 Aren't we due a royalty statement?

Charles, Prince of Wales 1948– : to his literary agent; Giles Gordon *Aren't We Due a Royalty Statement?* (1993)

Quotations

1 He liked those literary cooks
Who skim the cream of others' books;
And ruin half an author's graces
By plucking bon-mots from their places.

Hannah More 1745–1833: *Florio* (1786)

Advice for House of Commons quotations:
2 No Greek; as much Latin as you like: never French in any circumstance: no English poet unless he has completed his century.

Charles James Fox 1749–1806: J. A. Gere and John Sparrow (eds.) *Geoffrey Madan's Notebooks* (1981)

3 His works contain nothing worth quoting; and a book that furnishes no quotations is, *me judice*, no book—it's a plaything.

Thomas Love Peacock 1785–1866: *Crotchet Castle* (1831)

4 Next to the originator of a good sentence is the first quoter of it.

Ralph Waldo Emerson 1803–82: *Letters and Social Aims* (1876)

5 He wrapped himself in quotations—as a beggar would enfold himself in the purple of emperors.

Rudyard Kipling 1865–1936: *Many Inventions* (1893)

6 You must not treat my immortal works as quarries to be used at will by the various hacks whom you may employ to compile anthologies.

A. E. Housman 1859–1936: letter to his publisher Grant Richards, 29 June 1907

7 What a good thing Adam had. When he said a good thing he knew nobody had said it before.

Mark Twain 1835–1910: *Notebooks* (1935)

8 Anthologies are mischievous things. Some years ago there was a rage for chemically predigested food, which was only suppressed when doctors pointed out that since human beings had been given teeth and digestive organs they had to be used or they degenerated very rapidly. Anthologies are predigested food for the brain.

Rebecca West 1892–1983: in *The Clarion* 27 December 1912

9 Ah, yes! I wrote the 'Purple Cow'—
I'm sorry, now, I wrote it!
But I can tell you anyhow,
I'll kill you if you quote it!

Gelett Burgess 1866–1951: *The Burgess Nonsense Book* (1914) 'Confessional'

10 An anthology is like all the plums and orange peel picked out of a cake.

Walter Raleigh 1861–1922: letter to Mrs Robert Bridges, 15 January 1915

11 I know heaps of quotations, so I can always make quite a fair show of knowledge.

O. Douglas 1877–1948: *The Setons* (1917)

12 But I have long thought that if you knew a column of advertisements by heart, you could achieve unexpected felicities with them. You can get a happy quotation anywhere if you have the eye.

Oliver Wendell Holmes Jr. 1841–1935: letter to Harold Laski, 31 May 1923

13 For quotable good things, for pregnant aphorisms, for touchstones of ready application, the opinions of the English judges are a mine of instruction and a treasury of joy.

Benjamin N. Cardozo 1870–1938: *Law and Literature* (1931)

14 I always have a quotation for everything—it saves original thinking.

Dorothy L. Sayers 1893–1957: *Have His Carcase* (1932)

15 Misquotation is, in fact, the pride and privilege of the learned. A widely-read man never quotes accurately, for the rather obvious reason that he has read too widely.

Hesketh Pearson 1887–1964: *Common Misquotations* (1934) introduction

16 To-day I am a lamppost against which no anthologist lifts his leg.

James Agate 1877–1947: diary 21 August 1941

17 There is no reason why a book of quotations should be dull; it has its uses in idleness as well as in study.

H. L. Mencken 1880–1956: introduction to *H. L. Mencken's Dictionary of Quotations* (1942)

18 I...try much to my fury to find quotations in my own books for Doubleday Doran's *Dictionary of Quotations*. It doesn't work. I am not given to apophthegms. My gift is to explain things at length and convey atmosphere.

Harold Nicolson 1886–1968: diary 7 November 1948

19 I was both horrified and immeasurably flattered by your confession that you had in the past quoted from my work: horrified because unbeknownst to yourself, you ran the risk of verbal infection (the kind of words I use are liable to become imbedded and fester, like the steel wool housewives use).

S. J. Perelman 1904–79: letter to Betsy Drake, 1951

20 It seems pointless to be quoted if one isn't going to be quotable...It's better to be quotable than honest.

Tom Stoppard 1937– : in *Guardian* 21 March 1973

Religion See also *God*

1 Mr Doctor, that loose gown becomes you so well I wonder your notions should be so narrow.

Elizabeth I 1533–1603: to the Puritan Dr Humphreys, as he was about to kiss her hand on her visit to Oxford in 1566; F. Chamberlin *Sayings of Queen Elizabeth* (1923)

2 I am a Jew else; an Ebrew Jew.

William Shakespeare 1564–1616: *Henry IV, Part* 1 (1597)

3 God and the doctor we alike adore
But only when in danger, not before;
The danger o'er, both are alike requited,
God is forgotten, and the Doctor slighted.

John Owen c.1563–1622: *Epigrams*

At Oxford, to an angry crowd who thought she was Charles II's French Catholic mistress the Duchess of Portsmouth:
4 Pray, good people, be civil. I am the Protestant whore.

Nell Gwyn 1650–87: B. Bevan *Nell Gwyn* (1969)

5 No praying, it spoils business.

Thomas Otway 1652–85: *Venice Preserved* (1682)

6 A lady, if undressed at Church, looks silly,
One cannot be devout in dishabilly.

George Farquhar 1678–1707: *The Stage Coach* (1704)

7 As Sir Roger is landlord to the whole congregation, he keeps them in very good order, and will suffer nobody to sleep in it [the church] besides himself; for if by chance he has been surprised into a short nap at sermon, upon recovering out of it, he stands up, and looks about him; and if he sees anybody else nodding, either wakes them himself, or sends his servant to them.

Joseph Addison 1672–1719: *The Spectator* 9 July 1711

8 We have in England a particular bashfulness in every thing that regards religion.

Joseph Addison 1672–1719: *The Spectator* 15 August 1712

9 As I take my shoes from the shoemaker, and my coat from the tailor, so I take my religion from the priest.

Oliver Goldsmith 1730–74: James Boswell *Life of Samuel Johnson* (1934 ed.) 9 April 1773

10 This merriment of parsons is mighty offensive.

Samuel Johnson 1709–84: James Boswell *Life of Samuel Johnson* (1791) March 1781

11   As a priest,
A piece of mere church furniture at best.

William Cowper 1731–1800: 'Tirocinium' (1785)

12 The parson knows enough who knows a duke.

William Cowper 1731–1800: 'Tirocinium' (1785)

A rhyming marriage license, said to have been composed for an al fresco ceremony outside Lichfield:
13 Under an oak in stormy weather
I joined this rogue and whore together;
And none but he who rules the thunder
Can put this rogue and whore asunder.

Anonymous: has been attributed to Swift, but of doubtful authenticity; C. H. Wilson *Swiftiana* (1804)

14 When I turn thirty—I will turn devout—I feel a great vocation that way in Catholic churches—and when I hear the organ.

Lord Byron 1788–1824: letter to his publisher John Murray, 9 April 1817

15 I am always most religious upon a sunshiny day.

Lord Byron 1788–1824: 'Detached Thoughts' 15 October 1821

16 I have not the smallest influence over Lord Byron, in this particular, and if I had, I certainly should employ it to eradicate from his great mind the delusions of Christianity, which, in spite of his reason, seem perpetually to recur.

Percy Bysshe Shelley 1792–1822: letter 11 April 1822

17 A Curate—there is something which excites compassion in the very name of a Curate!!!

Sydney Smith 1771–1845: *Edinburgh Review* (1822) 'Persecuting Bishops'

18 Christians have burnt each other, quite persuaded That all the Apostles would have done as they did.

Lord Byron 1788–1824: *Don Juan* (1819–24)

19 *Merit*, indeed! ... We are come to a pretty pass if they talk of *merit* for a bishopric.

Lord Westmorland 1759–1841: Lady Salisbury diary 9 December 1835

20 I have seen nobody since I saw you, but persons in orders. My only varieties are vicars, rectors, curates, and every now and then (by way of turbot) an archdeacon.

Sydney Smith 1771–1845: letter to Miss Berry, 28 January 1843

21 As the French say, there are three sexes—men, women, and clergymen.

Sydney Smith 1771–1845: Lady Holland *Memoir* (1855)

22 Deserves to be preached to death by wild curates.

Sydney Smith 1771–1845: Lady Holland *Memoir* (1855)

23 I am just going to pray for you at St Paul's, but with no very lively hope of success.

Sydney Smith 1771–1845: Hesketh Pearson *The Smith of Smiths* (1934)

24 Things have come to a pretty pass when religion is allowed to invade the sphere of private life.

Lord Melbourne 1779–1848: on hearing an evangelical sermon; G. W. E. Russell *Collections and Recollections* (1898)

25 How can you expect to convert England if you use a cope like that?

Augustus Welby Pugin 1812–52: to an unidentified Catholic priest; Bernard Ward *The Sequel to Catholic Emancipation* (1915)

26 Dr Gwynne himself, though a religious man, was also a thoroughly practical man of the world, and he regarded with no favourable eye the tenets of anyone who looked on the two things as incompatible.

Anthony Trollope 1815–82: *Barchester Towers* (1857)

27 Is man an ape or an angel? Now I am on the side of the angels.

Benjamin Disraeli 1804–81: speech at Oxford, 25 November 1864

28 A Protestant, if he wants aid or advice on any matter, can only go to his solicitor.

Benjamin Disraeli 1804–81: *Lothair* (1870)

29 I was a pale young curate then.

W. S. Gilbert 1836–1911: *The Sorcerer* (1877)

30 Said Waldershare, 'Sensible men are all of the same religion.' 'And pray what is that?' ... 'Sensible men never tell.'

Benjamin Disraeli 1804–81: *Endymion* (1880)

31 THE ARCHDEACON: Her deafness is a great privation to her. She can't even hear my sermons now.

Oscar Wilde 1854–1900: *A Woman of No Importance* (1893)

32 The spirituality of man is most apparent when he is eating a hearty dinner.

W. Somerset Maugham 1874–1965: *A Writer's Notebook* (1949) written in 1897

33 There is only one religion, though there are a hundred versions of it.

George Bernard Shaw 1856–1950: preface to *Plays Pleasant and Unpleasant* (1898) vol. 2

34 That the Almighty would send down His wisdom on the Queen's Ministers, who sorely need it.

Dr Macgregor: prayer delivered in Crathie church, to Queen Victoria's amusement; Arthur Ponsonby *Henry Ponsonby* (1942)

35 Martyrdom ... the only way in which a man can become famous without ability.

George Bernard Shaw 1856–1950: *The Devil's Disciple* (1901)

36 Every reformation must have its victims. You can't expect the fatted calf to share the enthusiasm of the angels over the prodigal's return.

Saki 1870–1916: *Reginald* (1904)

37 People may say what they like about the decay of Christianity; the religious system that produced green Chartreuse can never really die.

Saki 1870–1916: *Reginald* (1904)

38 Gentlemen, I am a Catholic ... If you reject me on account of my religion, I shall thank God that He has spared me the indignity of being your representative.

Hilaire Belloc 1870–1953: speech to voters of South Salford, 1906

39 Wot prawce Selvytion nah?

George Bernard Shaw 1856–1950: *Major Barbara* (1907)

40 Christianity never got any grip of the world until it virtually reduced its claims on the ordinary citizen's attention to a couple of hours every seventh day, and let him alone on week-days.

George Bernard Shaw 1856–1950: preface to *Getting Married* (1911)

41 When suave politeness, tempering bigot zeal,
Corrected *I believe* to *One does feel.*

Ronald Knox 1888–1957: 'Absolute and Abitofhell' (1913)

42 'Oh, a cheque, I think,' said the rector; 'one can do so much more with it, after all.' 'Precisely,' said his father; he was well aware of many things that can be done with a cheque that cannot possibly be done with a font.

Stephen Leacock 1869–1944: *Arcadian Adventures with the Idle Rich* (1914)

43 God is a man, so it must be all rot.

Nancy Nicholson d. 1977: just before her marriage to Robert Graves in 1917; R. Graves *Goodbye to All That* (1929)

Mahaffy had been asked 'Are you saved?' by 'a zealot who cornered him in a railway carriage':
44 To tell you the truth, my good fellow, I am; but it was such a narrow squeak it does not bear talking about.

John Pentland Mahaffy 1839–1919: Oliver St John Gogarty *It Isn't This Time of Year at All* (1954)

In 1919 Archbishop Bernard resigned the archbishopric of Dublin to become Provost of Trinity:
45 He has sold the Thirty-Nine Articles for the thirty pieces of silver.

Oliver St John Gogarty 1878–1957: Ulick O'Connor *Oliver St John Gogarty* (1964)

46 'I know of no joy,' she airily began, 'greater than a cool white dress after the sweetness of confession.'

Ronald Firbank 1886–1926: *Valmouth* (1919)

47 Bernard always had a few prayers in the hall and some whiskey afterwards as he was rarther pious but Mr Salteena was not very addicted to prayers so he marched up to bed.

Daisy Ashford 1881–1972: *The Young Visiters* (1919)

48 Faith may be defined briefly as an illogical belief in the occurrence of the improbable.

H. L. Mencken 1880–1956: *Prejudices* (1922)

49 I remember the average curate at home as something between a eunuch and a snigger.

Ronald Firbank 1886–1926: *The Flower Beneath the Foot* (1923)

50 How can what an Englishman believes be heresy? It is a contradiction in terms.

George Bernard Shaw 1856–1950: *Saint Joan* (1924)

Of Dr Arnold when St Paul was by someone put above St John:
51 He burst into tears and begged that the subject might never again be mentioned in his presence.

A. C. Benson 1862–1925: George Lyttelton letter to Rupert Hart-Davis, 20 August 1958

52 There's no reason to bring religion into it. I think we ought to have as great a regard for religion as we can, so as to keep it out of as many things as possible.

Sean O'Casey 1880–1964: *The Plough and the Stars* (1926)

53 There is a species of person called a 'Modern Churchman' who draws the full salary of a beneficed clergyman and need not commit himself to any religious belief.

Evelyn Waugh 1903–66: *Decline and Fall* (1928)

54 The Bishop…was talking to the local Master of Hounds about the difficulty he had in keeping his vicars off the incense.

P. G. Wodehouse 1881–1975: *Mr. Mulliner Speaking* (1929)

55 The conversion of England was thus effected by the landing of St Augustine in Thanet and other places, which resulted in the country being overrun by a Wave

W. C. Sellar 1898–1951 and **R. J. Yeatman** 1898–1968: *1066 and All That* (1930)

of Saints. Among these were St Ive, St Pancra, the great
St Bernard (originator of the clerical collar), St Bee, St
Ebb, St Neot (who invented whisky), St Kit and St Kin,
and the Venomous Bead (author of *The Rosary*).

56 Broad of Church and 'broad of Mind',
Broad before and broad behind,
A keen ecclesiologist,
A rather dirty Wykehamist.

John Betjeman 1906–84: 'The Wykehamist' (1931)

57 The Church's Restoration
In eighteen-eighty-three
Has left for contemplation
Not what there used to be.

John Betjeman 1906–84: 'Hymn' (1931)

58 He was an embittered atheist (the sort of atheist who
does not so much disbelieve in God as personally dislike
Him), and took a sort of pleasure in thinking that human
affairs would never improve.

George Orwell 1903–50: *Down and Out in Paris and London* (1933)

59 I always claim the mission workers came out too early to
catch any sinners on this part of Broadway. At such an
hour the sinners are still in bed resting up from their
sinning of the night before, so they will be in good shape
for more sinning a little later on.

Damon Runyon 1884–1946: in *Collier's* 28 January 1933, 'The Idyll of Miss Sarah Brown'

60 I've been a sinner, I've been a scamp,
But now I'm willin' to trim my lamp,
So blow, Gabriel, blow!

Cole Porter 1891–1964: 'Blow, Gabriel, Blow' (1934)

61 King David and King Solomon
Led merry, merry lives,
With many, many lady friends,
And many, many wives;
But when old age crept over them—
With many, many qualms!—
King Solomon wrote the Proverbs
And King David wrote the Psalms.

James Ball Naylor 1860–1945: 'King David and King Solomon' (1935)

*On 23 March 1936, The Dean and Chapter of Liverpool had refused to
say prayers for the Cabinet during Evensong, as a protest against
British support for the French occupation of the Rhineland:*

62 The attitude of some of these clerics [to the army]...
makes me feel some sympathy with Henry II, who in
a moment of haste expressed an opinion which led to an
unexpected vacancy at Canterbury.

Duff Cooper 1890–1954: Artemis Cooper *Mr Wu and Mrs Stitch* (1991)

63 All moanday, tearsday, wailsday, thumpsday, frightday,
shatterday till the fear of the Law.

James Joyce 1882–1941: *Finnegans Wake* (1939)

64 An atheist is a man who has no invisible means of
support.

John Buchan 1875–1940: H. E. Fosdick *On Being a Real Person* (1943)

65 Lord Hugh Cecil preaching (Miss Goodford present) and
saying that eternal torment was almost certain: but
a very few might hope for merciful annihilation.

Lord Hugh Cecil 1869–1956: sermon at Eton, 25 November 1944; J. A. Gere and John Sparrow (eds.) *Geoffrey Madan's Notebooks* (1981)

66 Poor Uncle Harry
Having become a missionary

Noël Coward 1899–1973: 'Uncle Harry' (1946)

Found the natives' morals rather crude.
He and Aunt Mary
Quickly imposed an arbitrary
Ban upon them shopping in the nude.
They all considered this silly and they didn't take it well,
They burnt his boots and several suits and wrecked the
    Mission Hotel,
They also burnt his mackintosh, which made
    a disgusting smell...
Uncle Harry's not a missionary now.

67 The Revised Prayer Book: a sort of attempt to suppress
burglary by legalizing petty larceny.

Dean Inge 1860–1954: J. A. Gere
and John Sparrow (eds.) *Geoffrey
Madan's Notebooks* (1981)

68 'God knows how you Protestants can be expected to have
any sense of direction,' she said. 'It's different with us,
I haven't been to mass for years, I've got every mortal
sin on my conscience, but I know when I'm doing
wrong. I'm still a Catholic, it's there, nothing can take it
away from me.' 'Of course, duckie,' said Jeremy...'once
a Catholic always a Catholic.'

Angus Wilson 1913–91: *The Wrong
Set* (1949)

69 Puritanism. The haunting fear that someone, somewhere,
may be happy.

H. L. Mencken 1880–1956:
Chrestomathy (1949)

70   What after all
Is a halo? It's only one more thing to keep clean.

Christopher Fry 1907– : *The
Lady's not for Burning* (1949)

71 I rather wish the rising generation of clergy were more
intellectual; so many seem rather chumps.

Rose Macaulay 1881–1958: letter to
Father Johnson, 30 August 1950

72 In the course of one of his most rousing sermons,
fortunately at Evensong, he announced that it had
recently been revealed to him in a dream that there were
no women in heaven, the female part of mankind having
finally been judged incapable of salvation. While those of
his hearers who were acquainted with the Canon's wife
could quite appreciate the obvious satisfaction with
which the Vicar promulgated this new dogma, few
among a congregation that was largely female could be
expected to share it.

Osbert Lancaster 1908–80: *All
Done From Memory* (1953)

73 I went to Duff [Cooper]'s service—C of E at its most
uncompromising. Our Bishop is so low church that he
thinks singing hymns is idolatry so we sat while one was
played.

Nancy Mitford 1904–73: letter
8 January 1954

74 The two dangers which beset the Church of England are
good music and bad preaching.

Lord Hugh Cecil 1869–1956: K.
Rose *The Later Cecils* (1975)

75 It is now quite lawful for a Catholic woman to avoid
pregnancy by a resort to mathematics, though she is still
forbidden to resort to physics and chemistry.

H. L. Mencken 1880–1956:
Notebooks (1956) 'Minority Report'

76 If Evan gave *all* his reasons for joining the Church he'd be excommunicated.

Oliver St John Gogarty
1878–1957: of an acquaintance who had become a convert to Catholicism; Ulick O'Connor *Oliver St John Gogarty* (1964)

77 Evangelical vicar, in want of a portable, second-hand font, would dispose, for the same, of a portrait, in frame, of the Bishop, elect, of Vermont.

Ronald Knox 1888–1957: advertisement placed in a newspaper; W. S. Baring-Gould *The Lure of the Limerick* (1968)

78 Thanks to God, I am still an atheist.

Luis Buñuel 1900–83: *Le Monde* 16 December 1959

79 Having the chaplain around Headquarters all the time made the other officers uncomfortable. It was one thing to maintain liaison with the Lord, and they were all in favour of that; it was something else, though, to have Him hanging around twenty-four hours a day.

Joseph Heller 1923– : *Catch-22* (1961)

On the appointment of Michael Ramsey to succeed Geoffrey Fisher as Archbishop of Canterbury:
80 We have had enough of Martha and it is time for some Mary.

Harold Macmillan 1894–1986: attributed

81 A Consumer's Guide to Religion—The Best Buy—Church of England. It's a jolly friendly faith. If you are one, there's no onus to make everyone else join. In fact no one need ever know.

Robert Gillespie and **Charles Lewson**: *That Was The Week That Was* BBC television 1962

82 As for the British churchman, he goes to church as he goes to the bathroom, with the minimum of fuss and with no explanation if he can help it.

Ronald Blythe 1922– : *The Age of Illusion* (1963)

83 When Messiah comes,
He will say to us
'I apologise that I took so long,
But I had a little trouble finding you.
Over here a few and over there a few—
You were hard to reunite,
But everything is going to be all right.
Up in heaven there
How I wrang my hands
When they exiled you from the Promised Land.
In Babylon you went like castaways
On the first of many, many moving days.
What a day and what a blow,
How terrible I felt you'll never know!'

Sheldon Harnick 1924– : 'When Messiah Comes' (1964)

84 For a halo up in heaven
I have never been too keen.
Who needs another gadget
That a fellow has to clean?

E. Y. Harburg 1898–1981: 'The Man who has Everything' (1965)

85 No matter how I probe and prod
I cannot quite believe in God.
But oh! I hope to God that he
Unswervingly believes in me.

E. Y. Harburg 1898–1981: 'The Agnostic' (1965)

86 The orgasm has replaced the Cross as the focus of longing and the image of fulfilment.

Malcolm Muggeridge 1903–90: *Tread Softly* (1966)

87 I was told that the Chinese said they would bury me by the Western Lake and build a shrine to my memory. I have some slight regret that this did not happen as I might have become a god, which would have been very *chic* for an atheist.

Bertrand Russell 1872–1970: *Autobiography* (1968)

88 FOSTER: I'm still a bit hazy about the Trinity, sir. SCHOOLMASTER: Three in one, one in three, perfectly straightforward. Any doubts about that see your maths master.

Alan Bennett 1934– : *Forty Years On* (1969)

89 HANNAY: I don't think you understand. She is what we in the Church of England call a divorced woman. LEITHEN: God! it's filthy!

Alan Bennett 1934– : *Forty Years On* (1969)

90 Prove to me that you're no fool Walk across my swimming pool.

Tim Rice 1944– : 'Herod's Song' (1970)

91 Don't like bishops. Fishy lot. Blessed are the meek my foot! They're all on the climb. Ever heard of meekness stopping a bishop from becoming a bishop? Nor have I.

Maurice Bowra 1898–1971: in conversation while lunching at the Reform Club with a bishop at the next table; Arthur Marshall *Life's Rich Pageant* (1984)

92 I wonder whether Jesus did odd carpentry jobs around people's houses? 'I'm sorry, Mrs Cohen, I shan't be in for the next forty days. No. Not really a holiday. Just coming to terms with myself, really!'

Alan Bennett 1934– : *Getting On* (1972)

93 I was going to be a nun, but they wouldn't have me because I didn't believe...not about him being the son of God, for instance, that's the part that put paid to my ambition, that's where we didn't see eye to eye.

Tom Stoppard 1937– : *If You're Glad I'll Be Frank* (1973)

To a clergyman who thanked him for the enjoyment he'd given the world:
94 And I want to thank you for all the enjoyment you've taken out of it.

Groucho Marx 1895–1977: Joe Adamson *Groucho, Harpo, Chico and sometimes Zeppo* (1973)

95 Food was a very big factor in Christianity. What would the miracle of the loaves and fishes have been without it? And the Last Supper—how effective would that have been?

Fran Lebowitz 1946– : *Metropolitan Life* (1978)

96 Did you know they've scrapped the Holy Communion? They're experimenting with something called Series One, Series Two and Series Three. That doesn't sound like the Eucharist to me. That sounds like baseball.

Alan Bennett 1934– : *The Old Country* (1978)

97 Religions are manipulated by those who govern society and not the other way around. This is a brand-new thought to Americans, whether once or twice or never bathed in the Blood of the Lamb.

Gore Vidal 1925– : *Pink Triangle and Yellow Star* (1982)

98 Good manners can replace religious beliefs. In the Anglican Church they already have. Etiquette (and quiet, well-cut clothes) are devoutly worshipped by Anglicans.

P. J. O'Rourke 1947– : *Modern Manners* (1984)

99 The attitude that regards entanglement with religion as something akin to entanglement with an infectious disease must be confronted broadly and directly.

William J. Bennett 1943– : in *New York Times* 8 August 1985

100 The Bishops [in the House of Lords] treat everyone like patient peasants waiting to be told which way to vote.

Lord Hailsham 1907– : in an interview; John Mortimer *Character Parts* (1986)

101 'If Jesus were alive today, Mrs Whittaker, I think you'd find these were the type of shoes he would be wearing.' 'Not if his mother had anything to do with it.'

Alan Bennett 1934– : *Talking Heads* (1988)

102 For those of us who are baseball fans and agnostics, the [Baseball] Hall of Fame is as close to a religious experience as we may ever get.

Bill Bryson 1951– : *The Lost Continent* (1989)

103 Protestant women may take the pill. Roman Catholic women must keep taking The Tablet.

Irene Thomas: in *Guardian* 28 December 1990

104 The crisis of the Church of England is that too many of its bishops, and some would say of its archbishops, don't quite realise that they are atheists, but have begun to suspect it.

Clive James 1939– : *The Dreaming Swimmer* (1992)

105 Much as Field-Marshal Goering sought to confer Aryan status on the Jewish tenor Richard Tauber, so my mother spared Pat Bagott [her gardener] her usual strictures against Catholicism. Without knowing it, the spotless and particular Bagotts were granted a unique amnesty; in my mother's eyes at least they were honorary Protestants.

Barry Humphries 1934– : *More Please* (1992)

106 Redemption does, on the whole, play a rather important part in the Christian religion, and...the Founder of it was particularly taken with the idea.

Bernard Levin 1928– : *If You Want My Opinion* (1992)

107 Baptists are only funny underwater.

Neil Simon 1927– : *Laughter on the 23rd Floor* (1994)

Royalty

1 I had three concubines, who in three diverse properties diversely excelled. One, the merriest; another the wiliest; the third, the holiest harlot in my realm, as one whom no man could get out of the church lightly to any place but it were to his bed.

Edward IV 1442–83: Thomas More *The History of Richard III*, composed about 1513

On the debates in the House of Lords on Lord Ross's Divorce Bill:
2 Better than a play.

Charles II 1630–85: A. Bryant *King Charles II* (1931)

3 Here lies a great and mighty king
Whose promise none relies on;
He never said a foolish thing,
Nor ever did a wise one.

Lord Rochester 1647–80: 'The King's Epitaph' (an alternative first line reads: 'Here lies our sovereign lord the King')

4 This is very true: for my words are my own, and my
actions are my ministers'.

Charles II 1630–85: reply to 'The
King's Epitaph'; *Thomas Hearne:
Remarks and Collections* (1885–1921)
17 November 1706

When preaching before Charles II and his court:
5 My lord, you snore so loud you will wake the king.

Dr South 1634–1716: to Lord
Lauderdale; Arthur Bryant *King
Charles II* (rev. ed. 1964)

6 I've tried him drunk and I've tried him sober but there's
nothing in him.

Charles II 1630–85: of his niece
Anne's husband George of Denmark;
Gila Curtis *The Life and Times of
Queen Anne* (1972)

7 He had been, he said, an unconscionable time dying; but
he hoped that they would excuse it.

Charles II 1630–85: Lord Macaulay
History of England (1849)

8 Sire, your majesty seems to have won the race.

Lady Tyrconnel d. 1731: after the
Battle of the Boyne to James II, who
had complained that Lady Tyrconnel's
countrymen had run away; Elizabeth
Longford (ed.) *The Oxford Book of
Royal Anecdotes* (1989)

*England had declared war on France two weeks after the accession of
Queen Anne:*
9 It means I'm growing old when ladies declare war on
me.

Louis XIV 1638 1715: Gila Curtis
The Life and Times of Queen Anne
(1972)

10 Here thou, great Anna! whom three realms obey,
Dost sometimes counsel take—and sometimes tea.

Alexander Pope 1688–1744: *The
Rape of the Lock* (1714)

11 I hate all Boets and Bainters.

George I 1660–1727: John Campbell
Lives of the Chief Justices (1849) 'Lord
Mansfield'

12 I am his Highness' dog at Kew;
Pray, tell me sir, whose dog are you?

Alexander Pope 1688–1744:
'Epigram Engraved on the Collar of
a Dog which I gave to his Royal
Highness' (1738)

13 The Right Divine of Kings to govern wrong.

Alexander Pope 1688–1744: *The
Dunciad* (1742)

*Notice affixed to the gates of St James's Palace during one of George
II's absences in Hanover:*
14 Lost or strayed out of this house a man who has left
a wife and six children on the parish. .. [A reward of
four shillings and sixpence is offered] Nobody judging
him to deserve a crown.

Anonymous: Duke of Windsor 'My
Hanoverian Ancestors' (unpublished
reminiscences); Elizabeth Longford
(ed.) *The Oxford Book of Royal
Anecdotes* (1989)

When Queen Caroline, on her deathbed, urged him to marry again:
15 No, I shall have mistresses.

George II 1683–1760: John Hervey
Memoirs of the Reign of George II
(1848); the Queen replied, 'Oh, my
God! That won't make any difference'

Of the Emperor Gordian:

16 Twenty-two acknowledged concubines, and a library of sixty-two thousand volumes, attested the variety of his inclinations, and from the productions which he left behind him, it appears that the former as well as the latter were designed for use rather than ostentation. [Footnote] By each of his concubines the younger Gordian left three or four children. His literary productions were by no means contemptible.

Edward Gibbon 1737–94: *The Decline and Fall of the Roman Empire* (1776–88)

17 One of Edward's Mistresses was Jane Shore, who has had a play written about her, but it is a tragedy and therefore not worth reading.

Jane Austen 1775–1817: *The History of England* (written 1791)

On first seeing Caroline of Brunswick, his future wife:

18 Harris, I am not well; pray get me a glass of brandy.

George IV 1762–1830: Earl of Malmesbury *Diaries and Correspondence* (1844), 5 April 1795

19 I shall be an autocrat: that's my trade. And the good Lord will forgive me: that's his.

Catherine the Great 1729–96: attributed

20 Another damned, thick, square book! Always scribble, scribble, scribble! Eh! Mr Gibbon?

Duke of Gloucester 1743–1805: Henry Best *Personal and Literary Memorials* (1829); also attributed to the Duke of Cumberland and King George III

21 Not a fatter fish than he
Flounders round the polar sea.
See his blubber—at his gills
What a world of drink he swills...
By his bulk and by his size
By his oily qualities
This (or else my eyesight fails)
This should be the Prince of Wales.

Charles Lamb 1775–1834: anonymously written in 1812; Elizabeth Longford (ed.) *Oxford Book of Royal Anecdotes* (1989)

22 As Jordan's high and mighty squire
Her playhouse profits deigns to skim,
Some folks audaciously enquire:
If *he* keeps *her*, or *she* keeps *him*?

Anonymous: of the Duke of Clarence (later William IV) and his mistress, the actress Mrs Jordan; Philip Ziegler *King William IV* (1971)

Notice on a playbill sent to her former lover, the Duke of Clarence, refusing repayment of her allowance:

23 Positively no money refunded after the curtain has risen.

Mrs Jordan 1762–1816: Duke of Windsor 'My Hanoverian Ancestors' (unpublished reminiscences); Elizabeth Longford (ed.) *The Oxford Book of Royal Anecdotes* (1989)

After the death in childbirth of the Prince Regent's daughter Charlotte, four of the Regent's brothers married in an attempt to provide an heir to the throne:

24 Yoics! the Royal sport's begun!
I'faith but it is glorious fun,
For hot and hard each Royal pair
Are at it hunting for an heir.

Peter Pindar 1738–1819: Elizabeth Longford (ed.) *The Oxford Book of Royal Anecdotes* (1989)

The Duke of Clarence had told his father that he made his mistress Mrs Jordan an allowance of £1000 per year:

25 A thousand, a thousand; too much; too much! Five hundred quite enough! Quite enough!

George III 1738–1820: Brian Fothergill *Dorothy Jordan* (1965)

26 Most Gracious Queen, we thee implore
To go away and sin no more,
But if that effort be too great,
To go away at any rate.

Anonymous: epigram on Queen Caroline, quoted in a letter from Francis Burton to Lord Colchester, 15 November 1820

Caroline of Brunswick, estranged wife of George IV, while attending the debate in the House of Lords on the Bills of Pains and Penalties whereby George IV was attempting to divorce her, habitually fell asleep:

27 Her conduct at present no censure affords,
She sins not with courtiers but sleeps with the Lords.

Anonymous: Roger Fulford *The Trial of Queen Caroline* (1967)

It was said that during a cruise Caroline of Brunswick would sleep in a tent on deck with her majordomo, and take a bath in her cabin either with him or in his presence:

28 The Grand Master of St Caroline has found promotion's path;
He is made both Knight Companion and Commander of the Bath.

Anonymous: Roger Fulford *The Trial of Queen Caroline* (1967)

When forced by a mob to cheer George IV's wife Caroline of Brunswick:

29 God Save the Queen, and may all your wives be like her!

Duke of Wellington 1769–1852: Elizabeth Longford *Wellington: Pillar of State* (1972); also attributed to Lord Anglesey and others

Having been wakened with the news of his accession, William IV returned to bed:

30 To enjoy the novelty of sleeping with a queen.

William IV 1765–1837: Duke of Windsor 'My Hanoverian Ancestors' (unpublished reminiscences); Elizabeth Longford (ed.) *The Oxford Book of Royal Anecdotes* (1989)

William IV, on his way to dissolve Parliament, with uproar growing in both Houses over the Reform Bill and a cannon heralding his approach, asked his Lord Chancellor what the noise could be:

31 If you please, Your Majesty, it is the Lords debating.

Lord Brougham 1778–1868: *Works of Henry Lord Brougham* (1872)

32 'Where shall I begin, please your Majesty?' he asked. 'Begin at the beginning,' the King said, gravely, 'and go on till you come to the end: then stop.'

Lewis Carroll 1832–98: *Alice's Adventures in Wonderland* (1865)

33 There is a tale of Queen Victoria being shown over Trinity by the Master, Dr. Whewell, and saying, as she looked down over the bridge: 'What are all those pieces of paper floating down the river?' To which [recognizing them as lavatory paper], with great presence of mind, he replied, 'Those, ma'am, are notices that bathing is forbidden.'

Dr Whewell 1794–1866: G. Raverat *Period Piece* (1952)

34 I never deny; I never contradict; I sometimes forget.

Benjamin Disraeli 1804–81: of his dealings as Prime Minister with Queen Victoria; Elizabeth Longford *Victoria R.I.* (1964)

35 Everyone likes flattery; and when you come to Royalty you should lay it on with a trowel.

Benjamin Disraeli 1804–81: to Matthew Arnold; G. W. E. Russell *Collections and Recollections* (1898)

36 Lord Granville has not the courage of his opinions and therefore is of not the slightest use to the Queen.

Queen Victoria 1819–1901: letter to Sir Henry Ponsonby, 21 May 1882

37 The Queen is a good deal surprised and she must say annoyed at Mr. Gladstone's 'Progress'. He 'was not to cross the border' and yet he has been landing and receiving Addresses from many places in Scotland and is now off to Norway.

Queen Victoria 1819–1901: letter to Sir Henry Ponsonby, 16 September 1883

38 Fate wrote her a most tremendous tragedy, and she played it in tights.

Max Beerbohm 1872–1956: of Caroline of Brunswick, wife of George IV; *The Yellow Book* (1894)

To the Archbishop of Canterbury after the service of celebration at St Paul's for Queen Victoria's Diamond Jubilee in 1897:
39 I have no objection whatsoever to the notion of the Eternal Father, but every objection to the concept of an eternal mother.

Edward VII 1841–1910: attributed, perhaps apocryphal

40 He speaks to Me as if I was a public meeting.

Queen Victoria 1819–1901: of Gladstone; G. W. E. Russell *Collections and Recollections* (1898)

41 I am returning from your palace to my house.

Queen Victoria 1819–1901: to the Duchess of Sutherland after visiting Stafford House; Michael Hill (ed.) 'Right Royal Remarks' (unpublished compilation); in *Ned Sherrin in his Anecdotage* (1993)

42 How different, how very different from the home life of our own dear Queen!

Anonymous: comment overheard at a performance of Cleopatra by Sarah Bernhardt (probably apocryphal)

At the funeral of Edward VII the Kaiser asked Roosevelt to call on him the next day 'at two o'clock sharp—for I can give you only 45 minutes':
43 I will be there at two, but unfortunately I have just 20 minutes to give you.

Theodore Roosevelt 1858–1919: attributed, perhaps apocryphal

Edward VII was puzzled by the presence at a dinner to celebrate the new Dictionary of National Biography of Canon Ainger, author of the articles on Charles and Mary Lamb. The explanation 'he is a great authority on Lamb' confused him further:
44 On *lamb*!

Edward VII 1841–1910: Christopher Hibbert *Edward VII* (1976)

On being asked if Queen Victoria would be happy in heaven:
45 She will have to walk behind the angels—and she won't like that.

Edward VII 1841–1910: attributed, perhaps apocryphal

Housman had been asked to choose a selection of his poems for the library of Queen Mary's doll's house:

46 I selected the 12 shortest and least likely to fatigue the attention of dolls or members of the illustrious House of Hanover.

A. E. Housman 1859–1936: letter 4 May 1923

47 His Weariness the Prince entered the room in all his tinted orders.

Ronald Firbank 1886–1926: *The Flower Beneath the Foot* (1923)

Questionnaire for would-be Kings in the Wars of the Roses:

48 Are you Edmund Mortimer? If not, have you got him?

W. C. Sellar 1898–1951 and **R. J. Yeatman** 1898–1968: *1066 and All That* (1930)

49 He also invented a game called '*Bluff King Hal*' which he invited his ministers to play with him. The players were blindfolded and knelt down with their heads on a block of wood; they then guessed whom the King would marry next.

W. C. Sellar 1898–1951 and **R. J. Yeatman** 1898–1968: of Henry VIII; *1066 and All That* (1930)

50 The cruel Queen died and a post-mortem examination revealed the word 'CALLOUS' engraved on her heart.

W. C. Sellar 1898–1951 and **R. J. Yeatman** 1898–1968: of Mary Tudor; *1066 and All That* (1930)

51 Charles II was always very merry and was therefore not so much a king as a Monarch.

W. C. Sellar 1898–1951 and **R. J. Yeatman** 1898–1968: *1066 and All That* (1930)

52 The kings whose names are most firmly fixed in the national memory are those who continually did wrong, whether in a constitutional, political, social, moral, or religious sense; and I am quite sure that the familiar names of John, Charles, James, and Henry are at this moment present in your Lordships' minds.

A. P. Herbert 1890–1971: *Misleading Cases* (1935)

In conversation with Anthony Eden, 23 December 1935, following Samuel Hoare's resignation as Foreign Secretary:

53 I said to your predecessor: 'You know what they're all saying, no more coals to Newcastle, no more Hoares to Paris.' The fellow didn't even laugh.

George V 1865–1936: Earl of Avon *Facing the Dictators* (1962)

On a proposed State Visit to Holland:

54 Amsterdam, Rotterdam, and all the other dams. Damned if I do.

George V 1865–1936: Michael Hill (ed.) 'Right Royal Remarks' (unpublished compilation); in *Ned Sherrin in his Anecdotage* (1993)

55 Lousy but loyal.

Anonymous: London East End slogan at George V's Jubilee, 1935

Harold Nicolson had failed to recognize immediately that the 'dear little woman in black' to whom he was talking was the Duchess of York:

56 I steered my conversation onwards in the same course as before but with different sails: the dear old jib of comradeship was lowered and very slowly the spinnaker of 'Yes Ma'am' was hoisted in its place.

Harold Nicolson 1886–1968: diary 20 February 1936

57 King's Moll Reno'd in Wolsey's Home Town.

Anonymous: US newspaper headline on Wallis Simpson's divorce proceedings in Ipswich

Of the British people:
58 They 'ate 'aving no family life at Court.

J. H. Thomas 1874–1949: Harold Nicolson letter 26 February 1936

To Harold Nicolson on the Abdication crisis:
59 And now 'ere we 'ave this obstinate little man with 'is Mrs Simpson. Hit won't do, 'arold, I tell you that straight.

J. H. Thomas 1874–1949: Harold Nicolson letter 26 February 1936

On being asked, just after George VI's accession, if she had seen Chips Channon's new gold dinner service in his Belgravia home:
60 Oh no, we're not nearly grand enough to be asked there.

Queen Elizabeth, the Queen Mother 1900– : attributed, perhaps apocryphal

61 We saw Queen Mary looking like the Jungfrau, white and sparkling in the sun.

Chips Channon 1897–1958: diary 22 June 1937

62 Spirits of well-shot woodcock, partridge, snipe Flutter and bear him up the Norfolk sky.

John Betjeman 1906–84: 'Death of King George V' (1937)

63 The Queen, with her ever-ready, eager smile and bright popping eyes, is so pretty that she would make an ideal appendage to any chocolate shop.

Cecil Beaton 1904–80: of the exiled Queen of Albania; diary August 1940

To Brigadier Hinde, who had replied to the question, 'Have we met before?' with 'I don't think so':
64 You should bl-bloody well know.

George VI 1895–1952: Lord Carver *Out of Step* (1989)

The Queen, 'whose great gambit is always where do you come from', had greeted a Greek bishop visiting Buckingham Palace with the words, 'I suppose you come from Athens':
65 No Madam I am a Lesbian.

Anonymous: unnamed Greek bishop; Nancy Mitford letter 10 January 1945

66 Which King did you say?

Anonymous: BBC receptionist to King Haakon of Norway; in *Ned Sherrin in his Anecdotage* (1993)

67 It will be fun being 'In search of George'—but it will be hell writing the thing. I quite see that the Royal Family feel their myth is a piece of gossamer and must not be blown upon. So George VI will cut out all the jokes about George V.

Harold Nicolson 1886–1968: on his biography of George V; diary 9 September 1948

On being told that one of the Royal paintings was a Mercier, not by Nollekens:
68 We prefer the picture to remain as by Nollekens.

Queen Mary 1867–1953: Michael Hill (ed.) 'Right Royal Remarks' (unpublished compilation); in *Ned Sherrin in his Anecdotage* (1993)

69 She looked like a huge ball of fur on two well-developed legs. Shortest dress I ever saw and a Frenchman said it begins so low and ends so soon.

Nancy Mitford 1904–73: of Princess Margaret at a dinner in Paris; letter to Lady Redesdale, 28 April 1959

70 The Q, covered with barbed wire, looked SWEET and as cheerful as the other [Princess Margaret] was cross.

Nancy Mitford 1904–73: of the Queen at a dinner in Paris; letter to Lady Redesdale, 28 April 1959

71 What do the simple folk do?
...I have been informed
By those who know them well,
They find relief in quite a clever way.
When they're sorely pressed
They whistle for a spell:
And whistling seems to brighten up their day.
And that's what simple folk do;
So they say.

Alan Jay Lerner 1918–86: 'What Do the Simple Folk Do?' (1960)

72 Ma'am or Sir,
Sir or Ma'am
Makes every royal personage as happy as a clam.

Noël Coward 1899–1973: 'Sir or Ma'am' (1962)

73 LADY D: Is there anything in the newspaper this morning, Withers?
WITHERS: They have named another battleship after Queen Victoria, ma'am.
LADY D: Another? She must be beginning to think there is some resemblance.

Alan Bennett 1934– : *Forty Years On* (1969)

74 I told the Queen how moved I had been by Prince Charles's Investiture [as Prince of Wales], and she gaily shattered my sentimental illusions by saying that they were both struggling not to giggle because at the dress rehearsal the crown was too big and extinguished him like a candle-snuffer!

Noël Coward 1899–1973: diary 27 July 1969

75 I think everybody really will concede that on this, of all days, I should begin my speech with the words 'My husband and I'.

Elizabeth II 1926– : speech at Guildhall, London, on her 25th wedding anniversary

76 I left England when I was four because I found out I could never be King.

Bob Hope 1903– : from the Bob Hope Joke Files stored in two vaults of his Toluca Lake estate office; William Robert Faith *Bob Hope* (1983)

77 THE QUEEN: This ostrich egg was given us by the people of Samoa. It hasn't quite found its place yet.

Alan Bennett 1934– : *A Question of Attribution* (1989)

78 Ah'm sorry your Queen has to pay taxes. She's not a wealthy woman.

John Paul Getty 1892–1976: in *Ned Sherrin in his Anecdotage* (1993); attributed

79 My children are not royal, they just happen to have the Queen as their aunt.

Princess Margaret 1930– : Elizabeth Longford (ed.) *The Oxford Book of Royal Anecdotes* (1989)

Satisfaction and Discontent See also *Happiness and Unhappiness*

1 There was a jolly miller once,
Lived on the river Dee;
He worked and sang from morn till night;
No lark more blithe than he...

And this the burthen of his song,
For ever used to be,
I care for nobody, not I,
If no one cares for me.

Isaac Bickerstaffe 1733–*c*.1808: *Love in a Village* (1762)

2 You have delighted us long enough.

Jane Austen 1775–1817: *Pride and Prejudice* (1813)

3 Does he paint? He would fain write a poem.
Does he write? He would fain paint a picture.

Robert Browning 1812–89: 'One Word More' (1855)

4 If, of all words of tongue and pen,
The saddest are, 'It might have been,'
More sad are these we daily see:
'It is, but hadn't ought to be!'

Bret Harte 1836–1902: 'Mrs Judge Jenkins' (1867)

5 It's better to be looked over than overlooked.

Mae West 1892–1980: *Belle of the Nineties* (1934 film)

6 He spoke with a certain what-is-it in his voice, and I could see that, if not actually disgruntled, he was far from being gruntled.

P. G. Wodehouse 1881–1975: *The Code of the Woosters* (1938)

7 My life was simply hellish
I didn't stand a chance
I thought that I would relish
A tomb like General Grant's
But now I feel so swellish
So Elsa Maxwellish
That I'm giving a dance.

Cole Porter 1891–1964: 'I'm Throwing a Ball Tonight' (1940)

Comment made to Cecil Beaton by a lady-in-waiting to the exiled Queen Geraldine of Albania:

8 Of course, we'll go back there one day. Meanwhile, we have to make a new life for ourselves at the Ritz.

Anonymous: Cecil Beaton diary 1940

9 I test my bath before I sit,
And I'm always moved to wonderment
That what chills the finger not a bit
Is so frigid upon the fundament.

Ogden Nash 1902–71: 'Samson Agonistes' (1942)

10 Ice formed on the butler's upper slopes.

P. G. Wodehouse 1881–1975: *Pigs Have Wings* (1952)

11 I can tolerate without discomfort being waited on hand and foot.

Osbert Lancaster 1908–80: *All Done From Memory* (1953)

12 His strongest tastes were negative. He abhorred plastics, Picasso, sunbathing and jazz—everything in fact that had happened in his own lifetime.

Evelyn Waugh 1903–66: *The Ordeal of Gilbert Pinfold* (1957)

13 I ask very little. Some fragments of Pamphilides, a Choctaw blood-mask, the prose of Scaliger the Elder, a painting by Fuseli, an occasional visit to the all-in

Cyril Connolly 1903–74: *The Condemned Playground* 'Told in Gath', a parody of Aldous Huxley

wrestling, or to my meretrix; a cook who can produce a passable 'poulet à la Khmer', a Pong vase. Simple tastes, you will agree, and it is my simple habit to indulge them.

Science and Technology See also *Progress*

1 Multiplication is vexation,
  Division is as bad;
  The Rule of Three doth puzzle me,
  And Practice drives me mad.

Anonymous: in *Lean's Collectanea* (1904), possibly 16th-century

2 He had been eight years upon a project for extracting sun-beams out of cucumbers, which were to be put into vials hermetically sealed, and let out to warm the air in raw inclement summers.

Jonathan Swift 1667–1745: *Gulliver's Travels* (1726)

3 He put this engine [a watch] to our ears, which made an incessant noise like that of a water-mill; and we conjecture it is either some unknown animal, or the god that he worships; but we are more inclined to the latter opinion.

Jonathan Swift 1667–1745: *Gulliver's Travels* (1726)

4 Why sir, there is every possibility that you will soon be able to tax it!

Michael Faraday 1791–1867: to Gladstone, when asked about the usefulness of electricity; W. E. H. Lecky *Democracy and Liberty* (1899 ed.)

5 There is something fascinating about science. One gets such wholesale returns of conjecture out of such a trifling investment of fact.

Mark Twain 1835–1910: *Life on the Mississippi* (1883)

6 I never could make out what those damned dots meant.

Lord Randolph Churchill 1849–94: on decimal points; W. S. Churchill *Lord Randolph Churchill* (1906)

7 The Microbe is so very small
  You cannot make him out at all.
  But many sanguine people hope
  To see him through a microscope.

Hilaire Belloc 1870–1953: 'The Microbe' (1897)

8 The Scylla's cave which men of science are preparing for themselves to be able to pounce out upon us from it, and into which we cannot penetrate.

Samuel Butler 1835–1902: of scientific terminology; *Notebooks* (1912)

9 If they are worthy of the name, they are indeed about God's path and about his bed and spying out all his ways.

Samuel Butler 1835–1902: of scientists; *Notebooks* (1912)

10 Sir Humphrey Davy
   Abominated gravy.
   He lived in the odium
   Of having discovered Sodium.

Edmund Clerihew Bentley 1875–1956: 'Sir Humphrey Davy' (1905)

11 Why is it that the scholar is the only man of science of whom it is ever demanded that he should display taste and feeling?

A. E. Housman 1859–1936: 'Cambridge Inaugural Lecture' (1911)

12 Science becomes dangerous only when it imagines that it has reached its goal.

George Bernard Shaw 1856–1950: preface to *The Doctor's Dilemma* (1911)

13 When man wanted to make a machine that would walk he created the wheel, which does not resemble a leg.

Guillaume Apollinaire 1880–1918: *Les Mamelles de Tirésias* (1918)

14 There was a young lady named Bright,
Whose speed was far faster than light;
She set out one day
In a relative way
And returned on the previous night.

Arthur Buller 1874–1944: 'Relativity' (1923)

15 I read with infinite pleasure Eddington's *Nature of the Physical World* which for 24 hours almost persuaded me that I had caught a glimpse of what the new physics was really about. It wasn't, of course, true; but the sensation, while it lasted, was charming.

Harold Laski 1893–1950: letter to Oliver Wendell Holmes, 30 November 1928

16 Dr Strabismus (Whom God Preserve) of Utrecht has patented a new invention. It is an illuminated trouser-clip for bicyclists who are using main roads at night.

J. B. Morton 1893–1975: *Morton's Folly* (1933)

17 Her own mother lived the latter years of her life in the horrible suspicion that electricity was dripping invisibly all over the house.

James Thurber 1894–1961: *My Life and Hard Times* (1933)

18 The Doctor is said also to have invented an extraordinary weapon which will make war less brutal. It is described as a very powerful liquid which rots braces at a distance of a mile.

J. B. Morton 1893–1975: *Gallimaufry* (1936) 'Bracerot'

On being asked what he thought of Einstein's relativity:
19 Oh, that stuff! We never bother with that in our work.

Ernest Rutherford 1871–1937: in conversation; Stephen Leacock *The Boy I Left Behind Me* (1947)

To an elderly scientist who had bored her by talking interminably about the social organization of ants, which have 'their own police force and their own army':
20 No navy, I suppose?'

Mrs Patrick Campbell 1865–1940: James Agate diary 11 February 1944

21 It was Einstein who made the real trouble. He announced in 1905 that there was no such thing as absolute rest. After that there never was.

Stephen Leacock 1869–1944: *The Boy I Left Behind Me* (1947)

22 When Rutherford was done with the atom all the solidity was pretty well knocked out of it.

Stephen Leacock 1869–1944: *The Boy I Left Behind Me* (1947)

23 I have no more faith in men of science being infallible than I have in men of God being infallible, principally on account of them being men.

Noël Coward 1899–1973: diary 1 July 1946

24 Aristotle maintained that women have fewer teeth than men; although he was twice married, it never occurred to him to verify this statement by examining his wives' mouths.

Bertrand Russell 1872–1970: *Impact of Science on Society* (1952)

25 Molesworth 2...is inventing the wheel as he feel in science nothing should be accepted he is utterly wet.

Geoffrey Willans 1911–1958 and **Ronald Searle** 1920– : *Down with Skool!* (1953)

26 If I could remember the names of all these particles I'd be a botanist.

Enrico Fermi 1901–54: R. L. Weber *More Random Walks in Science* (1973)

27 Equations are more important to me, because politics is for the present, but an equation is something for eternity.

Albert Einstein 1879–1955: Stephen Hawking *A Brief History of Time* (1988)

28 The scientist who yields anything to theology, however slight, is yielding to ignorance and false pretences, and as certainly as if he granted that a horse-hair put into a bottle of water will turn into a snake.

H. L. Mencken 1880–1956: *Minority Report* (1956)

29 Technology...the knack of so arranging the world that we need not experience it.

Max Frisch 1911–91: *Homo Faber* (1957)

30 When I find myself in the company of scientists, I feel like a shabby curate who has strayed by mistake into a drawing room full of dukes.

W. H. Auden 1907–73: *The Dyer's Hand* (1963)

31 It is a good morning exercise for a research scientist to discard a pet hypothesis every day before breakfast.

Konrad Lorenz 1903–89: *On Aggression* (1966)

32 If an elderly but distinguished scientist says that something is possible he is almost certainly right, but if he says that it is impossible he is very probably wrong.

Arthur C. Clarke 1917– : in *New Yorker* 9 August 1969

33 Basic research is what I am doing when I don't know what I am doing.

Werner von Braun 1912–77: R. L. Weber *A Random Walk in Science* (1973)

34 It was absolutely marvellous working for Pauli. You could ask him anything. There was no worry that he would think a particular question was stupid, since he thought *all* questions were stupid.

Victor Weisskopf 1908– : in *American Journal of Physics* 1977

35 To err is human but to really foul things up requires a computer.

Anonymous: in *Farmers' Almanac for 1978*

36 My theory [is] that modern science was largely conceived of as an answer to the servant problem and that it is generally practised by those who lack a flair for conversation.

Fran Lebowitz 1946– : *Metropolitan Life* (1978)

37 Scientists are rarely to be counted among the fun people. Awkward at parties, shy with strangers, deficient in irony—they have had no choice but to turn their attention to the close study of everyday objects.

Fran Lebowitz 1946– : *Metropolitan Life* (1978)

38 The way botanists divide up flowers reminds me of the way Africa was divided into countries by politicians.

Miles Kington 1941– : *Nature Made Ridiculously Simple* (1983)

39 All I know about the becquerel is that, like the Italian lira, you need an awful lot to amount to very much.

Arnold Allen: in *Financial Times* 19 September 1986

40 I was right about the skate-board, I was right about *nouvelle cuisine*, and I'll be proved right about the digital watch. Digitals have got no class, you see. They're science and technology.

Tom Stoppard 1937– : *The Real Thing* (1988 rev. ed.)

41 Someone told me that each equation I included in the book would halve the sales.

Stephen Hawking 1942– : *A Brief History of Time* (1988)

42 JACKIE: (*very slowly*) Take Tube A and apply to Bracket D. VICTORIA: Reading it slower does not make it any easier to do.

Victoria Wood 1953– : *Mens Sana in Thingummy Doodah* (1990)

43 A modern computer hovers between the obsolescent and the nonexistent.

Sydney Brenner 1927– : in *Science* 5 January 1990; attributed

44 To mistrust science and deny the validity of the scientific method is to resign your job as a human. You'd better go look for work as a plant or wild animal.

P. J. O'Rourke 1947– : *Parliament of Whores* (1991)

45 Let's be frank, the Italians' technological contribution to humankind stopped with the pizza oven.

Bill Bryson 1951– : *Neither Here Nor There* (1991)

46 The thing with high-tech is that you always end up using scissors.

David Hockney 1937: in *Observer* 10 July 1994 'Sayings of the Week'

Scotland and the Scots See also *Countries and Peoples, Places*

1 *Oats*. A grain, which in England is generally given to horses, but in Scotland supports the people.

Samuel Johnson 1709–84: *A Dictionary of the English Language* (1755)

2 [BOSWELL:] I do indeed come from Scotland, but I cannot help it...
[JOHNSON:] That, Sir, I find, is what a very great many of your countrymen cannot help.

Samuel Johnson 1709–84: James Boswell *Life of Samuel Johnson* (1791) 16 May 1763

3 Norway, too, has noble wild prospects; and Lapland is remarkable for prodigious noble wild prospects. But, Sir, let me tell you, the noblest prospect which a Scotchman ever sees, is the high road that leads him to England!

Samuel Johnson 1709–84: James Boswell *Life of Samuel Johnson* (1791) 6 July 1763

4 That knuckle-end of England—that land of Calvin, oat-cakes, and sulphur.

Sydney Smith 1771–1845: Lady Holland *Memoir* (1855)

5 It requires a surgical operation to get a joke well into a Scotch understanding. Their only idea of wit... is laughing immoderately at stated intervals.

Sydney Smith 1771–1845: Lady Holland *Memoir* (1855)

6 There are few more impressive sights in the world than a Scotsman on the make.

J. M. Barrie 1860–1937: *What Every Woman Knows* (performed 1908)

7 A young Scotsman of your ability let loose upon the world with £300, what could he not do? It's almost appalling to think of; especially if he went among the English.

J. M. Barrie 1860–1937: *What Every Woman Knows* (1918)

8 No McTavish
Was ever lavish.

Ogden Nash 1902–71: 'Genealogical Reflection' (1931)

9 It is never difficult to distinguish between a Scotsman with a grievance and a ray of sunshine.

P. G. Wodehouse 1881–1975: *Blandings Castle and Elsewhere* (1935)

10 Can the United States ever become genuinely civilized? Certainly it is possible. Even Scotland has made enormous progress since the Eighteenth Century, when, according to Macaulay, most of it was on the cultural level of Albania.

H. L. Mencken 1880–1956: *Minority Report* (1956)

11 I had occasion, not for the first time, to thank heaven for that state of mind which cartographers seek to define as Scotland.

Claud Cockburn 1904–81: *Crossing the Line* (1958)

12 They christened their game golf because they were Scottish and revelled in meaningless Celtic noises in the back of the throat.

Stephen Fry 1957– : *Paperweight* (1992)

Self-Knowledge and Self-Deception See also *Character*

1 Satire is a sort of glass, wherein beholders do generally discover everybody's face but their own.

Jonathan Swift 1667–1745: *The Battle of the Books* (1704) preface

2 Lady Kill-Chairman, who is one of the greatest gossips in the kingdom, and knows everybody but herself.

Anonymous: in *The Female Tatler* December 1709

3 It exactly resembles a superannuated Jesuit...though my mind misgives me that it is hideously like. If it is—I can not be long for this world—for it overlooks seventy.

Lord Byron 1788–1824: of a bust of himself by Bartolini; letter 23 September 1822

4 'He has a profound contempt for human nature.'
'Of course, he is much given to introspection.'

Charles-Maurice de Talleyrand 1754–1838: of Fouché; Leon Harris *The Fine Art of Political Wit* (1965)

5 I don't at all like knowing what people say of me behind my back. It makes me far too conceited.

Oscar Wilde 1854–1900: *An Ideal Husband* (1895)

6 Our polite recognition of another's resemblance to ourselves.

Ambrose Bierce 1842–?1914: definition of admiration; *Cynic's Word Book* (1906)

7 A person of low taste, more interested in himself than in me.

Ambrose Bierce 1842–?1914: definition of an egotist; *Cynic's Word Book* (1906)

To a footman who had accidentally spilt cream over him:
8 My good man, I'm not a strawberry!

Edward VII 1841–1910: William Lanceley *From Hall-Boy to House-Steward* (1925)

9 The photograph is not quite true to my own notion of my gentleness and sweetness of nature, but neither perhaps is my external appearance.

A. E. Housman 1859–1936: letter 12 June 1922

Housman was a pall-bearer at Thomas Hardy's funeral:
10 A journalist present in the abbey says that my person proved as polished as my verse, after which I desire to be for ever invisible.

A. E. Housman 1859–1936: letter 24 January 1928

11 For self-revelation, whether it be a Tudor villa on the by-pass or a bomb-proof chalet at Berchtesgaden, there's no place like home.

Osbert Lancaster 1908–80: *Homes Sweet Homes* (1939)

12 The Crown Prince Umberto is charm itself, but has no great intelligence. He reminds me of myself.

Chips Channon 1897–1958: diary (undated entry); introduction to *Chips: the Diaries of Sir Henry Channon* (1993)

13   I tell you,
Miss, I knows an undesirable character
When I see one; I've been one myself for years.

Christopher Fry 1907– : *Venus Observed* (1950)

14 Long experience has taught me that to be criticized is not
always to be wrong.

Anthony Eden 1897–1977: speech at Lord Mayor's Guildhall banquet during the Suez crisis; in *Daily Herald* 10 November 1956

15 If it were an innocent, passive gullibility it would be
excusable; but all too clearly, alas, it is an active
willingness to be deceived.

Peter Medawar 1915–87: review of Teilhard de Chardin *The Phenomenon of Man* (1961)

16 Underneath this flabby exterior is an enormous lack of
character.

Oscar Levant 1906–72: *Memoirs of an Amnesiac* (1965)

17 I do not stare at myself in the mirror. For one thing
I can't see myself properly without my glasses and
because I can't bear looking at myself in glasses because
I look so terrible in them, I never look at myself at all.

Alan Ayckbourn 1939– : *Table Manners* (1975)

18 All my shows are great. Some of them are bad. But they
are all great.

Lew Grade 1906– : in *Observer* 14 September 1975

19 [I am] a doormat in a world of boots.

Jean Rhys c.1890–1979: in *Guardian* 6 December 1990

20 I'm the girl who lost her reputation and never missed it.

Mae West 1892–1980: P. F. Boller and R. L. Davis *Hollywood Anecdotes* (1988)

21 I am not the type who wants to go back to the land;
I am the type who wants to go back to the hotel.

Fran Lebowitz 1946– : *Social Studies* (1981)

22 My life, so far, seemed to have been a complete fiasco.
I had lived twenty-three endless years and what had I to
show for it? An unpublished novel, an inglorious war
and a disastrous love affair.

John Mortimer 1923– : *Clinging to the Wreckage* (1982)

23 I can put two and two together, you know. Do not think
you are dealing with a man who has lost his grapes.

Tom Stoppard 1937– : *Another Moon Called Earth* (1983)

24 I believe that Sir Isaiah Berlin is the only man in Britain
who talks more rapidly than I do, and even that is
a close-run thing.

Bernard Levin 1928– : *In These Times* (1986)

25 This piece of writing had all the characteristics of my
later work, namely that it was plagiarized, not very
funny and in slightly bad taste.

Michael Green 1927– : *The Boy Who Shot Down an Airship* (1988)

26 I am extraordinarily patient, provided I get my own way
in the end.

Margaret Thatcher 1925– : in *Observer* 4 April 1989

27 Without exactly *telling* them that I felt like a man
swimming towards a raft in a sea of circling fins,
I constructed a cry for help masterfully disguised as
a manifesto.

Clive James 1939– : *The Dreaming Swimmer* (1992)

28 Pavarotti is not vain, but conscious of being unique.

Peter Ustinov 1921– : in *Independent on Sunday* 12 September 1993

29 I had developed a reputation as a bit of a hatchet man, the sort of mean-spirited turnip whose work would never be allowed to grace the covers of such ferociously accommodating publications as *Entertainments Weekly*.

Joe Queenan: *If You're Talking To Me Your Career Must Be In Trouble* (1994)

Sex See also *Love, Marriage*

1 BARNARDINE: Thou hast committed—
BARABAS: Fornication? But that was in another country: and besides, the wench is dead.

Christopher Marlowe 1564–93: *The Jew of Malta* (c.1592)

2 Is it not strange that desire should so many years outlive performance?

William Shakespeare 1564–1616: *Henry IV, Part 2* (1597)

3 Your virginity, your old virginity, is like one of our French withered pears; it looks ill, it eats drily.

William Shakespeare 1564–1616: *All's Well that Ends Well* (1603–4)

Of Marina, a beautiful virgin:
4 She would serve after a long voyage at sea.

William Shakespeare 1564–1616: *Pericles* (1606–8)

5 No, no; for my virginity,
When I lose that, says Rose, I'll die:
Behind the elms last night, cried Dick,
Rose, were you not extremely sick?

Matthew Prior 1664–1721: 'A True Maid' (1718)

6 He in a few minutes ravished this fair creature, or at least would have ravished her, if she had not, by a timely compliance, prevented him.

Henry Fielding 1707–54: *Jonathan Wild* (1743)

7 It is true from early habit, one must make love mechanically as one swims, I was once very fond of both, but now as I never swim unless I tumble into the water, I don't make love till almost obliged.

Lord Byron 1788–1824: letter 10 September 1812

8 If people will stop at the first tense of the verb 'aimer' they must not be surprised if one finishes the conjugation with somebody else.

Lord Byron 1788–1824: letter 13 January 1814

9 Not tonight, Josephine.

Napoléon I 1769–1821: attributed, but probably apocryphal; R. H. Horne *The History of Napoleon* (1841) describes the circumstances in which the affront might have occurred

10 A little still she strove, and much repented,
And whispering 'I will ne'er consent'—consented.

Lord Byron 1788–1824: *Don Juan* (1819–24)

11 What men call gallantry, and gods adultery,
Is much more common where the climate's sultry.

Lord Byron 1788–1824: *Don Juan* (1819–24)

12 How can a bishop marry? How can he flirt? The most he can say is, 'I will see you in the vestry after service.'

Sydney Smith 1771–1845: Lady Holland *Memoir* (1855)

13 Do not adultery commit;
Advantage rarely comes of it.

Arthur Hugh Clough 1819–61: 'The Latest Decalogue' (1862)

14 Would you like to sin
With Elinor Glyn
On a tigerskin?
Or would you prefer

Anonymous: verse alluding to Elinor Glyn's romantic novel *Three Weeks* (1907); A. Glyn *Elinor Glyn* (1955)

To err
With her
On some other fur?

15 Enjoy your supper, Mr Percy, the port is on the chim-a-ney piece, and it's *still* adultery!

Lady Tree 1863–1937: on finding her husband Herbert Beerbohm Tree dining à deux with the young and handsome actor Esmé Percy; attributed, perhaps apocryphal

16 She kissed her way into society. I don't like her. But don't misunderstand me: my dislike is purely platonic.

Herbert Beerbohm Tree 1852–1917: of an actress whose reputation as a lover was higher than her reputation as an artist; Hesketh Pearson *Beerbohm Tree* (1956)

17 [CHAIRMAN OF MILITARY TRIBUNAL:] What would you do if you saw a German soldier trying to violate your sister? [STRACHEY:] I would try to get between them.

Lytton Strachey 1880–1932: in Robert Graves *Good-bye to All That* (1929); otherwise rendered as, 'I should interpose my body'

18 All this fuss about sleeping together. For physical pleasure I'd sooner go to my dentist any day.

Evelyn Waugh 1903–66: *Vile Bodies* (1930)

19 Let us honour if we can
The vertical man
Though we value none
But the horizontal one.

W. H. Auden 1907–73: 'To Christopher Isherwood' (1930)

20 The sexophones wailed like melodious cats under the moon.

Aldous Huxley 1894–1963: *Brave New World* (1932)

21 It's not the men in my life that counts—it's the life in my men.

Mae West 1892–1980: in *I'm No Angel* (1933 film)

22 Why don't you come up sometime, and see me?

Mae West 1892–1980: in *She Done Him Wrong* (1933 film); usually quoted 'Why don't you come up and see me sometime?'

23 You're the burning heat of a bridal suite in use.
You're the breasts of Venus,
You're King Kong's penis,
You're self abuse.
You're an arch
In the Rome collection
You're the starch
In a groom's erection.

Anonymous: parody version of Cole Porter's 'You're the Top' (1934), possibly by Porter

24 Surely the sex business isn't worth all this damned fuss? I've met only a handful of people who cared a biscuit for it.

T. E. Lawrence 1888–1935: on reading *Lady Chatterley's Lover*, in Christopher Hassall *Edward Marsh* (1959)

25 Home is heaven and orgies are vile,
But you *need* an orgy, once in a while.

Ogden Nash 1902–71: 'Home, 99⁴⁴/₁₀₀% Sweet Home' (1935)

26 'But what *is* the love life of newts, if you boil it right down? Didn't you tell me once that they just waggled their tails at one another in the mating season?'

P. G. Wodehouse 1881–1975: *The Code of the Woosters* (1938)

'Quite correct.'
I shrugged my shoulders.
'Well, all right, if they like it. But it's not my idea of
molten passion.'

On homosexuality:

27 It doesn't matter what you do in the bedroom as long as
you don't do it in the street and frighten the horses.

Mrs Patrick Campbell
1865–1940: Daphne Fielding *The
Duchess of Jermyn Street* (1964)

28 You should make a point of trying every experience once,
excepting incest and folk-dancing.

Anonymous: Arnold Bax *Farewell
My Youth* (1943), quoting 'a
sympathetic Scot'

29 Continental people have sex life; the English have hot-
water bottles.

George Mikes 1912– : *How to be
an Alien* (1946)

30 The House of Commons en bloc do it,
Civil Servants by the clock do it.

Noël Coward 1899–1973: 'Let's Do
It' (with acknowledgements to Cole
Porter) (1940s)

31 Sex is something I really don't understand too hot. You
never know *where* the hell you are. I keep making up
these sex rules for myself, and then I break them right
away.

J. D. Salinger 1919– : *The Catcher
in the Rye* (1951)

32 Nobody here [in England] talks about anything *at all*
except buggery it's too extraordinary. Half the public
wants it officially recognized and the other half wants
burning alive quartering etc. etc. to be restored as the
normal penalty.

Nancy Mitford 1904–73: letter
21 November 1953

33 Chasing the naughty couples down the grassgreen
gooseberried double bed of the wood.

Dylan Thomas 1914–53: *Under
Milk Wood* (1954)

34 Gomer Owen who kissed her once by the pig-sty when
she wasn't looking and never kissed her again although
she was looking all the time.

Dylan Thomas 1914–53: *Under
Milk Wood* (1954)

35 Birds do it, bees do it,
Even educated fleas do it.
Let's do it, let's fall in love.

Cole Porter 1891–1964: 'Let's Do It'
(1954; words added to the 1928
original)

36 In the licorice fields at Pontefract
My love and I did meet
And many a burdened licorice bush
Was blooming round our feet;
Red hair she had and golden skin,
Her sulky lips were shaped for sin,
Her sturdy legs were flannel-slack'd,
The strongest legs in Pontefract.

John Betjeman 1906–84: 'The
Licorice Fields at Pontefract' (1954)

37 In the Garden City Café with its murals on the wall
Before a talk on 'Sex and Civics' I meditated on the Fall.

John Betjeman 1906–84: 'Huxley
Hall' (1954)

38 Many years ago I chased a woman for almost two years,
only to discover that her tastes were exactly like mine:
we both were crazy about girls.

Groucho Marx 1895–1977: letter
28 March 1955

39 Thank God we're normal,
Yes, this is our finest shower!

John Osborne 1929– : *The
Entertainer* (1957)

40 On a sofa upholstered in panther skin
Mona did researches in original sin.

William Plomer 1903–73: 'Mews Flat Mona' (1960)

41 How long do you want to wait until you start enjoying life? When you're sixty-five you get social security, not girls.

Neil Simon 1927– : *Come Blow Your Horn* (1961)

42 Prostitution gives her an opportunity to meet people. It provides fresh air and wholesome exercise, and it keeps her out of trouble.

Joseph Heller 1923– : *Catch-22* (1961)

43 The trouble with a virgin is
She's always on the verge.
A virgin is the worst
Her method is reversed
She'll lead a horse to water
And then let him die of thirst.

E. Y. Harburg 1898–1981: 'Never Trust a Virgin' (1961)

44 [Peter O'Toole in *Lawrence of Arabia* is] far more attractive than Lawrence could ever hope to be. I said to him afterwards that if Lawrence had looked like him there would have been many more than twelve Turks queueing up for the buggering scene.

Noël Coward 1899–1973: diary 4 December 1962

45 When I was in Venice I thought that perhaps masked naked men, orgies and unlimited spying are an accompaniment of maritime powers in decline.

Nancy Mitford 1904–73: during the Profumo affair; letter 11 October 1963

46 'Ye'es, ye'es,' he finally observed with a certain dry relish, 'ye'es, I think I see some adulterers down there.'

Maurice Green 1906–87: in the Press Gallery of the House of Commons during the Profumo scandal, recorded by Colin Welch; Ned Sherrin *Cutting Edge* (1984)

47 When self-indulgence has reduced a man to the shape of Lord Hailsham, sexual continence requires no more than a sense of the ridiculous.

Reginald Paget: speech in the House of Commons during the Profumo affair, 17 June 1963

48 He said it was artificial respiration, but now I find I am to have his child.

Anthony Burgess 1917–93: *Inside Mr Enderby* (1963)

49 KATH: Can he be present at the birth of his child?...
ED: It's all any reasonable child can expect if the dad is present at the conception.

Joe Orton 1933–67: *Entertaining Mr Sloane* (1964)

50 Where is she at the moment? Alone with probably the most attractive man she's ever met. Don't tell me *that* doesn't beat hell out of hair curlers and the *Late Late Show*.

Neil Simon 1927– : *Barefoot in the Park* (1964)

51 I can't get no satisfaction
I can't get no girl reaction.

Mick Jagger 1943– and **Keith Richard** 1943– : '(I Can't Get No) Satisfaction' (1965)

52 A fast word about oral contraception. I asked a girl to go to bed with me and she said 'no'.

Woody Allen 1935– : at a night-club in Washington, April 1965

53 Your idea of fidelity is not having more than one man in bed at the same time.

Frederic Raphael 1931– : *Darling* (1965)

54 An orgy looks particularly alluring seen through the mists of righteous indignation.

Malcolm Muggeridge 1903-90: *The Most of Malcolm Muggeridge* (1966) 'Dolce Vita in a Cold Climate'

55 His second question was, 'How queer are you?' If I myself had small talent to amuse, I could at least make an effort to please. 'Oh, about twenty per cent.' 'Really! Are you? I'm ninety-five.'

John Osborne 1929- : recollection of a conversation with Noël Coward in 1966; *Almost a Gentleman* (1991)

56 MIKE: There's no word in the Irish language for what you were doing.
WILSON: In Lapland they have no word for snow.

Joe Orton 1933-67: *The Ruffian on the Stair* (rev. ed. 1967)

On her abortion:
57 It serves me right for putting all my eggs in one bastard.

Dorothy Parker 1893-1967: John Keats *You Might as well Live* (1970)

58 I became one of the stately homos of England.

Quentin Crisp 1908- : *The Naked Civil Servant* (1968)

59 You were born with your legs apart. They'll send you to the grave in a Y-shaped coffin.

Joe Orton 1933-67: *What the Butler Saw* (1969)

At a Confirmation class the vicar had put his hand over Coward's crotch:
60 Vicar, you are supposed to be preparing me for Confirmation. When I have received the gift of the Holy Spirit, if I'm in the mood, I'll telephone you.

Noël Coward 1899-1973: interview with David Frost in 1969

61 Masturbation is the thinking man's television.

Christopher Hampton 1946- : *The Philanthropist* (1970)

62 Time is short and we must seize
Those pleasures found above the knees.

Richard Eyre 1916-92: habitual comment made to his son Richard's girlfriends; Richard Eyre *Utopia and Other Places* (1993)

On being told he should not marry anyone as plain as his fiancée:
63 My dear fellow, buggers can't be choosers.

Maurice Bowra 1898-1971: Hugh Lloyd-Jones *Maurice Bowra: a Celebration* (1974)

64 I regret to say that we of the FBI are powerless to act in cases of oral-genital intimacy, unless it has in some way obstructed interstate commerce.

J. Edgar Hoover 1895-1972: Irving Wallace et al. *Intimate Sex Lives of Famous People* (1981)

65 I've been around so long, I knew Doris Day before she was a virgin.

Groucho Marx 1895-1977: Max Wilk *The Wit and Wisdom of Hollywood* (1972)

66 Is sex dirty? Only if it's done right.

Woody Allen 1935- : *Everything You Always Wanted to Know about Sex* (1972 film)

67 Ten years of courtship is carrying celibacy to extremes.

Alan Bennett 1934- : *Habeas Corpus* (1973)

68 There was a black-out. I saw his face only in the fitful light of a post-coital Craven A.

Alan Bennett 1934- : *Habeas Corpus* (1973)

69 We had a terrible experience coming down. We had to move our compartment three times to avoid a clergyman

Alan Bennett 1934- : *Habeas Corpus* (1973)

who was trying to look up her legs under cover of the *Daily Telegraph*.

70 Masturbation: the primary sexual activity of mankind. In the nineteenth century, it was a disease; in the twentieth, it's a cure.

Thomas Szasz 1920– : *The Second Sin* (1973)

On lesbianism:

71 I can understand two men. There is something to get hold of. But how do two insides make love?

Lydia Lopokova 1892–1981: A. J. P. Taylor letter 5 November 1973

72 I'm all for bringing back the birch, but only between consenting adults.

Gore Vidal 1925– : in *Sunday Times Magazine* 16 September 1973

73 Sexual intercourse began
In nineteen sixty-three
(Which was rather late for me)—
Between the end of the *Chatterley* ban
And the Beatles' first L.P.

Philip Larkin 1922–85: 'Annus Mirabilis' (1974)

74 I have a desire to put on my glasses and take off my clothes and dance naked on the grass for you, Tom. I'd put on my glasses not in order to improve the shape of my face, but in order to see your reaction, if any.

Alan Ayckbourn 1939– : *Round and Round the Garden* (1975)

75 Norman doesn't bother with secret signals. It was just wham, thump and there we both were on the rug.

Alan Ayckbourn 1939– : *Table Manners* (1975)

76 On bisexuality: It immediately doubles your chances for a date on Saturday night.

Woody Allen 1935– : in *New York Times* 1 December 1975

In 1951 the homosexual Labour politician Tom Driberg married a widow; he later complained:

77 She broke her marriage vows; she tried to sleep with me.

Tom Driberg 1905–76: in *Ned Sherrin in his Anecdotage* (1993)

78 Seduction is often difficult to distinguish from rape. In seduction, the rapist bothers to buy a bottle of wine.

Andrea Dworkin 1946– : *Letters from a War Zone* (1988)

79 If homosexuality were the normal way, God would have made Adam and Bruce.

Anita Bryant 1940– : in *New York Times* 5 June 1977

80 Don't knock masturbation. It's sex with someone I love.

Woody Allen 1935– : *Annie Hall* (1977 film, with Marshall Brickman)

81 That [sex] was the most fun I ever had without laughing.

Woody Allen 1935– : *Annie Hall* (1977 film, with Marshall Brickman)

82 It's an odd thing but travel broadens the mind in a way that the proverbialist didn't quite intend. It's only at airports and railway stations that one finds in oneself a curiosity about er—er—erotica, um, girlie magazines.

Tom Stoppard 1937– : *Professional Foul* (1978)

83 My mother used to say, Delia, if S-E-X ever rears its ugly head, close your eyes before you see the rest of it.

Alan Ayckbourn 1939– : *Bedroom Farce* (1978)

84 'My mother made me a homosexual.'
'If I send her the wool will she make me one?'

Anonymous: New York graffito of the 1970s

85 Enter the strumpet voluntary.

Kenneth Tynan 1927–80: of a guest at an Oxford party; attributed

86 I've no feeling in this arm and I can hardly see. Which
knocks out at least three erogenous zones for a kick-off.

Alan Bennett 1934– : *Enjoy* (1980)

87 It was the afternoon of my eighty-first birthday, and
I was in bed with my catamite when Ali announced that
the archbishop had come to see me.

Anthony Burgess 1917–93: *Earthly Powers* (1980); opening sentence

88 At Oxford after Dunkirk the fashion was to be
homosexual. It seems that it was only after the war, with
the return of the military, that heterosexuality came to
be completely tolerated.

John Mortimer 1923– : *Clinging to the Wreckage* (1982)

*At the age of ninety-seven, Blake was asked at what age the sex drive
goes:*

89 You'll have to ask somebody older than me.

Eubie Blake 1883–1983: in *Ned Sherrin in his Anecdotage* (1993)

90 Dating is a social engagement with the threat of sex at its
conclusion.

P. J. O'Rourke 1947– : *Modern Manners* (1984)

91 Sex is like having dinner: sometimes you joke about the
dishes, sometimes you take the meal seriously.

Woody Allen 1935– : attributed

92 Talking is excellent exercise for the mouth's all-important
oral sex muscles.

P. J. O'Rourke 1947– : *Modern Manners* (1984)

93 BONES: A consummate artist, sir. I felt it deeply when she
retired.
GEORGE: Unfortunately she retired from consummation
about the same time as she retired from artistry.

Tom Stoppard 1937– : *Jumpers* (rev. ed. 1986)

94 When people say, 'You're breaking my heart,' they do in
fact usually mean that you're breaking their genitals.

Jeffrey Bernard 1932– : in *The Spectator* 31 May 1986

95 I know it [sex] does make people happy, but to me it is
just like having a cup of tea.

Cynthia Payne: in *Observer* 8 February 1987 'Sayings of the Week'

96 Genitals are a great distraction to scholarship.

Malcolm Bradbury 1932– : *Cuts* (1987)

97 Nobody in their right minds would call me
a nymphomaniac. I only sleep with good-looking men.

Fiona Pitt-Kethley 1954– : in *Listener* 17 November 1988

98 I always thought music was more important than
sex–then I thought if I don't hear a concert for a year-
and-a-half it doesn't bother me.

Jackie Mason 1931– : in *Guardian* 17 February 1989

99 I wouldn't kidnap a man for sex—I'm not saying
I couldn't use someone to oil the mower.

Victoria Wood 1953– : *Mens Sana in Thingummy Doodah* (1990)

100 Our history master…was also known to possess a pair of
suede shoes, a sure sign in the Melbourne of this period
of sexual ambivalence.

Barry Humphries 1934– : *More Please* (1992)

101 Zeus performed acts with swans and heifers that would
debar him from every London club except the Garrick or
possibly the Naval and Military.

Stephen Fry 1957– : *Paperweight* (1992)

102 Before permissiveness came in, everyone everywhere was
at it like randy goats. But the moment the young started
to insist on talking about it all the time, you couldn't get
laid if you were a table at the Savoy. As soon as it

Stephen Fry 1957– : *The Hippopotamus* (1994)

becomes a Right you can't bloody do it any more. Self-consciousness, you see.

Sickness and Health See also *Medicine*

1 A custom loathsome to the eye, hateful to the nose, harmful to the brain, dangerous to the lungs, and in the black, stinking fume thereof, nearest resembling the horrible Stygian smoke of the pit that is bottomless.

James I 1566–1625: *A Counterblast to Tobacco* (1604)

2 The nurse sleeps sweetly, hired to watch the sick, Whom, snoring, she disturbs.

William Cowper 1731–1800: *The Task* (1785)

3 When men die of disease they are said to die from natural causes. When they recover (and they mostly do) the doctor gets the credit of curing them.

George Bernard Shaw 1856–1950: preface to *The Doctor's Dilemma* (1911)

4 The gonococcus is not an exclusively French microbe: the possiblity of sterilizing marriage is not bounded by the Channel, the Rhine, or the Alps.

George Bernard Shaw 1856–1950: preface to a collection of Brieux's plays in English translation (1911)

On hearing of the illness of Traill, who in 1904 had beaten him for the Provostship of Trinity Dublin:
5 Nothing trivial, I hope.

John Pentland Mahaffy 1839–1919: Ulick O'Connor *Oliver St John Gogarty* (1964)

6 My aunt died of influenza: so they said. But it's my belief they done the old woman in.

George Bernard Shaw 1856–1950: *Pygmalion* (1916)

7 In rural cottage life not to have rheumatism is as glaring an omission as not to have been presented at Court would be in more ambitious circumstances.

Saki 1870–1916: *The Toys of Peace* (1919)

8 To talk of diseases is a sort of *Arabian Nights* entertainment.

William Osler 1849–1919: Oliver Sacks *The Man Who Mistook his Wife for a Hat* (1985)

9 I enjoy convalescence. It is the part that makes illness worth while.

George Bernard Shaw 1856–1950: *Back to Methuselah* (1921)

10 This cough I've got is hacking, The pain in my head is wracking, I hardly need to mention my flu. The Board of Health has seen me They want to quarantine me, I might as well be miserable with you.

Howard Dietz 1896–1983: 'Miserable with You' (1931)

11 About five o'clock I am convinced, as of old, that I am suffering from a combination of D.T.'s and G.P.I. Think of making my will, but make some tea instead.

James Agate 1877–1947: diary 1 June 1943

12 In other words just from waiting around For that plain little band of gold A person...can develop a cold. You can spray her wherever you figure the streptococci lurk. You can give her a shot for whatever she's got but it just won't work.

Frank Loesser 1910–69: 'Adelaide's Lament' (1950)

If she's tired of getting the fish-eye from the hotel clerk,
A person...can develop a cold.

13 You can feed her all day with the vitamin A and the
   Bromo fizz,
   But the medicine never gets anywhere near where the
   trouble is,
   If she's getting a kind of a name for herself, and the
   name ain't his—
   A person...can develop a cough.

Frank Loesser 1910–69: 'Adelaide's
Lament', reprise (1950)

14 London is in the grip of a smog attack that makes
   anything we've ever seen look trifling; it's a wonder to
   me that everyone here isn't hospitalized with some kind
   of pulmonary illness, because breathing is like burying
   your head in a smokestack.

S. J. Perelman 1904–79: letter
13 December 1953

15 BUDDY: ...Do you feel any better?
   MOTHER: How do I know? I feel too sick to tell.

Neil Simon 1927– : Come Blow
Your Horn (1961)

16 I wish I had the voice of Homer
   To sing of rectal carcinoma,
   Which kills a lot more chaps, in fact,
   Than were bumped off when Troy was sacked.

J. B. S. Haldane 1892–1964:
'Cancer's a Funny Thing'; Ronald Clark
J. B. S. (1968)

17 My final word, before I'm done,
   Is 'Cancer can be rather fun'.
   Thanks to the nurses and Nye Bevan
   The NHS is quite like heaven
   Provided one confronts the tumour
   With a sufficient sense of humour.

J. B. S. Haldane 1892–1964:
'Cancer's a Funny Thing'; Ronald Clark
J. B. S. (1968)

18 When they catch some sickness—which they rarely do—
   usually they do not have to send for a doctor. They know
   the cure...horrified though the doctor might be if he
   heard what it was.

Flann O'Brien 1911–66: of the
older inhabitants of the Irish
Gaeltacht; Myles Away from Dublin
(1990)

19 A cripple of the worst sort, and consumptive into the
   bargain.

Alan Bennett 1934– : Forty Years
On (1969)

20 DENNIS: It's called Brett's Palsy.
   He shows her a medical book.
   MRS WICKSTEED: Tiredness, irritability, spots, yes. And
      generally confined to the Caucasus. If this germ is
      confined to the Caucasus what's it doing in Hove?

Alan Bennett 1934– : Habeas
Corpus (1973)

21 What's happened to the galloping consumption you had
   last Thursday? Slowed down to a trot I suppose.

Alan Bennett 1934– : Habeas
Corpus (1973)

22 He was a very fine doctor. Very little he couldn't put
   right when he set his mind to it. Rita's knee got the
   better of him, though.

Alan Ayckbourn 1939– : Sisterly
Feelings (1981)

23 Halitosis capable of de-scaling a kettle at fifty paces.

Alan Coren 1938– : Seems Like Old
Times (1989)

24 A cough so robust that I tapped into two new seams of
   phlegm.

Bill Bryson 1951– : Neither Here
Nor There (1991)

25 Up with thinking and feeling
   And stuff exercise.

Wendy Cope 1945– : 'Roger Bear's
Philosophical Pantoum' (1992)

26 The sexual revolution is over and the microbes won.

P. J. O'Rourke 1947– : *Give War a Chance* (1992)

27 I'm not unwell. I'm fucking dying.

Jeffrey Bernard 1932– : in conversation with Dominic Lawson; in *The Spectator* 19 February 1994

28 Piles are a Jewish man's affliction. Piles and mothers. What causes them?

Stephen Fry 1957– : *The Hippopotamus* (1994)

Singing See *Songs and Singing*

Sleep and Dreams

1 I have had a dream, past the wit of man to say what dream it was.

William Shakespeare 1564–1616: *A Midsummer Night's Dream* (1595–6)

2 I pray you, let none of your people stir me: I have an exposition of sleep come upon me.

William Shakespeare 1564–1616: *A Midsummer Night's Dream* (1595–6)

3 The eye of man hath not heard, the ear of man hath not seen, man's hand is not able to taste, his tongue to conceive, nor his heart to report, what my dream was.

William Shakespeare 1564–1616: *A Midsummer Night's Dream* (1595–6)

4 And so to bed.

Samuel Pepys 1633–1703: diary 20 April 1660

5 'It would make anyone go to sleep, that bedstead would, whether they wanted to or not.' 'I should think,' said Sam…'poppies was nothing to it.'

Charles Dickens 1812–70: *Pickwick Papers* (1837)

6 Many's the long night I've dreamed of cheese—toasted, mostly.

Robert Louis Stevenson 1850–94: *Treasure Island* (1883)

7 There ain't no way to find out why a snorer can't hear himself snore.

Mark Twain 1835–1910: *Tom Sawyer Abroad* (1894)

8 I haven't been to sleep for over a year. That's why I go to bed early. One needs more rest if one doesn't sleep.

Evelyn Waugh 1903–66: *Decline and Fall* (1928)

9 Men who are unhappy, like men who sleep badly, are always proud of the fact.

Bertrand Russell 1872–1970: *The Conquest of Happiness* (1930)

10 Try thinking of love, or something.
Amor vincit insomnia.

Christopher Fry 1907– : *A Sleep of Prisoners* (1951)

11 Last night I dreamt I was engaged to Lord Darnley, and was wondering how you would take it when I woke up and remembered that he is dead (to my relief I must add).

Nancy Mitford 1904–73: letter to Gaston Palewski, October 1955

12 I want something that will keep me awake thinking it was the food I ate and not the show I saw.

George S. Kaufman 1889–1961: after a disastrous preview; Howard Teichman *George S. Kaufman* (1973)

13 A gentleman…sleeps at his work. That's what work's for. Why do you think they have the SILENCE notices in the library? So as not to disturb me in my little nook behind the biography shelves.

Alan Ayckbourn 1939– : *Round and Round the Garden* (1975)

14 I love sleep because it is both pleasant and safe to use.

Fran Lebowitz 1946– : *Metropolitan Life* (1978)

15 Sleep appears to be rather addictive. Many find that they cannot do without it and will go to great lengths to ensure its possession. Such people have been known to neglect home, hearth, and even publishers' deadlines in the crazed pursuit of their objective.

Fran Lebowitz 1946– :
Metropolitan Life (1978)

16 SUSAN: Not really. I watch far too much television, if you can call that relaxing.
BILL: Oh, yes. Rather. Best sleeping draught there is.

Alan Ayckbourn 1939– : *Woman in Mind* (1986)

17 There is a school of thought that believes that sleep is for the night. You seem to be out to disprove them.

Alan Ayckbourn 1939– : *Woman in Mind* (1986)

18 It was a dream I had last week
And some kind of record seemed vital.
I knew it wouldn't be much of a poem
But I love the title.

Wendy Cope 1945– : 'Making Cocoa for Kingsley Amis' (1986)

Snobbery See also *Class*

1 Sir Walter Elliot, of Kellynch-hall, in Somersetshire, was a man who, for his own amusement, never took up any book but the Baronetage; there he found occupation for an idle hour, and consolation in a distressed one.

Jane Austen 1775–1817: *Persuasion* (1818)

2 Why cannot you go down to Bristol and see some of the third and fourth class people there, and they'll do just as well?

Lady Holland 1770–1845: to Charles Dickens, who had told her of his proposed trip to America; U. Pope-Hennessy *Charles Dickens* (1947)

3 Whenever he met a great man he grovelled before him, and my-lorded him as only a free-born Briton can do.

William Makepeace Thackeray 1811–63: *Vanity Fair* (1847–8)

As an undergraduate Curzon requested permission to be allowed to attend a ball in London in honour of the Empress Augusta of Germany:
4 I don't think much of Empresses. Good morning.

Benjamin Jowett 1817–93: Kenneth Rose *Superior Person* (1969)

Invitation issued by the Master of Balliol for 24 June 1893:
5 To meet members of the two Houses of Parliament and other members of the College.

Benjamin Jowett 1817–93: Kenneth Rose *Superior Person* (1969)

6 We have in England a curious belief in first-rate people, meaning all the people we do not know; and this consoles us for the undeniable second-rateness of the people we do know.

George Bernard Shaw 1856–1950: preface to *The Irrational Knot* (1905)

7 I am not quite a gentleman but you would hardly notice it but can't be helped anyhow.

Daisy Ashford 1881–1972: *The Young Visiters* (1919)

8 The bearer of this letter is an old friend of mine not quite the right side of the blanket as they say in fact he is the son of a first rate butcher but his mother was a decent family called Hyssopps of the Glen so you see he is not so bad and is desireus of being the correct article.

Daisy Ashford 1881–1972: *The Young Visiters* (1919)

9 Vulgarity has its uses. Vulgarity often cuts ice which refinement scrapes at vainly.

Max Beerbohm 1872–1956: letter 21 May 1921

10 I therefore send you my warm congratulations (from which I do not altogether exclude Sir William), and my earnest hope that you will not be stuck up.

A. E. Housman 1859–1936: letter to Lady Rothenstein on her husband's knighthood, 1 January 1931

On being told that Clare Boothe Luce was always kind to her inferiors:
11 And where does she find them?

Dorothy Parker 1893–1967: Marion Meade *What Fresh Hell is This?* (1988)

The Duchess of Devonshire had called on Queen Mary to apologize for her son's marrying the dancer Adele Astaire:
12 Don't worry. I have a niece called Smith.

Queen Mary 1867–1953: in *Times* 1 June 1994; obituary of Lady May Abel Smith

13 Yeats is becoming so aristocratic, he's evicting imaginary tenants.

Oliver St John Gogarty 1878–1957: Ulick O'Connor *Oliver St John Gogarty* (1964)

14 People like a bit of humbug. If a reader of this book heard that the King had appointed him Keeper of the Swans, he'd be all over town with it in a minute.

Stephen Leacock 1869–1944: *The Boy I Left Behind Me* (1947)

15 From Poland to polo in one generation.

Arthur Caesar D. 1953: of Darryl Zanuck; Max Wilk *The Wit and Wisdom of Hollywood* (1972)

16 [T. E.] Lawrence *was* an inverted show-off and I have myself heard him talk the most inconceivable balls. Even at the time I was inwardly aware of this, but his legend was too strong to be gainsaid and I, being a celebrity snob, crushed down my wicked suspicions.

Noël Coward 1899–1973: diary 19 March 1955

17 Sapper, Buchan, Dornford Yates, practitioners in that school of Snobbery with Violence that runs like a thread of good-class tweed through twentieth-century literature.

Alan Bennett 1934– : *Forty Years On* (1969)

18 Aunt Bess, a built-in snob and prig,
Considered all gnomes infra dig;
Not things one readily forgives
On lawns of true Conservatives.

Alan Melville 1910–83: *Gnomes and Gardens* (1983)

19 The trouble with Michael is that he had to buy all his furniture.

Michael Jopling 1930– : of Michael Heseltine; Alan Clark diary 17 June 1987

20 There is much to be said for the *nouveau riche* and the Reagans intend to say it all.

Gore Vidal 1925– : attributed

21 These are the same old fogies who doffed their lids and tugged the forelock to the British establishment.

Paul Keating 1944– : of Australian Conservative supporters of Great Britain, House of Representatives, 27 February 1992

Society and Social Life

1 The very pink of perfection.

Oliver Goldsmith 1730–74: *She Stoops to Conquer* (1773)

2 MRS CANDOUR: I'll swear her colour is natural—I have
seen it come and go—
LADY TEAZLE: I dare swear you have, ma'am; it goes of
a night and comes again in the morning.

Richard Brinsley Sheridan
1751–1816: *The School for Scandal*
(1777)

3 GERALD: I suppose society is wonderfully delightful!
LORD ILLINGWORTH: To be in it is merely a bore. But to be
out of it simply a tragedy.

Oscar Wilde 1854–1900: *A Woman
of No Importance* (1893)

4 The relations between the individual and society are like
a roulette table. Society is the banker. Individuals
sometimes win and sometimes lose; but the banker wins
always.

W. Somerset Maugham
1874–1965: *A Writer's Notebook* (1949)
written in 1896

5 Yes, dear Frank [Harris], we believe you: you have dined
in every house in London, *once*.

Oscar Wilde 1854–1900: William
Rothenstein *Men and Memories* (1931)

*On showing guests their rooms at Belvoir Castle, at a country-house
weekend at the turn of the century:*
6 If you are frightened in the night, Lord Kitchener, dear
Lady Salisbury is just next door.

Duchess of Rutland d. 1937:
Philip Ziegler *Diana Cooper* (1981)

7 MENDOZA: I am a brigand: I live by robbing the rich.
TANNER: I am a gentleman: I live by robbing the poor.

George Bernard Shaw
1856–1950: *Man and Superman* (1903)

8 When domestic servants are treated as human beings it
is not worth while to keep them.

George Bernard Shaw
1856–1950: *Man and Superman* (1903)
'Maxims: Servants'

9 Hail him like Etonians, without a single word,
Absolutely silent and indefinitely bored.

Ronald Knox 1888–1957: 'Magister
Reformator' (1906)

10 All decent people live beyond their incomes nowadays,
and those who aren't respectable live beyond other
peoples'.

Saki 1870–1916: *Chronicles of Clovis*
(1911)

11 I'm Burlington Bertie
I rise at ten thirty and saunter along like a toff,
I walk down the Strand with my gloves on my hand,
Then I walk down again with them off.

W. F. Hargreaves 1846–1919:
'Burlington Bertie from Bow' (1915)

12 I notice she likes lights and commotion, which goes to
show she has social instincts.

Ronald Firbank 1886–1926:
Valmouth (1919)

13 Though you would often in the fifteenth century have
heard the snobbish Roman say, in a would-be off-hand
tone, 'I am dining with the Borgias tonight,' no Roman
ever was able to say, 'I dined last night with the
Borgias.'

Max Beerbohm 1872–1956: *And
Even Now* (1920)

14 CECIL BEATON: What on earth can I become?
FRIEND: I shouldn't bother too much. Just become
a friend of the Sitwells and see what happens.

Anonymous: at the outset of Cecil
Beaton's career; Laurence Whistler *The
Laughter and the Urn* (1985)

15 Oh! Chintzy, Chintzy cheeriness,
Half dead and half alive!

John Betjeman 1906–84: 'Death in
Leamington' (1931)

16 You know I hate parties. My idea of hell is a very large
party in a cold room, where everybody has to play
hockey properly.

Stella Gibbons 1902–89: *Cold
Comfort Farm* (1932)

17 Children of the Ritz,
Mentally congealed
Lilies of the Field
We say just how we want our quails done,
And then we go and have our nails done.

Noël Coward 1899–1973: 'Children of the Ritz' (1932)

18 I've been to a marvellous party,
We didn't start dinner till ten
And young Bobbie Carr
Did a stunt at the bar
With a lot of extraordinary men.

Noël Coward 1899–1973: 'I've been to a Marvellous Party' (1938)

19 NINOTCHKA: Why should you carry other people's bags?
PORTER: Well, that's my business, Madame.
NINOTCHKA: That's no business. That's social injustice.
PORTER: That depends on the tip.

Charles Brackett 1892–1969 and **Billy Wilder** 1906– : *Ninotchka* (1939 film, with Walter Reisch)

20 To hear Alice [Keppel] talk about her escape from France, one would think she had swum the Channel, with her maid between her teeth.

Mrs Ronnie Greville d. 1942: Chips Channon diary 19 August 1940

21 It was a nice party, except for Joan Fontaine's titties which kept falling about, and a large rock python which was handed to me as a surprise.

Noël Coward 1899–1973: letter from Hollywood to Cole Lesley, 1948

22 Gaily into Ruislip Gardens
Runs the red electric train,
With a thousand Ta's and Pardon's
Daintily alights Elaine;
Hurries down the concrete station
With a frown of concentration,
Out into the outskirt's edges
Where a few surviving hedges
Keep alive our lost Elysium—rural Middlesex again.

John Betjeman 1906–84: 'Middlesex' (1954)

23 Milk and then just as it comes dear?
I'm afraid the preserve's full of stones;
Beg pardon, I'm soiling the doileys
With afternoon tea-cakes and scones.

John Betjeman 1906–84: 'How to get on in Society' (1954)

24 Phone for the fish-knives, Norman
As Cook is a little unnerved;
You kiddies have crumpled the serviettes
And I must have things daintily served.

John Betjeman 1906–84: 'How to get on in Society' (1954)

25 You can be in the Horseguards and still be common, dear.

Terence Rattigan 1911–77: *Separate Tables* (1954) 'Table Number Seven'

26 PLEASE ACCEPT MY RESIGNATION. I DON'T WANT TO BELONG TO ANY CLUB THAT WILL ACCEPT ME AS A MEMBER.

Groucho Marx 1895–1977: telegram; *Groucho and Me* (1959)

27 I'm a man more dined against than dining.

Maurice Bowra 1898–1971: John Betjeman *Summoned by Bells* (1960)

28 An office party is not, as is sometimes supposed, the Managing Director's chance to kiss the tea-girl. It is the tea-girl's chance to kiss the Managing Director.

Katharine Whitehorn 1926– : *Roundabout* (1962) 'The Office Party'

29 Radical Chic...is only radical in Style; in its heart it is part of Society and its tradition—Politics, like Rock, Pop, and Camp, has its uses.

Tom Wolfe 1931– : in *New York* 8 June 1970

30 Gee, what a terrific party. Later on we'll get some fluid and embalm each other.

Neil Simon 1927– : *The Gingerbread Lady* (1970)

31 A charity ball is like a dance except it's tax deductible.

P. J. O'Rourke 1947– : *Modern Manners* (1984)

32 I must say I take off my hat to you, coming home with Rembrandt place mats for your mother. It's those little touches that lift adultery out of the moral arena and make it a matter of style.

Tom Stoppard 1937– : *The Real Thing* (1988 rev. ed.)

33 Of course I don't want to go to a cocktail party...If I wanted to stand around with a load of people I don't know eating bits of cold toast I can get caught shoplifting and go to Holloway.

Victoria Wood 1953– : *Mens Sana in Thingummy Doodah* (1990)

34 The bar was like a funeral parlour with a beverage service.

Bill Bryson 1951– : *Neither Here Nor There* (1991)

35 Already at four years of age I had begun to apprehend that refinement was very often an extenuating virtue; one that excused and eclipsed almost every other unappetizing trait.

Barry Humphries 1934– : *More Please* (1992)

36 My particular nightmare is overdressing, and Glyndebourne has at least the advantage of particular rules of dress. Black tie or nothing. Though I suspect nothing would be frowned upon, if not barred outright.

Stephen Fry 1957– : *Paperweight* (1992)

Songs and Singing

1 Today if something is not worth saying, people sing it.

Pierre-Augustin Caron de Beaumarchais 1732–99: *Le Barbier de Séville* (1775)

2 It is a pity that the composer did not leave directions as to how flat he really did want it sung.

Anonymous: review in *West Wilts Herald* 1893; Ned Sherrin *Cutting Edge* (1984)

3 The first act of the three occupied two hours. I enjoyed that in spite of the singing.

Mark Twain 1835–1910: *What is Man?* (1906)

4 Nonsense. Has he not moved the Queen of Portugal to tears?

Violet Coward: when Noël was denied a place in the Chapel Royal School choir because his voice was unsuitable; Caryl Brahms and Ned Sherrin *Song by Song* (1984)

5 I lift up my finger and I say 'tweet tweet'.

Leslie Sarony 1897–1985: title of song (1929)

6 People are wrong when they say that the opera isn't what it used to be. It is what it used to be—that's what's wrong with it.

Noël Coward 1899–1973: *Design for Living* (1933)

7 In saloons and drab hallways
You are what I'll grab, always
Our love will be as grand
As Paul Whiteman's band
And will weigh as much as Paul weighs.
See how I dispense
Rhymes which are immense;
But do they make sense?
Not
Always.

Anonymous: a 1930s parody of
Irving Berlin's 'Always' in Lorenz Hart's
rhyming style; Ned Sherrin *Cutting
Edge* (1984)

On seeing a coloratura singer distinguished by her enormous jowl:
8 My God! She looks like I do in a spoon!

Mrs Patrick Campbell
1865–1940: James Agate diary
16 November 1944

9 LEW FIELDS: Ladies don't write lyrics.
DOROTHY FIELDS: I'm no lady, I'm your daughter.

Dorothy Fields 1905–74: to her
father; Caryl Brahms and Ned Sherrin
Song by Song (1984)

10 Opera is when a guy gets stabbed in the back and,
instead of bleeding, he sings.

Ed Gardner 1901–63: *Duffy's Tavern*
(US radio programme, 1940s)

11 I was just wondering, is this the place where I'm
supposed to be drowned by the waves or by the
orchestra?

John Coates 1865–1941: the tenor in
The Wreckers explaining to Sir Thomas
Beecham why he had stopped; C. Reid
Sir Thomas Beecham (1961)

12 A town-and-country soprano of the kind often used for
augmenting grief at a funeral.

George Ade 1866–1944: Nat
Shapiro (ed.) *An Encyclopedia of
Quotations about Music* (1978)

13 'Who wrote that song?'
'Rodgers and Hammerstein. If you can imagine it taking
two men to write one song.'

Cole Porter 1891–1964: of 'Some
Enchanted Evening' (1949); G. Eells
The Life that Late He Led (1967)

14 I do not mind what language an opera is sung in so long
as it is a language I don't understand.

Edward Appleton 1892–1965: in
Observer 28 August 1955

15 Opera in English is, in the main, just about as sensible as
baseball in Italian.

H. L. Mencken 1880–1956:
Laurence J. Peter (ed.) *Quotations for
our Time* (1977)

16 Tenors are usually short, stout men (except when they
are Wagnerian tenors, in which case they are large,
stout men) made up predominantly of lungs, rope-sized
vocal chords, large frontal sinuses, thick necks, thick
heads, tantrums and *amour propre*...It is certain that
they are a race apart, a race that tends to operate
reflexively rather than with due process of thought.

Harold Schonberg 1915– : in
Show December 1961

17 'Mr Nash, I can't hear you. Sing up!'
'How do you expect me to sing my best in this position,
Sir Thomas?'
'In that position, my dear fellow, I have given some of
my best performances.'

Thomas Beecham 1879–1961: to
a tenor in rehearsals for *La Bohème*
while lying on Mimi's bed; Ned Sherrin
Cutting Edge (1984)

18 The opera ain't over 'til the fat lady sings.

Dan Cook: in *Washington Post*
3 June 1978

19 A gender bender I,
A creature of illusion,
Of genital confusion,
A gorgeous butterfly.
My list of hits is long
Through every passion ranging,
To every fashion changing,
I tune my latent song.

Alistair Beaton and
Ned Sherrin 1931– :
a parody of
Gilbert and Sullivan's
'A Wandering Minstrel I' in
The Metropolitan Mikado (1985)

20 All the grittiness of *The Fantastics*.

Stephen Sondheim 1930– : of
one of his own lyrics; in conversation

Speeches and Speechmaking

1 ALEXANDER SMYTH: You, sir, speak for the present
generation, but I speak for posterity.
HENRY CLAY: Yes, and you seem resolved to speak until
the arrival of *your* audience.

Henry Clay 1777–1852: in the US
Senate; Robert V. Remini *Henry Clay*
(1991)

On Winston Churchill at a dinner at the London School of Economics:
2 He searched always to end a sentence with a climax. He
looked for antithesis like a monkey looking for fleas.

Harold Laski 1893–1950: letter to
Oliver Wendell Holmes, 7 May 1927

3 I fear I cannot make an amusing speech. I have just been
reading a book which says that 'all geniuses are devoid
of humour'.

Stephen Spender 1909– : speech
in a debate at the Cambridge Union,
January 1938

*At a dinner Winston Churchill was stirred by expressions of defeatism
into 'a magnificent oration' which evidently lasted for a considerable
time:*
4 We then change the subject and speak about the Giant
Panda.

Harold Nicolson 1886–1968: diary
14 June 1939

*With reference to William Jennings Bryan's speech at the Democratic
National Convention in 1896:*
5 Democracy seldom had a ruder shock than when
a phrase—you shall not crucify mankind upon a cross of
gold—nearly put an ignorant and conceited fool in the
White House.

W. Somerset Maugham
1874–1965: *A Writer's Notebook* (1949)
written in 1941

*Chairing the Press Conference in celebration of the completion of
Arnold Toynbee's* A Study of History, *Nicolson had made a speech
welcoming 'our more slender but no less weighty Gibbon':*
6 Not a smile does this quip evoke. I am hopeless at
making an amusing speech, since my jokes never seem to
the British public to be jokes at all. The only thing I am
at all good at is making funeral orations.

Harold Nicolson 1886–1968: diary
12 October 1954

7 I do not object to people looking at their watches when
I am speaking. But I strongly object when they start
shaking them to make certain they are still going.

Lord Birkett 1883–1962: in
Observer 30 October 1960

8 Reading a speech with his usual sense of discovery.

Gore Vidal 1925– : of ex-President Eisenhower at the Republican convention of 1964; in *New York Review of Books* 29 September 1983

9 Nixon's farm policy is vague, but he is going a long way towards slowing the corn surplus by his speeches.

Adlai Stevenson 1900–65: Bill Adler *The Stevenson Wit* (1966)

10 Someone must fill the gap between platitudes and bayonets.

Adlai Stevenson 1900–65: Leon Harris *The Fine Art of Political Wit* (1965)

11 I may not know much, but I know chicken shit from a chicken salad.

Lyndon Baines Johnson 1908–73: on a speech by Richard Nixon; Merle Miller *Lyndon* (1980)

Sports and Games

1 Football, wherein is nothing but beastly fury, and extreme violence, whereof proceedeth hurt, and consequently rancour and malice do remain with them that be wounded.

Thomas Elyot 1499–1546: *Book of the Governor* (1531)

2 Most of their discourse was about hunting, in a dialect I understand very little.

Samuel Pepys 1633–1703: diary 22 November 1663

3 Let spades be trumps! she said, and trumps they were.

Alexander Pope 1688–1744: *The Rape of the Lock* (1714)

4 It is very strange, and very melancholy, that the paucity of human pleasures should persuade us ever to call hunting one of them.

Samuel Johnson 1709–84: Hester Lynch Piozzi *Anecdotes of...Johnson* (1786)

5 'Unting is all that's worth living for—all time is lost wot is not spent in 'unting—it is like the hair we breathe—if we have it not we die—it's the sport of kings, the image of war without its guilt, and only five-and-twenty per cent of its danger.

R. S. Surtees 1805–64: *Handley Cross* (1843)

6 It ar'n't that I loves the fox less, but that I loves the 'ound more.

R. S. Surtees 1805–64: *Handley Cross* (1843)

7 The only athletic sport I ever mastered was backgammon.

Douglas Jerrold 1803–57: Walter Jerrold *Douglas Jerrold* (1914)

8 The English country gentleman galloping after a fox—the unspeakable in full pursuit of the uneatable.

Oscar Wilde 1854–1900: *A Woman of No Importance* (1893)

9 He suggested we should play 'Cutlets', a game we never heard of. He sat on a chair, and asked Carrie to sit on his lap, an invitation which dear Carrie rightly declined.

George Grossmith 1847–1912 and **Weedon Grossmith** 1854–1919: *The Diary of a Nobody* (1894)

10 The bigger they are, the further they have to fall.

Robert Fitzsimmons 1862–1917: prior to a fight, in *Brooklyn Daily Eagle* 11 August 1900 (similar forms found in proverbs since the 15th century)

11 His blade struck the water a full second before any other: the lad had started well. Nor did he flag as the race wore on...as the boats began to near the winning-post, his oar was dipping into the water nearly *twice* as often as any other.

Desmond Coke 1879–1931: *Sandford of Merton* (1903); often quoted 'All rowed fast, but none so fast as stroke'

12 Golf is a good walk spoiled.

Mark Twain 1835–1910: Alex Ayres *Greatly Exaggerated: the Wit and Wisdom of Mark Twain* (1988); attributed

On being approached for a contribution to W. G. Grace's testimonial:
13 It's not in support of cricket but as an earnest protest against golf.

Max Beerbohm 1872–1956: attributed

The umpire had called 'not out' after W. G. Grace was unexpectedly bowled first ball:
14 They have paid to see Dr Grace bat, not to see you bowl.

Anonymous: to the bowler; Harry Furniss *A Century of Grace* (1985); perhaps apocryphal

15 Never read print, it spoils one's eye for the ball.

W. G. Grace 1848–1915: habitual advice to his players; Harry Furniss *A Century of Grace* (1985)

16 The uglier a man's legs are, the better he plays golf—it's almost a law.

H. G. Wells 1866–1946: *Bealby* (1915)

17 Boxing is show-business with blood.

David Belasco: in 1915; Michael Parkinson *Sporting Lives* (1993); later also used by Frank Bruno

A dentist turned boxer, asked by Theodore Roosevelt why he had changed professions:
18 It pays me better to knock teeth out than put them in.

Frank Moran: Jonathon Green and Don Atyeo (eds.) *The Book of Sports Quotes* (1979)

19 Tall men come down to my height when I hit 'em in the body.

Jack Dempsey 1895–1983: in 1920; Jonathon Green and Don Atyeo (eds.) *The Book of Sports Quotes* (1979)

20 Golf...is the infallible test. The man who can go into a patch of rough alone, with the knowledge that only God is watching him, and play his ball where it lies, is the man who will serve you faithfully and well.

P. G. Wodehouse 1881–1975: *The Clicking of Cuthbert* (1922)

21 The least thing upset him on the links. He missed short putts because of the uproar of the butterflies in the adjoining meadows.

P. G. Wodehouse 1881–1975: *The Clicking of Cuthbert* (1922)

22 Personally, I have always looked upon cricket as organized loafing.

William Temple 1881–1944: view of a future archbishop of Canterbury in 1925; Michael Parkinson *Sporting Lives* (1993)

23 The fascination of shooting as a sport depends almost wholly on whether you are at the right or wrong end of a gun.

P. G. Wodehouse 1881–1975: attributed

On the golf course, on being asked by Nancy Cunard, 'What is your handicap?'

24 Drink and debauchery.

Lord Castlerosse 1891–1943: Philip Ziegler *Diana Cooper* (1981)

25 I have observed in women of her type a tendency to regard all athletics as inferior forms of foxhunting.

Evelyn Waugh 1903–66: *Decline and Fall* (1928)

26 To say that these men paid their shillings to watch twenty-two hirelings kick a ball is merely to say that a violin is wood and catgut, that *Hamlet* is so much paper and ink. For a shilling the Bruddersford United AFC offered you Conflict and Art.

J. B. Priestley 1894–1984: *Good Companions* (1929)

On being asked why he did not hunt:

27 I do not see why I should break my neck because a dog chooses to run after a nasty smell.

Arthur James Balfour 1848–1930: Ian Malcolm *Lord Balfour: A Memory* (1930)

After Jack Sharkey beat Max Schmeling (of whom Jacobs was manager) in the heavyweight title fight, 21 June 1932:

28 We was robbed!

Joe Jacobs 1896–1940: Peter Heller *In This Corner* (1975)

29 Although he is a bad fielder he is also a poor hitter.

Ring Lardner 1885–1933: of a baseball player; R. E. Drennan *Wit's End* (1973)

30 Men who would face torture without a word become blasphemous at the short fourteenth. It is clear that the game of golf may well be included in that category of intolerable provocations which may legally excuse or mitigate behaviour not otherwise excusable.

A. P. Herbert 1890–1971: *Misleading Cases* (1935)

After leaving his sick-bed in October 1935 to attend the World Baseball Series in Detroit, and betting on the losers:

31 I should of stood in bed.

Joe Jacobs 1896–1940: John Lardner *Strong Cigars* (1951)

32 Makes me want to yell from St Paul's steeple
The people I'd like to shoot are the shooting people.

Howard Dietz 1896–1983: 'By Myself' (1937)

33 His drive has gone to pieces, largely through having more hinges in it than a sardine tin. But he could always play his iron shots, and his never-ending chatter must be worth at least two holes to his side.

James Agate 1877–1947: diary 7 August 1938

34 A handicapper being a character who can dope out from the form what horses ought to win the races, and as long as his figures turn out all right, a handicapper is spoken of most respectfully by one and all, although of course when he begins missing out for any length of time as handicappers are bound to do, he is no longer spoken of respectfully, or even as a handicapper. He is spoken of as a bum.

Damon Runyon 1884–1946: *Take it Easy* (1938); 'All Horse Players Die Broke'

35 While tearing off
A game of golf
I may make a play for the caddy.
But when I do

Cole Porter 1891–1964: 'My Heart belongs to Daddy' (1938)

I don't follow through
'Cause my heart belongs to Daddy.

36 While Spider McCoy manages a number of fighters, he
never gets excited about anything but a heavyweight,
and this is the way all fight managers are. A fight
manager may have a lightweight champion of the world,
but he will get more heated up about some sausage who
scarcely knows how to hold his hands up if he is
a heavyweight.

Damon Runyon 1884–1946: *Take
It Easy* (1938)

37 He was once known along Broadway as a heavyweight
fighter and he was by no means a bad fighter in his day,
and he now has a pair of scrambled ears to prove it.
Furthermore he is bobbing slightly, and seems to have
a few marbles in his mouth, but he is greatly pleased to
see me.

Damon Runyon 1884–1946: *Take
It Easy* (1938)

When Goering's excuse for being late was a shooting party:
38 Animals, I hope.

Eric Phipps 1875–1945: Ned Sherrin
Cutting Edge (1984); attributed

39 SHE: Are you fond of riding, dear?
Kindly tell me, if so.
HE: Yes, I'm fond of riding, dear,
But in the morning, no.

Cole Porter 1891–1964: 'But in the
Morning, No' (1939)

40 Pam, I adore you, Pam, you great big mountainous
        sports girl,
Whizzing them over the net, full of the strength of five:
That old Malvernian brother, you zephyr and khaki
        shorts girl,
Although he's playing for Woking,
Can't stand up to your wonderful backhand drive.

John Betjeman 1906–84: 'Pot
Pourri from a Surrey Garden' (1940)

41 If you shout hooray for the Pennsylvania Dutchmen
Every team that they play will be carried away with
        a crutch when
They're out on the field if they're wearing the shield of
        the Dutchmen.

Hugh Martin and **Ralph Blane**:
'Buckle Down Winsocki' (1941)

42 He is also too daring for the majority of the black-beards,
the brown-beards and the no-beards, and the all-beards,
who sit in judgement on batsmen; in short, too daring
for those who have never known what it is to dare in
cricket. Only for those who have not yet grown to the
tyranny of the razor is Gimblett possibly not daring
enough.

R. C. Robertson-Glasgow
1901–65: on Harold Gimblett,
sometimes accused of being 'too
daring for the greybeards'; *Cricket
Prints* (1943)

43 He loved to walk sideways towards them, like a grimly
playful crab.

R. C. Robertson-Glasgow
1901–65: of George Gunn's approach
to faster bowlers; *Cricket Prints* (1943)

44 It is to be observed that 'angling' is the name given to
fishing by people who can't fish.

Stephen Leacock 1869–1944:
attributed

45 One of the chief duties of the fan is to engage in
arguments with the man behind him. This department of
the game has been allowed to run down fearfully.

Robert Benchley 1889–1945:
Ralph S. Graben *The Baseball Reader*
(1951)

46 You do not keep accounts and tell everybody that you think you are all square at the end of the year. You lie and you know it.

S. J. Simon 1904-48: *Why You Lose at Bridge* (1945)

47 Montherlant, the writer, who collaborated, is hiding in Paris but nobody bothers to look for him. Rather humiliating, like when one hides for sardines and nobody comes!

Nancy Mitford 1904-73: letter 4 November 1945

48 Miss J. Hunter Dunn, Miss J. Hunter Dunn, Furnish'd and burnish'd by Aldershot sun, What strenuous singles we played after tea, We in the tournament—you against me.

Love-thirty, love-forty, oh! weakness of joy, The speed of a swallow, the grace of a boy, With carefullest carelessness, gaily you won, I am weak from your loveliness, Joan Hunter Dunn.

John Betjeman 1906-84: 'A Subaltern's Love-Song' (1945)

Reflecting on the cricketer Billy Barnes who had made a century at Lord's while tipsy:

49 The modern professional cricketer does not get drunk a' Lord's or often get a century there, or anywhere else, before lunch.

Neville Cardus 1889-1975: *Autobiography* (1947)

50 All the arts, save one [music], were judged to be but enjoyable pastimes, more praiseworthy than bridge but less ennobling than riding.

Osbert Lancaster 1908-80: *All Done From Memory* (1953)

51 I remain of the opinion that there is no game from bridge to cricket that is not improved by a little light conversation; a view which...is shared only by a small and unjustly despised minority.

Osbert Lancaster 1908-80: *All Done From Memory* (1953)

52 Don't look back. Something may be gaining on you.

Satchel Paige 1906-82: a baseball pitcher's advice; in *Collier's* 13 June 1953

53 I don't know if it's good for baseball but it sure beats the hell out of rooming with Phil Rizzuto!

Yogi Berra 1925- : on the announcement of the marriage of Joe Di Maggio and Marilyn Monroe; Jonathon Green and Don Atyeo (eds.) *The Book of Sports Quotes* (1979)

54 A man described as a 'sportsman' is generally a bookmaker who takes actresses to night clubs.

Jimmy Cannon 1910-73: in *New York Post* c.1951-54 'Nobody Asked Me, But...'

55 If baseball goes for pay television, shouldn't the viewers be given a bonus for watching a ball game between Baltimore and Kansas City?

Jimmy Cannon 1910-73: in *New York Post* c.1951-54 'Nobody Asked Me, But...'

56 Oh wasn't it naughty of Smudges? Oh, Mummy, I'm sick with disgust. She threw me in front of the Judges And my silly old collarbone's bust.

John Betjeman 1906-84: 'Hunter Trials' (1954)

57 No one is more sensitive about his game than a weekend tennis player.

Jimmy Cannon 1910-73: in *New York Post* c.1955 'Nobody Asked Me, But...'

58 I hate all sports as rabidly as a person who likes sports hates common sense.

H. L. Mencken 1880–1956: Laurence J. Peter (ed.) *Quotations for our Time* (1977)

59 Vladimir, Vladimir, Vladimir Kuts
Nature's attempt at an engine in boots.

A. P. Herbert 1890–1971: on the Russian runner Vladimir Kuts in 1956; Ned Sherrin *Cutting Edge* (1984)

60 All winter long I am one for whom the bell is tolling
I can arouse no interest in basketball, indoor fly casting
   or bowling.
The sports pages are strictly no soap
And until the cry of 'Play Ball', I mope!

Ogden Nash 1902–71: in *Sports Illustrated* 1957

61 Do men who have got all their marbles go swimming in lakes with their clothes on?

P. G. Wodehouse 1881–1975: *Cocktail Time* (1958)

62 Oh, he's football crazy, he's football mad
And the football it has robbed him o' the wee bit sense
   he had.
And it would take a dozen skivvies, his clothes to wash
   and scrub,
Since our Jock became a member of that terrible football
   club.

Jimmy McGregor: 'Football Crazy' (1960)

63 Putting a fighter in the business world is like putting silk stockings on a pig.

Jack Hurley: in 1961, a boxing promoter's view; Jonathon Green and Don Atyeo (eds.) *The Book of Sports Quotes* (1979)

64 Rodeoing is about the only sport you can't fix. You'd have to talk to the bulls and the horses, and they wouldn't understand you.

Bill Linderman 1922–61: in 1961; Jonathon Green and Don Atyeo (eds.) *The Book of Sports Quotes* (1979)

65 It's a well-known fact that, when I'm on 99, I'm the best judge of a run in all the bloody world.

Alan Wharton 1923– : to Cyril Washbrook; Freddie Trueman *You Nearly Had Me That Time* (1978)

66 I figure I'll be champ for about ten years and then I'll let my brother take over—like the Kennedys down in Washington.

Muhammad Ali 1942– : before becoming world heavyweight champion in 1964; Jonathon Green and Don Atyeo (eds.) *The Book of Sports Quotes* (1979)

67 One who has to shout 'Fore' when he putts.

Michael Green 1927– : definition of a Coarse Golfer; *The Art of Coarse Golf* (1967)

George Best was often told by Matt Busby not to bother to turn up for Busby's team talks to Manchester United:

68 It wasn't worth his coming. It was a very simple team talk. All I used to say was: 'Whenever possible, give the ball to George.'

Matt Busby 1909–94: Michael Parkinson *Sporting Lives* (1993)

69 I need nine wickets from this match, and you buggers had better start drawing straws to see who I don't get.

Freddie Trueman 1931– : to an opposing team; in *Ned Sherrin in his Anecdotage* (1993)

70 I used to think the only use for it [sport] was to give small boys something else to kick besides me.

Katharine Whitehorn 1926– : *Observations* (1970)

71 Nothing there but basketball, a game which won't be fit for people until they set the umbilicus high and return the giraffes to the zoo.

Ogden Nash 1902–71: Jonathon Green and Don Atyeo (eds.) *The Book of Sports Quotes* (1979)

72 Some people think football is a matter of life and death... I can assure them it is much more serious than that.

Bill Shankly 1914–81: in *Guardian* 24 December 1973 'Sports Quotes of the Year'

73 I don't drop players. I make changes.

Bill Shankly 1914–81: a football manager's view; in *Guardian* 24 December 1973 'Sports Quotes of the Year'

74 All you have to do is keep the five players who hate your guts away from the five who are undecided.

Casey Stengel 1891–1975: a baseball manager's view in 1974; John Samuel (ed.) *The Guardian Book of Sports Quotes* (1985)

75 Every young sports writer starts out writing about the black athletes in the ghetto. They come back saying how articulate the black athlete is. What does that mean? That they can speak words?

Dick Young: a US sports writer's view in 1975; Jonathon Green and Don Atyeo (eds.) *The Book of Sports Quotes* (1979)

76 Maybe he thinks the gypsies have put a curse on me— He's very superstitious you know.

Stan Bowles 1948– : when Don Revie did not pick him for the England team in 1976; Jonathon Green and Don Atyeo (eds.) *The Book of Sports Quotes* (1979)

77 That man can't sing—he's the only nigger in the world ain't got rhythm.

Muhammad Ali 1942– : in 1976, of Joe Frazier; Jonathon Green and Don Atyeo (eds.) *The Book of Sports Quotes* (1979)

78 Another good reducing exercise consists in placing both hands against the table edge and pushing back.

Robert Quillen: Laurence J. Peter (ed.) *Quotations for our Time* (1977)

79 The BBC cameras picked up a solemn lady called Paula Fudge as she pounded along... with 'British Meat' written across her understandably heaving bosom. Sponsorship in sport is one thing but this was altogether a different kettle of offal.

Dennis Potter 1935–94: of athletics at the Crystal Palace; in *Guardian* 23 December 1978 'Sports Quotes of the Year'

80 Ron Pickering continued to overheat as usual. The mockery of my confreres had chided him out of saying 'he's pulling out the big one', and even 'he's whacking in the big one'; but the National Viewers' and Listeners' Association will cut off his tail with a carving knife for his new and shameless variant: 'If she hits the board and bangs a big one, that'll put her in the bronze medal position.'

Julian Barnes 1946– : in *Guardian* 23 December 1978 'Sports Quotes of the Year'

81 We're having a philosophical discussion about the yob ethics of professional footballers.

Tom Stoppard 1937– : *Professional Foul* (1978)

82 They're selling video cassettes of the Ali–Spinks fight for $89.95. Hell, for that money Spinks will come to your house.

Ferdie Pacheco: in *Guardian* 23 December 1978 'Sports Quotes of the Year'

83 When you're playing Richard, there's no satisfaction in beating him. He's more pleased if you win than if he does. At least if he wins he's apologetic about it. I mean. There's got to be some satisfaction in winning. Otherwise what's the point? He's the only person I know who enjoys genuine loser satisfaction.

Alan Ayckbourn 1939- : *Joking Apart* (1979)

84 Cricket—a game which the English, not being a spiritual people, have invented in order to give themselves some conception of eternity.

Lord Mancroft 1914- : *Bees in Some Bonnets* (1979)

85 Like a Volvo, Borg is rugged, has good after-sales service, and is very dull.

Clive James 1939- : in *Observer* 29 June 1980

86 I turned on the set hoping to see more rain, but instead found Nastase on his hands and knees banging his head against the turf. Then he...had a lengthy conversation with the electronic eye, a machine which threatens to crab his act, since he will be able to dispute no more line calls.

Clive James 1939- : in *Observer* 29 June 1980

87 The trouble with referees is that they just don't care which side wins.

Tom Canterbury: a US basketball player's view; in *Guardian* 24 December 1980 'Sports Quotes of the Year'

88 He just can't believe what isn't happening to him.

David Coleman: in *Guardian* 24 December 1980 'Sports Quotes of the Year'

89 DORCAS: I thought runners were all sportsmen and totally honest.
LEN: Not this lot. They're all as bent as hell.

Alan Ayckbourn 1939- : *Sisterly Feelings* (1981)

90 In *The Bob Hope Golf Classic*...the participation of President Gerald Ford was more than enough to remind you that the nuclear button was at one stage at the disposal of a man who might have either pressed it by mistake or else pressed it deliberately in order to obtain room service...a droll commentator remarked that the President had turned golf into a 'combat sport' and that the security men were coming in handy to keep track of the ball.

Clive James 1939- : in *Observer* 4 October 1981

91 I'm playing [golf] like Tarzan and scoring like Jane.

Chi Chi Rodrigues 1935- : Jonathon Green (ed.) *A Dictionary of Contemporary Quotations* (1982)

92 Loyalty to the school to which your parents pay to send you seemed to me like feeling loyal to Selfridges: consequently I never cared in the least which team won, but only prayed for the game to be over without the ball ever coming my way.

John Mortimer 1923- : *Clinging to the Wreckage* (1982)

93 Sport, as I have discovered, fosters international hostility and leads the audience, no doubt from boredom, to assault and do grievous bodily harm while watching it.

John Mortimer 1923- : *Clinging to the Wreckage* (1982)

94 In other sports, the lateral euphemism is still in its infancy (at Wimbledon, for example, they have only just

Julian Barnes 1946- : in *Observer* 4 July 1982

realized that 'perfectionist' can be used to represent 'extremely bad-tempered'). In soccer, the form of the encoded adjective is well developed. 'Tenacious', for example, always means 'small'.

95 I can't see who's in the lead but it's either Oxford or Cambridge.

John Snagge 1904- : C. Dodd *Oxford and Cambridge Boat Race* (1983)

96 Broken marriages, conflicts of loyalty, the problems of everyday life fall away as one faces up to Thomson.

Mike Brearley 1942- : on Jeff Thomson's bowling; Ned Sherrin *Cutting Edge* (1984)

97 New Yorkers love it when you spill your guts out there. Spill your guts at Wimbledon and they make you stop and clean it up.

Jimmy Connors 1952- : at Flushing Meadow; in *Guardian* 24 December 1984 'Sports Quotes of the Year'

98 I don't think I can be expected to take seriously any game which takes less than three days to reach its conclusion.

Tom Stoppard 1937- : a cricket enthusiast on baseball; in *Guardian* 24 December 1984 'Sports Quotes of the Year'

When playing in a Lancashire league game, Dennis Lillee's ball hit the batsman on the leg. Although given out, the batsman remained at the crease, and Lillee insisted forcefully that he must go:

99 I'd love to go Dennis but I daren't move. I think you've broken my bloody leg.

Anonymous: Michael Parkinson *Sporting Lives* (1993)

100 If I had the wings of a sparrow
If I had the arse of a crow
I'd fly over Tottenham tomorrow
And shit on the bastards below.

Anonymous: frequently sung on the Chelsea terraces; Ned Sherrin *Cutting Edge* (1984)

101 Football's football; if that weren't the case, it wouldn't be the game it is.

Garth Crooks 1958- : Barry Fantoni (ed.) *Private Eye's Colemanballs 2* (1984)

102 The only thing that Norwich didn't get was the goal that they finally got.

Jimmy Greaves 1940- : Barry Fantoni (ed.) *Private Eye's Colemanballs 2* (1984)

103 The sport of ski-ing consists of wearing three thousand dollars' worth of clothes and equipment and driving two hundred miles in the snow in order to stand around at a bar and get drunk.

P. J. O'Rourke 1947- : *Modern Manners* (1984)

104 There's been a colour clash: both teams are wearing white.

John Motson: in 'Colemanballs' column in *Private Eye*; Ned Sherrin *Cutting Edge* (1984)

105 Those people who had spent part of their childhood playing the delightful game of Charades found themselves at quite an advantage when joining up. It helped considerably, and here an experience of amateur dramatics was a bonus, to feel that you were merely acting a minor role in a rather long-running play.

Arthur Marshall 1910-89: *Life's Rich Pageant* (1984)

106 If people don't want to come out to the ball park, nobody's going to stop 'em.

Yogi Berra 1925- : of baseball games; attributed

107 That's the fastest time ever run—but it's not as fast as the world record.

David Coleman: Barry Fantoni (ed.) *Private Eye's Colemanballs 3* (1986)

108 If you think squash is a competitive activity, try flower arrangement.

Alan Bennett 1934– : *Talking Heads* (1988)

109 The thing about sport, any sport, is that swearing is very much part of it.

Jimmy Greaves 1940– : in *Observer* 1 January 1989 'Sayings of the Year'

110 Playing snooker gives you firm hands and helps to build up character. It is the ideal recreation for dedicated nuns.

Luigi Barbarito 1922– : view of the Pope's emissary, attending a sponsored snooker championship at Tyburn convent; in *Daily Telegraph* 15 November 1989

111 I want to keep fighting because it is the only thing that keeps me out of the hamburger joints. If I don't fight, I'll eat this planet.

George Foreman 1948– : in *Times* 17 January 1990

112 And I want to say anything is possible. Comma. You know.

Frank Bruno: in *Guardian* 24 December 1990 'Sports Quotes of the Year'

113 We didn't underestimate them. They were a lot better than we thought.

Bobby Robson 1933– : on Cameroon's football team; in *Guardian* 24 December 1990 'Sports Quotes of the Year'

114 Jogging is for people who aren't intelligent enough to watch television.

Victoria Wood 1953– : *Mens Sana in Thingummy Doodah* (1990)

115 [Gary Lineker is] the Queen Mother of football.

Arthur Smith and **Chris England**: *An Evening with Gary Lineker* (1990)

116 Baseball is very big with my people. It figures. It's the only way we can get to shake a bat at a white man without starting a riot.

Dick Gregory 1932– : D. H. Nathan (ed.) *Baseball Quotations* (1991)

117 There isn't much cricket in *Hamlet*...
There isn't much cricket in *Lear*.
I don't think there's any in *Paradise Lost*—
I haven't a copy right here.

Wendy Cope 1945– : 'The Cricketing Versions' (1992)

118 He mistrusts anyone who reads past the sports pages of the tabloids.

Peter Roebuck 1956– : of Michael Stewart, the former English Test team manager; in *Ned Sherrin in his Anecdotage* (1993)

119 I am here to propose a toast to the sports writers. It's up to you whether you stand or not.

Freddie Trueman 1931– : Michael Parkinson *Sporting Lives* (1993)

120 I couldn't bat for the length of time required to score 500. I'd get bored and fall over.

Denis Compton 1918– : to Brian Lara; in *Daily Telegraph* 27 June 1994

Success and Failure

1 Success is a science; if you have the conditions, you get the result.

Oscar Wilde 1854–1900: letter ?March–April 1883

2 Moderation is a fatal thing, Lady Hunstanton. Nothing succeeds like excess.

Oscar Wilde 1854–1900: *A Woman of No Importance* (1893)

Whistler had been found 'deficient in chemistry' in a West Point examination:

3 Had silicon been a gas, I would have been a major-general by now.

James McNeill Whistler 1834–1903: E. R. and J. Pennell *The Life of James McNeill Whistler* (1908)

4 I never climbed any ladder: I have achieved eminence by sheer gravitation.

George Bernard Shaw 1856–1950: preface to *The Irrational Knot* (1905)

5 Success. I don't believe it has any effect on me. For one thing I always expected it.

W. Somerset Maugham 1874–1965: *A Writer's Notebook* (1949) written in 1908

6 Success is the one unpardonable sin against our fellows.

Ambrose Bierce 1842–c.1914: *The Enlarged Devil's Dictionary* (1967)

7 She regretted that Fate had not seen its way to reserve for her some of the ampler successes for which she felt herself well qualified.

Saki 1870–1916: *The Toys of Peace* (1919)

8 Come forth, Lazarus! And he came fifth and lost the job.

James Joyce 1882–1941: *Ulysses* (1922)

9 Anybody seen in a bus over the age of 30 has been a failure in life.

Loelia, Duchess of Westminster 1902–93: in *The Times* 4 November 1993; habitual remark

10 The world is divided into people who do things and people who get the credit. Try, if you can, to belong to the first class. There's far less competition.

Dwight Morrow 1873–1931: letter to his son; Harold Nicolson *Dwight Morrow* (1935)

11 Be nice to people on your way up because you'll meet 'em on your way down.

Wilson Mizner 1876–1933: Alva Johnston *The Legendary Mizners* (1953)

12 Whom the gods wish to destroy they first call promising.

Cyril Connolly 1903–74: *Enemies of Promise* (1938)

13 If at first you don't succeed, try, try again. Then quit. No use being a damn fool about it.

W. C. Fields 1880–1946: attributed

14 How to succeed in business without really trying.

Shepherd Mead 1914– : title of book (1952)

15 The theory seems to be that as long as a man is a failure he is one of God's children, but that as soon as he succeeds he is taken over by the Devil.

H. L. Mencken 1880–1956: *Minority Report* (1956)

As the disastrous 1958 electoral results for the Canadian Liberal Party were announced, Lester Pearson's wife had comforted herself with the hope of 'an honourable if unflattering' exit from politics for her husband:

16 We've lost everything, we've even won our own constituency!

Maryon Pearson: Lester Pearson *Memoirs* (1975) vol. 3

17 David Frost has risen without trace.

Kitty Muggeridge 1903–94: said c.1965 to Malcolm Muggeridge

18 People who reach the top of the tree are only those who haven't got the qualifications to detain them at the bottom.

Peter Ustinov 1921– : interview with David Frost in 1969

19 Success took me to her bosom like a maternal boa constrictor.

Noël Coward 1899–1973: Sheridan Morley *A Talent to Amuse* (1969)

20 Whenever a friend succeeds, a little something in me dies.

Gore Vidal 1925– : in *Sunday Times Magazine* 16 September 1973

21 It is not enough to succeed. Others must fail.

Gore Vidal 1925– : G. Irvine *Antipanegyric for Tom Driberg* 8 December 1976

22 There is always time for failure.

John Mortimer 1923– : *Clinging to the Wreckage* (1982)

23 He turned being a Big Loser into a perfect triumph by managing to lose the presidency in a way bigger and more original than anyone else had ever lost it before.

Gore Vidal 1925– : of Richard Nixon; in *Esquire* December 1983

24 It's the story of my life, really. One day you've your name in lights—or on a begonia—the next, you're papering the spare room with rejection slips and worrying about your virility.

Alan Melville 1910–83: *Gnomes and Gardens* (1983)

25 In the end we are all sacked and it's always awful. It is as inevitable as death following life. If you are elevated there comes a day when you are demoted. Even Prime Ministers.

Alan Clark 1928– : diary 21 June 1983

26 I am that twentieth-century failure, a happy undersexed celibate.

Denise Coffey: Ned Sherrin *Cutting Edge* (1984)

27 There are three things you can't do in life. You can't beat the phone company, you can't make a waiter see you until he's ready to see you, and you can't go home again.

Bill Bryson 1951– : *The Lost Continent* (1989)

During a rehearsal at the Royal Court, Beckett encouraged an actor who had lamented, 'I'm failing':
28 Go on failing. Go on. Only next time, try to fail better.

Samuel Beckett 1906–89: Tony Richardson *Long Distance Runner* (1993)

29 If things had worked out differently it's strange to think *I* would now be Foreign Secretary and Douglas Hurd would be an assistant librarian.

Stephen Fry 1957– and **Hugh Laurie**: *A Bit More Fry and Laurie* (1991)

A choice of explanations for Dan Quayle's success at various critical points in his career:
30 His family knew people/calls were made/luck would have it.

Joe Queenan: *Imperial Caddy* (1992)

Taxes

1 *Excise*. A hateful tax levied upon commodities.

Samuel Johnson 1709–84: *A Dictionary of the English Language* (1755)

2 It was as true...as taxes is. And nothing's truer than them.

Charles Dickens 1812–70: *David Copperfield* (1850)

3 The average homebred Englishman...will shut his eyes to the most villainous abuses if the remedy threatens to add another penny in the pound to the rates and taxes which he has to be half cheated, half coerced into paying.

George Bernard Shaw 1856–1950: preface to *Plays Unpleasant* (1898)

4 I sincerely hope that increased taxation, necessary to meet the expenses of the war, will not fall upon the working classes; but I fear they will be most affected by the extra sixpence on beer.

Queen Victoria 1819–1901: letter to Lord Salisbury, 21 October 1899

5 What is the difference between a taxidermist and a tax collector? The taxidermist takes only your skin.

Mark Twain 1835–1910: *Notebook* 30 December 1902

6 Logic and taxation are not always the best of friends.

James C. McReynolds 1862–1946: concurring in *Sonneborn Bros. v. Cureton* 1923

7 Income Tax has made more Liars out of the American people than Golf.

Will Rogers 1879–1935: *The Illiterate Digest* (1924) 'Helping the Girls with their Income Taxes'

8 To be consistent the potato, introduced by Raleigh, would be extradited and smoking taxed as a foreign game.

Oliver St John Gogarty 1878–1957: on the introduction to the Irish Senate in 1932 of the Emergency Imposition of Duties Bill; Ulick O'Connor *Oliver St John Gogarty* (1964)

9 A bailiff acting for the Inland Revenue was struck and killed with a book of sermons while removing a wireless set belonging to the accused, and two rabbits, the property of a favourite daughter. The defence was that distress for income tax was a gross provocation comparable to the discovery of a wife in the arms of another.

A. P. Herbert 1890–1971: *Misleading Cases* (1935)

10 The collection of a lunatic and inequitable tax, however few the victims, must tend to breed an un-English dislike of taxation in general.

A. P. Herbert 1890–1971: *Misleading Cases* (1935)

11 Tax collectors who'll never know the invigorating joys of treading water in the deep end without a life belt.

Jeffrey Bernard 1932– : in *The Spectator* 3 March 1984

To the British:
12 Do anything you want with your poll tax but shut up about it, please. Not since John Lyly wrote *Euphues* has Britain provided the world with so much exhausting blather.

P. J. O'Rourke 1947– : *Parliament of Whores* (1991)

Technology See *Science and Technology*

Telegrams

1 The Queen has always telegraphed direct to her Generals and always will do so...She thinks Lord Hartington's

Queen Victoria 1819–1901: letter to Sir Henry Ponsonby, 24 January 1885

letter very officious and impertinent in tone. The Queen has a right to telegraph congratulations and enquiries to any one, and won't stand dictation. She won't be a machine.

2 FEAR I MAY NOT BE ABLE TO REACH YOU IN TIME FOR THE CEREMONY. DON'T WAIT.

James McNeill Whistler 1834–1903: telegram of apology for missing Oscar Wilde's wedding; E. J. and R. Pennell *The Life of James McNeill Whistler* (1908)

3 Along the electric wire the message came: He is not better—he is much the same.

Anonymous: parodic poem on the illness of the Prince of Wales, later King Edward VII, in F. H. Gribble *Romance of the Cambridge Colleges* (1913); sometimes attributed to Alfred Austin (1835–1913), Poet Laureate

Sent by a cricket-playing coroner, W. G. Grace's elder brother, to postpone an inquest:
4 PUT CORPSE ON ICE TILL CLOSE OF PLAY.

E. M. Grace d. 1911: A. A. Thomson *The Great Cricketer* (1957); perhaps apocryphal

5 At this point in the proceedings there was another ring at the front door. Jeeves shimmered out and came back with a telegram.

P. G. Wodehouse 1881–1975: *Carry On, Jeeves!* (1925)

As a young Times *correspondent in America, Claud Cockburn received a telegram authorizing him to report a murder in Al Capone's Chicago:*
6 BY ALL MEANS COCKBURN CHICAGOWARDS. WELCOME STORIES EX-CHICAGO NOT UNDULY EMPHASISING CRIME.

Anonymous: Claud Cockburn *In Time of Trouble* (1956)

7 So I sprang to a taxi and shouted 'To Aix!' And he blew on his horn and he threw off his brakes, And all the way back till my money was spent We rattled and rattled and rattled and rattled and rattled And rattled and rattled— And eventually sent a telegram.

W. C. Sellar 1898–1951 and **R. J. Yeatman** 1898–1968: 'How I Brought the Good News from Aix to Ghent (*Or Vice Versa*)' (1933)

Telegram to Mrs Sherwood on the arrival of her baby:
8 GOOD WORK, MARY. WE ALL KNEW YOU HAD IT IN YOU.

Dorothy Parker 1893–1967: Alexander Woollcott *While Rome Burns* (1934)

Cables were soon arriving... 'Require earliest name life story photograph American nurse upblown Adowa.' We replied:
9 NURSE UNUPBLOWN.

Evelyn Waugh 1903–66: *Waugh in Abyssinia* (1936)

Telegram to Irving Thalberg on the birth of his son:
10 CONGRATULATIONS ON YOUR LATEST PRODUCTION. AM SURE IT WILL LOOK BETTER AFTER IT'S BEEN CUT.

Eddie Cantor 1892–1964: Max Wilk *The Wit and Wisdom of Hollywood* (1972)

From G. K. Chesterton to his wife:

11 AM IN MARKET HARBOROUGH. WHERE OUGHT I TO BE?

G. K. Chesterton 1874–1936: *Autobiography* (1936)

Telegram sent to his partner Jack Wilson in New York in 1938 as the threat of war increased:

12 GRAVE POSSIBILITY WAR WITHIN FEW WEEKS OR DAYS MORE IF THIS HAPPENS POSTPONEMENT REVUE INEVITABLE AND ANNIHILATION ALL OF US PROBABLE.

Noël Coward 1899–1973: Sheridan Morley *A Talent to Amuse* (1969)

Despite the threat of war, arrangements for the revue Set to Music *went ahead:*

13 SUGGEST YOU ENGAGE EIGHT REALLY BEAUTIFUL SHOWGIRLS MORE OR LESS SAME HEIGHT NO REAL TALENT REQUIRED.

Noël Coward 1899–1973: telegram to Jack Wilson; Sheridan Morley *A Talent to Amuse* (1969)

Carl Laemmle Jr. had sent a telegram to his father, PLEASE WIRE MORE MONEY AM TALKING TO FRENCH COUNT RE MOVIE:

14 NO MONEY TILL YOU LEARN TO SPELL.

Carl Laemmle 1867–1939: Angus McGill and Kenneth Thomson *Live Wires* (1982)

15 Dear Mrs A.,
Hooray, hooray,
At last you are deflowered.
On this as every other day
I love you—Noel Coward.

Noël Coward 1899–1973: telegram to Gertrude Lawrence, 5 July 1940 (the day after her wedding)

In 1916 Norman Douglas had slipped bail on a charge of an indecent offence with a young man. He returned twenty-five years later, sending this telegram to a friend:

16 FEEL LIKE A BOY AGAIN.

Norman Douglas 1868–1952: Angus McGill and Kenneth Thomson *Live Wires* (1982)

17 I HAVE BEEN LOOKING AROUND FOR AN APPROPRIATE WOODEN GIFT AND AM PLEASED HEREBY TO PRESENT YOU WITH ELSIE FERGUSON'S PERFORMANCE IN HER NEW PLAY.

Alexander Woollcott 1887–1943: congratulatory telegram for George S. Kaufman's fifth wedding anniversary; Howard Teichman *George S. Kaufman* (1973)

Telegraph message on arriving in Venice:

18 STREETS FLOODED. PLEASE ADVISE.

Robert Benchley 1889–1945: R. E. Drennan *Wit's End* (1973)

19 LAST SUPPER AND ORIGINAL CAST COULDN'T DRAW IN THIS HOUSE.

George S. Kaufman 1889–1961: telegram to his father during a bad week with a stock company; Angus McGill and Kenneth Thomson *Live Wires* (1982)

20 LEGITIMATE AT LAST WONT MOTHER BE PLEASED.

Noël Coward 1899–1973: on Gertrude Lawrence's first straight role; Sheridan Morley *A Talent to Amuse* (1969)

21 HAVE MOVED HOTEL EXCELSIOR COUGHING MYSELF INTO A FIRENZE.

Noël Coward 1899–1973: telegram from Florence; Angus McGill and Kenneth Thomson *Live Wires* (1982)

*An estate agent in Bermuda told her that the house she was
considering came with a maid, a secretary and a chauffeur:*
22 AIRMAIL PHOTOGRAPH OF CHAUFFEUR.

Beatrice Lillie 1894–1989: Angus
McGill and Kenneth Thomson *Live
Wires* (1982)

Response to a telegraphic enquiry, HOW OLD CARY GRANT?:
23 OLD CARY GRANT FINE. HOW YOU?

Cary Grant 1904–86: R. Schickel
Cary Grant (1983)

The Theatre See also *Actors and Acting*

1 The most lamentable comedy, and most cruel death of
Pyramus and Thisby.

William Shakespeare 1564–1616:
A Midsummer Night's Dream (1595–6)

2 If this were played upon a stage now, I could condemn it
as an improbable fiction.

William Shakespeare 1564–1616:
Twelfth Night (1601)

3 *Exit, pursued by a bear.*

William Shakespeare 1564–1616:
stage direction in *The Winter's Tale*
(1610–11)

4 There still remains, to mortify a wit,
The many-headed monster of the pit.

Alexander Pope 1688–1744:
Imitations of Horace (1737)

5 I'll come no more behind your scenes, David; for the silk
stockings and white bosoms of your actresses excite my
amorous propensities.

Samuel Johnson 1709–84: James
Boswell *Life of Samuel Johnson* (1791)
1750; John Wilkes recalls the remark
[to Garrick] in the form: 'the silk
stockings and white bosoms of your
actresses do make my genitals to
quiver'

6 Prologues precede the piece—in mournful verse;
As undertakers—walk before the hearse.

David Garrick 1717–79: prologue
to Arthur Murphy's *The Apprentice*
(1756)

7 [John Gay's *The Beggar's Opera*]...was first offered to
Cibber and his brethren at Drury-Lane, and rejected; it
being then carried to Rich had the effect, as was
ludicrously said, of making Gay *rich*, and Rich *gay*.

Samuel Johnson 1709–84: *Lives of
the English Poets* (1779–81) 'John Gay'

8 It is better to have written a damned play, than no play
at all—it snatches a man from obscurity.

Frederic Reynolds 1764–1841: *The
Dramatist* (1789)

On Irving's revival of Macbeth *at the Lyceum, with Ellen Terry as Lady
Macbeth:*
9 Judging from the banquet, Lady Macbeth seems an
economical housekeeper and evidently patronises local
industries for her husband's clothes and the servants'
liveries, but she takes care to do all her shopping in
Byzantium.

Oscar Wilde 1854–1900: Rupert
Hart-Davis (ed.) *The Letters of Oscar
Wilde* (1962)

10 The play was a great success, but the audience was
a total failure.

Oscar Wilde 1854–1900: after the
first performance of *Lady
Windermere's Fan*; Peter Hay
Theatrical Anecdotes (1987)

On hearing the Cockney playwright Henry Arthur Jones reading his play Michael and his Lost Angel *(1896):*

11 But it's so *long*, Mr. Jones—even *without* the *h*'s.

Mrs Patrick Campbell 1865–1940: Margot Peters *Mrs Pat* (1984)

12 A buzz of recognition came from the front rows of the pit, together with a craning of necks on the part of those in less favoured seats. It heralded the arrival of Sherard Blaw, the dramatist who had discovered himself, and who had given so ungrudgingly of his discovery to the world.

Saki 1870–1916: *The Unbearable Bassington* (1912)

13 You don't expect me to know what to say about a play when I don't know who the author is, do you?

George Bernard Shaw 1856–1950: *Fanny's First Play* (1914)

14 Enter Michael Angelo. Andrea del Sarto appears for a moment at a window. Pippa passes.

Max Beerbohm 1872–1956: *Seven Men* (1919)

15 There is less in this than meets the eye.

Tallulah Bankhead 1903–68: of a revival of Maeterlinck's play 'Aglavaine and Selysette'; Alexander Woollcott *Shouts and Murmurs* (1922)

16 Mixed notices—they were good and rotten.

George S. Kaufman 1889–1961: after sharing a flop, *The Channel Road* (1929), with Alexander Woollcott; Howard Teichman *George S. Kaufman* (1973)

17 In fact, now that you've got me right down to it, the only thing I didn't like about *The Barretts of Wimpole Street* was the play.

Dorothy Parker 1893–1967: review in *New Yorker* 21 February 1931

18 'Ah,' I said to myself, for I love a responsive audience, 'so it's one of those plays.'

Dorothy Parker 1893–1967: review of A. A. Milne's *Give Me Yesterday* in *New Yorker* 14 March 1931

19 Shaw's plays are the price we pay for Shaw's prefaces.

James Agate 1877–1947: diary 10 March 1933

20 *House Beautiful* is play lousy.

Dorothy Parker 1893–1967: review in *New Yorker* 1933

21 *Rose and Glove* is Marlowe's Edward II re-written to prove that there was, in Stalky's phrase, 'no beastly Ericking' about the King and Piers Gaveston.

James Agate 1877–1947: diary 11 September 1934

The impresario Binkie Beaumont had been greatly impressed by The Wind of Heaven *(1945):*

22 BEAUMONT: I've read your new play, Emlyn, and I like it twice as much as your last.
WILLIAMS: Does that mean you're going to pay me twice my usual royalties?

Emlyn Williams 1905–87: James Harding *Emlyn Williams* (1987)

On the Company of Four's poorly attended revival of his play Spring 1600 *in 1945:*

23 The Lyric housed the Company of Four and the Audience of Two.

Emlyn Williams 1905–87: James Harding *Emlyn Williams* (1987)

24 Another pain where the ulcers grow,
Another op'nin' of another show.

Cole Porter 1891–1964: 'Another Op'nin', Another Show' (1948)

25 We open in Venice,
We next play Verona,
Then on to Cremona.
Lotsa laughs in Cremona.

Cole Porter 1891–1964: 'We Open in Venice' (1948)

26 Brush up your Shakespeare,
Start quoting him now.
Brush up your Shakespeare
And the women you will wow...

If she says your behaviour is heinous
Kick her right in the 'Coriolanus'.
Brush up your Shakespeare
And they'll all kowtow.

Cole Porter 1891–1964: 'Brush Up your Shakespeare' (1948)

27 The production [of *Private Lives*] is inept and the set is
hideous. The whole thing has all the chic of a whist drive
in Tulse Hill.

Noël Coward 1899–1973: diary 18 July 1949

28 Murder was one thing Hamlet sure did enjoy.
He was, how shall I say, quite a mischievious boy;
And the moral of this story was very, very plain;
You'd better get a mussle if you've got a great Dane!

Frank Loesser 1910–69: 'Hamlet' (1949)

29 The plot can be hot—simply teeming with sex,
A gay divorcee who is after her ex.
It could be Oedipus Rex,
Where a chap kills his father
And causes a lot of bother.
The clerk
Who is thrown out of work
By the boss
Who is thrown for a loss
By the skirt
Who is doing him dirt.
The world is a stage
The stage is a world of entertainment.

Howard Dietz 1896–1983: 'That's Entertainment' (1953)

30 Applause, applause!
Vociferous applause
From orchestra to gallery
Could mean a raise in salary.
Give out, give in!—
Be noisy, make a din!
(The manager, he audits our plaudits.)

Ira Gershwin 1896–1989: 'Applause, Applause' (1953)

31 Stop being gallant
And don't be such a bore,
Pack up your talent,
There's always plenty more
And if you lose hope
Take dope
And lock yourself in the John,
Why must the show go on?

Noël Coward 1899–1973: 'Why Must the Show Go On?' (1955)

32 *Moby Dick* nearly became the tragedy of a man who could not make up his nose.

Kenneth Tynan 1927–80: on Welles's production of *Moby Dick* in 1955, when his false nose fell off on the first night, alluding to the publicity for Olivier's *Hamlet* as 'the tragedy of a man who could not make up his mind'; *A View of the English Stage* (1975)

33 If any play has been produced only twice in three hundred years, there must be some good reason for it.

Rupert Hart-Davis 1907– : letter to George Lyttelton, 7 July 1957

34 Don't clap too hard—it's a very old building.

John Osborne 1929– : *The Entertainer* (1957)

35 I thought I heard one of the original lines of the show.

George S. Kaufman 1889–1961: of the Marx Brothers' ad-libbing; Howard Teichman *George S. Kaufman* (1973)

36 There was laughter in the back of the theatre, leading to the belief that someone was telling jokes back there.

George S. Kaufman 1889–1961: Howard Teichman *George S. Kaufman* (1973)

37 Well, Marc, there's only one thing we can do. We've got to call the audience in tomorrow morning for a ten o'clock rehearsal.

George S. Kaufman 1889–1961: to convince Marc Connelly that a line would not work; Howard Teichman *George S. Kaufman* (1973)

38 Satire is what closes Saturday night.

George S. Kaufman 1889–1961: Scott Meredith *George S. Kaufman and his Friends* (1974)

39 If someone tells you he is going to make a 'realistic decision', you immediately understand that he has resolved to do something bad.

Mary McCarthy 1912–89: *On the Contrary* (1961) 'American Realist Playwrights'

40 Something appealing,
Something appalling,
Something for everyone:
A comedy tonight!

Stephen Sondheim 1930– : 'Comedy Tonight' (1962)

On being asked 'What was the message of your play' after a performance of The Hostage:

41 Message? Message? What the hell do you think I am, a bloody postman?

Brendan Behan 1923–64: Dominic Behan *My Brother Brendan* (1965)

42 To sum up: your father, whom you love, dies, you are his heir, you come back to find that hardly was the corpse cold before his young brother popped onto his throne and into his sheets, thereby offending both legal and natural practice. Now why exactly are you behaving in this extraordinary manner?

Tom Stoppard 1937– : *Rosencrantz and Guildenstern Are Dead* (1967)

43 I can do you blood and love without the rhetoric, and I can do you blood and rhetoric without the love, and I can do you all three concurrent or consecutive, but I can't do you love and rhetoric without the blood. Blood is compulsory—they're all blood, you see.

Tom Stoppard 1937– : *Rosencrantz and Guildenstern are Dead* (1967)

44 It's about as long as *Parsifal*, and not as funny.

Noël Coward 1899–1973: on *Camelot*; Dick Richards *The Wit of Noël Coward* (1968)

45 And remember, this is the School play. You are not here to enjoy yourselves.

Alan Bennett 1934– : *Forty Years On* (1969)

46 This [*Oh, Calcutta!*] is the kind of show to give pornography a dirty name.

Clive Barnes 1927– : in *New York Times* 18 June 1969

47 Welcome to the Theatre,
To the magic, to the fun!
Where painted trees and flowers grow,
And laughter rings fortissimo,
And treachery's sweetly done.

Lee Adams: 'Welcome to the Theatre' (1970)

48 Shut up, Arnold, or I'll direct this play the way you wrote it!

John Dexter: to the playwright Arnold Wesker; in *Ned Sherrin in his Anecdotage* (1993)

49 'Who do I have to fuck to get out of this show?'
'Same person you fucked to get in!'

Stephen Sondheim 1930– : to Larry Kert during a technical rehearsal for the London production of *Company* in 1972; Ned Sherrin *Cutting Edge* (1984)

50 I was made to feel like a mud-wrestler being complimented by a Duchess.

John Osborne 1929– : on being complimented by Binkie Beaumont; *Almost a Gentleman* (1991)

51 If a director doesn't really want to do the *Shrew*, this is a pretty good way not to do it.

Stanley Kauffman 1916– : of a production at the American Conservatory Theatre in 1973; Diana Rigg *No Turn Unstoned* (1982)

52 I didn't like the play, but then I saw it under adverse conditions—the curtain was up.

Groucho Marx 1895–1977: ad-lib, attributed in an interview by Marx to George S. Kaufman; Peter Hay *Broadway Anecdotes* (1989)

53 I've never much enjoyed going to plays...The unreality of painted people standing on a platform saying things they've said to each other for months is more than I can overlook.

John Updike 1932– : George Plimpton (ed.) *Writers at Work* 4th Series (1977)

54 When you think about it, what other playwrights are there besides O'Neill, Tennessee and me?

Mae West 1892–1980: G. Eells and S. Musgrove *Mae West* (1989)

55 In the theatre words have to prove themselves immediately, by solid laughter which unites an audience, or by that attentive silence when even the most bronchial listeners forget to cough, which is the greatest compliment that can be paid to the writer.

John Mortimer 1923– : *Clinging to the Wreckage* (1982)

56 A play wot I wrote.

Eddie Braben: spoken by Ernie Wise; Gary Morecambe and Martin Stirling *Behind the Sunshine* (1994)

57 I have knocked everything but the knees of the chorus girls, and nature has anticipated me there.

Percy Hammond: Ned Sherrin *Cutting Edge* (1984)

58 I very much doubt the wisdom of exposing youngish persons to the plays of Racine and Corneille. It is possible to take the view that the plays of Racine and Corneille lack interest and attraction, and that if Racine and Corneille knew any jokes, they kept them to themselves.

Arthur Marshall 1910–89: *Life's Rich Pageant* (1984)

59 This place, you tell them you're interested in the arts, you get messages of sympathy.

Alan Ayckbourn 1939– : *Chorus of Disapproval* (1986)

60 The difficulty about a theatre job is that it interferes with party-going.

Barry Humphries 1934– : *More Please* (1992)

61 Crowds have always frightened and appalled me unless they happen to be in a theatre during one of my engagements. Then the noise they make is benign; a great ecstatic whoosh like a fire going up a chimney or the word 'yes' chanted by a heavenly host.

Barry Humphries 1934– : *More Please* (1992)

62 For so many people, going to the theatre is just a little bit of a nuisance. When going out to have a good old laugh gets worthy, the writing is on the wall.

Griff Rhys Jones 1953– : in *Daily Telegraph* 22 January 1994

Time

1 I'll be with you in the squeezing of a lemon.

Oliver Goldsmith 1730–74: *She Stoops to Conquer* (1773)

2 There was a pause—just long enough for an angel to pass, flying slowly.

Ronald Firbank 1886–1926: *Vainglory* (1915)

To a man in the street, carrying a grandfather clock:
3 My poor fellow, why not carry a watch?

Herbert Beerbohm Tree 1852–1917: Hesketh Pearson *Beerbohm Tree* (1956)

On arriving at Dublin Castle for the handover by British forces on 16 January 1922, and being told that he was seven minutes late:
4 We've been waiting 700 years, you can have the seven minutes.

Michael Collins 1880–1922: Tim Pat Coogan *Michael Collins* (1990); attributed, perhaps apocryphal

5 I am a sundial, and I make a botch
Of what is done much better by a watch.

Hilaire Belloc 1870–1953: 'On a Sundial' (1938)

6 'Twenty three and a quarter minutes past,' Uncle Matthew was saying furiously, 'in precisely six and three-quarter minutes the damned fella will be late.'

Nancy Mitford 1904–1973: *Love in a Cold Climate* (1949)

7 VLADIMIR: That passed the time.
ESTRAGON: It would have passed in any case.
VLADIMIR: Yes, but not so rapidly.

Samuel Beckett 1906–89: *Waiting for Godot* (1955)

8 Time spent on any item of the agenda will be in inverse proportion to the sum involved.

C. Northcote Parkinson 1909– : *Parkinson's Law* (1958)

9 We have passed a lot of water since then.

Sam Goldwyn 1882–1974: E. Goodman *The Fifty-Year Decline of Hollywood* (1961); attributed, possibly apocryphal

10 Eternity's a terrible thought. I mean, where's it all going to end?

On receiving an invitation for 9 a.m.:
11 Oh, are there two nine o'clocks in the day?

12 Life is too short to stuff a mushroom.

13 The ability of dandelions to tell the time is somewhat exaggerated, owing to the fact that there is always one seed that refuses to be blown off; the time usually turns out to be 37 o'clock.

14 Bureaucratic time, which is slower than geologic time but more expensive than time spent with Madame Claude's girls in Paris.

Tom Stoppard 1937– :
Rosencrantz and Guildenstern are Dead (1967)

Tallulah Bankhead 1903–68:
attributed, perhaps apocryphal

Shirley Conran 1932– :
Superwoman (1975)

Miles Kington 1941– : *Nature Made Ridiculously Simple* (1983)

P. J. O'Rourke 1947– : *Parliament of Whores* (1991)

Towns and Cities

1 Fleet-street has a very animated appearance; but I think the full tide of human existence is at Charing-Cross.

2 When a man is tired of London, he is tired of life; for there is in London all that life can afford.

3 One has no great hopes from Birmingham. I always say there is something direful in the sound.

4 So literary a little town is Oxford that its undergraduates see a newspaper nearly as seldom as the Venetians see a horse.

5 God made the harbour, and that's all right, but Satan made Sydney.

6 [Sydney] was all London without being London. Without any of the lovely old glamour that invests London. This London of the Southern hemisphere was all, as it were, made in five minutes, a substitute for the real thing. Just a substitute—as margarine is a substitute for butter.

7 It is sad to reflect that so much ingenuity should have been wasted on streets and estates which will inevitably become the slums of the future. That is, if a fearful and more sudden fate does not obliterate them prematurely; an eventuality that does much to reconcile one to the prospect of aerial bombardment.

8 New York, New York,—a helluva town,
The Bronx is up but the Battery's down,
And people ride in a hole in the ground:
New York, New York,—It's a helluva town.

9 A big hard-boiled city with no more personality than a paper cup.

Samuel Johnson 1709–84: James Boswell *Life of Samuel Johnson* (1791) 2 April 1775

Samuel Johnson 1709–84: James Boswell *Life of Samuel Johnson* (1791) 20 September 1777

Jane Austen 1775–1817: *Emma* (1816)

Max Beerbohm 1872–1956: letter May 1894

Anonymous: unnamed Sydney citizen; Mark Twain *More Tramps Abroad* (1897)

D. H. Lawrence 1885–1930:
Kangaroo (1923)

Osbert Lancaster 1908–80: *Pillar to Post* (1938)

Betty Comden 1919– and **Adolph Green** 1915– : 'New York, New York' (1945)

Raymond Chandler 1888–1959: *The Little Sister* (1949)

10 People don't talk in Paris; they just look lovely...and
eat.

Chips Channon 1897–1958: diary
22 May 1951

*It had been proposed that the trees lining the banks of the Liffey,
against which prostitutes entertained their clients, be cut down:*
11 Surely the trees are more sinned against than sinning.

Oliver St John Gogarty
1878–1957: attributed

12 If I were taken and pinioned for hours at a time in
a shuddering, jerking box of steel and glass, lights flashed
in my eyes, fumes blown up my nose and gas pumped
into my lungs, if this were to be done by the Chinese,
then I should be the subject of stern leaders in *The Times*
and the righteous anger of the *Daily Express*. Yet I submit
to this treatment of my own free will. I do it every week
and it's called driving down to London.

Alan Bennett 1934– : *Getting On*
(1972)

13 City of perspiring dreams.

Frederic Raphael 1931– : of
Cambridge; *The Glittering Prizes*
(1976)

14 The people of Berlin are doing very exciting things with
their city at the moment. Basically they had this idea of
just knocking it through.

Stephen Fry 1957– and **Hugh
Laurie**: *A Bit More Fry and Laurie*
(1991)

15 I still felt like an exile in Sydney. I was stranded among
people who could not even muster the glottal energy to
pronounce the 'd' in the name of their own city.

Barry Humphries 1934– : *More
Please* (1992)

16 Saigon is like all the other great modern cities of the
world. It's the mess left over from people getting rich.

P. J. O'Rourke 1947– : *Give War
a Chance* 1992)

Transport

1 What is better than presence of mind in a railway
accident? Absence of body.

Punch 1841–1992: vol. 16 (1849)

2 Sure, the next train has gone ten minutes ago.

Punch 1841–1992: vol. 60 (1871)

3 For you dream you are crossing the Channel, and tossing
about in a steamer from Harwich—
Which is something between a large bathing machine
and a very small second class carriage.

W. S. Gilbert 1836–1911: *Iolanthe*
(1882)

4 Aunt Jane observed, the second time
She tumbled off a bus,
'The step is short from the Sublime
To the Ridiculous.'

Harry Graham 1874–1936:
'Equanimity' (1899)

5 There once was an old man who said, 'Damn!
It is borne in upon me I am
An engine that moves
In determinate grooves,
I'm not even a bus, I'm a tram.'

Maurice Evan Hare 1886–1967:
'Limerick' (1905)

6 'Glorious, stirring sight!' murmured Toad, never offering
to move. 'The poetry of motion! The *real* way to travel!
The *only* way to travel! Here today—in next week
tomorrow! Villages skipped, towns and cities jumped—

Kenneth Grahame 1859–1932:
The Wind in the Willows (1908)

always somebody else's horizon! O bliss! O poop-poop!
O my! O my!'

7 Sir, Saturday morning, although recurring at regular and
well-foreseen intervals, always seems to take this railway
by surprise.

W. S. Gilbert 1836–1911: letter to
the station-master at Baker Street, on
the Metropolitan line; John Julius
Norwich *Christmas Crackers* (1980)

8 What is this that roareth thus?
Can it be a Motor Bus?
Yes, the smell and hideous hum
Indicat Motorem Bum! ...
How shall wretches live like us
Cincti Bis Motoribus?
Domine, defende nos
Contra hos Motores Bos!

A. D. Godley 1856–1925: letter to
C. R. L. Fletcher, 10 January 1914

9 Walk! Not bloody likely. I am going in a taxi.

George Bernard Shaw
1856–1950: *Pygmalion* (1916)

10 My inclination to go by Air Express is confirmed by the
crash they had yesterday, which will make them careful
in the immediate future.

A. E. Housman 1859–1936: letter
17 August 1920

11 Home James, and don't spare the horses.

Fred Hillebrand 1893– : Title of
song (1934)

12 The defendant is clearly one who insufficiently
appreciates the value of the motor car to the human
race. But we must not allow our natural detestation for
such an individual to cloud our judgment.

A. P. Herbert 1890–1971:
Misleading Cases (1935)

13 There is no juridical distinction between fire-arms, wild
beasts, and motor cars where the safety and peace of the
King's subjects on the King's highway are concerned.

A. P. Herbert 1890–1971:
Misleading Cases (1935)

14 Why is it no one ever sent me yet
One perfect limousine, do you suppose?
Ah no, it's always just my luck to get
One perfect rose.

Dorothy Parker 1893–1967: 'One
Perfect Rose' (1937)

15 He [Benchley] came out of a night club one evening and,
tapping a uniformed figure on the shoulder, said, 'Get me
a cab.' The uniformed figure turned around furiously and
informed him that he was not a doorman but a rear
admiral. 'O.K.,' said Benchley, 'Get me a battleship.'

Robert Benchley 1889–1945: in
New Yorker 5 January 1946

On seeing the Morris Minor prototype in 1945:
16 It looks like a poached egg—we can't make that.

Lord Nuffield 1877–1963:
attributed

On the choice of colour for the Model T Ford:
17 Any colour—so long as it's black.

Henry Ford 1863–1947: Allan
Nevins *Ford* (1957)

18 Take most people, they're crazy about cars. They worry if
they get a little scratch on them, and they're always
talking about how many miles they get to a gallon...
I don't even like *old* cars. I mean they don't even interest

J. D. Salinger 1919– : *The Catcher
in the Rye* (1951)

me. I'd rather have a goddam horse. A horse is at least *human*, for God's sake.

19 For sheer pleasure few methods of progression, one comes gradually to realise, can compare with the perambulator. The motion is agreeable, the range of vision extensive and one has always before one's eyes the rewarding spectacle of a grown-up maintaining prolonged physical exertion.

Osbert Lancaster 1908-80: *All Done From Memory* (1953)

Nancy was flying from Helsinki to Moscow:
20 It was a pretty little plane rather like a cottage all blue and white with plush curtains. No nonsense about fasten your safety belt—and no safety belt either.

Nancy Mitford 1904-73: letter 30 May 1954

21 'Take my camel, dear,' said my aunt Dot, as she climbed down from this animal on her return from High Mass.

Rose Macaulay 1881-1958: *The Towers of Trebizond* (1956)

22 That monarch of the road,
Observer of the Highway Code,
That big six-wheeler
Scarlet-painted
London Transport
Diesel-engined
Ninety-seven horse power
Omnibus!

Michael Flanders 1922-75 and **Donald Swann** 1923-94: 'A Transport of Delight' (c.1956)

23 The automobile changed our dress, manners, social customs, vacation habits, the shape of our cities, consumer purchasing patterns, common tastes and positions in intercourse.

John Keats 1920- : *The Insolent Chariots* (1958)

Of Bishop Patrick's fatal error in crossing the street:
24 The light of God was with him,
But the traffic light was not.

E. Y. Harburg 1898-1981: 'Lead Kindly Light' (1965)

25 I found myself going homewards the other evening, not in a cab but in that odd mobile apartment with the dun-coloured wall-paper, a brown study.

Flann O'Brien 1911-66: *The Best of Myles* (1968)

26 People who spend most of their natural lives riding iron bicycles over the rocky roadsteads of this parish get their personalities mixed up with the personalities of their bicycles as a result of the interchanging of the atoms of each of them and you would be surprised at the number of people in these parts who nearly are half people and half bicycles.

Flann O'Brien 1911-1966: *The Third Policeman* (1967)

27 The freeway is..the place where they [Angelenos] spend the two calmest and most rewarding hours of their daily lives.

Reynar Banham 1922-88: *Los Angeles: the Architecture of Four Ecologies* (1971)

28 It is up to the horseman to prevent his horse from touching the electric fence. I agree that horses do not have four-wheel brakes or a steering wheel, but I cannot say that I really support this amendment.

Lord Massereene and Ferrard 1914-93: speech on the Wildlife and Countryside Bill, House of Lords 19 February 1981

29 Q: If Mrs Thatcher were run over by a bus...?
LORD CARRINGTON: It wouldn't dare.

Lord Carrington 1919- : during the Falklands War; Russell Lewis *Margaret Thatcher* (1984)

On a car called by Macmillan 'Mrs Thatcher':

30 This car makes a noise if you don't fasten your seat belt, and a light starts flashing if you don't close the door. It's a *very bossy* car.

Harold Macmillan 1894–1986: Ludovic Kennedy *On My Way to the Club* (1989)

31 Those who think the war is dangerous have not seen the traffic in Beirut. It's a city of a million people with three stop lights and these aren't working.

P. J. O'Rourke 1947– : *Holidays in Hell* (1988)

32 Boston's freeway system...was clearly designed by a person who had spent his childhood crashing toy trains.

Bill Bryson 1951– : *The Lost Continent* (1989)

On the Channel Tunnel:

33 I have always been pro-tunnel, although I should have preferred a bridge. The people of Kent have been anti-tunnel, but I hope they will soon grow out of that.

Lord Massereene and Ferrard 1914–93: speech in the House of Lords, 26 March 1990

34 Traffic is like a bad dog. It isn't important to look both ways when crossing the street. It's important to not show fear.

P. J. O'Rourke 1947– : *Give War a Chance* (1992)

Travel and Exploration

On the Giant's Causeway:

1 Worth seeing, yes; but not worth going to see.

Samuel Johnson 1709–84: James Boswell *Life of Samuel Johnson* (1791) 12 October 1779

2 It is not worthwhile to go around the world to count the cats in Zanzibar.

Henry David Thoreau 1817–62: *Walden* (1854) 'Conclusion'

Of the Prince of Wales's trip to India:

3 Bertie's progresses lose a little interest and are very wearing—as there is such a constant repetition of elephants—trappings—jewels—illuminations and fireworks.

Queen Victoria 1819–1901: letter to the Crown Princess of Prussia, 2 February 1876

4 But the principal failing occurred in the sailing,
And the Bellman, perplexed and distressed,
Said he *had* hoped, at least, when the wind blew due East,
That the ship would *not* travel due West!

Lewis Carroll 1832–98: *The Hunting of the Snark* (1876) 'Fit the Second: The Bellman's Speech'

5 And bound on that journey you find your attorney (who started that morning from Devon);
He's a bit undersized, and you don't feel surprised when he tells you he's only eleven.

W. S. Gilbert 1836–1911: *Iolanthe* (1882)

6 In your shirt and your socks (the black silk with gold clocks), crossing Salisbury Plain on a bicycle.

W. S. Gilbert 1836–1911: *Iolanthe* (1882)

7 In these days of rapid and convenient travel...to come from Leighton Buzzard does not necessarily denote any great strength of character. It might only mean mere restlessness.

Saki 1870–1916: *The Chronicles of Clovis* (1911)

8 They say travel broadens the mind; but you must have the mind.

G. K. Chesterton 1874–1936: 'The Shadow of the Shark' (1921)

9 Nobody nowadays travels, even in Central America or Thibet, without bringing back a chapter on 'The Mind of Costa Rica', or on 'The Psychology of the Mongolian'. Even the gentler peoples, such as the Burmese, the Siamese, the Hawaiians, and the Russians, though they have no minds, are written up as souls.

Stephen Leacock 1869–1944: *My Discovery of England* (1922) 'Impressions of London'

10 In America there are two classes of travel—first class, and with children.

Robert Benchley 1889–1945: *Pluck and Luck* (1925)

On the difficulties of the Passport Regulations:
11 Drake himself, confronted with the same discouragements, might well have degenerated into a stay-at-home.

A. P. Herbert 1890–1971: *Misleading Cases* (1935)

12 The whistle shrilled and in a moment I was chugging out of Grand Central's dreaming spires followed only by the anguished cries of relatives who would now have to go to work. I had chugged only a few feet when I realized that I had left without the train, so I had to run back and wait for it to start.

S. J. Perelman 1904–79: *The Most of S. J. Perelman* (1959) 'Strictly from Hunger'

13 So think twice my friends, before you doubt Columbus,
Just imagine what happens to Posterity without
    Columbus.
No New York, and no skyscrapers,
No funnies in the papers,
No automat nickels,
No Heinz and his pickles,
No land of the Brave and the Free.

Ira Gershwin 1896–1983: 'The Nina, the Pinta, the Santa Maria' (1945)

14 Abroad is bloody.

George VI 1895–1952: W. H. Auden *A Certain World* (1970)

Supposedly quoting a letter from a Tyrolean landlord:
15 Standing among savage scenery, the hotel offers stupendous revelations. There is a French widow in every bedroom, affording delightful prospects.

Gerard Hoffnung 1925–59: speech at the Oxford Union, 4 December 1958

16 If only I could get down to Sidcup! I've been waiting for the weather to break. He's got my papers, this man I left them with, it's got it all down there, I could prove everything.

Harold Pinter 1930– : *The Caretaker* (1960)

17 Why do the wrong people travel, travel, travel,
When the right people stay back home?
What compulsion compels them
And who the hell tells them
To drag their cans to Zanzibar
Instead of staying quietly in Omaha?

Noël Coward 1899–1973: 'Why do the Wrong People Travel?' (1961)

Of someone suffering from sea-sickness:
18 His condition was not enhanced by the titters of passers-by, chiefly women who should in justice be far sicker than he.

Flann O'Brien 1911–66: *The Best of Myles* (1968)

Filling in an embarkation form on a channel crossing:
19 HAROLD NICOLSON: What age are you going to put, Osbert?

OSBERT SITWELL: What sex are you going to put, Harold?

Harold Nicolson 1886–1968: attributed, perhaps apocryphal

20 A person can be stranded and get by, even though she will be imperilled; two people with a German shepherd and no money are in a mess.

Andrea Dworkin 1946– : *Letters from a War Zone* (1988)

21 Commuter—one who spends his life
In riding to and from his wife;
A man who shaves and takes a train,
And then rides back to shave again.

E. B. White 1899–1985: 'The Commuter' (1982)

22 My first rule of travel is never to go to a place that sounds like a medical condition and Critz clearly was an incurable disease involving flaking skin.

Bill Bryson 1951– : *The Lost Continent* (1989)

23 What an odd thing tourism is. You fly off to a strange land, eagerly abandoning all the comforts of home, and then expend vast quantities of time and money in a largely futile attempt to recapture the comforts that you wouldn't have lost if you hadn't left home in the first place.

Bill Bryson 1951– : *Neither Here Nor There* (1991)

24 At my age travel broadens the behind.

Stephen Fry 1957– : *The Liar* (1991)

25 Everybody in fifteenth-century Spain was wrong about where China was and as a result, Columbus discovered Caribbean vacations.

P. J. O'Rourke 1947– : *Parliament of Whores* (1991)

26 Giannini and I were adhering to the two key rules of third world travel:
1. Never run out of whiskey.
2. Never run out of whiskey.

P. J. O'Rourke 1947– : *Give War a Chance* (1992)

27 On arrival in that loathsome land of frog-eatg. Toads, Pederasts and Dancing Masters, I went ashore with only Roderick as my companion. Grunge had got on the wrong boat at Dover and was now on his way to Sweden.

Michael Green 1927– : in *Daily Telegraph* 21 August 1993 'Squire Haggard's Journal'

Trust and Treachery

1 By this leek, I will most horribly revenge.

William Shakespeare 1564–1616: *Henry V* (1599)

2 *Pension.* Pay given to a state hireling for treason to his country.

Samuel Johnson 1709–84: *A Dictionary of the English Language* (1755)

The Emperor of Russia had spoken bitterly of those who had betrayed the cause of Europe:
3 That, Sire, is a question of dates.

Charles-Maurice de Talleyrand 1754–1838: Duff Cooper *Talleyrand* (1932)

4 There is a most indiscreet book of Mr C. Greville's... published. It is Mr. Reeve's intense indiscretion to publish it—and shows a nasty, most ill-conditioned disloyal

Queen Victoria 1819–1901: letter to the Crown Princess of Prussia, 25 October 1874

disposition towards my two Uncles in whose service he was and whose hospitality he enjoyed.

Discussing a friend with Robert Lajeunesse:

5 LAJEUNESSE: He deserves to be betrayed.
FEYDEAU: And even so, his wife has to help him.

Georges Feydeau 1862–1921: Caryl Brahms and Ned Sherrin *Ooh! La-La!* (1973)

The leader of the French delegation to the Disarmament Conference in Washington after the First World War had described the city as un Versailles nègre:

6 Thus (for you figure to yourself the reactions of Southern senators to whom his ill-timed if apt remark was, I need hardly tell you, instantly communicated) stabbing himself in the back, a performance singularly otiose in a city where so many stand only too eagerly ready to do it for you.

Willmott Lewis 1877–1950: Claud Cockburn *In Time of Trouble* (1957)

7 He that hath a Gospel
Whereby Heaven is won
(Carpenter, or Cameleer,
Or Maya's dreaming son),
Many swords shall pierce Him,
Mingling blood with gall;
But His Own Disciple
Shall wound Him worst of all!

Rudyard Kipling 1865–1936:
Limits and Renewals (1932)

8 To have betrayed two leaders—to have wrecked two historic parties—reveals a depth of infamy never previously reached, compared with which the Thugs of India are faithful friends and Judas Iscariot is entitled to a crown of glory.

John Burns 1858–1943: of Joseph Chamberlain; Leon Harris *The Fine Art of Political Wit* (1965)

9 He trusted neither of them as far as he could spit, and he was a poor spitter, lacking both distance and control.

P. G. Wodehouse 1881–1975:
Money in the Bank (1946)

10 Never take a reference from a clergyman. They always want to give someone a second chance.

Lady Selborne 1858–1950: K. Rose *The Later Cecils* (1975)

On Guy Burgess, who had defected to Russia:

11 So far as I [as Home Secretary] am concerned, he is perfectly free to come and go as he chooses. Of course, the fellows at MI5 may take a different view.

R. A. Butler 1902–82: attributed

12 The only recorded instance in history of a rat swimming *towards* a sinking ship.

Winston Churchill 1874–1965: of a former Conservative who proposed to stand as a Liberal; Leon Harris *The Fine Art of Political Wit* (1965)

13 Never trust a man who combs his hair straight from his left armpit.

Alice Roosevelt Longworth 1884–1980: of the careful distribution of hair on General MacArthur's balding head; Michael Teague *Mrs L* (1981)

14 Defectors are like grapes. The first pressings from them are the best. The third and fourth lack body.

Maurice Oldfield 1915–81: Chapman Pincher in *Mail on Sunday* 19 September 1982; attributed

15 Outside Shakespeare the word treason to me means nothing. Only, you pissed in our soup and we drank it.

Alan Bennett 1934– : *An Englishman Abroad* (1989)

16 It is rather like sending your opening batsmen to the crease only for them to find the moment that the first balls are bowled that their bats have been broken before the game by the team captain.

Geoffrey Howe 1926– : resignation speech as Deputy Prime Minister, House of Commons 13 November 1990

17 His absence wasn't a problem
But the corkscrew had gone as well.

Wendy Cope 1945– : 'Loss' (1992)

18 When I was at Cambridge it was, naturally enough I felt, my ambition to be approached in some way by an elderly homosexual don and asked to spy for or against my country.

Stephen Fry 1957– : *Paperweight* (1992)

Truth and Lies

1 'Tis strange—but true; for truth is always strange; Stranger than fiction.

Lord Byron 1788–1824: *Don Juan* (1819–24)

2 Something unpleasant is coming when men are anxious to tell the truth.

Benjamin Disraeli 1804–81: *The Young Duke* (1831)

3 There are three kinds of lies: lies, damned lies and statistics.

Benjamin Disraeli 1804–81: attributed to Disraeli in Mark Twain *Autobiography* (1924)

4 'The Adventures of Tom Sawyer'...was made by Mr Mark Twain, and he told the truth, mainly. There was things which he stretched, but mainly he told the truth.

Mark Twain 1835–1910: *The Adventures of Huckleberry Finn* (1884)

5 It is always the best policy to speak the truth—unless, of course, you are an exceptionally good liar.

Jerome K. Jerome 1859–1927: in *The Idler* February 1892

6 Untruthful! My nephew Algernon? Impossible! He is an Oxonian.

Oscar Wilde 1854–1900: *The Importance of Being Earnest* (1895)

7 The truth is rarely pure, and never simple.

Oscar Wilde 1854–1900: *The Importance of Being Earnest* (1895)

8 A thing is not necessarily true because a man dies for it.

Oscar Wilde 1854–1900: *Sebastian Melmoth* (1904 ed.)

9 The pursuit of truth is chimerical...What we should pursue is the most convenient arrangement of our ideas.

Samuel Butler 1835–1902: *Notebooks* (1912)

10 Matilda told such Dreadful Lies,
It made one Gasp and Stretch one's Eyes;
Her Aunt, who, from her Earliest Youth,
Had kept a Strict Regard for Truth,
Attempted to Believe Matilda:
The effort very nearly killed her.

Hilaire Belloc 1870–1953: 'Matilda' (1907)

11 For every time She shouted 'Fire!'
They only answered 'Little Liar!'
And therefore when her Aunt returned,
Matilda, and the House, were Burned.

Hilaire Belloc 1870–1953: 'Matilda' (1907)

12 A little inaccuracy sometimes saves tons of explanation.

Saki 1870–1916: *The Square Egg* (1924)

13 Never tell a story because it is true: tell it because it is a good story.

John Pentland Mahaffy 1839–1919: W. B. Stanford and R. B. McDowell *Mahaffy* (1971)

14 That branch of the art of lying which consists in very nearly deceiving your friends without quite deceiving your enemies.

Francis M. Cornford 1874–1943: of propaganda; *Microcosmographia Academica* (1922 ed.)

15 By the time you say you're his,
Shivering and sighing
And he vows his passion is
Infinite, undying—
Lady, make a note of this:
One of you is lying.

Dorothy Parker 1893–1967: 'Unfortunate Coincidence' (1937)

16 The 'Sunday Express' today published a most extraordinary paragraph to the effect that I am really 41 instead of 39, and hinted that I had faked my age in the reference books. The awful thing is that it is true.

Chips Channon 1897–1958: diary 19 June 1938

17 She [Lady Desborough] tells enough white lies to ice a wedding cake.

Margot Asquith 1864–1945: Lady Violet Bonham Carter 'Margot Oxford' in *Listener* 11 June 1953

18 I never give them [the public] hell. I just tell the truth, and they think it is hell.

Harry S. Truman 1884–1972: in *Look* 3 April 1956

Lord Normanbrook, BBC Chairman and Cabinet Secretary, in conversation with Sir Hugh Greene, BBC Director-General, at the time of the Suez crisis, Greene having remarked that one day presumably the whole truth would emerge:

19 Damned good care has been taken to see that the whole truth never does emerge.

Lord Normanbrook 1902–67: in *Guardian* 30 October 1986; attributed

20 I am suing Lord Beaverbrook for libel and hope for some lovely tax-free money in damages. He has very conveniently told some lies about me.

Evelyn Waugh 1903–66: letter to Lady Diana Cooper, March 1956

At the trial of Stephen Ward, 29 June 1963, on being told that Lord Astor claimed that her allegations, concerning himself and his house parties at Cliveden, were untrue:

21 He would, wouldn't he?

Mandy Rice-Davies 1944– : in *Guardian* 1 July 1963

22 He occasionally stumbled over the truth, but hastily picked himself up and hurried on as if nothing had happened.

Winston Churchill 1874–1965: of Stanley Baldwin; J. L. Lane (ed.) *The Sayings of Winston Churchill* (1992)

23 It reminds me of the small boy who jumbled his biblical quotations and said: 'A lie is an abomination unto the Lord, and a very present help in trouble.'

Anonymous: recalled by Adlai Stevenson; Billl Adler *The Stevenson Wit* (1966)

24 I don't think the son of a bitch knows the difference between telling the truth and lying.

Harry S. Truman 1884–1972: of Richard Nixon; Merle Miller *Plain Speaking* (1974)

25 In its natural state, the child tells the literal truth because it is too naive to think of anything else. Blurting out the complete truth is considered adorable in the

Judith Martin 1938– : *Miss Manners' Guide to Rearing Perfect Children* (1985)

young, right smack up to the moment that the child
says, 'Mommy, is this the fat lady you can't stand?'

26 Our old friend...economical with the *actualité*.

Alan Clark 1928– : under cross-
examination at the Old Bailey during
the Matrix Churchill case; in
Independent 10 November 1992

27 The New Year's maxim, for instance, was 'Kindness costs
nothing', a rather peculiar little lie.

Stephen Fry 1957– : *Paperweight*
(1992)

28 In exceptional circumstances it is necessary to say
something that is untrue in the House of Commons.

William Waldegrave 1946– : in
Guardian 9 March 1994

The Universe

1 Had I been present at the Creation, I would have given
some useful hints for the better ordering of the universe.

Alfonso, King of Castile
1221–84: on studying the Ptolemaic
system (attributed)

2 Twinkle, twinkle, little bat!
How I wonder what you're at!
Up above the world you fly!
Like a teatray in the sky.

Lewis Carroll 1832–98: *Alice's
Adventures in Wonderland* (1865)

On hearing that Margaret Fuller 'accepted the universe':
3 Gad! she'd better!

Thomas Carlyle 1795–1881:
William James *Varieties of Religious
Experience* (1902)

4 The world is disgracefully managed, one hardly knows to
whom to complain.

Ronald Firbank 1886–1926:
Vainglory (1915)

5 Now, my own suspicion is that the universe is not only
queerer than we suppose, but queerer than we *can*
suppose.

J. B. S. Haldane 1892–1964:
Possible Worlds (1927)

6 'I quite realized,' said Columbus,
'That the Earth was not a rhombus,
But I *am* a little annoyed
To find it an oblate spheroid.'

Edmund Clerihew Bentley
1875–1956: 'Columbus' (1929)

7   Listen: there's a hell
Of a good universe next door; let's go.

e. e. cummings 1894–1962: *1 x 1*
(1944)

8 The whole thing was so amazingly simple...Once started,
the nebulous world condensed into suns, the suns threw
off planets, the planets cooled, life resulted and presently
became conscious, conscious life got higher up and
higher up till you had apes, then Bishop Wilberforce, and
then Professor Huxley.

Stephen Leacock 1869–1944: *The
Boy I Left Behind Me* (1947)

9 If this planet is a sample,
Or a preview if you will,
Or a model demonstration
Of the great designer's stall,
I say without hesitation,
'Thank you, no reincarnation.'

E. Y. Harburg 1898–1981: 'Letter
to my Gaza' (1976)

10 To make the longest story terse,
Be it blessing, be it curse
The Lord designed the Universe
With built in obsolescence...

E. Y. Harburg 1898–1981: 'The Odds on Favourite' (1976)

11 This is the first convention of the Space Age—when a candidate can promise the moon and mean it.

David Brinkley: Laurence J. Peter (ed.) *Quotations for our Time* (1977)

12 The only lyric writer on the Broadway treadmill to get comic with the cosmic.

John Lahr 1941– : of E. Y. Harburg; Ned Sherrin *Cutting Edge* (1984)

13 Space is almost infinite. As a matter of fact, we think it is infinite.

Dan Quayle 1947– : in *Daily Telegraph* 8 March 1989

Virtue and Vice See also *Morality*

1 There is nothing in this world constant, but inconstancy.

Jonathan Swift 1667–1745: *A Critical Essay upon the Faculties of the Mind* (1709)

2 But if he does really think that there is no distinction between virtue and vice, why, Sir, when he leaves our houses, let us count our spoons.

Samuel Johnson 1709–84: James Boswell *Life of Samuel Johnson* (1791) 14 July 1763

3 An original something, fair maid, you would win me
To write—but how shall I begin?
For I fear I have nothing original in me—
Excepting Original Sin.

Thomas Campbell 1777–1844: 'To a Young Lady, Who Asked Me to Write Something Original for Her Album' (1843)

4 I think I could be a good woman if I had five thousand a year.

William Makepeace Thackeray 1811–63: *Vanity Fair* (1847–8)

5 The louder he talked of his honour, the faster we counted our spoons.

Ralph Waldo Emerson 1803–82: *The Conduct of Life* (1860)

6 Barring that natural expression of villainy which we all have, the man looked honest enough.

Mark Twain 1835–1910: *A Curious Dream* (1872) 'A Mysterious Visit'

7 If only the good were a little less heavy-footed!

W. Somerset Maugham 1874–1965: *A Writer's Notebook* (1949) written in 1896

8 I can resist everything except temptation.

Oscar Wilde 1854–1900: *Lady Windermere's Fan* (1892)

9 A little sincerity is a dangerous thing, and a great deal of it is absolutely fatal.

Oscar Wilde 1854–1900: 'The Critic as Artist' (1891)

10 Self-denial is not a virtue: it is only the effect of prudence on rascality.

George Bernard Shaw 1856–1950: *Man and Superman* (1903)

11 Decency is Indecency's conspiracy of silence.

George Bernard Shaw 1856–1950: *Man and Superman* (1903) 'Maxims: Decency'

12 A dead sinner revised and edited.

Ambrose Bierce 1842–c.1914: definition of a saint; *The Devil's Dictionary* (1911)

13 Temptations came to him, in middle age, tentatively and without insistence, like a neglected butcher-boy who asks

Saki 1870–1916: *The Chronicles of Clovis* (1911)

for a Christmas box in February for no more hopeful
reason than that he didn't get one in December.

14 I'm as pure as the driven slush.

Tallulah Bankhead 1903–68: in
Saturday Evening Post 12 April 1947

15 The rain, it raineth on the just
And also on the unjust fella:
But chiefly on the just, because
The unjust steals the just's umbrella.

Lord Bowen 1835–94: Walter Sichel
Sands of Time (1923)

16 All things are capable of excess. Absence of morbid
moisture is a Whig virtue. But morbid dryness is a Whig
vice.

Max Beerbohm 1872–1956: letter
July 1928

17 honesty is a good
thing but
it is not profitable to
its possessor
unless it is
kept under control.

Don Marquis 1878–1937: *archys
life of mehitabel* (1933) 'archygrams'

18 I do not look with favour on the collecting of first
editions and autographs, but it is a vice which is
sometimes found in otherwise virtuous persons.

A. E. Housman 1859–1936: letter
28 March 1933

19 I've been things and seen places.

Mae West 1892–1980: in *I'm No
Angel* (1933) film)

20 When I'm good, I'm very, very good, but when I'm bad,
I'm better.

Mae West 1892–1980: in *I'm No
Angel* (1933) film)

21 Between two evils, I always pick the one I never tried
before.

Mae West 1892–1980: in *Klondike
Annie* (1936 film)

*When dining with 'a lot of earnest and important Americans' Nancy
Mitford was asked to play a game defining 'the stone of insult':*
22 I said 'I see it as a very small diamond offered for ONE's
virtue.' They all rose to their feet and said it was time to
go home.

Nancy Mitford 1904–73: letter
29 May 1952

23 He that but looketh on a plate of ham and eggs to lust
after it, hath already committed breakfast with it in his
heart.

C. S. Lewis 1898–1963: letter
10 March 1954

On being discovered by his wife with a chorus girl:
24 I wasn't kissing her, I was just whispering in her mouth.

Chico Marx 1891–1961: Groucho
Marx and Richard J. Anobile *Marx
Brothers Scrapbook* (1973)

25 Like a monkey scratching for the wrong fleas, every age
assiduously seeks out in itself those vices which it does
not in fact have, while ignoring the large, red, beady-
eyed crawlers who scuttle around unimpeded.

Katharine Whitehorn 1926– :
Observations (1970)

26 In former days, everyone found the assumption of
innocence so easy; today we find fatally easy the
assumption of guilt.

Amanda Cross 1926– : *Poetic
Justice* (1970)

27 I am cultivating a new Vice for my old age. I go to bed
early—10.30 or so, eat half an orange, read about the
Tractarians and fall asleep.

Sylvia Townsend Warner
1893–1978: letter 21 January 1974

28 Beaverbrook, as it seemed to me, was a perfect example of the validity of the Faust myth; he really did believe he had sold his soul to the Devil, and was terrified of having to settle the account.

Malcolm Muggeridge 1903–90: *The Infernal Grove* (1975)

29 I used to be Snow White...but I drifted.

Mae West 1892–1980: Joseph Weintraub *Peel Me a Grape* (1975)

30 Lydia was tired of being good. She felt it didn't altogether suit her. It made her feel a little dowdy, as though she had taken up residence in the suburbs of morality.

Alice Thomas Ellis 1932– : *Unexplained Laughter* (1985)

31 Smoking is very bad for you and should only be done because it looks so good. People who don't smoke have a terrible time finding something polite to do with their lips.

P. J. O'Rourke 1947– : *Modern Manners* (1984)

32 Goodness never means simply acceding to everyone else's idea of what you ought to be doing (for them). Adult virtue includes being able to decide what you can do, in terms of the importance you assign a task and the cost to you of performing it.

Judith Martin 1938– : *Miss Manners' Guide to Rearing Perfect Children* (1985)

Wales and the Welsh See also *Countries and Peoples, Places*

1 Now I perceive the devil understands Welsh.

William Shakespeare 1564–1616: *Henry IV, Part 1* (1597)

2 Not for Cadwallader and all his goats.

William Shakespeare 1564–1616: *Henry V* (1599)

3 'I often think,' he continued, 'that we can trace almost all the disasters of English history to the influence of Wales!'

Evelyn Waugh 1903–66: *Decline and Fall* (1928)

4 The land of my fathers. My fathers can have it.

Dylan Thomas 1914–53: *Adam* December 1953

5 There are still parts of Wales where the only concession to gaiety is a striped shroud.

Gwyn Thomas 1913– : in *Punch* 18 June 1958

6 It profits a man nothing to give his soul for the whole world...But for Wales—!

Robert Bolt 1924– : *A Man for All Seasons* (1960)

A Board Member objecting to Richard Burton's candidature for leading a Welsh National Theatre Company, after hearing of Burton's international triumphs:

7 Yes, but what has he done for Wales?

Anonymous: in *Ned Sherrin's Theatrical Anecdotes* (1992)

War See also *The Armed Forces*

1 'Our armies swore terribly in Flanders,' cried my uncle Toby,—'but nothing to this.'

Laurence Sterne 1713–68: *Tristram Shandy* (1759–67)

2 There never was a good war, or a bad peace.

Benjamin Franklin 1706–90: letter to Josiah Quincy, 11 September 1783

3 As Lord Chesterfield said of the generals of his day, 'I only hope that when the enemy reads the list of their names, he trembles as I do.'

Duke of Wellington 1769–1852: letter, 29 August 1810, usually quoted 'I don't know what effect these men will have upon the enemy, but, by God, they frighten me'

Of Sir Charles Napier's conquest of Sindh:
4 *Peccavi*—I have Sindh.

Catherine Winkworth 1827–78: in *Punch* 18 May 1844, supposedly sent by Napier to Lord Ellenborough; reworking Latin *peccavi* I have sinned

5 Good-bye-ee!—Good-bye-ee!
Wipe the tear, baby dear, from your eye-ee.
Tho' it's hard to part, I know,
I'll be tickled to death to go.
Don't cry-ee—don't sigh-ee!
There's a silver lining in the sky-ee!
Bonsoir, old thing! cheerio! chin-chin!
Nahpoo! Toodle-oo! Good-bye-ee!

R. P. Weston 1878–1936 and **Bert Lee** 1880–1936: 'Good-bye-ee!' (c.1915)

6 Well, if you knows of a better 'ole, go to it.

Bruce Bairnsfather 1888–1959: *Fragments from France* (1915)

7 Kitchener is a great poster.

Margot Asquith 1864–1945: *More Memories* (1933)

8 I gave my life for freedom—This I know:
For those who bade me fight had told me so.

William Norman Ewer 1885–1976: 'Five Souls' (1917)

9 Though Waterloo was won upon the playing fields of Eton,
The next war will be photographed, and lost, by Cecil Beaton.

Noël Coward 1899–1973: 'Bright Young People' (1931)

10 The last European war (commonly called Great, as all wars are called by those concerned in them).

A. P. Herbert 1890–1971: *Misleading Cases* (1935)

11 Little girl...Sometime they'll give a war and nobody will come.

Carl Sandburg 1878–1967: *The People, Yes* (1936); 'Suppose They Gave a War and Nobody Came?' was the title of a 1970 film

12 Come, friendly bombs, and fall on Slough!
It isn't fit for humans now,
There isn't grass to graze a cow.
Swarm over, Death!

John Betjeman 1906–84: 'Slough' (1937)

13 If we'd had as many soldiers as that, we'd have won the war!

Margaret Mitchell 1900–49: on seeing the number of Confederate troops in *Gone with the Wind* at the 1939 premiere; W. G. Harris *Gable and Lombard* (1976)

On becoming aware of the Nazi threat:
14 I shall put warmonger on my passport.

Robert Byron 1905–41: *The Road to Oxiana* (1980 ed.); introduction

To Peter Quennell, who had been complaining that he had to do fire-watching:

15 Can't you get out of it on the ground that you have a child and three wives to support?

Cyril Connolly 1903–74: Harold Nicolson *Diaries* (1980 ed).

16 All the same, sir, I would put some of the colonies in your wife's name.

Joseph Herman Hertz 1872–1946: the Chief Rabbi to George VI, summer 1940; Chips Channon diary 3 June 1943

Of the retreat from Dunkirk, May 1940:

17 The noise, my dear! And the people!

Anonymous: Anthony Rhodes *Sword of Bone* (1942)

18 The day war broke out.

Robb Wilton 1881–1957: customary preamble to radio monologues in the role of a Home Guard, from c.1940

Evelyn Waugh, returning from Crete in 1941, was asked his impression of his first battle:

19 Like German opera, too long and too loud.

Evelyn Waugh 1903–66: Christopher Sykes *Evelyn Waugh* (1975)

20 I think from now on they're shooting without a script.

George S. Kaufman 1889–1961: comment on German strategy when the Germans invaded Russia; Howard Teichman *George S. Kaufman* (1973)

When Park Lane was bombed:

21 I was under the table with the telephone and Shakespeare.

Emerald Cunard: Chips Channon diary 20 March 1945

22 The nine o'clock news announced the discovery of the German blacklist. Among the people to be dealt with when England was invaded were Winston, Vic Oliver, Sybil Thorndyke, Rebecca West and me. What a cast!

Noël Coward 1899–1973: diary 13 September 1945

23 The quickest way of ending a war is to lose it.

George Orwell 1903–50: in *Polemic* May 1946 'Second Thoughts on James Burnham'

24 After each war there is a little less democracy to save.

Brooks Atkinson 1894–1984: *Once Around the Sun* (1951) 7 January

25 Fortunately, just when things were blackest, the war broke out.

Joseph Heller 1923– : *Catch-22* (1961)

26 I'd like to see the government get out of war altogether and leave the whole field to private industry.

Joseph Heller 1923– : *Catch-22* (1961)

27 The First World War had begun—imposed on the statesmen of Europe by railway timetables. It was an unexpected climax to the railway age.

A. J. P. Taylor 1906–90: *The First World War* (1963)

Of Viscount Montgomery:

28 In defeat unbeatable: in victory unbearable.

Winston Churchill 1874–1965: Edward Marsh *Ambrosia and Small Beer* (1964)

29 It was like winning, being captured. The war was still going on but I wasn't going to it any more.

Tom Stoppard 1937– : *A Separate Peace* (1969)

30 I have never understood this liking for war. It panders to instincts already catered for within the scope of any respectable domestic establishment.

Alan Bennett 1934– : *Forty Years On* (1969)

31 War is capitalism with the gloves off and many who go to war know it but they go to war because they don't want to be a hero.

Tom Stoppard 1937– : *Travesties* (1975)

32 The first step in having any successful war is getting people to fight it.

Fran Lebowitz 1946– : *Social Studies* (1981)

33 Like many men of my generation, I had an opportunity to give war a chance, and I promptly chickened out.

P. J. O'Rourke 1947– : *Give War a Chance* (1992)

Wealth   See also *Money, Poverty*

1 It was very prettily said, that we may learn the little value of fortune by the persons on whom heaven is pleased to bestow it.

Richard Steele 1672–1729: *The Tatler* 27 July 1710

2 £40,000 a year [is] a moderate income—such a one as a man might jog on with.

Lord Durham 1792–1840: Herbert Maxwell *The Creevey Papers* (1903); letter from Mr Creevey to Miss Elizabeth Ord, 13 September 1821

3 I am a Millionaire. That is my religion.

George Bernard Shaw 1856–1950: *Major Barbara* (1907)

4 To trust people is a luxury in which only the wealthy can indulge; the poor cannot afford it.

E. M. Forster 1879–1970: *Howards End* (1910)

5 I've a shooting box in Scotland,
I've a chateau in Touraine,
I've a silly little chalet
In the Interlaken Valley,
I've a hacienda in Spain,
I've a private fjord in Norway,
I've a villa close to Rome,
And in travelling
It's really quite a comfort to know
That you're never far from home!

Cole Porter 1891–1964: 'I've a Shooting Box in Scotland' (1916)

6 I have never seen any rich people. Very often I have thought that I had found them. But it turned out that it was not so. They were not rich at all. They were quite poor. They were hard up. They were pushed for money. They didn't know where to turn for ten thousand dollars.

Stephen Leacock 1869–1944: *Further Foolishness* (1917) 'Are the Rich Happy?'

7 It was a sumpshous spot all done up in gold with plenty of looking glasses.

Daisy Ashford 1881–1972: *The Young Visiters* (1919)

8 When I want a peerage, I shall buy it like an honest man.

Lord Northcliffe 1865–1922: Tom Driberg *Swaff* (1974)

9 I used to walk in the shade,
With those blues on parade,
But I'm not afraid.
This Rover crossed over.
If I never have a cent
I'll be rich as Rockefeller,

Dorothy Fields 1905–74: 'On the Sunny Side of the Street' (1930)

Gold dust on my feet,
On the sunny side of the street.

10 It is the wretchedness of being rich that you have to live with rich people.

Logan Pearsall Smith 1865–1946: *Afterthoughts* (1931)

11 To suppose, as we all suppose, that we could be rich and not behave as the rich behave, is like supposing that we could drink all day and keep absolutely sober.

Logan Pearsall Smith 1865–1946: *Afterthoughts* (1931)

12 It is very difficult to spend less than £200 a morning when one goes out shopping.

Chips Channon 1897–1958: diary 27 September 1934

13 Mrs Budge Bulkeley, worth £32,000,000, has arrived here [Isfahan] accompanied by some lesser millionairesses. They are in great misery because the caviare is running out.

Robert Byron 1905–41: on fellow travellers in Persia; *The Road to Oxiana* (1937)

14 The Hotel [in Lisbon] is full of spies, impoverished grandees and nondescript people, including Rothschilds down to their last two millions.

Chips Channon 1897–1958: diary 19 February 1941

15 If you would know what the Lord God thinks of money, you have only to look at those to whom he gives it.

Maurice Baring 1874–1945: Malcolm Cowley (ed.) *Writers at Work* (1958) 1st series

16 A rich man is nothing but a poor man with money.

W. C. Fields 1880–1946: attributed

17 A kiss on the hand may be quite continental,
But diamonds are a girl's best friend...

Men grow cold as girls grow old
And we all lose our charms in the end.
But square cut or pear shape,
These rocks won't lose their shape,
Diamonds are a girl's best friend.

Leo Robin 1900– : 'Diamonds are a Girl's Best Friend' (1949)

18 When I hear a rich man described as a colourful character I figure he's a bum with money.

Jimmy Cannon 1910–73: in *New York Post* c.1955 'Nobody Asked Me, But...'

19 HE: Who wants to be a millionaire?
SHE: I don't.
HE: Have flashy flunkeys ev'rywhere?
SHE: I don't...
HE: Who wants a marble swimming pool too?
SHE: I don't.
HE: And I don't,
BOTH: 'Cause all I want is you.

Cole Porter 1891–1964: 'Who Wants to be a Millionaire?' (1956)

20 Poor Harold, he can live on his income all right, but he no longer can live on the income from his income.

George S. Kaufman 1889–1961: of Harold Vanderbilt; Howard Teichman *George S. Kaufman* (1973)

21 There is no stronger craving in the world than that of the rich for titles, except perhaps that of the titled for riches.

Hesketh Pearson 1887–1964: *The Pilgrim Daughters* (1961)

22 Chapman insisted, however, that the poet should come along...holding that millionaires were necessarily personable folk whose friendship could be very beautiful.

Flann O'Brien 1911–66: *The Best of Myles* (1968)

23 I've been poor and I've been rich—rich is better.

Sophie Tucker 1884–1966:
attributed

24 I can walk. It's just that I'm so rich I don't need to.

Alan Bennett 1934– : *Forty Years On* (1969)

25 Where would the Rockefellers be today if sainted old John D. had gone on selling short-weight kerosene (paraffin to you) to widows and orphans instead of wisely deciding to mulct the whole country?

S. J. Perelman 1904–79: letter 25 October 1976

26 The meek shall inherit the earth, but not the mineral rights.

John Paul Getty 1892–1976:
Robert Lenzner *The Great Getty*;
attributed

27 I sometimes wished he would realize that he was poor instead of being that most nerve-racking of phenomena, a rich man without money.

Peter Ustinov 1921– : *Dear Me* (1977)

28 Wealth and power are much more likely to be the result of breeding than they are of reading.

Fran Lebowitz 1946– : on self-help books; *Social Studies* (1981)

29 I've got £700,000 in my Abbey National Crazy-High-Interest account. But what's the use?

Alan Clark 1928– : diary 24 December 1987

30 The Rich aren't like us—they pay less taxes.

Peter de Vries 1910–93: in *Washington Post* 30 July 1989

31 'Whatever happened to the good old-fashioned City gent?'
'He's helping police with their enquiries.'

Anonymous: graffito in City of London lavatory, 1980s.

32 I hold private-property rights to be sacred—in theory. Which is like saying I'm rich—in Bulgaria.

P. J. O'Rourke 1947– : *Parliament of Whores* (1991)

The Weather

1 Some are weather-wise, some are otherwise.

Benjamin Franklin 1706–90: *Poor Richard's Almanac* (1735) February

2 When two Englishmen meet, their first talk is of the weather.

Samuel Johnson 1709–84: *The Idler* 24 June 1758

3 The way to ensure summer in England is to have it framed and glazed in a comfortable room.

Horace Walpole 1717–97: letter to Revd William Cole, 28 May 1774

4 The English winter—ending in July,
To recommence in August.

Lord Byron 1788–1824: *Don Juan* (1819–24)

5 Summer has set in with its usual severity.

Samuel Taylor Coleridge 1772–1834: letter to Vincent Novello, 9 May 1826

6 Let no man boast himself that he has got through the perils of winter till at least the seventh of May.

Anthony Trollope 1815–82: *Doctor Thorne* (1858)

7 It was a wild and stormy night on the West Coast of Scotland. This, however, is immaterial to the present story, as the scene is not laid in the West of Scotland. For the matter of that the weather was just as bad on the East Coast of Ireland.

Stephen Leacock 1869–1944: *Nonsense Novels* (1911) 'Gertrude the Governess'

8 Winter is icummen in,
Lhude sing Goddamm,
Raineth drop and staineth slop,
And how the wind doth ramm!
Sing: Goddamm.

Ezra Pound 1885–1972: 'Ancient Music' (1917)

9 The Gulf Stream, as it nears the shores of the British Isles and feels the propinquity of Ireland, rises into the air, turns into soup, and comes down on London...London people are a little sensitive on the point and flatter their atmosphere by calling it a fog; but it is not: it is soup.

Stephen Leacock 1869–1944: *My Discovery of England* (1922) 'Impressions of London'

10 'Anyhow,' Mme de Cambremer went on, 'I have a horror of sunsets, they're so romantic, so operatic.'

Marcel Proust 1871–1922: *Sodome et Gomorrhe* (Cities of the Plain, 1922)

11 It was such a lovely day I thought it was a pity to get up.

W. Somerset Maugham 1874–1965: *Our Betters* (1923)

12 Thank heavens, the sun has gone in, and I don't have to go out and enjoy it.

Logan Pearsall Smith 1865–1946: *Afterthoughts* (1931)

13 It ain't a fit night out for man or beast.

W. C. Fields 1880–1946: adopted by Fields but claimed by him not to be original; letter 8 February 1944

On being asked why he never sunbathed in California instead of sitting under a sun-lamp:
14 And get hit by a meteor?

Robert Benchley 1889–1945: R. E. Drennan *Wit's End* (1973)

15 We sat on the front [at Deal] and watched the hardy English children and a few adults advancing, mauve with cold, into the cheerless waves.

Noël Coward 1899–1973: diary 1 July 1946

16 SHE: I really can't stay
HE: But baby it's cold outside.

Frank Loesser 1910–69: 'Baby, It's Cold Outside' (1949)

17 The most serious charge which can be brought against New England is not Puritanism but February.

Joseph Wood Krutch 1893–1970: *The Twelve Seasons* (1949) 'February'

18 April in Fairbanks
There's nothing more appealing
You feel your blood congealing
In April in Fairbanks.

Murray Grand: 'April in Fairbanks' (1952)

19 I am entirely with you in your obvious reluctance to rehearse on a morning as chilly and dismal as this—but please do try to keep in touch with us from time to time.

Thomas Beecham 1879–1961: Neville Cardus *Sir Thomas Beecham* (1961)

20 If this was Australia, this would be mid-winter. Think of that. Thick snow on the coolibah trees, koala bears rushing about in gum boots.

Alan Ayckbourn 1939– : *Table Manners* (1975)

21 By and large the world considers weather to be something, if not all, of a romantic—given to dashing about hither and yon raining and snowing and cooling and heating with a capriciousness astonishing if not downright ridiculous in one so mature.

Fran Lebowitz 1946– : *Metropolitan Life* (1978)

22 Any lone cloud in an otherwise clear sky has got some explaining to do. Very probably it has just got cut off from the main herd or has lost its mother, but

Miles Kington 1941– : *Nature Made Ridiculously Simple* (1983)

occasionally it is a rogue cloud looking for someone to rain on. I must say, if I looked down and saw an old poet mooning over some daffodils, I'd be very tempted.

23 Wet spring had merged imperceptibly into bleak autumn. For months the sky had remained a depthless grey. Sometimes it rained, but mostly it was just dull...It was like living inside Tupperware.

Bill Bryson 1951– : *The Lost Continent* (1989)

24 It was the wrong kind of snow.

Terry Worrall: explaining disruption on British Rail; in *The Independent* 16 February 1991

Wit and Wordplay See also *Humour*

1 It's hard not to write satire.

Juvenal AD c.60–c.130: *Satires*

2 I see a voice: now will I to the chink,
To spy an I can hear my Thisby's face.

William Shakespeare 1564–1616: *A Midsummer Night's Dream* (1595–6)

3 Away, you scullion! you rampallion! you fustilarian! I'll tickle your catastrophe.

William Shakespeare 1564–1616: *Henry IV, Part 2* (1597)

4 Most forcible Feeble.

William Shakespeare 1564–1616: *Henry IV, Part 2* (1597)

5 Comparisons are odorous.

William Shakespeare 1564–1616: *Much Ado About Nothing* (1598–9)

6 POLONIUS: What do you read, my lord?
HAMLET: Words, words, words.

William Shakespeare 1564–1616: *Hamlet* (1601)

7 Look, he's winding up the watch of his wit, by and by it will strike.

William Shakespeare 1564–1616: *The Tempest* (1611)

8 A wit should be no more sincere than a woman constant; one argues a decay of parts, as t'other of beauty.

William Congreve 1670–1729: *The Way of the World* (1700)

9 You beat your pate, and fancy wit will come:
Knock as you please, there's nobody at home.

Alexander Pope 1688–1744: 'Epigram: You beat your pate' (1732)

10 Illiterate him, I say, quite from your memory.

Richard Brinsley Sheridan 1751–1816: *The Rivals* (1775)

11 An aspersion upon my parts of speech!

Richard Brinsley Sheridan 1751–1816: *The Rivals* (1775)

12 He is the very pineapple of politeness!

Richard Brinsley Sheridan 1751–1816: *The Rivals* (1775)

13 If I reprehend any thing in this world, it is the use of my oracular tongue, and a nice derangement of epitaphs!

Richard Brinsley Sheridan 1751–1816: *The Rivals* (1775)

14 No caparisons, Miss, if you please!—Caparisons don't become a young woman.

Richard Brinsley Sheridan 1751–1816: *The Rivals* (1775)

15 She's as headstrong as an allegory on the banks of the Nile.

Richard Brinsley Sheridan 1751–1816: *The Rivals* (1775)

16 LADY SNEERWELL: There's no possibility of being witty without a little ill-nature; the malice of a good thing is the barb that makes it stick.

Richard Brinsley Sheridan 1751–1816: *The School for Scandal* (1777)

17 His wit invites you by his looks to come,
But when you knock it never is at home.

William Cowper 1731–1800:
'Conversation' (1782)

18 Staircase wit.

Denis Diderot 1713–84: the witty riposte one thinks of only when one has left the drawing-room and is already on the way downstairs, in *Paradoxe sur le Comédien* (written 1773–8, published 1830)

When his apparently flattering reference to Gibbon as the 'luminous' author of The Decline and Fall *was queried:*
19 Luminous! oh, I meant—voluminous.

Richard Brinsley Sheridan 1751–1816: during the trial of Warren Hastings in 1785; Samuel Rogers *Table Talk* (1903)

20 O lovely O most charming pug
Thy graceful air and heavenly mug...
His noses cast is of the roman
He is a very pretty weoman
I could not get a rhyme for roman
And was oblidged to call it weoman.

Marjory Fleming 1803–11: 'Sonnet'

21 'I can't see the Speaker,
Pray, Hal, do you?'
'Not see the Speaker, Bill?
Why I see *two*.'

Richard Brinsley Sheridan 1751–1816: recalling an epigram commemorating the drunkenness of Pitt and Henry Dundas in the House of Commons; Walter Jerrold *Bon-Mots* (1893)

22 Those who cannot miss an opportunity of saying a good thing...are not to be trusted with the management of any great question.

William Hazlitt 1778–1830: *Characteristics* (1823)

The American lexicographer Noah Webster was said to have been found by his wife embracing a chambermaid:
23 MRS WEBSTER: Noah, I'm surprised.
NOAH WEBSTER: No, my dear. You are amazed. It is we who are surprised.

Noah Webster 1758–1843: apocryphal; William Safire in *New York Times* 15 October 1973

On seeing his friend Mrs Grote in a huge rose-coloured turban:
24 Now I know the meaning of the word 'grotesque'.

Sydney Smith 1771–1845: Peter Virgin *Sydney Smith* (1994)

25 A man might sit down as systematically, and successfully, to the study of wit as he might to the study of mathematics...By giving up only six hours a day to being witty, he should come on prodigiously before midsummer.

Sydney Smith 1771–1845: *Sketches of Moral Philosophy* (1849)

On being told that the publisher of Bentley's Miscellany *had thought of calling it* The Wits' Miscellany:
26 You need not have gone to the other extremity.

Douglas Jerrold 1803–57: Charles Cowden Clarke *Recollections of Writers* (1878)

27 'Curiouser and curiouser!' cried Alice.

Lewis Carroll 1832–98: *Alice's Adventures in Wonderland* (1865)

28 'That's the reason they're called lessons,' the Gryphon remarked: 'because they lessen from day to day.'

Lewis Carroll 1832–98: *Alice's Adventures in Wonderland* (1865)

29 I summed up all systems in a phrase, and all existence in an epigram.

Oscar Wilde 1854–1900: letter, from Reading Prison, to Lord Alfred Douglas, January–March 1897

30 OSCAR WILDE: How I wish I had said that.
WHISTLER: You will, Oscar, you will.

James McNeill Whistler 1834–1903: in R. Ellman *Oscar Wilde* (1987)

31 'Sesquippledan,' he would say. 'Sesquippledan verboojuice.'

H. G. Wells 1866–1946: *The History of Mr Polly* (1909)

32 Impropriety is the soul of wit.

W. Somerset Maugham 1874–1965: *The Moon and Sixpence* (1919)

33 You have tasted your worm, you have hissed my mystery lectures, and you must leave by the first town drain.

William Archibald Spooner 1844–1930: to an undergraduate; *Oxford University What's What* (1948); attributed, perhaps apocryphal

34 To our queer old dean.

William Archibald Spooner 1844–1930: a toast; *Oxford University What's What* (1948); attributed, perhaps apocryphal

35 You will find as you grow older that the weight of rages will press harder and harder upon the employer.

William Archibald Spooner 1844–1930: William Hayter *Spooner* (1977)

On being asked how to make an epigram by a young man in the flying corps:
36 You merely loop the loop on a commonplace and come down between the lines.

W. Somerset Maugham 1874–1965: *A Writer's Notebook* (1949) written in 1933

37 I can answer you in two words, im-possible.

Sam Goldwyn 1882–1974: Alva Johnston *The Great Goldwyn* (1937); apocryphal

38 Many of us can still remember the social nuisance of the inveterate punster. This man followed conversation as a shark follows a ship.

Stephen Leacock 1869–1944: *The Boy I Left Behind Me* (1947)

On swimming in the sewage-laden Liffey, to which he had presented a pair of swans:
39 It was no more than going through the motions.

Oliver St John Gogarty 1878–1957: Ulick O'Connor *Oliver St John Gogarty* (1964)

40 Epigram: a wisecrack that played Carnegie Hall.

Oscar Levant 1906–72: in *Coronet* September 1958

Ira Gershwin had noticed two aged men entering the theatre:
41 GERSHWIN: That must be Gilbert and Sullivan coming to fix the show.
KAUFMAN: Why don't you put jokes like that into your lyrics?'

George S. Kaufman 1889–1961: Howard Teichman *George S. Kaufman* (1973)

42 The dusk was performing its customary intransitive operation of 'gathering'.

Flann O'Brien 1911–66: *The Best of Myles* (1968)

To the British actor Herbert Marshall who annoyed her by repeated references to his busy 'shedule':

43 I think you're full of skit.

Dorothy Parker 1893–1967: Marion Meade *What Fresh Hell Is This?* (1988)

44 You've got to take the bull between your teeth.

Sam Goldwyn 1882–1974: N. Zierold *Hollywood Tycoons* (1969)

45 There's an element of mockery here I don't like. I don't mind your tongue being in your cheek, but I suspect your heart is there with it.

Alan Bennett 1934– : *Forty Years On* (1969)

46 Wild horses on their bended knees would not get me out there.

Alan Bennett 1934– : *Forty Years On* (1969)

47 [*Shogun* ended with] almost everybody except Richard Chamberlain being killed in the city of Osaka. *Moral—* Never give Osaka an even break.

Herbert Kretzmer: review of the miniseries *Shogun*; Ned Sherrin *Cutting Edge* (1984)

48 The greatest thing since they reinvented unsliced bread.

William Keegan 1938– : in *Observer* 13 December 1987

Women and Woman's Role See also *Men and Women*

1 Ful weel she soong the service dyvyne,
Entuned in hir nose ful semely;
And Frenssh she spak ful faire and fetisly,
After the scole of Stratford atte Bowe,
For Frenssh of Parys was to hire unknowe.

Geoffrey Chaucer c.1343–1400: of the Prioress; *The Canterbury Tales* 'The General Prologue'

2 O! when she's angry she is keen and shrewd.
She was a vixen when she went to school:
And though she be but little, she is fierce.

William Shakespeare 1564–1616: *A Midsummer Night's Dream* (1595–6)

3 The lady doth protest too much, methinks.

William Shakespeare 1564–1616: *Hamlet* (1601)

4 The world is full of care, much like unto a bubble;
Woman and care, and care and women, and women and care and trouble.

Nathaniel Ward 1578–1652: epigram, attributed by Ward to a lady at the Court of the Queen of Bohemia; *The Simple Cobbler of Aggawam in America* (1647)

5 When once a woman has given you her heart, you can never get rid of the rest of her body.

John Vanbrugh 1664–1726: *The Relapse* (1696)

6 No woman can be a beauty without a fortune.

George Farquhar 1678–1707: *The Beaux' Stratagem* (1707)

7 A woman seldom writes her mind but in her postscript.

Richard Steele 1672–1729: *The Spectator* 31 May 1711

8 I have never had any great esteem for the generality of the fair sex, and my only consolation for being of that gender has been the assurance it gave me of never being married to anyone amongst them.

Lady Mary Wortley Montagu 1689–1762: letter to Mrs Calthorpe, 7 December 1723

9 I must have women. There is nothing unbends the mind like them.

John Gay 1685–1732: *The Beggar's Opera* (1728)

10 A woman's preaching is like a dog's walking on his hinder legs. It is not done well; but you are surprised to find it done at all.

Samuel Johnson 1709–84: James Boswell *Life of Samuel Johnson* (1791) 31 July 1763

11 When lovely woman stoops to folly
And finds too late that men betray,
What charm can soothe her melancholy,
What art can wash her guilt away?

Oliver Goldsmith 1730–74: *The Vicar of Wakefield* (1766)

12 There are worse occupations in this world than feeling a woman's pulse.

Laurence Sterne 1713–68: *A Sentimental Journey* (1768)

13 O'erjoy'd was he to find
That, though on pleasure she was bent,
She had a frugal mind.

William Cowper 1731–1800: 'John Gilpin' (1785)

14 My only books
Were woman's looks,
And folly's all they've taught me.

Thomas Moore 1779–1852: *Irish Melodies* (1807) 'The time I've lost in wooing'

15 A good uniform must work its way with the women, sooner or later.

Charles Dickens 1812–70: *Pickwick Papers* (1837)

16 She's the sort of woman...one would almost feel disposed to bury for nothing: and do it neatly, too!

Charles Dickens 1812–70: *Martin Chuzzlewit* (1844)

17 Women never look so well as when one comes in wet and dirty from hunting.

R. S. Surtees 1805–64: *Mr Sponge's Sporting Tour* (1853)

18 The Queen is most anxious to enlist every one who can speak or write to join in checking this mad, wicked folly of 'Woman's Rights', with all its attendant horrors, on which her poor feeble sex is bent, forgetting every sense of womanly feeling and propriety.

Queen Victoria 1819–1901: letter to Theodore Martin, 29 May 1870

19 Plain women he regarded as he did the other severe facts of life, to be faced with philosophy and investigated by science.

George Eliot 1819–80: *Middlemarch* (1871–2)

20 She may very well pass for forty-three
In the dusk with a light behind her!

W. S. Gilbert 1836–1911: *Trial by Jury* (1875)

21 I'm called Little Buttercup—dear Little Buttercup,
Though I could never tell why.

W. S. Gilbert 1836–1911: *HMS Pinafore* (1878)

22 To everybody's prejudice I know a thing or two;
I can tell a woman's age in half a minute—and I do!

W. S. Gilbert 1836–1911: *Princess Ida* (1884)

23 She who must be obeyed.

Rider Haggard 1856–1925: *She* (1887)

24 Many a woman has a past, but I am told that she has at least a dozen, and that they all fit.

Oscar Wilde 1854–1900: *Lady Windermere's Fan* (1892)

25 One should never trust a woman who tells one her real age. A woman who would tell one that, would tell one anything.

Oscar Wilde 1854–1900: *A Woman of No Importance* (1893)

26 When you get to a man in the case,
They're like as a row of pins—

Rudyard Kipling 1865–1936: 'The Ladies' (1896)

For the Colonel's Lady an' Judy O'Grady
Are sisters under their skins!

27 Could you not get Mrs Marshall to send down one of her
typewriting girls—women are the most reliable, as they
have no memory for the important.

Oscar Wilde 1854–1900: letter to
Robert Ross from Reading Prison,
1 April 1897

28 A woman can become a man's friend only in the
following stages—first an acquaintance, next a mistress,
and only then a friend.

Anton Chekhov 1860–1904: *Uncle
Vanya* (1897)

29 When a woman isn't beautiful, people always say, 'You
have lovely eyes, you have lovely hair.'

Anton Chekhov 1860–1904: *Uncle
Vanya* (1897)

30 The fickleness of the women I love is only equalled by the
infernal constancy of the women who love me.

George Bernard Shaw
1856–1950: *The Philanderer* (1898)

31 I will vote for it [female suffrage] when women have left
off making a noise in the reading-room of the British
Museum.

Samuel Butler 1835–1902:
Notebooks (1912)

32 I heard a man say that brigands demand your money *or*
your life, whereas women require both.

Samuel Butler 1835–1902: *Further
Extracts from Notebooks* (1934)

33 Zuleika, on a desert island, would have spent most of her
time in looking for a man's footprint.

Max Beerbohm 1872–1956: *Zuleika
Dobson* (1911)

34 I myself have never been able to find out precisely what
feminism is: I only know that people call me a feminist
whenever I express sentiments that differentiate me from
a doormat or a prostitute.

Rebecca West 1892–1983: in 1913;
The Young Rebecca (1982)

35 When lovely woman stoops to folly and
Paces about her room again, alone,
She smoothes her hair with automatic hand,
And puts a record on the gramophone.

T. S. Eliot 1888–1965: *The Waste
Land* (1922)

36 'O! help me, heaven,' she prayed, 'to be decorative and
to do right!'

Ronald Firbank 1886–1926: *The
Flower Beneath the Foot* (1923)

37 It's not 'cause I wouldn't,
It's not 'cause I shouldn't,
And, Lord knows, it's not 'cause I couldn't,
It's simply because I'm the laziest gal in town.

Cole Porter 1891–1964: 'The Laziest
Girl in Town' (1927)

38 Other people's babies—
That's my life!
Mother to dozens,
And nobody's wife.

A. P. Herbert 1890–1971: of
a nanny; 'Other People's Babies'
(1930)

39 I do see her in tough joints more than somewhat.

Damon Runyon 1884–1946: in
Collier's 22 May 1930 'Social Error'

40 Women do not find it difficult nowadays to behave like
men, but they often find it extremely difficult to behave
like gentlemen.

Compton Mackenzie 1883–1972:
Literature in My Time (1933)

41 A busted, disgusted cocotte am I,
Undesired on my tired little bottom, I,
While those fat femmes du monde
With the men whom once I owned
Splash around like hell-bound hippopotami.

Cole Porter 1891–1964: 'The
Cocotte' (1933)

42 Why do you rush through the fields in trains,
Guessing so much and so much.
Why do you flash through the flowery meads,
Fat-head poet that nobody reads;
And why do you know such a frightful lot
About people in gloves and such?

G. K. Chesterton 1874–1936: 'The
Fat White Woman Speaks' (1933); an
answer to Frances Cornford

43 Remember, you're fighting for this woman's honour...
which is probably more than she ever did.

Bert Kalmar 1884–1947 et al.: *Duck
Soup* (1933 film); spoken by Groucho
Marx

44 And there was that wholesale libel on a Yale prom. If all
the girls attending it were laid end to end, Mrs Parker
said, she wouldn't be at all surprised.

Dorothy Parker 1893–1967:
Alexander Woollcott *While Rome
Burns* (1934)

45 That woman speaks eighteen languages, and can't say
No in any of them.

Dorothy Parker 1893–1967:
Alexander Woollcott *While Rome
Burns* (1934)

46 There was a young belle of old Natchez
Whose garments were always in patchez.
When comment arose
On the state of her clothes,
She drawled, When Ah itchez, Ah scratchez.

Ogden Nash 1902–71: 'Requiem'
(1938)

47 I will not stand for being called a woman in my own
house.

Evelyn Waugh 1903–66: *Scoop*
(1938)

48 It was a blonde. A blonde to make a bishop kick a hole
in a stained glass window.

Raymond Chandler 1888–1959:
Farewell, My Lovely (1940)

49 I'm just a fool when lights are low,
I cain't be prissy and quaint,
I ain't the type thet c'n faint,
How c'n I be whut I ain't,
I cain't say no!

Oscar Hammerstein II
1895–1960: 'I Cain't Say No' (1943)

50 Other girls are coy and hard to catch,
But other girls ain't havin' any fun.
Ev'ry time I lose a wrestlin' match
I have a funny feelin' that I won.

Oscar Hammerstein II
1895–1960: 'I Cain't Say No' (1943)

51 When Grandma was a lassie
That tyrant known as man
Thought a woman's place
Was just the space
Around a fryin' pan.

It was good enough for Grandma
But it ain't good enough for us!

E. Y. Harburg 1898–1981: 'It was
Good Enough for Grandma' (1944)

52 The suffragettes were triumphant. Woman's place was in
the gaol.

Caryl Brahms 1901–82 and **S. J.
Simon** 1904–48: *No Nightingales*
(1944)

53 When women kiss it always reminds one of prize-fighters
shaking hands.

H. L. Mencken 1880–1956:
Chrestomathy (1949)

54 When she's narrow, she's narrow as an arrow
And she's broad, where a broad, should be broad.

Oscar Hammerstein II
1895–1960: 'Honey Bun' (1949)

55 'Always be civil to the girls, you never know who they may marry' is an aphorism which has saved many an English spinster from being treated like an Indian widow.

Nancy Mitford 1904–73: *Love in a Cold Climate* (1949)

56 I let go of her wrists, closed the door with my elbow and slid past her. It was like the first time. 'You ought to carry insurance on those,' I said.

Raymond Chandler 1888–1959: *The Little Sister* (1949)

57 Glitter and be gay,
That's the part I play.
Here I am, unhappy chance.
Forced to bend my soul
To a sordid role,
Victimized by bitter, bitter circumstance.

Richard Wilbur 1921– : 'Glitter and be Gay' (1956)

58 Thank heaven for little girls!
For little girls get bigger every day.

Alan Jay Lerner 1918–86: 'Thank Heaven for Little Girls' (1958)

59 The trouble with women in an orchestra is that if they are attractive it will upset my players and if they're not it will upset me.

Thomas Beecham 1879–1961: Harold Atkins and Archie Newman *Beecham Stories* (1978)

60 Starlet is the name for any woman under thirty not actively employed in a brothel.

Ben Hecht 1894–1964: E. Goodman *The Fifty-Year Decline and Fall of Hollywood* (1961)

61 I can stretch a greenback dollar from here to Kingdom Come.
I can play the numbers, pay my bills, an' still end up with some
I got a twenty dollar piece says
There ain't nothin' I can't do.
I can make a dress out of a feed bag an' I can make a man out of you.
'Cause I'm a woman
W-O-M-A-N
I'll say it again.

Jerry Leiber 1933– : 'I'm a Woman' (1962)

62 I'd the upbringing a nun would envy...Until I was fifteen I was more familiar with Africa than my own body.

Joe Orton 1933–67: *Entertaining Mr Sloane* (1964)

63 You can lead a horticulture, but you can't make her think.

Dorothy Parker 1893–1967: John Keats *You Might as well Live* (1970)

64 She's like the old line about justice—not only must be done, but must be seen to be done.

John Osborne 1929– : *Time Present* (1968)

65 Nature played a cruel trick on her by giving her a waxed moustache.

Alan Bennett 1934– : *Forty Years On* (1969)

66 Here's to the ladies who lunch—
Everybody laugh—
Lounging in their caftans and planning a brunch
On their own behalf...
Off to the gym
Then to a fitting
Claiming they're fat,
And looking grim
'Cause they've been sitting

Stephen Sondheim 1930– : 'The Ladies who Lunch' (1970)

Choosing a hat—
Does anyone still wear a hat?
I'll drink to that...

...Another long exhausting day,
Another thousand dollars
A Matinée, a Pinter play,
Perhaps a piece of Mahler's—
I'll drink to that.
And one for Mahler...

...A toast to that invincible bunch
The dinosaurs surviving the crunch
Let's hear it for the ladies who lunch.

67 I had never seen a naked woman, and the way things were going I was never likely to. My family owned land.

Tom Stoppard 1937– : *Artist Descending a Staircase* (1973)

68 One of the few lessons I have learned in life is that there is invariably something odd about women who wear ankle socks.

Alan Bennett 1934– : *The Old Country* (1978)

69 We are becoming the men we wanted to marry.

Gloria Steinem 1934– : in *Ms* July/August 1982

70 Surely that shove I feel between my shoulder blades isn't liberation?

Jill Tweedie 1936–93: *Letters From a Fainthearted Feminist* (1982)

71 Feminism is the result of a few ignorant and literal-minded women letting the cat out of the bag about which is the superior sex.

P. J. O'Rourke 1947– : *Modern Manners* (1984)

72 Miss Manners cannot think of a more succinct definition of a lady than 'someone who wants to punch another person in the nose, but doesn't.'

Judith Martin 1938– : *Miss Manners' Guide to Rearing Perfect Children* (1985)

73 I didn't fight to get women out from behind the vacuum cleaner to get them onto the board of Hoover.

Germaine Greer 1939– : in *Guardian* 27 October 1986

74 As the Prime Minister developed her case she, as it were, auto-fed her own indignation. It was a prototypical example of an argument with a woman—no rational sequence, associative, lateral thinking, jumping the rails the whole time.

Alan Clark 1928– : diary 14 June 1988

75 The sight of a woman at my public school was almost as rare as a Cockney accent in class; and if we spotted one it was, as often as not, a fierce and elderly matron.

John Mortimer 1923– : *Clinging to the Wreckage* (1982)

76 It's the last thing one would have expected of a woman who runs a donkey sanctuary—concubine to an opium addict.

Tom Stoppard 1937– : *The Dog It Was That Died* (1983)

77 How much fame, money, and power does a woman have to achieve on her own before you can punch her in the face?

P. J. O'Rourke 1947– : *Modern Manners* (1984)

78 There are a number of mechanical devices which increase sexual arousal, particularly in women. Chief among these is the Mercedes-Benz 380SL convertible.

P. J. O'Rourke 1947– : *Modern Manners* (1984)

79 Your concern for the rights of women
Is especially welcome news.

I'm sure you'd never exploit one;
I expect you'd rather be dead;
I'm thoroughly convinced of it—
Now can we go to bed?

Wendy Cope 1945– : 'From June to December' (1986)

80 I blame the women's movement for 10 years in a boiler suit.

Jill Tweedie 1936–93: attributed

81 The only options open for girls then were of course mother, secretary or teacher. At least that's what we all thought and were preparing ourselves for. Now, I must say how lucky we are, as women, to live in an age where 'Dental Hygienist' has been added to the list.

Roseanne Arnold 1953– : *Roseanne* (1990)

82 The thinking man's crumpet.

Frank Muir 1920– : of Joan Bakewell; attributed

83 It used to be almost the first question (just after 'Can you type?') in the standard female job interview: 'Are you now, or have you ever, contemplated marriage, motherhood, or the violent overthrow of the US government?'

Barbara Ehrenreich 1941– : *The Worst Years of our Lives* (1991)

84 A woman without a man is like a fish without a bicycle.

Gloria Steinem 1934– : attributed

Wordplay See *Wit and Wordplay*

Words See also *Language and Languages*

1 Words are like leaves; and where they most abound,
Much fruit of sense beneath is rarely found.

Alexander Pope 1688–1744: *An Essay on Criticism* (1711)

2 It's exactly where a thought is lacking
That, just in time, a word shows up instead.

Goethe 1749–1832: *Faust* (1808) pt 1

3 It is a pity that Chawcer, who had geneyus, was so unedicated. He's the wuss speller I know of.

Artemus Ward 1834–67: *Artemus Ward in London* (1867)

4 'There's glory for you!' 'I don't know what you mean by "glory",' Alice said. 'I meant, "there's a nice knock-down argument for you!" ' 'But "glory" doesn't mean "a nice knock-down argument",' Alice objected. 'When *I* use a word,' Humpty Dumpty said in a rather scornful tone, 'it means just what I choose it to mean—neither more nor less.'

Lewis Carroll 1832–98: *Through the Looking-Glass* (1872)

5 You see it's like a portmanteau—there are two meanings packed up into one word.

Lewis Carroll 1832–98: *Through the Looking-Glass* (1872)

6 Some word that teems with hidden meaning—like Basingstoke.

W. S. Gilbert 1836–1911: *Ruddigore* (1887)

7 In modern life nothing produces such an effect as a good platitude. It makes the whole world kin.

Oscar Wilde 1854–1900: *An Ideal Husband* (1895)

8 An average English word is four letters and a half. By hard, honest labour I've dug all the large words out of my vocabulary and shaved them down till the average is

Mark Twain 1835–1910: *Mark Twain's Speeches* (1923)

three and a half letters...I never write metropolis for seven cents because I can get the same money for city. I never write policeman, because I can get the same money for *Cop*.

9 Is there, can there be, such a word as *purposive*? There is: it was invented by a surgeon in 1855; and instead of being kept on the top shelf of an anatomical museum it is exhibited in both these volumes.

A. E. Housman 1859–1936: in *Cambridge Review* 1917

10 Make me a beautiful word for doing things tomorrow; for that surely is a great and blessed invention.

George Bernard Shaw 1856–1950: *Back to Methuselah* (1921)

11 He respects Owl, because you can't help respecting anybody who can spell TUESDAY, even if he doesn't spell it right; but spelling isn't everything. There are days when spelling Tuesday simply doesn't count.

A. A. Milne 1882–1956: *The House at Pooh Corner* (1928)

Prescription when J. H. Thomas complained of 'an 'ell of an 'eadache':
12 A couple of aspirates.

F. E. Smith 1872–1930: in *Ned Sherrin in his Anecdotage* (1993)

13 I often think how much easier life would have been for me and how much time I should have saved if I had known the alphabet. I can never tell where I and J stand without saying G, H to myself first.

W. Somerset Maugham 1874–1965: *A Writer's Notebook* (1949) written in 1941

14 Words are chameleons, which reflect the colour of their environment.

Learned Hand 1872–1961: in *Commissioner v. National Carbide Corp.* (1948)

15 My stomach turned over twice at the thought of you sitting in a hot little office in South Beverly Hills scratching adjectives. Or verbs. They are the least responsive, most ornery little critters in the world to work with, and I needn't tell you how exasperating, befuddling, and dismaying a full day of struggling with them can be.

S. J. Perelman 1904–79: letter to Betsy Drake, 12 May 1952

As a young serviceman Dennis Potter was summoned for help with spelling by an elderly Major:
16 How you do spell 'accelerator'? I've been all through the blasted 'Ex's' in this bloody dictionary.

Anonymous: related by Dennis Potter during the launch of his television show *Lipstick on Your Collar*, in *Ned Sherrin in his Anecdotage* (1993)

17 I understand your new play is full of single entendre.

George S. Kaufman 1889–1961: to Howard Dietz on *Between the Devil*; Howard Teichman *George S. Kaufman* (1973)

18 Man does not live by words alone, despite the fact that he sometimes has to eat them.

Adlai Stevenson 1900–65: *The Wit and Wisdom of Adlai Stevenson* (1965)

On the proposed use of the term casus belli:
19 Philologo-juridical obscurantism sits ill upon the mantle of Dame Justice and will not be permitted to besmirch the fair name of this court.

Flann O'Brien 1911–66: *The Best of Myles* (1968)

20 Harold [Acton], writing about *Sun King* [her biography of
Louis XIV], takes exception to the word Sodomite which,
he says, reminds him of Mr Odom and the Bishop of
Sodor and Man. I asked what I ought to call the
adherents of that cult and he says metallists. All right—
so long as one knows.

Nancy Mitford 1904–73: letter
28 November 1966

21 The present age shrinks from precision and 'understands'
only soft woolly words which really have no particular
meaning, like 'cultural heritage' or 'the exigent dictates
of modern traffic needs'.

Flann O'Brien 1911–66: *The Hair of
the Dogma* (1977)

22 Together they go places...Words make you think
a thought. Music makes you feel a feeling. A song makes
you feel a thought...The greatest romance in the life of
a lyricist is when the right word meets the right note;
often however, a Park Avenue phrase elopes with
a Bleeker Street chord resulting in a shotgun wedding
and a quickie divorce.

E. Y. Harburg 1898–1981: lecture
given at the New York YMCA in 1970

23 Excluding two-letter prepositions and 'an', I imagine *me*
is the most used two-letter word in Songdom. 'I' (leaving
out indefinite article 'a') is doubtless the most used one-
letter word (and everywhere else, for that matter). 'You'
(if definite article 'the' bows out) is the most frequent
three-letter word. 'Love' probably gets the four-letter nod
(referring strictly to songs that can be heard in the
home). In the five-letter stakes I would wager that 'heart'
and 'dream' photo-finish in a dead heat. As for words of
more than five letters, you're on your own.

Ira Gershwin 1896–1983: *Lyrics on
Several Occasions: A Brief
Concordance* (1977)

Work and Leisure

1 Anythin' for a quiet life, as the man said wen he took
the sitivation at the lighthouse.

Charles Dickens 1812–70: *Pickwick
Papers* (1837)

2 My life is one demd horrid grind!

Charles Dickens 1812–70: *Nicholas
Nickleby* (1839)

3 It's dogged as does it. It ain't thinking about it.

Anthony Trollope 1815–82: *The
Last Chronicle of Barset* (1867)

4 It is impossible to enjoy idling thoroughly unless one has
plenty of work to do.

Jerome K. Jerome 1859–1927: *Idle
Thoughts of an Idle Fellow* (1886) 'On
Being Idle'

5 I...recognized her as a woman who used to work years
ago for my old aunt at Clapham. It only shows how
small the world is.

George Grossmith 1847–1912 and
Weedon Grossmith 1854–1919:
The Diary of a Nobody (1894)

6 Work is the curse of the drinking classes.

Oscar Wilde 1854–1900: Hesketh
Pearson *Life of Oscar Wilde* (1946)

7 Mr Chamberlain loves the working man, he loves to see
him work.

Winston Churchill 1874–1965: of
Joseph Chamberlain in 1903; K. Halle
The Irrepressible Churchill (1985)

When criticized for continually arriving late for work:
8 But think how early I go.

Lord Castlerosse 1891–1943: while working in the City in 1919 for his uncle Lord Revelstoke; Leonard Mosley *Castlerosse* (1956); remark also claimed by Howard Dietz at MGM

9 I can think of few nobler callings for elderly persons with leisure than to provide unindexed books with indexes.

E. V. Lucas 1868–1938: *365 Days and One More* (1926)

10 Most memorable…was the discovery (made by all the rich men in England at once) that women and children could work twenty-five hours a day in factories without many of them dying or becoming excessively deformed. This was known as the Industrial Revelation.

W. C. Sellar 1898–1951 and **R. J. Yeatman** 1898–1968: *1066 and All That* (1930)

11 Being a specialist is one thing, getting a job is another.

Stephen Leacock 1869–1944: *The Boy I Left Behind Me* (1947)

12 A professional is a man who can do his job when he doesn't feel like it. An amateur is a man who can't do his job when he does feel like it.

James Agate 1877–1947: diary 19 July 1945

13 I will undoubtedly have to seek what is happily known as gainful employment, which I am glad to say does not describe holding public office.

Dean Acheson 1893–1971: in *Time* 22 December 1952

14 I suspect guys who say, 'I just send out for a sandwich for lunch,' as lazy men trying to impress me.

Jimmy Cannon 1910–73: in *New York Post* c.1955 'Nobody Asked Me, But…'

15 Why do men delight in work? Fundamentally, I suppose, because there is a sense of relief and pleasure in getting something done—a kind of satisfaction not unlike that which a hen enjoys on laying an egg.

H. L. Mencken 1880–1956: *Minority Report* (1956)

16 Work expands so as to fill the time available for its completion.

C. Northcote Parkinson 1909–93: *Parkinson's Law* (1958)

17 I understand. You work very hard two days a week and you need a five-day weekend. That's normal.

Neil Simon 1927– : *Come Blow Your Horn* (1961)

18 A secretary is not a toy.

Frank Loesser 1910–69: song title (1961)

19 I was proud to work with the great Gershwin, and I would have done it for nothing, which I did.

Howard Dietz 1896–1983: *Dancing in the Dark* (1974)

20 I saw newspapermen at work so I became a correspondent. I saw advertising men at work so I became an advertising man; publicity people at work, I went in for publicity. I saw painters at work, so I bought some canvases and covered them with oil. I saw musical shows I liked and I became a lyric writer.

Howard Dietz 1896–1983: *Dancing in the Dark* (1974)

21 How to be an effective secretary is to develop the kind of lonely self-abnegating sacrificial instincts usually possessed only by the early saints on their way to martyrdom.

Jill Tweedie 1936–93: *It's Only Me* (1980)

22 Employers have a very bad time these days, what with the Protection of Employment Act and various other acts. You may give your employees intructions but you cannot ensure that they are carried out.

Lord Massereene and Ferrard 1914–93: speech on the Wildlife and Countryside Bill, House of Lords 3 February 1981

23 It's true hard work never killed anybody, but I figure why take the chance?

Ronald Reagan 1911– : interview; in *Guardian* 31 March 1987

24 I realized I could have written two songs and made myself some money in that time.

Irving Berlin 1888–1989: after taking two days of piano lessons; Caryl Brahms and Ned Sherrin *Song by Song* (1984)

25 I have long been of the opinion that if work were such a splendid thing the rich would have kept more of it for themselves.

Bruce Grocott 1940– : in *Observer* 22 May 1988 'Sayings of the Week'

26 Astronomers, like burglars and jazz musicians, operate best at night.

Miles Kington 1941– : *Welcome to Kington* (1989)

27 If I am doing nothing, I like to be doing nothing to some purpose. That is what leisure means.

Alan Bennett 1934– : *A Question of Attribution* (1989)

28 I do nothing, granted. But I see the hours pass—which is better than trying to fill them.

E. M. Cioran 1911–95: in *Guardian* 11 May 1993

Writers and Writing See also *Books, Literature, Poetry and Poets*

1 In the mind, as in the body, there is the necessity of getting rid of waste, and a man of active literary habits will write for the fire as well as for the press.

Jerome Cardan 1501–76: William Osler *Aequanimites* (1904); epigraph

2 Authors are judged by strange capricious rules
The great ones are thought mad, the small ones fools.

Alexander Pope 1688–1744: prologue to *Three Hours after Marriage* (1717)

3 Read over your compositions, and where ever you meet with a passage which you think is particularly fine, strike it out.

Samuel Johnson 1709–84: quoting a college tutor; James Boswell *Life of Samuel Johnson* (1791) 30 April 1773

4 No man but a blockhead ever wrote, except for money.

Samuel Johnson 1709–84: James Boswell *Life of Samuel Johnson* (1791) 5 April 1776

5 I do think...the mighty stir made about scribbling and scribes, by themselves and others—a sign of effeminacy, degeneracy, and weakness. Who would write, who had any thing better to do?

Lord Byron 1788–1824: diary 24 November 1813

6 In general I do not draw well with literary men—not that I dislike them but—I never know what to say to them after I have praised their last publication.

Lord Byron 1788–1824: 'Detached Thoughts' 15 October 1821

7 I know no person so perfectly disagreeable and even dangerous as an author.

William IV 1765–1837: Philip Ziegler *King William IV* (1971)

8 An author who speaks about his own books is almost as bad as a mother who talks about her own children.

Benjamin Disraeli 1804–81: at a banquet given in Glasgow on his installation as Lord Rector, 19 November 1873

9 He never leaves off... and he always has two packages of manuscript in his desk, besides the one he's working on, and the one that's being published.

Rose Trollope 1820–1917: on her husband Anthony Trollope; Julian Hawthorne *Shapes that Pass: Memories of Old Days* (1928)

10 Mr. [Henry] James writes fiction as if it were a painful duty.

Oscar Wilde 1854–1900: 'The Decay of Lying' (1891)

11 Meredith! Who can define him? His style is chaos illuminated by flashes of lightning. As a writer he has mastered everything except language: as a novelist he can do everything except tell a story. As an artist he is everything, except articulate.

Oscar Wilde 1854–1900: 'The Decay of Lying' (1891)

12 As to the Adjective: when in doubt, strike it out.

Mark Twain 1835–1910: *Pudd'nhead Wilson* (1894)

Objecting to having been appointed a Companion of Honour without his consent:

13 How would you like it if you woke up and found yourself Archbishop of Canterbury?

Rudyard Kipling 1865–1936: letter to Bonar Law, 1917; Charles Carrington *Rudyard Kipling* (1978)

On the difficulties of reading the novels of Sir Walter Scott:

14 He shouldn't have written in such small print.

O. Douglas 1877–1948: *The Setons* (1917)

15 The humour of Dostoievsky is the humour of a bar-loafer who ties a kettle to a dog's tail.

W. Somerset Maugham 1874–1965: *A Writer's Notebook* (1949) written in 1917

16 Written English is now inert and inorganic: not stem and leaf and flower, not even trim and well-joined masonry, but a daub of untempered mortar.

A. E. Housman 1859–1936: in *Cambridge Review* 1917

17 E. M. Forster never gets any further than warming the teapot. He's a rare fine hand at that. Feel this teapot. Is it not beautifully warm? Yes, but there ain't going to be no tea.

Katherine Mansfield 1888–1923: diary May 1917

18 To read Swift is like being locked up on a desert island with Napoleon in the capacity of secretary. There is no prospect of relief.

Harold Laski 1893–1950: letter to Oliver Wendell Holmes, 12 January 1919

19 This of course is not what he was trying to say, but the pen is mightier than the wrist.

A. E. Housman 1859–1936: in *Classical Review* 1920

20 We writers all act and react on one another; and when I see a good thing in another man's book I react on it at once.

Stephen Leacock 1869–1944: *My Discovery of England* (1922) 'Impressions of London'

21 It is our national joy to mistake for the first-rate, the fecund rate.

Dorothy Parker 1893–1967: review of Sinclair Lewis *Dodsworth*; in *New Yorker* 16 March 1929

22 Whence came the intrusive comma on p. 4? It did not fall from the sky.

A. E. Housman 1859–1936: letter to the Richards Press, 3 July 1930

23 Poor Henry [James], he's spending eternity wandering round and round a stately park and the fence is just too high for him to peep over and they're having tea just too far away for him to hear what the countess is saying.

W. Somerset Maugham 1874–1965: *Cakes and Ale* (1930)

24 Every author really wants to have letters printed in the papers. Unable to make the grade, he drops down a rung of the ladder and writes novels.

P. G. Wodehouse 1881–1975: *Louder and Funnier* (1932)

25 If you steal from one author, it's plagiarism; if you steal from many, it's research.

Wilson Mizner 1876–1933: Alva Johnston *The Legendary Mizners* (1953)

26 Anyone could write a novel given six weeks, pen, paper, and no telephone or wife.

Evelyn Waugh 1903–66: Chips Channon diary 16 December 1934

Explaining why he wrote opinions while standing:
27 Nothing conduces to brevity like a caving in of the knees.

Oliver Wendell Holmes Jr. 1841–1935: Catherine Drinker Bowen *Yankee from Olympus* (1944); attributed

28 I met Aldous Huxley slinking out of a bank, as if he was afraid to be seen emerging from a capitalist institution, from where he had doubtless withdrawn large sums.

Chips Channon 1897–1958: diary 16 December 1935

29 The defendant, Mr. Haddock, is, among other things, an author, which fact should alone dispose you in the plaintiff's favour.

A. P. Herbert 1890–1971: *Misleading Cases* (1935)

30 No plagiarist can excuse the wrong by showing how much of his work he did not pirate.

Learned Hand 1872–1961: *Sheldon v. Metro-Goldwyn Pictures Corp.* 1936

31 Mr. Ruskin, whose distinction it was to express in prose of incomparable grandeur thought of an unparalleled confusion.

Osbert Lancaster 1908–80: *Pillar to Post* (1938)

His Intourist guide had protested that Shakespeare's plays could never have been written by a grocer from Stratford-upon-Avon:
32 They are exactly the sort of plays I would expect a grocer to write.

Robert Byron 1905–41: *The Road to Oxiana* (1980 ed.); introduction

33 There is no need for the writer to eat a whole sheep to be able to tell you what mutton tastes like. It is enough if he eats a cutlet. But he should do that.

W. Somerset Maugham 1874–1965: *A Writer's Notebook* (1949) written in 1941

A young admirer had asked if he might kiss the hand that wrote Ulysses:
34 No, it did lots of other things too.

James Joyce 1882–1941: Richard Ellmann *James Joyce* (1959)

35 It took me fifteen years to discover that I had no talent for writing, but I couldn't give it up because by that time I was too famous.

Robert Benchley 1889–1945: Nathaniel Benchley *Robert Benchley* (1955)

A. A. Milne had written a hostile letter to the Daily Telegraph on the report of Wodehouse's broadcasting from Germany:
36 My personal animosity against a writer never affects my opinion of what he writes. Nobody could be more anxious than myself, for instance, that Alan Alexander Milne should trip over a loose bootlace and break his bloody neck, yet I re-read his early stuff at regular intervals with all the old enjoyment.

P. G. Wodehouse 1881–1975: letter 27 November 1945

37 The only thing that goes missing in Nature is a pencil.

Robert Benchley 1889–1945: attributed, perhaps apocryphal

38 The biggest obstacle to professional writing is the necessity for changing a typewriter ribbon.

Robert Benchley 1889–1945: *Chips off the old Benchley* (1949)

Of the cramped office shared by Robert Benchley and Dorothy Parker:
39 One square foot less and it would be adulterous.

Robert Benchley 1889–1945: in *New Yorker* 5 January 1946

40 [Proust] is an exquisite writer but for pomposity and intricacy of style he makes Henry James and Osbert Sitwell look like Berta Ruck.

Noël Coward 1899–1973: diary 25 July 1950

41 To see him [Stephen Spender] fumbling with our rich and delicate language is to experience all the horror of seeing a Sèvres vase in the hands of a chimpanzee.

Evelyn Waugh 1903–66: in *The Tablet* 5 May 1951

42 A confessional passage has probably never been written that didn't stink a little bit of the writer's pride in having given up his pride.

J. D. Salinger 1919– : *Catcher in the Rye* (1951)

Asked how he became a writer:
43 In the same way that a woman becomes a prostitute. First I did it to please myself, then I did it to please my friends, and finally I did it for money.

Ferenc Molnar 1878–1972: Jonathon Green (ed.) *Contemporary Quotations* (1982)

44 Virginia Woolf, I enjoyed talking to her, but thought *nothing* of her writing. I considered her 'a beautiful little knitter'.

Edith Sitwell 1887–1964: letter to Geoffrey Singleton, 11 July 1955

45 The art of writing, like the art of love, runs all the way from a kind of routine hard to distinguish from piling bricks to a kind of frenzy closely related to delirium tremens.

H. L. Mencken 1880–1956: *Minority Report* (1956)

On lady novelists:
46 As artists they're rot, but as providers they're oil wells; they gush.

Dorothy Parker 1893–1967: Malcolm Cowley *Writers at Work* 1st Series (1958)

47 Dear Willie, you may well be right in thinking you write like Shakespeare. Certainly I have noticed during these last few months an adulation of your name in the more vulgar portions of the popular press. And one word of brotherly advice. *Do Not Attempt the Sonnets*.

Viscount Maugham d. 1958: letter to his brother Somerset Maugham, in *Ned Sherrin in his Anecdotage* (1993)

48 Tell them the author giveth and the author taketh away.

George S. Kaufman 1889–1961: to a playwright afraid to tell the cast of cuts he had made; Howard Teichman *George S. Kaufman* (1973)

49 The compulsion to make rhymes was born in me. For those sated readers of my work who wish ardently that I would stop, the future looks dark indeed.

Noël Coward 1899–1973: foreword to the *The Lyrics of Noel Coward* (1965)

50 THE EDITOR: We can't have much more of this, space must also be found for my stuff.
MYSELF: All right, never hesitate to say so. I can turn off the tap at will.

Flann O'Brien 1911–66: *The Best of Myles* (1968)

51 He's a writer for the ages—for the ages of four to eight.

Dorothy Parker 1893–1967: R. E. Drennan *Wit's End* (1973)

52 A New Jersey Nero who mistakes his pinafore for a toga.

Edna Ferber 1887–1968: of Alexander Woollcott; R. E. Drennan *Wit's End* (1973)

53 There are three reasons for becoming a writer. The first is that you need the money; the second, that you have something to say that you think the world should know; and the third is that you can't think what to do with the long winter evenings.

Quentin Crisp 1908– : *The Naked Civil Servant* (1968)

54 HANNEN SWAFFER: I have always said that you act much better than you write.
NOËL COWARD: How odd, I'm always saying the same about you.

Noël Coward 1899–1973: to the critic Hannen Swaffer; Sheridan Morley *A Talent to Amuse* (1969)

55 I had my fill of this dreamy abstract thing called business and I decided to face reality by writing lyrics...the capitalists saved me in 1929...I was left with a pencil and finally had to write for a living.

E. Y. Harburg 1898–1981: lecture given at the New York YMCA in 1970

56 If you can't annoy somebody with what you write, I think there's little point in writing.

Kingsley Amis 1922–95: in *Radio Times* 1 May 1971

57 The ideal reader of my novels is a lapsed Catholic and a failed musician, short-sighted, colour-blind, auditorily biased, who has read the books that I have read. He should also be about my age.

Anthony Burgess 1917–93: George Plimpton (ed.) *Writers at Work* 4th Series (1977)

58 Having recently seen *St Joan* in London and *Caesar and Cleopatra* in Sydney, it is clearer to me than ever that Shaw is the most fraudulent, inept writer of Victorian melodramas ever to gull a timid critic or fool a dull public. He writes like a Pakistani who had learned English when he was twelve years old in order to become a chartered accountant.

John Osborne 1929– : letter in *Guardian* 23 June 1977

59 I love being a writer. What I can't stand is the paperwork.

Peter de Vries 1910–93: Laurence J. Peter (ed.) *Quotations for our Time* (1977)

60 Writing, I explained, was mainly an attempt to out-argue one's past; to present events in such a light that battles lost in life were either won on paper or held to a draw.

Jules Feiffer 1929– : *Ackroyd* (1977)

61 The writer is to the real world what Esperanto is to the language world—funny, maybe, but not *that* funny.

Fran Lebowitz 1946– : *Metropolitan Life* (1978)

62 I am the kind of writer that people think other people are reading.

V. S. Naipaul 1932– : in *Radio Times* 14 March 1979

63 Let Shakespeare do it his way, I'll do it mine. We'll see who comes out better.

Mae West 1892–1980: G. Eells and S. Musgrove *Mae West* (1989)

64 What obsesses a writer starting out on a lifetime's work is the panic-stricken search for a voice of his own.

John Mortimer 1923– : *Clinging to the Wreckage* (1982)

65 What other culture could have produced someone like Hemingway and *not* seen the joke?

Gore Vidal 1925– : *Pink Triangle and Yellow Star* (1982)

66 No, on the whole I think all writers should be in prison.

Ralph Richardson 1902–83: on being asked to appear in a charity programme in support of imprisoned writers; in *Ned Sherrin in his Anecdotage* (1993)

67 The book of my enemy has been remaindered
And I rejoice...
What avail him now his awards and prizes,
The praise expended upon his meticulous technique,
His individual new voice?

Clive James 1939– : 'The Book of My Enemy has been Remaindered' (1986)

68 I learned to read and write with unusual speed, a facility the book-buying public would regret forty years later.

Michael Green 1927– : *The Boy Who Shot Down an Airship* (1988)

69 We shouldn't trust writers, but we should read them.

Ian McEwan 1948– : in BBC2 'Late Show' 7 February 1990

70 [David Merrick] liked writers in the way that a snake likes live rabbits.

John Osborne 1929– : *Almost a Gentleman* (1991)

71 The shelf life of the modern hardback writer is somewhere between the milk and the yoghurt.

Calvin Trillin 1935– : in *Sunday Times* 9 June 1991; attributed

72 Let alone re-write, he doesn't even re-read.

Clive James 1939– : *The Dreaming Swimmer* (1992)

73 Write to amuse? What an appalling suggestion!
I write to make people anxious and miserable and to worsen their indigestion.

Wendy Cope 1945– : 'Serious Concerns' (1992)

Of appreciations of other writers in Kingsley Amis's Memoirs:
74 It is as if Amis is swimming slowly but surely under water, carefully slogging through the praise stroke by stroke, when all of a sudden he feels he can't go any further without rising to the surface and taking a quick slug of the air of misanthropy.

Craig Brown 1957– : *Craig Brown's Greatest Hits* (1993)

Having been paid a 75000 dollar advance for a book:
75 The problem with writing is that there's not much money in it.

Cheryl Tiegs: a highly-paid model's view; in *Ned Sherrin in his Anecdotage* (1993)

76 Most people are vain, so I try to ensure that any author who comes to stay will find at least one of their books in their room.

Duke of Devonshire 1920– : in *The Spectator* 22 January 1994

Youth See also *Children, Middle Age, Old Age*

1 It's all that the young can do for the old, to shock them and keep them up to date.

George Bernard Shaw 1856–1950: *Fanny's First Play* (1914) 'Induction'

2 She's shy—of the Violet persuasion, but that's not a bad thing in a young girl.

Ronald Firbank 1886–1926: *The Flower Beneath the Foot* (1923)

3 It is better to waste one's youth than to do nothing with it at all.

Georges Courteline 1858–1929: *La Philosophie de Georges Courteline* (1948)

4 I am just an ingénue
And shall be till I'm eighty-two.

Noël Coward 1899–1973: 'Little Women' (1928)

5 The new generation has discovered the act by which it came into being and is happy in the discovery.

Oliver Wendell Holmes Jr. 1841–1935: letter to Harold Laski, 9 September 1929

6 What music is more enchanting than the voices of young people, when you can't hear what they say?

Logan Pearsall Smith 1865–1946: *Afterthoughts* (1931)

Houston Martin, a young American book-collector, had sent Housman an unauthorized US publication of A Shropshire Lad, *in the vain hope that Housman would autograph it:*

7 I congratulate you on your twentieth birthday and your approach, I hope, to years of discretion. I did not realize how frightfully young you were: it explains much and perhaps excuses much.

A. E. Housman 1859–1936: letter 26 September 1934

8 Give me a girl at an impressionable age, and she is mine for life.

Muriel Spark 1918– : *The Prime of Miss Jean Brodie* (1961)

9 One's prime is elusive. You little girls, when you grow up, must be on the alert to recognize your prime at whatever time of your life it may occur.

Muriel Spark 1918– : *The Prime of Miss Jean Brodie* (1961)

10 Being young is not having any money; being young is not minding not having any money.

Katharine Whitehorn 1926– : *Observations* (1970)

11 Bohemianism is like measles; it is something you should get over young.

Cyril Scott 1879–1970: D. A. Callard *Pretty Good for a Woman: the Enigmas of Evelyn Scott* (1985)

12 Remember that as a teenager you are at the last stage in your life when you will be happy to hear that the phone is for you.

Fran Lebowitz 1946– : *Social Studies* (1981)

13 Weird clothing is *de rigueur* for teenagers, but today's generation of teens is finding it difficult to be sufficiently weird. This is because the previous generation of teens, who went through adolescence in the sixties and seventies, used up practically all the available weirdness. After what went on in that twenty-year period, almost nothing looks strange to anyone.

P. J. O'Rourke 1947– : *Modern Manners* (1984)

14 I have been in a youth hostel. I know what they're like. You are put in a kitchen with seventeen venture scouts with behavioural difficulties and made to wash swedes.

Victoria Wood 1953– : *Mens Sana in Thingummy Doodah* (1990)

Indexes

Author Index

Murder 7
Music 30
Old Age 20, 24, 26
Past 5
People 38
Philosophy 5
Places 6
Religion 66
Royalty 72, 74
Science 23
Sex 30, 44, 60
Snobbery 16
Society 17, 18, 21
Songs 6
Success 19
Telegrams 12, 13, 15, 20, 21
Theatre 27, 31, 44
Travel 17
War 9, 22
Weather 15
Writers 40, 49, 54
Youth 4
Coward, Violet
Songs 4
Cowley, Malcolm (1898–1989)
Critics 37
Cowper, William (1731–1800)
Armed Forces 4
Country 2, 3
Crime 4
Family 4
Foolishness 8
Home 3
News 2
Religion 11, 12
Sickness 2
Wit 17
Women 13
Crabbe, George (1754–1832)
Poverty 4
Craigie, W. A. (1867–1967)
Dictionaries 5
Crawford, Cindy see Gere, Richard and Crawford, Cindy
Crèvecoeur, St John de (1735–1813)
Food 10
Crisp, Quentin (1908–)
Biography 30
Sex 58
Writers 53
Critchley, Julian (1930–)
Class 33

People 54
Politics 77
Power 10
Crompton, Richmal (1890–1969)
Children 25
Crooks, Garth (1958–)
Sports 101
Crosby, John (1912–)
News 52
Cross, Amanda (1926–)
Virtue 26
cummings, e. e. (1894–1962)
Epitaphs 13
Politicians 38
Universe 7
Cunard, Emerald
War 21
Curran, John Philpot (1750–1817)
Description 2
Curry, John (1949–94)
Fashion 30
Curtis, Richard (1959–) and **Elton, Ben**
Comedy 27
Progress 14
Curtis, Tony (1925–)
Cinema 36
Curtiz, Michael (1888–1962)
Cinema 11
Curzon, Lord (1859–1925)
Class 16, 24
Death 35

Dalton, Hugh (1887–1962)
People 24
Daninos, Pierre
Behaviour 28
England 36
Darling, Lord (1849–1936)
Crime 17
Darlington, W. A. (1890–1979)
Actors 42
Darrow, Clarence (1857–1938)
America 17
Certainty 9
God 20
Davies, Raymond Douglas
Fashion 23
Davies, Robertson (1913–)
Countries 60
Davies, Russell (1946–)
Broadcasting 14
Cinema 72

Davis, Sammy, Jnr. (1925–90)
Prejudice 10
Davy, William (d. 1780)
Law 4
Dean, Dizzy
Alcohol 74
de Gaulle, Charles (1890–1970)
Countries 44
Delafield, E. M. (1890–1943)
Books 22
Holidays 3
de Leon, Walter and **Jones, Paul M.**
Life 8
De Mille, Cecil B. (1881–1959)
Cinema 33
Dempsey, Jack (1895–1983)
Sports 19
Denning, Lord (1899–)
Law 73
Dennis, Patrick
Publishing 18
Derby, Lord (1799–1869)
Politics 8
Devonshire, Duke of (1920–)
Writers 76
de Vries, Peter (1910–93)
Love 40
Music 76
Politicians 76
Wealth 30
Writers 59
Dexter, John
Theatre 48
Diaghilev, Sergei (1872–1929)
Music 29
Diana, Princess of Wales (1961–)
Children 37
Dibdin, Charles (1745–1814)
Armed Forces 5
Love 8
Dickens, Charles (1812–70)
Actors 6, 7
Alcohol 11, 13, 14
Art and Artists 3
Body 6, 7
Bureaucracy 1
Character 5
Children 5
Countries 8
Crime 5
Death 12
Education 3, 4

Dickens, Charles (*cont.*)
  England 11
  Family 7, 10, 11
  Food 16, 17, 18, 19, 20
  Home 6
  Hope 2, 3
  Hypocrisy 4
  Language 2
  Law 6, 7, 8, 11
  Letters 5
  Life 2
  Literature 7
  Love 10, 11, 12
  Marriage 41, 47, 48
  Medicine 7
  Men and Women 6
  Mistakes 4
  Money 3
  Music 6
  Places 2
  Poetry 13
  Politics 7
  Sleep 5
  Taxes 2
  Women 15, 16
  Work 1, 2
Dickson, Paul (1939-)
  Betting 9
Diderot, Denis (1713-84)
  Wit 18
Dietz, Howard (1896-1983)
  Cinema 31
  Countries 24
  Description 24
  Family 29
  Fashion 14
  Music 75
  Old Age 25
  Sickness 10
  Sports 32
  Theatre 29
  Work 19, 20
Dinesen, Isak (1885-1962)
  Body 14
Disraeli, Benjamin (1804-81)
  Alcohol 15
  Argument 9
  Conversation 8
  Critics 8
  Death 16
  Democracy 2
  Description 3
  Foolishness 11
  Insults 12, 15
  Last Words 4, 5

Literature 9
Love 9
Marriage 51, 54
Mistakes 5
News 6
Old Age 5
People 6
Politicians 5, 6, 8, 9
Politics 5, 9, 10, 12, 14, 15
Praise 2, 3
Pride 4
Religion 27, 28, 30
Royalty 34, 35
Truth and Lies 2, 3
Writers 8
Dobbs, Michael (1948-)
  Comedy 28
Dodd, Ken (1931-)
  Humour 36
Donleavy, J. P. (1926-)
  Death 52
  Money 13
Donne, John (1572-1631)
  Family 3
Dorsey, Tommy (1905-56)
  Music 48
Douglas, Norman (1868-1952)
  Class 23
  Friends 18
  Government 26
  Progress 7
  Telegrams 16
Douglas, O. (1877-1948)
  Letters 11
  Quotations 11
  Writers 14
Douglas, Stephen A. (1813-61)
  Politicians 10
Douglas, William O. (1898-1980)
  Censorship 9
  Government 42
Douglas-Home, Caroline
(1937-)
  Class 28
Doyle, Arthur Conan
(1859-1930)
  Crime 12, 13
  Mind 7
Drake, Ervin
  America 34
Driberg, Tom (1905-76)
  Country 13
  Sex 77
Dryden, John (1631-1700)
  England 1

Marriage 16
Poetry 5
Dunne, Finley Peter (1867-1936)
  Alcohol 22
  America 5
  Libraries 2
Dunsany, Lord (1878-1957)
  Aristocracy 11
Durante, Jimmy (1893-1980)
  Music 80
Durham, Lord (1792-1840)
  Wealth 2
Dworkin, Andrea (1946-)
  Sex 78
  Travel 20

Eban, Abba (1915-)
  History 21
Ebb, Fred
  Life 15
Edelman, Maurice (1911-75)
  Censorship 16
Eden, Anthony (1897-1977)
  Self-Knowledge 14
Edgar, Marriott (1880-1951)
  Places 7
Edison, Thomas Alva (1847-1931)
  Intelligence 3
Edward IV (1442-83)
  Royalty 1
Edward VII (1841-1910)
  Fashion 9, 10
  Prejudice 3
  Royalty 39, 44, 45
  Self-Knowledge 8
Edward VIII (1894-1972)
  America 30
Edwards, Oliver (1711-91)
  Philosophy 1
Edwards, Sherman
  America 36
Ehrenreich, Barbara (1941-)
  Politicians 80
  Women 83
Einstein, Albert (1879-1955)
  Future 5
  Life 10
  Science 27
Eliot, George (1819-80)
  Humour 7
  Women 19
Eliot, T. S. (1888-1965)
  Poetry 22, 30
  Women 35

Hawking, Stephen (1942-)
  Science 41
Hawkins, Henry (1817-1907)
  God 10
Hawthorne, Nathaniel
(1804-64)
  Death 13
Hay, Ian (1876-1952)
  Handwriting 6
  Humour 15
Hazlitt, William (1778-1830)
  Letters 4
  Prejudice 1
  Wit 22
Headlam, Cuthbert Morley
(1876-1964)
  Publishing 10
Healey, Denis (1917-)
  Insults 52
Hecht, Ben (1894-1964)
  Women 60
Hedren, Tippi (1935-)
  Body 29
Heine, Heinrich (1797-1856)
  God 3
Heller, Joseph (1923-)
  America 33
  Armed Forces 23, 24
  Character 14
  Countries 42
  Critics 45
  Democracy 17
  God 28
  History 18
  Humour 26
  Insults 38
  Literature 31
  Medicine 21
  Mind 8
  Names 8, 9
  Places 10
  Politics 53
  Religion 79
  Sex 42
  War 25, 26
Helpmann, Robert (1909-86)
  Dance 12
Henahan, Donal
  Biography 32
Henley, Arthur W. D.
  Middle Age 2
Henry, O. (1862-1910)
  Crime 15

Henson, Herbert Hensley
(1863-1947)
  Insults 33
  Mistakes 17
Herbert, A. P. (1890-1971)
  Aristocracy 14
  Art and Artists 16
  Betting 2
  Censorship 5
  Country 7
  Democracy 8
  Education 27
  God 22
  Government 17, 20, 22, 23
  Language 21
  Law 38, 41, 42, 43, 44, 45,
  47
  Marriage 87, 88, 89
  Men and Women 33
  News 23
  Politics 31
  Royalty 52
  Sports 30, 59
  Taxes 9, 10
  Transport 12, 13
  Travel 11
  War 10
  Women 38
  Writers 29
Herbert, George (1593-1633)
  Music 2
Hertz, Joseph Herman
(1872-1946)
  War 16
Hewson, John (1946-)
  Insults 62
Heywood, John (c.1497-c.1580)
  Marriage 2
Hillebrand, Fred (1893-)
  Transport 11
Hislop, Ian (1960-)
  Law 80
Hitchcock, Alfred (1899-1980)
  Cinema 21
  Murder 11
Hobson, Harold (1904-)
  Critics 41
Hockney, David (1937)
  Science 46
Hoffnung, Gerard (1925-59)
  Travel 15
Hogg, Douglas (1945-)
  Government 46

Hoggart, Simon (1946-)
  Politicians 79
Holiday, Billie (1915-59)
  Parents 5
Holland, Lady (1770-1845)
  Snobbery 2
Holland, Lord (1705-74)
  Death 6
  Parents 2
Hollander, John (1929-)
  Mistakes 18
  Politicians 61
Holmes, Oliver Wendell, Jr.
(1841-1935)
  Certainty 8
  Crime 7
  God 11, 13
  Heaven 3
  Human Race 3
  Ideas 2
  Language 14
  Law 24
  Quotations 12
  Writers 27
  Youth 5
Home, Lord (1903-95)
  Aristocracy 18
  Politicians 83
Honegger, Arthur (1892-1955)
  Music 43
Hood, Thomas (1799-1845)
  Armed Forces 6, 7
  Countries 7
  Death 10
  Poetry 12
Hoover, J. Edgar (1895-1972)
  Sex 64
Hope, Anthony (1863-1933)
  Children 17
  Choice 2, 3
Hope, Bob (1903-)
  Democracy 16
  Money 14
  Royalty 76
Hornby, James John (1826-1909)
  Poetry 16
Horne, Kenneth (1900-69) *see*
Murdoch, Richard and Horne,
Kenneth
Housman, A. E. (1859-1936)
  America 10
  Argument 11
  Biography 16, 17
  Birds 24

Wit 38
Work 11
Writers 20
Lear, Amanda
Gossip 13
Lebowitz, Fran (1946–)
Appearance 15
Birds 54
Books 39
Broadcasting 8
Censorship 18
Children 35, 36
Conversation 25, 26
Countries 51
Education 49, 50
Fame 9
Fashion 25
Food 96, 97
Law 70
Letters 20
Life 21
Men and Women 69
Poetry 40
Religion 95
Science 36, 37
Self-Knowledge 21
Sleep 14, 15
War 32
Wealth 28
Weather 21
Writers 61
Youth 12
Lee, Bert (1880–1936) *see* Weston,
R. P. and Lee, Bert
Lehrer, Tom (1928–)
Countries 36
Future 11
Murder 9
Leiber, Jerry (1933–)
Dance 5
Women 61
Leiber, Jerry (1933–) and
Stoller, Mike (1933–)
Crime 26
Education 34
Love 35
Lerner, Alan Jay (1918–86)
Alcohol 54
Countries 39
Country 16
Language 35
Marriage 109
Men and Women 49, 51, 68
Old Age 21, 23

Royalty 71
Women 58
Levant, Oscar (1906–72)
Alcohol 57
Cinema 52
Love 31
Music 35, 67, 68
Self-Knowledge 16
Wit 40
Levin, Bernard (1928–)
Bureaucracy 19
Conversation 31
God 50
Literature 40
Murder 14
Nature 16
News 56, 66
Politics 86
Religion 106
Self-Knowledge 24
Levinson, Leonard Louis
Books 38
Lewis, C. S. (1898–1963)
Certainty 15
Virtue 23
Lewis, Willmott (1877 1950)
News 17
Trust 6
Lewson, Charles *see* Gillespie,
Robert and Lewson, Charles
Lichtenberg, Georg Christoph
(1742–99)
Body 4
Liebling, A. J. (1904–63)
Censorship 11
Lillie, Beatrice (1894–1989)
Fashion 24
Telegrams 22
Lincoln, Abraham (1809–65)
Armed Forces 8
Foolishness 13
Ideas 1
Law 9, 15
Politicians 11
Linderman, Bill (1922–61)
Sports 64
Linklater, Eric (1899–1974)
Marriage 81
Llewelyn-Davies, Jack
(1894–1959)
Children 15
Lloyd George, David (1863–1945)
Armed Forces 18
Death 33

Government 18
Money 10
Politicians 18, 20, 32, 40,
41, 42
Politics 26
Loesser, Frank (1910–69)
America 28
Betting 6, 7
Birds 39
Business 5
Countries 31
Law 54
Men and Women 48, 50, 53
Sickness 12, 13
Theatre 28
Weather 16
Work 18
Loewe, Frederick (1904–88)
Music 79
Long, Huey (1893–1935)
Government 21
Longford, Lord (1905–)
Pride 16
Longworth, Alice Roosevelt
(1884–1980)
Children 34
Description 27
Gossip 14
Insults 37
Trust 13
Loos, Anita (1893–1981)
America 11
Men and Women 23
Lopokova, Lydia (1892–1981)
Sex 71
Lorenz, Konrad (1903–89)
Science 31
Louis XIV (1638–1715)
Royalty 9
Lovelock, Terry
Alcohol 72
Lucas, E. V. (1868–1938)
Behaviour 17
England 18
Epitaphs 18
Work 9
Luce, Clare Boothe (1903–87)
Censorship 23
Lynn, Jonathan (1943–) and
Jay, Anthony (1930–)
Argument 23
Bureaucracy 20
Countries 55
Insults 57

Keyword Index

addicted Salteena was not very a. RELIGION 47
addictive appears to be rather a. SLEEP 15
address note down her a. ARISTOCRACY 12
addresses A. are given to us to conceal
PLACES 4
receiving A. ROYALTY 37
adds It a. a new terror INSULTS 22
adjective A.: when in doubt WRITERS 12
drinks than one German a. LANGUAGE 7
adjectives Beverly Hills scratching a. WORDS 15
adjudication bad case of premature a. LAW 78
adjust a. your dress before leaving
POLITICIANS 35
administrative will and the a. won't
ARGUMENT 23
admirable produced a wholly a. man
HUMAN RACE 12
admiral doorman but a rear a. TRANSPORT 15
admirals A. extolled for standing still
ARMED FORCES 4
admire cannot possibly a. them POVERTY 9
really a. about myself CRITICS 42
admired Sophistication is not an a. quality
BEHAVIOUR 38
admirer enthusiastic a. of mine LITERATURE 5
admit Whenever you're wrong, a. it
MARRIAGE 108
adorable a. pancreas APPEARANCE 9
adore Pam, I a. you SPORTS 40
We a. those sort of people BEHAVIOUR 31
adored I was a. once too LOVE 1
adornment from the a. of his person INSULTS 18
ads He watched the a. EPITAPHS 20
adult A. virtue includes being VIRTUE 32
with the a. world CHILDREN 44
adulterers see some a. down there SEX 46
adulterous less and it would be a. WRITERS 39
adultery a. out of the moral arena SOCIETY 32
Do not a. commit SEX 13
gallantry, and gods a. SEX 11
henceforward to the strictest a. MORALITY 3
it's *still* a. SEX 15
now as common as a. BIOGRAPHY 27
Only evidence of a. LAW 39
people have committed a. MARRIAGE 125
adults only between consenting a. SEX 72
advance say civilization don't a. PROGRESS 5
advanced In an a. state of nudity BODY 18
advancement useful for political a. POLITICS 86
advantage A. rarely comes of it SEX 13
affairs for private a. POLITICS 24
take a mean a. of them BEHAVIOUR 14
advantages I have not had your a.
EDUCATION 15

adversary mine a. had written a book BOOKS 1
advertise a. a book to any extent PUBLISHING 15
Sure I eat what I a. ALCOHOL 74
advertisement same as that of a. ADVERTISING 1
advertisements column of a. by heart
QUOTATIONS 12
thinks of those liquor a. ADVERTISING 5
writer of real estate a. BIOGRAPHY 32
advertisers proprietor's prejudices as the a.
NEWS 38
advertising A. is the rattling ADVERTISING 4
A. may be described ADVERTISING 2
revised spellings of the a. ADVERTISING 10
with lust and calls it a. ADVERTISING 11
advise STREETS FLOODED. PLEASE A. TELEGRAMS 18
would a. no man to marry MARRIAGE 30
advises It's my old girl that a. MARRIAGE 47
advocate called the art of the a. ARGUMENT 19
aesthete perfect a. logically ART AND ARTISTS 27
aesthetic a. sense override MORALITY 14
apostle in the high a. band ART AND ARTISTS 5
affair a. between Margot Asquith INSULTS 24
affairs public a. for private POLITICS 24
afford Can't a. them, Governor MORALITY 12
some man that can a. MEN AND WOMEN 16
affront a. to God POLITICS 46
afraid not that I'm a. to die DEATH 68
Africa A. was divided into countries SCIENCE 38
with A. than my own body WOMEN 62
Afro-Asian A. studies which consisted
COUNTRIES 59
after A. you, Claude COMEDY 4
afternoon With a. tea-cakes SOCIETY 23
again whimpering child a. MEN AND WOMEN 40
against all life is 6 to 5 a. BETTING 4
I always vote *a.* DEMOCRACY 12
most people vote a. DEMOCRACY 9
agapanthus Beware of the A. COUNTRY 17
age a. are you going to put TRAVEL 19
A. before Beauty INSULTS 46
a. is not estimable CHARACTER 4
a. to write an autobiography BIOGRAPHY 26
a. wipes the slate clean OLD AGE 37
door in the face of a. OLD AGE 20
every a. assiduously seeks VIRTUE 25
faked my a. in the reference TRUTH AND LIES 16
I can tell a woman's a. WOMEN 22
lie about his a. HUMOUR 26
tells one her real a. WOMEN 25
very attractive a. MIDDLE AGE 1
when the a. is in OLD AGE 1
you've the a. you're too old ACTORS 63
aged I saw an a., aged man OLD AGE 7

American (*cont.*)

A. names as Cathcart	NAMES	9
A. political system	AMERICA	43
A. president	GOVERNMENT	45
A.'s ears were used	AMERICA	44
A. woman has two souls	AMERICA	16
great lady of the A. stage	ACTORS	28
have a nod from an A.	AMERICA	2
living the A. dream	GENERATION GAP	10
play A. music	COUNTRIES	47
told bad news to the A.	POLITICIANS	78
unworthy, and A.	AMERICA	10

American Express To pay for my A.

	ADVERTISING	12
your VISA bill on your A.	MONEY	21

Americans A. born between 1890

	CINEMA	71
A. have a perfect right	AMERICA	8
A. with no Disneyland	COUNTRIES	58
bad A. are slobs	COUNTRIES	61
I have always liked A.	AMERICA	31
Never criticize A.	AMERICA	42
older A.	OLD AGE	38
personality is concerned, the A.	AMERICA	41
To A., English manners	AMERICA	27
what the A. were like here	AMERICA	20
when bad A. die	AMERICA	3

amoebae a. getting married	MARRIAGE	79
amor A. vincit insomnia	SLEEP	10
amorous actresses excite my a.	THEATRE	5
amuse Write to a.?	WRITERS	73
amused a. by its presumption	ALCOHOL	35
anaesthetic vasectomy without a.	MUSIC	83
Anantanarayanan Ah, A.	POETRY	35
anarchism A. is a game	POLITICS	25
anatomy a. from Arthur Mee's	EDUCATION	56
a. which would keep swinging	DANCE	12
studied a.	MARRIAGE	39
ancestors do with our pricey a.		
	GENERATION GAP	9
ancestry a. back to a protoplasmal		
	ARISTOCRACY	8
Andrea Doria A.	MISTAKES	18
anecdotes these deplorable a.	CENSORSHIP	5
angel a. to pass, flying slowly	TIME	2
a. travelling incognito	PEOPLE	34
Is man an ape or an a.	RELIGION	27
to the recording a.	MURDER	12
Who wrote like an a.	EPITAPHS	8
woman yet think him an a.		
	MEN AND WOMEN	10
angels a. over the prodigal's	RELIGION	36
have to walk behind the a.	ROYALTY	45
anger A. makes dull men witty	ANGER	2

Anglican he was a devout A.	POETRY	19
Anglicans devoutly worshipped by A.		
	RELIGION	98
angling 'a.' is the name	SPORTS	44
Anglish A. is what we don' know	LANGUAGE	42
Anglo-Irishman He was an A.	IRELAND	11
Anglo-Saxon A., pro-American God	GOD	28
angry a. she is keen and shrewd	WOMEN	2
I was a. with my friend	ANGER	3
when very a., swear	ANGER	4
animal He's an a. lover	HUMAN RACE	14
Only A. that Blushes	HUMAN RACE	4
vegetable, a., and mineral	ARMED FORCES	10
what a. would you like	BORES	11
animalculous names of beings a.		
	ARMED FORCES	10
animals All a. are equal	DEMOCRACY	11
A., I hope	SPORTS	38
Appreciation of Music Among A.	CRITICS	23
be more cruel to a.	BIRDS	6
British love affair with a.	BIRDS	59
distinguishes man from a.	MEDICINE	11
animosity a. against a writer	WRITERS	36
fervour of sisterly a.	BEHAVIOUR	6
ankle socks women who wear a.	WOMEN	68
annihilation A. ALL OF US PROBABLE	TELEGRAMS	12
hope for merciful a.	RELIGION	65
annoy A. 'im	GOD	16
He only does it to a.	CHILDREN	7
If you can't a. somebody	WRITERS	56
annoyance a. of a good example	CHARACTER	7
a. of one who would have	ACTORS	40
annuals a. are the ones that never	GARDENS	8
another that was in a country	SEX	1
answer Give them an a., I beg	MUSIC	32
inclination to a. letters back	CENSORSHIP	6
I thought of the a. after	CINEMA	66
answered They a., as they took	MEDICINE	8
answering persist in a. you in French		
	COUNTRIES	51
answers figure out the funny a.	HUMOUR	16
antagonistic a. governments everywhere		
	NEWS	27
antediluvian one of your a. families	CLASS	1
anthologies A. are predigested food		
	QUOTATIONS	8
may employ to compile a.	QUOTATIONS	6
anthologist no a. lifts his leg	QUOTATIONS	16
anthology a. is like all the plums	QUOTATIONS	10
anthrax a. bacillus can stand	HUMAN RACE	11
anthropology most familiar facts of a.		
	MARRIAGE	62
anticipates a. his century	OLD AGE	5

back (cont.)

gets stabbed in the b.	SONGS 10
in the small of the b.	DESCRIPTION 7
say of me behind my b.	SELF-KNOWLEDGE 5
stabbing himself in the b.	TRUST 6
to go b. to the hotel	SELF-KNOWLEDGE 21

backbone b. than a chocolate éclair

	POLITICIANS 14
backgammon I ever mastered was b.	SPORTS 7
backhand your wonderful b. drive	SPORTS 40
backing always b. into the limelight	PEOPLE 19
backward B. ran sentences	LANGUAGE 22
infant doing a b. somersault	CHILDREN 42
backwards I knew these lines b.	ACTORS 56
I'm walking b. for Christmas	CHRISTMAS 6
backyard somebody else's b.	NEWS 52
Bacon heard of a saying by B.	LAW 36
When their lordships asked B.	CRIME 20
bad Aren't things b. enough	LAW 50
babies can't be all b.	PEOPLE 20
b. as the play was	ACTORS 12
b. aunts and good aunts	FAMILY 31
b. Brits are snobs	COUNTRIES 61
b. poetry springs from	POETRY 17
b. times just around	HOPE 11
b. unhappily	BOOKS 10
Casuistry has got a b. name	ARGUMENT 17
dearth of b. pictures	CINEMA 15
how b. the picture is	CINEMA 32
I call you b., my little child	CHILDREN 12
If one hears b. music	CONVERSATION 9
reliance on his own b. taste	CRITICS 10
resolved to do something b.	THEATRE 39
She was not really b. at heart	CHILDREN 19
shocking b. hats	POLITICIANS 7
Some of them are b.	SELF-KNOWLEDGE 18
We are in for a b. time	BOOKS 17
when I'm b., I'm better	VIRTUE 20
written a b. cheque	DEBT 7
badgers not to bugger b.	BIRDS 60
bags carry other people's b.	SOCIETY 19
bailiff b. acting for the Inland	TAXES 9
bainters hate all Boets and B.	ROYALTY 11
Baked Alaska resembled a B.	DESCRIPTION 31
bald implies that you are b.	FASHION 29
Slightly b.	CINEMA 74
baldness far side of b.	GENERATION GAP 5
ball b. rolled out of her reach	PEOPLE 23
charity b. is like a dance	SOCIETY 31
give the b. to George	SPORTS 68
Play B.	SPORTS 60
real business of a b.	BEHAVIOUR 7
spoils one's eye for the b.	SPORTS 15
without the b. ever coming	SPORTS 92

ballet b. in the evening	DANCE 10
trained at the Russian b.	HANDWRITING 7
ball-point gave her a b.	DIPLOMACY 14
balls yesterday it was three brass b.	CLASS 20
Bambi B.—see the movie	FOOD 122
banana If this is justice, I am a b.	LAW 80
band high aesthetic b.	ART AND ARTISTS 5
prison b. was there	CRIME 26
Silver B. so nonplussed	DESCRIPTION 20
bands who pursue Culture in b.	
	ART AND ARTISTS 13
bank b. is a place that will	MONEY 14
Huxley slinking out of a b.	WRITERS 28
robbing a b. compared	CRIME 16
banker Society is the b.	SOCIETY 4
world as a Scotch b.	COUNTRIES 60
bankruptcy living on the edge of b.	
	ECONOMICS 7
banks In '29 when the b. went bust	
	ECONOMICS 8
banned *Pompadour* is b. in Ireland	CENSORSHIP 8
banquet Judging from the b.	THEATRE 9
Banquo unnerved by B.'s valet	ACTORS 49
baptismal Fell into the water b.	DEATH 50
Baptists B. are only funny underwater	
	RELIGION 107
bar b. was like a funeral parlour	SOCIETY 34
Did a stunt at the b.	SOCIETY 18
In a b. on the Piccola Marina	COUNTRIES 37
wrong b. or bed	MISTAKES 20
Barabbas B. was a much misunderstood	
	PUBLISHING 20
Now B. was a publisher	PUBLISHING 3
barb b. that makes it stick	WIT 16
barbecue Sue wants a b.	FOOD 73
barbed wire covered with b.	ROYALTY 70
barber b.'s chair that fits all	CHARACTER 1
I must to the b.'s	FASHION 1
Barbirolli B. has worked wonders	MUSIC 55
wrath of Sir John B.	MUSIC 70
barefoot b. boy from Wall Street	POLITICIANS 37
barged Bankhead b. down the Nile	ACTORS 25
Baring taken by Rothschild and B.	MONEY 5
bark you heard a seal b.	CERTAINTY 11
barking sound of Harold Hobson b.	CRITICS 33
Barkis B. is willin'	LOVE 12
baronet half mad b.	PEOPLE 48
No little lily-handed b.	ENGLAND 10
Baronetage any book but the B.	SNOBBERY 1
barracuda Man he eat the b.	NATURE 6
barrels slurp into the b.	MONEY 12
barrenness In b., at any rate	POETRY 20
Barrie Sir James B.'s cans	LITERATURE 16

barring B. that natural expression VIRTUE 6
barrister b.'s life who has not LAW 71
bars ooze through the b. BIRDS 24
  principal research in b. NEWS 59
barter finding b. cumbersome BUSINESS 14
baseball b. fans and agnostics RELIGION 102
  B. is very big with my people SPORTS 116
  If b. goes for pay television SPORTS 55
  if it's good for b. SPORTS 53
  sensible as b. in Italian SONGS 15
  That sounds like b. RELIGION 96
baseballs b. through the windows NEWS 29
bashful b. young potato ART AND ARTISTS 5
bashfulness in England a particular b.
                                                           RELIGION 8
Basingstoke meaning—like B. WORDS 6
basket eggs in one b. BUSINESS 2
basketball Nothing there but b. SPORTS 71
Basque B. or Navaho LANGUAGE 46
bass Slap that b. MUSIC 33
basta B. LANGUAGE 17
bastard all my eggs in one b. SEX 57
  pray to God...the b. GOD 27
bastards gods, stand up for b. CRIME 2
bat held his b. so straight CENSORSHIP 19
  Neither from owl or from b. BIRDS 5
  old sabre-toothed b. FAMILY 47
  paid to see Dr Grace b. SPORTS 14
  shake a b. at a white man SPORTS 116
  Twinkle, twinkle, little b. UNIVERSE 2
bath better in the b. overnight CINEMA 77
  between a cold b. NEWS 23
  cold douche after my warm b. MEDICINE 14
  Commander of the B. ROYALTY 28
  every morning, like a hot b. NEWS 41
  I test my b. before I sit SATISFACTION 9
  occur to a man in his b. IDEAS 7
  stepping from his b. PRIDE 13
bathing caught the Whigs b. POLITICIANS 6
  From the b. machine came a din ALCOHOL 51
  Girls Surprised while B. BODY 8
  large b. machine TRANSPORT 3
  notices that b. is forbidden ROYALTY 33
bathroom church as he goes to the b.
                                                           RELIGION 82
bats b. have been broken before TRUST 16
Battery B.'s down TOWNS 8
battledore B. and shuttlecock's a wery LAW 7
battleship Get me a b. TRANSPORT 15
  named another b. ROYALTY 73
baying county families b. ENGLAND 19
bayonets between platitudes and b. SPEECHES 10
BBC To goad the B. BROADCASTING 19

beak He takes in his b. BIRDS 19
bean home of the b. and the cod AMERICA 7
  not too French French b. ART AND ARTISTS 5
bear B. of Very Little Brain BIRDS 26
  embrace the Russian b. COUNTRIES 25
  Exit, pursued by a b. THEATRE 3
bearable b. to millions of people ALCOHOL 20
beard endure a husband with a b.
                                                           MEN AND WOMEN 2
  He had a thin vague b. APPEARANCE 3
bearer b. of this letter SNOBBERY 8
beast B. stands for strong mutually NEWS 27
  But fortunately a deaf b. INSULTS 20
  night out for man or b. WEATHER 13
beastly b. to the Bank POWER 10
  b. to the Germans COUNTRIES 26
beasts themselves as swans or wild b.
                                                           CENSORSHIP 5
  wild b., and motor cars TRANSPORT 13
beat b. him when he sneezes CHILDREN 7
  guys I'd like to b. up BODY 31
  quite a lot of breast to b. BODY 30
Beatles B.' first L.P SEX 73
beaut make a mistake, it's a b. LAW 51
beautiful b. and simple as all truly CRIME 15
  be b. than to be good APPEARANCE 1
  When a woman isn't b. WOMEN 29
beauty Age before B. INSULTS 46
  be a b. without a fortune WOMEN 6
  b. being only skin-deep APPEARANCE 9
  b. is only sin deep APPEARANCE 2
  B. school report EDUCATION 43
  My b. am faded APPEARANCE 20
Beaverbrook [B.] gets to Heaven HEAVEN 4
becquerel know about the b. SCIENCE 39
bed about his b. and spying SCIENCE 9
  And so to b. SLEEP 4
  any place but it were to his b. ROYALTY 1
  asked what she wore in b. FASHION 18
  b. fell on my father FAMILY 28
  b. people of below-stairs CLASS 38
  b. with my catamite SEX 87
  Dean of Durham in b. INSULTS 33
  girl to go to b. with me SEX 52
  gooseberried double b. SEX 33
  go to b. at least one night PARENTS 2
  housemaids sit on the b. ACTORS 23
  in b. at the same time SEX 53
  I should of stood in b. SPORTS 31
  Now can we go to b. WOMEN 79
  stay in b. all day MISTAKES 16
  still in b. resting RELIGION 59
  That's why I go to b. early SLEEP 8
  Who goes to b. with whom OLD AGE 22

bed (*cont.*)
wrong bar or b.   MISTAKES 20
bedfellows strange b.   MISTAKES 1
bedpost lose its flavour on the b.   FOOD 48
bedroom French widow in every b.   TRAVEL 15
what you do in the b.   SEX 27
bedtime likely to argue about b.   FAMILY 53
bee hero is a b.   BIRDS 20
Beecham's Pills B. are just the thing
                                                   MEDICINE 24
beef lamentations after b. and beer   COUNTRIES 3
Roast B., Medium   FOOD 37
beef tea b. down the noses   MEDICINE 30
been I've b. things and seen places   VIRTUE 19
beer b. to cry into   ALCOHOL 34
extra sixpence on b.   TAXES 4
I'm only a b. teetotaller   ALCOHOL 18
inseparable than B. and Britannia   ENGLAND 9
lamentations after beef and b.   COUNTRIES 3
to desire small b.   ALCOHOL 2
beers parts other b. cannot reach   ALCOHOL 72
Beethoven Anything but B.   CINEMA 62
What do you think of B.   MUSIC 66
where is B.   MUSIC 42
With Spohr and B.   MUSIC 18
would like to thank B.   MUSIC 47
before Broad b. and broad behind   RELIGION 56
begin B. at the beginning   ROYALTY 32
should b. at home   CENSORSHIP 23
beginning b. are tasteless   BEHAVIOUR 35
Movies should have a b.   CINEMA 69
begins Church of England b.   ENGLAND 39
begot were about when they b.   PARENTS 1
behave difficult to b. like gentlemen   WOMEN 40
behaving b. in this extraordinary   THEATRE 42
behaviour b. not otherwise excusable
                                                   SPORTS 30
privileges for good b.   BIRDS 49
behind dusk with a light b.   WOMEN 20
moment it will be b. me   LETTERS 10
no more b. your scenes   THEATRE 5
She has no bosom and no b.   ENGLAND 26
travel broadens the b.   TRAVEL 24
walk b. the angels   ROYALTY 45
beige It's just my colour: it's b.   ARCHITECTURE 8
Beirut seen the traffic in B.   TRANSPORT 31
Belgrave Square May beat in B.   ARISTOCRACY 5
belief b. in the occurrence   RELIGION 48
b. they done the old woman   SICKNESS 6
believe Attempted to B. Matilda
                                                   TRUTH AND LIES 10
b. all you read   NEWS 16
b. almost anything provided   INTELLIGENCE 15
b. what isn't happening   SPORTS 88

don't b. in Mother Goose   GOD 20
I b. I am between *both*   ARGUMENT 6
I b. to *One does feel*   RELIGION 41
I cannot quite b. in God   RELIGION 85
If you b. that, you'll   PEOPLE 5
only he doesn't b. in God   GOD 45
believed b. of any man whatsoever   ALCOHOL 26
I should not be b.   MARRIAGE 15
believers As belonged to b. in Clough
                                                   EPITAPHS 12
bell sexton tolled the b.   DEATH 10
bellman B., perplexed   TRAVEL 4
belly cask, in his b.   ALCOHOL 1
belly-tension b. between a man   MARRIAGE 82
belong B. TO ANY CLUB   SOCIETY 26
belongs animal b. to you   NAMES 12
beloved B. friends   HANDWRITING 10
below belt without hitting b.   POLITICIANS 43
below-stairs If you bed people of b.   CLASS 38
belt b. without hitting below   POLITICIANS 43
belted I've b. you and flayed you
                                                   ARMED FORCES 11
bench fancied he was on the b.   LAW 5
benighted knighted without being b.   IRELAND 6
benign noise they make is b.   THEATRE 61
Benois B....If 'e come   DANCE 4
bent all as b. as hell   SPORTS 89
bereaved b. if snobbery died   HUMOUR 22
Berlin B. are doing very exciting   TOWNS 14
Berliner *Ich bin ein B.*   COUNTRIES 43
Berlitz B.-school   LANGUAGE 17
Bernard B. always had a few prayers
                                                   RELIGION 47
berth b. of a railway compartment
                                                   MARRIAGE 96
which happened in his b.   DEATH 10
best b. of us being unfit   DEATH 13
misery in the b. of things   HAPPINESS 15
Reagan for his b. friend   CINEMA 43
best-seller b. is the gilded tomb   BOOKS 23
betrayed He deserves to be b.   TRUST 5
To have b. two leaders   TRUST 8
better b. part of biography   BIOGRAPHY 15
B. than a play   ROYALTY 2
b. to be looked over   SATISFACTION 5
Gad! she'd b.   UNIVERSE 3
He is not b.   TELEGRAMS 3
I expected b. manners   BEHAVIOUR 19
if they had been any b.   LITERATURE 27
know b. as they grow older   CHILDREN 24
lot b. than we thought   SPORTS 113
music is b. than it sounds   MUSIC 26
there was nothing *b.*   FOOD 25
things I'd been b. without   LOVE 24

We get b. justice   COUNTRIES 27
when I'm bad, I'm b.   VIRTUE 20
who had any thing b.   WRITERS 5
You're a b. man than I am   ARMED FORCES 11
better-class b. people get it apparently
    MEDICINE 34
between I believe I am b. *both*   ARGUMENT 6
I would try to get b. them   SEX 17
There is something b. us   BODY 22
Beulah B., peel me a grape   FOOD 58
Bevan [B.] enjoys prophesying   POLITICIANS 53
beverage funeral parlour with a b.   SOCIETY 34
beware B. of men bearing flowers
    MEN AND WOMEN 78
B. of the Agapanthus   COUNTRY 17
bewildered bothered and b.   MEN AND WOMEN 40
bewitched B., bothered   MEN AND WOMEN 40
bible dagger in one hand and a B.
    POLITICIANS 65
bicycle king rides a b.   COUNTRIES 53
like a fish without a b.   WOMEN 84
Salisbury Plain on a b.   TRAVEL 6
so is a b. repair kit   MARRIAGE 135
bicycles half people and half b.   TRANSPORT 26
bicyclists illuminated trouser-clip for b.
    SCIENCE 16
biennials b. are the ones that die   GARDENS 8
big he's pulling out the b. one   SPORTS 80
he was too b. for them   POLITICIANS 45
Hey! b. spender   MEN AND WOMEN 57
I am b. It's the pictures   CINEMA 26
bigamy And b., Sir, is a crime   MARRIAGE 64
B. is having one husband   MARRIAGE 130
maximum punishment for b.   MARRIAGE 61
big game Biography, like b. hunting
    BIOGRAPHY 11
bigger b. they are, the further   SPORTS 10
girls get b. every day   WOMEN 58
biggest b. industrial corporation   BUSINESS 3
bighead B.   COMEDY 22
bike Mind my b.   COMEDY 3
bikers one-word nickname for b.   MEDICINE 39
bill Someone had to pay the b.   PUBLISHING 24
billboard b. lovely as a tree   ADVERTISING 3
bills I have the b. to prove   MEN AND WOMEN 68
two things about b.   DEBT 8
Billy B., in one of his nice   DEATH 22
Bind B.-their-kings-in-chains-   NAMES 4
biographers love passes the love of b.
    BIOGRAPHY 3
biographical b. friend who has added
    BIOGRAPHY 4
biographies always liked reading b.
    BIOGRAPHY 33

biography B. is about Chaps   BIOGRAPHY 6
B., like big game hunting   BIOGRAPHY 11
B. should be written   BIOGRAPHY 12
first b. of Tennyson   BIOGRAPHY 40
Judas who writes the b.   BIOGRAPHY 5
no b. of Matthew Arnold   BIOGRAPHY 16
not the better part of b.   BIOGRAPHY 15
birch bringing back the b.   SEX 72
bird b. does not leave the nest   FASHION 19
Birdie lady whose name is B.   LETTERS 9
birds b. coughing in the trees   NATURE 11
b., wild flowers   POLITICS 28
one's eye for the high b.   POLITICIANS 28
very merciful to the b.   ARISTOCRACY 10
Birkenhead B. is very clever   INSULTS 31
Birmingham no great hopes from B.   TOWNS 3
birth at the b. of his child   SEX 49
b. of each child you lose   CHILDREN 43
birth control b. is flagrantly middle-class
    CLASS 26
she had not thought of b.   INSULTS 59
woman's craving for b.   PEOPLE 59
birthday afternoon of my eighty-first b.   SEX 87
biscuit people who cared for it   SEX 24
bisexuality On b.: It immediately doubles
    SEX 76
bishop b. with a moustache   PROGRESS 11
How can a b. marry   SEX 12
make a b. kick a hole   WOMEN 48
meekness stopping a b.   RELIGION 91
of the B., elect   RELIGION 77
bishopric talk of *merit* for a b.   RELIGION 19
Bishops B. [in the House   RELIGION 100
sotto voce to the B.   LAW 77
too many of its b.   RELIGION 104
bit b. in the corner   LIFE 14
bitch he's our son of a b.   POLITICIANS 31
bite *b.* some of my other generals
    ARMED FORCES 2
To b. his pen, and drop a tear   EPITAPHS 4
biting b. the hand that lays   CINEMA 13
I'm b. my knuckles   CINEMA 41
bits swallowed their b.   BIRDS 41
bitten b. in half by a shark   CHOICE 10
bitterness b. of life   BIRDS 12
Bizet I like Chopin and B.   MONEY 12
black Any colour—so long as it's b.
    TRANSPORT 17
articulate the b. athlete   SPORTS 75
bit of b. mackintosh   FOOD 56
b. blood makes a man coloured   PREJUDICE 7
study of mankind is *b.* man   PREJUDICE 12
unexpectedly turned b.   ACTORS 19
wear b. all the time   HAPPINESS 7

book adversary had written a b.	BOOKS 1	Have you read any good b.	COMEDY 11
any b. but the Baronetage	SNOBBERY 1	his b. were read	DEATH 34
because a b. is humorous	PUBLISHING 11	I hate b.; they only teach	BOOKS 2
b. about the Crusades	BOOKS 30	lot of b. in their houses	BOOKS 33
b.-buying public would regret	WRITERS 68	membership in the Great B. Club	
b. by a committee	BOOKS 40		INTELLIGENCE 17
b. flying a bullet	CRIME 19	my b. had been any worse	LITERATURE 27
b. in praise of parentage	CENSORSHIP 2	My only b.	WOMEN 14
b. of Job last night	BIBLE 6	No furniture so charming as b.	BOOKS 6
B. of Life begins	BIBLE 2	no point in writing b.	BOOKS 34
b. of my enemy has been	WRITERS 67	oddity of Oxford b.	PUBLISHING 25
B. of the Month choice	BOOKS 22	provided with no b.	BOOKS 31
b. that furnishes no quotations	QUOTATIONS 3	regular supply of b.	LIFE 7
b. which people praise	BOOKS 11	showed me his b.	LIBRARIES 5
b. with no alcohol	BOOKS 43	their b. in their room	WRITERS 76
b. would have been finished	FAMILY 24	unindexed b. with indexes	WORK 9
depraved by the b.	CENSORSHIP 20	world doesn't read its b.	BOOKS 26
get a lawyer—not a b.	LAW 70	writing b. about living men	BIOGRAPHY 17
I did so enjoy your b.	BIOGRAPHY 19	**bookseller** he once shot a b.	PUBLISHING 2
just cause for b. publication	BOOKS 39	**book-sharks** borrowers and b.	BOOKS 32
knocks me out is a b.	BOOKS 29	**bootboy** b. at Claridges	CRITICS 22
knows this out of the b.	EDUCATION 4	**bootlace** trip over a loose b.	WRITERS 36
like a b. in breeches	PEOPLE 4	**Boots** Books from B.'	ENGLAND 30
losing a b. from Bodley	LIBRARIES 4	**boots** Aristocrat who cleans the b.	CLASS 7
mentioning a single b.	LITERATURE 29	carries his heart in his b.	COUNTRY 7
moment I picked up your b.	LITERATURE 18	doormat in a world of b.	SELF-KNOWLEDGE 19
new b. on the lively arts	BOOKS 45	engine in b.	SPORTS 59
not a b. for the pundit	BOOKS 48	gentleman: look at his b.	CLASS 13
on which a b. is depicted	FASHION 27	legs when I take my b. off	BODY 7
read a b. before reviewing it	CRITICS 7	school without any b.	POLITICIANS 45
read one b. in my life	LITERATURE 28	top of his b.	ARMED FORCES 18
read the b. It's shorter	CRITICS 30	**booze** with b. until he's fifty	ALCOHOL 58
she'd rather read a b.	DANCE 6	**boozes** man who "b."	ALCOHOL 33
take the b. along with them	BOOKS 3	**bop** 'B.' is like scrabble	MUSIC 46
thick, square b.	ROYALTY 20	**bordello** doorkeeper of a b.	MUSIC 49
to publish it in b. form	BODY 19	**bore** be in it is merely a b.	SOCIETY 3
until he has written a b.	BOOKS 9	b. is a man who	BORES 5
What is the use of a b.	LITERATURE 6	b. is simply a nonentity	BORES 14
you only advertise a b.	PUBLISHING 15	b. you to sleep	BORES 13
bookmaker b. who takes actresses	SPORTS 54	capacity of human beings to b.	BORES 15
bookmaking increasing the tax on b.	BETTING 8	He is an old b.	BORES 9
bookmark thin end of the b.	LIBRARIES 11	not to b. yourself	BORES 19
Book of Kells Henry Ford produce the B.		proof that God is a b.	GOD 26
	BUSINESS 7	**bored** b. for England	BORES 16
books anti-feminist b. to review	NEWS 11	I'd get b. and fall over	SPORTS 120
b. [are] by his bed	PEOPLE 29	never in my life been b.	BORES 20
B. are well written	BOOKS 8	one gets so b. with good wine	ALCOHOL 15
B. from Boots'	ENGLAND 30	silent and indefinitely b.	SOCIETY 9
b. were written	BOOKS 14	**boredom** b. occasioned by too much	BORES 10
b. you don't read	BOOKS 49	b. threshold is low	BORES 18
cream of others' b.	QUOTATIONS 1	**bores** logical destiny of b.	BORES 22
do *you* read b. *through*	BOOKS 4	**Borgias** last night with the B.	SOCIETY 13
exist. In b. By men	MEN AND WOMEN 62	**boring** being a b. kind of guy	BORES 21
has written all the b.	GOD 7	Somebody's b. me	BORES 12

born b. an Englishman and remained

ENGLAND 37

b. in a cellar — CLASS 2
b. in Australia — COUNTRIES 15
b. sneering — ARISTOCRACY 8
b. with your legs apart — SEX 59
future refusing to be b. — FUTURE 10
man is b. in a stable — IRELAND 1
Never was b. — FAMILY 8
person b. who is so unlucky — MISTAKES 15
some men are b. great — PRIDE 1
That's b. into the world alive — POLITICS 16
borrow b. his body — BODY 31
b. the money to do it — HAPPINESS 3
didn't b. the words — DICTIONARIES 10
know well enough to b. from — FRIENDS 11
borrowers b. and book-sharks — BOOKS 32
borrows b. a detective story — BOOKS 26
Borstal it may have been B. — EDUCATION 45
bosom glimpsed the female b. — BODY 19
She has no b. and no behind — ENGLAND 26
understandably heaving b. — SPORTS 79
bosoms b. of your actresses excite — THEATRE 5
boss By the b. — THEATRE 29
bossy It's a *very* b. car — TRANSPORT 30
Boston And this is good old B. — AMERICA 7
B. social zones — CLASS 19
I met him in B. — AMERICA 25
botanist these particles I'd be a b. — SCIENCE 26
botanists b. divide up flowers — SCIENCE 38
botch I am a sundial, and I make a b. — TIME 5
bother B. it — LANGUAGE 6
b. with that in our work — SCIENCE 19
I never b. with people I hate — BEHAVIOUR 22
no time to b. — LETTERS 14
bothered b. and bewildered — MEN AND WOMEN 40
Botticelli B.'s a *cheese* — FOOD 30
B. were alive today — FASHION 20
bottle b. just going to sit — HOME 22
b. on the chimley-piece — ALCOHOL 13
cat to sit on the b. — ALCOHOL 77
great desire to a b. of hay — FOOD 2
little for the b. — LOVE 8
One green b. — NATURE 14
shake The catsup b. — FOOD 95
bottles English have hot-water b. — SEX 29
bottom But if, baby, I'm the b.

MEN AND WOMEN 32

Undesired on my tired little b. — WOMEN 41
Which will reach the b. first — CHILDREN 13
bottomless smoke of the pit that is b. — SICKNESS 1
Boule Little sticks of B. — ART AND ARTISTS 19
boundaries surrounded on all sides by b.

COUNTRIES 42

bounded Hollywood is b. on the north

CINEMA 53

bouquet b. is better than the taste — ALCOHOL 49
bourbon Wheaties with B. — ALCOHOL 74
Bovril made into B. when she dies — INSULTS 30
she does her hair with B. — FRIENDS 16
bow b., ye tradesmen — CLASS 6
bowel very lower b. of music — MUSIC 76
bowl b. with atrabilious — COUNTRIES 18
not to see you b. — SPORTS 14
bow-windows putting b. to the house — HOPE 3
bow-wows gone to the demnition b. — MISTAKES 4
box jerking b. of steel and glass — TOWNS 12
pianoforte is a harp in a b. — MUSIC 7
boxcar locked in a rolling b. — POLITICIANS 64
boxing B. is show-business — SPORTS 17
boy FEEL LIKE A B. AGAIN — TELEGRAMS 16
fifteen-year-old b. — PARENTS 8
mad about the b. — CINEMA 4
misfortunes can befall a b. — FAMILY 20
no longer a b. — CHARACTER 4
roughly to your little b. — CHILDREN 7
used to be a good b. — PAST 1
boys b. something else to kick — SPORTS 70
By office boys for office b. — NEWS 10
liked little b. too little — EDUCATION 37
Mealy b., and beef-faced — CHILDREN 5
braces liquid which rots b. — SCIENCE 18
brain around with b. surgeons — NEWS 44
Bear of Very Little B. — BIRDS 26
b. like Swiss cheese — CINEMA 38
b. of feathers — INSULTS 4
b. some rising young interior decorator

ART AND ARTISTS 15

electric b. can do it — BOOKS 34
harmful to the b. — SICKNESS 1
his b. and his expression — HUMOUR 34
If I only had a b. — INTELLIGENCE 10
leave that b. outside — POLITICS 17
My b.? It's my second favourite — BODY 25
brains b. are in the right place — DESCRIPTION 5
feet instead of their b. — MUSIC 31
inherits my body and your b.

MEN AND WOMEN 41

intelligence and no b. — CHARACTER 14
sometimes his b. go to his head — INSULTS 31
brakes b. or a steering wheel — TRANSPORT 28
brandy b. of the damned — MUSIC 22
must drink b. — ALCOHOL 9
pray get me a glass of b. — ROYALTY 18
brass b. plate on your door — HOME 7
braw b. bricht moonlicht nicht — ALCOHOL 23
Bray Vicar of B. — POLITICIANS 2

buttocks chair that fits all b.   CHARACTER 1
button Push de b.   PROGRESS 10
  you that the nuclear b.   SPORTS 90
buttresses insufficient flying b.   INSULTS 48
butty He's an oul' b. o' mine   MEN 10
buy b. all his furniture   SNOBBERY 19
  b. back my introduction   COMEDY 2
  b. it like an honest man   WEALTH 8
  consumerism is never to b.   BUSINESS 16
buying dinner only if he's b.   CHILDREN 35
by B. and by   EPITAPHS 17
Byron B.!—he would be all forgotten   PEOPLE 9
  movement needs a B.   POETRY 26
Byronic think all poets were B.   POETRY 42
Byzantium all her shopping in B.   THEATRE 9

cab Get me a c.   TRANSPORT 15
  theatre in a hired c.   PRIDE 10
cabaret Life is a C.   LIFE 15
cabbage c. with a college education   FOOD 29
Cabinet another to mislead the C.   POLITICS 30
  C. ministers are educated   LITERATURE 15
  getting into the C.   POLITICS 51
cabman position of a c.   LAW 28
Cabots Lowells talk to the C.   AMERICA 7
caddy make a play for the c.   SPORTS 35
Cadogan One-eighty-nine C. Square
                                             ENGLAND 30
cads second division are c.   CLASS 23
Cadwallader C. and all his goats   WALES 2
Caesars worship the C. and Napoleons
                                             POWER 4
cage natural to us than a c.   HOME 11
cake peel picked out of a c.   QUOTATIONS 10
  steak and a layer c.   FOOD 73
cakes no more c. and ale   MORALITY 1
calamities C. are of two kinds   MISTAKES 9
calamity extent of the individual c.   MISTAKES 2
  Oh, c.   COMEDY 16
  would be a c.   MISTAKES 5
calculating desiccated c. machine
                                             POLITICIANS 56
calculators child straight on to c.   EDUCATION 48
calculus integral and differential c.
                                             ARMED FORCES 10
calendar trick played on the c.   DEATH 74
calf c. to share the enthusiasm   RELIGION 36
  lion and the c. shall   BIRDS 50
  worshipped the Golden C.   MONEY 8
California C. is a fine place to live   AMERICA 19
Californication C. of Ireland   CENSORSHIP 12
call C. Me God   GOVERNMENT 38
  Let's c. the whole thing off   FOOD 61

May I c. you 338   LETTERS 12
Will you c. me, Noël   ACTORS 57
you can c. Paul Keating   INSULTS 62
called Dick and Harry is c. Arthur   NAMES 10
callous c.   ROYALTY 50
calls c. were made   SUCCESS 30
  If anybody c.   ARCHITECTURE 2
  took her curtain c.   ACTORS 53
calmest c. and most rewarding hours
                                             TRANSPORT 27
calumny history of human c.   HUMAN RACE 13
calves susceptible to c.   MEN AND WOMEN 26
Calvin broken the heart of John C.   FASHION 12
  that land of C.   SCOTLAND 4
Cambridge C. was the first stopping   PLACES 16
  For C. people rarely smile   PLACES 5
  When I was at C. it was   TRUST 18
camel c. has a single hump   BIRDS 32
  c. is a horse designed   BUSINESS 13
  If you come on a c.   COUNTRIES 40
  Take my c.   TRANSPORT 21
camelopardalis killed a c.   BIRDS 3
campaigning years organizing and c.   POWER 7
Campbell breaks the C.'s back   NAMES 7
can C. I do you now, sir   COMEDY 5
  guy says the horse c. do   BETTING 6
  He who c., does   EDUCATION 10
  I c. do that   AMERICA 39
  think you c.   FUTURE 4
Canada C. as a country torn   COUNTRIES 60
  C. keeps up the appeal   COUNTRIES 27
  C., Our Good Neighbour   PUBLISHING 26
Canadian little time left to be C.   COUNTRIES 50
Canadians C. are Americans with no
                                             COUNTRIES 58
Canaletto stare at C.   ART AND ARTISTS 29
Canalettos Then the C. go   POLITICS 81
canaries C., caged in the house, do it   BIRDS 25
can-can Baby, you can c. too   DANCE 9
cancer C. can be rather fun   SICKNESS 17
candidate c. talking to a rich person   POLITICS 71
  when a c. can promise   UNIVERSE 11
candidates when c. appeal   POLITICS 36
candle c. in that great turnip   POLITICIANS 46
  I care not a farthing c.   MUSIC 5
candy C. Is dandy   ALCOHOL 32
canned American c. food   FOOD 69
cannibal Said the c. as he cut   FOOD 86
cannibalism C. went right out   FOOD 69
  Like c., a matter of taste   FOOD 60
cannibals c. in the country   POLITICIANS 44
cannon-ball c. took off his legs   ARMED FORCES 6

cant c. of criticism   HYPOCRISY 1
Canterbury unexpected vacancy at C.
                                        RELIGION 62
canting canted in this c. world   HYPOCRISY 1
cap Housman's c.   DESCRIPTION 8
capable c. of higher things   LITERATURE 21
c. of reigning if only   POWER 1
capacity c. must be shown   LAW 23
caparisons No c., Miss   WIT 14
cape Risorgimento c. of hers   APPEARANCE 14
capital c. is always timid   NEWS 34
c. outlays were involved   POVERTY 22
capitalism definition of c.   AMERICA 38
War is c. with the gloves   WAR 31
capitalist emerging from a c. institution
                                         WRITERS 28
captain by the team c.   TRUST 16
there's nobody like the C.   NEWS 4
captured like winning, being c.   WAR 29
car afford to keep a motor c.   ENGLAND 22
It's a *very bossy* c.   TRANSPORT 30
motor c. to the human race   TRANSPORT 12
caravan stationary c. at Cleethorpes
                                         HAPPINESS 18
carbuncle monstrous c.   ARCHITECTURE 11
carcases And our c.   BODY 5
carcinoma To sing of rectal c.   SICKNESS 16
card c. to play for Honours   LITERATURE 15
cards send funny greetings c.   CHRISTMAS 8
care c. where the water goes   ALCOHOL 25
I c. for nobody   SATISFACTION 1
I find that I c. less and less   OLD AGE 22
Take c. of him   MARRIAGE 116
taken better c. of myself   OLD AGE 35
women and c. and trouble   WOMEN 4
career Good c. move   DEATH 75
loyal to his own c.   PEOPLE 24
careful c. in the choice   FRIENDS 6
c. in the immediate future   TRANSPORT 10
carelessness lose both looks like c. FAMILY 19
With carefullest c.   SPORTS 48
Caribbean Columbus discovered C.   TRAVEL 25
caricature With a c. of a face   OLD AGE 9
Carlyle very good of God to let C.   MARRIAGE 55
carnation We all wear a green c.   MEN 11
Carnegie wisecrack that played C.   WIT 40
Carnera C. hadn't stunted his growth BODY 13
car park c. till twenty to one
                                         MEN AND WOMEN 43
carpentry whether Jesus did odd c.   RELIGION 92
carpeting c. he treats me like underlay
                                         MEN AND WOMEN 76
carpets Instead of fitted c.   MONEY 12

carriage very small second class c. TRANSPORT 3
carrots c. are acceptable as food   FOOD 96
carry can't make your children c.   BUSINESS 16
cars reduce the speed of motor c.
                                         GOVERNMENT 22
they're crazy about c.   TRANSPORT 18
wild beasts, and motor c.   TRANSPORT 13
cart-horse like a damned old c.   MUSIC 39
cartographers c. seek to define   SCOTLAND 11
Cary OLD C. GRANT FINE   TELEGRAMS 23
Casanova would like to be, a C.   MEN 12
case civil servant a good c.   BUREAUCRACY 16
heard one side of the c.   GOD 7
In c. it is one of mine   PARENTS 6
working on a c. of Scotch   ALCOHOL 30
cases only two types of c.   MEDICINE 31
cash C. grew on trees   PAST 17
C. that goes therewith   HYPOCRISY 7
she needs good c.   MIDDLE AGE 8
cask c., in his belly   ALCOHOL 1
cassock C., band, and hymn-book   BIRDS 7
cassowary If I were a c.   BIRDS 7
cast c. the first rock   MEN AND WOMEN 23
everyone else in the c.   ACTORS 50
see the movie! Eat the c.   FOOD 122
What a c.   WAR 22
Castlereagh mask like C.   MURDER 1
castrati reviving the *c.*   MUSIC 45
castration c. of sex offenders   CENSORSHIP 15
casuistry C. has got a bad name   ARGUMENT 17
cat bowels of the c.   HYPOCRISY 2
c. detained briefly   PEOPLE 61
c. hung up by its tail   MUSIC 9
c. to sit on the bottle   ALCOHOL 77
endow a college, or a c.   DEATH 3
I never do swing a c.   HOME 6
intestines of the agile c.   MUSIC 15
part to tear a c. in   ACTORS 1
room enough to swing a c.   POVERTY 3
terrible account of your c.   BIRDS 45
catalogue carefully through the c.   BOOKS 12
catamite I was in bed with my c.   SEX 87
catamount c. is nonplussed   BIRDS 42
catapult only time I fired a c.   CRIME 29
catastrophe between education and c.
                                         HISTORY 6
c. is still there   GOVERNMENT 50
I'll tickle your c.   WIT 3
catch c. diseases but at least   BIRDS 56
something you can c.   BODY 32
Catch-22 as good as C.   CRITICS 45
one catch and that was C.   MIND 8
catching Come away; poverty's c.   POVERTY 2

She was an aggravating c.   CHILDREN 19
whimpering c. again   MEN AND WOMEN 40
With the birth of each c.   CHILDREN 43
your c. for the future   EDUCATION 49
childbirth Death and taxes and c.   DEATH 40
childhood C. is Last Chance Gulch   CHILDREN 32
what my lousy c. was like   BIOGRAPHY 22
childminder certainly underpaid as a c.
    EDUCATION 54
children be very good with c.   INSULTS 53
bored by c.   BORES 18
breeds contempt—and c.   FAMILY 21
can't make your c. carry   BUSINESS 16
C. always assume the sexual   CHILDREN 31
C. and zip fasteners do   POWER 6
c. are a bitter disappointment   CHILDREN 10
C. are given us to discourage   CHILDREN 16
C. begin by loving   CHILDREN 11
C. can be awe-inspiringly   CHILDREN 33
C. from the age of five   FAMILY 53
C. must be considered   MARRIAGE 141
c. must be extra polite   BEHAVIOUR 16
C. of the Ritz   SOCIETY 17
c. only scream in a low voice   CHILDREN 3
C. with Hyacinth's temperament   CHILDREN 24
C. you destroy together   MARRIAGE 123
discussing sex with small c.   CHILDREN 36
Everybody knows how to raise c.   FAMILY 54
first class, and with c.   TRAVEL 10
interest of the c.   FAMILY 32
Myself and c. three   FAMILY 4
parents obey their c.   AMERICA 30
sleepless c.'s hearts are glad   CHRISTMAS 5
talks about her own c.   WRITERS 8
taught to our defenceless c.   EDUCATION 27
teach their c. how to speak   LANGUAGE 35
telling you I liked c.   CHILDREN 2
There are six evacuated c.   CHRISTMAS 3
till the c. are settled   LOVE 43
Too many are like c.   PUBLISHING 12
we would love c. just   CHILDREN 38
women and c. could work   WORK 10
Chile earthquake in C.   NEWS 35
chilly although the room grows c.   DEATH 22
chimney port is on the c.   SEX 15
SIXTY HORSES WEDGED IN C.   NEWS 39
chimpanzee vase in the hands of a c.
    WRITERS 41
chin he had a c.   APPEARANCE 3
China On a slow boat to C.   COUNTRIES 31
story laid in C.   MUSIC 34
where C. was   TRAVEL 25
Chinese C. dinner at six   FOOD 63
C. wouldn't dare   ENGLAND 23

chinks fill hup the c. wi' cheese   FOOD 22
chintzy Chintzy, C. cheeriness   SOCIETY 15
chip c. of the old block   POLITICIANS 3
chipolata dozen acorns and a c.   BODY 23
chippy cheap and c. chopper   CRIME 9
chocolate appendage to any c. shop   ROYALTY 63
c. cream soldier   ARMED FORCES 14
It's called c.   FOOD 116
choice c. between the lesser   CHOICE 7
measure and the c.   CHOICE 1
choose c. between these persons   GOVERNMENT 18
hardly expect to pick and c.   MARRIAGE 73
choosers buggers can't be c.   SEX 63
chop c. your poppa up   MURDER 8
when we c. a tree   NATURE 3
Chopin between Dorothy and C.   MUSIC 37
I like C. and Bizet   MONEY 12
chopper c. on a big black block   CRIME 9
chorus knees of the c. girls   THEATRE 57
chosen English are of course the c.   ENGLAND 17
Christ author as C. or Faust   BOOKS 13
C. crucified Pontius Pilate   POLITICIANS 19
Christian tiger that hadn't *got* a C.   BIRDS 8
Christianity C. never got any grip   RELIGION 40
mind the delusions of C.   RELIGION 16
very big factor in C.   RELIGION 95
Christians C. have burnt each other
    RELIGION 18
Christmas C. begins about the first   CHRISTMAS 7
C.-morning bells say   CHRISTMAS 5
C. should fall out   CHRISTMAS 1
C., that time of year when   CHRISTMAS 10
I'm walking backwards for C.   CHRISTMAS 6
Merry C. to all my friends   CHRISTMAS 4
sent me the insulting C. card   CHRISTMAS 2
something from them for C.   CHRISTMAS 3
chuck C. it, Smith   HYPOCRISY 7
chum front-page news or Thor's c.   BIRDS 31
chumps C. always make the best   MARRIAGE 75
so many seem rather c.   RELIGION 71
chundered c. in the old Pacific sea   ALCOHOL 62
church bit like the c.   MEDICINE 33
Broad of C.   RELIGION 56
C.'s Restoration   RELIGION 57
get me to the c. on time   MARRIAGE 109
get out of the c. lightly   ROYALTY 1
he goes to c. as he goes   RELIGION 82
mere c. furniture at best   RELIGION 11
One is a c. to God   ARCHITECTURE 5
ought never to go to c.   ARMED FORCES 17
Churchill C. from John of Marlborough
    ARISTOCRACY 7
Randolph C. went into hospital   MEDICINE 26

churchman As for the British c. RELIGION 82
Modern C. RELIGION 53
Church of England Best Buy—C. RELIGION 81
crisis of the C. RELIGION 104
dangers which beset the C. RELIGION 74
ends and the C. begins ENGLAND 39
churchyards gloomy c. DESCRIPTION 15
chutzpa C. is that quality enshrined FAMILY 45
cigarette c. is the perfect type HAPPINESS 5
Cinderella C. and her ugly FAMILY 51
cinema attendance at the c. LANGUAGE 21
cinemas On the screens at c. CINEMA 1
circulation assists the c. of their blood
GENERATION GAP 4
circumcision breast-feeding, c. CHILDREN 29
circumlocution C. Office was beforehand
BUREAUCRACY 1
circumstance Victimized by bitter, bitter c.
WOMEN 57
circumstantial c. evidence is very strong
LAW 10
circus celebrated Barnum's c. POLITICIANS 26
cistern Cold the seat and loud the c.
OLD AGE 40
cities other great modern c. TOWNS 16
shape of our c. TRANSPORT 23
city c. with no more personality TOWNS 9
enough to stay in the c. COUNTRY 14
good old-fashioned C. gent WEALTH 31
Up and down the C. Road POVERTY 7
civil Always be c. to the girls WOMEN 55
good people, be c. RELIGION 4
civilities groundless c. BEHAVIOUR 3
civilization can't say c. don't advance
PROGRESS 5
Is this C.? I'm only thankful PROGRESS 12
menace to c. PROGRESS 7
not even the veneer of c. HOME 29
civilizations We used to build c. HUMAN RACE 17
civilized c. man has built a coach PROGRESS 1
ever become genuinely c. SCOTLAND 10
civil servant c. doesn't make jokes
BUREAUCRACY 8
Give a c. a good case BUREAUCRACY 16
Here lies a c. He was civil BUREAUCRACY 11
civil servants about c. written by a rabbit
BOOKS 42
c. are human beings BUREAUCRACY 12
C. by the clock do it SEX 30
civil service c. has finished drafting
BUREAUCRACY 5
claiming c. to be Major Brabazon-Plank
ARGUMENT 16

clap Don't c. too hard THEATRE 34
clappers he moves like the c. INSULTS 54
claret C. is the liquor for boys ALCOHOL 9
Claridges body of the bootboy at C. CRITICS 22
clarinet Gentlemen in the c. department
MUSIC 32
Clark C. isn't here to see it PROGRESS 12
class better c. of enemy FRIENDS 22
Britain is a c.-ridden CLASS 36
c. distinction between APPEARANCE 17
C. War Correspondent PEOPLE 8
Digitals have got no c. SCIENCE 40
free of c. distinctions CLASS 22
free passes, c. distinction ENGLAND 30
Infants' Bible C. EDUCATION 30
classes better c. are born concussed CLASS 27
Clashing of C. POLITICS 67
c. which need sanctuary POLITICS 28
divisible into two great c. CLASS 15
classic 'C' A book BOOKS 11
'c.' is a synonym LITERATURE 37
C. music is th'kind MUSIC 25
classical At c. Monday Pops MUSIC 18
classroom c. cool and slow EDUCATION 34
clatter c. of Sir James Barrie's LITERATURE 16
Claude After you, C. COMEDY 4
clauses c. all embedded CONVERSATION 31
claws panes of glass with its c. MUSIC 9
clean c., verb active EDUCATION 4
I like things c. PARENTS 7
one more thing to keep c. RELIGION 70
which engine-drivers c. DESCRIPTION 8
cleaned c. the windows LAW 17
Cleethorpes stationary caravan at C.
HAPPINESS 18
Cleopatra Nile last night as C. ACTORS 25
clergy c. were more intellectual RELIGION 71
clergyman c. who was trying to look SEX 69
salary of a beneficed c. RELIGION 53
take a reference from a c. TRUST 10
clergymen women, and c. RELIGION 21
clerk c. Who is thrown THEATRE 29
clever c. men at Oxford EDUCATION 11
I'm so terribly c. CRITICS 42
provided he is c. enough INTELLIGENCE 15
Some parts were c. DICTIONARIES 3
cleverness C. is a quality INTELLIGENCE 9
cliché c. and an indiscretion DIPLOMACY 8
c.-avoidance BROADCASTING 14
used every c. except POLITICIANS 35
clichés he'll wreck it with c. BUREAUCRACY 16
Let's have some new c. CINEMA 58
cliff Drive off that c. GOVERNMENT 32

climax end a sentence with a c.   SPEECHES 2
    works its way up to a c.   CINEMA 60
Clive What I like about C.   DEATH 28
clock after my dining room c.   BROADCASTING 2
close c. your eyes before you   SEX 83
    ON ICE TILL C. OF PLAY   TELEGRAMS 4
closed Philadelphia, but it was c.   AMERICA 21
closes Satire is what c. Saturday   THEATRE 38
clothes C. by a man who doesn't   FASHION 17
    gollywog and his c.   APPEARANCE 6
    had no c.   FASHION 15
    not quite enough c.   FASHION 6
    poured into his c.   DESCRIPTION 13
    She wears her c., as if   FASHION 2
    take off my c. and dance   SEX 74
    walked away with their c.   POLITICIANS 6
clothing sheep in sheep's c.   INSULTS 43
    Weird c. is *de rigueur*   YOUTH 13
    you know why c. exists   CHILDREN 42
cloud c. looking for someone   WEATHER 22
clouds I've found more c. of grey   LOVE 20
Clough poor poet named C.   EPITAPHS 12
cloven out pops the c. hoof   FAMILY 31
club ANY C. THAT WILL ACCEPT   SOCIETY 26
    c. except the Garrick   SEX 101
    most exclusive c.   ENGLAND 27
    say this place is a c.   INSULTS 26
CMG rise from C.   GOVERNMENT 38
coach civilized man has built a c.   PROGRESS 1
coach and six indifference and a c.   HOME 2
coachman c.'s a privileged individual
                                        MEN AND WOMEN 6
coal c. and surrounded by fish   BUREAUCRACY 3
coals no more c. to Newcastle   ROYALTY 53
coarse In a c., rather Corsican way
                                        MARRIAGE 98
    one of them is rather c.   BIRDS 27
coast East C. of Ireland   WEATHER 7
coat hung on to his c. tails   PARENTS 3
coca c. bushes   PAST 17
cocaine C. habit-forming   LIFE 11
cock C. and a Bull   CONVERSATION 3
cockatoo cage is natural to a c.   HOME 11
Cocklecarrot C. began the hearing   LAW 49
cockroaches C. have been given a bad
                                        HOME 27
cocksure c. of anything as Tom Macaulay
                                        CERTAINTY 2
    c. of many things   CERTAINTY 8
cocktail c. parties of the geriatric   DEATH 73
    want to go to a c. party   SOCIETY 33
cocoa C. is a vulgar beast   FOOD 41
    nice cup of c. really   CINEMA 3

cocotte busted, disgusted c.   WOMEN 41
cod bean and the c.   AMERICA 7
code obey the country c.   COUNTRY 18
codfish like an embattled c.   DESCRIPTION 18
coffee c. than make their programmes
                                        BROADCASTING 22
    if this is c., I want   FOOD 34
    nail each other to c. tables   MEN AND WOMEN 77
    put poison in your c.   INSULTS 34
coffer Sow and close her in a c.   BIRDS 1
coffin becomes his c.   DEATH 5
    grave in a Y-shaped c.   SEX 59
    Like the silver plate on a c.   DESCRIPTION 2
coins on the c. of the country   GOD 9
    Our c. still read   ECONOMICS 8
cold baby it's c. outside   WEATHER 16
    because my bath is c.   MEDICINE 14
    c. as yesterday's mashed   MEN AND WOMEN 34
    C. the seat and loud   OLD AGE 40
    mauve with c.   WEATHER 15
    person...can develop a c.   SICKNESS 12
    straight past the common c.   MEDICINE 32
Coleridge poet C.   BODY 15
Coliseum You're the C.   PRAISE 7
collaborated had ever c. on anything
                                        MARRIAGE 84
collapse institutions on the point of c.
                                        BUREAUCRACY 10
collarbone my silly old c.'s bust   SPORTS 56
colleague execution of a senior c.   POLITICS 83
collecting c. of first editions   VIRTUE 18
college cabbage with a c. education   FOOD 29
    C. with such fury   MARRIAGE 78
    endow a c., or a cat   DEATH 3
    other members of the C.   SNOBBERY 5
    second oldest c.   EDUCATION 32
    stupidity sent to c.   FOOLISHNESS 34
colonel C.'s Lady   WOMEN 26
colonies c. in your wife's name   WAR 16
colour Any c.—so long as it's black
                                        TRANSPORT 17
    effective c. schemes   MORALITY 14
    swear her c. is natural   SOCIETY 2
    There's been a c. clash   SPORTS 104
    unreceptive to c.   FASHION 25
coloured makes a man c.   PREJUDICE 7
colours nailing his c. to the fence   CERTAINTY 20
Columbus before you doubt C.   TRAVEL 13
    C. discovered Caribbean   TRAVEL 25
    laughed at Christopher C.   PROGRESS 6
    said C.   UNIVERSE 6
columnist temper at a newspaper c.   NEWS 58
columnists When the political c. say
                                        POLITICS 36

columns between the Doric c. ARCHITECTURE 10
coma c. without the worry BROADCASTING 17
state of resentful c. EDUCATION 16
come C., friendly bombs WAR 12
c. out long before MUSIC 19
c. out to the ball park SPORTS 106
c. up and see me SEX 22
I go—I c. back COMEDY 8
Oh, it needn't c. to that POETRY 14
they'll c. out DEATH 55
war and nobody will c. WAR 11
comedies Our c. are not to be laughed
CINEMA 49
comedy [C. is] the kindly contemplation
HUMOUR 30
C., like sodomy HUMOUR 29
c. tonight THEATRE 40
c. to those that think HUMAN RACE 1
important aspect of c. HUMOUR 38
most lamentable c. THEATRE 1
tragedy, c., history ACTORS 3
comes c. again in the morning SOCIETY 2
just as it c. SOCIETY 23
comfort not ecstasy but it was c. MARRIAGE 48
comfortable c. estate of widowhood
MARRIAGE 23
comfortably lived c. so long together
MARRIAGE 22
comforts recapture the c. TRAVEL 23
comic get c. with the cosmic UNIVERSE 12
comical I often think it's c. POLITICS 16
comma Whence came the intrusive c.
WRITERS 22
commander C. of the Bath ROYALTY 28
commandments first nine c. CINEMA 76
his teeth like the Ten C. PREJUDICE 5
release it as *The Five C.* CINEMA 33
satisfied with Ten C. POLITICIANS 16
ten c. in every stroke HANDWRITING 3
why there are only ten c. BIBLE 5
commences after it c. MUSIC 19
commendably speaking c. CONVERSATION 1
comment C. is free but facts NEWS 47
I couldn't possibly c. COMEDY 28
commentators As learned c. view CRITICS 2
commerce obstructed interstate c. SEX 64
commercial you're labelled c. MUSIC 69
commercialism [C. is] BUSINESS 9
commercials appearing in television c.
BIRDS 54
commit refusing to c. oneself BEHAVIOUR 13
committed c. breakfast with it VIRTUE 23
committee book by a c. BOOKS 40
c. discussions and decisions BUREAUCRACY 20

c.'s idea of what apples DESCRIPTION 29
horse designed by a c. BUSINESS 13
common c. where the climate's SEX 11
Horseguards and still be c. SOCIETY 25
man is a c. murderer FOOD 42
members of the c. throng ARISTOCRACY 4
commonplace loop the loop on a c. WIT 36
Commons C. must bray like an ass
ARISTOCRACY 14
common sense great c. and good taste PEOPLE 7
importance of things which c. LITERATURE 20
never ascribe c. to God GOD 23
Nothing but c. LAW 63
Use your c., avoid logic PEOPLE 18
who likes sports hates c. SPORTS 58
commotion she likes lights and c. SOCIETY 12
communication however, is c. CONVERSATION 28
Communist C. Manifesto in the Queen's
IDEAS 8
commuter C.—one who spends his life
TRAVEL 21
companion advertise for a holiday c.
HOLIDAYS 9
company by the c. he chooses ALCOHOL 33
C. of Four and the Audience THEATRE 23
in married life three is c. MARRIAGE 60
I play it the c. way BUSINESS 5
Punctual Delivery C. FOOD 19
steal out of your c. CRIME 1
comparisons C. are odorous WIT 5
compassion c. in the very name RELIGION 17
compensate c. people for the damage
LITERATURE 39
competition We have to fight home c.
HUMOUR 19
competitive c. spirit is an ethos EDUCATION 60
squash is a c. activity SPORTS 108
complain being in no position to c. NEWS 66
hardly knows to whom to c. UNIVERSE 4
complainings constant c. ARISTOCRACY 16
compliance by a timely c. SEX 6
compliment c. that can be paid THEATRE 55
pay a woman a c. today MEN AND WOMEN 63
they believe any c. automatically PRAISE 9
composer c. and *not* homosexual MUSIC 29
c. did not leave directions SONGS 2
c. is to be dead MUSIC 43
movie about a blind c. CINEMA 62
composers don't like c. who think MUSIC 75
compromise c. with being swallowed CHOICE 10
compulsion What c. compels them TRAVEL 17
computer c. hovers between SCIENCE 43
foul things up requires a c. SCIENCE 35

cripple c. of the worst sort — SICKNESS 19
c. without talking about — CONVERSATION 14
crisis cannot be a c. next week — DIPLOMACY 10
Party only panics in a c. — POLITICS 63
real c. on your hands — NATURE 9
critic c. is a man who knows — CRITICS 35
c. said that the author — CRITICS 26
c. spits on what is done — POETRY 12
cry of the c. for five — ART AND ARTISTS 4
man is a dramatic c. — CRITICS 25
set up in honour of a c. — CRITICS 28
critical c. period in matrimony — MARRIAGE 89
criticism cant of c. is the most — HYPOCRISY 1
c. as a good dutiful boy — CRITICS 6
C. is a study by which men — CRITICS 3
c. is ever inhibited by ignorance — POLITICS 59
C. is not only medicinally — CRITICS 13
criticize Never c. Americans — AMERICA 42
criticized c. is not always to be wrong
— SELF-KNOWLEDGE 14
have never c. your plays — CRITICS 12
critics Appreciation of Music Among C.
— CRITICS 23
become mass murderers or c.
— ART AND ARTISTS 36
C. are like eunuchs — CRITICS 34
C. search for ages — CRITICS 40
lot of c. is to be remembered — CRITICS 9
You know who the c. are — CRITICS 8
critique Non, je suis c. — CRITICS 41
crochet c. week in Rhyl — HOLIDAYS 8
crocodiles trap-door to the waiting c.
— HYPOCRISY 11
crook you told him he was a c. — CRIME 21
crooning c. like a bilious pigeon — LANGUAGE 13
cross adjective 'c.' — ANGER 5
C. as the focus of longing — RELIGION 86
rule of taste about c. dressing — FASHION 28
so dreadfully c. and what about — ANGER 7
un-nailed from the c. — ACTORS 53
cross-examination c. is not the art — LAW 52
cross-gartered to see thee ever c. — PRIDE 3
crossing double c. of a pair of heels — LOVE 27
crossroads mankind faces a c. — CHOICE 8
crotchet c. which deranges the whole
— GOVERNMENT 4
crow If I had the arse of a c. — SPORTS 100
crowd c. will never buy you lunch — PEOPLE 58
crowds C. have always frightened — THEATRE 61
crown c. of thorns and the thirty — POLITICS 45
c. was too big — ROYALTY 74
judging him to deserve a c. — ROYALTY 14
crown court except in a C. — CLASS 37

Croydon Chartreuse over South C. — NEWS 32
Crucifixion anticlimax after the C. — CINEMA 68
cruel more c. to animals — BIRDS 6
Such c. glasses — INSULTS 40
cruelty given up due to the c. — FOOD 118
crumpet Hot Muffin and C. — FOOD 19
thinking man's c. — WOMEN 82
Crusades book about the C. — BOOKS 30
crushed c. life is what I lead — MARRIAGE 110
crutch want to kick in the c. — ANGER 9
crutches their c. at the doctor — GOVERNMENT 25
cry beer to c. into — ALCOHOL 34
with a c. brief and dismal — DEATH 50
cryptogram charm of a c. — BIOGRAPHY 23
cuckoo c. clock — COUNTRIES 32
cucumber c. should be well sliced — FOOD 8
when c. is added to it — FOOD 52
cucumbers c. and the castration — CENSORSHIP 15
extracting sun-beams out of c. — SCIENCE 2
cuddlesome seeing nature as c. — NATURE 13
cuddly women as kissable, c.
— MEN AND WOMEN 79
culture c. could have produced — WRITERS 65
whole vast intuitive c. — COUNTRIES 48
who pursue C. in bands — ART AND ARTISTS 13
cultured wonder if they're real or c. — FAME 2
cunning I have a c. plan — COMEDY 27
curable Love's a disease. But c. — LOVE 18
curate average c. at home — RELIGION 49
c. made out of pink marzipan — APPEARANCE 7
c. who has strayed by mistake — SCIENCE 30
c. with eyes like rubies — FRIENDS 23
I was a pale young c. then — RELIGION 29
very name of a C. — RELIGION 17
curates preached to death by wild c.
— RELIGION 22
curb snaffle and the c. — LITERATURE 19
cure in the twentieth, it's a c. — SEX 70
no C. for this Disease — MEDICINE 8
They know the c. — SICKNESS 18
cured C. yesterday of my disease — MEDICINE 3
cures like c. like — BORES 8
No herb ever c. anything — MEDICINE 35
curiosity C. — HISTORY 16
c. about the future has — BIOGRAPHY 26
Love, c., freckles, and doubt — LOVE 24
curiouser C. and curiouser — WIT 27
curse c. of the drinking classes — WORK 6
gypsies have put a c. — SPORTS 76
journalistic c. of Eve — NEWS 11
curtail c. undue freedom of speech
— CENSORSHIP 18
curtain after the c. has risen — ROYALTY 23
c. was up — THEATRE 52

day (*cont.*)
D. will break   FOOD 49
Doris D. before she was a virgin   SEX 65
During the d.   MARRIAGE 115
people write every other d.   LETTERS 11
days Organization in five or six d.   POLITICS 37
daytime You know d. television

                                               BROADCASTING 16
dead all our best men are d.   LITERATURE 11
besides, the wench is d.   SEX 1
blooming well d.   DEATH 37
character d. at every word   GOSSIP 3
composer is to be d.   MUSIC 43
d. for the next two months   LETTERS 8
d. sinner revised and edited   VIRTUE 12
deal to be said For being d.   DEATH 28
dropping d. at the top   DEATH 39
Either he's d., or my watch   DEATH 45
healthy and wealthy and d.   DEATH 46
if I am d. he would like to see   DEATH 6
Lady Dalhousie are d.   DEATH 25
Lord Jones D.   NEWS 12
Ned Sherrin is d.   BROADCASTING 10
not divorced, but d.   MARRIAGE 37
Not many d.   NEWS 35
or himself must be d.   DEATH 9
pleasure we'd rather be d.   HOLIDAYS 2
regular readers were d.   NEWS 66
remembered that he is d.   SLEEP 11
rot the d. talk   DEATH 41
servant's cut in half; he's d.   DEATH 21
sort of Mayfair of the d.   DEATH 70
wait until we drop down d.   HOPE 11
we'd have been seen d. with   DEATH 47
When I am d., I hope   DEATH 34
Who was alive and is d.   EPITAPHS 6
deaded I told you I'd be d.   DEATH 53
deadlines d. in the crazed pursuit   SLEEP 15
deadlock Holy d.   MARRIAGE 87
deadly other seven d. virtues   MORALITY 5
they are more d.   EDUCATION 5
deaf d. man to a blind woman   MARRIAGE 40
fortunately a d. beast   INSULTS 20
longing to be absolutely d.   MUSIC 20
man's getting d. as well   OLD AGE 27
deafness d. is a great privation   RELIGION 31
dean D. of Christ Church   PRIDE 5
D. of Durham in bed   INSULTS 33
To our queer old d.   WIT 34
dear D. 338171   LETTERS 12
dearth d. of bad pictures   CINEMA 15
death added a new terror to d.   BIOGRAPHY 4
continuously until d. do them part

                                                MARRIAGE 69
D. and marriage are raging   MARRIAGE 78

d. and taxes   DEATH 8
D. and taxes and childbirth   DEATH 40
D. has got something   DEATH 71
D. is always a great pity   DEATH 78
[D. is] nature's way   DEATH 57
D. is the most convenient time   DEATH 33
d. of a political economist   ECONOMICS 1
d. of a proprietor   HYPOCRISY 12
d. of Little Nell without   CRITICS 14
d., sex and jewels   ART AND ARTISTS 38
enormously improved by d.   DEATH 32
Even d. is unreliable   DEATH 80
everything nowadays, except d.   DEATH 18
His d., which happened   DEATH 10
Hovering between wife and d.   DEATH 59
loving ourselves to d.   POLITICS 90
makes d. a long-felt want   INSULTS 22
no drinking after d.   ALCOHOL 5
no place in his d.   DEATH 27
old maid is like d. by drowning   OLD AGE 31
preached to d. by wild curates   RELIGION 22
put the worst to d.   DEATH 13
Reports of my d.   DEATH 19
Swarm over, D.   WAR 12
teaching me my d. duties   DEATH 42
thought of d. has now   DEATH 63
debating it is the Lords d.   ROYALTY 31
debauchery Drink and d.   SPORTS 24
debt laziness and d.   ART AND ARTISTS 34
mechanism for accumulating d.

                                              BROADCASTING 18
National D. is a very Good Thing   DEBT 3
debts creditors press you for d.   DEBT 5
get caught up on your d.   CINEMA 44
If I hadn't my d.   DEBT 1
début one's d. with a scandal   OLD AGE 10
decadence d. of the present day   OLD AGE 11
Everywhere one looks, d.   PROGRESS 11
decay one argues a d. of parts   WIT 8
deceived active willingness to be d.

                                         SELF-KNOWLEDGE 15
deceiving d. your friends without

                                           TRUTH AND LIES 14
decency D. is Indecency's conspiracy   VIRTUE 11
his d. is sort of secret   CHARACTER 20
decent d. people live beyond   SOCIETY 10
decipherable individual word was d.

                                            HANDWRITING 5
deciphering d. *her* invitations   HANDWRITING 9
decision important illegal d.   POLITICIANS 80
monologue is not a d.   POLITICS 55
realistic d.   THEATRE 39
decisions d. he is allowed to take

                                             BUREAUCRACY 9

desperation quality of coy d.   ARCHITECTURE 10
despised d. Mr Tattle of all things MARRIAGE 14
destiny logical d. of bores   BORES 22
destroy Whom the gods wish to d. SUCCESS 12
destruction d. by Fire/Brimstone GOD 50
destructive are essentially d. POLITICIANS 12
detect I think I d. sarcasm ARGUMENT 22
detective it borrows a d. story BOOKS 26
detectives our d. improved MURDER 4
deteriorate d. in a really alarming OLD AGE 15
detest d. him more than cold boiled FRIENDS 5
detested d. him for 23 years BEHAVIOUR 24
dethrimental it would be d. ANGER 6
Deuteronomy washes it down with D.
   PEOPLE 29
Devil apology for the D. GOD 7
  d. and the Holy See CENSORSHIP 12
  D. sends cooks FOOD 9
  d. understands Welsh WALES 1
  I believe in the D. PEOPLE 40
  sacrifice to God of the d.'s leavings OLD AGE 2
  sold his soul to the D. VIRTUE 28
  sooner vote for the d. DEMOCRACY 1
  taken over by the D. SUCCESS 15
Devon started that morning from D. TRAVEL 5
devoured this time been d. by mice BOOKS 15
devout cannot be d. in dishabilly RELIGION 6
Dewar D. from somewhere ALCOHOL 68
diabetes triumph of sugar over d. PEOPLE 33
diagonally lie d. in his bed MARRIAGE 27
dialect d. I understand SPORTS 2
diameter organ of prodigious d. POETRY 45
diamond d. and safire bracelet AMERICA 11
  d. offered for ONE's virtue VIRTUE 22
diamonds D. are a girl's best friend WEALTH 17
Diana It's awf'lly bad luck on D. BIRDS 41
diaries d. of men who enjoy DIARIES 3
diary d.-writing isn't wholly good DIARIES 6
  dull than a discreet d. DIARIES 4
  keep a d. and some day DIARIES 5
  never travel without my d. DIARIES 2
  To write a d. every day DIARIES 8
Dick Any Tom, D. or Harry MARRIAGE 99
Dickens put to D. as children LITERATURE 35
dictation at d. speed what he knew LIFE 23
  won't stand d. TELEGRAMS 1
dictionaries bad business, opening d.
   DICTIONARIES 8
  d. are nothing but storerooms DICTIONARIES 12
  d. defining what is unknown DICTIONARIES 9
  Short d. should be improved DICTIONARIES 11
  writer of d., a harmless DICTIONARIES 1
dictionary Architect's D. DICTIONARIES 13
  D. has not attempted DICTIONARIES 5

in this bloody d. WORDS 16
Oxford D. of Quotations NEWS 56
  time I ever made the d. DICTIONARIES 6
  two pages of the *New Oxford D.* DICTIONARIES 4
die at least they d. happier BIRDS 56
  back to America…to d. AMERICA 9
  D., and endow a college DEATH 3
  d. beyond my means DEATH 23
  D., my dear Doctor LAST WORDS 3
  d. there unnecessarily BIRDS 22
  fifteen-year-old boy until *they* d. PARENTS 8
  For tomorrow we shall d. DEATH 44
  he had to d. in my week DEATH 62
  I'm sorry—but we all must d. EPITAPHS 4
  not that I'm afraid to d. DEATH 68
  persons d. before they sing DEATH 11
  they choose to d. MEDICINE 6
  unfit to d. DEATH 13
  We d. sooner MEN AND WOMEN 72
  wise shall d. ere he thrive MARRIAGE 2
died d. last night of my physician MEDICINE 3
  d. laughing over one HUMOUR 19
  he d. too soon DEATH 61
dies into Bovril when she d. INSULTS 30
  little something in me d. SUCCESS 20
  One d. only once DEATH 1
  true because a man d. for it TRUTH AND LIES 8
diesel D.-engined TRANSPORT 22
diet d. unparalleled EDUCATION 3
  important part of a balanced d. FOOD 97
difference d. between Ford and Carter
   POLITICIANS 72
  d. of taste in jokes HUMOUR 7
  greatly exaggerate the d. MEN AND WOMEN 19
different arguing from d. premises ARGUMENT 7
  d. from the home life ROYALTY 42
  d. sense of morality MORALITY 20
  only on d. subjects FOOLISHNESS 22
  other naturs thinks d. COUNTRIES 8
differential integral and d. calculus
   ARMED FORCES 10
difficult D. do you call it MUSIC 3
  Luckily, this is not d. MEN AND WOMEN 54
difficulties little local d. POLITICS 48
digest wholesome to d. FOOD 38
digesting D. it BEHAVIOUR 29
digests It d. all things but itself FOOD 4
digitals D. have got no class SCIENCE 40
dignity d. tends to increase BUREAUCRACY 2
  room with silent d. MISTAKES 6
digressions D., incontestably BOOKS 3
dilly-dally Don't d. on the way HOME 14

dime Of a shiny new d.   POVERTY 17
dine going to d. with some men   ARCHITECTURE 2
dined d. in every house in London   SOCIETY 5
   d. last night with the Borgias   SOCIETY 13
   I have d. to-day   FOOD 23
   more d. against than dining   SOCIETY 27
dinner After a good d. one can forgive
                                FAMILY 17
   best number for a d. party   FOOD 85
   d. only if he's buying   CHILDREN 35
   had a better d.   FOOD 7
   have a sherry before d.   ALCOHOL 52
   he is eating a hearty d.   RELIGION 32
   no longer separate after d.   MARRIAGE 140
   Sex is like having d.   SEX 91
   sometimes better than the d.   MARRIAGE 36
   too hungry for d. at eight   BEHAVIOUR 22
   What are you doing for d. tonight
                           BEHAVIOUR 29
Dior Never darken my D. again   FASHION 24
diplomat d. is that he can say no   DIPLOMACY 11
   d. these days is nothing   DIPLOMACY 9
direct d. this play the way you   THEATRE 48
director if a d. doesn't really want   THEATRE 51
direful something d. in the sound   TOWNS 3
dirty call d. in our pictures   CINEMA 47
   give pornography a d. name   THEATRE 46
   In a d. glass   FOOD 72
   Is sex d.   SEX 66
   paid to have d. minds   CENSORSHIP 10
Dirty Dick At D.'s and Sloppy Joe's   ALCOHOL 40
disagreeable d. and even dangerous   WRITERS 7
disappeared it's d. without trace   MARRIAGE 137
disappointed been d. as often
                       MEN AND WOMEN 79
   he shall never be d.   HOPE 1
   Sir! you have d. us   POLITICIANS 15
disappointing he'll be the least d.   POLITICS 52
disappointment children are a bitter d.
                         CHILDREN 10
   damped by ceaseless d.   CHARACTER 19
   d. to their children   CHILDREN 26
disasters d. of English history   WALES 3
   treat all d. as incidents   MARRIAGE 122
disbelief kind of ferocious d.   DESCRIPTION 32
disciple But His Own D.   TRUST 7
   d. of Bernard Shaw   MORALITY 8
disciples man nowadays has his d.   BIOGRAPHY 5
discipline D. must be maintained   MARRIAGE 47
   may be difficult to d.   PARENTS 12
discomfort tolerate without d.   SATISFACTION 11
discourage Children are given us to d.
                         CHILDREN 16

discouragements confronted with the same d.
                           TRAVEL 11
discover d. that I had no talent   WRITERS 35
discovered dramatist who had d.   THEATRE 12
discovery d. of a new dish   FOOD 13
   Medicinal d.   MEDICINE 32
   with his usual sense of d.   SPEECHES 8
discreet more dull than a d. diary   DIARIES 4
discretion D. is not the better part BIOGRAPHY 15
discussing d. on the same level   DIPLOMACY 6
   d. sex with small children   CHILDREN 36
discussion d. programmes   BROADCASTING 15
   government by d.   DEMOCRACY 15
disdain my dear Lady D.   INSULTS 1
disease Cured yesterday of my d.   MEDICINE 3
   d. involving flaking skin   TRAVEL 22
   d. that afflicts amateurs   ART AND ARTISTS 12
   entanglement with an infectious d.
                          RELIGION 99
   if they cannot ascertain a d.   MEDICINE 5
   Love's a d. But curable   LOVE 18
   nineteenth century, it was a d.   SEX 70
   sexually transmitted d.   LIFE 25
   There is no Cure for this D.   MEDICINE 8
   When men die of d.   SICKNESS 3
diseases d. are innumerable   FOOD 1
   lists of fatal d.   MEDICINE 21
   People may catch d.   BIRDS 56
   scientific treatment for all d.   MEDICINE 10
   To talk of d.   SICKNESS 8
disgrace It's no d. t'be poor   POVERTY 14
   Its private life is a d.   BIRDS 21
disgruntled if not actually d.   SATISFACTION 6
disguise that made him d. himself   PEOPLE 42
   Tory in d. is a Whig   POLITICS 5
disgusting description, it is always d.
                         DESCRIPTION 1
dish discovery of a new d.   FOOD 13
dishabilly One cannot be devout in d.
                         RELIGION 6
dishes there's no washing of d.   EPITAPHS 10
disinherited d. by the out of pocket   MIND 12
disinheriting damned d. countenance
                        CHARACTER 3
disinterred sometimes be d. by chance   LAW 72
dislike d. which people not too   FRIENDS 2
   much as we d. him   LAW 45
   my d. is purely platonic   SEX 16
disliked would have d. him   PEOPLE 21
disloyal d. disposition towards   TRUST 4
dismal awake with a d. headache   LANGUAGE 8
Disneyland Americans with no D.   COUNTRIES 58
dispoged when I am so d.   ALCOHOL 13

dispute d. no more line calls   SPORTS 86
disputing d. a line call at Wimbledon   ANGER 12
dissected d. at the least one woman

          MARRIAGE 39
distinction d. between virtue and vice   VIRTUE 2
   few escape that d.   PRIDE 6
   merciless class d.   APPEARANCE 17
   see you were a man of d.   MEN AND WOMEN 57
distinctions free of class d.   CLASS 22
   unused to making fine d.   PEOPLE 41
distraction great d. to scholarship   SEX 96
diver Don't forget the d.   COMEDY 6
divided d. by a common language

          COUNTRIES 34
divine by D. Inadvertence   MISTAKES 17
   Right D. of Kings to govern wrong   ROYALTY 13
   You look d. as you advance   APPEARANCE 5
division D. is as bad   SCIENCE 1
divisions How many d. has *he* got   POWER 3
divorce Children must be considered in a d.

          MARRIAGE 141
   from a good d.   MARRIAGE 142
   Mention d.   MARRIAGE 129
   terrible thing, isn't it? D.   MARRIAGE 119
   when I d. I keep the house   MARRIAGE 139
divorced call a d. woman   RELIGION 89
   If Gloria hadn't d. me   FAMILY 59
   my fault that we got d.   MARRIAGE 118
   not d., but dead   MARRIAGE 37
   those of us who are d.   LIFE 16
divorcee gay d. who is after her ex   THEATRE 29
do Can I d. you now, sir   COMEDY 5
   Civil Servants by the clock d. it   SEX 30
   d. the perfectly correct thing   BEHAVIOUR 15
   d. what I want to do   LAW 29
   Hit won't d., 'arold   ROYALTY 59
   horse can d.   BETTING 6
   I can d. that   AMERICA 39
   Let's d. it, let's fall   COUNTRIES 20
   Let's d. it, let's fall   SEX 35
   so long as they d. what I say   GOVERNMENT 44
   way I d. it   CINEMA 67
doctor d. being always in the right   MEDICINE 9
   d. gets the credit of curing   SICKNESS 3
   d. whispers in the hospital   MEDICINE 29
   God and the d. we alike adore   RELIGION 3
   horrified though the d. might be   SICKNESS 18
   kind of d. I want   MEDICINE 23
   throw their crutches at the d.   GOVERNMENT 25
   you are the regimental d.   FASHION 4
doctored I knew he'd been d.   INSULTS 39
documents d. and trusted friends   FRIENDS 27
dodge science nor an art, but a d.   ARGUMENT 10

do-ers d. and the done-by   LAST WORDS 9
doffed d. their lids   SNOBBERY 21
dog characteristics of a d. except loyalty

          INSULTS 14
   d. ate my homework   DIPLOMACY 12
   d. chooses to run after   SPORTS 27
   d.'s walking on his hinder legs   WOMEN 10
   door is what a d.   BIRDS 40
   engine of pollution, the d.   BIRDS 51
   fleas is good fer a d.   BIRDS 16
   if a man bites a d.   NEWS 14
   nothin' but a hound d.   LOVE 35
   sourest-natured d.   BIRDS 2
   This business is d. eat dog   CINEMA 57
   Traffic is like a bad d.   TRANSPORT 34
   whose d. are you   ROYALTY 12
dogged It's d. as does it   WORK 3
dogma serve to beat a d.   ARGUMENT 12
dogs All bachelors love d.   CHILDREN 38
   Cats and d. amicably embracing   BIRDS 52
   D. are interested in fleas   POLITICIANS 81
   D. look up to us   BIRDS 47
   d., who are the companions   BIRDS 6
   D. who earn their living   BIRDS 54
   Don't let's go to the d. tonight   BETTING 2
   go to the d. or the Radicals   POLITICIANS 13
   hates d. and babies   PEOPLE 20
   hates d. and loves whisky   ALCOHOL 43
   Mad d. and Englishmen   ENGLAND 23
   more one values d.   BIRDS 4
doileys I'm soiling the d.   SOCIETY 23
doing don't know what I am d.   SCIENCE 33
   see what she's d.   CHILDREN 9
doll only doing it for some d.

          MEN AND WOMEN 48
dollar D. lolly   COMEDY 22
dollars looks like a million d.   MARRIAGE 81
   turn for ten thousand d.   WEALTH 6
   you leave him with two d.   MEN AND WOMEN 66
dolls fatigue the attention of d.   ROYALTY 46
doll's house d. that some bullying skinhead

          DESCRIPTION 30
dolphin publicly eat an entire d.   NATURE 16
Domesday Book D. to come out   LIBRARIES 12
domestic except in his d. life   ARMED FORCES 11
   Hatred of d. work   HOME 12
   respectable d. establishment   WAR 30
domine D., defende nos   TRANSPORT 8
don Remote and ineffectual D.   LITERATURE 13
done Apostles would have d.   RELIGION 18
   d. very well out of the war   POLITICIANS 17
   getting something d.   WORK 15
   should not be d. at all   BUSINESS 9
   surprised to find it d. at all   WOMEN 10

dynamite tons of d. are set off   CINEMA 24

each e. claiming to be Major   ARGUMENT 16
eagle In and out the E.   POVERTY 7
ear e. of man hath not seen   SLEEP 3
   purse out of your wife's e.   BIRDS 30
   scientist were to cut his e.   ART AND ARTISTS 28
earl e. and a knight   POLITICIANS 51
   fourteenth e. is concerned   ARISTOCRACY 18
Earl Grey Burnt E. omelettes   FOOD 110
early But think how e. I go   WORK 8
   E. to rise and early   DEATH 46
   had it been e., had been kind   INSULTS 7
earn do least to e. it   HAPPINESS 16
earrings e. probably won't last   BUSINESS 17
ears E. like bombs   CHILDREN 28
   e. make him look like a taxi-cab   CINEMA 48
   man of distinction has long e.   APPEARANCE 12
   phase out his e. completely   AMERICA 44
   scrambled e. to prove it   SPORTS 37
earth E. was not a rhombus   UNIVERSE 6
   Lie heavy on him, E.   EPITAPHS 5
   meek shall inherit the e.   PRIDE 12
   meek shall inherit the e.   WEALTH 26
   Reformation, E., Dust   NAMES 1
earthquake Small e. in Chile   NEWS 35
   starts with an e.   CINEMA 60
easier e. job like publishing   PUBLISHING 23
eat e. an entire dolphin   NATURE 16
   E. the cast   FOOD 122
   e. wisely but not too well   CONVERSATION 13
   I'll e. this planet   SPORTS 111
   I see what I e.   CONVERSATION 7
   look lovely...and e.   TOWNS 10
   Man he e. the barracuda   NATURE 6
   sometimes has to e. them   WORDS 18
   Sure I e. what I advertise   ALCOHOL 74
   you can kill and e. them   BIRDS 57
eating introduce the subject of e.   CONVERSATION 6
eats gentleman never e.   CLASS 12
ebullient someone who's e.   LIFE 20
eccentricity E., to be socially acceptable   BEHAVIOUR 25
eccentrics possible number of salaried e.   NEWS 36
ecclesiologist keen e.   RELIGION 56
echelons confined to the lower e.   CLASS 34
echo waiting for the e.   POETRY 28
echoes e. the sails of yachts   PLACES 12
éclair backbone than a chocolate é.   POLITICIANS 14

ecology new term 'e.'   NATURE 4
economical e. with the *actualité*   TRUTH AND LIES 26
economics more about e.   BUREAUCRACY 4
economist death of a political e.   ECONOMICS 1
economists if e. could manage   ECONOMICS 5
economy E. is going without something   CHOICE 3
   E. was always 'elegant'   MONEY 4
   fear of Political E.   DEBT 3
   Political E. has, quite   ECONOMICS 4
   Principles of Political E.   ECONOMICS 3
ecstasy not e. but it was comfort   MARRIAGE 48
Eden E.'s dread probationary tree   NEWS 2
   report from Anthony E.   POLITICIANS 35
edible e. and the readable   FOOD 108
edition first e. limited to one   BOOKS 19
editions first e. and autographs   VIRTUE 18
   understand e.   BOOKS 5
editor brilliant writer in the e.'s chair   NEWS 30
   E.: a person employed   NEWS 13
   e. did it when I was away   NEWS 68
   If you are E. [of *The Times*]   NEWS 55
editors e., and people with tapeworms   LANGUAGE 11
   lazy e. from working   CRITICS 16
educated Cabinet ministers are e.   LITERATURE 15
   government by the badly e.   GOVERNMENT 24
education between e. and catastrophe   HISTORY 6
   cabbage with a college e.   FOOD 29
   E. in those elementary subjects   EDUCATION 27
   e. is what is left when   EDUCATION 40
   e. produces no effect whatsoever   FOOLISHNESS 16
   E. with socialists   EDUCATION 44
   hatred of any branch of e.   EDUCATION 29
   higher e. of men   EDUCATION 7
   intelligence, e., taste   BEHAVIOUR 34
   Soap and e. are not   EDUCATION 5
   that is not what I call e.   EDUCATION 35
   what I call a liberal e.   EDUCATION 39
   What poor e. I have received   EDUCATION 15
educational in and out of e. establishments   EDUCATION 58
educator ludicrously overpaid as an e.   EDUCATION 54
Edwardians E., on the contrary   HOLIDAYS 4
eel e. out of a tub of water   HUMOUR 20
Eeyore E., the old grey Donkey   BIRDS 23
effect believe it has any e. on me   SUCCESS 5
   to get the full e.   APPEARANCE 16
effort But if that e. be too great   ROYALTY 26

enemies attempt to locate his e.   POLITICIANS 75
  choice of his e.   FRIENDS 6
  forgiving one's e.   FRIENDS 7
  friends conciliates e.   FRIENDS 13
  People wish their e. dead   FRIENDS 3
  quite deceiving your e.   TRUTH AND LIES 14
  time for making new e.   LAST WORDS 1
enemy better class of e.   FRIENDS 22
  effect these men will have upon the e.   WAR 3
  e. has been remaindered   WRITERS 67
  e. is not only out to steal   POLITICS 46
  e. of good art   MARRIAGE 91
  hasn't an e. in the world   FRIENDS 10
  Morrison was his own worst e.   POLITICIANS 47
  sleeps with the e.   MARRIAGE 144
  written by an acute e.   BIOGRAPHY 12
  your e. and your friend, working   FRIENDS 8
energy glottal e. to pronounce   TOWNS 15
engaged e. to Miss Joan Hunter
                                          MEN AND WOMEN 43
engagement sort of eternal e.   MARRIAGE 131
engine e. [a watch] to our ears   SCIENCE 3
  e.-drivers clean their hands   DESCRIPTION 8
  e. in boots   SPORTS 59
  e. that moves   TRANSPORT 5
  unsavoury e. of pollution   BIRDS 51
engineer be an e. or such like   EDUCATION 9
England between France and E.   COUNTRIES 9
  bored for E.   BORES 16
  E. and America are two countries
                                             COUNTRIES 34
  expect to convert E.   RELIGION 25
  Good evening, E.   ENGLAND 31
  I left E. when I was four   ROYALTY 76
  in E. a particular bashfulness   RELIGION 8
  In E. people actually try   BORES 4
  In E., you see, age wipes   OLD AGE 37
  Merrie E. in the time   ACTORS 13
  no amusements in E.   ENGLAND 8
  really *like* dowdiness in E.   ENGLAND 42
  road that leads him to E.   SCOTLAND 3
  stately homos of E.   SEX 58
  summer in E.   WEATHER 3
  taken for granted in E.   COUNTRY 19
  they that rule in E.   GOVERNMENT 16
English by virtue of its not being E.
                                              LANGUAGE 41
  can't the E. teach their children   LANGUAGE 35
  E. are busy   ENGLAND 3
  E. are inclined to be more cruel   BIRDS 6
  E. are of course the chosen race   ENGLAND 17
  E. as to the manner born   CONVERSATION 31
  E. belief that if a thing is unpleasant
                                               ENGLAND 29

E. can be explained   ENGLAND 36
E. completely disappears   LANGUAGE 35
E. have hot-water bottles   SEX 29
E. is now inert and inorganic   WRITERS 16
E. manners are far more frightening
                                                  AMERICA 27
E. may not like music   ENGLAND 38
E., not being a spiritual people   SPORTS 84
E. up with which I will not put   LANGUAGE 31
if he went among the E.   SCOTLAND 7
Larkin was so E.   ENGLAND 44
learned E. when he was twelve   WRITERS 58
Leslie [Howard] was E.   PEOPLE 26
like all other E. servants   COUNTRIES 3
no E. poet unless   QUOTATIONS 2
No one working in the E. language   PRIDE 17
Not to be E.   ENGLAND 34
Opera in E.   SONGS 15
speaking to you in E.   ENGLAND 31
standard of E. here   LANGUAGE 38
talent of our E. nation   ENGLAND 1
teach the E. how to talk   CONVERSATION 11
think of the E. for a thing   LANGUAGE 5
translated into E.   CENSORSHIP 2
Englishman average E. pretends desperately
                                                  ENGLAND 40
  broad-shouldered genial E.   ENGLAND 10
  E. a combination of qualities   ENGLAND 11
  E. among the under-dogs   ENGLAND 33
  E. believes be heresy   RELIGION 50
  E. does not travel to see   ENGLAND 6
  E., even if he is alone   ENGLAND 32
  E. is to belong   ENGLAND 27
  E.'s house is his hospital   ENGLAND 24
  E. thinks he is moral   ENGLAND 16
  E. who can look his gnu   ENGLAND 20
  E. will give his mind   ENGLAND 22
  He is an E.   ENGLAND 12
  He is a typical E.   ENGLAND 14
  He remains an E.   COUNTRIES 12
  He was born an E.   ENGLAND 37
Englishmen E. never will be slaves   ENGLAND 15
  E. of the right type reserve   ENGLAND 43
  Mad dogs and E.   ENGLAND 23
  qualified as honorary E.   COUNTRIES 35
  When two E. meet   WEATHER 2
English-speaking anthropomorphic, E.   GOD 28
Englishwoman This E. is so refined   ENGLAND 26
enjoy except how to e. it   LITERATURE 31
  have to go out and e. it   WEATHER 12
  I did so e. your book   BIOGRAPHY 19
  I e. convalescence   SICKNESS 9
  You are not here to e.   THEATRE 45

enjoyment e. you've taken out   RELIGION 94
   extract from it a low e.   BOOKS 21
   their own e. of a good meal   FOOD 32
enjoyments if it were not for its e.   HAPPINESS 2
enlightenment generous urge to spread e.
                                        EDUCATION 31
ennobling less e. than riding   SPORTS 50
enough Five hundred quite e.   ROYALTY 25
entanglement e. with religion   RELIGION 99
entendre play is full of single e.   WORDS 17
entertain e. an idea   IDEAS 5
entertained e. by some of your grosser
                                        LETTERS 15
entertainment Pictures are for e.   CINEMA 61
   sort of *Arabian Nights* e.   SICKNESS 8
   stage is a world of e.   THEATRE 29
enthusiasm e. for a pointless variety BORES 10
environment humdrum issues like the e.
                                        NATURE 9
epic very *e*. appearance   PEOPLE 2
epicure e. would say   FOOD 23
epiglottis My e. filled him with glee MEDICINE 13
epigram all existence in an e.   WIT 29
   E.: a wisecrack that played   WIT 40
   Impelled to try an e.   LITERATURE 22
   until it purrs like an e.   NEWS 26
epitaphs nice derangement of e.   WIT 13
Epstein E. for his representation
                                        ART AND ARTISTS 25
equal All shall e. be   CLASS 7
equality e. in the servants' hall   CLASS 10
   true sexual e.   MEN AND WOMEN 80
equals Judas Iscariot would be e.   LAW 30
equanimity No man can face with e.   POLITICS 18
equation e. I included in the book   SCIENCE 41
   e. is something for eternity   SCIENCE 27
equipment only item of essential e.
                                        MARRIAGE 143
equity E. does not demand   LAW 40
erection In a groom's e.   SEX 23
Ericking no beastly E.   THEATRE 21
erogenous e. zones for a kick-off   SEX 86
   We retain our zones e.   OLD AGE 29
erotic And you're an erratic e.
                                        MEN AND WOMEN 55
err to e. is human but to really   SCIENCE 35
   To e. With her   SEX 14
errands e. for the Ministers   GOVERNMENT 8
erratic For I'm a neurotic e.   MEN AND WOMEN 55
erroneous e. opinion of their position
                                        HUMAN RACE 2
error confessions of e.   BEHAVIOUR 37
escape few e. that distinction   PRIDE 6

Eskimos corset to the E.   BUSINESS 8
Esperanto E. is to the language world
                                        WRITERS 61
   unless the poet writes in E.   POETRY 21
essential only item of e. equipment
                                        MARRIAGE 143
esses so many e. in it   NAMES 8
establishment forelock to the British e.
                                        SNOBBERY 21
estate dealing with e. workers   CLASS 28
esteem grow old in my own e.   CHARACTER 4
estimable my esteem age is not e.   CHARACTER 4
eternal concept of an e. mother   ROYALTY 39
eternity equation is something for e. SCIENCE 27
   E.'s a terrible thought   TIME 10
   some conception of e.   SPORTS 84
ethics e. of professional footballers SPORTS 81
etiquette E. (and quiet well-cut clothes)
                                        RELIGION 98
   E., sacred subject of   BEHAVIOUR 36
   isn't e. to cut any one   BEHAVIOUR 9
Eton boys of E. must not be encouraged
                                        CENSORSHIP 5
   during the holidays from E.   EDUCATION 24
   wearing an E. Ramblers' tie   POLITICIANS 83
Etonians Hail him like E.   SOCIETY 9
Ettie E. is an ox   INSULTS 30
Eucharist sound like the E. to me   RELIGION 96
Eumenides E. and not the humanities
                                        ACTORS 45
eunuch between a e. and a snigger   RELIGION 49
   prerogative of the e.   GOVERNMENT 39
eunuchs Critics are like e.   CRITICS 34
   seraglio of e.   POLITICS 62
euphemism lateral e. is still   SPORTS 94
Europe Britain was no part of E.   COUNTRIES 38
   In E., when a rich woman   MEN AND WOMEN 56
European E. view of a poet   POETRY 21
   every E. language except one   LANGUAGE 24
Eutopia We rose to bring about E.   IRELAND 9
evacuated e. children in our house   CHRISTMAS 3
evah Well, did you e.   MARRIAGE 93
evasive take e. action   POLITICIANS 75
even e. terror of their lives   PREJUDICE 11
evening never get away for an e.   NEWS 55
evenings with the long winter e.   WRITERS 53
eventide perfect e. home   OLD AGE 32
events e., mostly unimportant   HISTORY 4
   removed from the centre of e.
                                        MEN AND WOMEN 73
   shape and direct e.   HISTORY 22
ever Well, did you e.   MARRIAGE 93

every E. thinking man   POLITICS 36
everybody You know e. is ignorant
   FOOLISHNESS 22
everything e. in its place   POLITICIANS 34
   E. is funny as long as   HUMOUR 10
   e. that other people want   ARISTOCRACY 9
   Tom Macaulay is of e.   CERTAINTY 2
everywhere his behaviour e.   COUNTRIES 1
evidence e. of life after death   POLITICS 73
   gave e. to the effect   CENSORSHIP 19
   it's not e.   LAW 6
   Only e. of adultery   LAW 39
   Some circumstantial e.   LAW 10
   would never hear the e.   LAW 57
evil don't think that he's e.   GOD 38
   must return good for e.   MORALITY 2
evils Between two e.   VIRTUE 21
   enamoured of existing e.   POLITICS 20
   greatest of e.   POVERTY 12
evolution e. may well phase out   AMERICA 44
exaggerate e. the difference   MEN AND WOMEN 19
exaggerated death have been greatly e.
   DEATH 19
exalting object of e. their authors   HISTORY 9
examinations e. those who do not wish
   EDUCATION 18
examiners about economics than my e.
   BUREAUCRACY 4
example annoyance of a good e.   CHARACTER 7
   don't set us a good e.   CLASS 9
   e. he sets to this Infants'   EDUCATION 30
   e. of everything I didn't   GENERATION GAP 11
   their duty to set a good e.   PARENTS 14
exams rigorous judging e.   LAW 58
exception I'll be glad to make an e.   INSULTS 47
excess Nothing succeeds like e.   SUCCESS 2
excise E. A hateful tax   TAXES 1
excite e. my amorous propensities   THEATRE 5
excitin' too e. to be pleasant   LAW 7
excommunicated he'd be e.   RELIGION 76
excuse E. My Dust   EPITAPHS 16
   e. not to play football   MEN AND WOMEN 69
excuses perhaps e. much   YOUTH 7
   several e. are always less convincing
   ARGUMENT 13
execution e. of a senior colleague   POLITICS 83
exercise And stuff e.   SICKNESS 25
   Talking is excellent e.   SEX 92
exhalted whoever wrote the praise e.
   APPEARANCE 8
exhausted range of e. volcanoes   DESCRIPTION 3
exhausting e. condition continuously
   MARRIAGE 69

exhaustion reduces me to a pudding of e.
   OLD AGE 18
exhibition ingredients for a successful e.
   ART AND ARTISTS 38
exist He doesn't e.   GOD 27
   Laski that He doesn't e.   GOD 31
   off-chance that God does e.   GOD 44
   perfect right to e.   AMERICA 8
existence all e. in an epigram   WIT 29
exit E., pursued by a bear   THEATRE 3
   Such a graceful e.   BEHAVIOUR 32
expect e. if the dad is present   SEX 49
expected I always e. it   SUCCESS 5
   I e. better manners   BEHAVIOUR 19
expects e. the Spanish Inquisition   COMEDY 20
   man who e. nothing   HOPE 1
expenditure e. nineteen nineteen six   MONEY 3
   E. rises to meet income   ECONOMICS 6
expense at your e.   POLITICIANS 57
   repay the trouble and e.   BIRDS 14
   Would be at the e. of two   GOD 4
expenses facts are on e.   NEWS 47
expensive extremely e. it is to be poor
   POVERTY 20
   most e. face in history   POLITICS 41
experience e. has taught me   SELF-KNOWLEDGE 14
   giving Robert some legal e.   FAMILY 42
   I have e.   MARRIAGE 17
   never had much e.   HOPE 7
   triumph of hope over e.   MARRIAGE 28
   world that we need not e. it   SCIENCE 29
expert against the educated e.   LAW 18
explain e. why it didn't happen   POLITICIANS 60
explaining e. to do to the recording   MURDER 12
explanation reason for and e. of everything
   CERTAINTY 3
   sometimes saves tons of e.   TRUTH AND LIES 12
   with no e.   RELIGION 82
exploit I'm sure you'd never e. one   WOMEN 79
exposed intellect is improperly e.   MIND 2
exposing e. himself in Sainsbury's   FAMILY 56
exposition e. of sleep come upon me   SLEEP 2
express down e. in the small   DESCRIPTION 7
expression between his brain and his e.
   HUMOUR 34
extensive are so delightfully e.   HOME 5
exterior this flabby e.   SELF-KNOWLEDGE 16
exterminator your e. called   ADVERTISING 8
extinct I am e.   OLD AGE 17
extinction constant complainings of e.
   ARISTOCRACY 16
   to total e.   CHOICE 8
extra add some e., just for you   PARENTS 10

family planning f. leaflet in the other

           MEN AND WOMEN 63

famous become f. without ability RELIGION 35

 by that time I was too f.   WRITERS 35

 have a f. relation   FAME 5

 he'll be rich, or f.   NEWS 58

fan chief duties of the f.   SPORTS 45

 female sex has no greater f.

           MEN AND WOMEN 68

fanatics f. are on top there GOVERNMENT 35

fancy young man's f.   LOVE 38

fantastics grittiness of *The F.* SONGS 20

far he had not f. to go   FOOLISHNESS 10

 see as f. as Marlow   MISTAKES 10

 you're never f. from home WEALTH 5

farce longest running f. GOVERNMENT 43

 nothing about f. until I read HUMOUR 32

 wine was a f.   FOOD 79

farm f. is an irregular patch COUNTRY 14

 Nixon's f. policy is vague SPEECHES 9

farmer F. will never be happy COUNTRY 7

farmers aid to anyone but f. POLITICS 53

 protect their inefficient f. COUNTRIES 55

farming F. is so charming COUNTRY 9

farmyard f. of humanity INSULTS 63

fart acoustic would make a f. MUSIC 84

 can't f. and chew gum INSULTS 51

 Love is the f.   LOVE 2

fashion dedicated follower of f. FASHION 23

 in my f.   MEN AND WOMEN 45

 passion of a vegetable f. ART AND ARTISTS 5

 To every f. changing   SONGS 19

fast f. word about oral contraception SEX 52

 none so f. as stroke   SPORTS 11

 Stealing too f.   BUSINESS 10

 who will not f. in peace POVERTY 4

fastest That's the f. time ever run SPORTS 107

fastidiousness f. a quality useful POLITICS 86

fat f. greedy owl of the Remove CHILDREN 22

 f. is something you can catch BODY 32

 if you're f., is a minefield LIFE 26

 Imprisoned in every f. man BODY 10

 like all stout women she is very f. BODY 20

 'til the f. lady sings   SONGS 18

 which their f. was fried MARRIAGE 72

fatal I am a f. man MEN AND WOMEN 8

 it is absolutely f.   VIRTUE 9

fate F. cannot harm me   FOOD 23

 F. had not seen its way SUCCESS 7

 f. worse than marriage MARRIAGE 131

 F. wrote her a most tremendous ROYALTY 38

 I have a bone to pick with F. MIDDLE AGE 3

 wagged contempt at F. EPITAPHS 19

fat-head F. poet that nobody reads WOMEN 42

father As my poor f. used to say

         ART AND ARTISTS 16

 because your f.'s an actor BEHAVIOUR 16

 either my f. or my mother PARENTS 1

 f. had an accident there BIRDS 17

 f. was so ignorant GENERATION GAP 3

 Had it been his f.   EPITAPHS 6

 man whose f. was a dragon FAMILY 13

 night the bed fell on my f. FAMILY 28

 seduction by his f. BEHAVIOUR 35

 She gave her f. forty-one MURDER 5

 whistle your f.   FAMILY 50

 wise f. that knows his own child FAMILY 1

 your f., whom you love THEATRE 42

fathers F. should be neither seen FAMILY 18

 My f. can have it   WALES 4

Father William You are old, F. OLD AGE 6

fathom f. the inscrutable workings

         ARGUMENT 14

fatigue f. the attention of dolls ROYALTY 46

fattening immoral, or f. HAPPINESS 12

fault It has no kind of f. or flaw LAW 19

 nothing is anybody's f. EDUCATION 61

faults with the f. they had PARENTS 10

Faust author as Christ or F. BOOKS 13

 validity of the F. myth VIRTUE 28

favour be said in f. iv dhrink ALCOHOL 22

favourite It's my second f. organ BODY 25

fax fox from a f.-machine COUNTRY 23

faxed proposal which my secretary f. LOVE 44

FBI F. are powerless to act SEX 64

fear f. of finding something worse CHILDREN 20

 important to not show f. TRANSPORT 34

 till the f. of the Law RELIGION 63

feast Marriage is a f. MARRIAGE 36

feather-footed F. through the plashy fen

         LANGUAGE 25

feathers three white f. CLASS 20

February not Puritanism but F. WEATHER 17

fecund first-rate, the f. rate WRITERS 21

fee For a small f. in America AMERICA 29

feeble Most forcible F. WIT 4

feed F. the brute MARRIAGE 56

 flock of starlings could f. DESCRIPTION 28

feel F. LIKE A BOY AGAIN. TELEGRAMS 16

 how the Taj Mahal must f. MARRIAGE 128

 It makes me f. good ALCOHOL 57

 One does f. RELIGION 41

 song makes you f. a thought WORDS 22

 that I don't f. worse MORALITY 16

 tragedy to those that f. HUMAN RACE 1

 when he doesn't f. like it WORK 12

forge man can't f. his own will | CRIME 11
forget Don't f. the diver | COMEDY 6
   f. the names of our own children | NAMES 11
   I never f. a face | INSULTS 47
   I sometimes f. | ROYALTY 34
forgetting actresses f. their lines | OLD AGE 26
forgive After a good dinner one can f.
   | FAMILY 17
   F., O Lord, my little jokes | GOD 29
   f. the British | COUNTRIES 33
   good Lord will f. me | ROYALTY 19
   rarely, if ever, do they f. them | CHILDREN 11
forgiving f. one's enemies | FRIENDS 7
forgot then f. to tell us why | BIRDS 33
forgotten f. all you have ever learned
   | EDUCATION 40
   he would be all f. today | PEOPLE 9
fork lost it with his f. | MEDICINE 19
   When he left off using a f. | BEHAVIOUR 12
formula 'f.' of the atomic bomb | FOOLISHNESS 30
   f., the ritual | HOPE 6
Forster F. never gets any further | WRITERS 17
forte macaroni are their f. | COUNTRIES 6
fortissimo F. at last | NATURE 1
fortnight f. in a stationary caravan
   | HAPPINESS 18
fortunate should have been more f. | NAMES 3
fortune beauty without a f. | WOMEN 6
   good f. to others | MISTAKES 2
   her f. by way of marriage | MARRIAGE 24
   little value of f. | WEALTH 1
   made his f. with the knife | MEDICINE 19
   possession of a good f. | MARRIAGE 31
forty At f. I lost my illusions | OLD AGE 28
   loves a fairy when she's f. | MIDDLE AGE 2
forty-three very well pass for f. | WOMEN 20
forward looking f. to the past | PAST 6
foul to really f. things up | SCIENCE 35
founding compared with f. a bank | CRIME 16
fount sacred f. of learning | FOOLISHNESS 13
fountain Thou f., at which drink | NEWS 2
fountain-pen f. filler into pots | GOSSIP 8
four Company of F. | THEATRE 23
   count f. | ANGER 4
   F. legs good, two legs bad | BIRDS 36
   f. with paper hats | ARMED FORCES 22
   Kiss them on all f. cheeks | DIPLOMACY 3
fourteen Wilson requires F. Points
   | POLITICIANS 16
fourteenth F. Amendment | GOVERNMENT 42
   f. Mr Wilson | ARISTOCRACY 18
fourth class third and f. people | SNOBBERY 2
fox ar'n't that I loves the f. | SPORTS 6
   f. from a fax-machine | COUNTRY 23

gentleman galloping after a f. | SPORTS 8
My God! They've shot our f. | POLITICS 40
when the metaphysical f. | CONVERSATION 30
foxed I was even almost f. | ALCOHOL 6
fox-hunting inferior forms of f. | SPORTS 25
   prefer f. | POLITICS 38
frailty therefore more f. | BODY 1
framed to have it f. | WEATHER 3
France between F. and England | COUNTRIES 9
   his round hose in F. | COUNTRIES 1
   repopulate F. | CENSORSHIP 2
   this matter better in F. | COUNTRIES 2
Francesca di Rimini F., miminy | MEN 4
frank many f. words | POLITICIANS 57
Frankenstein Didn't F. get married
   | EDUCATION 28
freckles Love, curiosity, f., and doubt | LOVE 24
Fred Here lies F. | EPITAPHS 6
free Ev'rything f. in America | AMERICA 29
   f. expression provided | CENSORSHIP 13
   F. speech, free passes | ENGLAND 30
   f. speech in the slack moments | CENSORSHIP 4
   F. speech is not to be regulated | CENSORSHIP 9
   f. to ask whatever questions | DEMOCRACY 17
   f. verse as play tennis | POETRY 34
   Give a man a f. hand | MEN AND WOMEN 35
   they are f. to do whatever | ENGLAND 15
   They bring it to you, f. | DEATH 71
   This is a f. country | BEHAVIOUR 27
   where the press is f. | CENSORSHIP 1
freedom curtail undue f. of speech
   | CENSORSHIP 18
   fight for f. and truth | FASHION 5
   f. may not be a good thing | CENSORSHIP 15
   F. of the press in Britain | NEWS 38
   F. of the press is guaranteed | CENSORSHIP 11
   I gave my life for f. | WAR 8
   vacant f. and indeterminate progress
   | PROGRESS 8
free-gift F., Reformation | NAMES 1
freemasonry have a kind of bitter f. | LOVE 16
freeway Boston's f. system | TRANSPORT 32
   f. is the place where | TRANSPORT 27
French answering you in F. | COUNTRIES 51
   exclusively F. microbe | SICKNESS 4
   F. are awful | COUNTRIES 57
   F. are masters | DIPLOMACY 12
   F. dinner at nine | FOOD 63
   F. of Parys was to hire | WOMEN 1
   F., or Turk, or Proosian | COUNTRIES 12
   F. went in to protect | COUNTRIES 55
   F. widow in every bedroom | TRAVEL 15
   how it's improved her F. | LANGUAGE 20
   never F. in any circumstance | QUOTATIONS 2

French (cont.)

not too French F. bean	ART AND ARTISTS	5
professor of F. letters	FRIENDS	12
reading a F. novel	CRITICS	27
sauces which serve the F.	FOOD	39
something fishy about the F.	COUNTRIES	22
Speak in F. when you can't	LANGUAGE	5
speaking F. fluently	LANGUAGE	29
what F. people are saying	LANGUAGE	47
worst F. novels	NEWS	5
Frenchmen fifty million F.	FOOD	62
frenzy f. closely related	WRITERS	45
fresh noted for f. air and fun	PLACES	7
Freud investigations of Herr F.	ART AND ARTISTS	18
trouble with F.	HUMOUR	36
Freudian It's a F. nightmare	FAMILY	44
fried their fat was f.	MARRIAGE	72
friend breaking it in for a f.	NAMES	13
f. of the Sitwells	SOCIETY	14
F. of Womanhood	MEN	15
goodnatured f. or another	FRIENDS	4
if your f. is not standing	DEMOCRACY	1
I was angry with my f.	ANGER	3
lay down his wife for his f.	FRIENDS	12
terrific f. of yours	BOOKS	29
To find a f. one must close	FRIENDS	18
Whenever a f. succeeds	SUCCESS	20
woman can become a man's f.	WOMEN	28
your enemy and your f.	FRIENDS	8
friends about two real f.	LIFE	7
Beloved f.	HANDWRITING	10
Christmas to all my f.	CHRISTMAS	4
deserting f. conciliates enemies	FRIENDS	13
did it to please my f.	WRITERS	43
documents and trusted f.	FRIENDS	27
f. of the author	ADVERTISING	9
His f. he loved	EPITAPHS	19
lay down his f. for his life	FRIENDS	21
make f. fall out	MARRIAGE	9
Money couldn't buy f.	FRIENDS	22
nearly deceiving your f.	TRUTH AND LIES	14
none of his f. like him	FRIENDS	10
no true f. in politics	POLITICS	84
only two f. in the world	FRIENDS	24
our f. are true	FUTURE	1
Seek younger f.	OLD AGE	17
friendship f. called slight	FRIENDS	11
f. could be very beautiful	WEALTH	22
frighten by God, they f. me	WAR	3
f. the horses	SEX	27
frightened f. them all into fits	BIRDS	41
If you are f. in the night	SOCIETY	6
frivolity how precious is f.	LITERATURE	21

frivolous memoirs of the f.	BIOGRAPHY	18
frivolously ability to make love f.	LOVE	30
frocks Her f. are built in Paris	FASHION	8
Frogs F....are slightly better	COUNTRIES	29
front-page f. news or Thor's chum	BIRDS	31
frown Say that she f.	MEN AND WOMEN	1
With a scowl and a f.	HOPE	11
frugal She had a f. mind	WOMEN	13
fruit f. is a vegetable	FOOD	111
like a delicate exotic f.	FOOLISHNESS	16
frustration nothing like sexual f.	FRIENDS	25
fuck Fish f. in it	FOOD	71
f. to get out of this show	THEATRE	49
They f. you up, your mum	PARENTS	10
fugues Of masses and f.	MUSIC	18
fule As any f. kno	FOOLISHNESS	25
fulfilment image of f.	RELIGION	86
full f. tide of human existence	TOWNS	1
Serenely f., the epicure	FOOD	23
fuller f.'s earth for reputations	MONEY	1
fume stinking f. thereof	SICKNESS	1
fun Cancer can be rather f.	SICKNESS	17
certainly damps the f.	HOME	16
counted among the f. people	SCIENCE	37
f. in any Act of Parliament	GOVERNMENT	23
girls ain't havin' any f.	WOMEN	50
Not a f. person really	PEOPLE	49
[sex] was the most f.	SEX	81
Swiss have no concept of f.	COUNTRIES	62
fundament so frigid upon the f.	SATISFACTION	9
funeral also helps pay for the f.	PARENTS	13
At his f. in Omaha	DEATH	48
bar was like a f. parlour	SOCIETY	34
f. expenses	DEATH	17
f. for sharpening the appetite	DEATH	77
making f. orations	SPEECHES	6
next day there's a f.	MEDICINE	29
refused to attend his f.	DEATH	29
funny anything so f. in my life	ACTORS	10
Everything is f. as long	HUMOUR	10
f. greetings cards on birthdays	CHRISTMAS	8
Funny-peculiar or f. ha-ha	HUMOUR	15
I don't think that's f.	HUMOUR	24
It's a f. old world	LIFE	8
maybe, but not *that* f.	WRITERS	61
not very f.	SELF-KNOWLEDGE	25
funny-peculiar F. or funny ha-ha	HUMOUR	15
fur huge ball of f.	ROYALTY	69
On some other f.	SEX	14
Three kinds of f.	CLASS	29
furnish'd F. and burnish'd	SPORTS	48
furniture f. on the deck of the Titanic	POLITICS	68
f. that used to be in the saloon	POLITICS	81

he had to buy all his f.   SNOBBERY 19
I had twice as much f.   HOME 23
No f. so charming as books   BOOKS 6
piece of mere church f.   RELIGION 11
useless and cumbersome f.   HOME 13
further f. they have to fall   SPORTS 10
fury nothing but beastly f.   SPORTS 1
fuss f. about sleeping together   SEX 18
minimum of f.   RELIGION 82
fustian whose f.'s so sublimely bad   POETRY 7
future curiosity about the f.   BIOGRAPHY 26
f. is the phallus   FUTURE 7
f. looks dark indeed   WRITERS 49
f. on both sides   DEATH 66
f. refusing to be born   FUTURE 10
I never think of the f.   FUTURE 5
preparing your child for the f.   EDUCATION 49
futures market in cream f.   PEOPLE 53
fwowed which Tonstant Weader f. up
                                                           CRITICS 24

Gabor G. marrying Freddie Ayer   MARRIAGE 147
Gabriel blow, G., blow   RELIGION 60
Gaelic hard to restore the old G.   IRELAND 8
gaiety concession to g.   WALES 5
gaily G. into Ruislip Gardens   SOCIETY 22
gainful known as g. employment   WORK 13
gaining Something may be g.   SPORTS 52
Galatians There's a great text in G.   BIBLE 1
gallant Stop being g.   THEATRE 31
gallantry What men call g.   SEX 11
galleon Stately as a g.   DANCE 13
galloping g. consumption you had   SICKNESS 21
gallows upon the g. or of the pox   INSULTS 9
galoshes He wears a vest and g.   CHARACTER 17
gamble g. at terrible odds   LIFE 17
gamblers g. are as happy as most   BETTING 1
game always played the g.   POLITICIANS 24
Anarchism is a g.   POLITICS 25
g. which takes less than three days   SPORTS 98
no g. from bridge to cricket   SPORTS 51
prayed for the g. to be over   SPORTS 92
Socratic method is a g.   EDUCATION 46
wouldn't be the g. it is   SPORTS 101
gamma g. quotient was stepped   MISTAKES 19
gamut g. of the emotions   ACTORS 20
Gandhi [G.] knew the cost   POVERTY 19
gaol Woman's place was in the g.   WOMEN 52
gap g. between Dorothy   MUSIC 37
g. between platitudes   SPEECHES 10
garbage second week of the g. strike
                                                           APPEARANCE 11

garbled Rather g.   MARRIAGE 127
Garbo one sees in G. sober   PEOPLE 36
unwelcoming Greta G.   MEN AND WOMEN 67
garden g. is a loathsome thing   GARDENS 4
g. path by the Taoiseach   DIPLOMACY 15
man and a woman in a g.   BIBLE 2
Garden City G. Café with its murals   SEX 37
gardeners g. possess a keen sense   GARDENS 5
Mad fools of g. go out   GARDENS 14
gardening British magazines cover g.   NEWS 62
when Shakespeare's g.   GARDENS 6
gardens Irish g. beat *all* for horror   GARDENS 7
gas g. pumped into my lungs   TOWNS 12
G. smells awful   DEATH 43
Had silicon been a g.   SUCCESS 3
gas-meter How to read the g.   EDUCATION 31
gate a-sitting on a g.   OLD AGE 7
gathering operation of 'g.'   WIT 42
gauze shoot her through g.   CINEMA 46
gay Gay *rich*, and Rich *g.*   THEATRE 7
Glitter and be g.   WOMEN 57
So g. the band   DANCE 13
geisha Get yourself a G.   COUNTRIES 24
gender g. bender I   SONGS 19
g. right for Christsakes   GOD 47
general g. called Anthea   MEN AND WOMEN 80
G. was essentially a man   ARMED FORCES 13
generals *bite* some of my other g.
                                                           ARMED FORCES 2
wooden swords we're all G.   ARMED FORCES 22
generation From Poland to polo in one g.
                                                           SNOBBERY 15
g. of citizens who buy   POWER 14
g. of English kids   EDUCATION 52
Had it been the whole g.   EPITAPHS 6
new g. has discovered the act   YOUTH 5
generations g. of inbreeding   BEHAVIOUR 25
generosity g. even approach this sum
                                                           GOVERNMENT 52
geniality g. of the politician   POLITICIANS 30
genitals G. are a great distraction   SEX 96
make my g. to quiver   THEATRE 5
you're breaking their g.   SEX 94
genius amount almost to g.   CRITICS 27
G. is one per cent inspiration   INTELLIGENCE 3
Men of g. are so few   INTELLIGENCE 4
nothing to declare except my g.   INTELLIGENCE 2
stronger than g.   BORES 6
geniuses all g. are devoid of humour
                                                           SPEECHES 3
genteel g. hermitage   CENSORSHIP 24
Gentile dense as the normal G.   POLITICIANS 62
gentleman Every other inch a g.   INSULTS 36
g. falls in love with his dogs   COUNTRY 1

gentleman (*cont.*)

g. never eats	CLASS 12
g....sleeps at his work	SLEEP 13
g. than a journalist	NEWS 15
g. who was generally spoken	POVERTY 8
He's a g.: look at his boots	CLASS 13
I am a g.: I live by robbing	SOCIETY 7
I am not quite a g.	SNOBBERY 7
No real English g.	ECONOMICS 1
talking about being a g.	CLASS 4
teach you to be a g. there	EDUCATION 9
write no memoirs. I'm a g.	BIOGRAPHY 9
gentlemanly werry g. ideas	ALCOHOL 12
gentlemen difficult to behave like g.	WOMEN 40
first division are g.	CLASS 23
G. do not take soup at luncheon	CLASS 24
Most g. don't like love	LOVE 29
what most of the g. does	CLASS 17
gently g. as any sucking dove	ACTORS 2
gentry aristocracy and landed g.	ARISTOCRACY 16
genuine springs from g. feeling	POETRY 17
genuineness Lawrence's g.	PEOPLE 25
geography G. is about Maps	BIOGRAPHY 6
geologic slower than g. time	TIME 14
George G. the Third Ought never	MISTAKES 11
give the ball to G.	SPORTS 68
later by G. the Fourth	HOME 15
Georgian all the G. silver goes	POLITICS 81
geriatric cocktail parties of the g.	DEATH 73
g. home in Weston-super-Mare	HAPPINESS 19
germ g. is confined to the Caucasus	SICKNESS 20
German always reason with a G.	ARGUMENT 24
far better to be G.	COUNTRIES 35
G. Foreign Minister	POLITICIANS 57
G. soldier trying to violate	SEX 17
one G. adjective	LANGUAGE 7
Waiting for the G. verb	LANGUAGE 37
Germans all G. went to heaven	COUNTRIES 17
Don't let's be beastly to the G.	COUNTRIES 26
G. went in to cleanse themselves	COUNTRIES 55
They're G. Don't mention	COUNTRIES 49
Germany his bonnet in G.	COUNTRIES 1
Gershwin G. songs	MONEY 12
Gertie public lying-in-state for G.	DEATH 49
gerund Save the g.	LANGUAGE 48
get g. anywhere in a marriage	MARRIAGE 114
g. out of these wet clothes	ALCOHOL 28
g. where I am today	COMEDY 21
only thing that Norwich didn't g.	SPORTS 102
ghastly G. good taste	ARCHITECTURE 4
ghost can't give up the g.	OLD AGE 28
g. of a crazy younger son	MURDER 7
never mind Banquo's g.	ACTORS 49
gibberish original g. into Arabic	LANGUAGE 44

Gibbon Eh! Mr G.	ROYALTY 20
giblet He liked thick g. soup	FOOD 46
giddy So g. the sight	DANCE 13
Gide [André G.]	PEOPLE 34
gifts g. over the value of £125	GOVERNMENT 52
gigolo I'm a famous g.	MEN AND WOMEN 27
Gilbert G. and Sullivan coming	WIT 41
gin at least two g.-and-limes	FOOD 74
definite flavour of g.	ALCOHOL 51
flavour of g. for hours	ALCOHOL 67
g. before breakfast	ALCOHOL 44
G. was mother's milk to her	ALCOHOL 27
if g. will make them run	FASHION 16
sooner we can get out the g.	FOOD 78
ginger-beer only g.	POLITICIANS 8
gingerbread Off the g.	HOME 16
giraffe camelopardalis or g.	BIRDS 3
g. stamping on the genitals	BROADCASTING 14
giraffes return the g.	SPORTS 71
girdle g. when your hips stick	
	MEN AND WOMEN 46
girl first rock at a g.	MEN AND WOMEN 23
g. at an impressionable age	YOUTH 8
g. needs good parents	MIDDLE AGE 8
I can't get no g. reaction	SEX 51
When I'm not near the g.	LOVE 33
girlie g. magazines	SEX 82
girls At g. who wear glasses	MEN AND WOMEN 36
both were crazy about g.	SEX 38
g. in slacks remember Dad	CHRISTMAS 5
g. turn into American women	AMERICA 38
In Little G. is slamming Doors	CHILDREN 18
Men grow cold as g. grow old	WEALTH 17
options opened for g.	WOMEN 81
other g. are coy	WOMEN 50
social security, not g.	SEX 41
Watching all the g. go by	MEN AND WOMEN 50
gist and sum of it	MEN AND WOMEN 37
give g. the public something	DEATH 55
I couldn't g. it up	WRITERS 35
intends to g. nothing away	POLITICIANS 70
given g. to government	FAMILY 11
giveth author g.	WRITERS 48
G.K.C. Poor G., his day is past	EPITAPHS 18
glad g. I'm not young	OLD AGE 23
just g. to see me	MEN AND WOMEN 64
gladioli G., especially flesh-pink	NATURE 15
Gladstone G. fell into the Thames	MISTAKES 5
G....spent his declining years	IRELAND 5
Mr G. may perspire	POLITICIANS 12
glare To protect you from the g.	ENGLAND 23
Glasgow G. Empire on a Saturday	HUMOUR 36
glasheen for a modest g.	ALCOHOL 63

Goddamm Lhude sing G.   WEATHER 8
godmother g. of my literary agent   CHILDREN 39
Godot We're waiting for G.   CERTAINTY 13
gods comfort of all other G.   HAPPINESS 13
   g. wish to destroy   SUCCESS 12
   run by a board of g.   GOD 25
goes Anything g.   BEHAVIOUR 20
   g. of a night and comes   SOCIETY 2
going certain they are still g.   SPEECHES 7
   cheerful as keeps me g.   COMEDY 9
   g. on already without reading   NEWS 49
gold all done up in g.   WEALTH 7
   G. dust on my feet   WEALTH 9
golden hand that lays the g. egg   CINEMA 13
   In good King Charles's g. days   POLITICIANS 2
   Red hair she had and g. skin   SEX 36
Goldsmith Here lies Nolly G.   EPITAPHS 8
Goldwyn streets are paved with G.   CINEMA 16
golf American people than G.   TAXES 7
   better he plays g.   SPORTS 16
   earnest protest against g.   SPORTS 13
   g. because they were Scottish   SCOTLAND 12
   G. is a good walk spoiled   SPORTS 12
   G....is the infallible test   SPORTS 20
   g. may well be included   SPORTS 30
   like a suburban g. course   GARDENS 7
   tearing off A game of g.   SPORTS 35
   too young to take up g.   MIDDLE AGE 4
   turned g. into a 'combat sport'   SPORTS 90
gollywog g. and his clothes   APPEARANCE 6
gondola down the Avon in a g.   INTELLIGENCE 13
gone g. to the demnition bow-wows   MISTAKES 4
gongs struck regularly, like g.
              MEN AND WOMEN 28
gonococcus g. is not an exclusively   SICKNESS 4
good amazed he was such a g. shot   DEATH 65
   annoyance of a g. example   CHARACTER 7
   anything g. to say   GOSSIP 14
   be g. than to be ugly   APPEARANCE 1
   being really g. all the time   HYPOCRISY 6
   be thought half as g.   MEN AND WOMEN 54
   can be g. in the country   COUNTRY 5
   g. and rotten   THEATRE 16
   g. ended happily   BOOKS 10
   g. enough for Grandma   WOMEN 51
   G. evening, England   ENGLAND 31
   G. manners are a combination   BEHAVIOUR 34
   g. politician is quite   POLITICIANS 22
   G. *Thing*   ENGLAND 21
   g. time who had been had by all   CHARACTER 11
   g. to some man   MEN AND WOMEN 16
   g. were a little less heavy-footed   VIRTUE 7
   g. woman if I had five thousand   VIRTUE 4
   must return g. for evil   MORALITY 2

natural man is naturally g.   CHILDREN 41
   privileges for g. behaviour   BIRDS 49
   unpleasant it is automatically g.   ENGLAND 29
   used to be a g. hotel   PAST 1
   Was one a g. year   ALCOHOL 61
   What earthly g. can come of it
              MEN AND WOMEN 37
   When he said a g. thing   QUOTATIONS 7
   When I'm g., I'm very   VIRTUE 20
goodbye Before I kiss the world g.   OLD AGE 25
   G., moralitee   ART AND ARTISTS 16
   he did not say g.   PUBLISHING 5
good-bye-ee G.! —Good-bye-ee   WAR 5
Good Friday Court might sit on G.   LAW 4
goodness G. never means simply acceding
              VIRTUE 32
   their own terrific g.   MORALITY 19
gooseberried g. double bed   SEX 33
gospel He that hath a G.   TRUST 7
gossamer their myth is a piece of g.   ROYALTY 67
gossip g. about people you don't know
              GOSSIP 16
   g. columnist's business   GOSSIP 9
   G. is what you say about   GOSSIP 15
   reading rabble for g.   GOSSIP 5
gossips greatest g. in the kingdom
              SELF-KNOWLEDGE 2
gossipy g. interest in the living   BIOGRAPHY 33
got If not, have you g. him   ROYALTY 48
Goth G. swaggering around Rome   PEOPLE 56
Götterdämmerung rhythmical changes in G.
              MUSIC 39
gourmet g. can tell from the flavour   FOOD 94
gout give them the g.   FRIENDS 3
govern g. New South Wales   POLITICIANS 15
   How can you g. a country   COUNTRIES 44
   those who g. society   RELIGION 97
government Be glad to help the G.   HISTORY 23
   going to get good g.   GOVERNMENT 21
   G. and public opinion allow   ENGLAND 15
   g. by discussion   DEMOCRACY 15
   g. by the uneducated   GOVERNMENT 24
   g. does it to somebody   GOVERNMENT 51
   g. doesn't work and then   GOVERNMENT 49
   g. get out of war altogether   WAR 26
   G. I despise for ends   GOVERNMENT 14
   g. is a parliament of whores   DEMOCRACY 19
   g. is the organization   GOVERNMENT 10
   g. is too unglamorous   BUREAUCRACY 21
   G. of the United States   AMERICA 32
   g. to adopt and enforce   GOVERNMENT 34
   g. which robs Peter   GOVERNMENT 27
   G. will be fearfully blamed   GOVERNMENT 5
   hands of the general g.   GOVERNMENT 2

growed I s'pect I g.   CHILDREN 6

growing price to pay for g. up   MIDDLE AGE 10

growling g., prowling, scowling   BIOGRAPHY 37

grown-up g. maintaining prolonged

     TRANSPORT 19

grown-ups When g. pretend   MIDDLE AGE 13

growth stunted his g.   BODY 13

grunt g. which is technically   BEHAVIOUR 13

gruntled far from being g.   SATISFACTION 6

guaranteed Freedom of the press is g.

     CENSORSHIP 11

guess g. that he was born   COUNTRIES 15

     Medical Men g.   MEDICINE 5

guessed g. whom the King would   ROYALTY 49

guessing G. so much and so much   WOMEN 42

guest g. who had outstayed   HOME 7

guests classes: hosts and g.   CLASS 15

guides g. cannot master the subtleties

     HUMOUR 6

Guido G. Natso is natso g.   INSULTS 45

guile packed with g.   PLACES 5

guilt easy the assumption of g.   VIRTUE 26

     either for a sign of g.   BEHAVIOUR 1

     What art can wash her g. away   WOMEN 11

guilty g. never escape unscathed   LAW 64

guineas you ask two hundred g.

     ART AND ARTISTS 10

Gulf G. Stream, as it nears   WEATHER 9

gum can't fart and chew g.   INSULTS 51

gun right or wrong end of a g.   SPORTS 23

     We have got The Maxim G.   POWER 2

Gunga better man than I am, G. Din

     ARMED FORCES 11

guns G. are always the best method   DEATH 76

     G. aren't lawful   DEATH 43

gurgle with undercurrents of g.   PEOPLE 15

gush they're oil wells; they g.   WRITERS 46

guts Spill your g. at Wimbledon   SPORTS 97

gutter so I lay down in the g.   ALCOHOL 33

guy g.'s only doing it   MEN AND WOMEN 48

guys g. are not equipped   MEN 15

gypsies g. have put a curse   SPORTS 76

h *without* the *h*'s   THEATRE 11

habit-forming Cocaine h.?   LIFE 11

habits changing social h.   CLASS 19

     Inhibit their h.   BIRDS 35

hack h. can find to louse up   GOVERNMENT 33

Hackensack I took a trip to H.   AMERICA 12

had good time who had been h.   CHARACTER 11

     WE ALL KNEW YOU H. IT   TELEGRAMS 8

haddock *Quotations* and a very large h.

     NEWS 56

sausage and h.   FOOD 65

hail H. him like Etonians   SOCIETY 9

hair Archbishop of Canterbury's h.   NEWS 60

     At fifty I lost my h.   OLD AGE 28

     beat hell out of h. curlers   SEX 50

     does her h. with Bovril   FRIENDS 16

     h. has become very white   OLD AGE 6

     h. is dirty   FASHION 29

     h. is like that of a gollywog   APPEARANCE 6

     h. straight from his left armpit   TRUST 13

     let his h. grow   LAW 66

     like the h. we breathe   SPORTS 5

     pin up my h. with prose   LETTERS 2

     Reagan doesn't dye his h.   APPEARANCE 18

     smoothes her h.   WOMEN 35

     you have lovely h.   WOMEN 29

haircut His h. will be crew   FAMILY 36

haircuts stuck with the jobs and h.

     GENERATION GAP 10

hairpieces about as reliable as his h.

     BIOGRAPHY 43

hairs h. weakly curled and clustered

     APPEARANCE 3

hairy marvellous h. about the face   FASHION 1

half finished in h. the time   FAMILY 24

     H. dead and half alive   SOCIETY 15

     h. mad baronet, half beautiful   PEOPLE 48

     h. that's got my keys   DEATH 21

halitosis H. capable of de-scaling   SICKNESS 23

hall Meet her in the h.   MURDER 7

Hallé worked wonders with the H.   MUSIC 55

halo For a h. up in heaven   RELIGION 84

     h.? It's only one more thing   RELIGION 70

ham fried h. tasting   FOOD 64

     when there's h.   MEDICINE 7

Hamlet H. in invisible pince-nez   ACTORS 36

     H. is so much paper   SPORTS 26

     H. like a demented typewriter   ACTORS 42

     Murder was one thing H.   THEATRE 28

     There isn't much cricket in *H.*   SPORTS 117

hammer carpenter's h.   MUSIC 4

hand biting the h. that lays   CINEMA 13

     Give a man a free h.   MEN AND WOMEN 35

     hair with automatic h.   WOMEN 35

     h. is not able to taste   SLEEP 3

     h. of Nature   NATURE 2

     H. that rocked the cradle   DEATH 81

     h. that wrote Ulysses   WRITERS 34

     kiss on the h. may be quite   WEALTH 17

     lily in your medieval h.   ART AND ARTISTS 4

     other h. he picks my pocket   FRIENDS 17

handbag hitting it with her h.   POWER 10

Handel For either of them, or for H.   MUSIC 5

handicap so terrible a h.   ENGLAND 34
   What is your h.   SPORTS 24
handicapper h. is spoken of   SPORTS 34
handkerchief damp h.   FOOD 52
   scent on a pocket h.   POLITICIANS 20
handle h. of the big front door   LAW 17
hand press h. once dropped   BOOKS 47
hands h. against the table edge   SPORTS 78
   Holding h. at midnight   LOVE 28
   prize-fighters shaking h.   WOMEN 53
   so much ice on your h.   FASHION 30
handwriting h. like a fly   HANDWRITING 7
   Indistinct and very small h.   HANDWRITING 2
   legibility in his h.   HANDWRITING 6
   your own h., dear   HANDWRITING 4
handy both h. and cheap   FAMILY 37
hang h. the panel   LAW 15
   they h. a man first   LAW 2
hanged be h. in a fortnight   DEATH 7
   got myself burnt or h.   HUMOUR 11
hanging h. prevents a bad marriage
                                             MARRIAGE 5
   one of them is my h.   ARISTOCRACY 11
hangover hard to see hope with a h.   HOPE 12
happen accidents which started to h.
                                             MISTAKES 15
   foretell what is going to h.   POLITICIANS 60
happened I wonder what h. to him
                                          ARMED FORCES 21
   things after they have h.   FUTURE 9
happening can't believe what isn't h.
                                              SPORTS 88
happens be there when it h.   DEATH 68
happier at least they die h.   BIRDS 56
happily h. a woman may be married
                                            MARRIAGE 103
happiness But a lifetime of h.   HAPPINESS 10
   Last Chance Gulch for h.   CHILDREN 32
   man in pursuit of h.   MARRIAGE 32
   Money won't buy h.   MONEY 19
   our h. is assured   FUTURE 1
   result h.   MONEY 3
   sacrifice one's own h.   HAPPINESS 6
happy All h. families resemble   FAMILY 14
   can be h. with any woman   MEN AND WOMEN 13
   conspiracy to make you h.   AMERICA 40
   Farmer will never be h.   COUNTRY 7
   gamblers are as h. as most   BETTING 1
   How h. could I be with either   LOVE 5
   keep unemployed people h.   BROADCASTING 16
   never going to be h.   LITERATURE 41
   policeman's lot is not a h. one   HAPPINESS 4
   She hasn't led a very h. life   FAMILY 23
   someone, somewhere, may be h.   RELIGION 69

harbour God made the h.   TOWNS 5
hard Arnold, you're a h. man   PRAISE 6
   h. man is good to find   MEN 13
   very h. guy, indeed   BETTING 3
hard-boiled h. city   TOWNS 9
hard-faced lot of h. men   POLITICIANS 17
harem like eunuchs in a h.   CRITICS 34
hark H.! the herald angels sing   MEDICINE 24
harlot holiest h. in my realm   ROYALTY 1
   prerogative of the h.   NEWS 20
harp pianoforte is a h. in a box   MUSIC 7
Harpic As I read the H. tin   OLD AGE 40
Harris this is the *present* Mrs H.   MARRIAGE 85
Harrow H. man, I expect   EDUCATION 28
   head boy at H. survived   EDUCATION 51
   I wish Shelley had been at H.   POETRY 16
Harry Any Tom, Dick or H.   MARRIAGE 99
Harvard He was from H.   AMERICA 25
harvest she laughs with a h.   COUNTRIES 10
Harwich in a steamer from H.   TRANSPORT 3
haste they repent in h.   MARRIAGE 12
hat brim of her floppy h.   MEN AND WOMEN 67
   put on his cocked h. for him   ALCOHOL 10
   right h. to wear   FASHION 7
   Wearing a h. implies   FASHION 29
hate bother with people I h.   BEHAVIOUR 22
   five players who h. your guts   SPORTS 74
   If h. killed men   GARDENS 2
   I h. all Boets and Bainters   ROYALTY 11
   I h. men   MEN AND WOMEN 44
   I h. music   MUSIC 80
hated h. it somehow pleased them
                                          ARMED FORCES 29
hates hateful h.   LOVE 26
   h. dogs and babies   PEOPLE 20
   h. them for it   HOPE 4
   man who h. his mother   MARRIAGE 138
hating But h., my boy, is an art   FRIENDS 14
hatred Oxford's instinctive h.   EDUCATION 29
hats h. were nearly all   FASHION 21
   so many shocking bad h.   POLITICIANS 7
   they have h. like plates   ENGLAND 23
haunt certain to h. her   FAMILY 5
haut-ton h. was gone for ever   BEHAVIOUR 39
Haworth We also saw H.   DESCRIPTION 15
hay desire to a bottle of h.   FOOD 2
   eating h. when you're faint   FOOD 25
   So *that's* what h. looks like   COUNTRY 10
Haydn Some cry up H.   MUSIC 5
hazardous without actually being h.   FOOD 115
he H. would, wouldn't he   TRUTH AND LIES 21
head for your good h.   BODY 3
   h. more full of undesirable fluids   BODY 33
   his brains go to his h.   INSULTS 31

head (cont.)

ideas of its "h."	POLITICS 12
incessantly stand on your h.	OLD AGE 6
On my h.	POLITICIANS 5
psychiatrist should have his h.	MEDICINE 28
put my h. in a moose	CINEMA 56
rears its ugly h.	SEX 83
wrong man's h. off	CRIME 5

headache awake with a dismal h. LANGUAGE 8
rather like a popular h. ACTORS 37
headline h. has not turned up yet NEWS 39
headmaster made H. of Westminster PAST 7
not going to be my h. CHOICE 5
headnotes H. arranged vertically LIBRARIES 4
headquarters chaplain around H. RELIGION 79
h. where his hindquarters ARMED FORCES 8
heads I talk over people's h. POLITICIANS 49
lay their h. together INSULTS 11
headstrong h. as an allegory WIT 15
head-waiter h. who's allowed to sit

	DIPLOMACY 9

health interests of my h. ALCOHOL 78
When you have both it's h. MONEY 13
healths drink one another's h. ALCOHOL 17
healthy h. and wealthy and dead DEATH 46
hear can h. my Thisby's face WIT 2
can't h. what they say YOUTH 6
h. it through their feet MUSIC 31
one must h. several times MUSIC 11
read music but can't h. it MUSIC 58
heard be neither seen nor h. FAMILY 18
h. one of the original lines THEATRE 35
h. one side of the case GOD 7
neither h., read, talked about MURDER 2
hearse h. drivers must smoke DEATH 79
walk before the h. THEATRE 6
heart except for an occasional h. attack

	HUMOUR 13
Fourteen h. attacks	DEATH 62
get your h.'s desire	HAPPINESS 9
'h.' and 'dream' photo-finish	WORDS 23
h. is on the left	MEDICINE 2
'h.' lies much lower	BODY 4
h. of lead	INSULTS 4
h. of stone to read the death	CRITICS 14
h. to poke poor Billy	DEATH 22
He carries his h. in his boots	COUNTRY 7
Irishman's h. is nothing	IRELAND 2
mending a broken h.	LOVE 37
my h. belongs to Daddy	SPORTS 35
My h. has made its mind up	LOVE 46
nor his h. to report	SLEEP 3
suspect your h. is there	WIT 45
woman has given you her h.	WOMEN 5
You're breaking my h.	SEX 94

hearts h. and house-keepings LOVE 10
H. just as pure and fair ARISTOCRACY 5
hidden in each other's h. CHARACTER 5
heat h. of a bridal suite SEX 23
heaven all Germans went to h. COUNTRIES 17
[Beaverbrook] gets to H. HEAVEN 4
h. is pleased to bestow WEALTH 1
H. sends us good meat FOOD 9
H. will protect a working-girl POVERTY 13
H. would be too dull EPITAPHS 22
it's the Hebrew in H. LANGUAGE 19
leave to h. the measure CHOICE 1
leaving mercy to h. CRIME 3
My idea of h. is, eating HEAVEN 2
NHS is quite like h. SICKNESS 17
no women in h. RELIGION 72
sudden journey to h. HEAVEN 5
who to h. might have gone EPITAPHS 15
heavy-footed good were a little less h. VIRTUE 7
heavyweight about anything but a h.

	SPORTS 36
h. fighter and he was	SPORTS 37
tabloid feel like a h.	BROADCASTING 19

Hebrew it's the H. in Heaven LANGUAGE 19
Hebrews H. 13.8 CRITICS 31
hedgehog like a h. all in primroses FASHION 22
hedges Where a few surviving h. SOCIETY 22
heels crossing of a pair of h. LOVE 27
heifers acts with swans and h. SEX 101
height MORE OR LESS SAME H. TELEGRAMS 13
my h. when I hit 'em SPORTS 19
Heineken H. refreshes the parts ALCOHOL 72
heir at it hunting for an h. ROYALTY 24
held h. his bat so straight CENSORSHIP 19
hell h. is a very large party SOCIETY 16
H. is full of musical amateurs MUSIC 22
h. of a lot of things COUNTRIES 28
h. on earth HAPPINESS 10
H. would not be Hell if EPITAPHS 22
I say the h. with it FOOD 53
I want to go to H. HEAVEN 3
May he rot in h. LAW 67
merger between Heaven and H. HEAVEN 4
re-designed H. HEAVEN 6
they think it is h. TRUTH AND LIES 18
Whatever you do, life is h. LIFE 27
hellhound h. is always a h. CHARACTER 9
hellish My life was simply h. SATISFACTION 7
helluva New York,—a h. town TOWNS 8
helmet much football without a h. INSULTS 50
help acknowledges the technical h. CRITICS 47
go to Hell I will h. them HEAVEN 3
h. masterfully disguised SELF-KNOWLEDGE 27
h. me, heaven WOMEN 36

his wife has to h. him   TRUST 5
place where h. wasn't hired   EPITAPHS 10
Scotland Yard for generous h.   CRIME 34
sick enough to call for h.   MEDICINE 17
very present h. in trouble   TRUTH AND LIES 23
you can't h. it   INSULTS 25
your countrymen cannot h.   SCOTLAND 2
helped can't be h.   CRIME 5
helping h. police with their enquiries   WEALTH 31
Hemingway H. and *not* seen the joke
    WRITERS 65
hen been a gentle useful h.   FOOD 10
h. is only an egg's way   BIRDS 9
h. you ran over the other day   MARRIAGE 110
Henery I'm H. the Eighth   MARRIAGE 70
hen-pecked have they not h. you all
    INTELLIGENCE 1
hens h. who've earned privileges   BIRDS 49
herald Hark! the h. angels sing   MEDICINE 24
herb No h. ever cures anything   MEDICINE 35
herds H. of wildebeeste   PLACES 11
here H. at last in Asia   PLACES 8
want you to be h. and sexy   MARRIAGE 115
heresy Englishman believes be h.   RELIGION 50
hermaphroditism h. of being both writer
    MUSIC 40
hermitage some kind of genteel h.
    CENSORSHIP 24
hero be the H. of a novel yet   LITERATURE 5
h. is a bee   BIRDS 20
h. is the author as Christ   BOOKS 13
no man is a valet to his h.   CLASS 11
they don't want to be a h.   WAR 31
who aspires to be a h.   ALCOHOL 9
Herod character of H.   CHILDREN 2
Oh, for an hour of H.   CHILDREN 17
heroes h. were good through   BOOKS 18
heroine when a h. goes mad   MIND 1
heron H. flies in a slow leisurely   BIRDS 34
h.'s eggs whipped   FOOD 50
Herr German Foreign Minister, H.
    POLITICIANS 57
herring plague o' these pickle h.   FOOD 3
Herveys women, and H.   ARISTOCRACY 2
Herzog thought Moses H.   MIND 9
hesitate h. and halt so in his talk   POLITICIANS 8
heterodox It would have been less h.   LETTERS 18
heterodoxy h. is another man's doxy
    BEHAVIOUR 4
heterosexuality h. came to be completely
    SEX 88
hick Sticks nix h. pix   NEWS 24
hidden h. in each other's hearts   CHARACTER 5
teems with h. meaning   WORDS 6

hide His h. is sure to flatten 'em   BIRDS 13
Minister has nothing to h.   PRIDE 13
hideous horrid, h. notes of woe   MISTAKES 3
hides when one h. for sardines   SPORTS 47
high her h. days and low days   MEDICINE 33
h. altar on the move   DESCRIPTION 25
h. road that leads   SCOTLAND 3
I'm getting h.   ALCOHOL 66
She's the Broad and I'm the H.   PRIDE 5
highballs Three h. and I think   ALCOHOL 37
highbrow What is a h.   INTELLIGENCE 6
higher capable of h. things   LITERATURE 21
High Mass Like H. without the vestments
    BUSINESS 12
high-minded with being innocent or h.
    MORALITY 18
high-tech h. is that you always end   SCIENCE 46
high-water h. mark of my youth   FAMILY 28
Hilda it's needed H.   MUSIC 45
himself interested in h. than in me
    SELF-KNOWLEDGE 7
hindquarters headquarters where his h.
    ARMED FORCES 8
hindsight H. is always twenty-twenty   PAST 11
hinges more h. in it   SPORTS 33
hippopotami like hell-bound h.   WOMEN 41
hippopotamus I shoot the H.   BIRDS 13
hips armchairs tight about the h.   DESCRIPTION 4
when your h. stick   MEN AND WOMEN 46
hired They h. the money   DEBT 4
hireling h. for treason to his country   TRUST 2
historians H. repeat each other   HISTORY 7
historical h. films with Sacha Guitry   CINEMA 29
history all the h. worth bothering about
    HISTORY 25
American h. is as good   HISTORY 18
comedy, h., pastoral   ACTORS 3
definition of h.   HISTORY 4
disasters of English h.   WALES 3
duty we owe to h. is to rewrite   HISTORY 1
entitled to telescope h.   CRITICS 26
falsification of h.   HISTORY 8
great deal of h. to produce   LITERATURE 8
h. becomes more and more a race   HISTORY 6
H. came to a .   HISTORY 11
H. gets thicker   HISTORY 20
H. is more or less bunk   HISTORY 5
H. is not what you thought   HISTORY 10
H. is to console the reader   HISTORY 9
H., like wood, has a grain   HISTORY 22
H. repeats itself   HISTORY 7
H. started badly and hav   HISTORY 15
h. without the people   BOOKS 40
interruption in British h.   ECONOMICS 7

history (cont.)

more h. than they can consume	COUNTRIES	16
more to shape h.	HISTORY	17
People who make h. know	HISTORY	12
What will h. say	HISTORY	3

hit my height when I h. 'em — SPORTS 19

Hitler H. had killed six *million* — PREJUDICE 13

It's like kissing H. — CINEMA 36

much in common with H. — PEOPLE 38

hits list of h. is long — SONGS 19

hitter also a poor h. — SPORTS 29

ho What h. — CONVERSATION 16

hoarder I am a h. of two things — FRIENDS 27

Hoare H. was certified — DIPLOMACY 4

Hoares no more H. to Paris — ROYALTY 53

Hobson H. barking up the wrong — CRITICS 33

hoe tickle her with a h. — COUNTRIES 10

hoedown break into a lively h. — OLD AGE 30

Hoffa H.'s most valuable contribution

DEATH 69

hog disadvantage of being a h. — BIRDS 30

hogamus H., higamous — MARRIAGE 68

hokum h. with which this country — CLASS 22

hold h. a man is in your arms

MEN AND WOMEN 65

hole bishop kick a h. — WOMEN 48

knows of a better h. — WAR 6

people ride in a h. — TOWNS 8

sub-normallest h. I have ever struck — PLACES 9

holiday advertise for a h. companion

HOLIDAYS 9

flight of time when on a h. — HOLIDAYS 3

holidays during the h. from Eton — EDUCATION 24

recollections of our earlier h. — HOLIDAYS 5

Holland H....lies so low — COUNTRIES 7

Holloway shoplifting and go to H. — SOCIETY 33

Hollywood English butler in H. — EDUCATION 51

H. Boulevard crosses Vine — AMERICA 34

H. is a place where people from Iowa

CINEMA 28

H. is plagiarism — CINEMA 45

H. money isn't money — CINEMA 35

H.: They know only one word — CINEMA 64

I'm not very keen on H. — CINEMA 3

invited to H. — LITERATURE 27

Lunch H.-style — FOOD 88

phoney tinsel of H. — CINEMA 52

holy H. deadlock — MARRIAGE 87

Holy See between the devil and the H.

CENSORSHIP 12

Holy Spirit received the gift of the H. — SEX 60

homage h. which they pay to Virtue

HYPOCRISY 3

Home [H.] is used to dealing with — CLASS 28

home all the comforts of h. — TRAVEL 23

begin at h. — CENSORSHIP 23

H. is heaven and orgies — SEX 25

H. James, and don't spare — TRANSPORT 11

h. keeps you from living — FAMILY 52

H. life as we understand it — HOME 11

h. life of our own dear Queen — ROYALTY 42

h. of the bean and the cod — AMERICA 7

h. of the literal — AMERICA 35

it never is at h. — WIT 17

little h. will be quaint — MONEY 12

more years in a geriatric h. — HAPPINESS 19

murder into the h. — MURDER 11

never far from h. — WEALTH 5

refuge from h. — HOME 9

there's nobody at h. — WIT 9

What's the good of a h. — HOME 8

you can't go h. again — SUCCESS 27

Homer H. sometimes sleeps — LITERATURE 4

In Homer more than H. knew — CRITICS 2

I wish I had the voice of H. — SICKNESS 16

homes Stately H. of England — ARISTOCRACY 13

homework dog ate my h. — DIPLOMACY 12

homicidal great h. classics — LITERATURE 32

homos stately h. of England — SEX 58

homosexual composer and *not* h. — MUSIC 29

My mother made me a h. — SEX 84

homosexuality h. were the normal way — SEX 79

homosexuals six hundred thousand h.

PREJUDICE 13

honest be quotable than h. — QUOTATIONS 20

buy it like an h. man — WEALTH 8

man looked h. enough — VIRTUE 6

Men are so h. — MEN AND WOMEN 51

unthinkable as an h. burglar — POLITICIANS 22

urged you to be h. — LAW 25

honesty h. is a good thing — VIRTUE 17

honey month of h. — MARRIAGE 42

honeymooning h. husband — MARRIAGE 96

honorary h. Protestants — RELIGION 105

honour fighting for this woman's h. — WOMEN 43

h. is almost greater — PUBLISHING 13

Let us h. if we can — SEX 19

louder he talked of his h. — VIRTUE 5

set up in h. of a critic — CRITICS 28

Though loss of h. was a wrench — LANGUAGE 20

honourable designs were strictly h.

MARRIAGE 24

honours good card to play for H. — LITERATURE 15

hoof-beats h. of a galloping relative — FAMILY 30

Hoover onto the board of H. — WOMEN 73

hop I made the little buggers h. — DANCE 11

hope h. that keeps up a wife's spirits

MARRIAGE 23

people of this town need is H.   HOPE 13
see h. with a hangover   HOPE 12
triumph of h. over experience   MARRIAGE 28
hopeless h. passion is my destiny

    MEN AND WOMEN 8
hopelessness despair and utter h.   CHOICE 8
hopes great h. from Birmingham   TOWNS 3
hops cherries, h., and women   PLACES 2
horizontal But the h. one   SEX 19
h. desire   DANCE 8
Horlicks positively reeking of H.   PEOPLE 35
horrible can be awe-inspiringly h.   CHILDREN 33
There is this h. idea   CHILDREN 41
horror I have a h. of sunsets   WEATHER 10
I was h. and struck   CINEMA 23
horse does not make him a h.   IRELAND 1
feeds the h. enough oats   ECONOMICS 10
hair of the h. to the bowels   HYPOCRISY 2
heard no h. sing a song   MUSIC 73
h. designed by a committee   BUSINESS 13
h. is at least *human*   TRANSPORT 18
I know two things about the h.   BIRDS 27
like a h. and carriage   MARRIAGE 107
Ninety-seven h. power   TRANSPORT 22
phone, a h. or a broad   PEOPLE 44
tail of the noble h.   MUSIC 15
where's the bloody h.   LITERATURE 19
horseback On h. after we   FAMILY 4
Horseguards H. and still be common

    SOCIETY 25
horses Bring on the empty h.   CINEMA 11
don't spare the h.   TRANSPORT 11
eat h. instead of ride them   FOOD 62
generally given to h.   SCOTLAND 1
h. do not have four-wheel brakes

    TRANSPORT 28
SIXTY H. WEDGED IN CHIMNEY   NEWS 39
street and frighten the h.   SEX 27
Wild h. on their bended knees   WIT 46
horseshoe h. hanging over his door

    CERTAINTY 10
horticulture You can lead a h.   WOMEN 63
Hoskin He's loo-vely, Mrs H.   COMEDY 14
hospital doctor whispers in the h.   MEDICINE 29
Englishman's house is his h.   ENGLAND 24
h. in Ireland   MEDICINE 27
hospitality whose h. I have enjoyed

    BIOGRAPHY 9
host have been under the h.   ALCOHOL 64
hostages accompanied by the taking of h.

    BROADCASTING 8
hostility All humour is based on h.   HUMOUR 40
hosts h. and guests   CLASS 15

hot It's Rome, it's h.   CINEMA 30
hot dog h. and vintage wine   FOOD 88
hotel h. is that it's a refuge   HOME 9
h. offers stupendous revelations   TRAVEL 15
used to be a good h.   PAST 1
wants to go back to the h.   SELF-KNOWLEDGE 21
hound I loves the h. more   SPORTS 6
nothin' but a h. dog   LOVE 35
hour occupation for an idle h.   SNOBBERY 1
Oh, for an h. of Herod   CHILDREN 17
spring comes her h.   NATURE 2
hours been going three h.   MUSIC 81
calmest and most rewarding h.   TRANSPORT 27
I see the h. pass   WORK 28
house called a woman in my own h.

    WOMEN 47
COULDN'T DRAW IN THIS H.   TELEGRAMS 19
Englishman's h. is his hospital   ENGLAND 24
from your palace to my h.   ROYALTY 41
gets you out of the h.   LAW 48
had a mind to sell his h.   HOME 1
have dined in every h.   SOCIETY 5
H. at Pooh Corner   CRITICS 24
H. Beautiful is play lousy   THEATRE 20
h. for fools and mad   EPITAPHS 3
H. of Peers, throughout   GOVERNMENT 6
h. rose like magic   ACTORS 17
h. that has got over all its troubles   HOME 10
I divorce I keep the h.   MARRIAGE 139
Keeping h. is as unpleasant   HOME 28
man in the h. is worth two   MEN AND WOMEN 31
so in the way in the h.   FAMILY 9
Spinks will come to your h.   SPORTS 82
swell h.   PROGRESS 3
houseguests h. were as well behaved   HOME 27
householder housekeeper think she's a h.

    MARRIAGE 92
housekeeper bribe to make a h.   MARRIAGE 92
economical h.   THEATRE 9
housekeeping He taught me h.   MARRIAGE 139
house-keepings jining of hearts and h.   LOVE 10
housemaids Only h. sit on the bed   ACTORS 23
house-moving definitive work on h.   HOME 25
House of Commons Advice for H. quotations

    QUOTATIONS 2
his attendance at the H.   MARRIAGE 54
H. be blowed   GOVERNMENT 20
H. en bloc do it   SEX 30
H. is trying to become   GOVERNMENT 9
libraries of the H.   LIBRARIES 6
that is untrue in the H.   TRUTH AND LIES 28
House of Lords H., an illusion   GOVERNMENT 39
H. is a perfect eventide home   OLD AGE 32
H. is the British Outer Mongolia   POLITICIANS 58

important make him feel i. MARRIAGE 116
more i. things going on PAST 8
no memory for the i. WOMEN 27
impossible if he says that it is i. SCIENCE 32
ignoring i. instructions ARMED FORCES 28
i. for God GOD 8
i. to enjoy idling thoroughly WORK 4
in two words, i. WIT 37
I wish it were i. MUSIC 3
impotence I. and sodomy are socially CLASS 26
impresarios i. and interior decorators
ART AND ARTISTS 36
impresses i. me most about America
AMERICA 30
impressionable Give me a girl at an i. age
YOUTH 8
impressive i. sights in the world SCOTLAND 6
imprisoned I. in every fat man BODY 16
improbable occurrence of the i. RELIGION 48
improper its subject was too i. CENSORSHIP 2
impropriety I. is the soul of wit WIT 32
indulge in, without i. LANGUAGE 8
improved enormously i. by death DEATH 32
improvement schemes of political i. POLITICS 1
in i. it is merely a bore SOCIETY 3
wrong bits are i. CRITICS 46
inaccuracy i. sometimes saves tons
TRUTH AND LIES 12
inadvertence by Divine I. MISTAKES 17
inbreeding five generations of i. BEHAVIOUR 25
incense keeping his vicars off the i. RELIGION 54
incest excepting i. and folk-dancing SEX 28
wrong with a little i. FAMILY 37
inch Every other i. a gentleman INSULTS 36
Inchbold mad artist named I. HOME 7
inches talk about the seven i. BODY 27
incidents treat all disasters as i. MARRIAGE 122
inclined I am i. to think MIND 7
include Gentlemen, i. me out CINEMA 9
incognito fallen angel travelling i. PEOPLE 34
income Annual i. twenty pounds MONEY 3
Expenditure rises to meet i. ECONOMICS 6
£40,000 a year a moderate i. WEALTH 2
live on the i. from his i. WEALTH 20
organism to live beyond its i. PROGRESS 4
incomes beyond their i. nowadays SOCIETY 10
income tax I. adjusterers begat POLITICS 39
I. has made more Liars TAXES 7
i. was a gross provocation TAXES 9
incommunicado i. with him BROADCASTING 12
incomplete man in love is i. MARRIAGE 112
in-conceivable family pride is something i.
ARISTOCRACY 8

incongruous contemplation of the i.
HUMOUR 30
inconsolable i. widower for three months
GENERATION GAP 1
inconstancy constant, but i. VIRTUE 1
inconveniences all the modern i. PROGRESS 3
inconvenient i. to be poor CRIME 4
it is confoundedly i. POVERTY 5
increasing reward for i. the tax BETTING 8
indecency Decency is I.'s conspiracy VIRTUE 11
indecent sent down for i. behaviour CLASS 17
indecisive He used to be fairly i. CERTAINTY 18
independence i. of party by writing
FOOLISHNESS 9
independent i. is a guy who wants POLITICS 60
index don't find it in the I. BOOKS 12
i. is a great leveller BOOKS 28
I. to see if my name occurs BIOGRAPHY 14
look for myself in the i. BOOKS 45
preparing the i. wrong BOOKS 20
reorganized the Main I. LIBRARIES 10
Indexers I., Society of BOOKS 44
indexes unindexed books with i. WORK 9
India created Viceroy of I. HEAVEN 5
I., what does the name COUNTRIES 28
never go to I. after reading it COUNTRIES 45
Indian treated like an I. widow WOMEN 55
Indians Give it back to the I. AMERICA 18
talking about the brown I. PREJUDICE 6
Indies augmentation of the I. PRIDE 2
indifference i. and a coach and six HOME 2
i. closely bordering INSULTS 16
i. on the subject altogether POLITICS 3
only another name for i. PREJUDICE 2
indifferent been delayed till I am i. INSULTS 7
indigestion worsen their i. WRITERS 73
indignation mists of righteous i. SEX 54
indignity He has spared me the i. RELIGION 38
indiscreet most i. book of Mr C TRUST 4
indiscretion air of witty i. POLITICIANS 70
between a cliché and an i. DIPLOMACY 8
individual extent of the i. calamity MISTAKES 2
indoors 'Er i. COMEDY 23
industrial biggest i. corporation BUSINESS 3
I. archaeology PAST 14
known as the I. Revelation WORK 10
industry whole field to private i. WAR 26
inebriated i. with the exuberance INSULTS 15
ineffective be a drunk to be i. POLITICIANS 82
ineffectual Remote and i. Don LITERATURE 13
inert useless when i. CENSORSHIP 16
inexperienced young and i. house HOME 10
infallible men of science being i. SCIENCE 23
only i. rule we know CLASS 4

jellybeans by his way of eating j.   CHARACTER 18
je-ne-sais-quoi *J.* young man   MEN 4
Jesuit its J. practitioners   ARGUMENT 17
  resembles a superannuated J.

                SELF-KNOWLEDGE 3
Jesus J. Christ and Napoleon   POLITICIANS 18
  J. did odd carpentry jobs   RELIGION 92
  J. fails to meet any rational   HUMAN RACE 12
  know J. wasn't married   MARRIAGE 126
Jew I am a J. else   RELIGION 2
  J. sitting and listening   CONVERSATION 32
jewels death, sex and j.   ART AND ARTISTS 38
Jewish half J. and yet sometimes   POLITICIANS 62
  It'll be good J. music   MUSIC 34
  J. man with parents alive   PARENTS 8
Jew-ish Just J. Not the whole   COUNTRIES 41
Jews But spurn the J.   GOD 15
  killed six *million* J.   PREJUDICE 13
  place was run by J.   EPITAPHS 15
  To choose The J.   GOD 14
jining j. of hearts and house-keepings   LOVE 10
Job I read the book of J.   BIBLE 6
job Always suspect any j. men

             MEN AND WOMEN 70
  By offering them your j.   GOVERNMENT 46
  came fifth and lost the j.   SUCCESS 8
  difficulty about a theatre j.   THEATRE 60
  do his j. when he doesn't feel   WORK 12
  easier j. like publishing   PUBLISHING 23
  female j. interview   WOMEN 83
  getting a j. is another   WORK 11
  he's doing a grand j.   COMEDY 17
  husband a whole-time j.   MARRIAGE 74
  man to give her his j.   MEN AND WOMEN 71
  resign your j. as a human   SCIENCE 44
  sort of j. all working-class   POLITICS 88
jogging J. is for people   SPORTS 114
John do not christen him J.   NAMES 3
Johnson literature, Samuel J.   PEOPLE 1
  no arguing with J.   ARGUMENT 5
join J. it   POETRY 15
joint minute you walked in the j.

             MEN AND WOMEN 57
  Remove the j.   BEHAVIOUR 9
joints tough j. more than somewhat   WOMEN 39
joke Hemingway and *not* seen the j.   WRITERS 65
  j. must transform real life   HUMOUR 41
  j.'s a very serious thing   HUMOUR 4
  j. was to lie about his age   HUMOUR 26
  j. well into a Scotch understanding

                  SCOTLAND 5
  j. with a double meaning   HUMOUR 31
  subtleties of the American j.   HUMOUR 6
  you tell an Iowan a j.   HUMOUR 34

jokes all the j. about George V   ROYALTY 67
  Another day gone and no j.   HUMOUR 27
  apocryphal j. I never made   DEATH 51
  civil servant doesn't make j.   BUREAUCRACY 8
  Corneille knew any j.   THEATRE 58
  difference of taste in j.   HUMOUR 7
  j. like that into your lyrics   WIT 41
  j. never seem to the British   SPEECHES 6
  J. which have to do with   CENSORSHIP 7
  my little j. on Thee   GOD 29
  over one of his own j.   HUMOUR 19
  telling j. back there   THEATRE 36
  things which are not j.   ARISTOCRACY 11
jolly j. of you to suggest it   LAST WORDS 8
  wish I thought *What J. Fun!*   HUMAN RACE 7
Jones Lord J. Dead   NEWS 12
Josephine Not tonight, J.   SEX 9
jostle Philistines may j.   ART AND ARTISTS 5
journal dear j., this unworthy   DIARIES 7
  decided to keep a full j.   DIARIES 9
  J. is like a cake of portable   DIARIES 1
journalism first law of j.   NEWS 45
  j. is to exploit the moral   NEWS 42
  J. is unreadable, and literature   NEWS 9
  J. largely consists in saying   NEWS 12
  Rock J. is people who can't   NEWS 50
journalist British j.   NEWS 19
  hack j. half as old as time   CRITICS 38
  More like a gentleman than a j.   NEWS 15
journalists j. have infiltrated   NEWS 61
  We j. don't have to step   NEWS 63
journey On a j. North   HOME 15
Jovelike description of his J. wrath   ANGER 5
  J. side to his character   FAMILY 40
Judas betting odds in favour of J.   LAW 30
  J. who writes the biography   BIOGRAPHY 5
judge after a time they j. them   CHILDREN 11
  best j. of a run   SPORTS 65
  j. goes to the lawyer   CINEMA 18
  j. had slept through   LAW 5
  mail that cheque to the J.   LAW 68
  talking J. is like   LAW 36
  want to know who the j. is   LAW 75
judgement died of an undelivered j.   DEATH 54
  not give his j. rashly   ARGUMENT 1
judges j. are a mine of instruction

              QUOTATIONS 13
  J. commonly are elderly   LAW 24
  She threw me in front of the J.   SPORTS 56
judging had the Latin for the j.   LAW 58
Judy O'Grady Colonel's Lady an' J.   WOMEN 26
jug it git loose fum de j.   ALCOHOL 16
juice j. of two quarts of whisky   ALCOHOL 48

lines (*cont.*)

l. having similar sounds	POETRY 38
one of the original l.	THEATRE 35
lingering Something l.	CRIME 10
linguistic L. analysis	LANGUAGE 45
linoleum shoot me through l.	CINEMA 46
lion achieve a l. by hearsay	DESCRIPTION 21
l. and the calf shall lie	BIRDS 50
l. in a den of Daniels	FRIENDS 9
lionized spoilt by being l.	HUMAN RACE 6
lip Stiff upper l.	ENGLAND 25
lips l. to it when I am so dispoged	ALCOHOL 13
l. were shaped for sin	SEX 36
polite to do with their l.	VIRTUE 31
lipstick you've got on too much l.	
	MEN AND WOMEN 46
liquid l. which rots braces	SCIENCE 18
liquor bowl with atrabilious l.	COUNTRIES 18
bumper of good l.	ALCOHOL 8
But l. Is quicker	ALCOHOL 32
I don't drink l.	ALCOHOL 57
l. advertisements which boast	ADVERTISING 5
L. talks mighty loud	ALCOHOL 16
made l. for temptation	ALCOHOL 54
We drank our l. straight	ALCOHOL 40
lira like the Italian l.	SCIENCE 39
lisped I l. in numbers	CHILDREN 1
list I've got a little l.	CRIME 8
listen Irish how to l.	CONVERSATION 11
people don't l.	CONVERSATION 12
when you wish him to l.	BORES 7
women who l. to it	MUSIC 13
listener Shaw's wife was a good l.	
	CONVERSATION 21
listening talking about him ain't l.	ACTORS 44
lit these courts must be l.	MURDER 4
whole Fleet's l. up	ALCOHOL 36
literacy l. is in the United States	MARRIAGE 125
literal home of the l.	AMERICA 35
literal-minded l. women letting the cat	
	WOMEN 71
literary godmother of my l. agent	CHILDREN 39
head of the l. profession	PRAISE 3
He liked those l. cooks	QUOTATIONS 1
l. a little town is Oxford	TOWNS 4
l. gift is a mere accident	LITERATURE 12
l. man—*with* a wooden leg	LITERATURE 7
l. offspring is not to die young	CHILDREN 14
l. productions were by no means	ROYALTY 16
nonstop l. drinker	ALCOHOL 56
not draw well with l. men	WRITERS 6
Of all the l. scenes	POETRY 24
personality in a l. article	AMERICA 10
literate If, with the l., I am	LITERATURE 22

literature failed in l. and art	CRITICS 8
great Cham of l.	PEOPLE 1
history to produce a little l.	LITERATURE 8
ideas of their own about l.	PUBLISHING 7
knew everything about l. except	LITERATURE 31
life had been ruined by l.	LITERATURE 36
L., alas, has no place	DEATH 27
l. is not read	NEWS 9
L.'s always a good card	LITERATURE 15
l. they have produced about him	POETRY 29
louse in the locks of l.	CRITICS 11
litigant l. drawn to the United	LAW 73
littered l. under Mercury	CHARACTER 2
St. Paul's had come down and l.	
	ARCHITECTURE 1
little I ask very l.	SATISFACTION 13
it was a very l. one	CHILDREN 4
l. local difficulties	POLITICS 48
l. may be diffused	DIARIES 1
L. to do, and plenty to get	LAW 6
Thank heaven for l. girls	WOMEN 58
though she be but l.	WOMEN 2
live gonna l. this long	OLD AGE 35
leave sack, and l. cleanly	ARISTOCRACY 1
l. for others and not for myself	MORALITY 11
l. in the twentieth century	PAST 16
l. on now is macaroni	OLD AGE 14
l. well on nothing a year	POVERTY 6
l. with a good conscience	HYPOCRISY 9
l. with rich people	WEALTH 10
thank-you-God-for-not-making-me-l.-here	
	PLACES 15
they sometimes l. apart	GOVERNMENT 12
You might as well l.	DEATH 43
lived never l. his life at all	LIFE 6
liver l. is on the right	MEDICINE 2
lives l. have been taken away	DEATH 26
living But who calls dat l.	OLD AGE 13
Dogs who earn their l.	BIRDS 54
finally had to write for a l.	WRITERS 55
gossipy interest in the l.	BIOGRAPHY 33
I *love* l.	LIFE 19
Lady Disdain, are you yet l.	INSULTS 1
l. for one's diary instead	DIARIES 6
writing books about l. men	BIOGRAPHY 17
Lizzie Borden L. took an axe	MURDER 5
Lloyd George [L.] did not seem to care	
	POLITICIANS 59
loaded I practise when I'm l.	MUSIC 82
loaf l. with a field	FOOD 28
loafing cricket as organized l.	SPORTS 22
loathsome garden is a l. thing	GARDENS 4
lobster tonic of a small l.	FOOD 15

love (*cont.*)

L. is the delusion	LOVE 34
L. is the fart	LOVE 2
l. life of newts	SEX 26
L. makes the world go round	ALCOHOL 46
'L.' probably gets	WORDS 23
L.'s a disease. But curable	LOVE 18
L.'s like the measles	LOVE 13
l. slops out all over	LOVE 47
l. the noise it makes	ENGLAND 38
L.-thirty, love-forty	SPORTS 48
l. without the rhetoric	THEATRE 43
l. you instead of laughing	HUMOUR 17
made l. as though they were	LOVE 40
make l. frivolously	LOVE 30
make l. mechanically	SEX 7
Make l. to every woman you meet	LOVE 21
men have got l. well weighed	LOVE 36
more of l. than matrimony	MARRIAGE 26
Most gentlemen don't like l.	LOVE 29
My l. and I did meet	SEX 36
Of soup and l.	FOOD 5
passes the l. of biographers	BIOGRAPHY 3
sex with someone I l.	SEX 80
tender l. scene is burning	CINEMA 65
To keep my l. alive	MARRIAGE 94
Try thinking of l.	SLEEP 10
two insides make l.	SEX 71
What is commonly called l.	LOVE 7
When l. congeals	LOVE 27
With l. to lead the way	LOVE 20
loved I wish I l. the Human Race	HUMAN RACE 7
Out upon it, I have l.	LOVE 3
loveliness I am weak from your l.	SPORTS 48
that is a miracle of l.	BODY 9
lovely He's l., Mrs Hoskin	COMEDY 14
Hurry! It's l. up here	COUNTRY 16
l. day I thought it was	WEATHER 11
When l. woman stoops to folly	WOMEN 11
You have l. eyes	WOMEN 29
lover former l. worry	LOVE 42
Scratch a l., and find a foe	FRIENDS 15
Such a constant l.	LOVE 3
what is left of a l.	MARRIAGE 76
loves Chamberlain l. the working man	WORK 7
l. the fox less	SPORTS 6
loving lovely l. and the hateful hates	LOVE 26
l. ourselves to death	POLITICS 90
l. the land that has taught	COUNTRIES 5
low begins so l.	ROYALTY 69
Lowells L. talk to the Cabots	AMERICA 7
lower confined to the l. echelons	CLASS 34
immorality of the l. classes	CLASS 5
l. case to banish any lurking	GOD 40
l. classes had such white skins	CLASS 16

l. orders don't set us	CLASS 9
l. than the fourth waistcoat	BODY 4
lowest l. rank	BUREAUCRACY 17
lowly As in the l. air	ARISTOCRACY 5
loyal Lousy but l.	ROYALTY 55
l. to his own career	PEOPLE 24
loyalties by their l. and ambitions	MONEY 11
loyalty characteristics of a dog except l.	
	INSULTS 14
conflicts of l.	SPORTS 96
I want l.	POWER 8
L. to the school	SPORTS 92
luck always just my l. to get	TRANSPORT 14
awf'lly bad l. on Diana	BIRDS 41
door would bring him l.	CERTAINTY 10
l. was his light-o'-love	MEN AND WOMEN 18
l. would have it	SUCCESS 30
lucky man's l. if he gets out	LIFE 8
lucrative When it's so l. to cheat	CRIME 6
lugger once aboard the l.	MARRIAGE 44
luminous L.! oh, I meant	WIT 19
lump L. the whole thing	COUNTRIES 11
lunatics devoted to idiots and l.	MARRIAGE 88
l. have taken charge	CINEMA 2
lunch ask him to l. in advance	OLD AGE 20
crowd will never buy you l.	PEOPLE 58
Here's to the ladies who l.	WOMEN 66
L. Hollywood-style	FOOD 88
regrets she's unable to l.	BEHAVIOUR 21
took the cork out of my l.	ALCOHOL 38
with an hour off for l.	GOVERNMENT 37
your l. is probably being	NEWS 61
lunched l. with it	LIFE 6
luncheon do not take soup at l.	CLASS 24
lunches l. of fifty-seven years	FOOD 51
lungs dangerous to the l.	SICKNESS 1
lust eggs to l. after it	VIRTUE 23
l. and calls it advertising	ADVERTISING 11
lusty call l. in foreign films	CINEMA 47
luxury accounted a l.	MEN AND WOMEN 33
l. the accomplished sofa	HOME 3
l. was lavished on you	CHILDREN 29
To trust people is a l.	WEALTH 4
lying branch of the art of l.	TRUTH AND LIES 14
l. awake with a dismal headache	LANGUAGE 8
One of you is l.	TRUTH AND LIES 15
telling the truth and l.	TRUTH AND LIES 24
lying-in-state public l. for Gertie	DEATH 49
Lyme old man of L.	MARRIAGE 64
lyric I became a l. writer	WORK 20
lyrics like that into your l.	WIT 41

Ma'am M. or Sir   ROYALTY 72
Yes M.   ROYALTY 56
macaroni m. and memorial services   OLD AGE 14
  m. are their forte   COUNTRIES 6
MacArthur General Douglas M.   GOD 24
Macaulay [M.] has occasional flashes
                                            CONVERSATION 5
  [M.] is like a book in breeches   PEOPLE 4
Macbeth Consider M.'s friends   FAMILY 51
  Little Nell and Lady M.   PEOPLE 17
  M. as the messenger   ACTORS 64
machine desiccated calculating m.
                                            POLITICIANS 56
  I have tested your m.   INSULTS 22
  ingenious m. for turning   BODY 14
  m. that would walk   SCIENCE 13
  Man is a beautiful m.   HUMAN RACE 10
  She won't be a m.   TELEGRAMS 1
mackintosh bit of black m.   FOOD 56
  evening like a damp m.   DESCRIPTION 22
  They also burnt his m.   RELIGION 66
mad great ones are thought m.   WRITERS 2
  half of the nation is m.   ENGLAND 4
  house for fools and m.   EPITAPHS 3
  How m. I am, sad I am   LOVE 32
  I'm m. about the boy   CINEMA 4
  M. dogs and Englishmen   ENGLAND 23
  m. till you have your mistresses   MEN 3
  when a heroine goes m.   MIND 1
madness be not love, it is m.   LOVE 4
  sort of m. [Bolshevism]   POLITICS 29
Mafia restaurants it's the M.   CRIME 28
magazine furbish falsehoods for a m.   NEWS 3
  m. was a transformed resurrection
                                             LITERATURE 26
magazines British m. cover gardening   NEWS 62
  girlie m.   SEX 82
  graves of little m.   POETRY 24
magic house rose like m.   ACTORS 17
  m. in a pint bottle   MARRIAGE 48
  m. of first love   LOVE 9
magnificent It's more than m.   CINEMA 54
maid aboard the lugger and the m.
                                             MARRIAGE 44
  old m. is like death   OLD AGE 31
  with her m. between her teeth   SOCIETY 20
mail downstairs to get the m.   LETTERS 20
majesty M.'s library in every county   LIBRARIES 1
major M. Major it had been all   INSULTS 38
major-general very model of a modern M.
                                          ARMED FORCES 10
majority big enough m. in any town
                                           FOOLISHNESS 14
  m. is always the best repartee   DEMOCRACY 2

  m. of MPs on your side   POLITICS 76
  silent, unfancied m.   APPEARANCE 17
  would admit to be the m.   DEMOCRACY 13
make it'll m. a woman of you   ARMED FORCES 26
  Scotsman on the m.   SCOTLAND 6
  to m. it up   MIND 3
  You cannot m. him out at all   SCIENCE 7
maker he adores his m.   PEOPLE 6
male middle-aged m.   GOD 48
  quite so bright as the m.   MEN AND WOMEN 42
  so that a m. servant   MEN AND WOMEN 33
males coarser m. grew angry   BIRDS 22
malice m. of a good thing   WIT 16
  measured m. of music   MUSIC 4
malignant not m. and remove it   MEDICINE 20
Mall kicked down the M.   DESCRIPTION 30
Malvernian That old M. brother   SPORTS 40
mama m. of dada   LITERATURE 30
mammals aspects of the woollier m.
                                         ART AND ARTISTS 20
Mammon serve both God and M.   GOD 21
man Clothes by a m. who doesn't   FASHION 17
  companions of m.   BIRDS 6
  everyone has sat except a m.   POLITICIANS 38
  fit night out for m. or beast   WEATHER 13
  get to a m. in the case   WOMEN 26
  Give a m. a free hand   MEN AND WOMEN 35
  God is a m., so it must   RELIGION 43
  hard m. is good to find   MEN 13
  hold a m. is in your arms   MEN AND WOMEN 65
  if a m. bites a dog   NEWS 14
  If a m. runs after money   MONEY 16
  make a m. by standing a sheep   MEN 8
  makes a m. coloured   PREJUDICE 7
  makes m. and wife one flesh   MARRIAGE 13
  m. can be happy   MEN AND WOMEN 13
  M. does not live by words   WORDS 18
  M. he eat the barracuda   NATURE 6
  m. in love is incomplete   MARRIAGE 112
  m. in the house is worth   MEN AND WOMEN 31
  M. is a beautiful machine   HUMAN RACE 10
  M. is Nature's sole mistake   MEN 6
  M. is one of the toughest   HUMAN RACE 11
  m. . . . . is *so* in the way   FAMILY 9
  M. is the Only Animal   HUMAN RACE 4
  m. made the town   COUNTRY 3
  m. more dined against   SOCIETY 27
  m. shouldn't fool with booze   ALCOHOL 58
  m. to a worm   FOOD 38
  m. who "boozes"   ALCOHOL 33
  m. who's untrue to his wife   INTELLIGENCE 12
  married at all . . . I'm a m.   MARRIAGE 111
  no m. ever shall put asunder   MARRIAGE 71
  No m. in his heart is quite   MEN AND WOMEN 15

means *(cont.)*
  live within our m.   HAPPINESS 3
  m. just what I choose   WORDS 4
mean-spirited m. turnip   SELF-KNOWLEDGE 29
meant manage to say what we m.   LANGUAGE 45
measles Bohemianism is like m.   YOUTH 11
  Love's like the m.   LOVE 13
measure to heaven the m.   CHOICE 1
meat British M.   SPORTS 79
  Eastern country they *are* m.   BIRDS 54
  Heaven sends us good m.   FOOD 9
  If you give him m. no woman   PEOPLE 12
  new cheese or very old m.   FOOD 87
  Well, no m.   FOOD 118
mechanical m. devices   WOMEN 78
mechanics M., not microbes   PROGRESS 7
mechanism m. for accumulating debt
                                                        BROADCASTING 18
media m. It sounds like   BROADCASTING 7
medical in advance of m. thought   ALCOHOL 29
  sounds like a m. condition   TRAVEL 22
medicinal M. discovery   MEDICINE 32
medicinally not only m. salutary   CRITICS 13
medicine desire to take m.   MEDICINE 11
  home studying m.   MEDICINE 23
  m. by a completely new method   MEDICINE 2
  m. hath done me little honesty   MEDICINE 1
  m. never gets anywhere near   SICKNESS 13
  M. never really got anywhere   MEDICINE 18
  No patent m. was ever put   GOVERNMENT 42
medieval lily in your m. hand   ART AND ARTISTS 5
mediocre m. judges and people   LAW 62
  more than magnificent, it's m.   CINEMA 54
  Some men are born m.   INSULTS 38
  writes m. verse   POETRY 29
mediocrity m. thrust upon them   INSULTS 38
Mediterranean ever taken from the M.
                                                            COUNTRIES 48
medium Roast Beef, M.   FOOD 37
  we call it a m.   BROADCASTING 3
medley m. of extemporanea   LOVE 25
Mee anatomy from Arthur M.'s   EDUCATION 56
meek m. shall inherit the earth   PRIDE 12
  m. shall inherit the earth   WEALTH 26
meekness m. stopping a bishop   RELIGION 91
meet m. from time to time   GOVERNMENT 18
  opportunity to m. people   SEX 42
meeting seeing, hearing, or m.   HOME 5
megalomaniacally client is not m. insane
                                                                   LAW 81
Meir illegitimate son of Golda M.   GOSSIP 10
melancholy What charm can soothe her m.
                                                              WOMEN 11
melons raiser of huge m.   ENGLAND 10

member ACCEPT ME AS A M.   SOCIETY 26
members m. of the common throng
                                                       ARISTOCRACY 4
membership m. in the Great Books Club
                                                      INTELLIGENCE 17
memoirists Of political m.   BIOGRAPHY 39
memoirs Like all good m.   BIOGRAPHY 29
  m. of the frivolous   BIOGRAPHY 18
  parody the m. of politicians   POLITICIANS 84
  To write one's m.   BIOGRAPHY 20
  write no m.   BIOGRAPHY 9
memoranda read these m. of yours
                                                        GOVERNMENT 29
memorandum m. is written not to inform
                                                       BUREAUCRACY 14
memorial macaroni and m. services   OLD AGE 14
memory fixed in the national m.   ROYALTY 52
  My mother lost her m.   FAMILY 49
  no m. for the important   WOMEN 27
men all our best m. are dead   LITERATURE 11
  don't have to bother with m.   PRAISE 9
  higher education of m.   EDUCATION 7
  If m. could get pregnant   MEN AND WOMEN 60
  If m. had to have babies   CHILDREN 37
  I hate m.   MEN AND WOMEN 44
  In books. By m.   MEN AND WOMEN 62
  in the m.'s room whenever   POLITICIANS 80
  many kinds of awful m.   MEN AND WOMEN 74
  m. and nations behave wisely   HISTORY 21
  m. are unaccountable things   MEN 3
  M. grow cold as girls grow old   WEALTH 17
  m. have got love well weighed   LOVE 36
  m. in my life that counts   SEX 21
  M. seldom make passes   MEN AND WOMEN 36
  m. we wanted to marry   WOMEN 69
  m., women, and clergymen   RELIGION 21
  m., women and Herveys   ARISTOCRACY 2
  more I see of m.   BIRDS 4
  never take away from m.   MEN AND WOMEN 72
  no reference to m.   BOOKS 43
  Some m. are born mediocre   INSULTS 38
  They say that m. suffer   MEN 14
  too late that m. betray   WOMEN 11
  unscrupulous m. for unhealthy
                                                      ART AND ARTISTS 21
mending ways of m. a broken heart   LOVE 37
mental It's not m., in fact   MEDICINE 34
mention Don't m. the war   COUNTRIES 49
  resolved not to m. Oscar Wilde
                                                       CONVERSATION 17
  Will m. the matter to God   GOD 34
mentioned might never again be m.   RELIGION 51

menu waiters discuss the m.   FOOD 101
Mercedes-Benz M. 380SL convertible
                                                    WOMEN 78
merciful hope for m. annihilation   RELIGION 65
  very m. to the birds   ARISTOCRACY 10
Mercury littered under M.   CHARACTER 2
mercy Hae m. o' my soul, Lord God   EPITAPHS 11
  leaving m. to heaven   CRIME 3
  like God's infinite m.   POLITICS 85
  like his m., it seemed   GOD 10
Meredith M.'s a prose Browning   LITERATURE 10
  M., we're in   COMEDY 1
merger m. between Heaven and Hell   HEAVEN 4
merit have only one m.   CRITICS 15
  m. for a bishopric   RELIGION 19
merrie M. England in the time   ACTORS 13
merriment m. of parsons   RELIGION 10
Merry M. Christmas to all   CHRISTMAS 4
mess m. left over from people   TOWNS 16
  that's why I'm a m.   FAMILY 41
message M.? What the hell   THEATRE 41
  take a m. to Albert   LAST WORDS 5
messages m. should be delivered   CINEMA 61
  you get m. of sympathy   THEATRE 59
messenger hit in *Macbeth* as the m.   ACTORS 64
met Have we m. before   ROYALTY 64
  how first he m. her   MEN AND WOMEN 11
metallists he says m.   WORDS 20
metaphor multipurpose m.   POLITICIANS 77
metaphors cure for mixed m.   LITERATURE 40
metaphysical m. fox has gone to earth
                                     CONVERSATION 30
metaphysics threw m. overboard   MEDICINE 18
meteor get hit by a m.   WEATHER 14
meters very lame—no m.   OLD AGE 33
Methodist with the morals of a M.   HYPOCRISY 5
Methuselah M. is my favourite saint
                                           OLD AGE 23
  M. live nine hundred years   OLD AGE 13
metric m. system   EDUCATION 52
metropolis m. for seven cents   WORDS 8
mezzanine down into the m. floor   FOOD 51
mice devoured by m.   BOOKS 15
  minding m. at crossroads   INSULTS 44
Michael Angelo Italy from designs by M.
                                         COUNTRIES 11
Mickey Mouse make the M. brand   CINEMA 10
  You're M.   PRAISE 7
microbe exclusively French m.   SICKNESS 4
  M. is so very small   SCIENCE 7
microbes Mechanics, not m.   PROGRESS 7
  m. won   SICKNESS 26
microscope m. at a drop of pond water
                                         MARRIAGE 79

middle beginning, a m. and an end   CINEMA 69
  can be sure about the m.   BEHAVIOUR 35
  M. is a dispiritingly practical age
                                        MIDDLE AGE 12
  stay in the m. of the road   POLITICS 43
middle age dead centre of m.   MIDDLE AGE 4
  Temptations came to him, in m.   VIRTUE 13
middle ages In the m., I should probably
                                           HUMOUR 11
middle class birth control is flagrantly m.
                                             CLASS 26
  m. male prerogative   CLASS 32
  M. was quite prepared   POLITICIANS 15
  that's m. morality   MORALITY 11
  What is m. morality   MORALITY 13
  What rituals does the m. have   CLASS 35
  with a powerful m.   POLITICS 14
middle classes Bow, bow, ye lower m.   CLASS 6
Middlesex rural M. again   SOCIETY 22
midnight Holding hands at m.   LOVE 28
mid-winter this would be m.   WEATHER 20
MI5 M. may take a different   TRUST 11
might Britons alone use 'M.'   ENGLAND 28
  It m. have been   SATISFACTION 4
mightier pen is m. than the wrist   WRITERS 19
migrate They don't m.   FAMILY 55
mild brought reg'lar and draw'd m.   ALCOHOL 14
  I should prefer m. hale   ALCOHOL 12
military Doing the M. Two-step   DANCE 13
  unfit for m. service   ARMED FORCES 24
  When the m. man approaches
                                    ARMED FORCES 16
milk between the m. and the yoghurt
                                           WRITERS 71
  find a trout in the m.   LAW 10
  Gin was mother's m. to her   ALCOHOL 27
  M. and then just as it comes   SOCIETY 23
  m. of human kindness   LITERATURE 16
  m.'s leap toward immortality   FOOD 80
  One end is moo, the other, m.   BIRDS 28
  white curd of ass's m.   INSULTS 3
Mill John Stuart M.   ECONOMICS 3
million first ten m. years   PAST 12
millionaire I am a M. That is my religion
                                            WEALTH 3
  m. has just as good   DEMOCRACY 16
  old-fashioned m.   MONEY 12
  Who wants to be a m.   WEALTH 19
millionaires m. were necessarily personable
                                           WEALTH 22
millionairesses accompanied by some lesser m.
                                           WEALTH 13
millions down to their last two m.   WEALTH 14
  opinion against that of m.   MUSIC 79

mists m. of righteous indignation · SEX 54
misunderstood Barabbas was a much m.
    PUBLISHING 20
Mitty Walter M., the undefeated · CHARACTER 10
moanday All m., tearsday, wailsday
    RELIGION 63
mob do what the m. do · POLITICS 7
Moby Dick M. nearly became the tragedy
    THEATRE 32
mock m. anything of value · HUMOUR 37
model m. of a modern Major-General
    ARMED FORCES 10
  unreliable male m. from Spain
    MEN AND WOMEN 80
moderate m. income · WEALTH 2
moderation M. in all things · LIFE 13
  M. is a fatal thing · SUCCESS 2
modern all the m. inconveniences · PROGRESS 3
  good temper of most m. men · MEN 7
  model of a m. Major-General · ARMED FORCES 10
  M. Churchman · RELIGION 53
  m. cities of the world · TOWNS 16
  m. hardback writer is somewhere · WRITERS 71
  will never make a m. poet · POETRY 23
modest m. man who has a good deal
    INSULTS 35
  M.? My word · PRIDE 15
modesty time to cultivate m. · PRIDE 14
moi Pretentious? M. · COMEDY 24
molasses M. to Rum · AMERICA 36
moll King's M. Reno'd · ROYALTY 57
moments Wagner has lovely m. · MUSIC 10
Mona M. did researches in original sin · SEX 40
Mona Lisa On the M. · MEN AND WOMEN 32
monarch so much a king as a M. · ROYALTY 51
  That m. of the road · TRANSPORT 22
monarchy Tudor m. plus telephones · POLITICS 72
Monday At classical M. Pops · MUSIC 18
money bleeding hearts mean is M. · HOPE 13
  bum with m. · WEALTH 18
  distrusted the use of m. · BUSINESS 14
  earning some serious m. · ARCHITECTURE 14
  ever wrote, except for m. · WRITERS 4
  finally I did it for m. · WRITERS 43
  for that m. Spinks will come · SPORTS 82
  German shepherd and no m. · TRAVEL 20
  Hollywood m. isn't money · CINEMA 35
  If a man runs after m. · MONEY 16
  lend you m. if you can prove · MONEY 14
  Lord God thinks of m. · WEALTH 15
  lost m. by underestimating · INTELLIGENCE 5
  made myself some m. · WORK 24
  make a little m. · CINEMA 44
  M. couldn't buy friends · FRIENDS 22

M. gives me pleasure all · MONEY 6
M. is better than poverty · MONEY 18
M. is what you'd get on · MONEY 20
m. wall to wall · MONEY 12
M. was exactly like sex · MONEY 15
m. was handed out freely · EDUCATION 55
M., wife, is the true fuller's earth · MONEY 1
M. won't buy happiness · MONEY 19
no m. refunded after the curtain · ROYALTY 23
NO M. TILL YOU LEARN TO SPELL · TELEGRAMS 14
only interested in m. · CINEMA 14
parting a fool and his m. · BETTING 11
poor man with m. · WEALTH 16
quality of needing the m. · ACTORS 65
rich man without m. · WEALTH 27
rub up against m. · MONEY 7
sordid preoccupation with m. · DIARIES 7
there's not much m. in it · WRITERS 75
They hired the m., didn't they · DEBT 4
way the m. goes · POVERTY 7
we have to borrer the m. · HAPPINESS 3
When you have m. · MONEY 13
you need the m. · WRITERS 53
young is not having any m. · YOUTH 10
your m. or your life · WOMEN 32
monkey attack the m. when the organ
    POLITICIANS 54
  m. looking for fleas · SPEECHES 2
monogamous Woman m. · MARRIAGE 68
monogamy M. is the same · MARRIAGE 130
monologue m. is not a decision · POLITICS 55
monosyllabic nothing so m. as to cheat
    LANGUAGE 34
monotony long m. of marriage · MARRIAGE 82
monster many-headed m. of the pit · THEATRE 4
  regard some m. at the Zoo · LAW 44
monstrous m. carbuncle · ARCHITECTURE 11
Month Arrival of Book of the M. · BOOKS 22
  if they wait for a m. · LETTERS 11
  m. of honey with a life · MARRIAGE 42
monument immense m. to modern
    BUREAUCRACY 7
moo One end is m., the other, milk · BIRDS 28
mood m. of the Party · POLITICS 83
moon candidate can promise the m. · UNIVERSE 11
  melodious cats under the m. · SEX 20
moonlight in the wasted m. · MARRIAGE 128
Moor highly educated M. · ACTORS 19
moose put my head in a m. · CINEMA 56
moral adultery out of the m. arena · SOCIETY 32
  Englishman thinks he is m. · ENGLAND 16
  government is often the most m.
    GOVERNMENT 35
  law is not a m. profession · LAW 20

moral (*cont.*)

m. or an immoral book	BOOKS 8
override one's m. sense	MORALITY 14

morality attitude towards personal m.

	COUNTRIES 54
different sense of m.	MORALITY 20
Goodbye, m.	ART AND ARTISTS 16
I don't believe in m.	MORALITY 8
middle-class m. all the time	MORALITY 13
residence in the suburbs of m.	VIRTUE 30
that's middle-class m.	MORALITY 11

morals either m. or principles ARISTOCRACY 7

Have you no m., man	MORALITY 12
nation's m. are like its teeth	MORALITY 9
with the m. of a Methodist	HYPOCRISY 5

morbid m. dryness is a Whig vice VIRTUE 16

most m. of the Tennysons FAMILY 12

more m. equal than others DEMOCRACY 11

Please, sir, I want some m.	FOOD 17
take *m.* than nothing	FOOD 24
which is probably m.	WOMEN 43

morning Good m., sir COMEDY 12

grey dawn of the m. after	ALCOHOL 19
I'm getting married in the m.	MARRIAGE 109
who started that m. from Devon	TRAVEL 5

Mornington present of M. Crescent ACTORS 17

Morocco we're M. bound DICTIONARIES 7

moron consumer isn't a m. ADVERTISING 7

morphia like a taste for m. ARCHITECTURE 7

Morris [William M.] ART AND ARTISTS 22

mortality Take away that emblem of m.

	DEATH 16

mortar daub of untempered m. WRITERS 16

mortgaged frequently m. to the hilt HOME 16

Mortimer Are you Edmund M. ROYALTY 48

Moses face shining like M. PREJUDICE 5

this pocket edition of M.	MONEY 8
Was persuaded to leave M.	CINEMA 17

mother And her m. came too PARENTS 4

concept of an eternal m.	ROYALTY 39
drum out of the skin of his m.	POLITICIANS 40
either my father or my m.	PARENTS 1
For m. will be there	BETTING 2
gave her m. forty whacks	MURDER 5
his m. was a decent family	SNOBBERY 8
I threw my m. into it	PARENTS 3
killed his m. and father	FAMILY 45
man who hates his m.	MARRIAGE 138
m. has just been broadcast	FAMILY 39
M. to dozens	WOMEN 38
m. who talks about her own children	
	WRITERS 8
My m. made me a homosexual	SEX 84
never been a M. or a Wife	FAMILY 23
Not if his m. had anything to do	RELIGION 101

really affectionate m.	FAMILY 20
What have you done with your m.	FAMILY 26
WONT M. BE PLEASED	TELEGRAMS 20

Mother Goose don't believe in M. GOD 20

mother-in-law given pleasure to my m.

	FAMILY 5
man said when his m. died	DEATH 17
savage contemplates his m.	MARRIAGE 62

mothers m. go on getting blamed PARENTS 9

m. of large families	BIRDS 14
Piles and m.	SICKNESS 28
women become like their m.	
	MEN AND WOMEN 14
women dress like their m.	MEN AND WOMEN 58

mothers-in-law m. and Wigan Pier

	BUREAUCRACY 6
Two m.	MARRIAGE 61

motion poetry of m. TRANSPORT 6

motions going through the m. WIT 39

motoribus Cincti Bis M. TRANSPORT 8

motto that is my m. HOPE 9

mountain In a m. greenery COUNTRY 8

mountaineer philosopher is like a m.

	PHILOSOPHY 2

mountainous great big m. sports girl

	SPORTS 40

mourn don't m. for me never EPITAPHS 10

mourner like a m. peeling onions HAPPINESS 17

mourning I'm in m. for my life HAPPINESS 7

in such very deep m.	DEATH 9
laugh in m.	PEOPLE 32

mouse Anything except that damned M.

	CHOICE 4

moustache Big chap with a small m.

	DESCRIPTION 16
by giving her a waxed m.	WOMEN 65
man who *didn't* wax his m.	MEN AND WOMEN 12
saw a bishop with a m.	PROGRESS 11
with Hitler, only no m.	PEOPLE 38

mouth cathedral in your m. PEOPLE 60

hand over that man's m.	ACTORS 46
his suede shoes in his m.	ANGER 10
just whispering in her m.	VIRTUE 24
keep your m. shut and appear stupid	
	FOOLISHNESS 19
keeping your m. shut	LIFE 10
silver foot in his m.	PEOPLE 55
talk out of the m.	LANGUAGE 26

mouths examining his wives' m. SCIENCE 24

move high altar on the m. DESCRIPTION 25

I daren't m.	SPORTS 99
things that can m. about	COUNTRY 18

movie make a m. out of BOOKS 38

wanted to be m. stars CINEMA 71

naïve He made 'em both a little n.

    FOOLISHNESS 24

  n. domestic Burgundy ALCOHOL 35

naked never seen a n. woman WOMEN 67

  opportunities to meet n. women

    ART AND ARTISTS 30

name alien, distasteful n. NAMES 9

  Casuistry has got a bad n. ARGUMENT 17

  colonies in your wife's n. WAR 16

  Democracy is the n. DEMOCRACY 5

  don't wish to sign my n. LETTERS 6

  If my n. had been Edmund NAMES 3

  Index to see if my n. BIOGRAPHY 14

  n. in such large letters PRIDE 11

  n. is not in the obits DEATH 64

  n. that sounded so nice PLACES 3

  n. to catch out borrowers BOOKS 32

  what does the n. *not* suggest COUNTRIES 28

  you've your n. in lights SUCCESS 24

names American n. as Cathcart NAMES 9

  Cats' n. are more for human NAMES 12

  n. of all these particles SCIENCE 26

  when you forget the n. NAMES 11

nap into a short n. at sermon RELIGION 7

Napoleon between Jesus Christ and N.

    POLITICIANS 18

  desert island with N. WRITERS 18

  N.'s armies always used ARMED FORCES 19

Napoleons worship the Caesars and N.

    POWER 4

narcotic synonym for 'n.' LITERATURE 37

narrow its neck is n. BIRDS 44

  notions should be so n. RELIGION 1

nasty everybody is as n. as himself HOPE 4

  Nice guys, when we turn n. CHARACTER 22

  Something n. in the woodshed MISTAKES 14

Natchez young belle of old N. WOMEN 46

nation No n. wanted it so much EPITAPHS 3

  Still better for the n. EPITAPHS 6

  top n. HISTORY 11

  what our N. stands for ENGLAND 30

national N. Debt is a very Good DEBT 3

nations Other n. use 'force' ENGLAND 28

  To belong to other n. COUNTRIES 12

native interest in n. things PEOPLE 41

natives Britons were only n. ENGLAND 21

  n.' morals rather crude RELIGION 66

Natso Guido N. is n. guido INSULTS 45

natural I do it more n. FOOLISHNESS 1

  n. to us than a cage HOME 11

  On the stage he was n. ACTORS 4

  swear her colour is n. SOCIETY 2

  twice as n. LIFE 3

nature autobiographical n. BIOGRAPHY 16

  hand of N. and we women NATURE 2

  Man is N.'s sole mistake MEN 6

  N. always does contrive POLITICS 16

  n. has anticipated me THEATRE 57

  N. has no cure for this POLITICS 29

  N. is creeping up ART AND ARTISTS 11

  N. played a cruel trick WOMEN 65

  n. replaces it with NATURE 5

  n.'s way of telling you DEATH 57

  seeing n. as cuddlesome NATURE 13

  She is a phenomenon of n. CINEMA 40

  their position in n. HUMAN RACE 2

  Whenever n. creates something NATURE 10

  Writing a lot about n. COUNTRY 22

natures those terribly weak n. CHARACTER 8

naughty n. of Smudges SPORTS 56

Navaho Basque or N. LANGUAGE 46

naval about n. tradition ARMED FORCES 25

navy No n., I suppose SCIENCE 20

  Ruler of the Queen's N. LAW 17

  struggle by the Irish N. ARMED FORCES 27

Nazi N. war criminals CRIME 33

near When I'm not n. the girl LOVE 33

necessarily It ain't n. so BIBLE 3

necessity old invention—N. POVERTY 18

  Thus first n. invented stools HOME 3

neck both his legs round his n. ANGER 10

  break his bloody n. WRITERS 36

  break my n. because a dog chooses SPORTS 27

  its n. is narra BIRDS 44

need people whenever we n. them DEMOCRACY 5

  unless I n. him CINEMA 59

needing quality of n. the money ACTORS 65

needle darning n. is broader POLITICIANS 29

neglect n. of his duties INSULTS 18

  perfectly understandable n.

    MEN AND WOMEN 53

neglected Reformers are always finally n.

    BIOGRAPHY 18

negotiable N. Cow LAW 47

Negro drop of N. blood PREJUDICE 7

  N. could never *hope* PREJUDICE 10

Negroes consequence of a weakness for N.

    LOVE 17

  culture of the N. MUSIC 36

neighbour *Our Good N.* PUBLISHING 26

neighbourhood lived in a better n.

    MARRIAGE 100

neighbours N. you annoy together

    MARRIAGE 123

  when our n. do wrong CRIME 7

Nell Little N. and Lady Macbeth PEOPLE 17

  Little N. without laughing CRITICS 14

no *(cont.)*

say n. in such a way	DIPLOMACY 11
Noah Like N.'s Ark	EDUCATION 47
N. he often said	ALCOHOL 25
Nobel you deserve the N. Prize	OLD AGE 37
noble disposed towards n. authors	
	ARISTOCRACY 3
noblemen n. who have gone wrong	
	ARISTOCRACY 4
noblest n. prospect which a Scotchman	
	SCOTLAND 3
nobly Spurn not the n. born	ARISTOCRACY 6
nobody But n.'s chasing me	MEN AND WOMEN 47
give a war and n. will come	WAR 11
I care for n.	SATISFACTION 1
n. knew what was going on	MUSIC 35
n.'s going to stop 'em	SPORTS 106
Well, n.'s perfect	MARRIAGE 111
nod n. from an American	AMERICA 2
n. their heads with a fraudulent air	
	CONVERSATION 32
noise absolutely love the n.	ENGLAND 38
loud n. at one end	CHILDREN 27
n. in the reading-room	WOMEN 31
n. like that of a water-mill	SCIENCE 3
n., my dear! And the people	WAR 17
n. they make is benign	THEATRE 61
noises meaningless Celtic n.	SCOTLAND 12
Nollekens remain as by N.	ROYALTY 68
nomadic on the contrary, were n.	HOLIDAYS 4
non compos I was n. penis	CRITICS 21
nonentity simply a n. who resents	BORES 14
nonexistent obsolescent and the n.	SCIENCE 43
nonplussed seen a Silver Band so n.	
	DESCRIPTION 20
Norfolk bear him up the N. sky	ROYALTY 62
Very flat, N.	PLACES 6
normal homosexuality were the n. way	SEX 79
Thank God we're n.	SEX 39
Norwegian N. television	BROADCASTING 17
Norwegians I don't like N. at all	COUNTRIES 23
nose another person in the n.	WOMEN 72
could not make up his n.	THEATRE 32
Entuned in hir n. ful semely	WOMEN 1
Had a very shiny n.	BIRDS 38
hateful to the n.	SICKNESS 1
How haughtily he lifts his n.	FOOLISHNESS 4
miss the insinuated n.	EPITAPHS 19
Must often wipe a bloody n.	ARGUMENT 2
N. to Nose	DANCE 5
thing is not a n. at all	BODY 10
nose-painting n., sleep, and urine	ALCOHOL 3
noses forcing beef tea down the n.	MEDICINE 30
His n. cast is of the roman	WIT 20

nostalgia N. isn't what it used	PAST 10
not N. while I'm alive he ain't	POLITICIANS 47
notebook down herself in a n.	PEOPLE 14
nothing absolutely n. could be said	IRELAND 12
Black tie or n.	SOCIETY 36
doing n. to some purpose	WORK 27
doing n. with a deal of skill	ARMED FORCES 4
do n. for ever and ever	EPITAPHS 10
easy to take *more* than n.	FOOD 24
God did n., and ever since	GOD 19
How to live well on n. a year	POVERTY 6
I do n., granted	WORK 28
intends to give n. away	POLITICIANS 70
n. a-year, paid quarterly	POVERTY 8
N. for nothink 'ere	ECONOMICS 2
n. on in the photograph	PEOPLE 28
say there was n. *better*	FOOD 25
Tar-baby ain't sayin' n.	BIRDS 11
when there's n. to be said	FOOLISHNESS 6
Worked myself up from n.	POVERTY 16
would have done it for n.	WORK 19
notice n. which you have been	INSULTS 7
notices Mixed n.	THEATRE 16
pretty good n.	MUSIC 35
notions n. should be so narrow	RELIGION 1
nouveau riche said for the *n.*	SNOBBERY 20
novel first n. the hero is the author	BOOKS 13
Hero of a n.	LITERATURE 5
n. about civil servants	BOOKS 42
n. was self-administered	LITERATURE 23
unpublished n.	SELF-KNOWLEDGE 22
write a n. given six weeks	WRITERS 26
novelists old n. who saw people	BOOKS 18
novels each child you lose two n.	CHILDREN 43
ideal reader of my n.	WRITERS 57
worst French n.	NEWS 5
novelties fall in love with n.	LAW 24
novelty n. of sleeping with a queen	ROYALTY 30
novice n. brought into the world	
	MEN AND WOMEN 22
now If they could see me n.	CLASS 29
nuclear n. button was at one stage	SPORTS 90
nude n. infant doing a backward	CHILDREN 42
nudity In an advanced state of n.	BODY 18
n. ought not to be published	DIARIES 3
nuisance title is really rather a n.	ARISTOCRACY 9
null N. an' Void	LAW 34
number n. for a dinner party	FOOD 85
numbers lisped in n.	CHILDREN 1
nun extremely rowdy N.	MURDER 7
If N., write *None*	FAMILY 26
I was going to be a n.	RELIGION 93
nuns recreation for dedicated n.	SPORTS 110

nurse always keep a-hold of N.   CHILDREN 20
  n. sleeps sweetly   SICKNESS 2
  N. UNUPBLOWN   TELEGRAMS 9
nuts where the n. come from   FAMILY 16
nylon Curtains in orange n.   HOME 29
nymphomaniac call me a n.   SEX 97

oafish o. louts remember Mum   CHRISTMAS 5
OAP O. with a temper like   OLD AGE 36
oat-cakes Calvin, o., and sulphur   SCOTLAND 4
oats feeds the horse enough o.   ECONOMICS 10
  O. A grain   SCOTLAND 1
Obadiah O. Bind-their-kings   NAMES 4
obesity O. is really widespread   BODY 26
obeyed She who must be o.   WOMEN 23
obits my name is not in the o.   DEATH 64
obituaries o. every day   DEATH 63
obituary o. in serial form   BIOGRAPHY 30
  read o. in the Times   DEATH 20
object o. to people looking   SPEECHES 7
objecting What I am o. to is the use
    CENSORSHIP 14
objections o. to seeing trees   COUNTRY 21
objectivity code of Olympian o.   NEWS 63
objects shouldn't be treated like o.   PEOPLE 50
oblate To find it an o. spheroid   UNIVERSE 6
obscurantism o. sits ill upon the mantle
    WORDS 19
obscurity snatches a man from o.   THEATRE 8
observation o. told him   BOOKS 33
observer keen o. of life   INTELLIGENCE 12
obsolescence With built in o.   UNIVERSE 10
obsolescent o. and the nonexistent   SCIENCE 43
obstacle o. racing   HOME 13
  o. to professional writing   WRITERS 38
obstetrician Brutus is like an o.   INSULTS 27
occasional o. heart attack   HUMOUR 13
occupation found o. for an idle hour   SNOBBERY 1
  o. of buildings   BROADCASTING 8
  some sort of o. nowadays   DEBT 1
occupations pleasurable of imaginable o.
    NEWS 29
occurred Ought never to have o.   MISTAKES 11
o'clock turns out to be 37 o.   TIME 13
o'clocks are there two nine o.   TIME 11
odd How o. Of God   GOD 14
  It's an o. job, making   HUMOUR 1
  Must think it exceedingly o.   GOD 17
  Not o. Of God   GOD 16
  not so o. As those who choose   GOD 15
odds gamble at terrible o.   LIFE 17
  o. are five to six   BETTING 9

odium He lived in the o.   SCIENCE 10
odorous Comparisons are o.   WIT 5
Odysseus Like O., the President   GOVERNMENT 15
Oedipus It could be O. Rex   THEATRE 29
off down again with them o.   SOCIETY 11
off-chance o. that God does exist   GOD 44
offend And others doth o.   LOVE 2
offenders society o.   CRIME 8
offending o. both legal and natural   THEATRE 42
offensive You are extremely o.   INSULTS 25
offer o. he can't refuse   POWER 5
office By office boys for o. boys   NEWS 10
  country in which the o. is held   BUREAUCRACY 2
  except public o.   GOVERNMENT 31
  o. boy to an Attorney's firm   LAW 17
  O. hours are from 12 to 1   GOVERNMENT 37
  o. party is not   SOCIETY 28
  o. shared by Robert Benchley   WRITERS 39
  O. tends to confer a dreadful   GOVERNMENT 53
  Whig in o.   POLITICS 5
  with an o. party   CHRISTMAS 7
officers ministers and staff o.   GOVERNMENT 4
official This high o., all allow   GOVERNMENT 17
officials persistence of public o.   BUREAUCRACY 19
officiously O. to keep alive   DEATH 15
offspring If the literary o. is not   CHILDREN 14
off-the-record leaders an o. briefing   GOD 46
oil as providers they're o. wells   WRITERS 46
  sound of o. wells   MONEY 12
  with boiling o. in it   CRIME 10
oilcloth o. pockets so he can steal   CINEMA 7
old Alas o. animals   BIRDS 45
  conservative when o.   POLITICS 32
  getting so o. anyway   CRIME 33
  Growing o. is like being increasingly
    OLD AGE 34
  grow o. in my own esteem   CHARACTER 4
  HOW O. CARY GRANT   TELEGRAMS 23
  interest to one's o. age   OLD AGE 10
  journalist half as o. as time   CRITICS 38
  Men grow cold as girls grow o.   WEALTH 17
  never mind, he was very o.   BIRDS 58
  new Vice for my o. age   VIRTUE 27
  o. age crept over them   RELIGION 61
  o. age is always fifteen years older   OLD AGE 19
  o. beast of the jungle   POLITICIANS 75
  o. gentleman with iron-grey   PEOPLE 9
  o. have reminiscences   GENERATION GAP 2
  o. heads on your young shoulders
    EDUCATION 36
  o. maid is like death by drowning   OLD AGE 31
  o. when ladies declare war   ROYALTY 9
  staff to my father's o. age   PARENTS 3
  terrifying fact about o. people   OLD AGE 39

old (cont.)

too o. to rush up to the net	MIDDLE AGE	4
Very o.—very lame	OLD AGE	33
virtuous in their o. age	OLD AGE	2
What a sad o. age	OLD AGE	4
You are o., Father William	OLD AGE	6
young can do for the o.	YOUTH	1
you've the age you're too o.	ACTORS	63
older always fifteen years o.	OLD AGE	19
As I grow o. and older	OLD AGE	22
ask somebody o. than me	SEX	89
o. Americans	OLD AGE	38
o. we do not get any younger	MIDDLE AGE	5
oldest o. established permanent	BETTING	7
second o. college in Oxford	EDUCATION	32
old-fashioned I want an o. house	MONEY	12
So make it another o., please	ALCOHOL	39
'ole knows of a better o.	WAR	6
Omaha staying quietly in O.	TRAVEL	17
ombibulous more simply, o.	ALCOHOL	53
omelettes Burnt Earl Grey o.	FOOD	110
make o. properly	FOOD	55
omnibibulous I am o.	ALCOHOL	53
omnibus horse power O.	TRANSPORT	22
omniscience o. his foible	INSULTS	10
on Chico was always o.	PEOPLE	44
Onanism his is the O. of poetry	POETRY	11
Onassis O. would not have married	HISTORY	24
once can only be killed o.	POLITICS	58
every house in London, o.	SOCIETY	5
I was adored o. too	LOVE	1
oncoming headlight of an o. train	BETTING	9
one-sided This contract is so o.	LAW	61
onions like a mourner peeling o.	HAPPINESS	17
ooze o. through the bars	BIRDS	24
open it was an o. cow	LAW	47
Jed, your fly is o.	APPEARANCE	10
We o. in two weeks	ACTORS	55
We o. in Venice	THEATRE	25
you o. that Pandora's Box	DIPLOMACY	7
opening Another o. of another show	THEATRE	24
o. dictionaries	DICTIONARIES	8
opera echoing o. houses	PLACES	12
language an o. is sung in	SONGS	14
Like German o., too long	WAR	19
o. ain't over 'til	SONGS	18
O. in English	SONGS	15
o. isn't what it used to be	SONGS	6
O. is when a guy gets stabbed	SONGS	10
o. that starts at six o'clock	MUSIC	81
operas now return to making o.	COUNTRIES	6
o. sung by Swedish artists	LANGUAGE	15
operatic so romantic, so o.	WEATHER	10

operational at least they were o.	POLITICS	41
Ophelia she is not O.	INSULTS	28
opinion His o. of himself	PRIDE	9
o. against that of millions	MUSIC	79
public o. is generally	POLITICS	15
opinions high quality of early o.	BOOKS	31
music of our own o.	LAW	59
not the courage of his o.	ROYALTY	36
opium Coleridge? He smoked o.	BODY	15
concubine to an o. addict	WOMEN	76
opportunities o. to meet naked women	ART AND ARTISTS	30
opportunity commit when he had the o.	MEN	9
manhood was an o.	MEN	16
o. of saying a good thing	WIT	22
with the maximum of o.	MARRIAGE	66
oppose o. everything	POLITICS	8
opposite o. of talking is waiting	CONVERSATION	26
we're the o. of people	ACTORS	54
opposition duty of an O.	POLITICS	8
It's called o.	GOVERNMENT	54
optimism unquestioning o.	NATURE	15
optimist o. is a guy	HOPE	7
options o. opened for girls	WOMEN	81
oracular use of my o. tongue	WIT	13
oral all-important o. sex muscles	SEX	92
word about o. contraception	SEX	52
oral-genital cases of o. intimacy	SEX	64
orange he's just prematurely o.	APPEARANCE	18
you happen to be an o.	AMERICA	19
oranges boy flew at the o.	FOOD	43
orations making funeral o.	SPEECHES	6
oratorio more disgusting than an o.	MUSIC	8
oratorios o. being sung in the costume	MUSIC	27
orchestra by the waves or by the o.	SONGS	11
finest chamber o.	MUSIC	55
rules for an o.	MUSIC	63
she endows an o. for him	MEN AND WOMEN	56
squeak's heard in the o.	MUSIC	15
trouble with women in an o.	WOMEN	59
orchestras O. only need to be sworn at	LANGUAGE	33
order following in o. of importance	CHOICE	9
not necessarily in that o.	CINEMA	69
They o., said I, this matter	COUNTRIES	2
ordering better o. of the universe	UNIVERSE	1
orders don't take o. from you	ARGUMENT	21
ordinary o. name	NAMES	7
organ mellering to the o.	MEDICINE	4
my second favourite o.	BODY	25
o. grinder is present	POLITICIANS	54

o. of prodigious diameter POETRY 45
same length as my male o. BIOGRAPHY 41
when I hear the o. RELIGION 14
organism o. to live beyond its income
PROGRESS 4
organization o. of idolatry GOVERNMENT 10
organize o. her own immortality PEOPLE 14
organized cricket as o. loafing SPORTS 22
organizing o. and campaigning POWER 7
organs o. have been transplanted OLD AGE 29
o. of beasts and fowls FOOD 46
orgasm o. has replaced the Cross RELIGION 86
orgies Home is heaven and o. are vile SEX 25
o. and unlimited spying SEX 45
orgy But you *need* an o. SEX 25
o. looks particularly alluring SEX 54
Oriental Like an O. tart ARCHITECTURE 3
original heard one of the o. lines THEATRE 35
I have nothing o. in me VIRTUE 3
it saves o. thinking QUOTATIONS 14
none of the o. ideas is sound POLITICS 54
o. idea IDEAS 9
originality without o. or moral courage
PEOPLE 7
originator o. of a good sentence QUOTATIONS 4
orphan mercy of the court as an o. FAMILY 45
orphaned rather late to be o. OLD AGE 24
orthodoxy O. is my doxy BEHAVIOUR 4
Osaka Never give O. an even break WIT 47
Oscar We all assume that O. said it
LITERATURE 22
You will, O., you will WIT 30
ostentation use rather than o. ROYALTY 16
ostrich O. roams the great Sahara BIRDS 44
Othello man of affairs like O. ACTORS 18
O. had the naturalness ACTORS 19
other did lots of o. things too WRITERS 34
Every o. inch a gentleman INSULTS 36
happened to o. people PROGRESS 14
think o. people are reading WRITERS 62
Were t'o. dear charmer away LOVE 5
others O. must fail SUCCESS 21
ought It is, but hadn't o. to be SATISFACTION 4
WHERE O. I TO BE TELEGRAMS 11
'ound that I loves the o. more SPORTS 6
our he's o. son of a bitch POLITICIANS 31
out include me o. CINEMA 9
say he is o. of touch CLASS 28
out-argue attempt to o. one's past WRITERS 60
Outer Mongolia British O. POLITICIANS 58
out-of-date throwing away o. files
BUREAUCRACY 13
outside baby it's cold o. WEATHER 16
o. pissing in POWER 9

ovaltine art to be like o. ART AND ARTISTS 35
oven got a self-cleaning o. HOME 30
over opera ain't o. SONGS 18
try to put it all o. you MEN AND WOMEN 35
overachiever conversational o.
CONVERSATION 25
overdraft o. to buy 500 begonias BETTING 10
overdressing nightmare is o. SOCIETY 36
overkill it looks like o. night BROADCASTING 13
overlooked looked over than o. SATISFACTION 5
overpaid Is grossly o. GOVERNMENT 17
overthrow o. the Government AMERICA 32
owe For in truth we o. everybody NAMES 2
owes o. me ninety-seven dollars DEBT 2
owl fat greedy o. of the Remove CHILDREN 22
He respects O. WORDS 11
Neither from o. or from bat BIRDS 5
owling prowling, scowling and o. BIOGRAPHY 37
own guaranteed only to those who o.
CENSORSHIP 11
my words are my o. ROYALTY 4
o. back from erring nephews FAMILY 38
provided I get my o. way SELF-KNOWLEDGE 26
ox [Lady Desborough] is an o. INSULTS 30
Oxfam O. ever return anything POVERTY 21
Oxford clever men at O. EDUCATION 11
either O. or Cambridge SPORTS 95
exercise that right in O. AMERICA 8
I hated O.—the rudest PLACES 9
literary a little town is O. TOWNS 4
nice sort of place, O. EDUCATION 9
oddity of O. books PUBLISHING 25
O.'s instinctive hatred EDUCATION 29
O. that has made me insufferable EDUCATION 8
published by the O. University Press
PUBLISHING 13
secret in the O. sense GOSSIP 12
So poetry, which is in O. made POETRY 5
Oxonian Impossible! He is an O.
TRUTH AND LIES 6
oyster open an o. at sixty paces DESCRIPTION 16
typewriter full of o. shells PLACES 12
oysters o. in a month that has FOOD 112
poverty and o. FOOD 16

paces open an oyster at sixty p. DESCRIPTION 16
Pacific P. Ocean was a body PLACES 10
pack keep running with the p. POLITICS 75
Paddington As London is to P. POLITICIANS 4
pagan something p. in me CERTAINTY 1
page allowed P. 3 to develop NEWS 68
moral law all over the p. HANDWRITING 3
p. on which I write BOOKS 32

pageant life's rich p.   DICTIONARIES 10
  part of life's rich p.   LIFE 9
pages fills about thirty-five p.   BIOGRAPHY 38
  through six hundred p.   BIOGRAPHY 34
paid if not p. *before*   LAW 9
pain on your threshold of p.   FAMILY 43
  p. in my head is wracking   SICKNESS 10
pains p. a man when 'tis kept   LOVE 2
paint would fain p. a picture   SATISFACTION 3
painted P., too, didn't he   ART AND ARTISTS 8
  unreality of p. people   THEATRE 53
painter Our p.! He never got under
    ART AND ARTISTS 17
  p.'s eye is to him   ART AND ARTISTS 2
pairs they always come in p.   EDUCATION 47
Pakistani P. who had learned English
    WRITERS 58
palace from your p. to my house   ROYALTY 41
palaces live in p.   HOME 17
pale I was a p. young curate   RELIGION 29
palsy strucken wid de p.   OLD AGE 8
Pam P., I adore you   SPORTS 40
pamphleteer p. on guano   ENGLAND 10
pancreas adorable p.   APPEARANCE 9
panda speak about the Giant P.   SPEECHES 4
Pandora If you open that P.'s Box   DIPLOMACY 7
panegyric P. he may keep vices out   BIOGRAPHY 1
panel more ready to hang the p.   LAW 15
panics Party only p. in a crisis   POLITICS 63
pansy p. with a stammer   BEHAVIOUR 23
pants your lower limbs in p.   APPEARANCE 5
paper as p. all they provide   NEWS 51
  more personality than a p. cup   TOWNS 9
  on both sides of the p.   EDUCATION 25
  on both sides of the p.   LAW 61
  p. appears dull   BORES 1
  p. floating down the river   ROYALTY 33
  verbal contract isn't worth the p.   CINEMA 12
  waiting for the p.   NEWS 60
paperback Book to come out in p.   LIBRARIES 12
paperbacks fat p., intended to while   BOOKS 41
papering p. the spare room   SUCCESS 24
papers He's got my p., this man   TRAVEL 16
  I never read the p.   NEWS 49
  letters printed in the p.   WRITERS 24
  P. are power   GOVERNMENT 47
  they will go to the p.   CLASS 38
paperwork I can't stand is the p.   WRITERS 59
  p. down to a minimum   BOOKS 35
paradise people living in a fool's p.
    FOOLISHNESS 27
  squeeze into P.   BODY 5
  up to a passport to P.   HEAVEN 1

parasol quaint as an old p.   MONEY 12
pardon God will p. me   GOD 3
  With a thousand Ta's and P.'s   SOCIETY 22
parent p. who could see his boy   CHILDREN 23
  To lose one p., Mr Worthing   FAMILY 19
parentage book in praise of p.   CENSORSHIP 2
  P. is a very important profession   FAMILY 32
parents begin by loving their p.   CHILDREN 11
  girl needs good p.   MIDDLE AGE 8
  gratify their p.   EDUCATION 59
  Jewish man with p. alive   PARENTS 8
  job all working-class p. want   POLITICS 88
  living with your p.   FAMILY 52
  our p. won   GENERATION GAP 10
  p. did for me as a child   GENERATION GAP 11
  P.—especially step-parents   CHILDREN 26
  p. finally realize   FAMILY 48
  P. have the idea that it is their duty
    PARENTS 14
  p. may be difficult to discipline   PARENTS 12
  p. obey their children   AMERICA 30
  P. should be given only   PARENTS 13
  p. were very pleased   ARMED FORCES 29
  sexual lives of their p.   CHILDREN 31
  what their p. do not wish   CHILDREN 10
Paris Americans die they go to P.   AMERICA 3
  frocks are built in P.   FASHION 8
  no more Hoares to P.   ROYALTY 53
  People don't talk in P.   TOWNS 10
parish six children on the p.   ROYALTY 14
park come out to the ball p.   SPORTS 106
  To poison a pigeon in the p.   MURDER 9
Parker [Dorothy P.]   PEOPLE 17
parliament [p.] are a lot of hard-faced men
    POLITICIANS 17
  p. of whores   DEMOCRACY 19
  P. to do things at eleven   ALCOHOL 20
  rabble who are elected to P.   DEMOCRACY 8
parliamentarian safe pleasure for a p.
    POLITICS 77
parody p. the memoirs of politicians
    POLITICIANS 84
parrots largely inhabited by p.   FOOLISHNESS 17
Parsifal It's about as long as P.   THEATRE 44
parsley P. Is gharsley   FOOD 67
parson p. knows enough who knows
    RELIGION 12
  would have made a good p.   GOD 45
parsons This merriment of p.   RELIGION 10
part I read p. of it   BOOKS 37
  p. to tear a cat in   ACTORS 1
  prepared to play a p.   POLITICIANS 53

peel Beulah, p. me a grape · FOOD 58
plums and orange p. · QUOTATIONS 10
peer old P. raise his robes · ARISTOCRACY 12
peerage When I want a p. · WEALTH 8
You should study the P. · ENGLAND 13
peers House of P., throughout · GOVERNMENT 6
Peke supply of books, and a P. · LIFE 7
Peking Supermarket in Old P. · COUNTRIES 40
Pekingese bitty like a P.'s tongue · FOOD 121
P. is a more common name · BIRDS 58
pelican wondrous bird is the p. · BIRDS 19
pen every stroke of the p. · HANDWRITING 3
far less brilliant p. · HISTORY 2
p. is mightier than the wrist · WRITERS 19
prevents his holding a p. · LETTERS 5
To bite his p. · EPITAPHS 4
pencil left with a p. · WRITERS 55
missing in Nature is a p. · WRITERS 37
penetrate into which we cannot p. · SCIENCE 8
penetrating p. sort of laugh · HUMOUR 9
penis I was non compos p. · CRITICS 21
think a *p.* was phallic · CRITICS 43
You're King Kong's p. · SEX 23
pension *P.* Pay given to a state · TRUST 2
Pentagon P., that immense monument
· BUREAUCRACY 7
pentameter his rhythm—Iambic P. · POETRY 45
people bludgeoning of the p. · DEMOCRACY 4
half p. and half bicycles · TRANSPORT 26
half the p. are right · DEMOCRACY 10
history without the p. · BOOKS 40
noise, my dear! And the p. · WAR 17
p. are only human · HUMAN RACE 9
p. is first what it eats · ENGLAND 36
p. know what they want · DEMOCRACY 6
P. shouldn't be treated · PEOPLE 50
p. who do things · SUCCESS 10
Politicians *are* interested in p. · POLITICIANS 81
protect the p. from the press · NEWS 7
we're the opposite of p. · ACTORS 54
peppered Shepherd's pie p. · FOOD 98
perambulator compare with the p.
· TRANSPORT 19
percentage It's a reasonable p. · CERTAINTY 14
perennials P. are the ones that grow
· GARDENS 8
perfect Nobody's p. · HUMAN RACE 18
None of us are p. · PRIDE 8
Well, nobody's p. · MARRIAGE 111
perfection P. of planned layout · BUREAUCRACY 10
very pink of p. · SOCIETY 1
performance FERGUSON'S P. · TELEGRAMS 17
it takes away the p. · ALCOHOL 3
so many years outlive p. · SEX 2

performances some of my best p. · SONGS 17
performing faint aroma of p. seals · LOVE 27
period p. would need a far less · HISTORY 2
permissiveness Before p. came · SEX 102
perpendicular p. expression · DANCE 8
railings leaning out of the p. · HANDWRITING 1
perpetrators p. of these deeds · BROADCASTING 8
persecuted generally p. when living · OLD AGE 5
persistence p. of public officials · BUREAUCRACY 19
person adornment of his p. · INSULTS 18
only one p. at a time · GOSSIP 12
p....can develop a cold · SICKNESS 12
p....can develop a cough · SICKNESS 13
p. proved as polished · SELF-KNOWLEDGE 10
p. you and I took me for · MARRIAGE 35
personal large dose of p. prejudice · BOOKS 25
personality From 35 to 55, good p.
· MIDDLE AGE 8
no more p. than a paper cup · TOWNS 9
p. in a literary article · AMERICA 10
where p. is concerned · AMERICA 41
perspiration ninety-nine per cent p.
· INTELLIGENCE 3
perspire that Mr Gladstone may p.
· POLITICIANS 12
perspiring City of p. dreams · TOWNS 13
perverse transform real life in some p.
· HUMOUR 41
pessimist Do you know what a p. is · HOPE 4
I am a life-enhancing p. · PEOPLE 45
pet And kept it for a p. · BIRDS 15
only possible p. is a cow · BIRDS 57
petal p. down the Grand Canyon · POETRY 28
Peter Pan has been wholly in P. · PEOPLE 37
petite Marcus prefers p. women
· MEN AND WOMEN 75
petulance p. is not sarcasm · INSULTS 12
pews Talk about the p. and steeples · HYPOCRISY 7
phagocytes stimulate the p. · MEDICINE 10
phallic you'd think a *penis* was p. · CRITICS 43
phallus future is the p. · FUTURE 7
pharynx went wild about my p. · MEDICINE 13
pheasant For P. *read* Peasant · MISTAKES 12
p., the pheasant · FOOD 21
phenomenon describe the infant p. · ACTORS 6
She is a p. of nature · CINEMA 40
Philadelphia rather be living in P. · EPITAPHS 14
went to P., but it was closed · AMERICA 21
philanthropy not trade. It is p. · BUSINESS 8
Philippines In the P., there are lovely
· ENGLAND 23
philistines Though the P. may jostle
· ART AND ARTISTS 5

politics (cont.)

take the p. out of politics	POLITICS 60
poll with your p. tax	TAXES 12
pollution unsavoury engine of p.	BIRDS 51
polo p. in one generation	SNOBBERY 15
polygamous Man is p.	MARRIAGE 68
polytechnic In the P. they teach you	
	EDUCATION 9
Pompey wars of P. the Great	ARMED FORCES 1
pomposity p. and intricacy of style	WRITERS 40
ponies p. have swallowed	BIRDS 41
Pontefract In the licorice fields at P.	SEX 36
poodle briefly in a p. parlour	PEOPLE 61
recollect the Alington p.	BIRDS 43
Pooh P. began to feel a little	BIRDS 26
pool Walk across my swimming p.	RELIGION 90
poop-poop O bliss! O p.	TRANSPORT 6
poor As for the virtuous p.	POVERTY 9
expensive it is to be p.	POVERTY 20
inconvenient to be p.	CRIME 4
I've been p. and I've been rich	WEALTH 23
live by robbing the p.	SOCIETY 7
marry a rich woman as a p.	
	MEN AND WOMEN 7
murmuring p., who will not fast	POVERTY 4
no disgrace t'be p.	POVERTY 14
object is p. or obscure	FRIENDS 11
one of the undeserving p.	MORALITY 13
p. cannot afford it	WEALTH 4
p. man with money	WEALTH 16
realize that he was p.	WEALTH 27
pop P. goes the weasel	POVERTY 7
p. my cork for every guy	MEN AND WOMEN 57
Pope P.! How many divisions	POWER 3
P. will grieve a month	EPITAPHS 4
recovered from Alexander P.	POETRY 27
poppa chop your p. up	MURDER 8
poppies p. was nothing to it	SLEEP 5
popping sound of a p. cork	ALCOHOL 76
poppy Piccadilly with a p. or a lily	
	ART AND ARTISTS 5
pops At classical Monday P.	MUSIC 18
population pubs per head of the p.	ALCOHOL 75
porcelain Little bits of p.	ART AND ARTISTS 19
pork eat p. and take birth control	FOOD 117
not a word about P. Chops	FOOD 68
pornographic nothing p. about them	NEWS 62
pornography give p. a dirty name	THEATRE 46
p. up to the present day	LIBRARIES 13
port It would be p. if it could	ALCOHOL 7
p., for men	ALCOHOL 9
p. is on the chim-a-ney	SEX 15
porter decompose in a barrel of p.	DEATH 52
that of a drunken p.	GOVERNMENT 1

portmanteau it's like a p.	WORDS 5
portrait p., in frame	RELIGION 77
P. painters tend to regard	ART AND ARTISTS 37
two styles of p. painting	ART AND ARTISTS 3
position In that p., my dear fellow	SONGS 17
possession p. of a good fortune	MARRIAGE 31
possible something is p.	SCIENCE 32
post-coital light of a p. Craven A	SEX 68
poster Kitchener is a great p.	WAR 7
posterity I speak for p.	SPEECHES 1
P. is as likely to be wrong	FUTURE 3
p. talking bad grammar	LAST WORDS 4
Why should I write for p.	FUTURE 12
postman think I am, a bloody p.	THEATRE 41
post mortem p. re-appearance	MIND 10
post office p. to buy a stamp	MIDDLE AGE 7
postponement P. REVUE INEVITABLE	TELEGRAMS 12
postscript all the pith is in the p.	LETTERS 4
her mind but in her p.	WOMEN 7
pot *make them in the one p.*	FOOD 47
potato bashful young p.	ART AND ARTISTS 5
glass-hard roast p.	FOOD 64
To be consistent the p.	TAXES 8
You like p. and I like po-tah-to	FOOD 61
potatoes serves instant mash p.	GOSSIP 11
yesterday's mashed p.	MEN AND WOMEN 34
potency p. in his electoral address	POLITICIANS 9
potent Extraordinary how p. cheap music	
	MUSIC 30
Potter This is Gillie P. speaking	ENGLAND 31
pounce p. out upon us from it	SCIENCE 8
poured p. into his clothes	DESCRIPTION 13
poverty Come away; p.'s catching	POVERTY 2
except p. and toothache	LOVE 41
Money is better than p.	MONEY 18
p. and oysters	FOOD 16
P. is no disgrace to a man	POVERTY 5
p. knows how extremely	POVERTY 20
setting him up in p.	POVERTY 19
state of extreme p.	POVERTY 16
Testament in praise of p.	POVERTY 10
wedded to P.	POVERTY 11
worst of crimes is p.	POVERTY 12
power Papers are p.	GOVERNMENT 47
p. on a plate	POWER 11
P. without responsibility	NEWS 20
responsibility without p.	GOVERNMENT 39
Wealth and p. are much	WEALTH 28
powers p. into the hands	GOVERNMENT 2
pox gallows or of the p.	INSULTS 9
practical Commends a most p. plan	FUTURE 4
thoroughly p. man of the world	RELIGION 26
practice God knows she had plenty of p.	
	CONVERSATION 21

P. drives me mad   SCIENCE 1
p. of writing books about   BIOGRAPHY 17
practise I p. when I'm loaded   MUSIC 82
   would p. this without me   ACTORS 5
praise people p. and don't read   BOOKS 11
   p. as a greedy boy takes   CRITICS 6
   p. stroke by stroke   WRITERS 74
   wrote the p. exhalted   APPEARANCE 8
praised p. their last publication   WRITERS 6
praises to sound his own p.   POLITICIANS 40
praiseworthy more p. than bridge   SPORTS 50
pram p. in the hall   MARRIAGE 91
prattle how pleasantly they p.   CONVERSATION 10
prawn I'd swallowed the last p.   ALCOHOL 62
   p. sandwich from Marks   BUSINESS 17
pray I p. for the country   GOVERNMENT 11
   p. for you at St Paul's   RELIGION 23
   p. to Him I find I'm talking   GOD 33
Prayer Book Revised P.   RELIGION 67
prayers Bernard always had a few p.

                       RELIGION 47
praying No p., it spoils business   RELIGION 5
preached p. to death by wild curates

                       RELIGION 22
preaching good music and bad p.   RELIGION 74
   p. and got myself burnt   HUMOUR 11
   woman's p. is like a dog   WOMEN 10
precedency p. between a louse   POETRY 9
pre-christian described as a p. cemetery

                       IRELAND 4
precision age shrinks from p.   WORDS 21
predict p. things after they have   FUTURE 9
predigested Anthologies are p. food

                     QUOTATIONS 8
preface contained a scurrilous p.   BOOKS 21
prefaces price we pay for Shaw's p.   THEATRE 19
prefer Or would you p.   SEX 14
pregnancies note of six p.   MUSIC 59
pregnancy p. by a resort to mathematics

                     RELIGION 75
pregnant If men could get p.

              MEN AND WOMEN 60
prejudice aid of p. and custom   PREJUDICE 1
   confirm existing p.   NEWS 45
   large dose of personal p.   BOOKS 25
   popular p. runs   BODY 6
   result of PRIDE AND P.   LITERATURE 2
   To everybody's p.   WOMEN 22
prejudices moral p. of the reader   NEWS 42
   p. as the advertisers don't   NEWS 38
   reviewing it; it p. a man   CRITICS 7
premature case of p. adjudication   LAW 78
prematurely he's just p. orange   APPEARANCE 18

premises arguing from different p.   ARGUMENT 7
prerogative p. of the eunuch   GOVERNMENT 39
   p. of the harlot   NEWS 20
presence indication of your p.   MUSIC 52
   p. of mind in a railway   TRANSPORT 1
present decadence of the p.   OLD AGE 11
   flattery when they aren't p.   GOSSIP 15
   know nothing but the p.   PAST 4
   people were p.   HUMOUR 39
   p. of Mornington Crescent   ACTORS 17
presents it were not for the p.   MARRIAGE 63
preserve p.'s full of stones   SOCIETY 23
presidency lose the p.   SUCCESS 23
   p. is a Tudor monarchy   POLITICS 72
   wants the p. so much   POWER 7
president anybody could become P.   AMERICA 17
   any boy may become P.   AMERICA 26
   Manhattan Bank, the American p.

                   GOVERNMENT 45
   more than any other P.   GOVERNMENT 19
   P. of the Board of Trade   GOVERNMENT 17
   p. to treat the post   POLITICIANS 79
presidential P. Office is not power   BIOGRAPHY 31
presidents Only p., editors   LANGUAGE 11
press Freedom of the p. in Britain   NEWS 38
   Freedom of the p. is guaranteed   CENSORSHIP 11
   god of our idolatry, the p.   NEWS 2
   I enclose my p. cuttings   ACTORS 59
   p. as a Pulitzer Prize   NEWS 64
   p. can show extraordinary   HYPOCRISY 12
   protect the people from the p.   NEWS 7
   racket is back in its p.   LOVE 32
   well as for the p.   WRITERS 1
   where the p. is free   CENSORSHIP 1
   with you on the free p.   NEWS 48
pressure Blood p.   HANDWRITING 10
presumption amused by its p.   ALCOHOL 35
Pretender James II, and the Old P.   LITERATURE 17
pretending p. to be wicked   HYPOCRISY 6
pretentious No to p. rubbish   CRITICS 29
   P.? *Moi*   COMEDY 24
prettiness characteristic of Victorian p.

                   PEOPLE 22
pretty He is a very p. weoman   WIT 20
   p. can get away with   BEHAVIOUR 30
   so p. that she would make   ROYALTY 63
previous no P. Chapters   BOOKS 16
prey quarry, the destined p.   MEN AND WOMEN 17
price I won't put a p. on him

              MEN AND WOMEN 39
   p. of everything   CHARACTER 6
   p. which in Europe only   ART AND ARTISTS 6
   whose insane initial p.   BOOKS 46
   Wot p. Selvytion nah   RELIGION 39

refined This Englishwoman is so r.   ENGLAND 26
refinement often cuts ice which r.   SNOBBERY 9
  r. was very often an extenuating   SOCIETY 35
reform mention the word r.   MEDICINE 37
  R.! Aren't things bad   LAW 50
reformation end of satire is r.   HUMOUR 2
  Free-gift, R., Earth   NAMES 1
  plotting some new r.   ENGLAND 1
  r. must have its victims   RELIGION 36
reformer r. is a guy who rides   CINEMA 6
reformers All R., however strict   HYPOCRISY 8
  R. are always finally neglected   BIOGRAPHY 18
refreshes r. the parts other beers   ALCOHOL 72
refuge r. and a home for the largest   NEWS 36
  r. from home   HOME 9
refunded no money r.   ROYALTY 23
refuse offer he can't r.   POWER 5
regimental you are the r. doctor   FASHION 4
regret book-buying public would r.   WRITERS 68
  r. in the theatre   ACTORS 32
regrets r. she's unable to lunch   BEHAVIOUR 21
regular brought r. and draw'd mild   ALCOHOL 14
regulated speech is not to be r.   CENSORSHIP 9
rehearsal ten o'clock r.   THEATRE 37
rehearse obvious reluctance to r.   WEATHER 19
reigned if only he had not r.   POWER 1
reindeer Rudolph, the Red-Nosed R.   BIRDS 38
reinvented they r. unsliced bread   WIT 48
reject If you r. me on account   RELIGION 38
rejection spare room with r. slips   SUCCESS 24
relation have a famous r.   FAME 5
  r. to do the business   FAMILY 6
relations God's apology for r.   FRIENDS 19
  supporting company are all r.   DANCE 7
relative hoof-beats of a galloping r.   FAMILY 30
  In a r. way   SCIENCE 14
relativity thought of Einstein's r.   SCIENCE 19
reliable r. as his hairpieces   BIOGRAPHY 43
reliance r. on his own bad taste   CRITICS 10
relic meaningless r. of Empire   COUNTRIES 64
relied now be absolutely r. upon   NEWS 8
religion all of the same r.   RELIGION 30
  bring r. into it   RELIGION 52
  entanglement with r.   RELIGION 99
  every thing that regards r.   RELIGION 8
  fox-hunting—the wisest r.   POLITICS 38
  in England but vice and r.   ENGLAND 8
  in place of a state r.   FOOD 39
  Millionaire. That is my r.   WEALTH 3
  reject me on account of my r.   RELIGION 38
  r. is allowed to invade   RELIGION 24
  take my r. from the priest   RELIGION 9
  There is only one r.   RELIGION 33

religions R. are manipulated by those
    RELIGION 97
religious between a cold bath and a r.   NEWS 23
  commit himself to any r. belief   RELIGION 53
  I am all for a r. cry   POLITICS 10
  manners can replace r.   RELIGION 98
  r. system that produced   RELIGION 37
  r. upon a sunshiny day   RELIGION 15
  though a r. man, was also   RELIGION 26
reluctance r. to rehearse   WEATHER 19
remainder r. shops by the direct   BOOKS 46
remaindered my enemy has been r.   WRITERS 67
remarkable This very r. man   FUTURE 4
remedy r. for the sorrows   HAPPINESS 14
remember I r. it well   OLD AGE 21
remembered r. by what they failed   CRITICS 9
  r. for a very long time   DEATH 26
  r. that he is dead   SLEEP 11
remind you to r. me of my age   OLD AGE 41
reminiscence best-selling r.   BIOGRAPHY 31
reminiscences old have r. of what
    GENERATION GAP 2
  r. of Mrs Humphrey Ward   BIOGRAPHY 8
  some of your grosser r.   LETTERS 15
remorse R.! Those dry Martinis   ALCOHOL 19
remote R. and ineffectual Don   LITERATURE 13
removal like the r. men   HOME 25
remove fat greedy owl of the R.   CHILDREN 22
  not malignant and r. it   MEDICINE 26
removed r. from the centre of events
    MEN AND WOMEN 73
Renaissance recovered from the R.   POETRY 27
  R. was just something   PROGRESS 14
Reno'd King's Moll R.   ROYALTY 57
rent They r. out my room   FAMILY 48
repartee majority is always the best r.
    DEMOCRACY 2
  r. in a wife more keenly   MARRIAGE 77
repay Will find a Tiger well r.   BIRDS 14
repeat Historians r. each other   HISTORY 7
repent we may r. at leisure   MARRIAGE 12
repented she strove, and much r.   SEX 10
repetition constant r. of elephants   TRAVEL 3
replied r. to your letter   LETTERS 16
report Beauty school r.   EDUCATION 43
reports R. of my death   DEATH 19
repose r. is not the destiny   HUMAN RACE 3
  r. is taboo'd by anxiety   LANGUAGE 8
represent We don't r. anybody   ARISTOCRACY 14
representation entitled to a little r.   LAW 62
representative indignity of being your r.
    RELIGION 38
reptile r. all the rest   INSULTS 2

republic r. is like a chicken   ARISTOCRACY 17

Republican R. and Santa Claus   AMERICA 43

Republicans I like a lot of R.   GOVERNMENT 31

    make a bargain with the R.   POLITICS 42

    R. are the party that says   GOVERNMENT 49

    R. talk of cutting taxes   GOVERNMENT 32

repulsive Right but R.   DESCRIPTION 12

reputation anything except a good r.   DEATH 18

    At ev'ry word a r. dies   CRITICS 1

    I owe my deplorable r.   ARGUMENT 11

    lost her r. and never missed

       SELF-KNOWLEDGE 20

reputations sit upon the murdered r.   GOSSIP 2

    true fuller's earth for r.   MONEY 1

re-read he doesn't even r.   WRITERS 72

    yet I r. his early stuff   WRITERS 36

rescuers sinking ship firing on the r.   ACTORS 33

research dignify by the name of r.   EDUCATION 16

    my principal r. in bars   NEWS 59

    r. is what I am doing when   SCIENCE 33

    r. staff to study the problem   MONEY 19

    steal from many, it's r.   WRITERS 25

resemblance recognition of another's r.

       SELF-KNOWLEDGE 6

    think there is some r.   ROYALTY 73

resented Who r. it   MURDER 7

resentful That state of r. coma   EDUCATION 16

resents nonentity who r.   BORES 14

reserved R. for the second Lady Curzon

       DEATH 35

resignation Always threatening r.

       POLITICIANS 50

    holy r. and an iron constitution   MEDICINE 27

    humorous r.   HAPPINESS 8

resist r. everything except temptation   VIRTUE 8

resort infinite mercy, a last r.   POLITICS 85

respect loved by a man I r.   MEN AND WOMEN 53

    r. for the character   CHILDREN 2

    Thieves r. property   CRIME 14

    without losing one's r.   FASHION 11

respectability floral symbols of r.   NATURE 15

respectable r. live beyond other peoples'

       SOCIETY 10

respective words in our r. languages

       POLITICIANS 57

respiration said it was artificial r.   SEX 48

responsibility I am absolved of r.   NEWS 63

    lowest rank of technical r.   BUREAUCRACY 17

    no sense of r.   CHILDREN 27

    Power without r.   NEWS 20

    r. without power   GOVERNMENT 39

responsible by all r. men   FOOLISHNESS 31

responsive I love a r. audience   THEATRE 18

rest Australia is a huge r. home   COUNTRIES 56

    more r. if one doesn't sleep   SLEEP 8

    such thing as absolute r.   SCIENCE 21

restaurant anywhere except to a good r.

       FOOD 102

    get a table at a good r.   FAME 9

restaurants four r. it's the Mafia   CRIME 28

restlessness might only mean mere r.   TRAVEL 7

restoration Church's R.   RELIGION 57

restraint r. is always preferable   BORES 10

    r. with which they write   LITERATURE 19

result conditions, you get the r.   SUCCESS 1

    r. happiness   MONEY 3

retainer r. of the Chase Manhattan

       GOVERNMENT 45

retired r. from consummation   SEX 93

retirement greenroom after final r.   POLITICS 64

    otherwise blank days of r.   POLITICIANS 79

retraction newspaper can always print a r.

       NEWS 40

retreating Have you seen yourself r.

       APPEARANCE 5

retrieve they could be taught to r.   CHILDREN 38

return Oxfam ever r. anything   POVERTY 21

    r. to earth as the doorkeeper   MUSIC 49

returned r. on the previous night   SCIENCE 14

reunite You were hard to r.   RELIGION 83

revelations hotel offers stupendous r.   TRAVEL 15

    It ends with R.   BIBLE 2

revenge Gerald Ford as his r.   POLITICIANS 71

    I will most horribly r.   TRUST 1

    r. by the culture of the Negroes   MUSIC 36

review anti-feminist books to r.   NEWS 11

    have your r. before me   LETTERS 10

    r. may spoil your breakfast   CRITICS 44

    R. of Reviews of Reviews   NEWS 18

reviewing book before r. it   CRITICS 7

reviews no more r. of any kind   CRITICS 5

revival since the r. of letters   BIRDS 3

    there is a Peacock r.   LITERATURE 38

    think we're doing a r.   MUSIC 50

reviving r. the *castrati*   MUSIC 45

revolution daring that amounts to r.   ACTORS 43

    sexual r. is over   SICKNESS 26

    want a self-limiting r.   PROGRESS 13

    war break out first, or the r.   FUTURE 8

revolutions R. are not made with rosewater

       POLITICS 13

revue POSTPONEMENT R. INEVITABLE   TELEGRAMS 12

reward r. for increasing the tax   BETTING 8

rewrite Let alone r., he doesn't   WRITERS 72

    owe to history is to r.   HISTORY 1

rewritten r. to prove that there   THEATRE 21

rogue this r. and whore together   RELIGION 13
rogues couple of r.   ART AND ARTISTS 1
role poor r. models   PARENTS 14
   r. in a rather long-running play   SPORTS 105
roles r. this quality of needing   ACTORS 65
rolled apparently r. along on wheels

     MEN AND WOMEN 26
roller skates Like running up hill in r.   BORES 17
Roman His noses cast is of the r.   WIT 20
   no R. ever was able to say   SOCIETY 13
   R. Conquest was   ENGLAND 21
   R.-style buildings   ARCHITECTURE 13
romance fine r. with no kisses

     MEN AND WOMEN 34
   R.—finis   MEN AND WOMEN 40
   Twenty years of r. make   MARRIAGE 58
romances on all these torrid r.   CENSORSHIP 17
romantic For something r.   LITERATURE 34
   R.? In your mother's clean   LOVE 39
   r. surroundings are the worst   LETTERS 7
   something, if not all, of a r.   WEATHER 21
Rome It's R., it's hot   CINEMA 30
roof on a corrugated tin r.   MUSIC 61
room although the r. grows chilly   DEATH 22
   bastard back into my r. again   CINEMA 59
   find my way across the r.   PREJUDICE 1
   r. enough to lay a hat   HOME 21
   r. to swing a cat there   HOME 6
   sitting in the smallest r.   LETTERS 10
rooming r. with Phil Rizzuto   SPORTS 53
Roosevelt Once we had a R.   AMERICA 37
Rooshans may be R., and others may

     COUNTRIES 8
Roosian For he might have been a R.

     COUNTRIES 12
roots drought is destroying his r.   COUNTRY 7
rope Brother, can you spare a r.   AMERICA 37
   Like a rat up a r.   ACTORS 60
Rosalind R. was a gay and giddy   ACTORS 37
rose dropping a r. petal down   POETRY 28
   One perfect r.   TRANSPORT 14
   R., were you not extremely sick   SEX 5
rose-coloured r. glasses with special   HOME 24
rose-red r. sissy half as old as time

     DESCRIPTION 17
roses smells like r.   POWER 8
   would like my r. to see you   MEN AND WOMEN 5
rosewater Revolutions are not made with r.

     POLITICS 13
Rosie Too many rings around R.

     MEN AND WOMEN 25
rot As artists they're r.   WRITERS 46
   knew the living talked r.   DEATH 41
   May he r. in hell   LAW 67

   R. them for a couple   ART AND ARTISTS 1
   so it must be all r.   RELIGION 43
Rothschild taken by R. and Baring   MONEY 5
Rothschilds R. down to their last two

     WEALTH 14
rots liquid which r. braces   SCIENCE 18
rotted Or simply r. early   MIDDLE AGE 3
rotten they were good and r.   THEATRE 16
   You r. swines   DEATH 53
rouge too much r. last night   FASHION 6
roulette society are like a r. table   SOCIETY 4
round R. up the usual suspects   CRIME 22
Roundheads R. (Right but   DESCRIPTION 12
roundly r., but hollowly   CONVERSATION 20
routine r. hard to distinguish   WRITERS 45
row likes better than a good r.   ARGUMENT 18
Rowe R.'s Rule   BETTING 9
rowed All r. fast, but none   SPORTS 11
rows not lugged into Family R.   FAMILY 22
royal R. Family feel their myth   ROYALTY 67
royalties pay me twice my usual r.   THEATRE 22
royalty Aren't we due a r. statement

     PUBLISHING 27
   When you come to R.   ROYALTY 35
rub if you r. up against   MONEY 7
rubbish all they provide is r.   NEWS 51
   powerful heap of r.   LIBRARIES 3
   saying No to pretentious r.   CRITICS 29
rude Because a manner r. and wild   CHILDREN 12
   But only rather r. and wild   CHILDREN 19
   r. to some of the most   PUBLISHING 22
Rudolph R., the Red-Nosed Reindeer   BIRDS 38
rug we both were on the r.   SEX 75
ruin increasingly to resemble a r.   MARRIAGE 133
   woman look like a r.   MARRIAGE 58
ruined had been r. by literature   LITERATURE 36
Ruislip Gaily into R. Gardens   SOCIETY 22
rule And they that r. in England   GOVERNMENT 16
   only infallible r. we know   CLASS 4
   other party is unfit to r.   DEMOCRACY 14
   Rowe's R.   BETTING 9
   R. of Three doth puzzle me   SCIENCE 1
ruler R. of the Queen's Navee   LAW 17
rulers are brought about by r.   HISTORY 4
rules believer in r. and regulations   GOD 48
   by strange capricious r.   WRITERS 2
   golden r. for an orchestra   MUSIC 63
   r. of British conduct   BEHAVIOUR 28
   simple little r. and few   BIRDS 15
   these sex r. for myself   SEX 31
rum Molasses to R.   AMERICA 36
   r., sodomy, and the lash   ARMED FORCES 25
   so r. it might not be true   CERTAINTY 12

rumours I hate to spread r.	GOSSIP 13	**salads** always say about your s.	FOOD 92
Rumpole R. could've got me out	CRIME 30	**sale** day of a great white s.	MIND 5
run best judge of a r.	SPORTS 65	**sales** book would halve the s.	SCIENCE 41
They get r. down	POLITICS 43	**Salisbury Plain** crossing S. on a bicycle	
runners r. were all sportsmen	SPORTS 89		TRAVEL 6
running r. up hill in roller skates	BORES 17	**salmon** like a short stout s.	DESCRIPTION 10
takes all the r. *you* can do	PROGRESS 2	s. standing on its tail	PEOPLE 46
rural r. cottage life	SICKNESS 7	**salon** s. for his agents	ARCHITECTURE 5
rush r. through the fields	WOMEN 42	**salt** Not enough s.	FOOD 66
rushes Tsar of all the r.	CINEMA 34	s. left in my shaker	OLD AGE 25
Ruskin doubt that art needed R.		**Salteena** Mr S. was an elderly man	OLD AGE 12
	ART AND ARTISTS 32	S. was not very addicted	RELIGION 47
Russian embrace the R. bear	COUNTRIES 25	**salutary** not only medicinally s.	CRITICS 13
For he might have been a R.	COUNTRIES 12	**salvation** Wot prawce S. nah	RELIGION 39
R. Ambassador would ever cross	DIPLOMACY 5	**Sam** wouldn't have a Willie or a S.	
Russians Americans is liable to like R.			MARRIAGE 70
	AMERICA 31	**same** he is much the s.	TELEGRAMS 3
may be R., and others may	COUNTRIES 8	make all the s. mistakes	LIFE 18
rustle r. in your dying throat	DEATH 36	s. thing in different words	CRITICS 32
ruts treading in r.	HUMAN RACE 5	saying the s. about you	WRITERS 54
rye Just make it a straight r.	ALCOHOL 39	usually the s. day	FUTURE 13
		sample If this planet is a s.	UNIVERSE 9
		sanctuary three classes which need s.	
s so many s's in it	NAMES 8		POLITICS 28
sabbatical already have a s. system		**sand** s. in the porridge	HOLIDAYS 2
	GOVERNMENT 54	**sandwich** ask for a watercress s.	FOOD 28
sabre-toothed old s. bat upstairs	FAMILY 47	cheaper than a prawn s.	BUSINESS 17
sack leave s., and live cleanly	ARISTOCRACY 1	Life is a shit s.	LIFE 22
sacked s. and it's always awful	SUCCESS 25	s. named after me	FAME 4
sacrament abortion would be a s.		send out for a s. for lunch	WORK 14
	MEN AND WOMEN 60	sort of gritty this s.	FOOD 100
sacrifice s. one's own happiness	HAPPINESS 6	**sandwiches** green s.	FOOD 87
s. to God of the devil's leavings	OLD AGE 2	**Sandy** this is my friend, S.	COMEDY 18
sad How mad I am, s. I am	LOVE 32	**sane** no s. person would do at eleven	
s. old age you are preparing	OLD AGE 4		ALCOHOL 20
Saddam that S. [Hussein]	POLITICIANS 83	**sanitary** glorified s. engineer	PEOPLE 11
saddens s. me over my demise	DEATH 51	**Santa Claus** S. is a Democrat	AMERICA 43
sadness s. that steals over	OLD AGE 11	S. is preferable to God	GOD 49
safe no woman in London will be s.	PEOPLE 12	**sarcasm** I think I detect s.	ARGUMENT 22
pleasant and s. to use	SLEEP 14	**sardine** hinges in it than a s. tin	SPORTS 33
safety fasten your s. belt	TRANSPORT 20	**sardines** like opening a tin of s.	LIFE 14
said if I had s. it myself	CONVERSATION 2	like when one hides for s.	SPORTS 47
might be s. on both sides	ARGUMENT 1	**sashes** one of his nice new s.	DEATH 22
nobody had s. it before	QUOTATIONS 7	**sat** everyone has s. except a man	POLITICIANS 38
sailing failing occurred in the s.	TRAVEL 4	**Satan** S. made Sydney	TOWNS 5
sailor s. who has contrivance	ARMED FORCES 3	S. probably wouldn't have	GOD 43
sailors S. ought never to go	ARMED FORCES 17	**satire** end of s. is reformation	HUMOUR 2
three young s. from Messina	COUNTRIES 37	It's hard not to write s.	WIT 1
sails with different s.	ROYALTY 56	S. is a sort of glass	SELF-KNOWLEDGE 1
saint she could make of me a s.	LOVE 6	S. is what closes Saturday	THEATRE 38
saints overrun by a Wave of S.	RELIGION 55	S. or sense, alas	INSULTS 3
s. on their way to martyrdom	WORK 21	**satiric** showed, by one s. touch	EPITAPHS 3
salad I can't bear s.	FOOD 91	**satirist** s. like a cheetah laughing	HUMOUR 23
shit from a chicken s.	SPEECHES 11	would-be s., a hired buffoon	NEWS 3

satisfaction genuine loser s.   SPORTS 83
  I can't get no s.   SEX 51
satisfied S. great success   MUSIC 72
  s. until he's assassinated   ACTORS 51
satisfying s. a voracious appetite   LOVE 7
Saturday date on S. night   SEX 76
  Glasgow Empire on a S.   HUMOUR 36
  Satire is what closes S. night   THEATRE 38
  S. morning, although recurring   TRANSPORT 7
sausage s. and haddock   FOOD 65
savage s. contemplates his mother-in-law
    MARRIAGE 62
  Standing among s. scenery   TRAVEL 15
savaged s. by a dead sheep   INSULTS 52
save But we'll s. the planet   NATURE 14
  little less democracy to s.   WAR 24
  S. your money, dress better   MARRIAGE 83
saved Are you s.   RELIGION 44
saw I s. you do it   ACTORS 54
say denying anything I did not s.   CERTAINTY 19
  I s. the hell with it   FOOD 53
  I s., you fellows   CHILDREN 21
  manage to s. what we meant   LANGUAGE 45
  Reagans intend to s. it all   SNOBBERY 20
  s. of me behind my back   SELF-KNOWLEDGE 5
  s. the perfectly correct   BEHAVIOUR 15
  should s. what you mean   CONVERSATION 7
  so long as they do what I s.   GOVERNMENT 44
  someone else has got to s.   ARGUMENT 8
  way I s. it   CINEMA 67
  you have something to s.   WRITERS 53
saying if something is not worth s.   SONGS 1
  In stories s. it brings   LITERATURE 41
  miss an opportunity of s.   WIT 22
  rage for s. something   FOOLISHNESS 6
sayings s. are generally like women's   LETTERS 4
scamp I've been a s.   RELIGION 60
scandal make one's début with a s.   OLD AGE 10
  s. is the second breath   BIOGRAPHY 10
scarlet His sins were s.   DEATH 34
scenery Standing among savage s.   TRAVEL 15
  Where God paints the s.   COUNTRY 8
scenes no more behind your s.   THEATRE 5
scent s. on a pocket handkerchief
    POLITICIANS 20
schedule his busy s.   WIT 43
  My s. is already full   DIPLOMACY 10
schemes s. of political improvement   POLITICS 1
scherzando S.! ma non troppo ppp   MUSIC 12
schizo It's so S.   CLASS 31
Schleswig-Holstein S. question   DIPLOMACY 2
scholar s. is the only man of science   SCIENCE 11
scholars s. to argue against me   ARGUMENT 11

scholarship great distraction to s.   SEX 96
school Baby, I went to night s.
    MEN AND WOMEN 59
  Beauty s. report   EDUCATION 43
  given to s. bursars   EDUCATION 53
  he's been to a good s.   EDUCATION 13
  Loyalty to the s.   SPORTS 92
  master at a pubic s.   BROADCASTING 11
  s. without any boots   POLITICIANS 45
  this is the S. play   THEATRE 45
  vixen when she went to s.   WOMEN 2
  woman at my public s.   WOMEN 75
schoolboy To tell what every s. knows
    FOOLISHNESS 4
School for Scandal seen the S. in its glory
    OLD AGE 3
schoolmaster you'll be becoming a s.   CLASS 17
schools We class s., you see   EDUCATION 22
schoolteacher s. is certainly underpaid
    EDUCATION 54
Schopenhauer I was reading S. last
    INTELLIGENCE 11
science investigated by s.   WOMEN 19
  scholar is the only man of s.   SCIENCE 11
  S. becomes dangerous only   SCIENCE 12
  S. is his forte, and omniscience   INSULTS 10
  s. of arresting human intelligence
    ADVERTISING 2
  s. was largely conceived   SCIENCE 36
  something fascinating about s.   SCIENCE 5
  Success is a s.   SUCCESS 1
  They're s. and technology   SCIENCE 40
  typical triumph of modern s.   MEDICINE 26
scientific Idiot Boy of the S.   ECONOMICS 4
  s. names of beings animalculous
    ARMED FORCES 10
  validity of the s. method   SCIENCE 44
scientist s. says that something   SCIENCE 32
  s. to discard a pet hypothesis   SCIENCE 31
  s. were to cut his ear off   ART AND ARTISTS 28
  s. who yields anything to theology   SCIENCE 28
scientists in the company of s.   SCIENCE 30
  S. are rarely to be counted   SCIENCE 37
scissors always end up using s.   SCIENCE 46
  by a larger pair of s.   FASHION 27
scones afternoon tea-cakes and s.   SOCIETY 23
score s. one more time before   MUSIC 50
  time required to s. 500   SPORTS 120
scoring s. like Jane   SPORTS 91
scorn Nor treat with virtuous s.   ARISTOCRACY 6
Scotch Being S., he didn't mind   FUTURE 6
  get a joke well into a S.   SCOTLAND 5
  S. banker   COUNTRIES 60
  working on a case of S.   ALCOHOL 30

Scotchman noblest prospect which a S.

                                    SCOTLAND 3

Scotland cartographers seek to define as S.

                                 SCOTLAND 11

do indeed come from S.   SCOTLAND 2

inferior sort of S.   COUNTRIES 4

in S. supports the people   SCOTLAND 1

offered him Labour-voting S. DIPLOMACY 14

on the West Coast of S.   WEATHER 7

S. has made enormous progress SCOTLAND 10

very much the same in S.   COUNTRIES 33

Scotsman S. of your ability SCOTLAND 7

S. on the make   SCOTLAND 6

S. with a grievance   SCOTLAND 9

Scott Fell half so flat as Walter S. CRITICS 4

S. has not read a review   CRITICS 5

wrong part wrote S.   DICTIONARIES 3

scout S. movement was a case EDUCATION 38

scouts s. with behavioural difficulties YOUTH 14

scowling s. and owling   BIOGRAPHY 37

scrabble s. with all the vowels MUSIC 46

scratch all you can do is s. it MUSIC 62

S. a lover, and find a foe   FRIENDS 15

scratchez When Ah itchez, Ah s. WOMEN 46

scratching I'm only s. the surface HOME 25

s. of pimples on the body   CRITICS 22

scream children only s.   CHILDREN 3

s. till I'm thick   CHILDREN 25

screens On the s. at cinemas CINEMA 1

scribble Always s., scribble ROYALTY 20

scribbler s. of some low lampoon NEWS 3

script they're shooting without a s. WAR 20

scullery i.e. the s.   CLASS 30

scullion Away, you s.   WIT 3

sculptor last refuge of the s. ART AND ARTISTS 24

s. only acquainted   DESCRIPTION 21

scurrilous s. preface   BOOKS 21

scurvy getting s.   FOOD 74

sea France and England is—the s. COUNTRIES 9

into a s. of platitudes CONVERSATION 15

never go to s.   ARMED FORCES 9

seal mistook you for the Great S. LAW 16

you heard a s. bark   CERTAINTY 11

sealing wax just throw s. and red tape

                             MARRIAGE 132

search s. for a voice of his own WRITERS 64

sea-sickness someone suffering from s.

                             TRAVEL 18

seasonal S. verse   CHRISTMAS 9

seasons S. return, and today MIDDLE AGE 5

seat s. on a bus to a woman MEN AND WOMEN 71

seated looked wiser when he was s.

                             GOVERNMENT 15

seaweed [S.'s] only natural enemies FOOD 103

second round the grounds for a s. time

                             GARDENS 1

s. oldest profession   POLITICS 70

years of playing s. fiddle   POWER 13

second-rate many s. ones of our own MUSIC 64

second-rateness s. of the people we do

                             SNOBBERY 6

secret bother with s. signals SEX 75

his decency is sort of s. CHARACTER 20

I know that's a s.   GOSSIP 1

I'll keep your s.   ACTORS 58

neurosis is a s.   MIND 11

s. dies with me   LIBRARIES 10

s. in the Oxford sense   GOSSIP 12

secretary effective s.   WORK 21

Napoleon in the capacity of s. WRITERS 18

s. is not a toy   WORK 18

secrets disclosing musical s. MUSIC 68

security expose airport s. NEWS 61

seduction In s., the rapist bothers SEX 78

s. by his father   BEHAVIOUR 35

see I can hardly s.   SEX 86

If they could s. me now   CLASS 29

I'll come and s. you   ACTORS 48

I'll s. you later   PUBLISHING 5

I s. a voice   WIT 2

I s. what I eat   CONVERSATION 7

I think that I shall never s. ADVERTISING 3

not worth going to s.   TRAVEL 1

s. as far as Marlow   MISTAKES 10

seed s. that refuses to be blown TIME 13

seediness depths of s. DESCRIPTION 28

seen be neither s. nor heard FAMILY 18

degree of justice must be s. MURDER 13

have been s. dead   DEATH 47

s. one Western   CINEMA 63

sees s. and hears all we do MARRIAGE 53

self-administered novel was s. in private

                           LITERATURE 23

self-assertion s. abroad NEWS 27

self-cleaning I've got a s. oven HOME 30

self-confidence he exudes s. PEOPLE 56

self-defence s. manual in one hand

                        MEN AND WOMEN 63

self-denial S. is not a virtue VIRTUE 10

self-indulgence s. has reduced a man SEX 47

self-limiting s. revolution PROGRESS 13

self-made Bright was a s. man PEOPLE 6

s. grammar school lass POLITICS 78

self-respect starves your s. POLITICS 89

self-revelation For s., whether it

                        SELF-KNOWLEDGE 11

self-righteous s. stubbornness — PEOPLE 57
self-sacrifice devoted s. — BUREAUCRACY 15
self-sufficiency S. at home — NEWS 27
sell *after* it's beginning to s. — PUBLISHING 15
I'll s. him — CHILDREN 23
s. them in the street — FOOD 26
to s. his house — HOME 1
sells Queen, she s. — CINEMA 50
semicolon telephoned a s. — NEWS 21
semi-house-trained s. polecat — POLITICIANS 68
senators look at the s. and I pray — GOVERNMENT 11
senna-tea good dutiful boy takes s. — CRITICS 6
sensation Awaiting the s. of a short — CRIME 9
sensations s. of its "tail" — POLITICS 12
sense different s. of morality — MORALITY 20
have a s. of humour — ENGLAND 18
Satire or s., alas — INSULTS 3
s. beneath is rarely found — WORDS 1
senses should they come to their s. — POLITICIANS 1
sensibilité word equivalent to s. — LANGUAGE 3
sensible S. men are all of the same — RELIGION 30
sensitivity show extraordinary s. — HYPOCRISY 12
sensual be Catholic and s. — COUNTRIES 19
sentence end a s. with a climax — SPEECHES 2
her husband finish a s. — MARRIAGE 124
Marriage isn't a word…it's a s. — MARRIAGE 80
originator of a good s. — QUOTATIONS 4
s. containing anything — CONVERSATION 31
s. he [George Bush] manages — LANGUAGE 50
S. structure is innate — LANGUAGE 43
s., that dignified entity — LANGUAGE 40
s. with seven grammatical errors — EPITAPHS 13
sentenced s. in my absence — DEATH 56
sentences Backward ran s. — LANGUAGE 22
s. is like plodding over — CRITICS 19
sentencing s. a man for one crime — CRIME 27
sentiment generally public s. — POLITICS 15
sentimental All the s. crap of it — AMERICA 24
Of its s. value — BODY 17
s. passion of a vegetable — ART AND ARTISTS 5
separate no longer s. after dinner — MARRIAGE 140
separated they cannot be s. — MARRIAGE 45
seraglio s. of eunuchs — POLITICS 62
serial obituary in s. form — BIOGRAPHY 30
series something called S. One — RELIGION 96
serious joke's a very s. thing — HUMOUR 4
much more s. — SPORTS 72
Murder is a s. business — MURDER 6
s. and the smirk — ART AND ARTISTS 3
seriously S., though, he's doing — COMEDY 17
seriousness S. is stupidity sent to college — FOOLISHNESS 34

sermon into a short nap at s. — RELIGION 7
It was a divine s. — GOD 10
sermons can't even hear my s. now — RELIGION 31
killed with a book of s. — TAXES 9
S. and soda-water — HAPPINESS 1
servant answer to the s. problem — SCIENCE 36
cracked lookingglass of a s. — ART AND ARTISTS 14
male s., as such — MEN AND WOMEN 33
s. to the devil — BUREAUCRACY 11
topic was the s. problem — COUNTRY 13
Your s.'s cut in half — DEATH 21
servants equality in the s.' hall — CLASS 10
like all other English s. — COUNTRIES 3
s. are treated as human — SOCIETY 8
serve And s. him right — DEATH 31
s. both God and Mammon — GOD 21
service good after-sales s. — SPORTS 85
she soong the s. dyvyne — WOMEN 1
unfit for military s. — ARMED FORCES 24
serviettes crumpled the s. — SOCIETY 24
sesquippledan S. verboojuice — WIT 31
set s. fair — PRIDE 9
Vilely s. — BOOKS 47
which he had a complete s. — LIBRARIES 5
settled till the children are s. — LOVE 43
seven Even the Almighty took s. — POLITICS 37
old man had learned in s. years — GENERATION GAP 3
talk about the s. inches — BODY 27
Seven Dials Of S. — ARISTOCRACY 5
seventh couple of hours every s. day — RELIGION 40
seventy-five fifty-fifty proposition as s. — CRIME 21
several hear s. times — MUSIC 11
severity set in with its usual s. — WEATHER 5
sew s. rings on the new curtains — INSULTS 28
sewage pump all his s. out to sea — HUMAN RACE 15
sewer s. in a glass-bottomed boat — CINEMA 6
sex changed her s. — MEN AND WOMEN 22
Continental people have s. life — SEX 29
death, s. and jewels — ART AND ARTISTS 38
discussing s. with small children — CHILDREN 36
exactly like s. — MONEY 15
Is s. dirty — SEX 66
kidnap a man for s. — SEX 99
more dangerous than s. — FOOD 114
more important than s. — SEX 98
newspaper prints a s. crime — NEWS 22
no alcohol, no s. — BOOKS 43
poor feeble s. is bent — WOMEN 18
practically conceal its s. — BIRDS 29
S. and Civics — SEX 37
s. business isn't worth — SEX 24

S. ever rears its ugly head	SEX 83	[S.] hasn't an enemy	FRIENDS 10
S. is like having dinner	SEX 91	S. is the most fraudulent	WRITERS 58
S. is something I really	SEX 31	S.'s plays are the price	THEATRE 19
s., smoking dope, rioting	EDUCATION 57	vegetarian George Bernard S.	PEOPLE 12
s. the way British magazines	NEWS 62	**she** S. who must be obeyed	WOMEN 23
[s.] was the most fun	SEX 81	**shears** resembles a pair of s.	MARRIAGE 45
s. with someone I love	SEX 80	**she-camels** rode none but s.	BIRDS 22
short-legged sex the fair s.	MEN AND WOMEN 9	**sheep** mountain s. are sweeter	FOOD 12
threat of s. at its conclusion	SEX 90	savaged by a dead s.	INSULTS 52
What s. are you going to put	TRAVEL 19	s. in sheep's clothing	INSULTS 43
When you have money, it's s.	MONEY 13	s. painted by Raphael	PEOPLE 22
which is the superior s.	WOMEN 71	s. to achieve a lion	DESCRIPTION 21
sexes All the s.	LOVE 22	standing a s. on its hind legs	MEN 8
there are three s.	RELIGION 21	which men share with s.	HUMAN RACE 5
sexophones s. wailed	SEX 20	writer to eat a whole s.	WRITERS 33
sexton s. tolled the bell	DEATH 10	**shelf** have in a libry is a s.	LIBRARIES 2
sexual period of s. ambivalence	SEX 100	s. life of the modern hardback	WRITERS 71
primary s. activity	SEX 70	**shell-cases** making s. instead	MUSIC 24
s. continence requires	SEX 47	**Shelley** S. under the impression	POETRY 19
s. equality will come when		**shepherd** s. and no money	TRAVEL 20
	MEN AND WOMEN 80	S.'s pie peppered	FOOD 98
s. frustration to give	FRIENDS 25	**sherry** have a s. before dinner	ALCOHOL 52
S. intercourse began	SEX 73	kitchen with the cooking s.	ALCOHOL 56
s. lives of their parents	CHILDREN 31	**shield** s. of the Dutchmen	SPORTS 41
s. revolution is over	SICKNESS 26	**shimmered** Jeeves s. out	TELEGRAMS 5
which increase s. arousal	WOMEN 78	**shimmy** s. like my sister Kate	DANCE 2
sexually s. transmitted disease	LIFE 25	**ship** desert a sinking s.	CERTAINTY 16
sexy want you to be here and s.	MARRIAGE 115	Has anybody seen our s.	ARMED FORCES 20
Shah mention the S. out loud	NAMES 5	s. firing on the rescuers	ACTORS 33
shaken To be well s.	MEDICINE 4	s. is being in a jail	ARMED FORCES 3
Shakespeare Brush up your S.	THEATRE 26	s. would *not* travel due West	TRAVEL 4
'I know' said S.	ACTORS 31	swimming *towards* a sinking s.	TRUST 12
Let S. do it his way	WRITERS 63	**ships** drawing s., making quips	BIOGRAPHY 22
S. is so tiring	ACTORS 38	**Shiraz** wine of S. into urine	BODY 14
S.'s gardening fit	GARDENS 6	**shirt** In your s. and your socks	TRAVEL 6
S. Sonnets to the blind	ACTORS 21	**shit** And s. on the bastards below	SPORTS 100
thinking you write like S.	WRITERS 47	Life is a s. sandwich	LIFE 22
with the telephone and S.	WAR 21	s. from a chicken salad	SPEECHES 11
shaking s. them to make certain	SPEECHES 7	**shits** knew who the s. were	GOVERNMENT 48
shame secret s. destroyed my peace	POETRY 36	**shiver** s. looking for a spine	INSULTS 61
s. and humiliation is now	FAME 8	**shivers** s. like the jelly	DANCE 2
still have to ask...s. on you	MUSIC 71	**shock** sensation of a short, sharp s.	CRIME 9
shape rocks won't lose their s.	WEALTH 17	s. them and keep them	YOUTH 1
s. of Lord Hailsham	SEX 47	**shoe** banging his s. on the desk	LANGUAGE 36
shares s. are a penny	MONEY 5	**shoemaker** take my shoes from the s.	
shark bitten in half by a s.	CHOICE 10		RELIGION 9
followed conversation as a s.	WIT 38	**shoes** his suede s. in his mouth	ANGER 10
that it is leading the s.	NEWS 65	It's better with your s. off	COUNTRIES 24
sharks s.' fins navigating unhappily	FOOD 63	s. he would be wearing	RELIGION 101
We are all s. circling	POLITICS 84	s. with high heels	FASHION 12
shaved s. as close as a bridegroom	GARDENS 10	**shome** S. mishtake, shurely	COMEDY 25
shaves man who s. and takes a train	TRAVEL 21	**shoot** I s. the Hippopotamus	BIRDS 13
Shaw disciple of Bernard S.	MORALITY 8	Please do not s. the pianist	MUSIC 16
labour to the S. clan	ALCOHOL 21	s. me in my absence	DEATH 56

shoot (cont.)

s. me through linoleum	CINEMA 46
shooting being late was a s. party	SPORTS 38
I've a s. box in Scotland	WEALTH 5
shoot are the s. people	SPORTS 32
s. as a sport depends	SPORTS 23
Stop s. now	CINEMA 33
they're s. without a script	WAR 20
shopkeepers weakness, it is for s.	CLASS 33
shoplifting caught s.	SOCIETY 33
shopping Now we build s. malls	HUMAN RACE 17
when one goes out s.	WEALTH 12
short Life is too s. to stuff	TIME 12
sensation of a s. sharp shock	CRIME 9
S. dictionaries should	DICTIONARIES 11
s. of Acetylmethyl...	MEDICINE 15
shortage s. of coal and fish	BUREAUCRACY 3
shorter read the book. It's s.	CRITICS 30
s. than they should have been	BODY 11
time to make it s.	LETTERS 1
shortest s. and least likely	ROYALTY 46
shorts khaki s. girl	SPORTS 40
shot amazed he was such a good s.	DEATH 65
he once s. a bookseller	PUBLISHING 2
s. at for sixpence a-day	ARMED FORCES 5
They've s. our fox	POLITICS 40
young Sahib s. divinely	ARISTOCRACY 10
shoulder-blade s. that is a miracle	BODY 9
shoulders heads on your young s.	
	EDUCATION 36
shouldn't It's not 'cause I s.	WOMEN 37
shout S. with the largest	POLITICS 7
show Another op'nin' of another s.	THEATRE 24
food I ate and not the s.	SLEEP 12
fuck to get out of this s.	THEATRE 49
Let's go on with the s.	ACTORS 35
s. to give pornography	THEATRE 46
Sullivan coming to fix the s.	WIT 41
Why must the s. go on	THEATRE 31
show-business Boxing is s. with blood	
	SPORTS 17
showgirls S. MORE OR LESS SAME HEIGHT	
	TELEGRAMS 13
show-off inverted s.	SNOBBERY 16
shows All my s. are great	SELF-KNOWLEDGE 18
shrew really want to do the S.	THEATRE 51
shrieks s. to pitying heav'n	DEATH 2
shrimp life in it as a potted s.	CRITICS 32
shroud gaiety is a striped s.	WALES 5
shudder awake with a s. despairing	MONEY 5
shut mouth s. and appear stupid	FOOLISHNESS 19
only we can get Man to s. up	GOD 39
Whenever you're right, s. up	MARRIAGE 108
shutters we'd need keep the s. up	CHARACTER 5

shuttlecock Battledore and s.'s a wery	LAW 7
shy feeling nervous and s.	MIDDLE AGE 7
She's s.—of the Violet	YOUTH 2
shyness s. and a longing for anonymity	
	PEOPLE 42
shysters s. out of their profession	LAW 46
sick hired to watch the s.	SICKNESS 2
I am s. of both	INSULTS 8
I feel too s. to tell	SICKNESS 15
I'll be s. tonight	CHILDREN 15
I'm s. with disgust	SPORTS 56
Pass the s. bag, Alice	COMEDY 26
s. enough to call for help	MEDICINE 17
thcream till I'm s.	CHILDREN 25
were you not extremely s.	SEX 5
sicker justice be far s.	TRAVEL 18
Sidcup I could get down to S.	TRAVEL 16
side don't care which s. wins	SPORTS 87
his own s. in a quarrel	POLITICS 56
Now I am on the s.	RELIGION 27
sides everyone changes s.	GENERATION GAP 6
life holding on to the s.	CHARACTER 21
might be said on both s.	ARGUMENT 1
on both s. of the paper	EDUCATION 25
sidestep I never s. skunks	INSULTS 13
sideways walk s. towards them	SPORTS 43
siesta Englishmen detest a s.	ENGLAND 23
sight each other at first s.	FRIENDS 2
sights more impressive s.	SCOTLAND 6
sign don't wish to s. my name	LETTERS 6
would give me some clear s.	GOD 36
signalling thin one is wildly s.	BODY 16
signature one's style is one's s.	LETTERS 6
signed he never s. off	POLITICIANS 50
not yet s. her contract	ACTORS 39
significance Of social s.	POLITICS 33
silence easy step to s.	POLITICS 4
Indecency's conspiracy of s.	VIRTUE 11
occasional flashes of s.	CONVERSATION 5
resulting in a momentary s.	ARGUMENT 16
s. notices in the library	SLEEP 13
s. when even the most bronchial	THEATRE 55
with the conspiracy of s.	POETRY 15
silent 'g' is s.	INSULTS 58
God is s., now if only	GOD 39
s. and indefinitely bored	SOCIETY 9
t is s., as in *Harlow*	INSULTS 32
silicon Had s. been a gas	SUCCESS 3
silk s. hat at a private view	FASHION 9
s. makes the difference	CLASS 3
s. purse out of your wife's ear	BIRDS 30
s. stockings	THEATRE 5
What? that thing of s.	INSULTS 3

silken s. rope and speculation	ARISTOCRACY 11
silly or I shall be getting s.	BIBLE 5
silver About a s. lining	HOPE 11
all the Georgian s.	POLITICS 81
s. foot in his mouth	PEOPLE 55
s. lining in the sky-ee'	WAR 5
s. plate on a coffin	DESCRIPTION 2
thirty pieces of s.	POLITICS 45
thirty pieces of s.	RELIGION 45
simple It was beautiful and s.	CRIME 15
rarely pure, and never s.	TRUTH AND LIES 7
S. tastes, you will agree	SATISFACTION 13
What do the s. folk do	ROYALTY 71
simplicity elegant s. of the three	MONEY 2
sin autobiography is a s.	BIOGRAPHY 8
beauty is only s. deep	APPEARANCE 2
Excepting Original S.	VIRTUE 3
lips were shaped for s.	SEX 36
not generally a social s.	HYPOCRISY 10
one unpardonable s.	SUCCESS 6
researches in original s.	SEX 40
To go away and s. no more	ROYALTY 26
Would you like to s.	SEX 14
sincere s. than a woman constant	WIT 8
sincerity s. is a dangerous thing	VIRTUE 9
Sindh *Peccavi*—I have S.	WAR 4
sing never heard no horse s.	MUSIC 73
persons die before they s.	DEATH 11
s. my best in this position	SONGS 17
unless, of course, they could s.	PREJUDICE 15
worth saying, people s. it	SONGS 1
young lady who cannot s.	ACTORS 11
singers well-known s.	MUSIC 45
singing in spite of the s.	SONGS 3
single s. man in possession	MARRIAGE 31
singles s. we played after tea	SPORTS 48
sings instead of bleeding, he s.	SONGS 10
With every word it s.	DESCRIPTION 9
sink cake standing over the s.	HOME 20
s. my boats	MARRIAGE 117
sinking kind of alacrity in s.	BODY 2
s. ship firing on the rescuers	ACTORS 33
swimming *towards* a s. ship	TRUST 12
whether to desert a s. ship	CERTAINTY 16
sinned more s. against	TOWNS 11
sinner dead s. revised and edited	VIRTUE 12
I've been a s.	RELIGION 60
Or I of her a s.	LOVE 6
sinners s. on this part of Broadway	RELIGION 59
sinning more s. a little later	RELIGION 59
sins His s. were scarlet	DEATH 34
s. not with courtiers	ROYALTY 27
Sir Ma'am or S.	ROYALTY 72

sissy s. stuff that rhymes	POETRY 31
sister Had it been his s.	EPITAPHS 6
My s. and my sister's child	FAMILY 4
trying to violate your s.	SEX 17
want one to bury my s.	DEATH 60
sisterly fervour of s. animosity	BEHAVIOUR 6
sisters And so do his s.	FAMILY 15
s. that come in triplicate	FAMILY 51
s. under their skins	WOMEN 26
sit anyone come and s. by me	GOSSIP 14
chance to s. down	ACTORS 38
head-waiter who's allowed to s.	DIPLOMACY 9
Here I s., alone and sixty	OLD AGE 40
sitar frantic s.-playing	MUSIC 83
sits Sometimes I s. and thinks	PHILOSOPHY 3
sitting My dear, you're s. on it	CINEMA 21
stay s. down	MIDDLE AGE 14
Sitwells become a friend of the S.	SOCIETY 14
six forget the s. feet	BODY 27
sixpence by the extra s. on beer	TAXES 4
nothing above s.	POLITICIANS 34
precious little for s.	ECONOMICS 2
sixties s. is rather late	OLD AGE 24
sixty Here I sit, alone and s.	OLD AGE 40
sixty-five s. you get social security	SEX 41
size Because of their s.	PARENTS 12
skating always s. on thin ice	ACTORS 27
skay s. is only seen	ACTORS 14
skeletons s. copulating	MUSIC 61
ski-ing s. consists of wearing	SPORTS 103
skill nothing with a deal of s.	ARMED FORCES 4
skin s. has unexpectedly turned	ACTORS 19
taxidermist takes only your s.	TAXES 5
skinhead some bullying s.	DESCRIPTION 30
skins sisters under their s.	WOMEN 26
such white s.	CLASS 16
skipping by dint of s.	MEN AND WOMEN 22
skirt By the s.	THEATRE 29
skit I think you're full of s.	WIT 43
Skugg Here S. Lies snug	EPITAPHS 7
skunks I never sidestep s.	INSULTS 13
sky s. is only seen	ACTORS 14
skyrockets s. to folk hero status	POLITICS 65
slab Beneath this s.	EPITAPHS 20
slacks girls in s. remember Dad	CHRISTMAS 5
slain swain getting s.	CINEMA 31
slam s. the door in the face	OLD AGE 20
slamming In Little Girls is s. Doors	CHILDREN 18
slander s. you and the other	FRIENDS 8
slang s. which he heard	LANGUAGE 16
slap S. that bass	MUSIC 33
slashed usual s.-wrist shot	CINEMA 27
slashing For a s. article, sir	NEWS 4
your damned cutting and s.	PUBLISHING 1

slate age wipes the s. clean .... OLD AGE 37
 his thoughts upon a s. .... POETRY 12
slave most beautiful s.-quarters .... CINEMA 37
slaves Englishmen never will be s. .... ENGLAND 15
 Molasses to Rum to S. .... AMERICA 36
sleep been to s. for over a year .... SLEEP 8
 calf won't get much s. .... BIRDS 50
 exposition of s. came upon .... SLEEP 2
 I love s. because .... SLEEP 14
 I s. easier now .... MIDDLE AGE 6
 like men who s. badly .... SLEEP 9
 nose-painting, s., and urine .... ALCOHOL 3
 ordinary s. is not enough .... MEDICINE 36
 she tried to s. with me .... SEX 77
 S. appears to be rather addictive .... SLEEP 15
 s. is for the night .... SLEEP 17
 s. is so deep .... LIBRARIES 6
 sleep where I shouldn't s. .... MEN AND WOMEN 40
 suffer nobody to s. in it .... RELIGION 7
 when you can't get to s. .... LIFE 21
 who will bore you to s. .... BORES 13
 would make anyone go to s. .... SLEEP 5
sleep-in s. maids .... HOME 19
sleeping Best s. draught .... SLEEP 16
 fuss about s. together .... SEX 18
 novelty of s. with a queen .... ROYALTY 30
sleepless S. themselves .... POETRY 8
sleeps Homer sometimes s. .... LITERATURE 4
 She s. alone at last .... EPITAPHS 21
 s. at his work .... SLEEP 13
 s. with the enemy .... MARRIAGE 144
 s. with the Lords .... ROYALTY 27
sleeve lacy s. with a bottle of vitriol .... PEOPLE 17
sleigh wolves had overtaken a s. .... DESCRIPTION 20
slept hearing that a judge had s. .... LAW 5
 s. more than any other .... GOVERNMENT 19
slice S. him where you like .... CHARACTER 9
slight friendship called s. .... FRIENDS 11
slightly he was S. in *Peter Pan* .... PEOPLE 37
slime doin' 'The S.' .... DANCE 5
sling s. out the fish-knives .... BEHAVIOUR 39
slink probably s. off by itself .... MUSIC 53
slobs bad Americans are s. .... COUNTRIES 61
slopes on the butler's upper s. .... SATISFACTION 10
sloppy divorced, broke and s. .... LIFE 16
Sloppy Joe At Dirty Dick's and S.'s .... ALCOHOL 40
slops when love s. out all over .... LOVE 47
Slough fall on S. .... WAR 12
slow consuming was s. poison .... ALCOHOL 41
 On a s. boat to China .... COUNTRIES 31
 s. dissolve in ten years .... CINEMA 42
 telling you to s. down .... DEATH 57

slower Reading it s. does not .... SCIENCE 42
slowly angel to pass, flying s. .... TIME 2
sluicing excellent browsing and s. .... FOOD 44
slum swear-word in a rustic s. .... LITERATURE 14
slumbering s. consciousness .... LAW 41
slums become the s. of the future .... TOWNS 7
 gay intimacy of the s. .... EDUCATION 23
slurp As they s., slurp, slurp .... MONEY 12
slush pure as the driven s. .... VIRTUE 14
small express in the s. of the back .... DESCRIPTION 7
 Microbe is so very s. .... SCIENCE 7
 no such thing as a s. whisky .... ALCOHOL 55
 pictures that got s. .... CINEMA 26
 shows how s. the world is .... WORK 5
smallest s. room of my house .... LETTERS 10
small-scale well suited to the s. plot .... POLITICIANS 69
small-talking this s. world .... LANGUAGE 32
smart Don't get s. alecksy .... PROGRESS 9
 Dull Alec versus S. Alec .... CHOICE 6
smarter who thought themselves s. .... POLITICIANS 51
smell run after a nasty s. .... SPORTS 27
 s. and hideous hum .... TRANSPORT 8
 s. too strong of the lamp .... LITERATURE 1
smells tell me it s. like roses .... POWER 8
smile Cambridge people rarely s. .... PLACES 5
 occasions for a s. .... DICTIONARIES 5
 s. bathed us like warm .... DESCRIPTION 26
 s. his face into more lines .... PRIDE 2
 s. on the face of the tiger .... BIRDS 46
 s. playing about his lips .... CHARACTER 10
 You're the s. .... MEN AND WOMEN 32
smirk serious and the s. .... ART AND ARTISTS 3
Smith Chuck it, S. .... HYPOCRISY 7
 have a niece called S. .... SNOBBERY 12
smog s. attack that makes anything .... SICKNESS 14
smoke hearse drivers must s. .... DEATH 79
 People who don't s. .... VIRTUE 31
 s. of the pit that is bottomless .... SICKNESS 1
smokestack burying your head in a s. .... SICKNESS 14
smoking s. taxed as a foreign .... TAXES 8
smut sex crime, it is s. .... NEWS 22
snaffle s. and the curb all right .... LITERATURE 19
snails s. without the added delicacies .... FOOD 104
snake handy in case I see a s. .... ALCOHOL 45
 more to this s. of a poem .... POETRY 10
 s. control in Ireland .... POLITICIANS 73
 S. is living yet .... BIRDS 15
 writers in the way that a s. .... WRITERS 70
snapper-up s. of unconsidered trifles .... CHARACTER 2

snatch when you s. Bookie Bob — BETTING 3
snatches s. a man from obscurity — THEATRE 8
sneering I was born s. — ARISTOCRACY 8
sneezes And beat him when he s. — CHILDREN 7
snigger between a eunuch and a s.
— RELIGION 49
snipe you could shoot s. — CHARACTER 12
snobbery bereaved if s. died — HUMOUR 22
S. with Violence — SNOBBERY 17
snobs bad Brits are s. — COUNTRIES 61
snooker Playing s. gives you — SPORTS 110
snore snorer can't hear himself s. — SLEEP 7
s. so loud you will wake — ROYALTY 5
snored Coolidge only s. — GOVERNMENT 19
snoring Whom, s., she disturbs — SICKNESS 2
snow It's congealed s. — CINEMA 35
no word for s. — SEX 56
s. on the coolibah trees — WEATHER 20
wrong kind of s. — WEATHER 24
Snow White I used to be S. — VIRTUE 29
snuff-box s. from an Emperor — AMERICA 2
snuff-boxes s. on my return — DIPLOMACY 5
snug Lies s. — EPITAPHS 7
soap S. and education are not — EDUCATION 5
s. box down in Union Square — NATURE 3
used your s. two years ago — PRAISE 4
soap opera refer to the television s.
— BIOGRAPHY 40
sober covered by s. journalists — NEWS 67
different when you're s. — HOME 23
he that will go to bed s. — ALCOHOL 4
I've tried him s. — ROYALTY 6
keep absolutely s. — WEALTH 11
one sees in Garbo s. — PEOPLE 36
so s. as to be able to pick — ALCOHOL 10
tomorrow I shall be s. — INSULTS 42
when I was one-third s. — ALCOHOL 33
sobriety language to express s. — IRELAND 10
s. from mild intoxication — ALCOHOL 47
social Boston s. zones — CLASS 19
English s. mill grinds slowly — LETTERS 17
not generally a s. sin — HYPOCRISY 10
Of s. significance — POLITICS 33
show she has s. instincts — SOCIETY 12
socialism creeping s. — POLITICS 53
socialist I am a S., an Atheist — POETRY 19
want a s. world — POLITICS 44
socialists Education with s. — EDUCATION 44
social security sixty-five you get s. — SEX 41
social services by the s. department
— BUREAUCRACY 15
society Britain is a class-ridden s. — CLASS 36
by those who govern s. — RELIGION 97
known as Indexers, S. — BOOKS 44

primitive s. — PREJUDICE 8
s. has had a taste of me — FOOD 54
S. is the banker — SOCIETY 4
s. is wonderfully delightful — SOCIETY 3
sociological it is a s. study — NEWS 22
socks In your shirt and your s. — TRAVEL 6
s. compelled one's attention — FASHION 11
Socratic S. method is a game — EDUCATION 46
sod till he got under the s. — ART AND ARTISTS 17
soda-water Sermons and s. — HAPPINESS 1
sodium Of having discovered S. — SCIENCE 10
sodomite exception to the word S. — WORDS 20
sodomy Comedy, like s. — HUMOUR 29
Impotence and s. — CLASS 26
s., and the lash — ARMED FORCES 25
sofa luxury the accomplished s. — HOME 3
s. upholstered in panther skin — SEX 40
softest s. thing about him — BETTING 3
Soho He was glued to S. — PLACES 13
soiling I'm s. the doileys — SOCIETY 23
soldier Ben Battle was a s. bold — ARMED FORCES 6
chocolate cream s. — ARMED FORCES 14
For a s. I listed — ARMED FORCES 5
s. can stand up to anything — ARMED FORCES 15
s. is no more exempt — FOOLISHNESS 7
Tomb of the Well-Known S. — GOVERNMENT 36
what the s. said — LAW 6
soldiers as many s. as that — WAR 13
s., mostly fools — HISTORY 4
solicitor can only go to his s. — RELIGION 28
haven't got the right s. — MARRIAGE 119
solidity with the atom all the s. — SCIENCE 22
solitary ennui of a s. existence — MARRIAGE 52
till I am s., and cannot — INSULTS 7
Solomon King S. wrote the Proverbs
— RELIGION 61
solution failed to seek a peaceful s.
— CHARACTER 13
s. for the problem of habitual — MISTAKES 16
solvent When newspapers became s. — NEWS 34
some s., alas, with Kate — ALCOHOL 40
somebodee When every one is s. — CLASS 8
someone s., somewhere — RELIGION 69
somersault s. you know why clothing
— CHILDREN 42
something it actually tells you s. — POETRY 39
S. for everyone — THEATRE 40
S. may be gaining on you — SPORTS 52
was there s. — COMEDY 12
somewhat tough joints more than s. — WOMEN 39
somewhere If you want to get s. — PROGRESS 2
son good idea—s. — COMEDY 22
our s. of a bitch — POLITICIANS 31

song I tune my latent s.   SONGS 19
  Sing us a s.   POLITICS 33
  s. makes you feel a thought   WORDS 22
  two men to write one s.   SONGS 13
songdom used two-letter word in S.   WORDS 23
songs written two s.   WORK 24
son-in-law My s.   FAMILY 36
sonnets *Do Not Attempt the S.*   WRITERS 47
  written s. all his life   MARRIAGE 38
sons Yes, we have two s.   MARRIAGE 84
soon begins so low and ends so s.   ROYALTY 69
sooner same mistakes—only s.   LIFE 18
  We die s.   MEN AND WOMEN 72
sophistication S. is not an admired quality
    BEHAVIOUR 38
soporific lettuce is 's.'   FOOD 36
soprano s. of the kind often used   SONGS 12
sorrows no remedy for the s.   HAPPINESS 14
  Then all my s. are at an end   MARRIAGE 21
sorry I'm s., now, I wrote it   QUOTATIONS 9
soul have a discreet s.   DIARIES 4
  iron has entered his s.   POLITICIANS 42
  one's s. shine through   APPEARANCE 15
  sold his s. to the Devil   VIRTUE 28
  s. for the whole world   WALES 6
  s. gets snapped up   BUREAUCRACY 15
  s. of reading   BOOKS 3
souls American woman has two s.   AMERICA 16
  are written up as s.   TRAVEL 9
  Most people sell their s.   HYPOCRISY 9
sound other not very s.   ENGLAND 4
  something direful in the s.   TOWNS 3
  s. ideas is original   POLITICS 54
  s. of a popping cork   ALCOHOL 76
  s. of English county families   ENGLAND 19
  s. of oil wells   MONEY 12
sounds music is better than it s.   MUSIC 26
  similar s. at their ends   POETRY 38
  unconnected, unset s.   MUSIC 4
soup cannot make a good s.   FOOD 14
  learnt to consume like s.   POETRY 32
  like a cake of portable s.   DIARIES 1
  not take s. at luncheon   CLASS 24
  Of s. and love   FOOD 5
  pockets so he can steal s.   CINEMA 7
  turns into s.   WEATHER 9
  you pissed in our s.   TRUST 15
sourest s.-natured dog   BIRDS 2
South African S. police would leave
    PREJUDICE 11
sovereign Here lies our s. lord the King
    ROYALTY 3
sow S. and close her in a coffer   BIRDS 1

soya gigantic field of s. beans   PHILOSOPHY 8
space convention of the S. Age   UNIVERSE 11
  S. is almost infinite   UNIVERSE 13
  s. must also be found   WRITERS 50
  s. where nobody is   AMERICA 14
spade I have never seen a s.   INSULTS 19
  s. is never so merely   LANGUAGE 34
spades Let s. be trumps   SPORTS 3
Spain given S. a miss this year   HOLIDAYS 8
  Go to S. and get killed   POETRY 26
  Rain in S. stays mainly   COUNTRIES 39
Spanglish S. is langlish we know   LANGUAGE 42
Spanish Cheapish, reddish and S.   ALCOHOL 69
  expects the S. Inquisition   COMEDY 20
  S. is seldom spoken   LANGUAGE 19
spanner their throats with a s.   BIRDS 41
spare Brother, can you s. a rope   AMERICA 37
  don't s. the horses   TRANSPORT 11
spared has s. me the indignity   RELIGION 38
sparerib Any s. that I can spare   FOOD 81
sparrow If I had the wings of a s.   SPORTS 100
sparrows road for the s.   ECONOMICS 10
speak cannot sing, dance or s.   ACTORS 11
  learn to s. it   IRELAND 8
  s. ill of everybody except   BIOGRAPHY 20
  S. roughly to your little boy   CHILDREN 7
  their children how to s.   LANGUAGE 35
  will not s. a word   MEN AND WOMEN 1
Speaker Not see the S., Bill   WIT 21
speaking Is he s. to you yet   BROADCASTING 12
  s. commendably of anybody   CONVERSATION 1
  their watches when I am s.   SPEECHES 7
  You have no s. voice, dear   DESCRIPTION 9
speaks s. to Me as if I was   ROYALTY 40
spearmint s. lose its flavour   FOOD 48
specialist Being a s. is one thing   WORK 11
species hates an unmistakable s.   NATURE 10
  s. I wouldn't mind seeing vanish   BIRDS 48
  they were an endangered s.   LOVE 40
spectacle I wanted an intimate s.   CINEMA 55
speculator I was raised by a s.   FAMILY 8
speech aspersion upon my parts of s.   WIT 11
  curtail undue freedom of s.   CENSORSHIP 18
  make a s. on conservation   NATURE 7
  Reading a s. with his usual   SPEECHES 8
  s. by Chamberlain is like   POLITICIANS 34
  s. to finish being invented   LANGUAGE 51
speeches corn surplus by his s.   SPEECHES 9
speed reduce the s. of motor cars
    GOVERNMENT 22
spell anybody who can s. TUESDAY   WORDS 11
  foreigners always s. better   LANGUAGE 4
  his utter inability to s.   HANDWRITING 6
  How you do s.   WORDS 16

star (cont.)

not exactly a big s.	FAME 4
Wet, she was a s.	CINEMA 25
starch You're the s.	SEX 23
stark No, Sir; s. insensibility	EDUCATION 1
starlet S. is the name for any woman	
	WOMEN 60
starlings s. could feed off him	DESCRIPTION 28
stars mistake each other for s.	CINEMA 28
self-importance of fading s.	FAME 7
start s. together and finish	MUSIC 63
started I can't get s. with you	AMERICA 15
who s. that morning from Devon	TRAVEL 5
starter Few thought he was even a s.	
	POLITICIANS 51
starvation Night s.	MEDICINE 36
stately S. as a galleon	DANCE 13
S. Homes of England	ARISTOCRACY 13
s. homos of England	SEX 58
s. park and the fence	WRITERS 23
statement ink on the publisher's s.	
	PUBLISHING 16
statesman s. is a politician who's	
	POLITICIANS 55
s. is that he be dull	GOVERNMENT 41
s. who is enamoured	POLITICS 20
statesmen requires grave s.	POLITICS 14
station Hurries down the concrete s.	SOCIETY 22
ideas above her s.	LANGUAGE 23
TV s., for a man	BROADCASTING 18
statistics damned lies and s.	TRUTH AND LIES 3
statue s. has never been set up	CRITICS 28
staves set about them with s.	CONVERSATION 32
stay S. away from the neighbourhood	
	CINEMA 32
s. up all night or eat	CHILDREN 40
stay-at-home degenerated into a s.	TRAVEL 11
steadfastness Could s. go further	NEWS 53
steal if you s. from many	WRITERS 25
preferred to s.	BUSINESS 14
so he can s. soup	CINEMA 7
s. out of your company	CRIME 1
Thou shalt not s.; an empty	CRIME 6
stealing S. too fast	BUSINESS 10
steam-engine like a s. in trousers	PEOPLE 3
steamer about in a s. from Harwich	
	TRANSPORT 3
steel s. in a velvet glove	PEOPLE 17
step s. is short from the Sublime	TRANSPORT 4
step-parents Parents—especially s.	
	CHILDREN 26
St Francis I think I'm S.	ALCOHOL 37
S. of Assisi I am wedded	POVERTY 11
stick barb that makes it s.	WIT 16
S. close to your desks	ARMED FORCES 9

s. inside a swill bucket	ADVERTISING 4
sticks S. nix hick pix	NEWS 24
stiff S. upper lip	ENGLAND 25
stigma Any s., as the old saying	ARGUMENT 12
still If you s. have to ask	MUSIC 71
not very s. lives	ART AND ARTISTS 37
stimulant s. handy in case I see	ALCOHOL 45
s. to the industry	ART AND ARTISTS 34
stimulate s. the phagocytes	MEDICINE 10
stockings commended thy yellow s.	PRIDE 3
stole who s. the college plate	PAST 7
stol'n had I s. the whole	PRIDE 7
stomach healthy s. is nothing if not	FOOD 33
s. must digest its waistcoat	FOOD 11
stomachs must not think of our s.	NATURE 8
used to march on their s.	ARMED FORCES 19
stone For underneath this s. do lie	EPITAPHS 1
give them the s.	FRIENDS 3
heart of s. to read the death	CRITICS 14
s. of insult	VIRTUE 22
stood I should of s. in bed	SPORTS 31
stools first necessity invented s.	HOME 3
stop come to the end: then s.	ROYALTY 32
nobody's going to s. 'em	SPORTS 106
s. everyone from doing it	LAW 38
s. or I shall be getting silly	BIBLE 5
S. shooting now	CINEMA 33
stop press S. At 3.55 pm	NEWS 32
storerooms dictionaries are nothing but s.	
	DICTIONARIES 12
stories In s. saying it	LITERATURE 41
stormy s. night on the West Coast	WEATHER 7
story realize your life's s.	BIOGRAPHY 38
s. because it is true	TRUTH AND LIES 13
s. of a purple man	BIOGRAPHY 7
s. that begins with a cancerous	
	BROADCASTING 14
They used the basic s.	CINEMA 51
stout s. on a Sunday night	ALCOHOL 59
s. women she is very fat	BODY 20
usually short, s. men	SONGS 16
stove see eye to eye with a s.	FOOD 99
St Pancras Towers of S. Station	MUSIC 60
St Paul's Say I am designing S.	ARCHITECTURE 2
S. had come down and littered	ARCHITECTURE 1
St Petersburg knew of S.	FOOLISHNESS 21
Strabismus Dr S.	SCIENCE 16
straight held his bat so s.	CENSORSHIP 19
strain there will be a sense of s.	ARGUMENT 16
Strand walk down the S.	SOCIETY 11
strange be very s. and well-bred	BEHAVIOUR 2
stranger From the wiles of the s.	FAMILY 27
S. than fiction	TRUTH AND LIES 1

his t. like the Ten Commandments

	PREJUDICE 5
morals are like its t.	MORALITY 9
pays me better to knock t. out	SPORTS 18
t. like splinters	CHILDREN 28
women have fewer t.	SCIENCE 24

teetotaller I'm only a beer t. ALCOHOL 18
telegram eventually sent a t. TELEGRAMS 7
telegraph Queen has a right to t. TELEGRAMS 1
telephone covering a teapot or a t.

	APPEARANCE 14
I'll t. you	SEX 60
no t. or wife	WRITERS 26
with the t. and Shakespeare	WAR 21

telephoned t. a semicolon NEWS 21
t. by the *Sunday Express* NEWS 31
telephones Tudor monarchy plus t. POLITICS 72
televised first live t. war NEWS 67
television appearing in t. commercials

	BIRDS 54
daytime t.	BROADCASTING 16
dead I switch on the t.	BROADCASTING 10
I don't watch t.	BROADCASTING 20
intelligent enough to watch t.	SPORTS 114
make a movie out of for t.	BOOKS 38
Norwegian t.	BROADCASTING 17
refer to the t. soap opera	BIOGRAPHY 40
rich person on t.	POLITICS 71
T. has brought back murder	MURDER 11
T. is for appearing on	BROADCASTING 5
T. is simultaneously blamed	BROADCASTING 9
T.? The word is half	BROADCASTING 1
thinking man's t.	SEX 61
watch far too much t.	SLEEP 16
watch more t.	FAMILY 53

tell How can they t. DEATH 38
I'll t. thee everything I can OLD AGE 7
t. her she mustn't CHILDREN 9
those who cannot t. EDUCATION 18
you never can t. CERTAINTY 5
tells actually t. you something POETRY 39
ask him how he is, t. you BORES 5
temper arrogant t. to which ARGUMENT 11
good t. of most modern men MEN 7
never lose me t. till ANGER 6
permanently in a most filthy t. CLASS 32
snappish OAP with a t. OLD AGE 36
t. at a newspaper columnist NEWS 58
temptation combines the maximum of t.

	MARRIAGE 66
resist everything except t.	VIRTUE 8
You oughtn't to yield to t.	CHOICE 2

temptations But in spite of all t. COUNTRIES 12
T. came to him, in middle age VIRTUE 13

tempting I see nothing very t. HEAVEN 1
Ten like the T. Commandments PREJUDICE 5
satisfied with T. Commandments

| | POLITICIANS 16 |

tenants he's evicting imaginary t. SNOBBERY 13
tendency Groucho t. POLITICS 61
tender t. love scene is burning CINEMA 65
tennis play t. with the net down POETRY 34
weekend t. player SPORTS 57
Tennyson biography of T. BIOGRAPHY 40
tenors T. are usually short SONGS 16
tent inside the t. pissing out POWER 9
share a small t. LIFE 20
tents To your t., O Israel FAMILY 25
term I served a t. LAW 17
terminology of scientific t. SCIENCE 8
there is some nicety of t. CONVERSATION 22
terrible isn't life a t. thing LIFE 12
T. Vaudeville BROADCASTING 3
that t. football club SPORTS 62
terrified t. to death MIDDLE AGE 13
terrifying t. during rehearsals ACTORS 55
t. fact about old people OLD AGE 39
terror added a new t. to death BIOGRAPHY 4
adds a new t. to life INSULTS 22
even t. of their lives PREJUDICE 11
Tesco T., you could understand it FAMILY 56
test infallible t. SPORTS 20
testators T. would do well to provide

| | POLITICS 31 |

Texan T. turned out to be good-natured

| | AMERICA 33 |

Texas Next to T. I love you AMERICA 22
text great t. in Galatians BIBLE 1
textbooks chance that in legal t. MARRIAGE 88
T. arranged alphabetically LIBRARIES 4
thank t. heaven for little girls WOMEN 58
t.-you-God-for-not-making-me PLACES 15
would like to t. Beethoven MUSIC 47
thanked t. the Lord for what GOD 35
thanks t. are also due BOOKS 20
Thatcher 'Mrs T.': This car TRANSPORT 30
spread abroad about Mrs T. GOSSIP 11
[T.] has been beastly to the Bank POWER 10
T. were run over by a bus TRANSPORT 29
thcream t. and thcream CHILDREN 25
theatre beautiful t. in a hired cab PRIDE 10
going to the t. THEATRE 62
I like the t., but never BEHAVIOUR 22
My only regret in the t. ACTORS 32
t. job is that it interferes THEATRE 60
t. words have to prove THEATRE 55
Welcome to the T. THEATRE 47

That passed the t.   TIME 7
t. available plus half an hour   HOME 26
T. is the one thing you have   GENERATION GAP 7
T. shall moult away his wings   LOVE 3
T. spent on any item   TIME 8
t. to cultivate modesty   PRIDE 14
t. when on a holiday   HOLIDAYS 3
trends of our t.   BROADCASTING 8
unconscionable t. dying   ROYALTY 7
We are in for a bad t.   BOOKS 17
timely by a t. compliance   SEX 6
times able letters to *The T.*   PEOPLE 9
bad t. just around the corner   HOPE 11
timetables Europe by railway t.   WAR 27
timid capital is always t.   NEWS 34
Timothy T. Winters comes to school
                                        CHILDREN 28
tin opening a t. of sardines   LIFE 14
tinkling t., silvery laugh   HUMOUR 14
tinsel t. of Hollywood lies   CINEMA 52
tip straight t. from a business   PUBLISHING 7
That depends on the t.   SOCIETY 19
they're t. mad   COUNTRIES 57
tipsy t. that I was obliged   ALCOHOL 10
tire t. of a lecture   EDUCATION 17
tired I'm t. of Love   MONEY 6
round him has always t. me
                                   ART AND ARTISTS 22
When a man is t. of London   TOWNS 2
woman who always was t.   EPITAPHS 10
tiring Shakespeare is so t.   ACTORS 38
Titanic furniture on the deck of the T.
                                        POLITICS 68
title banned because of the t.   CENSORSHIP 8
But I love the t.   SLEEP 18
marvellous what a good t. does   BOOKS 27
No need to change t.   PUBLISHING 17
t. from a better man   PRIDE 7
t. is really rather a nuisance   ARISTOCRACY 9
title-pages understand editions and t. BOOKS 5
titles that of the rich for t.   WEALTH 21
t. put you off for years   BOOKS 49
titties t. which kept falling about   SOCIETY 21
Toad As intelligent Mr T.   EDUCATION 11
toast eating bits of cold t.   SOCIETY 33
I had never had a piece of t.   FOOD 27
t. to the sports writers   SPORTS 119
today didn't get where I am t.   COMEDY 21
Here t.—in next week tomorrow   TRANSPORT 6
T. I feel like thirty cents   ALCOHOL 19
toddler t. knows this is nonsense   CHILDREN 41
toes drying between his t.   IDEAS 7
T. to Toes   DANCE 5

toff saunter along like a t.   SOCIETY 11
toga mistakes his pinafore for a t.   WRITERS 52
together comfortably so long t.   MARRIAGE 22
concerts you enjoy t.   MARRIAGE 123
Imagine signing a lease t.   MARRIAGE 97
toilet onyx t. seat for a collar   PEOPLE 56
remember to order T. PAPER   HOME 18
t. trained at five months   PARENTS 7
toilet-roll t. holder just to prove MEDICINE 38
told I t. you so   MISTAKES 3
tolerance T. is only another name   PREJUDICE 2
tolerant being t. for nothing   PREJUDICE 9
tolerate t. without discomfort   SATISFACTION 11
tolerated came to be completely t.   SEX 88
t. the Right Honourable Gentleman
                                      DEMOCRACY 7
Tom Any T., Dick or Harry   MARRIAGE 99
Every T., Dick and Harry   NAMES 10
tomato t. and I like to-mah-to   FOOD 61
tomatoes like a couple of hot t.
                                   MEN AND WOMEN 34
tomb t. of a mediocre talent   BOOKS 23
tomorrow For t. we shall die   DEATH 44
in next week t.   TRANSPORT 6
jam t.   PAST 2
Lookin' for t.   FAMILY 33
T. every Duchess in London   POLITICIANS 25
T., in my experience   FUTURE 13
word for doing things t.   WORDS 10
Tom Thumb thought about T.   CONVERSATION 4
tone that t. of voice   INSULTS 17
tongs t. and the bones   MUSIC 1
tongue bitty like a Pekingese's t.   FOOD 121
Have some t., like cures like   BORES 8
his t. to conceive   SLEEP 3
t. being in your cheek   WIT 45
use of my oracular t.   WIT 13
what the lawyer's t.   ART AND ARTISTS 2
tonic Use it like a t.   MUSIC 33
wicked as a ginless t.   POETRY 42
tonight comedy t.   THEATRE 40
Not t., Josephine   SEX 9
tooth Front t. broken off   OLD AGE 33
toothache except poverty and t.   LOVE 41
Music helps not the t.   MUSIC 2
toothpaste t. is out of the tube   POLITICS 66
top dropping dead at the t.   DEATH 39
People who reach the t.   SUCCESS 18
You're the t.   MEN AND WOMEN 32
topics you have but two t.   INSULTS 8
Tories are T. born wicked   POLITICS 19
T. by a self-made grammar   POLITICS 78
torment eternal t. was almost certain
                                        RELIGION 65

treat Nor t. with virtuous scorn   ARISTOCRACY 6
treatment scientific t. for all diseases

                                   MEDICINE 10
tree any dumber, he'd be a t.   POLITICIANS 67
   billboard lovely as a t.   ADVERTISING 3
   If he finds that this t.   GOD 17
   when we chop a t.   NATURE 3
   would cut down a redwood t.   NATURE 7
trees birds coughing in the t.   NATURE 11
   I think of the poor t.   NEWS 51
   objections to seeing t.   COUNTRY 21
   selected the felling of t.   POLITICIANS 12
   t. are more sinned against   TOWNS 1
   t. are taken for granted   COUNTRY 19
trembles he t. as I do   WAR 3
trick Nature played a cruel t.   WOMEN 65
   t. played on the calendar   DEATH 74
   T. that everyone abhors   CHILDREN 18
trickle T.-down theory   ECONOMICS 10
tried one I never t. before   VIRTUE 21
trifles snapper-up of unconsidered t.

                                   CHARACTER 2
Trinity bit hazy about the T.   RELIGION 88
   God also is a T. man   GOD 6
trip t. through a sewer   CINEMA 6
triplicate sisters that come in t.   FAMILY 51
triste jamais t. archy   HOPE 9
triumph t. of hope over experience   MARRIAGE 28
   t. of modern science   MEDICINE 26
   t. of the embalmer's art   PEOPLE 47
trivial diversion of t. men   POLITICS 47
   Nothing t., I hope   SICKNESS 5
Trojan T. 'orses will jump out   DIPLOMACY 7
trot down to a t. I suppose   SICKNESS 21
trouble very present help in t.   TRUTH AND LIES 23
   women and care and t.   WOMEN 4
troubled t. with her lonely life   MARRIAGE 7
troubles has got over all its t.   HOME 10
   our t. from our old kitbag   HOPE 11
trouser-clip t. for bicyclists   SCIENCE 16
trousers like a steam-engine in t.   PEOPLE 3
   t. off and those that don't   MEDICINE 31
   t. on when you go out   FASHION 5
   t. so copiously flared   FASHION 31
   t. that cling to him   MEN AND WOMEN 40
trout you find a t. in the milk   LAW 10
trowel should lay it on with a t.   ROYALTY 35
   t. and a pile of bricks   ARCHITECTURE 6
truck he apologizes to the t.   ENGLAND 41
truckman t., the trashman   INSULTS 37
true absolutely and entirely t.   GOSSIP 7
   And is it t.   CHRISTMAS 5
   But I'm always t. to you   MEN AND WOMEN 45
   newspapers is ever t.   NEWS 6

   no matter how t.   PAST 9
   so rum it might not be t.   CERTAINTY 12
   story because it is t.   TRUTH AND LIES 13
   t. because a man dies for it   TRUTH AND LIES 8
truer And nothing's t.   TAXES 2
trumpets to the sound of t.   HEAVEN 2
trumps Let spades be t.   SPORTS 3
trust To t. people is a luxury   WEALTH 4
   We shouldn't t. writers   WRITERS 69
   would t. them with anything   GOVERNMENT 31
trusted it is not to be t.   POWER 7
   t. neither of them as far   TRUST 9
   t. two persons whom I knew   PEOPLE 25
trusting t. in the Lord and a good   CRIME 31
truth anxious to tell the t.   TRUTH AND LIES 2
   Blurting out the complete t.   TRUTH AND LIES 25
   fight for freedom and t.   FASHION 5
   I just tell the t.   TRUTH AND LIES 18
   mainly he told the t.   TRUTH AND LIES 4
   Ministers are wedded to the t.   GOVERNMENT 12
   Now God will know the t.   EPITAPHS 18
   occasionally stumbled over the t.

                                     TRUTH AND LIES 22
   policy to speak the t.   TRUTH AND LIES 5
   see that the whole t.   TRUTH AND LIES 19
   Strict Regard for T.   TRUTH AND LIES 10
   telling the t. about them   POLITICS 42
   telling the t. and lying   TRUTH AND LIES 24
   t. is always strange   TRUTH AND LIES 1
   t. is rarely pure   TRUTH AND LIES 7
   t. may sometimes be disinterred   LAW 72
   t. universally acknowledged   MARRIAGE 31
truthful more t. than factual   HUMOUR 35
try t. again   SUCCESS 13
   t. him afterwards   LAW 2
   T. thinking of love   SLEEP 10
trying business without really t.   SUCCESS 14
   I am t. to be   INSULTS 25
Tsar T. of all the rushes   CINEMA 34
tuba t. is certainly the most   MUSIC 76
tube toothpaste is out of the t.   POLITICS 66
Tudor presidency is a T. monarchy   POLITICS 72
Tuesday T. simply doesn't count   WORDS 11
tummy ache He'll get a t. too   FOOD 73
tun would he had a t. of wine   ALCOHOL 1
tune thinkin'll turn into a t.   MUSIC 25
   we complain about the t.   POLITICIANS 54
tunes I only know two t.   MUSIC 17
tunnel always been pro-t.   TRANSPORT 33
   light at the end of the t.   BETTING 9
   train going into a t.   HUMOUR 9
Tupperware like living inside T.   WEATHER 23
turbot by way of t.   RELIGION 20
   T., Sir   FOOD 56

turd rymyng is nat worth a t.   POETRY 1

Turk French, or T., or Proosian   COUNTRIES 12

Turkish popular T. music is like   MUSIC 83

Turks T. queueing up   SEX 44

turned in case anything t. up   HOPE 3

Turner he resembled a T. sunset   DESCRIPTION 6

  surprised to see what T.   BODY 8

turnip candle in that great t.   POLITICIANS 46

  sort of mean-spirited t.   SELF-KNOWLEDGE 29

turtle Slow but sure the t.   BIRDS 42

  t. lives 'twixt plated decks   BIRDS 29

TV T.—a clever contraction   BROADCASTING 3

  T. station, for a man   BROADCASTING 18

tweed not wear t. nightgowns   ENGLAND 35

tweet t. tweet   SONGS 5

twelve At t. noon, the natives swoon

                                                                           ENGLAND 23

  learned English when he was t.   WRITERS 58

twentieth live in the t. century   PAST 16

  that t.-century failure   SUCCESS 26

twenty T. years of romance make   MARRIAGE 58

twenty-twenty Hindsight is always t.   PAST 11

twice I like it t. as much   THEATRE 22

  they must do t. as well   MEN AND WOMEN 54

twinkle Twinkle, t., little bat   UNIVERSE 2

twins Clara threw the t. she nursed   CHILDREN 13

two Audience of T.   THEATRE 23

  Between t. evils, I always   VIRTUE 21

  t. and two would continue   ART AND ARTISTS 4

  T. for a woman   MEDICINE 24

  t. meanings packed up into   WORDS 5

  t. men to write one song   SONGS 13

  t. nine o'clocks   TIME 11

  t. people miserable instead   MARRIAGE 55

  t. people with a German shepherd   TRAVEL 20

  t. things about the horse   BIRDS 27

  t. things that will be believed   ALCOHOL 26

  Why I see t.   WIT 21

  worth t. in the street   MEN AND WOMEN 31

type Englishmen of the right t.   ENGLAND 43

typewriter changing a t. ribbon   WRITERS 38

  Hamlet like a demented t.   ACTORS 42

  t. full of oyster shells   PLACES 12

typewriting t. machine, when played   MUSIC 21

typhoid exactly like a t. germ   BIRDS 43

typical Carter is your t. smiling   POLITICIANS 72

tyranny t. of the razor   SPORTS 42

ubiquitous by being at any rate u.

                                                                     INTELLIGENCE 4

uglier u. a man's legs are   SPORTS 16

ugly be good than to be u.   APPEARANCE 1

  Bessie, you're u.   INSULTS 42

  knowing he is u.   LAW 13

  so u. that he should donate   INSULTS 49

Ulysses hand that wrote U.   WRITERS 34

umbilicus set the u. high   SPORTS 71

'umble We are so very u.   HYPOCRISY 4

umbrella unjust steals the just's u.   VIRTUE 15

unattractive most u. old thing   OLD AGE 9

unawareness u. of the world of ideas   IDEAS 4

unbearable in victory u.   WAR 28

unbeatable In defeat u.   WAR 28

unbends nothing u. the mind like   WOMEN 9

unbribed man will do u.   NEWS 19

uncertainty at least, great u.   MARRIAGE 73

uncivilized kept unconquered, and u.

                                                                          ENGLAND 2

uncle u. who lives there   FAMILY 34

uncles u. when they see a chance   FAMILY 38

uncomfortable moral when he is only u.

                                                                         ENGLAND 16

uncommon very u. cook   FOOD 42

unconquered kept u., and uncivilized

                                                                          ENGLAND 2

unconscionable u. time dying   ROYALTY 7

unconsidered snapper-up of u. trifles

                                                                     CHARACTER 2

undecided from the five who are u.   SPORTS 74

  u. whether to desert   CERTAINTY 16

undelivered died of an u. judgment   DEATH 54

under I'd have been u. the host   ALCOHOL 64

  talk u. their feet   POLITICIANS 49

underachiever basically he's an u.   GOD 38

under-dogs Englishman among the u.

                                                                         ENGLAND 33

underestimate We didn't u. them   SPORTS 113

underestimating u. the intelligence

                                                                  INTELLIGENCE 5

undergraduates employments of the u.

                                                                      EDUCATION 2

underlay he treats me like u.

                                                          MEN AND WOMEN 76

undersexed As I'm slightly u.

                                                          MEN AND WOMEN 27

  happy u. celibate   SUCCESS 26

undersized could call the u.   MEN AND WOMEN 9

  He's a bit u.   TRAVEL 5

understand really don't u. too hot   SEX 31

  what they failed to u.   CRITICS 9

  won't u. a word she says   ACTORS 28

understanding likely to propagate u.

                                                                       MARRIAGE 30

  they pass all u.   POETRY 2

  which passeth all u.   GOD 10

undertakers As u.—walk before   THEATRE 6

  nothing against u. personally   DEATH 60

underwater Baptists are only funny u.
RELIGION 107

undeserving I'm one of the u. poor   MORALITY 13

undesirable I knows an u. character
SELF-KNOWLEDGE 13

un-done John Donne, Anne Donne, U.   FAMILY 3

unearned u. increment   MONEY 10

uneasy reader need not become u.   BIOGRAPHY 21

uneatable full pursuit of the u.   SPORTS 8

uneducated government by the u.
GOVERNMENT 24

unemployed keep u. people happy
BROADCASTING 16

un-English So very u.   ART AND ARTISTS 25
u. dislike of taxation   TAXES 10

unexpectedness which I call *u.*   GARDENS 1

unfit u. for military service   ARMED FORCES 24
u. for public business   DIPLOMACY 4

unforgiving u. eye, and a damned   CHARACTER 3

unfurnished write 'u.'   FOOLISHNESS 9

unglamorous government is too u.
BUREAUCRACY 21

ungrammatical invariably u.   LANGUAGE 9
unmetrical, and the u.   INSULTS 21

unhappily result of being u. married   POLITICS 49

unhappy cosmopolitan—u. anywhere
COUNTRIES 50
instinct for being u.   HAPPINESS 11
Men who are u.   SLEEP 9
mourning for my life, I'm u.   HAPPINESS 7
u. family is u. in its own way   FAMILY 14

unhealthy men for u. women   ART AND ARTISTS 21

uniform u. 'e wore   ARMED FORCES 12
u. must work its way   WOMEN 15

uninteresting u. to be really dangerous
MEN AND WOMEN 20

union u. of a deaf man to a blind   MARRIAGE 40

unique conscious of being u.   SELF-KNOWLEDGE 28

united U. Metropolitan Improved   FOOD 19

United States Can the U. ever become
SCOTLAND 10
Government of the U.   AMERICA 32
litigant drawn to the U.   LAW 73

universe accepted the u.   UNIVERSE 3
better ordering of the u.   UNIVERSE 1
good u. next door   UNIVERSE 7
imagine the u. run by a wise   GOD 25
u. is not only queerer   UNIVERSE 5

universities u. such as the one   EDUCATION 60

University At the U., I saw many men
EDUCATION 59
French letters to the u.   FRIENDS 12
gained in the U. of Life   EDUCATION 15
they call it the U.   EDUCATION 2

We are the U.   PRIDE 5

unjust u. steals the just's umbrella   VIRTUE 15

unkind saying witty, u. things   FOOLISHNESS 23

unknown buried the U. Prime Minister
POLITICIANS 23
from the known and the u.   PHILOSOPHY 6
something equally u.   DICTIONARIES 9

unlike So u. anything else   LIFE 5

unlucky who is so u.   MISTAKES 15

unmarried keep u. as long as he can
MARRIAGE 65

unmetrical u., and the ungrammatical
INSULTS 21

un-nailed been u. from the cross   ACTORS 53

unnatural boundaries, usually u.   COUNTRIES 42
like sodomy, is an u. act   HUMOUR 29

unnerved be u. by Banquo's valet   ACTORS 49

unnoticed pass u. through London   PEOPLE 42

unpardonable Success is the one u. sin
SUCCESS 6

unpleasant Something u. is coming
TRUTH AND LIES 2
u. it is automatically good   ENGLAND 29

unprinted only one u. masterpiece   BOOKS 15

unreadable Journalism is u.   NEWS 9

unreality u. of painted people   THEATRE 53

unreliable Even death is u.   DEATH 80

unremitting u. humanity soon had me
LITERATURE 35

unrequited what u. affection is   BODY 7

unsatisfied it leaves one u.   HAPPINESS 5

unscrupulous racket run by u. men
ART AND ARTISTS 21

unspeakable u. in full pursuit   SPORTS 8

'unting u. is all that's worth living   SPORTS 5

untrue man who's u. to his wife   INTELLIGENCE 12
u. in the House of Commons   TRUTH AND LIES 28

untrustworthy publishers are u.   PUBLISHING 6

untruthful U.! My nephew Algernon
TRUTH AND LIES 6

untutored u. savage contemplates   MARRIAGE 62

unupblown NURSE U.   TELEGRAMS 9

unwell I'm not u. I'm fucking dying   SICKNESS 27

unworthy his family was not u.   PRIDE 4

up curtain was u.   THEATRE 52
U. and down the City Road   POVERTY 7
u. is where to grow   COUNTRY 16
U. to a point, Lord Copper   NEWS 28

upper butler's u. slopes   SATISFACTION 10
Like many of the U. Class   CLASS 18
Stiff u. lip   ENGLAND 25
To prove the u. classes   ARISTOCRACY 13
u. class have always associated   BEHAVIOUR 37
You may tempt the u. classes   POVERTY 13

upper-class Labour is led by an u.   POLITICS 78
upright anywhere: and that is, u.
                                            ART AND ARTISTS 23
uproar u. of the butterflies   SPORTS 21
upset it will u. my players   WOMEN 59
   It won't u. her   ARGUMENT 18
upside u. down if there's no theory
                                                ARGUMENT 15
upstairs came u. into the world   CLASS 2
   Some went u. with Margery   ALCOHOL 40
Urals swept down from the U.   PLACES 16
urban Being u., squat, and packed   PLACES 5
   u. sort of person   COUNTRY 23
urine nose-painting, sleep, and u.   ALCOHOL 3
   tang of faintly scented u.   FOOD 46
   wine of Shiraz into u.   BODY 14
use But what's the u.   WEALTH 29
   not the slightest u. to the Queen ROYALTY 36
   u. rather than ostentation   ROYALTY 16
used It is what it u. to be   SONGS 6
   most u. two-letter word   WORDS 23
   since then I have u. no other   PRAISE 4
useful trying to become u.   GOVERNMENT 9
useless u. when inert   CENSORSHIP 16
usen't u. you to be J. B. Priestley   BIOGRAPHY 36

v with a "V" or a "W"   LANGUAGE 2
vacancy unexpected v. at Canterbury
                                                RELIGION 62
vacation lawyer's v.   LAW 14
vacations no v., and diet unparalleled
                                                EDUCATION 3
vacuum out from behind the v.   WOMEN 73
   v. is a hell of a lot better   NATURE 5
vain Most people are v.   WRITERS 76
   Pavarotti is not v.   SELF-KNOWLEDGE 28
valet no man is a v. to his hero   CLASS 11
   unnerved by Banquo's v.   ACTORS 49
valuable They aren't that v.   PEOPLE 50
value mock anything of v.   HUMOUR 37
   Though we v. none   SEX 19
   v. of fortune by the persons   WEALTH 1
   v. of nothing   CHARACTER 6
van Follow the v.   HOME 14
Vanbrugh John V.'s house of clay   EPITAPHS 5
Van Eyck younger V.   MISTAKES 8
Vanguard with the V. Press   PUBLISHING 18
vanity Being an MP feeds your v.   POLITICS 89
varicose would term Victorian V.
                                            ARCHITECTURE 12
variety enthusiasm for a pointless v.   BORES 10
vase v. in the hands of a chimpanzee
                                                WRITERS 41

vasectomy v. without anaesthetic   MUSIC 83
vaudeville Terrible V.   BROADCASTING 3
veal more than cold boiled v.   FRIENDS 5
   pounds of condemned v.   ACTORS 61
vegetable fruit is a v. with looks   FOOD 111
   passion of a v. fashion   ART AND ARTISTS 5
   v., animal, and mineral   ARMED FORCES 10
vegetarian Atheist and a V.   POETRY 19
velvet steel in a v. glove   PEOPLE 17
Venice We open in V.   THEATRE 25
venom pots of oily v.   GOSSIP 8
venomous V. Bead   RELIGION 55
Venus You're the breasts of V.   SEX 23
verb first tense of the v.   SEX 8
   v. chasing its own tail   LANGUAGE 50
   Waiting for the German v.   LANGUAGE 37
verbal friends with its own v. music   MUSIC 41
   risk of v. infection   QUOTATIONS 19
   v. abuse would have sufficed   INSULTS 56
   v. contract isn't worth   CINEMA 12
verboojuice Sesquippledan v.   WIT 31
verbose v. in fewer words   POLITICIANS 76
verbosity exuberance of his own v.   INSULTS 15
verdurer Laissez v.   LAST WORDS 9
verge She's always on the v.   SEX 43
Versailles city as *un V. nègre*   TRUST 6
verse Of all my v., like not   PRIDE 7
   Only with those in v.   LETTERS 2
   proved as polished as my v. SELF-KNOWLEDGE 10
   Seasonal v.   CHRISTMAS 9
   that is not v. is prose   POETRY 3
   Who died to make v. free   POETRY 24
   write free v. as play tennis   POETRY 34
verses Non-navigational V.   MISTAKES 18
versions hundred v. of it   RELIGION 33
vertical v. man   SEX 19
very V. interesting...but stupid   COMEDY 19
vest wears a v. and galoshes   CHARACTER 17
vestments High Mass without the v.
                                                BUSINESS 12
vestry v. after service   SEX 12
vexation Multiplication is v.   SCIENCE 1
vicar Evangelical v., in want   RELIGION 77
   I will be the V. of Bray, sir   POLITICIANS 2
vicars his v. off the incense   RELIGION 54
vice distinction between virtue and v.   VIRTUE 2
   England but v. and religion   ENGLAND 8
   new V. for my old age   VIRTUE 27
   sure that v. Will in a trice   CRIME 24
vices *Panegyric* he may keep v.   BIOGRAPHY 1
vicious expect a boy to be v. till   EDUCATION 13
victim v. must be found   CRIME 8
victims reformation must have its v.
                                                RELIGION 36

victor But my shock-headed v.   LOVE 32
Victorian V. age was simply an interruption
        ECONOMICS 7
  would term V. Varicose   ARCHITECTURE 12
Victorians said in favour of the V.
        ARCHITECTURE 6
  V. had not been anxious   HOLIDAYS 4
victory in v. unbearable   WAR 28
view I have no point of v.   BUSINESS 5
  may take a different v.   TRUST 11
viewers v. be given a bonus   SPORTS 55
views political v. of Attila   ANGER 11
villains their v. wholly bad   BOOKS 18
villainy v. which we all have   VIRTUE 6
Vinci V. and pronounce it Vinchy   LANGUAGE 4
Vine Hollywood Boulevard crosses V.
        AMERICA 34
vinegar honey with a life of v.   MARRIAGE 42
vines his client to plant v.   ARCHITECTURE 9
violence beastly fury, and extreme v.   SPORTS 1
  school of Snobbery with V.   SNOBBERY 17
  threat of physical v.   MEN AND WOMEN 62
violent always dull and usually v.   ENGLAND 14
  influence of the most v.   MARRIAGE 69
violet V. persuasion   YOUTH 2
violin hears v. music   HYPOCRISY 2
  v. is wood and catgut   SPORTS 26
violins appeal from the second v.   MUSIC 32
virgin Doris Day before she was a v.   SEX 65
  trouble with a v.   SEX 43
virginity just a little more v.   ACTORS 15
  No, no; for my v.   SEX 5
  your old v., is like one   SEX 3
virtue Adult v. includes being   VIRTUE 32
  despair, disguised as a v.   HOPE 5
  distinction between v. and vice   VIRTUE 2
  homage which they pay to V.   HYPOCRISY 3
  newspaper is what v.   NEWS 40
  Self-denial is not a v.   VIRTUE 10
virtues other seven deadly v.   MORALITY 5
virtuous because thou art v.   MORALITY 1
  grow v. in their old age   OLD AGE 2
  Nor treat with v. scorn   ARISTOCRACY 6
VISA V. bill on your American   MONEY 21
visit Sole purpose of v.   AMERICA 32
vita all aqua, no v.   PEOPLE 10
vitality redolent, and full of v.   CRITICS 32
vitriol sleeve with a bottle of v.   PEOPLE 17
vixen v. when she went to school   WOMEN 2
vocabulary It shows a lack of v.   LANGUAGE 39
vogue charming to totter into v.   FASHION 3
  he'd be working for V.   FASHION 20
voice for good the supplicating v.   CHOICE 1
  Her v. is so beautiful   ACTORS 28

I see a v.   WIT 2
look at me in that tone of v.   INSULTS 17
most lovely v. I know   PEOPLE 15
panic-stricken search for a v.   WRITERS 64
v. of bottled thunder   ADVERTISING 5
v. of Doris Day   MONEY 12
You have no speaking v.   DESCRIPTION 9
voices v. of young people   YOUTH 6
vole passes the questing v.   LANGUAGE 25
volubility Then I'll commend her v.
        MEN AND WOMEN 1
volumes two hundred thousand v.   LIBRARIES 3
voluminous I meant—v.   WIT 19
voluntary Enter the strumpet v.   SEX 85
volunteer v. his men for any target
        ARMED FORCES 23
vomit returning to one's own v.   DIARIES 8
vomiting making v. courteous   BEHAVIOUR 33
vote be told which way to v.   RELIGION 100
  I never v. *for* anybody   DEMOCRACY 12
  most people v. against somebody
        DEMOCRACY 9
  sooner v. for the devil   DEMOCRACY 1
  V. for the man who promises least   POLITICS 52
  v. just as their leaders tell 'em to   POLITICS 17
voted always v. at my party's call   DEMOCRACY 3
voter Every intelligent v.   POLITICS 36
voting not the v. that's democracy
        DEMOCRACY 18
vowels scrabble with all the v.   MUSIC 46
voyage after a long v. at sea   SEX 4
vulgar Cocoa is a v. beast   FOOD 41
  let the v. stuff alone   LANGUAGE 10
  spending always 'v.'   MONEY 4
  v. and worthless life captured   LITERATURE 42
vulgarity V. often cuts ice   SNOBBERY 9
vulture treacherous brain-damaged old v.
        POLITICIANS 63

w spell it with a "V" or a "W"   LANGUAGE 2
wagged tail that w. contempt   EPITAPHS 19
Wagner Brahms, W., Strauss   MUSIC 47
  I love W., but the music   MUSIC 9
  W. has lovely moments   MUSIC 10
  W.'s music is better   MUSIC 26
waistcoat lower than the fourth w. button
        BODY 4
  stomach must digest its w.   FOOD 11
  yolk runs down the w.   FOOD 18
wait CEREMONY. DON'T W.   TELEGRAMS 2
  who have to w. for them   BEHAVIOUR 17
waited without discomfort being w. on
        SATISFACTION 11

watercress I ask for a w. sandwich FOOD 28
Watergate This we learn from W. HISTORY 23
Waterloo On W.'s ensanguined plain CRITICS 4
  W. was being filmed PEOPLE 43
  W. was won upon the playing WAR 9
water-mill noise like that of a w. SCIENCE 3
water rat with a vicious 200-pound w.
                                    POLITICIANS 64
Watlington W., which combined ALCOHOL 75
Watson Elementary, my dear W. CRIME 13
Wattle ever hear of Captain W. LOVE 8
wave overrun by a W. of Saints RELIGION 55
waves into the cheerless w. WEATHER 15
wax *didn't* w. his moustache MEN AND WOMEN 12
wax fruit excited about making w. PAST 8
way have it your own w. CERTAINTY 11
  nice to people on your w. up SUCCESS 11
  pretty good w. not to do it THEATRE 51
  provided I get my own w. SELF-KNOWLEDGE 26
  Shakespeare do it his w. WRITERS 63
  they kill you in a new w. PROGRESS 5
  w. I do it CINEMA 67
  which w. he travelled POLITICIANS 59
we use the editorial 'w.' LANGUAGE 11
weak He is very w. and you MORALITY 4
  Like all w. men he laid CERTAINTY 7
  w. from your loveliness SPORTS 48
  w. natures that are not CHARACTER 8
weakness oh! w. of joy SPORTS 48
  [Thatcher] has a w. CLASS 33
wealth He gave the little w. he had EPITAPHS 3
  W. and power are much more WEALTH 28
wealthy business of the w. DEATH 31
  w. rather than passionate MEN AND WOMEN 27
wean w. our child straight EDUCATION 48
weaned had been w. on a pickle DESCRIPTION 14
weapon Our chief w. is surprise COMEDY 20
  warmly recommend it as a w.
                                    CONVERSATION 29
wear such qualities as would w. MARRIAGE 25
weariness W. the Prince entered ROYALTY 47
wearing w. armchairs tight about
                                    DESCRIPTION 4
wears she w. them FASHION 8
weasel w. took the cork out ALCOHOL 38
weather considers w. to be something
                                    WEATHER 21
  first talk is of the w. WEATHER 2
weather-forecasting into w. devices FOOD 103
weather-wise Some are w. WEATHER 1
Webster Like W.'s Dictionary DICTIONARIES 7
  W. struck me much like PEOPLE 3
wedded I have w. fyve MARRIAGE 1
  Ministers are w. to the truth GOVERNMENT 12

weddeth w. or he be wise shall MARRIAGE 2
wedding as she did her w. gown MARRIAGE 25
  knocked over the w. cake BIRDS 53
  man on top of the w. cake POLITICIANS 39
  My face looks like a w. cake APPEARANCE 13
  white lies to ice a w. cake TRUTH AND LIES 17
weddings anybody's w. just so long
                                    MARRIAGE 120
wedlock in w. wake MARRIAGE 20
Wednesday it was not W. HANDWRITING 8
wee There's a w. wifie waitin' ALCOHOL 23
week he had to die in my w. DEATH 62
  know where you are next w. ACTORS 48
  takes me as much as a w. MIND 3
weekend anxious to go away for the w.
                                    HOLIDAYS 4
  w. in the country HOLIDAYS 6
  w. tennis player SPORTS 57
  you need a five-day w. WORK 17
weeks We open in two w. ACTORS 55
weep W. not for little Léonie LANGUAGE 20
weevils between the lesser of two w. CHOICE 7
weighs It w. too much BIOGRAPHY 25
weight Same as her w. INTELLIGENCE 14
  w. of rages will press WIT 35
weird W. clothing is *de rigueur* YOUTH 13
welcome w. in the library LIBRARIES 11
  W. the sixte MARRIAGE 1
  W. to Holiday Inn HOLIDAYS 7
  W. to the Theatre THEATRE 47
well doing w. that which should not BUSINESS 9
  It is not done w. WOMEN 10
  not feeling very w. myself LITERATURE 11
  talk w. but not too wisely CONVERSATION 13
  that's as w. said CONVERSATION 2
well-bred cynical as a w. woman
                                    MEN AND WOMEN 15
  w. as if we were not married BEHAVIOUR 2
well-connected scorn The w. ARISTOCRACY 6
well-known Tomb of the W. Soldier
                                    GOVERNMENT 36
Welsh devil understands W. WALES 1
welshes w. on the deal COUNTRY 15
wench w. is dead SEX 1
Werther W. had a love for Charlotte
                                    MEN AND WOMEN 11
West Go W., young man NAMES 6
  running farce in the W. End GOVERNMENT 43
  would *not* travel due W. TRAVEL 4
Western delivered by W. Union CINEMA 61
  when you've seen one W. CINEMA 63
wet get out of these w. clothes ALCOHOL 28
  so w. you could shoot snipe CHARACTER 12
  W., she was a star CINEMA 25

withdrew I w. my attention   CONVERSATION 4
witness question put to a w.   LAW 14
   w. usually finds that   MARRIAGE 104
witty refrain from saying w.   FOOLISHNESS 23
   six hours a day to being w.   WIT 25
wives And many, many w.   RELIGION 61
   may all your w. be like her   ROYALTY 29
   three w. to support   WAR 15
   Translations (like w.)   MARRIAGE 101
wobbles good spelling but it W.   LANGUAGE 18
woe hideous notes of w.   MISTAKES 3
woke w. up and found yourself   WRITERS 13
Woking Although he's playing for W.
   SPORTS 40
Wolsey in W.'s Home Town   ROYALTY 57
wolves w. had overtaken a sleigh
   DESCRIPTION 20
woman American w. has two souls   AMERICA 16
   argument with a w.   WOMEN 74
   As w.'s love   MEN AND WOMEN 3
   Being a w. is of special interest
   MEN AND WOMEN 69
   body of a young w.   BODY 21
   books Were w.'s looks   WOMEN 14
   called a w. in my own house   WOMEN 47
   'Cause I'm a w.   WOMEN 61
   cynical as a well-bred w.   MEN AND WOMEN 15
   difference between one young w.
   MEN AND WOMEN 19
   every w. should marry   MARRIAGE 51
   flattering a w.   PRAISE 9
   good w. if I had five thousand   VIRTUE 4
   happily a w. may be married   MARRIAGE 103
   I am a w. of the world   BEHAVIOUR 15
   identify a w. writer   CRITICS 36
   If you were not a w.   BORES 11
   it'll make a w. of you   ARMED FORCES 26
   let a w. in your life   MEN AND WOMEN 49
   lovely w. stoops to folly   WOMEN 11
   lovely w. stoops to folly   WOMEN 35
   man can be happy with any w.
   MEN AND WOMEN 13
   Many a w. has a past   WOMEN 24
   never seen a naked w.   WOMEN 67
   No w. can be a beauty without   WOMEN 6
   no w. in London will be safe   PEOPLE 12
   No w. is worth more than   LOVE 15
   one w. differs from another   LOVE 34
   they done the old w. in   SICKNESS 6
   w. be more like a man   MEN AND WOMEN 51
   w. can become a man's friend   WOMEN 28
   w. drove me to drink   ALCOHOL 42
   w. has given you her heart   WOMEN 5
   w.'s age in half a minute   WOMEN 22

w.'s business to get married   MARRIAGE 65
w. seldom writes her mind   WOMEN 7
W.'s place Was in the gaol   WOMEN 52
w.'s place was just the space   WOMEN 51
w.'s preaching is like   WOMEN 10
W.'s Rights   WOMEN 18
w. to provide for herself   MEN AND WOMEN 16
w. who always was tired   EPITAPHS 10
w. who has the political views   ANGER 11
w. who tells one her real age   WOMEN 25
w. who writes is always given   NEWS 11
w. with fair opportunities   MARRIAGE 46
w. without a man is like   WOMEN 84
w. yet think him an angel   MEN AND WOMEN 10
womanhood Friend of W.   MEN 15
womankind packs off its w.   ARMED FORCES 16
wombat until I clasp my w.   BIRDS 5
women apples, cherries, hops, and w.   PLACES 2
   concern for the rights of w.   WOMEN 79
   constancy of the w. who love me   WOMEN 30
   girls turn into American w.   AMERICA 38
   have any w. got a right mind   MARRIAGE 148
   humour from w.   HUMOUR 17
   I must have w.   WOMEN 9
   Let us have wine and w.   HAPPINESS 1
   like w.'s letters   LETTERS 4
   man who doesn't know w.   FASHION 17
   married beneath me, all w. do   INSULTS 41
   men, w., and clergymen   RELIGION 21
   men, w., and Herveys   ARISTOCRACY 2
   more about w. than married men
   MARRIAGE 102
   more interesting than w.   INTELLIGENCE 6
   no w. in heaven   RELIGION 72
   opportunities to meet naked w.
   ART AND ARTISTS 30
   Plain w. he regarded   WOMEN 19
   prefers petite w.   MEN AND WOMEN 75
   Some w....enjoy tremendously
   MEN AND WOMEN 62
   Steadily towards drink and w.   EDUCATION 19
   thought of w. as kissable   MEN AND WOMEN 79
   unscrupulous men for unhealthy w.
   ART AND ARTISTS 21
   we w. cannot escape it   NATURE 2
   When w. go wrong   MEN AND WOMEN 29
   When w. kiss it always reminds   WOMEN 53
   w. and care and trouble   WOMEN 4
   w. and children could work   WORK 10
   w. are the most reliable   WOMEN 27
   w. become like their mothers
   MEN AND WOMEN 14
   w. can be divided into two groups
   MEN AND WOMEN 61

w. by the public and read   BOOKS 14
W. English is now inert   WRITERS 16
w. in such small print   WRITERS 14
wromantic Wrong but W.   DESCRIPTION 12
wrong ages for the w. word   CRITICS 40
   difference between right and w.   MORALITY 17
   he is very probably w.   SCIENCE 32
   Kings to govern w.   ROYALTY 13
   noblemen who have gone w.   ARISTOCRACY 4
   not always to be w.   SELF-KNOWLEDGE 14
   people will think it w.   LAW 21
   Posterity is as likely to be w.   FUTURE 3
   right or w. end of a gun   SPORTS 23
   so w. that only a very intelligent   IDEAS 3
   usually gets it all w.   POLITICIANS 27
   Whenever you're w., admit it   MARRIAGE 108
   when our neighbours do w.   CRIME 7
   When women go w., men go
                MEN AND WOMEN 29
   who continually did w.   ROYALTY 52
   w. bar or bed at the w. time   MISTAKES 20
   w. bits are in   CRITICS 46
   w. boat at Dover   TRAVEL 27
   W. but Wromantic   DESCRIPTION 12
   w. kind of snow   WEATHER 24
   w. people travel   TRAVEL 17
wrote blockhead ever w.   WRITERS 4
   this play the way you w. it   THEATRE 48
   Who w. like an angel   EPITAPHS 8
Wykehamist rather dirty W.   RELIGION 56

yachts echoes the sails of y.   PLACES 12
yaks lot of y. jumping about   MUSIC 56
Yale wholesale libel on a Y. prom   WOMEN 44
Yankee Doodle Y.   MUSIC 17
Yanks Y., through and through   AMERICA 6
yarooh groo—y.   CHILDREN 21
yawn You y. at one another   MEN AND WOMEN 38
yawns Even the grave y.   BORES 9
year next y. I shall be sixty-two   MIDDLE AGE 5
   Was one a good y.   ALCOHOL 61
yearns y. so hungrily   ACTORS 41
years additional dozen y.   MEDICINE 16
   Methus'lah live nine hundred y.   OLD AGE 13
   10 y. in a boiler suit   WOMEN 80
   well stricken in y.   OLD AGE 16
   We've been waiting 700 y.   TIME 4

Yeats Y. is becoming so aristocratic
                SNOBBERY 13
yes word 'y.' chanted   THEATRE 61
   y. without having asked   BEHAVIOUR 26
ying Y. tong iddle I po   COMEDY 15
yob y. ethics of professional   SPORTS 81
yolk y. runs down the waistcoat   FOOD 18
you Yet I get a kick out of y.   MEN AND WOMEN 30
   'Y.' (if definite article   WORDS 23
young as y. as he feels   OLD AGE 16
   dared be radical when y.   POLITICS 32
   denunciation of the y.   GENERATION GAP 4
   enchanting than the voices of y.   YOUTH 6
   frightfully y. you were   YOUTH 7
   I'm so glad I'm not y.   OLD AGE 23
   old heads on your y. shoulders   EDUCATION 36
   strength for it, you're too y.   ACTORS 63
   too y. to take up golf   MIDDLE AGE 4
   y. can do for the old   YOUTH 1
   y. have aspirations   GENERATION GAP 2
   y. is not having any money   YOUTH 10
younger older we do not get any y.
                MIDDLE AGE 5
   Seek y. friends   OLD AGE 17
   y. than a twenty-four-year-old girl
                MEN AND WOMEN 52
yourself you fall in love with y.   LOVE 31
youth been in a y. hostel   YOUTH 14
   better to waste one's y.   YOUTH 3
   I must look after my y.   BEHAVIOUR 31
   Y. are boarded, clothed   EDUCATION 3
   y. is dull as paint   OLD AGE 23
   y. of America   AMERICA 4
Yucatan I had an Aunt in Y.   BIRDS 15

Zanzibar count the cats in Z.   TRAVEL 2
   To drag their cans to Z.   TRAVEL 17
zeal not the slightest z.   LIFE 1
   tempering bigot z.   RELIGION 41
zest z. goes out of a beautiful   DANCE 13
Zeus Z. performed acts with swans   SEX 101
   Z. 'the God of Wine   GOD 51
zip Children and z. fasteners   POWER 6
   Z.! I was reading Schopenhauer
                INTELLIGENCE 11
zones We retain our z. erogenous   OLD AGE 29
zoo some monster at the Z.   LAW 44
Zuleika Z., on a desert island   WOMEN 33